Marquee Series

Office
Microsoft®

Brief Edition
2010

Nita Rutkosky

Pierce College at Puyallup, Puyallup, Washington

Denise Seguin

Fanshawe College, London, Ontario

Audrey Rutkosky Roggenkamp

Pierce College at Puyallup, Puyallup, Washington

Paradigm
PUBLISHING
St. Paul • Los Angeles • Indianapolis

Managing Editor	Sonja Brown
Developmental Editor	Brenda Palo
Supplements Developmental Editor	Brenda Owens
Production Editor	Donna Mears
Cover and Text Designer	Leslie Anderson
Copy Editors	Susan Capecchi and Laura Nelson
Desktop Production	Ryan Hamner and Jack Ross
Proofreader	Laura Nelson
Testers	Carley Bomstad, Amy McGuire, Rob Neilly, and Lindsay Ryan
Indexers	Ina Gravitz and Sandi Schroeder

The authors, editors, and publisher thank the following instructors for their helpful suggestions during the planning and development of the Marquee Office 2010 series: James Cutietta, Cuyahoga Community College—Metro Campus, Cleveland, OH; Carol Decker, Montgomery College, Rockville, MD; Shawna DePlonty, Sault College, Sault Ste. Marie, Ontario; Brian Fox, Santa Fe Community College, Gainesville, FL; Dr. Wade Graves, Grayson Community College, Denison, TX; Sherry Howard-Spreitzer, Northwestern Michigan College, Traverse City, MI; Vicki Johns, Florida Community College at Jacksonville, Jacksonville, FL; Jan Jordan, Paris Junior College, Paris, TX; Dan Kamradt, Southwestern Michigan College, Dowagiac, MI; Valerie Kasay, Southeastern Technical College, Vidalia, GA; Gajen Ramanathan, St. Cloud Technical College, St. Cloud, MN; Pat Serrano, Scottsdale Community College, Scottsdale, AZ; Cristy Stamps, Northwest Arkansas Community College, Bentonville, AR; Wilma Thomason, Mid-South Community College, West Memphis, AR; William Tucker, Austin Community College, Austin, TX; Mandy Wright, Altamaha Technical College, Jessup, GA.

Text: ISBN 978-0-76383-770-9
Text & CD: ISBN 978-0-76383-772-3

© 2011 by Paradigm Publishing, Inc.
875 Montreal Way
St. Paul, MN 55102
Email: educate@emcp.com
Website: www.emcp.com

Contents

iii

EXCEL 2010

ACCESS 2010

Preface

Marquee Series, Microsoft Office 2010 prepares students to work with Microsoft Office 2010 in a business office or for personal use. Incorporating an accelerated, step-by-step, project-based approach, this text builds student competency in Word, Excel, Access, and PowerPoint 2010 and the essential features of Windows 7 and Internet Explorer 8.0.

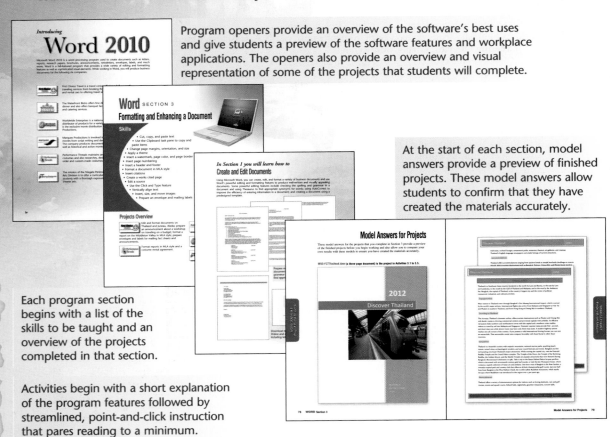

Program openers provide an overview of the software's best uses and give students a preview of the software features and workplace applications. The openers also provide an overview and visual representation of some of the projects that students will complete.

At the start of each section, model answers provide a preview of finished projects. These model answers allow students to confirm that they have created the materials accurately.

Each program section begins with a list of the skills to be taught and an overview of the projects completed in that section.

Activities begin with a short explanation of the program features followed by streamlined, point-and-click instruction that pares reading to a minimum.

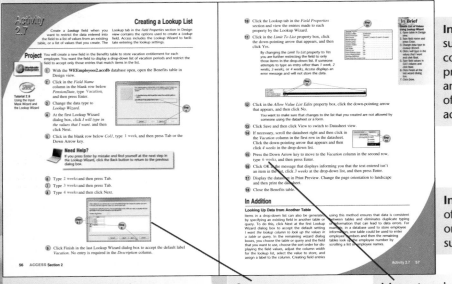

In Brief—Bare-bones summaries of major commands and features provide instant review and a quick reference of the steps required to accomplish a task.

In Addition—Sidebars offer extra information on key features and subfeatures.

Need Help?—Troubleshooting hints anticipate common obstacles or missteps and redirect students toward success.

Screen captures correlated with activity steps provide instant reinforcement.

Magenta color highlights text to be typed.

Features Summary—Commands taught in the section are listed with button, ribbon tab, Quick Access toolbar, and keyboard actions.

Skills Review—Completing these hands-on computer exercises reinforces students' learning of key features and skills. These activities include some guidance, but less than is provided for the intrasection projects.

Knowledge Check—Objective completion exercises allow students to assess their comprehension and recall of program features, terminology, and functions.

Skills Assessment—Framed within a workplace project perspective, these assessments evaluate students' abilities to apply section skills and concepts in solving realistic problems. They require demonstrating program skills as well as decision-making skills and include a Help activity, Internet-based activities, and an Individual Challenge.

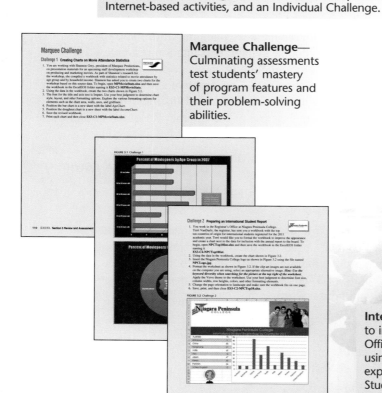

Marquee Challenge—Culminating assessments test students' mastery of program features and their problem-solving abilities.

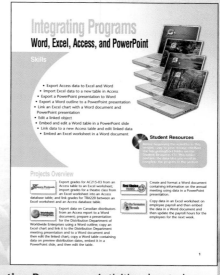

Integrating Programs—Activities devoted to integrating information among Microsoft Office 2010 programs highlight the benefits of using the Office suite. Projects include copying, exporting, linking, and embedding data. Students learn how to manage data efficiently in the business office or for personal use.

Student Courseware

Student Resources CD Each textbook comes with a Student Resources CD that contains typed documents and files required for completing activities and exercises. The first page of every section of the book provides instructions for accessing student data files from a specific folder on the Student Resources CD. The student will need to copy this folder of files from the CD to a storage medium before beginning the section activities. *(See the inside back cover for instructions on copying a folder.)*

Internet Resource Center Additional material for students preparing to work in the business office is available at the book-specific website at www.emcp.net/Marquee10. Here students will find the same resources that are on the Student Resources CD along with study tools, web links, and other information specifically useful in the workplace.

SNAP Training and Assessment SNAP is a web-based program offering an interactive venue for learning Microsoft Office 2010, Windows 7, and Internet Explorer 8.0. SNAP course work is comprised of a web-based learning management system, multimedia tutorials, performance skill items, document-based assessments, a concepts test bank, an online grade book, and a set of course planning tools. A CD of tutorials teaching the basics of Office, Windows, and Internet Explorer is also available if instructors wish to assign additional SNAP tutorial work without using the web-based SNAP program.

eBook For students who prefer studying with an eBook, the texts in the Marquee Series are available in an electronic form. The web-based, password-protected eBooks feature dynamic navigation tools, including bookmarking, a linked table of contents, and the ability to jump to a specific page. The eBook format also supports helpful study tools, such as highlighting and note taking.

Instructor Resources

Instructor's Guide and CD Instructor support for the Marquee Series includes an *Instructor's Guide* and Instructor Resources CD package. This resource includes planning information, such as Lesson Blueprints, teaching hints, and sample course syllabi; presentation resources, such as PowerPoint slide shows; and assessment resources, including an overview of available assessment venues, live and PDF model answers for section activities, and live and PDF model answers for end-of-section exercises. Contents of the *Instructor's Guide* and Instructor Resources CD package are also available on the password-protected section of the Internet Resource Center for this title at www.emcp.net/Marquee10.

Computerized Test Generator Instructors can use the **EXAM**VIEW® Assessment Suite and test banks of multiple-choice items to create customized web-based or print tests. The **EXAM**VIEW® Assessment Suite and test banks are provided on the Instructor Resources CD.

Blackboard Cartridge This set of files allows instructors to create a personalized Blackboard website for their course and provides course content, tests, and the mechanisms for establishing communication via e-discussions and online group conferences. Available content includes a syllabus, test banks, PowerPoint presentations, and supplementary course materials. Upon request, the files can be available within 24–48 hours. Hosting the site is the responsibility of the educational institution.

Information Technology Essentials

The Information Processing Cycle

Computers process information in the same way that humans make decisions. We use our eyes and ears to read or "input" facts and data into our brains. We use our brains to "process" that data and organize it into information. The resulting "output" is a thought or decision that we can display or present by drawing it, writing it, or making a voice recording of it. If we decide to keep the results for future use, we "store" the paper or recording in a file cabinet.

As shown in Figure 1, the information processing cycle can be divided into four segments: input, processing, output, and storage. It relies on computer hardware to mimic the human procedure. Hardware refers to the devices you can physically see and touch in and on the computer.

Input

Input involves getting data into the computer so that it can be processed. Some commonly used input devices are described in the following sections.

Keyboard Based on the layout of keys on a typewriter, the keyboard is primarily used for typing text. Although numbers are found in a row above the letters, most PC keyboards also include a calculator-style number pad for the convenience of bookkeepers, accountants, and others who work with numbers a lot.

Twelve keys labeled F1 through F12, as well as several other named keys, can be programmed to perform special functions in software applications. For example, the F1 key usually displays a help window where you might type a request for instructions on how to print what has just been typed. The Home key might move the cursor to the left side of a line in one program, but to the upper left corner of the page in another. (The cursor is the flashing bar, dash, or other symbol that indicates where the next character you type will appear on the screen.)

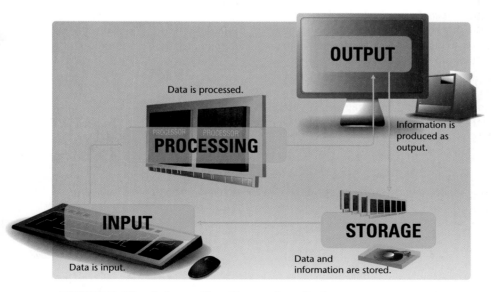

FIGURE 1 The Information Processing Cycle

Mouse A mouse is a pointing device used for issuing commands and selecting text or files for processing. Moving the mouse on the desktop causes a pointer to move on the screen. If you point to the File tab at the top left corner of the Microsoft Word screen, for example, then click the left mouse button, a drop-down menu will appear, allowing you to click *Open* if you want to access a file you have previously saved.

If you want to delete several words or lines, you can point to the beginning of the first word, then hold down the left mouse button, "drag" the mouse to highlight the text, and then click the Delete key to remove the text from the document.

A keyboard and mouse are examples of common input devices.

Touch Pad Most laptop computers provide a touch pad instead of a mouse as a pointing device. You move your forefinger across the pad to position the cursor, then use your thumb to press the equivalent of the mouse "button."

Touch Screen A touch screen allows you to select an item and input commands by physically touching a specific area of the monitor. You have probably used one if you use ATM machines for banking. They are also used at information kiosks to provide an easy-to-use way to select items of interest, without the necessity of a keyboard. Servers at restaurants use them to place orders. (Touch screens are much easier to clean than keyboards, and they can be used with only one hand.)

Commonly used at airport check-in counters, touch screens allow travelers to obtain boarding passes and check luggage by touching options on the monitor.

Scanner A scanner works like a photocopier to transfer pictures or text into the computer. If you don't have a digital camera, you can scan your photos into a PC, then organize or enhance them with photo editing software.

A scanner is a tool to input either pictures or text.

Digitizing Pen and Drawing Tablet Although a mouse can be used for drawing designs and pictures, it is very clumsy. Better detail can be achieved with a digitizing pen and drawing tablet. Some handheld and laptop computers now accept "handwritten" input with a digitizing pen called a stylus.

Engineers, architects, and designers often use a very sophisticated type of graphics tablet to make precise drawings such as those used in building construction and the manufacture of circuit boards for computers. Such graphics tablets are made up of hundreds of tiny intersecting wires forming an electronic matrix embedded in the tablet surface. A stylus or crosshair cursor activates these intersection points, which collectively represent the image.

Tablet PCs are useful for handwriting notes when in a meeting or on the road.

Joystick A joystick is an input device (named after the control lever used to fly fighter planes) consisting of a small box that contains a vertical lever that, when pushed in a certain direction, moves the graphics cursor correspondingly on the screen. Most often used to control fast-moving images in computer games, joysticks can also be used by people who have difficulty using a mouse.

A joystick is an input device used for moving objects on a computer screen and is a common input device for computer gaming.

Digital Camera Digital cameras can be used to transfer still and moving pictures into the computer. Webcams are a popular example of a video camera that can be used in combination with headphones and a microphone to communicate by "video phone" with people in all corners of the world.

A digital camera captures images in a digital format and often contains an output device for viewing those images.

A webcam is a digital camera that can be controlled remotely over the Internet.

Microphone With a microphone you can add a "sound bite" to a computerized slide presentation or speak to a friend over the Internet. Microphones can stand on the desk or be worn as part of a headset.

Bar Code Reader Bar code readers are used for entering the Universal Product Code (UPC) found on items in grocery and retail stores. They also are used to track medication administration in hospitals.

Dual Purpose Devices Although usually thought of as storage devices, compact discs (CDs), digital video discs (DVDs), flash drives, and hard drives all allow you to reenter data into the computer quickly and easily, without having to retype it. Floppy diskettes were once widely used in PCs, but have become obsolete because they can only hold 1.44 megabytes (MB)—that is, 1,440,000 characters—of data. The other devices mentioned will be discussed in the "Storage" section.

A bar code reader scans a UPC and resulting input can be used to check a patient's identity and medication requirements.

Processing

A computer's central function is to process data. Processing can involve calculating numbers, editing text, modifying pictures, and other information management tasks. The central processing unit (CPU) is the brain of the computer that handles those tasks. The rate at which the CPU can process data is known as the "clock speed."

Processors Most IBM-compatible PCs use a central processing unit made by Intel or AMD. They process data at clock speeds from 2.0 to 4.0 gigahertz (GHz). (One gigahertz equals one billion cycles per second.) The first Apple Macintosh computers ran on Motorola 68000 processors, but now use Intel processors and can run IBM-compatible PC operating systems.

Many CPUs include multiple processors on a single chip. These dual-core processors can process multiple instructions simultaneously for better performance. Some CPUs have four processors in one (quad-core). Single-core processors use a technique called "multitasking" in which one processor switches back and forth between programs so quickly that the user doesn't perceive any interruption, but both programs are actually running more slowly than they would with two separate processors, or with one dual-core processor.

Flash drives are small, easy-to-handle, portable storage devices that many people use to carry important data with them wherever they go.

Memory Chips Memory chips are the hardware that provides the workspace for the data and instructions the computer is processing. The user workspace is called random access memory (RAM) because the CPU has quick access to it and does not have to search through it "page by page." Having a large amount of RAM is like having a large work table where you can spread out books, papers, pencils, a calculator, and other tools you need to do your work. RAM is considered volatile or temporary "storage" because it disappears completely when the power to the computer is shut off.

The amount of RAM a personal computer needs depends on the operating system it runs. A Windows XP computer needs 512 megabytes (MB) of RAM; a Windows 7 or Windows Vista system requires 1 gigabyte (GB). A gigabyte equals about one billion bytes.

A processor chip (a CPU) performs the calculations in a computer.

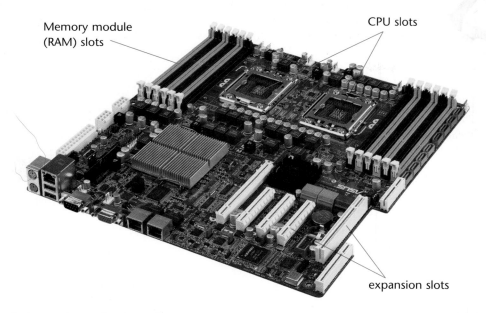

Memory module (RAM) slots

CPU slots

expansion slots

FIGURE 2 Motherboard Layout
The motherboard is a container for the computer's CPU and RAM, and contains slots for adding expansion cards.

Read only memory (ROM) is sometimes confused with RAM due to the similarity of their names. ROM is nonvolatile and contains the getting-started instructions that the PC needs when the power is first turned on. As its name implies, ROM can only be used as programmed by the PC manufacturer. You can't make any changes to it; you can only cause its contents to be "read" into the computer.

Figure 2 shows a typical motherboard layout.

Output

Output is processed data that can be used immediately or stored in computer-usable form for later use. Output may be produced in either hard copy or soft copy, or in both forms. Hard copy is a permanent version of output, such as a letter printed on paper using a printer. Soft copy is a temporary version and includes any output that cannot be physically handled. Soft copy output devices include monitors and speakers.

Monitor A monitor is the screen used for displaying graphics and text. Although older picture-tube type cathode ray tube (CRT) monitors are still in use, new PCs are sold with flat screen, liquid crystal display (LCD) monitors. In an LCD, liquid crystals are sandwiched between two sheets of material. Electric current passing through the crystals causes them to twist. This twisting effect blocks some light waves and allows other light waves to pass through, creating images on the screen.

Printer Printers provide hard copy printouts on paper. There are several printing technologies available, including ink-jet, which uses liquid ink squirted on the paper, and laser, which fuses powdered toner to the paper.

A flat screen, LCD monitor is the most commonly used output device.

Speakers and Headphones Speakers and headphones provide audio output in stereo for movies, radio programs, streaming video, online learning courses, and telephone calls.

Storage

The storage portion of the information processing cycle refers to recording output so that it will be available after the computer has been shut off and RAM has been erased.

Output can be stored for future use on hard drives, CDs, DVDs, and flash drives. A drive is a PC device that can read and write data onto the surface of a round platter (disk) as it spins. Hard disk platters are made of metal; compact and digital video discs are made of plastic. Flash drives and solid-state hard drives store data in nonvolatile RAM; they have no moving parts, but they provide the same function as conventional drives.

Hard drives contain a stack of metal platters (disks), a drive motor, and read/write heads that are positioned to access the top and bottom of each platter. Hard drive capacities vary; an average desktop PC might have a hard drive that holds 200 GB.

Data CDs are made of the same material that is used for music CDs. In fact, you can play your favorite music CDs in the CD drive of your PC. They can hold about 700 MB of data. DVDs can hold from 4 GB to 8 GB, depending on whether they can record on both sides and on one or two layers per side. Blu-ray discs are used both for high-definition video and for data; a Blu-ray disc can hold 25 GB to 50 GB.

The flash drives on the market today can hold from 128 megabytes to 256 gigabytes of data on a printed circuit board inside a protective plastic case. They are the size and shape of a person's thumb or a package of chewing gum. Some drives even provide fingerprint authorization. Flash drives connect directly to a USB port and thus do not require the installation of any device driver programs to support them.

System Unit Ports

Ports are the "sockets" that the input, output, and storage devices plug into (see Figure 3). In the early days of personal computing, serial, parallel, and printer cables and ports were found on all PCs. Today, most "peripheral" devices use Universal Serial Bus (USB) cables and ports. USB cables and connector plugs are smaller, thinner, and more flexible. They transmit data at up to 480 megabits per second (Mbps) for a USB 2.0 port. As many as 127 devices can be connected to the computer host at once through a daisy-chain–style connection setup.

USB hubs provide extra connection options for computers with only one or two USB ports. You might even discover that you can make backup copies of your data to an external hard drive that is connected to your computer via the USB port on your keyboard!

Computer speakers provide sound output.

Portable external hard drives are available in a variety of sizes, styles, and colors.

This flash drive storage device has a USB connector that fits into a standard USB port.

EXPLORING TECHNOLOGY

1

Identify the processor, clock speed, and amount of random access memory (RAM) in a computer you often use. *Hint: With Windows 7 or Windows Vista, follow* **Start > Control Panel > System and Maintenance > System.** *For Windows XP, follow* **Start > Control Panel > Performance and Maintenance > System.** *In either operating system, if the control panel is displayed using Classic view, double-click the* **System icon.**

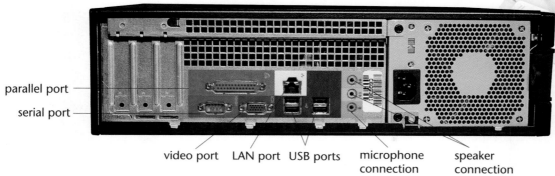

parallel port ——————
serial port ——————

video port   LAN port   USB ports   microphone   speaker
                                        connection   connection

FIGURE 3 System Unit Ports

Identify the hardware you have on your computer and categorize each piece as input, output, or both.

EXPLORING
TECHNOLOGY

2

Computer Software

Software refers to the operating instructions and applications that allow computers to process the numbers, pictures, sounds, and text we enter into them. We can touch the disk that contains the software, but not the lines of programming code that make up the software.

Personal Computer Operating Systems

The original personal computer operating system, MS-DOS (Disk Operating System), used a command-line interface. You typed commands into a text prompt, and the computer returned text output to the monitor. Today, most operating systems have Graphical User Interfaces (GUIs), in which a mouse is used to manipulate graphic objects such as icons and windows onscreen.

If a PC has an older CPU with a clock speed that is too slow, or not enough RAM, the PC will run slowly or it won't be able to run the operating system at all. Windows 7 requires, at a minimum, a CPU that runs at 1 GHz and has 1 GB of RAM. Windows Vista requires an 800 MHz CPU and 512 MB of RAM; Windows XP requires a 233 MHz CPU and 128 MB of RAM.

The Windows 7 operating system requires a CPU that runs at 1 GHz.

The Mac OS X operating system can run on IBM-compatible PCs.

The operating system for the Apple Macintosh is Mac OS. The tenth version of the Mac operating system is called Mac OS X. Since its initial introduction in 2005, several updates to it have been released, each one with an animal code name. The Snow Leopard (version 10.6) was released in 2009. Previous versions included Leopard, Tiger, and Panther.

Applications

People with no technical knowledge of how a PC works can use it to balance their checkbooks or to insert a photograph into a personalized greeting card, print it out, and send it to a friend. The thousands of software applications available provide the instructions that empower users to perform these and other tasks from the mundane to the outright amazing.

In this section we will present the most common types of computer programs on the market today.

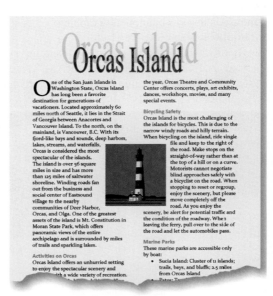

Microsoft Word is a word processing program that includes several formatting features that can be applied to words, lines, paragraphs, pages, or entire documents.

Word Processing Word processing software was originally designed as a replacement for the typewriter. Now a word processing program such as Microsoft Word can support photos and drawings, mathematical calculations, text in table format, text in varying sizes, shapes, and colors—and even sound bites.

Spreadsheet Spreadsheet software such as Microsoft Excel can be used for both simple and very complex calculations. Current versions can also support graphics and perform some database tasks, such as sorting. A series of keystrokes which perform several steps of a repetitive task can be saved as a "macro" and programmed to run at the click of an icon.

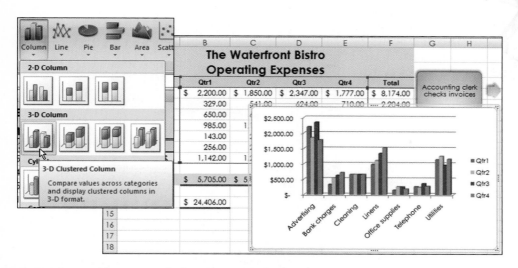

An Excel spreadsheet can calculate elements of a business proposal, such as operating expenses, and display them in a chart.

Because formulas are used to create calculations, you can ask, "If I spend only $2 per day on coffee instead of $5, how much money will I save at the end of the month?" When you replace one value with another, the program will recalculate your budget automatically.

Database Database software such as Microsoft Access is designed to keep track of information. It allows you to rearrange data alphabetically, numerically, or chronologically. Or you can filter the data to display only those items that match your criteria, such as the names of customers who spent more than $500 at your online music store last year. Database software can easily do simple calculations, such as showing monthly subtotals and an annual total for each of your customers, but complex math is usually best left to the spreadsheets.

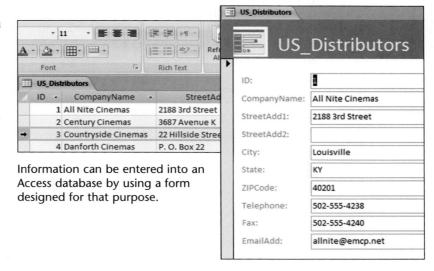

Information can be entered into an Access database by using a form designed for that purpose.

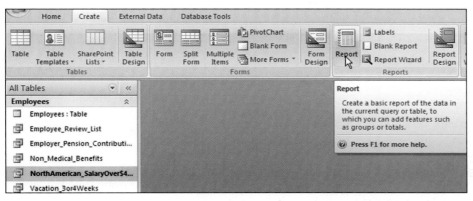

An Access database report is a selection of data in a database. The user chooses which types of information should be included in the report, and the database automatically finds and organizes the corresponding data.

Presentation Presentation software such as Microsoft PowerPoint allows users to create slide shows that can be viewed on the computer or projected onto a large screen. The shows can include clip art, graphs and charts, photos, drawings, video clips, sound, and text. Features such as arrows and boxes that "fly" into the screen and slide transition effects provide the attention-getting movement that appeals to sales people and teachers.

Audio, Video, and Photo Editing Photo editing software is used for organizing, retouching, and editing photographs and videos that have been saved on CDs and DVDs, scanned in, or transferred directly from the camera to the PC. PaintShop Pro and Photo Explosion allow you to edit photographs and crop out unwanted

PowerPoint can combine text, graphics, sounds, and videos.

"strangers," remove the red-eye effect, or put one person's head on another person's body. You can also create your own slide shows with background audio, then email the results to friends and family or copy them to a CD or DVD and display them on your TV set.

Video editing software such as ArcSoft VideoImpression can be used to edit video clips to remove the scenes you took of your feet when you forgot to stop recording, or to add music, or to rearrange the scenes to create a more logical flow—or a more creative one. You can also edit the audio tracks. With some relatively inexpensive products, you can fine-tune the sound and achieve a professional level of quality.

Nero StartSmart is an audio editing program that lets you transfer music from cassette tapes and vinyl records to CDs, iPods, and MP3 players. With it you can remove noise, clicks, and crackle; add reverb and other effects; remove the vocals by using a Karaoke filter; and tweak various other sound qualities.

Graphics and Drawing Applications such as CorelDraw, Adobe Illustrator, SmartDraw, Microsoft Paint, and Paint Show Pro are popular software packages that provide the tools to design graphical images that can be used for web pages, posters, marketing brochures, and greeting cards. Visio is a graphics application that focuses more on technical and business drawings, flow charts, and organizational charts to illustrate complex processes. Visio is vector graphics-based, meaning that it

Paint is a basic image-editing program included with Windows.

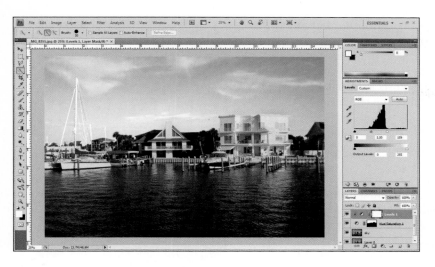

Adobe Photoshop is a high-end image-editing program used by graphics professionals.

uses points, lines, curves, and geometric shapes to create images. Another method is "raster-based," which uses groups of pixels (picture elements) to make an image. If you can see tiny squares when you magnify an image, you are viewing its individual elements.

A digitized pen and tablet may seem to be a requirement for using drawing applications, but you can do amazing things with a mouse by picking a circle from a group of shapes and making it larger or smaller or turning it into an oval. Free graphics and drawing software includes Inkscape, Skencil, and Open Office DRAW.

Suites Software applications are often bundled into packages called "suites." Widely used versions of the Microsoft Office suite contain the word processor, Word; the spreadsheet, Excel; the database manager, Access; and the presentation manager, PowerPoint.

Money Management Quicken and Microsoft Money are two software applications with an interface that resembles a checkbook. Users can not only write and print checks, but also track their spending habits, create a budget, generate cash flow reports, download their credit card charges, and keep track of their savings and investments.

TurboTax and TaxCut are income tax preparation programs that prompt you to enter your tax information, then print a duplicate of the state and federal forms with your data on the appropriate lines. They also let you file your tax returns electronically and direct your refund to your bank account.

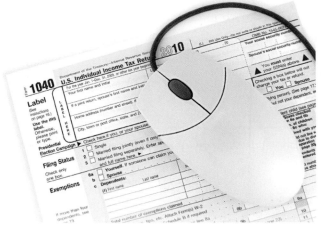

Money management software enables users to manage their money by helping them pay bills, balance checkbooks, keep track of income and expenses, maintain investment records, and other financial activities.

Tax preparation software allows users to efficiently fill out state and federal tax forms and submit them electronically.

Personal Information Management Microsoft Outlook and Lotus Organizer are examples of personal information management (PIM) programs that keep track of your to-do list, address book, and personal calendar. Many PIMs also contain a scheduler with an alarm to alert you of a meeting, whether it occurs daily, weekly, or only once. Smartphones and handheld devices can synchronize with your computer's PIM program so you can carry your information everywhere you go.

Collaboration Businesses often find the need to have several people collaborate on a project. Collaborative software or groupware, such as Lotus Notes and Microsoft Office SharePoint, provides a way to keep track of who has made or suggested changes to documents or plans and to distribute everything electronically. A calendar feature allows users to schedule meetings at times when others are free. Both email and instant messaging (IM) functions are used, providing real-time communication among team members wherever they are in the world. SharePoint allows direct editing of documents through Word, Excel, or PowerPoint and also provides controlled access to shared documents via the Web.

Smartphones such as this Blackberry include PDA software that tracks appointments and stores contact information.

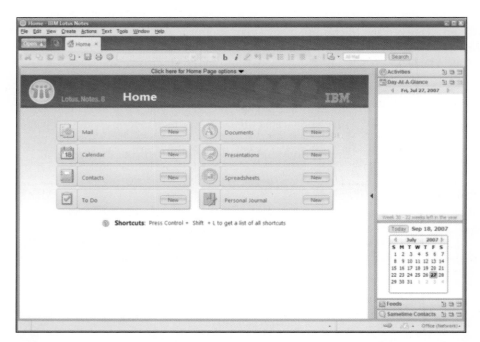

Collaboration software (groupware) can help team members stay connected.

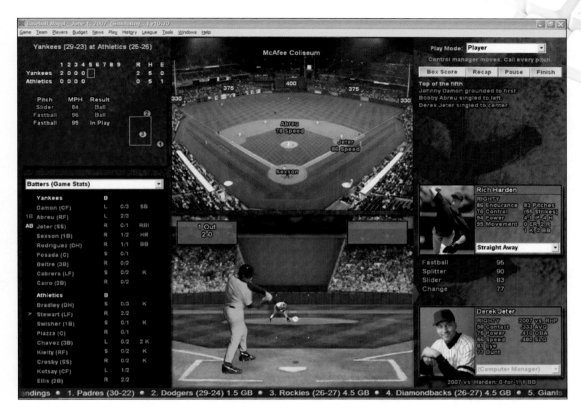

Entertainment and gaming software can be so lifelike they look like actual TV broadcasts.

Gaming Computer games have come a long way since the Solitaire program included in the first versions of Windows. Today's games contain high-quality 3D animations, sound, and action that is very realistic. Baseball and football games, auto racing, and fantasy worlds are just a small part of a fast growing industry. You can even play games over the Internet with players in other cities and countries.

Some games, especially those that include realistic simulations, require a lot of computing power. You will need a fast CPU and plenty of RAM for the best performance.

Open-Source Open-source software is the general term for applications that are provided completely free of charge, with no license fees or restrictions, and no copyrights to worry about. You can download the software, copy it, and give it to your friends. The programming source code is also provided without charge and anyone is allowed to modify and improve it. For further details, go to www.opensource.org.

OpenOffice is a suite of applications that are considered open source and includes a word processor, a spreadsheet, a presentation application, a drawing application, and a database manager. These applications can save and open data files from Microsoft Office, and provide many of the same capabilities as the equivalent retail products. OpenOffice can be downloaded for free from www.openoffice.org.

Identify the operating system version running on your computer. Has it been updated with a Service Pack? *Hint: Use the same method you used in the first exercise.*

EXPLORING
TECHNOLOGY

3

List and categorize the major applications installed on your computer using the terms mentioned in this section. *Hint: If you don't see icons for them on the Desktop, click the Start button.*

EXPLORING
TECHNOLOGY

4

Networks

Computer networks are created when people want to share something such as a printer, an Internet connection, the specific information within the confines of their business, or the wide and abundant variety of information found on the Web. The network allows computers to communicate and to share these resources.

Local Area Networks

The Local Area Network (LAN) illustrated in Figure 4 consists of several computers that are physically connected to one another via a central hub called a switch. The network also includes a server (a computer that manages the network) and a shared printer.

Most LANs are not stand-alone systems; they connect to the Internet as well, so users can take advantage of online resources such as the Web and email.

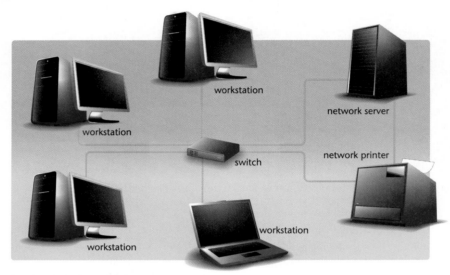

FIGURE 4 A Local Area Network

Wide Area Networks

A company might have several LANs, each in a different location or branch office. LANs can be connected to one another to form Wide Area Networks (WANs) as shown in Figure 5. The key difference between a LAN and a WAN is that, in a WAN, the company does not own all the pathways between the computers. The data has to go out in "public" to reach its destination, whether that is a leased phone line or the Internet. Leaving the protected local area carries security risks, but also connectivity benefits.

Large companies lease dedicated phone lines (T1 or T3 lines) or satellite connections to connect their LANs; many smaller companies find it more affordable to connect their branch offices via the existing Internet infrastructure.

Network Components

Computer networks require specialized hardware and software designed for the sharing of information and other collaborative functions. The various components are explained in this section.

Clients Clients are the computer workstations where end users run the various applications necessary for them to do their jobs. In a client-server network, clients request information from the servers. Figure 6 shows an example of a client-server architecture. In this type of network architecture structure, the networking paths allow a network client computer to send information to a server, which then can relay the information back to the client computer or to another client on the same network. In this network, fax machines and laser printers can be shared resources, available through their respective servers. In addition, the file server can provide access to a shared hard disk.

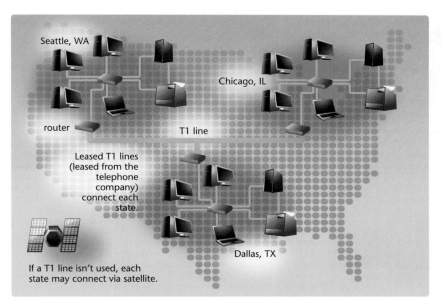

FIGURE 5 A Wide Area Network

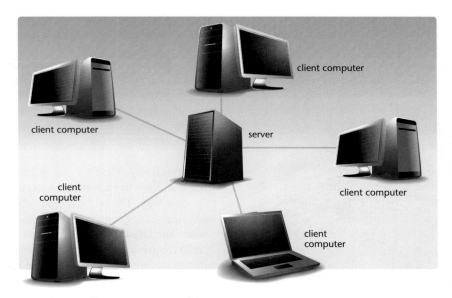

FIGURE 6 Client-Server Architecture

Servers Servers are data providers that are often larger and more powerful computers than clients. They house the network operating system software that organizes the sharing of data among the end users' PCs. They can hold large databases of information that users access to compile the reports that keep their organizations running smoothly. Servers might also be used as the storage location for everything every user creates, so that everyone else has easy access to it.

For small networks, the same computer can function as both client and server in a peer-to-peer network where all computers are equal and each one is both data requester and data provider (see Figure 7).

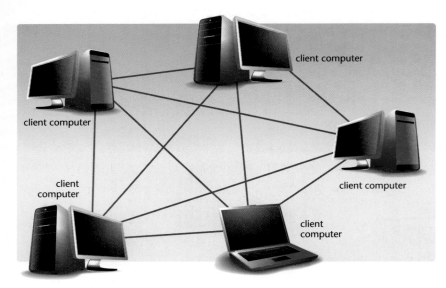

client computer

client computer

client
computer

client computer

client
computer

FIGURE 7 Peer-to-Peer Architecture

Switches and Routers Within a LAN, all the computers and other network-enabled devices (such as printers) must have a way of communicating with one another. Switches and routers serve as central hubs for that communication.

A switch is a box into which each computer connects via a cable. A switch that connects devices via radio waves (RF) rather than via cables is called a wireless access point. A router is a more sophisticated version of a switch. A router can pass data from one LAN to another, and throughout the Internet. Routers can be wired, wireless, or both.

A switch provides a central connection place for cables from multiple computers.

A router enables you to join two or more networks, or to join your LAN to the Internet.

Connectivity The PCs that make up a network have to be connected to each other in some way. The original method uses physical cables containing several strands of wire. The latest method is wireless and uses radio frequencies to carry data over short distances from a PC to a switch or router. All the devices are often located in the same room, but the signals are strong enough to penetrate the types of walls found in homes and offices.

The most commonly used network cable is unshielded twisted pair cable (UTP). UTP cable is rated by category, with higher categories of cable needed for faster networks. Standard home networks use Cat 5 or Cat 5e cables; for business use, Cat 6 cable is the norm.

Wireless connections are used where cables are difficult to install or where the users are mobile or not close to a switch or router. Commonly called Wi-Fi, these connections are known by their technical 802.11 protocol specifications. See the following section for details on them.

Protocols A protocol is a generally accepted agreement on how to behave in a certain situation. For example, in many countries it is considered proper protocol to stand at the playing of the national anthem. Computer protocols are international agreements on how to manufacture hardware and software, and how to send data from one computer to another.

As wireless connectivity finds its way into the home computer market, more and more people are becoming aware of its associated technical labels. The following is a list of common protocols.

- 802.11n is the current Wi-Fi standard. It has a maximum data rate of 150 Mbps and a range of about 70 meters indoors or 250 meters outdoors.

- 802.11g is an earlier Wi-Fi standard; many 802.11g devices are still in use today. It has a maximum data rate of 54 Mbps and a range of 38 meters indoors or 140 meters outdoors.

- 802.11b and 802.11a are now obsolete Wi-Fi standards, with a maximum data rate of 54 Mbps and 11 Mbps, respectively.

- **TCP/IP** (Transmission Control Protocol/Internet Protocol) defines the rules for sending and receiving data between network devices. Each device has a unique IP address, which is a series of four numbers between 0 and 255, separated by periods, like this: 192.168.0.1.

- **HTTP** (HyperText Transfer Protocol) defines the rules for sending and receiving web pages (hypertext) on the Internet. For example, you might see http://emcp/myschool.edu on the uniform resource locator (URL) or Address line of your Internet browser. Figure 8 shows how data travels across the Internet.

- **HTTPS** (HyperText Transfer Protocol Secure Sockets) encrypts data before sending it over the Web. You can see the letters *https* on the URL line when you reach a web page asking for your credit card number or when you are paying your bills online, such as https://emcp/mybank.com/myaccount.

- **POP3** is the current version of Post Office Protocol for receiving email. POP is a store-and-forward system in which your email waits on the mail server until you pick it up via an email application such as Outlook; then it forwards it to that application.

- **SMTP** (Simple Mail Transfer Protocol) enables you to send email. The message is transferred to the recipient's mail server on the Internet, where it waits for the user to pick it up via his or her email application.

- **FTP** (File Transfer Protocol) provides an efficient, fast way to transfer files between computers. It is commonly used for files that are too large for email attachments, and for large repositories of files.

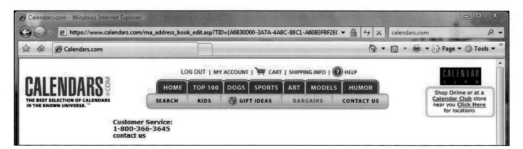

HTTPS is a protocol that protects your personal data. Note the padlock at the right of the address bar at the top of the screen.

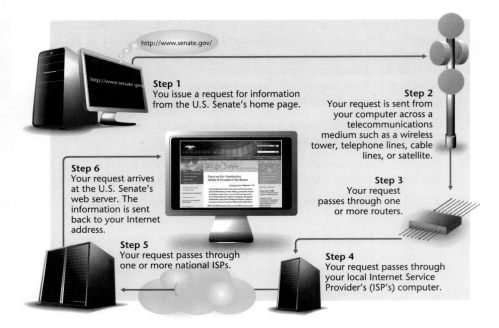

Step 1
You issue a request for information from the U.S. Senate's home page.

Step 2
Your request is sent from your computer across a telecommunications medium such as a wireless tower, telephone lines, cable lines, or satellite.

Step 6
Your request arrives at the U.S. Senate's web server. The information is sent back to your Internet address.

Step 3
Your request passes through one or more routers.

Step 5
Your request passes through one or more national ISPs.

Step 4
Your request passes through your local Internet Service Provider's (ISP's) computer.

FIGURE 8 The Infrastructure of the Internet
Data moves across the Internet by traveling through a collection of physical objects.

Connectors and Ports Wired network connections commonly use RJ-45 connectors. These are similar to telephone connectors (which are RJ-11 or RJ-14) but they use eight wires instead of the usual 2 or 4. An RJ-45 connector is slightly wider than its telephone counterpart.

EXPLORING TECHNOLOGY 5

If you have Windows 7 or Windows Vista, click the Start button, type *network*, and then click *Network* on the list that appears. A list of the computers and other devices in your LAN appears. Then open the Network and Sharing Center and explore the icons and links there to learn more about your network. What protocols are installed? What is your connection speed? *Hint: If you have a dial-up modem connection to the Internet, you may not see any references to a "network," but if you have a DSL or cable modem connection, you probably will—even if you have only one computer in your environment.*

EXPLORING TECHNOLOGY 6

Ask your instructor if your school has wireless connectivity. If yes, find out where wireless is active and then go to that area and see if you can locate the wireless access point(s) (antennas) that are installed. For example, if the school cafeteria has wireless connectivity, you may be able to see, mounted on the ceiling or walls, the hardware that provides the access to the Internet.

The Internet

The Internet is a global network of computers that allows data of all types and formats to be passed freely from one computer to another (see Figure 9). The Web, email, and FTP are different parts of the Internet.

World Wide Web

The World Wide Web is a collection of hypertext files, containing graphics, audio, and video that can be accessed on the Internet. The Web is only a part of the Internet, albeit a very large one.

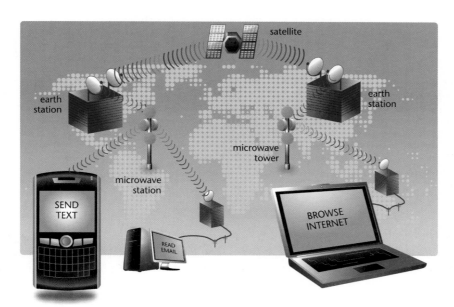

FIGURE 9 The Internet Network
Communications systems include computer hardware and communications software that allow computer users to exchange data around the house or around the world.

Electronic Mail

Electronic mail (email) uses its own protocols (such as SMTP and POP3) to route a message between computers on the Internet and hold it at a destination mail server until the recipient picks it up.

Many, but not all sites on the World Wide Web start with the three letters "www."

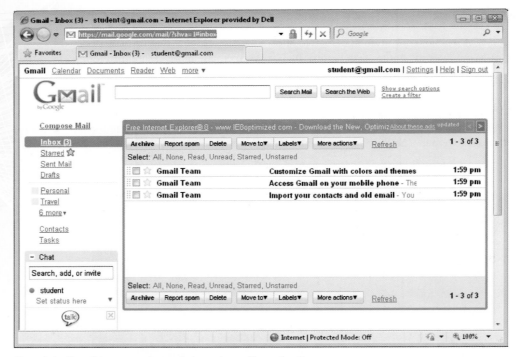

Google's Gmail is a popular web-based email application.

File Transfer Protocol

Like email and the Web, File Transfer Protocol (FTP) is an information workspace on the Internet. It is used for file transfer and was originally used for exchanging data between incompatible mainframe systems, such as those made by IBM and those made by UNIVAC.

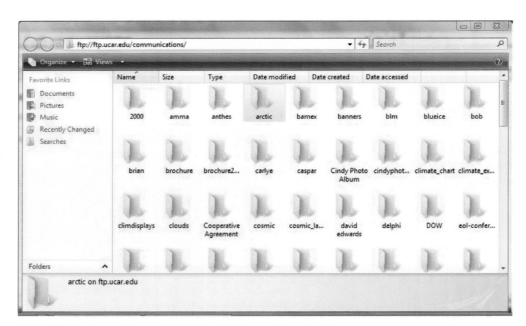

This FTP site shows files available for viewing or downloading.

Security Issues

Malware is a relatively new term describing computer programs that have a malicious intent. Viruses, worms, spyware, and adware programs, discussed in this section, all fall into this category.

Viruses

A computer virus is a string of code written by someone who wants to hurt others by damaging or destroying their computer files or making their computer experience difficult. Viruses are stored in executable (program) files; when the program runs, the virus code executes, causing damage and copying itself into the computer's memory, where it infects other programs (see Figure 10). A virus is typically spread via an email attachment. Some viruses send themselves out via automatically generated emails to everyone in your address book.

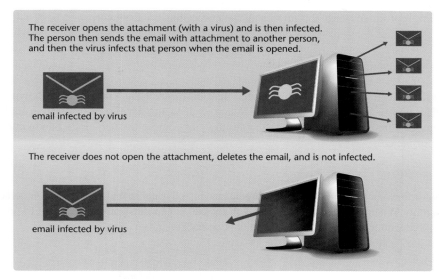

FIGURE 10 How a Virus Attacks
When you forward an email with an attachment such as a picture, you may be spreading a damaging virus.

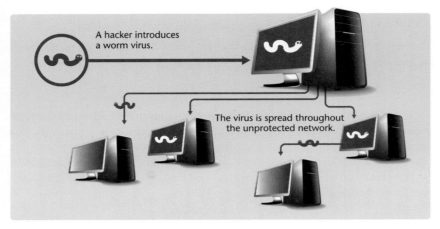

FIGURE 11 How a Worm Attacks
A worm reproduces itself and attacks all the computers on a network.

Worms

A worm is a self-replicating computer program that distributes itself via a network, as shown in Figure 11. Unlike a virus, it does not necessarily attach itself to another file. Worms are usually designed to damage a network, in many cases by simply clogging up the network's bandwidth and slowing its performance.

Trojan

Named after the infamous Trojan horse of the Greek legend, a Trojan is malware that masquerades as a useful program. When you run the program, you let the Trojan into your system (see Figure 12). Trojans open a "back door" to your system for malicious hackers.

Spyware

Spyware tracks your activity as you surf the Internet and reports it to companies that want to sell you their products—or steal your identity. Spyware takes advantage of cookies, the small files that websites put on your computer to remember who you are on your next visit.

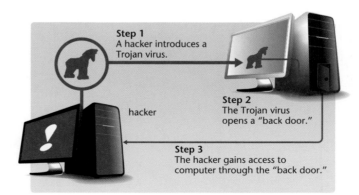

FIGURE 12 How a Trojan Attacks
A Trojan pretends to be a useful program but ends up opening your system to hackers.

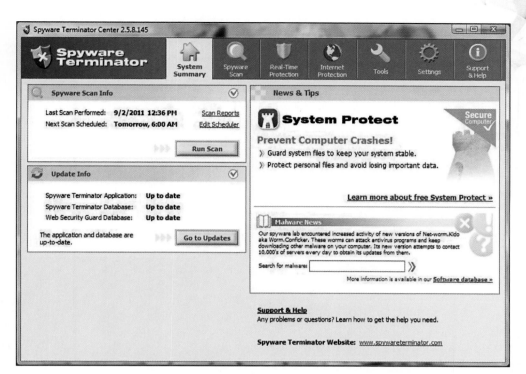

Products such as Spyware Terminator scan your computer for malware and help prevent it from downloading in the first place.

Adware

Adware looks at files on your computer and then sends pop-up advertisements that try to sell you products and services. Although annoying, adware is not usually destructive, but it can slow down your processor and your Internet access significantly.

Privacy Threats and Information Theft

Spyware programs can steal your personal information and tell it or sell it to other people who might be able to impersonate you and take money from your bank account or charge large purchases to your credit card.

   Phishing is a method of convincing people to reveal their passwords, credit card numbers, social security numbers, and other private or confidential information. Phishers pretend to be representatives of the victim's bank or a government agency by sending official-looking emails with obscure links back to websites that look exactly like the real website. The information they gather is then used in schemes involving identity theft that allow them to gain access to the victim's bank account, which they empty of its funds.

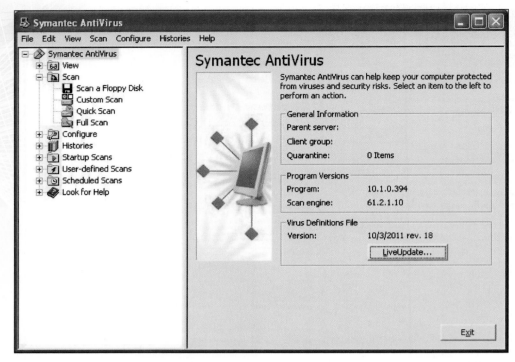

The installation of an antivirus software program such as Symantec AntiVirus is essential for computers connected to the Internet. Keeping these virus definitions up to date will significantly help in the fight against viruses.

Protection Software

Several computer programs are available to provide protection from virus attacks and from the installation of spyware or adware on your computer. Some examples are McAfee VirusScan and Symantec AntiVirus for viruses; and Spybot Search & Destroy, SpySweeper, AdAware, and Spyware Detector for spyware and adware. Windows 7 and Windows Vista include an anti-spyware program called Windows Defender.

To minimize infection, always update your computer with the latest security patches as they become available. Keep your protection software up to date by downloading the latest "signature" files of known viruses.

EXPLORING TECHNOLOGY

7

Explore the programs on your computer and identify what protection software is installed. Verify that the protection software is active while you are working and is up-to-date, and that a regular scan of all files takes place.

Email Etiquette and Computer Ethics

Two types of rules govern and guide behavior: etiquette and ethics. Etiquette refers to the rules that govern courteous behavior, such as holding the door open for someone, or saying "please" and "thank you." We often think of etiquette in terms of knowing which fork to use in a fancy restaurant, but etiquette also involves the rules for language appropriate in a businesslike environment. "Fighting words" are embarrassing to some people, and they can also lead to anger and violence. Showing proper etiquette is a way of showing a person respect. If you show disrespect to someone, that is not proper etiquette. When applied to computer communication, improper etiquette can result in serious misunderstandings or ill will among coworkers. It can even lead to the loss of a lucrative business contract or the loss of a job.

Ethics are the moral principles that govern behavior. In the news, we often see reports about corporate executives who have been charged or convicted of funneling company money into their own personal bank accounts. Politicians are accused of taking bribes from lobbyists in return for a favorable vote on a piece of legislation that will be profitable for the lobbyist's organization. Taxpayers claim tax deductions they are not entitled to. Students submit reports that were written by someone else. People offer to copy the latest music CD or software program they just purchased and give it to their friends. Where do you stand on these ethical issues?

Both etiquette and ethics have direct application to computers, especially in relation to email and copyright issues.

Email Etiquette

Everyone—friends, relatives, schoolmates, coworkers, employers, teachers, businesses, government officials, and sales and marketing departments—is sending email these days. Speedy communication with other people all over the world can be fun, exciting, and productive. However, it can also cause problems. What you

Ethics are the rules we use to determine what is right and wrong, and these rules help guide our choices and actions, both in our personal lives and in our business lives.

write in an email message can hurt someone's feelings, be misinterpreted, or might accidentally be sent to the wrong person. You can cause yourself embarrassment or even get yourself fired.

Here are ten rules of email etiquette. You might want to add a few of your own.

1. Be brief and to the point. Emails are supposed to be a fast way to communicate. Don't slow down the process.
2. Don't use ALL CAPITAL letters. It looks and feels like you're shouting or angry.
3. Remember to attach the attachment. Mentioning what you are "enclosing" in any type of letter is a good idea. Get in the habit of stopping as soon as you type the phrase "I am attaching…" and immediately clicking the Attach button.
4. Use the spelling check (even if you're a great speller). Using the spelling check feature only takes a few seconds and it shows that you care about quality. But watch out! It is very easy to click "Change" instead of "Ignore" and change a person's name to a common word and that, whether humorous or not, is an embarrassing mistake.
5. Reread what you wrote from the perspective of the receiver. Ask yourself how the recipient is likely to interpret your words. Did you leave out or misspell a word that completely changes the meaning?
6. Double-check the address in the *To* box. Confirm that you clicked the correct name in your address list. Once you click the Send button, there is *no* way to stop the message or undo an address mistake.
7. Watch your language. Profanity can come back to haunt you.
8. Assume your email will be read by *lots* of other people. Emails are often forwarded so others can take action or to inform a supervisor. Avoid cute or friendly asides and comments that you only want a close friend to see.
9. Always put something in the *Subject* line. A well-written subject will help the receiver decide where to file your message and whether to read it now or wait until later.
10. Privacy does not exist in emails, especially those in a corporate environment. The email administrator can potentially see the contents of any email. Company policy may allow checking emails to ensure that no company secrets are exposed, or to stop harassing or abusive email.

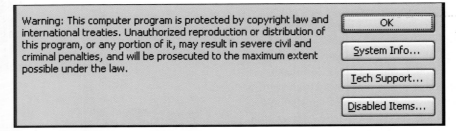

Software manufacturers usually obtain a copyright that prohibits the illegal copying and distribution of software. Warnings such as this one are designed to remind users of the copyright law.

Software Piracy and Copyright Infringement

When you install a software application, you must agree to accept the license agreement that describes the legal contract between the user (you) and the software developer. If you click the *No, I don't accept this agreement* box, the installation process will stop. By accepting the agreement, you agree with everything it says. The contract often covers the number of people who may use the program at the same time. That would usually be one person, but organizations can purchase agreements that cover a specific number of users.

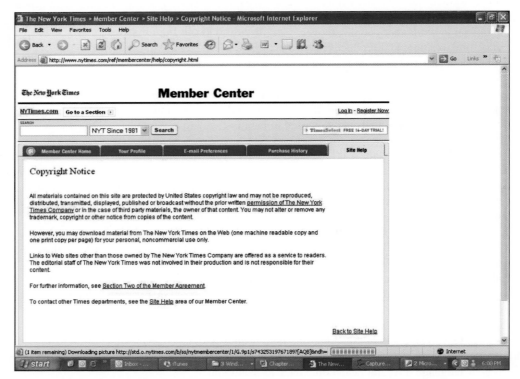

The copyright notice on *The New York Times* home page reminds visitors that the content of the site is copyrighted.

Most software is copyrighted. The exception is open source software mentioned earlier. Copyright laws in the United States and most (but not all) other countries state that authors, music composers, TV show and movie creators, artists, and publishers own the works they create and distribute; no one is allowed to use or copy their work without specific permission. Software license agreements might specify that you can make one backup copy, but you cannot give that copy to a friend. The same rules apply to all copyrighted material including music CDs, DVDs, and songs available on the Web. Infringing on a copyright is illegal, and this law is enforced.

Formerly known as the Software Publishers Association, the Software & Information Industry Association (SIIA, www.siia.net) encourages people who witness software piracy to inform them so that they can investigate the situation. Once they gather enough evidence, they will contact the organization's executives, ask them to prove they have enough licenses, and encourage them to purchase the software legally. In most cases the pressure works, but if necessary, the SIIA may take legal action.

Software piracy is a felony, but even if it was not, other compelling reasons exist for why you should not copy programs, music, or DVDs. It hurts the people who spend a lot of time and money creating products for your enjoyment. They do research. They buy computers, musical instruments, or video cameras. They pay money for studio time to record their songs, and then more money to advertise them and ship them to music stores. They may sell their creations to publishing companies who agree to pay them royalties based on sales. Will you send money to your favorite band every time you give a friend a copy of their latest CD? If graphic artists and musicians can't pay their expenses and cover the cost of making the songs, movies, computer games, and other software you enjoy, how can an individual artist, or even a large company, continue to create more?

Check to see who is the registered user of each of the applications on your computer by running it and watching for the name on the startup screen. If it isn't registered to your organization, your department, or yourself, ask a supervisor why not. Your action could actually help save your organization from costly litigation and potential fines.

EXPLORING
TECHNOLOGY
8

Navigate to www.siia.net and click the *Report Piracy* icon. Read about what you can do to help stop software piracy.

EXPLORING
TECHNOLOGY
9

Use your word processor to write the explanation you will use when you decline to give or receive a copy of a music CD, software program, DVD, or any other copyrighted material.

EXPLORING
TECHNOLOGY
10

Knowledge Check

Completion: On a separate piece of paper, indicate the correct term(s).

1. What are the four segments of the information processing cycle?
2. Besides the keyboard, mouse, and storage devices, list five devices that can be used to enter information into a computer.
3. What part of the computer handles the tasks of calculating formulas and editing documents?
4. What advantage do dual-core and quad-core processors have over single-core processors?
5. What is the technical name for the volatile computer workspace that is erased whenever the power is turned off?
6. Which storage device has no motor or other moving parts?
7. What type of port allows up to 127 hardware devices to be connected to the computer host at 480 Mbps?
8. What type of software can be copied freely and has no license agreement?
9. What is the basic purpose for a computer network?
10. What two terms describe the "data requester" and "data provider" in a LAN?
11. What is the name of the connector used on a network cable?
12. What is the basic protocol that allows all computers on the Internet to interact?
13. Which protocol and application can you use if you need to transfer a file that is too large to email?
14. List at least three types of malware.
15. What term describes the act of illegally sharing a software application with someone else?

GLOSSARY

For these and additional terms and definitions, go to this text's Internet Resource Center at www.emcp.net/Marquee10. A Spanish glossary is also available.

802.11 protocol a protocol for wireless LAN technology that specifies an over-the-air interface between the wireless client device and a server, or between two wireless devices, approved by the IEEE in 1997; also called Wi-Fi

802.11g protocol approved in June 2003, this protocol for wireless LAN technology operates in the same frequency range as 802.11b but with transfer rates similar to 802.11a

802.11n protocol this protocol for wireless LAN technology provides for speeds of up to 150 Mbps at a range of up to 250 meters (820 feet)

adware software that tracks the websites that a user visits in order to collect information for marketing or advertising

audio data relating to sound, including speech and music

bar code reader an electronic device that uses photo technology to read the lines in a bar code; the lines and spaces contain symbols that the computer translates into information

cathode ray tube (CRT) monitor a large, sealed glass tube housed in a plastic case; the most common type of monitor for desktop computers

central processing unit (CPU) the part of a computer that interprets and carries out instructions that operate the computer and manages the computer's devices and resources; consists of components, each of which performs specific functions; also called the microprocessor or processor

client a smaller computer, terminal, or workstation capable of sending data to and from a larger computer (host computer) in a network

client/server architecture a type of network architecture in which a personal computer, workstation, or terminal (called a client) is used to send information or a request to another computer (called a server) that then relays the information back to the user's client computer, or to another computer (another client)

collaboration software programs that enable people at separate PC workstations to collaborate on a single document or project, such as designing a new automobile engine; also called groupware

compact disc (CD) a plastic disc 4.75 inches in diameter and about 1/20th of an inch thick; uses laser technologies to store information and data

connectivity refers to the ability to link with other programs and devices

copyright the legal protection of an individual's or business's original work, such as applications software, music, and books, that prohibits others from duplicating or illegally using such work or products; an artist or author whose work is copyrighted has the right to charge others for its use

database a computer application in which data is organized and stored in a way that allows for specific data to be accessed, retrieved, and used

digital camera a type of camera that records and stores images, including people, scenery, documents, and products, in a digitized form that can be entered into and stored by a computer

digital versatile disc (DVD) an extremely high-capacity optical disc; also called a digital video disc (DVD)

digitizing the process of converting analog information to digital information; sometimes referred to as going digital

digitizing pen an electronic pen device, resembling a standard writing pen, used with a drawing tablet to simulate drawing on paper

drawing tablet a tablet with wires under the surface that, when used with a digitizing pen, allows the user to create and capture drawings that can be entered and stored on a computer

dual-core processor a central processing unit (CPU) chip that contains two complete processors along with their cache memory

electronic mail (email) a text, voice, or video message sent or received remotely, over a computer network or the system by which such a message is sent

ethics rules we use to determine the right and wrong things to do in our lives

etiquette rules governing courteous behavior

file allocation table (FAT) a filing system used on disks to keep track of the disk's content; there are two versions, 16-bit (FAT) and 32-bit (FAT32)

File Transfer Protocol (FTP) a transmission standard that enables a user to send and receive large files, such as reports, over the Internet

flash drive storage device with a USB connector

flash memory a type of read-only memory that can be erased and reprogrammed quickly, or updated; also called flash ROM

gigabyte unit of memory equal to 1,073,741,824 bytes

graphical user interface (GUI) a computer interface that enables a user to control the computer and launch commands by pointing and clicking at graphical objects such as windows, icons, and menu items

graphics computer-generated picture produced on a computer screen, paper, or film, ranging from a simple line or bar chart to a detailed, colorful image or picture; also called graphical image

graphics tablet a flat tablet used together with a pen-like stylus or a crosshair cursor; to capture an image, the user grasps a stylus or crosshair cursor and traces an image or drawing placed on the tablet surface

hard copy a permanent, tangible version of output, such as a letter printed on paper

hard drive a device for reading and writing to the magnetic storage medium known as a hard disk; consists of one or more rigid metal platters (disks) mounted on a metal shaft in a container that contains an access mechanism

Hypertext Transfer Protocol (HTTP) the communications standard used to transfer documents on the World Wide Web

information processing cycle a cycle during which a computer enters, processes, outputs, and/or stores information

ink-jet printer a nonimpact printer that forms images by spraying thousands of tiny droplets of electrically charged ink onto a page the printed images are in dot-matrix format, but of a higher quality than images printed by dot-matrix printers

input data that is entered into a computer or other device or the act of reading in such data

input device any hardware component that enables a computer user to enter data and programs into a computer system; keyboards, point-and-click devices, and scanners are among the more popular input devices, and a desktop or laptop computer system may include one or more input devices

Internet a worldwide network of computers linked together via communications software and media for the purpose of sharing information; the largest and best-known network in the world; also called the Net

Internet service provider (ISP) an organization that has a permanent connection to the Internet and provides temporary access to individuals and others for free or for a fee

joystick an input device (named after the control lever used to fly fighter planes) consisting of a small box that contains a vertical lever that, when pushed in a certain direction, moves the graphics cursor correspondingly on the screen; it is often used for computer games

keyboard an electronically controlled hardware component used to enter alphanumeric data (letters, numbers, and special characters); the keys on most keyboards are arranged similarly to those on a typewriter

laser printer a nonimpact printer that produces output of exceptional quality using a technology similar to that of photocopy machines

liquid crystal display (LCD) a display device in which liquid crystals are sandwiched between two sheets of material

local area network (LAN) a computer network physically confined to a relatively small geographical area, such as a single building or a college campus

malware malicious software

master file table (MFT) the internal table used on disks formatted with the NTFS file system to keep track of the disk's content; NTFS is used in Windows 2000 and higher

megabyte a unit of memory that stores approximately one million bytes

memory a chip-based data storage system in which each bit of data is represented by a binary on/off state, a series of 1s and 0s

monitor the screen, or display device, on which computer output appears

motherboard the main circuit board inside a personal computer to which other circuit boards can be connected; contains electrical pathways, called traces, etched onto it that allows data to move from one component to another

mouse an input device that, when moved about on a flat surface, causes a pointer on the screen to move in the same direction

multitasking the ability of an operating system to run more than one software program at a time; the use of different areas in Windows RAM makes this possible

network a group of two or more computers, software, and other devices that are connected by means of one or more communications media

New Technology File System (NTFS) the default disk file system for Windows 2000 and higher; offers improvements in storage and retrieval over the older FAT and FAT32 systems

nonvolatile storage that retains its data even when there is no power being supplied to it; a hard disk and a flash drive are both nonvolatile

open-source software program software whose programming code is owned by the original developer but made available free to the general public, who is encouraged to experiment with the software, make improvements, and share the improvements with the user community

operating system (OS) a type of software that creates a user interface and supports the workings of computer devices and software programs that perform specific jobs

output information that is written or displayed as a result of computer processing; also the act of writing or displaying such data

peer-to-peer architecture a network design in which each PC or workstation comprising the network has equivalent capabilities and responsibilities

personal digital assistant (PDA) a handheld, wireless computer, also known as a handheld PC or HPC, used for such purposes as storing schedules, calendars, and telephone numbers and for sending e-mail or connecting to the Internet

personal information manager (PIM) software that helps users organize contact information, appointments, tasks, and notes

phishing an activity characterized by attempts to fraudulently acquire another person's sensitive information, such as a credit card number

port a plug-in slot on a computer to which you can connect a device, such as a printer or, in the case of accessing the Internet, a telephone line; also called an interface

Post Office Protocol (POP) server a special type of server that holds e-mail messages until they are accessed and read by recipients of the messages

presentation graphics software an application program that allows one to create a computerized presentation of slides

printer the most common type of hard-copy output device that produces output in a permanent form

processing the manipulation of data by the computer's electrical circuits

processor the part of a computer that interprets and carries out instructions that operate the computer and manages the computer's devices

and resources; consists of components, each of which performs specific functions; also called the central processing unit (CPU)

protocol a set of rules and procedures for exchanging information between network devices and computers

quad-core processor a CPU that contains four complete processors in a single chip

random access memory (RAM) a computer chip or group of chips containing the temporary, or volatile, memory in which programs and data are stored while being used by a computer

read-only memory (ROM) a computer chip on the motherboard of a computer containing permanent, or nonvolatile, memory that stores instructions

router a hardware device that connects two or more networks

scanner a light-sensing electronic device that can read and capture printed text and images, such as photographs and drawings, and convert them into a digital form a computer can understand; once scanned, the text or image can be displayed on the screen, edited, printed, stored on a disk, inserted into another document, or sent as an attachment to an email message; also called an optical scanner

server a computer and its associated storage devices that users access remotely over a network

Simple Mail Transfer Protocol (SMTP) a communications protocol installed on the ISP's or online service's mail server that determines how each message is to be routed through the Internet and then sends the message

soft copy a temporary version of output, typically the display of data on a computer screen

software programs containing instructions that direct the operation of the computer system and the written documentation that explains how to use the programs; types include system software and application software

software piracy the act of copying or using a piece of software without the legal right to do so

software suite a combination of applications programs (usually integrated) bundled as a single package; may contain applications such as word processing, spreadsheet, database, and possibly other programs

spreadsheet software a productivity program that provides a user with a means of organizing, calculating, and presenting financial, statistical, and other numeric information; used to manipulate numbers electronically instead of using a pencil and paper

spyware software that tracks the activity of Internet users for the benefit of a third party

stylus a sharp, pointed instrument used for writing or marking

switch a small hardware device that joins multiple computers together within one local area network (LAN)

T1 line a high-speed telephone line that allows for both voice and data transmission and can carry data at a speed of 1.544 megabits per second

touch pad an input device that enables a user to enter data and make selections by moving a finger across the pad; also called a track pad

touch screen an input device that allows the user to choose options by pressing a finger (or fingers) on the appropriate part of the screen

Transmission Control Protocol/Internet Protocol (TCP/IP) protocol that governs how packets are constructed and sent over the Internet to their destination

Universal Product Code (UPC) a type of code printed on products and packages consisting of lines and spaces that a computer translates into a number; the computer then uses this number to find information about the product or package, such as its name and price, in a computerized database

Universal Serial Bus (USB) port a type of port that is widely used for connecting high-speed modems, scanners, and digital cameras to a computer; a single USB port can accommodate several peripheral devices connected together in sequence

video editing software software that allows users to edit sound and video and output it in various digital formats

virus a program that is designed to harm computer systems and/or any users, typically sent via email

volatile storage that loses its data when power is lost; the RAM on a motherboard is volatile, for example

webcam a digital video camera that captures real-time video for transmission to others via a web server or an instant messaging tool

wide area network (WAN) a network that spans a large geographical area

Windows a Microsoft-developed GUI operating system for personal computers.

word processing software a type of computer application that allows the user to create, edit, manipulate, format, store, and print a variety of documents, including letters, memos, announcements, and brochures

World Wide Web (www) a global system of linked computer networks that allows users to jump from one site to another by way of programmed links on web pages; also called the Web

worm a program that actively transmits copies of itself over the Internet, using up resources and causing other problems; also called a software worm

---

Photo Credits

Marquee Series

Microsoft® Windows 7

Nita Rutkosky

Pierce College at Puyallup, Puyallup, Washington

Denise Seguin

Fanshawe College, London, Ontario

Audrey Rutkosky Roggenkamp

Pierce College at Puyallup, Puyallup, Washington

Paradigm PUBLISHING

St. Paul • Los Angeles • Indianapolis

Contents

Managing Editor	Sonja Brown
Developmental Editor	Brenda Palo
Supplements Developmental Editor	Brenda Owens
Production Editor	Donna Mears
Cover and Text Designer	Leslie Anderson
Copy Editors	Susan Capecchi and Laura Nelson
Desktop Production	Ryan Hamner and Jack Ross
Proofreader	Laura Nelson
Testers	Amy McGuire, Rob Neilly, and Lindsay Ryan
Indexers	Ina Gravitz and Sandi Schroeder

Windows® 7 SECTION 1

Exploring Windows 7

Skills

- Navigate the Windows 7 desktop
- Perform the following actions using the mouse: point, click, double-click, and drag
- Start and close a program
- Open and close a window
- Shut down Windows 7
- Move a window
- Minimize, maximize, and restore a window
- Stack and cascade windows
- Use the snap feature to position windows on the desktop
- Change the date and time
- Use components of a dialog box
- Adjust the volume using the Speaker's slider bar
- Customize the Taskbar
- Add a gadget to the desktop
- Use the Help and Support feature
- Turn on the display of file extensions

Projects Overview

Your department at Worldwide Enterprises has received new computers with the Windows 7 operating system. You will explore the Windows 7 desktop; open, close, and manipulate windows; open a program; customize the Taskbar; add gadgets to the desktop; explore the online help for Windows 7; and turn on the display of file extensions.

Activity 1.1

Exploring the Windows 7 Desktop

The screen that displays when Windows 7 starts is called the *desktop*. This desktop can be compared to the top of a desk in an office. A person places necessary tools—such as pencils, pens, paper, files, calculator—on his or her desktop to perform functions. Similarly, the Windows 7 desktop contains tools for operating the computer. These tools are logically grouped and placed in dialog boxes or windows that can be accessed using the icons located on the desktop.

Project

Tutorial 1.1
Exploring the
Windows 7 Desktop

At your department, new computers have been installed with the Windows 7 operating system. You decide to take some time to explore the desktop to familiarize yourself with this new operating system.

1 Complete the step(s) needed to display the Windows 7 desktop.

Check with your instructor to determine the specific step(s) required to display Windows 7 on your computer at your school. You may need a user name and password to log on to the computer system. When Windows 7 is started, you will see a desktop similar to the one shown in Figure 1.1. Your desktop may contain additional icons or have a different background than the desktop shown in Figure 1.1.

2 Move the mouse on the desk and notice how the corresponding pointer moves in the Windows desktop.

The *mouse* is a device that controls the pointer that identifies your location on the screen. Move the mouse on the desk (preferably on a mouse pad) and the pointer moves on the screen. For information on mouse terms, refer to Table 1.1 and for information on mouse icons, refer to Table 1.2.

FIGURE 1.1 Windows 7 Desktop

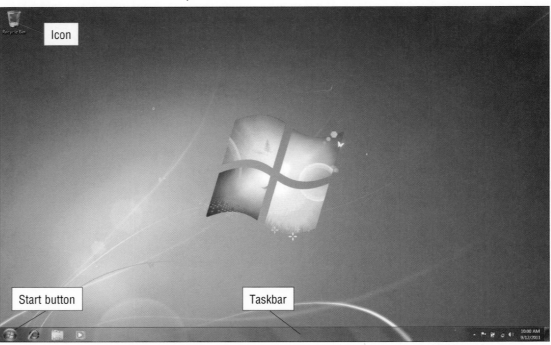

TABLE 1.1 Mouse Terms and Actions

Term	Action
point	Position the mouse pointer on the desired item.
click	Quickly tap a button, usually the left button, on the mouse once.
double-click	Tap the left mouse button twice in quick succession.
drag	Press and hold down the left mouse button, move the mouse pointer to a specific location, and then release the mouse button.

TABLE 1.2 Mouse Icons

Icon	Description
I	The mouse appears as an I-beam pointer in a program screen where you enter text (such as Microsoft Word) and also in text boxes. You can use the I-beam pointer to move the insertion point or select text.
⬉	The mouse pointer appears as an arrow pointing up and to the left (called the arrow pointer) on the Windows desktop and also in other program Title bars, Menu bars, and toolbars.
⬂⬈ ↕↔	The mouse pointer becomes a double-headed arrow (either pointing left and right, up and down, or diagonally) when performing certain functions such as changing the size of a window.
✥	Select an object in a program such as a picture or image and the mouse pointer becomes a four-headed arrow. Use this four-headed arrow pointer to move the object left, right, up, or down.
⬉	When you position the mouse pointer inside selected text in a document (such as a Microsoft Word document) and then drag the selected text to a new location in the document, the pointer displays with a gray box attached, indicating that you are moving the text.
⬉○	When a request is being processed or a program is being loaded, the mouse pointer may display with a moving circle icon beside it. The moving circle means "please wait." When the process is completed, the moving circle disappears.
☝	When you position the mouse pointer on certain icons or hyperlinks, it turns into a hand with a pointing index finger. This image indicates that clicking the icon or hyperlink will display additional information.

3 Move the mouse pointer to the bottom right of the desktop where the current day and time displays at the far right side of the Taskbar. After approximately one second, a pop-up box appears with the current day of the week as well as the current date.

To identify the location of the Taskbar, refer to Figure 1.1.

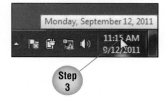

continues

4 Position the mouse pointer on the Start button  on the Taskbar and then click the left mouse button.

> Clicking the Start button causes the Start menu to display. The Start menu contains a list of software programs and other options available on your computer. The menu is divided into two columns. Links to programs display in the left column and links to folders, the Control Panel, Devices and Printers, Default Programs, and Help and Support display in the right column. The bottom of the right column Start menu contains options for shutting down, restarting, or logging off the computer.

5 At the Start menu, point to *All Programs* and then click *Accessories* in the left column.

> To point to a menu option, simply position the mouse pointer on the option. Do not click a mouse button. Pointing to *All Programs* causes the left Start column to be replaced with a list of available programs. If the list does not immediately appear, click the mouse button. You may need to scroll down the list if the list is long to locate all available programs. Some programs in the list, such as *Accessories*, display with a folder icon. Clicking a program name with a folder icon expands the list to reveal the individual applications associated with the program.

6 Move the mouse pointer to *Calculator* in the expanded menu and then click the left mouse button.

> Clicking *Calculator* causes the Calculator tool to open and display on the desktop.

7 Close the Calculator by clicking the Close button ▭ that displays at the upper right corner of the program.

Step 7

8 At the Windows 7 desktop, position the mouse pointer on the *Recycle Bin* icon and then double-click the left mouse button.

> Icons provide an easy method for opening programs or documents. Double-clicking the *Recycle Bin* icon displays the Recycle Bin window. When you open a program, a defined work area, referred to as a **window**, appears on the screen.

Recycle Bin

Step 8

9 Close the Recycle Bin window by clicking the Close button that displays at the upper right corner of the window.

10 Shut down Windows 7 by clicking the Start button and then clicking the Shut down button located at the bottom of the right column.

Options available from the right-pointing arrow next to the Shut down button include: switch to a different user account; log off or lock the computer; shut down and then immediately restart Windows (Restart); and place the computer in sleep mode or hibernate mode. Wait for Windows to power off the computer automatically. Important data is stored in memory while Windows is running and this data needs to be written to the hard disk before turning off the computer. In some cases, updates that have been downloaded automatically to your computer are installed during a shut down.

In Brief

Start Program
1. Click Start button.
2. Point to *All Programs*.
3. Click desired program.

Shut Down Windows
1. Click Start button.
2. Click Shut down.

Need Help?

Check with your instructor before shutting down Windows 7. If you are working in a computer lab at your school, a shared computer lab policy may prevent you from shutting down the computer. In this case, proceed to the next activity.

In Addition

Putting the Computer to Sleep

In Windows 7, Sleep mode saves all of your work and places the computer in a low power state by turning off the monitor and hard disk. A light on the outside of the computer case blinks or turns color to indicate Sleep mode is active. Reactivate the computer by pressing the Power button on the front of the computer case, or by moving the mouse. After logging on, the screen will display exactly as you left it when you activated Sleep mode. Sleep mode causes Windows to automatically save your work whereas shutting down does not save. Hibernate is an option designed primarily for laptops and is the lowest power setting. Hibernate saves open documents and programs to the hard disk and then turns off the computer.

Activity 1.2

Opening and Manipulating Windows

When you open a program, a defined work area, referred to as a *window*, appears on the screen. You can move a window on the desktop and change the size of a window. The top of a window is called the Title bar and generally contains buttons at the right side for closing the window and minimizing, maximizing, or restoring the size of the window. More than one window can be open at a time and open windows can be cascaded or stacked. The Snap feature in Windows 7 causes a window to "stick" to the edge of the screen when the window is moved to the left or right. When the window is moved to the top of the screen, the window is automatically maximized and when a maximized window is dragged down, the window is automatically restored down.

Project You will continue your exploration of the Windows 7 desktop by opening and manipulating windows.

Worldwide Enterprises

SNAP

Tutorial 1.2
Opening and Using Windows

① If necessary, turn on the power to your computer to start Windows. At the Windows 7 desktop, double-click the *Recycle Bin* icon.

Step 1

This opens the Recycle Bin window on the desktop. If the Recycle Bin window fills the entire desktop, click the Restore Down button 🗗, which is the second button from the right (immediately left of the Close button) located at the upper right corner of the window.

② Move the window on the desktop. To do this, position the mouse pointer on the window Title bar (the bar along the top of the window), hold down the left mouse button, drag the window to a different location on the desktop, and then release the mouse button.

③ Click the Start button on the Taskbar and then click *Computer* in the right column at the Start menu.

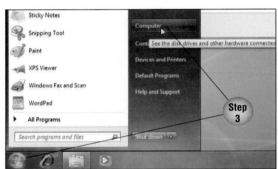
Step 3

If the Computer window fills the entire desktop, click the Restore Down button, which is the second button from the right (immediately left of the Close button) located at the upper right corner of the window. You now have two windows open on the desktop—Computer and Recycle Bin.

④ Make sure the Title bar of the Recycle Bin window is visible (if not, move the Computer window) and then click the Recycle Bin Title bar.

Clicking the Recycle Bin Title bar makes the Recycle Bin window active, moving it in front of the Computer window.

⑤ Minimize the Recycle Bin window to the Taskbar by clicking the Minimize button ▭ (located toward the right side of the Recycle Bin Title bar).

Step 5

The minimized Recycle Bin window is positioned below the Windows Explorer button (displays as a group of file folders) on the Taskbar. Notice the Windows Explorer button now appears with a button stacked below it.

⑥ Minimize the Computer window to the Taskbar below the Windows Explorer button by clicking the Minimize button located at the right side of the Title bar.

⑦ Move the pointer over the Windows Explorer button (displays as a group of file folders) located near the left side of the Taskbar.

The two minimized windows are stacked below the Windows Explorer button. Resting the pointer on the Windows Explorer button causes a Thumbnail Preview of each window to display.

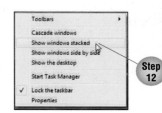

Step 7

Step 8

(8) Click the Thumbnail Preview for the Computer window to redisplay the window on the desktop.

(9) Rest the pointer over the Windows Explorer button on the Taskbar and then click the Thumbnail Preview for the Recycle Bin window.

(10) Drag the Title bar for the Recycle Bin window to the top of the desktop until the window fills the entire screen and then release the mouse button.

> Dragging a window to the top of the desktop causes the window to automatically maximize. You may need to drag the window up toward the top of the screen for a few seconds until the shape of the window automatically expands to fill the entire desktop area. The Snap feature allows you to resize a window by dragging the window to the edge of a screen. You can also Maximize the window by clicking the Maximize button (displays as a square) adjacent to the Close button at the right end of the Title bar.

(11) Drag the Title bar for the Recycle Bin window down from the top of the desktop to restore the window to its previous size before the window was maximized.

(12) Right-click on a blank, unused section of the Taskbar and then click *Show windows stacked* at the shortcut menu.

Step 12

> The Taskbar shortcut menu provides three options to display windows: *Cascade windows,* which places each window in a fanned, single stack with the title bars of each open window visible; *stacked,* which places windows in a horizontal stack with a portion of each window visible; or *side by side,* which places open windows next to each other.

(13) Right-click on a blank, unused section of the Taskbar and then click *Cascade windows* at the shortcut menu.

(14) Drag the Recycle Bin window off the right edge of the screen until the window resizes to fill one-half the width of the screen and then release the mouse button.

(15) Drag the Computer window off the left edge of the screen until the window resizes to fill the remaining width of the screen and then release the mouse button.

> The two windows are placed side-by-side. The Snap feature automatically resizes each window to fill one-half the screen.

(16) Close each of the two windows by clicking the Close button (contains a white X) located at the right side of the Title bar.

In Brief

Move Window
1. Position mouse pointer on window Title bar.
2. Hold down left mouse button.
3. Drag window to desired position.
4. Release mouse button.

Stack Windows
1. Right-click an unused section of Taskbar.
2. Click *Show windows stacked* at shortcut menu.

Cascade Windows
1. Right-click an unused section of Taskbar.
2. Click *Cascade windows* at shortcut menu.

In Addition

Sizing a Window

Using the mouse, you can increase or decrease the size of a window. To change the width, position the mouse pointer on the border at the right or left side of the window until it turns into a left- and right-pointing arrow. Hold down the left mouse button, drag the border to the right or left, and then release the mouse button. Complete similar steps to increase or decrease the height of the window using the top or bottom border. To change the width and height of the window at the same time, position the mouse pointer at the left or right corner of the window until the pointer turns into a diagonally pointing double-headed arrow and then drag in the desired direction to change the size.

Activity 1.3

Exploring the Taskbar, Gadgets, and Dialog Box Components

The bar that displays at the bottom of the desktop is called the **Taskbar** and it is divided into three sections: the Start button, the task button area, and the notification area. Click the Start button to start a program, use the Help and Support feature, change settings, open files, or shut down the computer. Open programs display as task buttons in the task button area of the Taskbar. You can right-click a blank, unused portion of the Taskbar to display a shortcut menu with options for customizing the Taskbar. The notification area displays at the right side of the Taskbar and contains a clock and the program icons for programs that run in the background on your computer. Gadgets are mini programs you can add to the desktop that provide information at a glance. Display a gadget for information that you frequently use such as a weather update for your area.

Project

As you continue exploring Windows 7, you want to learn more about the features available on the Taskbar and you also decide to experiment with adding a gadget to the desktop.

Tutorial 1.3
Exploring the Taskbar

1 At the Windows 7 desktop, click the current time that displays at the far right side of the Taskbar and then click *Change date and time settings*.

> Figure 1.2 identifies the components of the Taskbar. Clicking *Change date and time settings* causes the Date and Time dialog box to display. Please refer to Table 1.3 for information on dialog box components.

2 Check to make sure the correct date and time display in the Date and Time dialog box.

> If the date is incorrect, click the Change date and time button. At the Date and Time Settings dialog box, click the correct day in the calendar box. If necessary, use the left- or right-pointing arrows to change the calendar display to a different month. To change the time, double-click the hour, minutes, or seconds and then type the correct entry or use the up- and down-pointing arrows to adjust the time. Click OK when finished.

3 Click the Additional Clocks tab located toward the top of the Date and Time dialog box.

> At this tab you can add the ability to show the current time for a second clock when you hover or click the mouse over the current time in the Taskbar. For example, you could show the time for Cairo, Egypt in addition to the current time for your time zone.

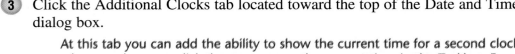

FIGURE 1.2 Taskbar

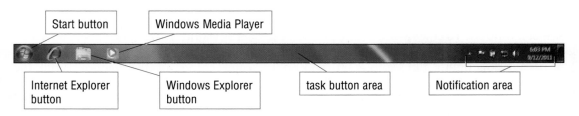

Start button

Windows Media Player

Internet Explorer button

Windows Explorer button

task button area

Notification area

TABLE 1.3 Dialog Box Components (Each component will not be present in every dialog box.)

Name	Image	Function
tabs	Date and Time | Additional Clocks | Internet Time	Click a dialog box tab and the dialog box options change.
text box	6:14:37 PM	Type or edit text in a text box. A text box may contain up- or down-pointing arrows to allow you to choose a number or an option instead of typing it in.
drop-down list box	M/d/yyyy, M/d/yy, MM/dd/yy, MM/dd/yyyy, yy/MM/dd, yyyy-MM-dd, dd-MMM-yy	Click the down-pointing arrow at the right side of a drop-down list box and a list of choices displays.
list box	Normal Select, Help Select, Working In Background, Busy, Precision Select	A list box displays a list of options.
check boxes	Desktop icons — Computer, User's Files, Network, ✓ Recycle Bin, Control Panel	If a check box contains a check mark, the option is active; if the check box is empty, the option is inactive. In some cases, any number of check boxes can be active.
option buttons	Smaller - 100% (default), Medium - 125%, Larger - 150%	Only one option button in a dialog box section can be selected at any time. An active option button contains a dark or colored circle.
command buttons	OK Cancel Apply	Click a command button to execute or cancel a command. If a command button name is followed by an ellipsis (. . .), clicking the button will open another dialog box.
slider	Select a pointer speed: Slow —— Fast	Using the mouse, drag a slider to increase or decrease the number, speed, or percentage of the option.
scroll bar	Time zone: (UTC-05:00) Eastern Time (US & Canada)	A scroll bar displays when the amount of information in a window is larger than can fit in a single window.

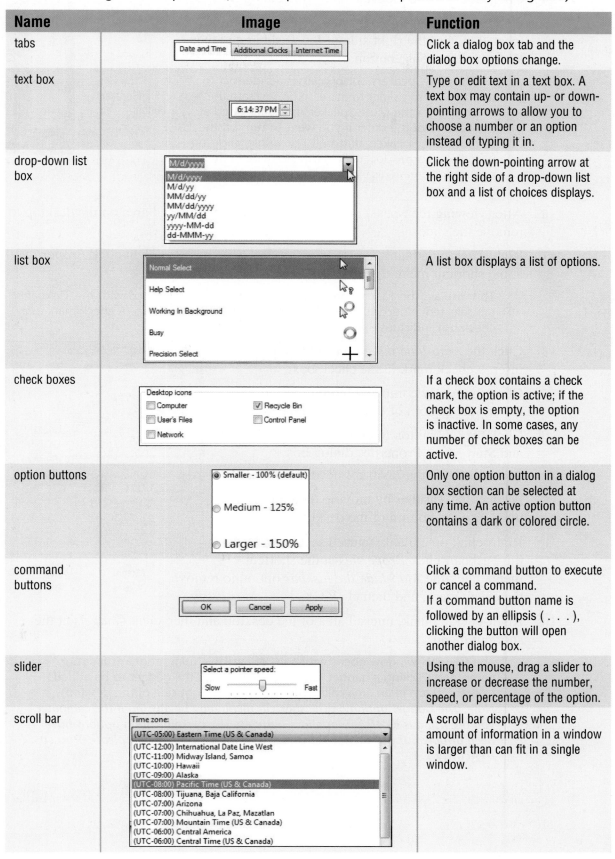

continues

④ Click OK to close the Date and Time dialog box.

⑤ Position the mouse pointer on the Speakers button 🔊 located toward the right side of the Taskbar and then click the left mouse button.

> Clicking the Speakers button causes a slider bar to display. Use this slider to increase or decrease the volume. Click the Mute Speakers button located at the bottom of the slider if you want to turn off the sound. If the Speakers button is not visible, click the up-pointing arrow located near the left side of the notification area. This expands the area to show hidden icons.

⑥ After viewing the Speakers slider, click in a blank, unused area on the desktop to remove the slider.

⑦ Right-click on a blank, unused section of the Taskbar and then click *Properties* at the shortcut menu that displays.

> This displays the Taskbar and Start Menu Properties dialog box with the Taskbar tab selected. Notice that the dialog box contains check boxes. A check mark in a check box indicates that the option is active.

⑧ Click the *Auto-hide the taskbar* option to insert a check mark in the check box.

⑨ Click the Apply command button located toward the bottom of the dialog box.

⑩ Click the OK button to close the Taskbar and Start Menu Properties dialog box.

> Notice that the Taskbar is no longer visible.

⑪ Display the Taskbar by moving the mouse pointer to the bottom of the desktop.

⑫ Right-click on a blank, unused section of the Taskbar, click *Properties* at the shortcut menu, click the *Auto-hide the taskbar* option to remove the check mark, and then click OK.

⑬ Right-click a blank, unused area of the desktop and then click *Gadgets* at the shortcut menu.

> The Gadgets window opens with a list of available mini programs for your computer. Clicking a gadget in the window causes the gadget to be added to the desktop in an area called the *Sidebar* (the right side of the desktop). *Note: The Gadget option on the shortcut menu may be missing if the computer you are using is located in a school setting where customization options have been disabled. If you do not see **Gadget** on the shortcut menu, please proceed to Activity 1.4.*

14 Double-click the *Calendar* gadget.

> The Calendar program is added to the desktop with the current date displayed. By default, gadgets snap to the edge of the screen.

Step 15

Step 14

In Brief

Display Date and Time Properties Dialog Box
Click current time at right side of Taskbar and click *Change date and time settings*.

Display Speakers Slider
Click Speakers button on Taskbar.

Display Taskbar and Start Menu Properties Dialog Box
1. Right-click an unused section on Taskbar.
2. Click *Properties* at shortcut menu.

15 Click the Close button in the Gadget window.

16 Move the mouse pointer over the Calendar gadget to view the gadget customization buttons.

> Customization options are dependent on the gadget program and some gadgets may not have any customization options.

17 Click the Larger size button (displays as an upward-pointing diagonal arrow) next to the Calendar gadget.

> The Calendar expands to show the month above the current date.

Step 17

In Addition

Using Gadgets While You Work

Additional gadgets are available from the Microsoft website. Click the link to Get more gadgets online in the Gadgets window to view a list of available gadgets that can be downloaded to your computer from the Windows website. For example, consider the following gadgets that can help you be productive at work:

- Add a gadget to show your upcoming appointments from Outlook.

- Add a traffic gadget to provide you with real time traffic conditions.

- Add a clock and customize the clock to display the current time for a different time zone if you regularly communicate with someone on the other side of the country or world.

Activity 1.4

Getting Help in Windows; Displaying File Extensions

Windows 7 includes an on-screen reference guide, called Windows Help and Support, that provides information, explanations, and interactive help on learning Windows features. The Windows Help and Support feature contains complex files with hypertext used to access additional information by clicking a word or phrase. Display the Windows Help and Support window by clicking the Start button on the Taskbar and then clicking *Help and Support* at the Start menu. At the Windows Help and Support window, you can perform such actions as choosing a specific help topic, searching for a keyword or topic, and displaying a Contents list of help topics.

Project

Tutorial 1.4
Getting Help

You decide to use the Windows Help and Support feature to learn how to customize the mouse. You will also turn on the display of file extensions to prepare for the next section with file management projects.

1. Display the Windows Help and Support window by clicking the Start button and then clicking *Help and Support*.

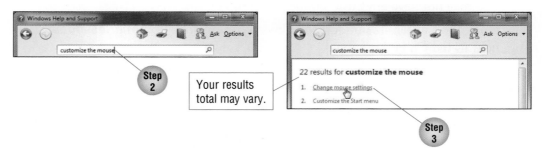

2. At the Windows Help and Support window with the insertion point positioned in the Search Help text box, type **customize the mouse** and press Enter.

3. Click the <u>Change mouse settings</u> hyperlink in the search results list.

4. Read the paragraph below the title *Change mouse settings* describing the options for customizing the mouse.

5. Click the <u>Go to the Windows website to watch the video (1:56)</u> hyperlink.

> You will need headphones to listen to the audio if you are watching this video in a computer lab that does not have speakers. If necessary, skip to Step 7 if you do not have headphones or cannot hear audio on the computer you are using.

6. At the Change mouse settings Windows web page, click the Play button positioned on the video player screen and watch the video.

7. Return to the Change mouse settings Windows Help and Support window by closing the Internet Explorer window when the video is completed.

8 Click the <u>To change how the mouse pointer looks</u> hyperlink.

> The Help topic is expanded below the hyperlink to show the steps for changing the pointer appearance.

9 Read the steps and then click the <u>To change how the mouse pointer looks</u> hyperlink a second time to hide the content.

10 Close the Windows Help and Support window by clicking the Close button located in the upper right corner of the window.

> Worldwide Enterprises requires that employees work with the display of file extensions turned on. This practice helps employees identify source applications associated with a file and often prevents an employee from accidentally opening a file attachment in an email that is likely to contain harmful data.

11 Click the Start button on the Taskbar and then click *Computer* at the Start menu.

12 Click the Organize button in the toolbar and then click *Folder and search options* at the drop-down list.

13 Click the View tab at the Folder Options dialog box.

14 Click the *Hide extensions for known file types* check box in the *Advanced settings* list box to clear the check mark and then click OK. ***Note: If the check box appears with no check mark in it, then file extensions are already turned on—click the Cancel button.***

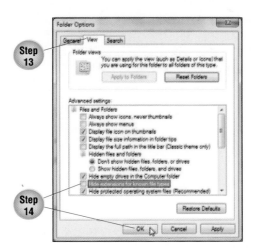

15 Close the Computer window by clicking the Close button located at the right side of the Title bar.

In Addition

Browsing Help by Topic Lists

You can locate Help information by browsing the Contents list of topics instead of typing key words in the *Search Help* text box. Click the Browse Help button (located next to the Print button) in the Windows Help and Support window toolbar. This displays the Contents list of Help topics. Click the hyperlink to a topic category in the Contents list and then continue clicking hyperlinks until you find the information you need.

Features Summary

Feature	Button	Action
close window	X	Click Close button on Title bar.
Computer window		Click Start button, click *Computer*.
Date and Time dialog box		Click time on Taskbar, click *Change date and time settings*.
Gadgets		Right-click unused area on desktop, click *Gadgets*.
maximize window	▢	Drag window to top of screen or click Maximize button on Title bar.
minimize window	▬	Click Minimize button on Title bar.
move window on desktop		Drag window Title bar.
restore window	▣	Drag maximized window down or click Restore Down button on Title bar.
shut down computer		Click Start button, click *Shut Down*.
Start menu	🪟	Click Start button on Taskbar.
Taskbar and Start Menu Properties dialog box		Right-click unused location on Taskbar, click *Properties* at shortcut menu.
Taskbar shortcut menu		Right-click unused location on Taskbar.
Speakers slider	🔊	Click Speakers button on Taskbar.
Windows Help and Support window		Click Start button, click *Help and Support*.

Knowledge Check

Completion: In the space provided at the right, indicate the correct term, command, or option.

1. This mouse term refers to tapping the left mouse button twice in quick succession. _____
2. Click this button on a window Title bar to reduce the window to a task button on the Taskbar. _____
3. Click this button on a window Title bar to expand the window so it fills the entire screen. _____
4. Click the time located at the right side of the Taskbar and then click this option to open the Date and Time dialog box. _____
5. This is the name of a mini program that you can display on the desktop for information at a glance, such as a calendar. _____
6. Windows Help and Support is accessed from this button on the Taskbar. _____

Skills Review

Review 1 Opening and Manipulating Windows

1. At the Windows 7 desktop, click the Start button on the Taskbar and then click *Documents*. (If the Documents window fills the desktop, drag the window down from the top of the screen or click the Restore Down button located in the upper right corner of the window.)
2. Click the Start button on the Taskbar and then click *Computer*. (If the Computer window fills the desktop, drag the window down from the top of the screen or click the Restore Down button.)
3. Position the mouse pointer on the Computer Title bar, hold down the left mouse button, and then drag the Computer window so the Documents Title bar is visible.
4. Click the Documents Title bar to make it the active window.
5. Right-click on a blank, unused section on the Taskbar and then click *Cascade windows* at the shortcut menu.
6. Click the Minimize button (located toward the right side of the Title bar) on the Documents Title bar to reduce the window to a task button below the Windows Explorer button on the Taskbar.
7. Click the Minimize button on the Computer window to reduce the window to a task button on the Windows Explorer button on the Taskbar.
8. Point to the Windows Explorer button on the Taskbar and then click the Thumbnail preview for the Computer window to restore the Computer window on the desktop.
9. Point to the Windows Explorer button on the Taskbar and then click the Thumbnail preview for the Documents window to restore the Documents window on the desktop.
10. Drag the Documents window to the top of the screen until the window expands to fill the entire screen and then release the mouse button.

11. Drag the Documents window down from the top of the screen to restore the window to its previous size and then release the mouse button.
12. Drag the Documents window off the right edge of the screen until the window snaps to the right edge and fills approximately one-half the width of the screen and then release the mouse button.
13. Drag the Computer window off the left edge of the screen until the window snaps to the left edge and fills the remaining width of the screen and then release the mouse button.
14. Close the Documents window.
15. Close the Computer window.

Review 2 Exploring the Taskbar and Gadgets

1. At the Windows 7 desktop, click the time that displays in the notification area at the right side of the Taskbar and then click *Change date and time settings*.
2. At the Date and Time dialog box, click the Change date and time button. Click the right arrow in the calendar to display the next month (from the current month).
3. Click the OK button twice.
4. Click the Start button, point to *All Programs*, click *Accessories*, and then click *Notepad*. Notepad is a program used for creating and editing text files.
5. Close Notepad by clicking the Close button located at the right side of the Notepad Title bar.
6. Right-click a blank, unused section of the desktop, and click *Gadgets*. Double-click the clock gadget to add a clock to the desktop and then close the Gadgets window.
   Note: If you do not see **Gadgets** *on the shortcut menu, then customization options have been disabled on the computer you are using. You will not be able to add a gadget to the desktop.*

Skills Assessment

Assessment 1 Manipulating Windows

1. Click the Start button and then click *Pictures*. (If the Pictures window fills the entire desktop, drag the window down from the top of the screen or click the Restore Down button.)
2. Click the Start button and then click *Music*. (If the Music window fills the entire desktop, drag the window down from the top of the screen or click the Restore Down button.)
3. Stack the two windows.
4. Make the Pictures window the active window and then reduce it to a task button on the Taskbar.
5. Reduce the Music window to a task button on the Taskbar.
6. Restore the Pictures window.
7. Restore the Music window.
8. Arrange the two windows side-by-side on the desktop with each window filling one-half the width of the screen.
9. Close the Music window and then close the Pictures window.

Assessment 2 **Customizing the Taskbar and Adding a Gadget**

1. At the Windows 7 desktop, display the Date and Time dialog box.
2. Change the current hour one hour ahead and then close the dialog box.
3. Display the Speakers slider bar, drag the slider to increase the volume, and then click the desktop outside the slider to close it.
4. Display the Taskbar and Start Menu Properties dialog box, change the Taskbar location on screen to *Top*, and then close the dialog box. (Notice that the Taskbar is now positioned along the top edge of the screen.)
5. Open the Gadgets window and add a gadget of your choosing to the desktop. *Note: Skip Steps 5–6 if* **Gadgets** *are not available on the computer you are using.*
6. Customize the gadget by dragging the *gadget* icon to another location on the desktop. If necessary, change other gadget options depending on the gadget you added. For example, if you added the Weather gadget, change the weather update to display the weather for your geographic location.

Assessment 3 **Restoring the Taskbar and Removing a Gadget**

1. At the Windows 7 desktop, display the Date and Time dialog box and change the date and time to today's date and the current time.
2. Display the Speakers slider bar and then drag the slider to the original position that the volume was at before you increased the volume in Assessment 2.
3. Display the Taskbar and Start Menu Properties dialog box and change the Taskbar location back to *Bottom*.
4. Remove the gadgets that you have added to the desktop in this section by right-clicking each gadget and then clicking *Close gadget*, or by moving the mouse over the gadget and then clicking the Close button that appears at the top right of the gadget.

Windows 7 SECTION 2

Maintaining Files and Customizing Windows

Skills

- Browse the contents of storage devices
- Change folder and view options
- Create a folder
- Rename a folder or file
- Select, move, copy, and paste folders or files
- Delete files/folders to and restore files/folders from the Recycle Bin
- Explore the Control Panel
- Use Search tools to find programs, folders and/or files
- Customize the desktop
- Change screen resolution

Student Resources

Before beginning the activities in Windows Section 2, copy to your storage medium the Windows folder on the Student Resources CD. This folder contains the data files you need to complete the projects in Windows Section 2.

Projects Overview

You will explore options for browsing and viewing folders and files and then organize folders and files for your department at Worldwide Enterprises. This organization includes creating and renaming folders and moving, copying, renaming, deleting, and restoring files. You will also search for specific files and customize your desktop to the corporate computer standard.

Organize files for Performance Threads including creating folders and copying, moving, renaming, and deleting files.

Organize files for First Choice Travel including creating folders and copying, moving, renaming, and deleting files. Assist your supervisor by searching for information on setting up a computer for multiple users and how to work with libraries.

19

Activity 2.1

Browsing Storage Devices and Files in a Computer Window

Open a Computer window to view the various storage devices connected to your computer. The Content pane of the Computer window displays an icon for each hard disk drive and each removable storage medium such as a CD, DVD, or USB device. Next to each storage device icon, Windows provides the amount of storage space available as well as a bar with the amount of space used up shaded with color. This visual cue allows you to see at a glance the proportion of space available relative to the capacity of the device. Double-click a device icon in the Content pane to change the display to show the contents stored on the device. You can display contents from another device or folder using the Navigation pane or the Address bar of the Computer window.

Project

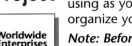

Worldwide Enterprises

You decide to explore the contents of the various storage devices on the computer you are using as you become familiar with the Windows 7 environment and are getting ready to organize your filing system.

Note: Before beginning the projects in this section, make sure you have copied the WindowsS2 folder from the Student Resources CD to your storage medium. If necessary, refer to the inside back cover of this textbook for instructions on how to copy a folder from the Student Resources CD to your storage medium such as a USB flash drive.

SNAP

Tutorial 2.1
Browsing Devices and Files

1. If necessary, insert into an empty USB port the storage medium that you are using for the files in this course. If an AutoPlay window opens with options for viewing the content on the drive, close the window by clicking the Close button located at the right end of the Title bar.

FIGURE 2.1 Computer Window

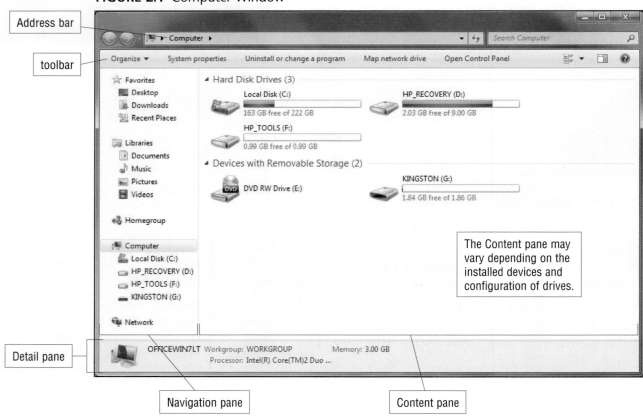

Address bar

toolbar

Detail pane

Navigation pane

Content pane

The Content pane may vary depending on the installed devices and configuration of drives.

In Brief

Display Computer Window
1. Click Start button
2. Click Computer.

2 At the Windows desktop, click the Start button on the Taskbar and then click *Computer* at the Start menu.

> The Computer window displays similar to the one shown in Figure 2.1.

3 Double-click the icon for the hard disk drive named *Local Disk (C:)*.

> The Computer window changes to show you the files and folders in the Content pane that are stored on the local hard disk drive assigned drive letter C:. Notice also that the Address bar in the Computer window updates to show the location where you are viewing *Local Disk (C:)* within *Computer*. You can navigate back using either the Back button or by clicking *Computer* in the Address bar.

4 Click the Back button to return to the previous list.

5 Double-click the icon for the storage medium upon which you copied the WindowsS2 folder. *Note: The screens shown in this section show* **KINGSTON (G:)** *as the storage medium in the Computer window. Your icon label and drive letter may vary.*

> USB flash drives are shown in the section of the Content pane labeled Devices with Removable Storage. Each device is assigned an alphabetic drive letter by Windows, usually starting at F or G and continuing through the alphabet depending on the number of removable devices that are currently in use. For example, if you had two removable devices inserted into two USB ports at the same time, one might be labeled G and the other H. Next to the drive letter, a label is shown depending on the manufacturer of the USB flash drive. If no manufacturer label is present, Windows displays *Removable Disk*.

6 Double-click the *WindowsS2* folder to view the contents of the folder in the Content pane.

7 Look at the Address bar and notice how the Address bar displays the path to the current content list: Computer ▶ KINGSTON (G:) ▶ WindowsS2. *Note: Your drive name and letter next to* **Computer** *may vary.*

> You can navigate to any other device or folder using the Address bar by clicking a drive or folder name, or by clicking the right-pointing black arrow to view a drop-down list of folders or other devices.

8 Click *Computer* in the Address bar.

9 Click the right-pointing arrow ▶ next to *Computer* in the Address bar (the arrow becomes a down-pointing arrow when clicked) and then click the drive letter representing the removable storage device with the WindowsS2 folder. For example, *KINGSTON (G:)*.

10 Click *Desktop* in the *Favorites* section of the Navigation pane.

> You can also change what is displayed in the Content pane by clicking the device or folder name in the Navigation pane. Click the white right-pointing arrow next to a device or folder name in the Content pane to expand the list and view what is stored within the item.

11 Close the Computer window.

Activity 2.2

Changing Folder and View Options

You can change the view to show the contents in various ways such as by size of icon, by list, by tiles, or by content. With the Content pane in Details view, you can click a column heading to sort the list or change from ascending order to descending order. In Activity 1.4, you displayed file extensions by opening the Folder Options dialog box and clearing the check mark for the *Hide extensions* for known file types option on the View tab. This turned on the display of file extensions when you were viewing a list of files. File extensions are helpful for identifying the program with which the file was created. Other ways in which you can customize the environment at the Folder Options dialog box include having each folder open in its own window, opening an item with a single-click, and applying the current view option to all folders.

Project You decide to experiment with various folder and view options as you continue to become acquainted with the Windows 7 environment and get ready to organize your filing system.

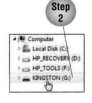

1 Click the Windows Explorer button ▨ on the Taskbar.

The Libraries window opens. For a description of libraries, please refer to the In Addition section at the end of this activity.

2 Click the drive letter representing your storage medium in the *Computer* section in the Navigation pane.

Tutorial 2.2
Creating a Folder

3 Double-click the *WindowsS2* folder in the Content pane.

4 Click the down-pointing arrow next to the Views button located at the right end of the toolbar (displays with the ScreenTip *More options*).

5 Drag the slider to the *Large Icons* option and then release the mouse button.

6 Click the Views button once (click on the button and not on the down-pointing arrow) to change the current view.

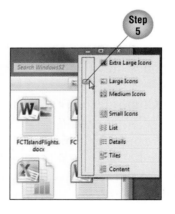

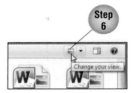

7 Click the Views button again to change to another view.

Each time you click the Views button you change the current view by cycling through five view options: Large Icons, List, Details, Tiles, and Content.

8 With the folder now displayed in Details view, click the *Name* column heading to change the view to sort the list in descending order by name.

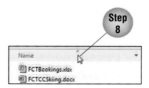

9. Click the *Name* column again to restore the list to ascending order by name.

10. Click the Organize button on the toolbar and then click *Folder and search options* at the drop-down list to open the Folder Options dialog box.

11. Click the *Open each folder in its own window* option in the *Browse folders* section of the General tab and then click OK.

12. Close the Computer window.

13. Click the Windows Explorer button on the Taskbar and then click the drive representing your storage medium in the *Computer* section in the Navigation pane.

14. Double-click the *WindowsS2* folder.

   Notice that this time a new window opened with the WindowsS2 content list layered on top of the original window.

15. Close the WindowsS2 folder window.

16. Click the Organize button, click *Folder and search options*, click the Restore Defaults button located near the bottom of the General tab, and then click OK.

17. Close the Computer window.

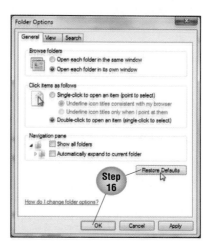

In Brief

Change Current View
Click down-pointing arrow next to Views button and drag slider to desired view.

Change Folder and View Options
1. Click Organize button
2. Click *Folder and search options.*
3. Click desired option(s).
4. Click OK.

In Addition

Windows Libraries

While browsing the Computer window you may have noticed a section in the Navigation pane with the title *Libraries*. Libraries are new to Windows 7 and are a tool you can use to keep track of and/or organize files that have something in common regardless of where they are stored. A library does not store the actual file but instead keeps track of locations where the source files are stored. When you click the library name in the Navigation pane, the library displays all of the files in the locations that it is keeping track of associated with that library. For example, in the Pictures library you could have Windows show you the contents of a Pictures folder on the local disk, from another folder on an external hard disk, and from a folder on a networked computer. Four default libraries are created when Windows 7 is installed: Documents, Music, Pictures, and Videos. You can create your own library and customize the locations associated with the default libraries. You will explore Libraries more in an Assessment at the end of this section.

Changing the Default View for All Folders

You can set a view to display by default for all folders of a similar type (such as all disk drive folders or all Documents folders). To do this, change the current view to the desired view for the type of folder that you want to set, such as a disk drive folder or a documents folder. Next, click the Organize button, click *Folder and search options*, and then click the View tab at the Folder Options dialog box. Click the Apply to Folders button in the *Folder views* section and click OK. Click Yes at the Folder Views message asking if you want all folders of this type to match this folder's view settings.

Activity 2.3

Creating a Folder; Renaming a Folder or File

As you begin working with programs, you will create files in which data (information) is saved. A file might be a Word document, an Excel workbook, or a PowerPoint presentation. Files on your computer may also be pictures or videos that you transferred from your digital camera. As you begin creating files, developing a system in which to organize those files becomes important so that you can easily retrieve a document or photo- graph when you need it. The first step in organizing your files is to create folders. Creating a folder is like creating a separate container in which you can place similar types of files.

File management tasks such as creating a folder, renaming a folder or file, and copying and moving files and folders can be completed at a variety of locations including at the Computer and Documents windows.

Project You need to organize files for your department at Worldwide Enterprises by first creating a folder.

Tutorial 2.3
Selecting, Copying, Moving, and Renaming Files

1. At the Windows desktop, click the Start button on the Taskbar and then click *Computer* at the Start menu.

2. Double-click the icon representing your storage medium on which you copied the WindowsS2 folder.

3. Click the New folder button New folder on the toolbar.

   A new folder icon is added in the Content pane with the text New folder already selected.

4. With the text *New folder* already selected next to the folder icon, type **Revenue** and then press Enter. Note that as soon as you type the *R* in *Revenue*, the existing text *New Folder* is immediately deleted.

   This changes the folder name from New Folder to Revenue.

5. You can also create a new folder using a shortcut menu. To begin, right-click in a blank, unused area in the Content pane, point to *New*, and then click *Folder*.

6. With the text *New folder* already selected next to the folder icon, type **Contracts** and then press Enter.

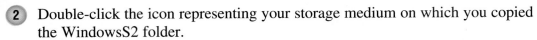

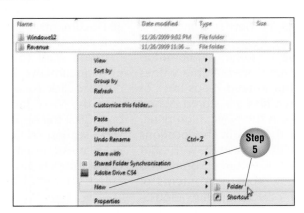

7. Click once on the *Revenue* folder to select the folder.

8 Click the Organize button on the toolbar and then click *Rename* at the drop-down list.

9 With the Revenue folder already selected, type **Income** and then press Enter.

> You can also use the shortcut menu to rename a file or folder.

10 Right-click the *Contracts* folder and then click *Rename* at the shortcut menu.

11 With the Contracts folder already selected, type **Administration** and then press Enter.

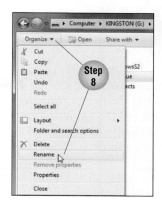

12 Double-click the *WindowsS2* folder.

13 Right-click the file *FCTExcelSalesCom.xlsx* and then click *Rename* at the shortcut menu.

14 Type **FCTSalesCommissions** and then press Enter.

> Notice when you rename a file that Windows does not select the file extension. Programs such as Microsoft Word and Microsoft Excel automatically assign a file extension to each document or workbook. These file extensions should remain intact. If you rename or remove a file extension by accident, Windows prompts you with a message that the file may no longer be usable and asks you if you are sure.

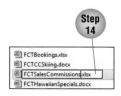

15 Close the Computer window.

In Addition

More about Organizing Files into Folders

Think of folders on the computer the same way you think of file folders in which you would store paper documents in your filing cabinet. Generally, you put similar types of documents into the same folder. For example, all of your rent receipts might be placed inside a file folder on which you have written the label *Rent* on the folder tab. Similarly, on the computer, you could create a folder named *Rent* and store all of the electronic copies of all of your rental documents within that folder. On the computer, a folder can have another folder stored inside it. The

folder within the folder is referred to as a *subfolder*. For example, you may have thousands of pictures stored on your computer. Saving all of the pictures in one folder named *Pictures* would be too cumbersome when the content list contains thousands of images. You would be scrolling a long time to locate a particular picture. Instead, consider creating subfolders in the Pictures folder so that related pictures are grouped together in one place.

Activity 2.4

Selecting and Copying Folders and Files

In addition to creating and renaming files and folders, file management activities include selecting, moving, copying, or deleting files or folders. Open a Computer or Documents library window to perform file management tasks. You can use options in the Organize button drop-down list or shortcut menu options. More than one file or folder can be moved, copied, or deleted at one time. Select adjacent files/folders using the Shift key and select nonadjacent files/folders using the Ctrl key. When selecting multiple files or folders, you may want to change the view in the Computer window.

Project

Tutorial 2.3
Selecting, Copying, Moving, and Renaming Files

Continuing to organize files for your department, you will copy files to the Income folder you created.

1. At the Windows desktop, open the Computer window.

2. Double-click the icon representing your storage medium on which you copied the WindowsS2 folder.

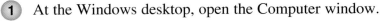
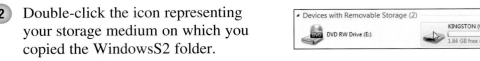

3. Double-click the *WindowsS2* folder in the Content pane.

4. Click the down-pointing arrow next to the Views button located at the right end of the toolbar (displays with the ScreenTip *More options*) and then drag the slider to *List* at the pop-up list.

5. Click the file named ***WEExcelRevenues.xlsx*** in the Content pane.

> Click once to select a file. Windows displays file properties in the Details pane at the bottom of the Computer window for a selected file and provides options to add or modify property information.

6. Hold down the Shift key, click the file named ***WETable02.docx***, and then release the Shift key.

> Clicking ***WETable02.docx*** while holding down the Shift key causes all files from ***WEExcelRevenues.xlsx*** through ***WETable02.docx*** to be selected.

7. Position the mouse pointer within the selected group of files, right-click, and then click *Copy* at the shortcut menu.

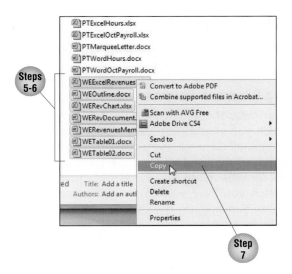

8 Click the Back button located left of the Address bar.

9 Double-click the *Income* folder.

10 Right-click in the Content pane and click *Paste* at the shortcut menu.

When a large file or large group of files is copied, Windows displays a message box with a progress bar to indicate the approximate time required to copy the files. The message box closes when the copy is complete.

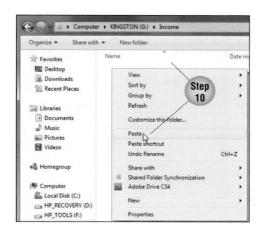
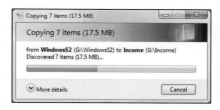

11 Click in a blank area of the Content pane to deselect the file names.

12 Close the Computer window.

In Brief

Copy Adjacent Files to New Folder
1. Display Computer window.
2. Navigate to desired drive and/or folder.
3. If necessary, change current view to *List*.
4. Click first file name.
5. Hold down Shift key and then click last file name.
6. Right-click in selected group of files and click *Copy*.
7. Navigate to desired destination drive and/or folder.
8. Right-click in blank area of Content pane and click *Paste*.

In Addition

Copying by Dragging

You can copy a file or folder to another location using a drag-and-drop technique. To do this, open a Computer or Documents library window and display the desired file or folder in the Content pane. Position the mouse pointer on the file or folder to be copied, hold down the left mouse button, drag to the destination drive or folder name in the *Favorites, Libraries,* or *Computer* list, and then release the mouse button. By default, if you drag a file from one disk drive to another, Windows uses a Copy command. If you are dragging from one folder to another on the same disk drive, hold down the Ctrl key while dragging to Copy. Alternatively, you could open two windows and arrange them side-by-side on the desktop. In one window, display the files that you want to copy. In the other window, display the destination folder. Select the files to be copied and then hold down the Ctrl key while dragging the selected files to the destination window.

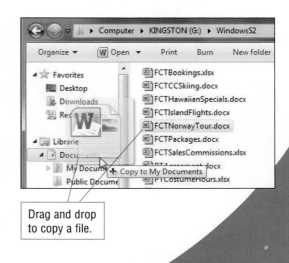

Drag and drop to copy a file.

Activity 2.5

Moving Folders and Files

Move files in a Computer or Documents library window in a manner similar to copying files. Select the file(s)/folder(s) that you want to move, position the mouse pointer over the selected file(s)/folder(s), right-click, and then click *Cut* at the shortcut menu. Navigate to the desired destination location, right-click a blank area in the Content pane, and then click *Paste* at the shortcut menu. You can also use the *Cut* and *Paste* options from the Organize button drop-down list.

Project

Tutorial 2.3
Selecting, Copying, Moving, and Renaming Files

After further review of the files you copied into the Income folder, you decide to create another folder and move some of the files from the Income folder into the new folder.

1 At the Windows desktop, display the Computer window.

2 Double-click the icon representing your storage medium on which you copied the WindowsS2 folder.

3 Click the New folder button on the toolbar.

4 Type **Distribution** and then press Enter.

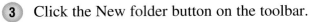

5 Double-click the *Income* folder.

6 Change the current view to *List*.

7 Click once on **WEOutline.docx**.

> Clicking once on the file selects the file name to identify the item that you want to move; double-clicking the file would instruct Windows to open Word and then open the document.

8 Hold down the Ctrl key, click once on **WETable01.docx**, click once on **WETable02.docx**, and then release the Ctrl key.

> Using the Ctrl key, you can select nonadjacent files.

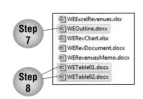

9 Click the Organize button in the toolbar and then click *Cut* at the drop-down list.

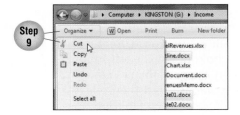

10 Click the Back button at the left of the Address bar.

11 Double-click the *Distribution* folder.

12 Click the Organize button in the toolbar and then click *Paste* at the drop-down list.

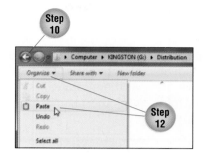

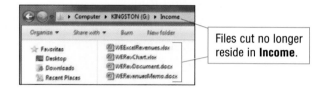

In Brief

Move Nonadjacent Files to New Folder
1. Display Computer window.
2. Navigate to desired drive and/or folder.
3. If necessary, change current view to *List*.
4. Click first file name.
5. Hold down Ctrl key, click each additional file name, and then release Ctrl key.
6. Click Organize button and click *Cut*.
7. Navigate to desired destination drive and/or folder.
8. Click Organize button and click *Paste*.

13 Click in a blank area of the Content pane to deselect the file names.

14 Click the Back button at the left of the Address bar.

15 Double-click the *Income* folder.

Notice the three files **WEOutline.docx**, **WETable01.docx**, and **WETable02.docx** no longer reside in the Income folder since Cut and Paste moves the files.

16 Close the Computer window.

In Addition

Displaying Disk or Drive Properties

Information such as the amount of used space and free space on a disk or drive and the disk or drive hardware is available at the Properties dialog box. To display the Local Disk (C:) Properties dialog box, similar to the one shown at the right, display a Computer window. At the Computer window, right-click *Local Disk (C:)* and then click *Properties* at the shortcut menu. With the General tab selected, information displays about used and free space on the drive. Click the Tools tab to display error-checking, backup, and defragmentation options. The Hardware tab displays the name and type of all disk drives as well as the device properties. The Sharing tab displays options for sharing folders and you can change user permissions at the Security tab. To enable quota management where you can assign space limits for each user click the Quota tab. View restore points at the Previous Versions tab.

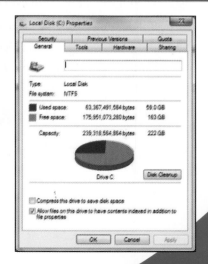

Activity 2.6

Deleting Folders and Files to the Recycle Bin

Deleting the wrong file can be a disaster, but Windows helps protect your work with the Recycle Bin. The Recycle Bin acts just like an office wastepaper basket; you can "throw away" (delete) unwanted files, but you can "reach in" to the Recycle Bin and take out (restore) a file if you threw it away by accident. Files or folders deleted from a hard disk drive are automatically sent to the Recycle Bin. Files or folders deleted from a removable disk, such as your USB flash drive, are deleted permanently. To delete a file or folder, display a Computer or Documents library window and then display in the Content pane the file(s) and/or folder(s) you want deleted. Select the file(s) and/or folder(s) and then press the Delete key on the keyboard, or right-click the selected files and click *Delete* at the shortcut menu. At the message asking you to confirm the deletion, click the Yes button.

Project

Tutorial 2.3
Selecting, Copying, Moving, and Renaming Files

Tutorial 2.4
Using the Recycle Bin

Continuing to organize your files, you will copy a file and a folder from your storage medium to the My Documents folder on the hard drive and then delete a file and folder to the Recycle Bin.

1. At the Windows desktop, display the Computer window.

2. Double-click the icon representing your storage medium on which you copied the WindowsS2 folder.

3. Click once to select the *Distribution* folder.

4. Position the mouse pointer over the selected folder name, hold down the left mouse button, drag to *Documents* in the *Libraries* section of the Navigation pane, and then release the mouse.

   As you point to the Documents library in the Navigation pane, Windows displays the ScreenTip *Copy to My Documents*.

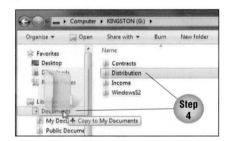

5. Double-click the *Income* folder.

6. Click once to select the **WERevDocument.docx** file.

7. Position the mouse pointer over the selected file name, hold down the left mouse button, drag to *Documents* in the *Libraries* section of the Navigation pane, and then release the mouse.

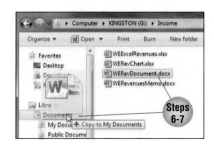

8 Click *Documents* in the *Libraries* section of the Navigation pane to display the files and folders associated with the Documents library in the Content pane.

> The Documents library displays the contents of two folders by default: My Documents and another folder named Public Documents. My Documents is the default folder in which files and folders are stored that are associated with the Documents library. You can add and remove folders associated with a library. You will learn more about libraries in an assessment at the end of this section.

9 Click once to select the *Distribution* folder.

Step 9

10 Press the Delete key on the keyboard.

11 At the Delete Folder message asking if you are sure you want to move this folder to the Recycle Bin, click Yes.

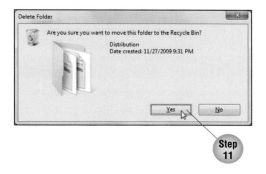

Step 11

12 Right-click **WERevDocument.docx** in the Content pane and then click *Delete* at the shortcut menu.

13 Click Yes at the Delete File message asking if you are sure you want to move this file to the Recycle Bin.

14 Close the Documents library window.

In Addition

Dragging and Dropping Files/Folders

Another method for deleting a file or folder is to drag the file or folder to the *Recycle Bin* icon on the desktop. This drops the file you are dragging into the Recycle Bin. You can also select multiple files or folders and then drag and drop the selected items in the *Recycle Bin* icon on the desktop.

Activity 2.7

Restoring Folders and Files; Emptying Files from the Recycle Bin

A file or folder deleted to the Recycle Bin can be restored. Restore a file or folder with options at the Recycle Bin window. Display this window by double-clicking the *Recycle Bin* icon on the Windows desktop. A restored file or folder is removed from the Recycle Bin and returned to its original location. Just like a waste-paper basket can become overfilled with too much waste, the Recycle Bin can have too many files and folders stored in it. Emptying the Recycle Bin permanently deletes all files and folders. You can also delete a single file or folder from the Recycle Bin (rather than all files and folders).

Project

You decide to experiment with the Recycle Bin and learn how to restore a file and then empty the Recycle Bin.

Worldwide Enterprises

1 At the Windows desktop, display the contents of the Recycle Bin by double-clicking the *Recycle Bin* icon.

Step 1

The Recycle Bin window displays similar to the one shown in Figure 2.2.

2 At the Recycle Bin window, change the current view to *List*.

3 Click once to select **WERevDocument.docx**.

Tutorial 2.4
Using the Recycle Bin

Depending on the contents of the Recycle Bin, you may need to scroll down the Recycle Bin list to display this document.

Step 4

Step 3

FIGURE 2.2 Recycle Bin Window

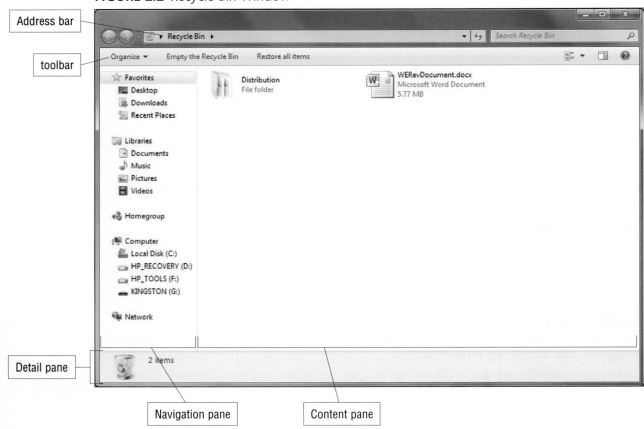

Address bar

toolbar

Detail pane

Navigation pane   **Content pane**

④ Click the Restore this item button on the toolbar.

> The file is removed from the Recycle Bin and returned to the location from which it was deleted. Once a file or folder is moved into the Recycle Bin you are limited to the following options: Restore, Cut, or Delete.

⑤ Click once to select the *Distribution* folder.

⑥ Click the Restore this item button on the toolbar.

⑦ Close the Recycle Bin window.

⑧ At the Windows desktop, open the Computer window.

⑨ Click *Documents* in the *Libraries* section of the Navigation pane.

> Notice that the file and folder that you had deleted have been restored from the Recycle Bin.

⑩ Delete the file and folder you restored. To do this, click once on the *Distribution* folder, hold down the Ctrl key, click once on the **WERevDocument.docx** file name, and then release the Ctrl key.

⑪ Press the Delete key.

⑫ At the Delete Multiple Items message box asking if you are sure you want to move these 2 items to the Recycle Bin, click Yes.

⑬ Close the Documents library window.

⑭ At the Windows desktop, double-click the *Recycle Bin* icon.

⑮ Click once on the *Distribution* folder, hold down the Ctrl key, click once on the **WERevDocument.docx** file name, and then release the Ctrl key.

⑯ Click the Organize button and then click *Delete* at the drop-down list.

⑰ At the Delete Multiple Items message box asking if you are sure you want to permanently delete these 2 items, click Yes.

> To empty the entire contents of the Recycle Bin, click the Empty the Recycle Bin button on the toolbar. At the message asking you to confirm the deletion, click Yes.

⑱ Close the Recycle Bin window.

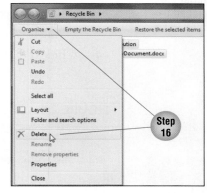

In Brief

Restore File/Folder from Recycle Bin
1. At Windows desktop, double-click *Recycle Bin* icon.
2. At Recycle Bin window, click file/folder to select it (or select multiple files/folders).
3. Click Restore this item button on toolbar.

Delete File/Folder from Recycle Bin
1. At Windows desktop, double-click *Recycle Bin* icon.
2. At Recycle Bin window, click file/folder to select it (or select multiple files/folders).
3. Press Delete key.
4. At confirmation message, click Yes.

In Addition

Showing or Hiding the Recycle Bin on the Desktop

You can choose whether the Recycle Bin icon displays on the desktop or not. By default, the Recycle Bin is shown on the desktop. To remove it, right-click a blank area on the desktop and then click *Personalize* at the shortcut menu. At the Control Panel, All Control Panel Items, Personalization window, click *Change desktop icons* in the left pane. At the Desktop Icon Settings dialog box shown at the right, clear the check mark in the *Recycle Bin* check box and then click OK. Note the other desktop icons you can choose to show or hide at this dialog box.

Activity 2.8

Exploring the Control Panel

The Control Panel offers a variety of categories each containing icons you can use to customize the appearance and functionality of your computer. Display the Control Panel window by clicking the Start button and then clicking *Control Panel* at the Start menu. At the Control Panel window, available categories display in the Content pane. (By default, the Control Panel window opens in Category view. If your window opens in Large icons view or Small icons view, click the down-pointing arrow next to *View by* located near the top right of the Control Panel window and then click *Category* at the drop-down menu.) Click a category or hyperlinked option below the category and a list of tasks, a list of icons, or a separate window displays.

Project

You want to know how to customize your computer so you decide to explore the Control Panel window.

1. At the Windows desktop, click the Start button and then click *Control Panel* at the Start menu.

   The Control Panel window displays similar to the one shown in Figure 2.3.

Tutorial 2.5
Exploring the Control Panel

2. At the Control Panel window, click the <u>Appearance and Personalization</u> hyperlink.

3. After viewing the tasks and icons available in the Appearance and Personalization category, click the Back button.

4. Click the <u>Hardware and Sound</u> hyperlink.

FIGURE 2.3 Control Panel Window

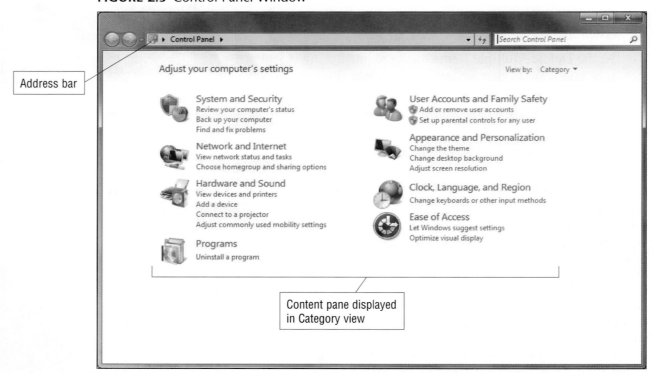

5 Click the <u>Mouse</u> hyperlink in the Devices and Printers category.

> This displays the Mouse Properties dialog box.

Step 5

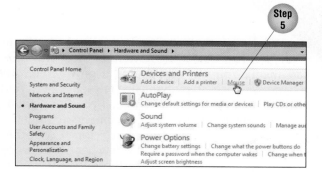

6 At the Mouse Properties dialog box, click each tab and review the available options.

7 Click the Cancel button to close the Mouse Properties dialog box.

8 Click the Back button.

9 Click the <u>Programs</u> hyperlink in the Content pane.

Step 9

10 At the Programs window, click the <u>Programs and Features</u> hyperlink.

> This is where you would uninstall a program on your computer.

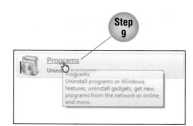

11 Click the Back button twice.

12 Click the <u>System and Security</u> hyperlink.

13 Click the <u>System</u> hyperlink.

14 Maximize the window.

15 Close the Control Panel window.

Step 13

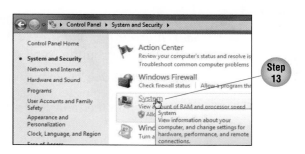

In Addition

Changing the Control Panel View

By default, the Control Panel window displays categories of tasks in what is called Category view. This view can be changed to *Large icons* or *Small icons*. In the Large icons view shown at the right, options for the control panel are shown alphabetically by icon name. To change from Category view to Large icons or Small icons, click the down-pointing arrow next to *View by* located near the top right of the Control Panel window (just below the Search text box) and then click the desired option at the drop-down list.

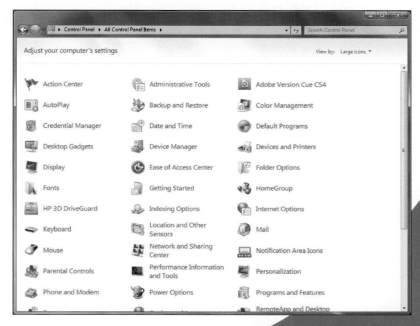

Activity 2.9

Using Windows Search Tools

Windows includes a *Search programs and files* text box at the bottom of the Start menu. You can quickly find a program or document by typing the first few letters of the program or document name. If your computer has many programs and documents stored on the hard disk, using the search tool allows you to locate what you need in a few seconds and with minimal mouse clicks. At the right of the Address bar in a Computer or Documents library window is a Search text box. Type the first few letters of a document you need to locate in this text box and the Content pane is filtered instantly to display items that match your criterion.

Windows performs fast searching because the operating system maintains an index in the background in which all of the key words associated with the programs and files on your computer are referenced. This index is constantly updated as you work. When you type an entry in a Search text box, Windows consults the index rather than conducting a search of the entire hard drive.

Project

You want to experiment with the Search capabilities of Windows to see how you can locate programs and documents more quickly in the future.

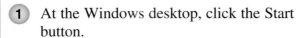

SNAP

Tutorial 2.6
Searching for a File or a Folder

1. At the Windows desktop, click the Start button.

2. With an insertion point blinking in the *Search programs and files* text box located just above the Start button, type **calc**.

> As soon as you begin typing an entry in the *Search programs and files* text box, Windows begins to display in the left column programs and/or documents that begin with the same letters that you type or that are associated with the same letters in a keyword. Notice that the Calculator program is shown below the heading *Programs* at the top of the list. Depending on the contents stored in the computer you are using, additional items may be displayed below *Calculator*.

3. Click *Calculator* in the *Programs* list at the top of the Start menu.

4. Close the Calculator window.

5. Click the Start button.

6. Type **snip** in the *Search programs and files* text box.

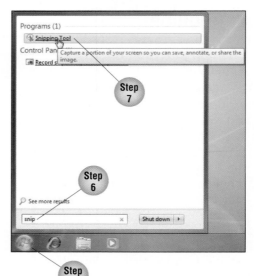

> Windows lists all file elements stored on the computer you are using that are associated with the text *snip*, including the snipping tool, which is a program that you can use to create and save images from your screen.

7. Point to <u>Snipping Tool</u> displayed in the *Programs* list and read the ScreenTip that appears. Point to any other items in the list and read the ScreenTip.

8. Press the Esc key.

> Pressing Esc clears the search results list and the *Search programs and files* text box.

9. Click *Computer* to open a Computer window.

10 Double-click the icon representing your storage medium on which you copied the WindowsS2 folder.

11 Double-click the *WindowsS2* folder and then change the current view to Large Icons.

12 Click in the *Search WindowsS2* text box located at the right of the Address bar.

13 Type **werev**.

As soon as you begin typing in the *Search WindowsS2* text box, Windows filters the list of files in the Content pane to those that begin with the letters that you type. Notice that the Address bar displays *Search Results in WindowsS2* to indicate that the files displayed that match your criteria were limited to the current folder. If you want to search other locations or by other file properties, click one of the option buttons located at the bottom of the Content pane below the title *Search again in*.

In Brief

Search for Programs or Document from Start Menu
1. Click Start button.
2. Type search criteria in *Search programs and files* text box.

Search for Document
1. Open Computer or Documents library window.
2. Type search criteria in Search text box.

Step 13

search results for files that begin with **werev**

14 With the insertion point still positioned in the Search text box, press the Backspace key to remove *werev* and then type **pte**.

The list of files in the Content pane is updated to display those files that begin with *PTE*.

15 Double-click the file named ***PTExcelOctPayroll.xlsx***.

The file opens in Microsoft Excel.

16 Close Microsoft Excel by clicking the Close button at the right end of the Title bar.

17 Close the Computer window.

In Addition

Using a Wildcard Character in a Search

When conducting a search you can type an asterisk (*) in place of any number of letters, numbers, or symbols within a file name to find files based on a pattern of characters. For example, typing ***hours*** would locate the files listed at the right in your WindowsS2 folder. Notice the pattern is that all files have *hours* in the middle of the file name but any number of other characters before and after *hours*.

PTWordHours.docx
PTExcelHours.xlsx
PTCostumeHours.xlsx

Activity 2.10

Customizing the Desktop

The Windows operating environment is very customizable. You can change background patterns and colors; specify a screen saver that will display when the screen sits idle for a specific period of time; or change the scheme for windows, title bars, and system fonts. Make these types of changes at the Control Panel Personalization window. Many companies adopt a corporate computer standard for display properties.

Project

Worldwide Enterprises

Tutorial 2.7
Customizing the Desktop

You decide to look at the customization options available for the desktop and set the screen resolution to the corporate standard in place for computers at Worldwide Enterprises.

Note: Before completing this activity, check with your instructor to determine if you can customize the desktop. If necessary, practice these steps on your home computer.

1. At the Windows desktop, position the arrow pointer on a blank area of the desktop, right-click the mouse, and then click *Personalize* at the shortcut menu.

2. At the Control Panel, All Control Panel Items, Personalization window, click the <u>Desktop Background</u> hyperlink located along the bottom of the window.

> Make a note of the current background.

3. If necessary, scroll up or down the available images, click an image that you like, and click the Save changes button.

Click an image that you like at Step 3.

4. Click the <u>Screen Saver</u> hyperlink.

> Make a note of the current screen saver name.

5. Click the button below *Screen saver* and then click *Photos* at the drop-down list.

> A preview of the screen saver displays in the screen located toward the top of the dialog box.

6. Click the up- or down-pointing arrow next to the *Wait* text box until *1* displays.

7. Click OK.

8 Click the <u>Window Color</u> hyperlink.

> Make a note of the color next to *Current color* below the color boxes.

9 Click the *Ruby* color box (last option in top row) and click the Save changes button. ***Note: Skip this step if your window does not display as shown below.***

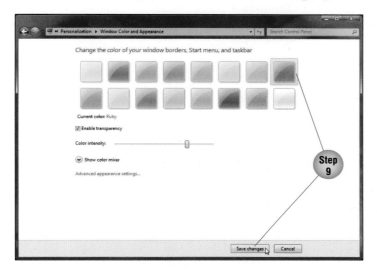

10 Close the Control Panel window. Let the screen remain idle for one minute until the screen saver displays.

11 Move the mouse to deactivate the screen saver and then double-click the *Recycle Bin* icon.

> Notice the Ruby color scheme applied to the Taskbar and the window borders.

12 Close the Recycle Bin window.

13 Reinstate the original desktop settings by right-clicking a blank area of the desktop, clicking *Personalize* at the shortcut menu, and then returning the Desktop Background, Screen Saver, and Window Color to the original settings.

> In the next steps, you will set the screen resolution to *1280 × 800 pixels,* which is the corporate standard for all desktops at Worldwide Enterprises. Standardizing display properties is considered a best practice in large companies that support many computer users.

14 Right-click a blank area of the desktop and click *Screen resolution* at the shortcut menu.

15 At the All Control Panel Items, Display, Screen Resolution window, look next to *Resolution* at the current setting displayed on the button. For example, your screen may be currently set at *1440 × 900.* If your screen is already set to *1280 × 800,* click OK to close the window and complete this activity.

> Screen resolution is set in pixels. ***Pixel*** is the abbreviation of *picture element* and refers to a single dot or point on the display monitor. Changing the screen resolution to a higher number of pixels means that more information can be seen on the screen as items are scaled to a smaller size.

continues

16 Click the button next to *Resolution* and then drag the slider bar up or down as necessary until the screen resolution is set to *1280 × 800*. If necessary, check with your instructor for alternate instructions.

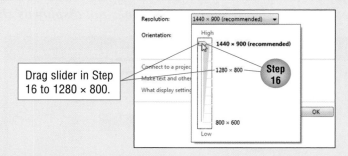

Drag slider in Step 16 to 1280 × 800.

Step 16

17 Click in the window outside the slider box, click OK, and then click the Keep Changes button at the Display Settings message box asking if you want to keep the display settings.

The screens in this textbook use 1280 × 800 screen resolution. If the computer you are using has a different screen resolution, what you will see on your screen may not match the textbook illustrations. For additional information, refer to the In Addition below.

In Addition

Windows Screen Resolution and the Microsoft Office Ribbon

Before you begin learning the applications in the Microsoft Office 2010 suite, take a moment to check the display settings on the computer you are using. The ribbon in the Microsoft Office suite adjusts to the screen resolution setting of your computer monitor. Computer monitors set at a high resolution will have the ability to show more buttons in the ribbon than will a monitor set to a low resolution. The illustrations in this textbook were made with a screen resolution display set at 1280 x 800 pixels. Below, the Word ribbon is shown three ways: at a lower screen resolution (1024 x 768 pixels), at the screen resolution featured throughout this textbook, and at a higher screen resolution (1440 x 900 pixels). Note the variances in the ribbon in all three examples. If possible, set your display to 1280 x 800 pixels to match the illustrations you will see in this textbook.

Appearance of Microsoft Word ribbon with computer monitor set at:

1024 x 768 screen resolution

1280 x 800 screen resolution (featured in this textbook)

1440 x 900 screen resolution

Features Summary

Feature	Button/Icon	Action
Computer window		Click Start button, click *Computer*.
Control Panel window		Click Start button, click *Control Panel*.
copy selected files/folders		At Computer or Documents library window, select files/folders to be copied, right-click in selected group, click *Copy*, navigate to destination folder, right-click in Content pane, click *Paste*.
create new folder	New folder	At Computer or Documents library window, right-click, point to *New*, click *Folder*.
delete selected files/folders		At Computer or Documents library window, select files to be deleted, press Delete key, click Yes.
folder options		Click Organize button, click *Folder and search options*.
move selected files/folders		At Computer or Documents library window, select files/folders to be moved, right-click in selected group, click *Cut*, navigate to destination folder, right-click in Content pane, click *Paste*.
Recycle Bin	Recycle Bin	Double-click *Recycle Bin* icon.
rename file/folder		At Computer or Documents library window, right-click file or folder, click *Rename,* type new name, press Enter.
restore files/folders from Recycle Bin	Restore this item	At Recycle Bin, select desired files/folders, click *Restore this item* button in toolbar.
search for programs or documents	Search programs and files	Click Start button, type search criterion in *Search programs and files* text box; or, open Computer or Documents library window, type search criterion in Search text box.
select adjacent files/folders		Click first file/folder, hold down Shift key, click last file/folder.
select nonadjacent files/folders		Click first file/folder, hold down Ctrl key, click any other files/folders.

Knowledge Check

Completion: In the space provided at the right, indicate the correct term, command, or option.

1. Navigate to any other device or folder from the current device and folder using the Navigation pane or this bar in the Computer window. _____

2. Specify the option to open each folder in its own window at this dialog box. _____

3. Click this button on the toolbar to create a new folder in the Computer window. _____

4. Change the display of files and folders in the Computer window to List or Details using this button on the toolbar. _____

5. To select adjacent files, click the first file, hold down this key, and then click the last file. _____

6. To select nonadjacent files, click the first file, hold down this key, and then click any other desired files. _____

7. Click this button to display in the Content pane the files in the previous folder viewed. _____

8. Click this option at the Organize button drop-down list to move the selected files. _____

9. Files deleted from the hard drive are sent here. _____

10. Open this window to display a list of categories or icons in which you can customize the appearance and functionality of your computer. _____

11. Type a search criterion in this text box at the Start menu to locate a program. _____

12. Customize the desktop by changing the background, screen saver, and color option at this window. _____

Skills Review

Review 1 Browsing Devices and Changing the View

1. Open the Computer window.
2. Change the view to *Large Icons*.
3. Change the folder option to open each folder in its own window.
4. Display the contents of your storage medium.
5. Display the contents of the WindowsS2 folder.
6. Change the view to *Details*.
7. Close the WindowsS2 window.
8. Close the window for your storage medium.
9. Change the folder option to open each folder in the same window.
10. Change the view to *Tiles* and then close the Computer window.

Review 2 Creating a Folder

1. Open the Computer window.
2. Display the contents of your storage medium.
3. Right-click a blank area in the Content pane, point to *New*, and then click *Folder*.
4. Type **Worksheets** and then press Enter.
5. Close the window.

Review 3 Selecting, Copying, Moving, and Deleting Files

1. Open the Computer window.
2. Display the contents of your storage medium.
3. Display the contents of the WindowsS2 folder.
4. Change the current view to *List* if the display is not already set to List.
5. Click once on *FCTBookings.xlsx* to select it, hold down the Shift key, and then click *FCTPackages.docx*.
6. Right-click within the selected group of files and click *Copy*.
7. Click the Back button.
8. Double-click the *Worksheets* folder.
9. Right-click in the Content pane, click *Paste*, and then click in a blank area to deselect the files.
10. Click the Back button and then double-click *WindowsS2*.
11. Click *WEExcelRevenues.xlsx* in the Content pane, hold down the Ctrl key, and then click *WERevChart.xlsx*.
12. Click the Organize button and then click *Cut* at the drop-down list.
13. Click the Back button and then double-click *Worksheets*.
14. Click the Organize button and then click *Paste* at the drop-down list.
15. Click the right-pointing arrow next to your storage medium in the Address bar and then click *WindowsS2* at the drop-down list.
16. Click *FCTCCSkiing.docx* in the Content pane, hold down the Ctrl key, and then click *FCTNorwayTour.docx*.
17. Press the Delete key and then click Yes at the Delete Multiple Items confirmation message.
18. Close the Computer window.

Review 4 Renaming a File

1. Open the Computer window.
2. Display the contents of your storage medium.
3. Display the contents of the WindowsS2 folder.
4. Right-click *WETable01.docx* and then click *Rename*.
5. Type **WEPreviewDistribution** and then press Enter.
6. Right-click *WETable02.docx* and then click *Rename*.
7. Type **WEGeneralDistribution** and then press Enter.
8. Close the Computer window.

Review 5 Searching for Files

1. Open the Computer window.
2. Display the contents of the WindowsS2 folder on your storage medium.
3. Type *rev* in the *Search WindowsS2* text box.
4. Press the Esc key until the filter is cleared and all files are redisplayed.
5. Type *excel* in the *Search WindowsS2* text box.
6. Close the Computer window.
7. Click the Start button.
8. Type *word* in the *Search programs and files* text box. Notice the programs and files displayed in the Start menu.
9. Click in the desktop outside the Start menu to close the menu.

Skills Assessment

Assessment 1 Managing Folders and Files

1. Create a new folder on your storage medium named PerformanceThreads.
2. Display the contents of the WindowsS2 folder.
3. If necessary, change the view to List.
4. Copy all files beginning with *PT* to the PerformanceThreads folder.
5. If necessary, display the contents of the PerformanceThreads folder and change the view to List.
6. Create a new folder within PerformanceThreads named Payroll. (A folder created within a folder is referred to as a subfolder.)
7. Move **PTExcelOctPayroll.xlsx** and **PTWordOctPayroll.docx** from the PerformanceThreads folder into the Payroll subfolder.
8. Delete **PTMarqueeLetter.docx** from the PerformanceThreads folder.
9. Rename the file named **PTAgreement.docx** located in the PerformanceThreads folder to **CostumeAgreement.docx**.

Assessment 2 Managing Folders and Files

1. Display the contents of your storage medium.
2. Create a new folder named FirstChoiceTravel.
3. Display the contents of the WindowsS2 folder.
4. Copy all files beginning with FCT to the FirstChoiceTravel folder.
5. If necessary, display the contents of the FirstChoiceTravel folder and change the view to List.
6. Create a new folder within FirstChoiceTravel named Accounting.
7. Create a new folder within the Accounting folder named Commissions.
8. Move **FCTBookings.xlsx** from the FirstChoiceTravel folder into the Accounting subfolder.
9. Move **FCTSalesCommissions.xlsx** from the FirstChoiceTravel folder into the Commissions subfolder.
10. Delete **FCTIslandFlights.docx** from the FirstChoiceTravel folder.
11. Rename the file named **FCTPackages.docx** located in the FirstChoiceTravel folder to **FCTOregonNevadaPkgs.docx**.

Assessment 3 Managing Folders and Files

1. Display the contents of your storage medium.
2. Create a new folder named WorldwideEnt.
3. Display the contents of the WindowsS2 folder.
4. Copy all files beginning with *WE* to the WorldwideEnt folder.
5. If necessary, display the contents of the WorldwideEnt folder and change the view to List.
6. Delete **WEOutline.docx** from the WorldwideEnt folder.
7. Rename the folder named WorldwideEnt to WorldwideEnterprises.

Assessment 4 Deleting Folders and Files

Note: Check with your Instructor before completing this Assessment in case you need to show him or her that you completed the Activities within this section before deleting the folders.

1. Display the contents of your storage medium.
2. Delete the folder named Administration.
3. Delete the folder named Distribution.
4. Delete the folder named Income.

Assessment 5 Copying Folders from the Student CD to Your Device

1. Display the contents of the Marquee student CD that accompanies this textbook in the Computer window.
2. Display the contents of the Word folder in the Content pane.
3. Select all of the subfolders in the Word folder and copy them to your storage medium.
4. Display the contents of the Excel folder in the Content pane and then copy all of the subfolders in the Excel folder to your storage medium.
5. Display the contents of the Access folder in the Content pane and then copy all of the subfolders in the Access folder to your storage medium.
6. Display the contents of the PowerPoint folder in the Content pane and then copy all of the subfolders in the PowerPoint folder to your storage medium.
7. Copy the AudioandVideo folder to your storage medium.
8. Display the contents of the Integrating folder and then copy all of the subfolders to your storage medium.

Assessment 6 Searching for Information on User Accounts

1. You have been asked by your supervisor at First Choice Travel to learn about sharing your computer with other users. Your supervisor is considering adding an evening shift and wants to find out how existing computer equipment can be set up for other users. Using the Windows Help and Support feature, search for information on user accounts. *Hint: Type user accounts in the* **Search Help** *text box and press Enter. Consider reading the topic* **What is a user account?** *as your first step*.
2. Locate topics with information about the three types of user accounts: *Standard*, *Administrator*, and *Guest*. Specifically, your supervisor is interested in which type of account would be best suited for day-to-day work and why this type of account is your recommendation.
3. Create a new folder on your storage medium named WindowsEOS.
4. Using WordPad or Word, compose a memo to your instructor that describes the differences between the three types of user accounts and then provide your recommendation for which type of account should be used for individual users on each shift.
5. Save the memo and name it **WS2-UserAccounts** in the WindowsEOS folder.
6. Print the memo.

Assessment 7 Searching for Information on Windows Libraries

1. You have been asked by your supervisor at First Choice Travel to learn about a new feature in Windows 7 called Libraries. Your supervisor is not sure about the difference between a library and a normal folder for managing folders and files. She wants you to find out how a library can be useful to her and how to create her own library and add folders to it. She also wonders if the default libraries Windows created can have other folders added to them. Using the Windows Help and Support feature, search for information on libraries. *Hint: Type libraries in the* **Search Help** *text box and press Enter. Consider reading the topic* **Working with libraries** *as your first step*.
2. Locate topics with information about libraries.
3. Using WordPad or Word, compose a memo to your instructor that provides her with answers to the following questions:
    a. What is the difference between a library and a folder?
    b. How can I create my own library?
    c. How can I add or remove folders in a library?
    d. What is the limit on the number of folders that can be added to a library?
4. Save the memo and name it **WS2-Libraries** in the WindowsEOS folder.
5. Print the memo.

Marquee Series

Internet
Microsoft®
Explorer 8.0

Nita Rutkosky

Pierce College at Puyallup, Puyallup, Washington

Denise Seguin

Fanshawe College, London, Ontario

Audrey Rutkosky Roggenkamp

Pierce College at Puyallup, Puyallup, Washington

Paradigm
PUBLISHING

St. Paul • Los Angeles • Indianapolis

Contents

Managing Editor	Sonja Brown
Developmental Editor	Brenda Palo
Production Editor	Donna Mears
Cover and Text Designer	Leslie Anderson
Copy Editors	Susan Capecchi and Laura Nelson
Desktop Production	Ryan Hamner and Jack Ross
Proofreader	Laura Nelson
Testers	Amy McGuire, Rob Neilly, and Lindsay Ryan
Indexers	Ina Gravitz and Sandi Schroeder

Internet Explorer
Browsing the Internet Using Internet Explorer 8.0

Skills

- Visit sites by typing a web address
- Use hyperlinks to navigate to web pages
- Search for information using search tools
- Narrow a search using advanced search options
- Download content from a web page
- Evaluate content found on a web page

Projects Overview

Visit websites for two national parks. Search for websites pertaining to historical costume design. Use advanced search options to locate information on skydiving companies in the state of Oregon. Locate and save images of Banff National Park. Find information on Apollo lunar missions and evaluate the source and date of publication of the information.

Visit the home pages for the *New York Times* and *USA Today* and read a current article.

Search for and locate the web page for the Theatre Department at York University and the web page for the Department of Drama at New York University.

Locate a website for a snow skiing resort in Utah and then download an image from the web page.

1

Activity 1.1

Navigating the Internet Using Web Addresses

In today's world, the Internet is used for a variety of tasks including locating information about any topic one could imagine, communicating with others through email or social networking sites, and buying and selling goods and services. In this section, you will use Microsoft's Internet Explorer web browser to locate information on the Internet. A *web browser* is a software program that allows you to view the text, images, and other content that has been stored on a web page on the Internet. *Uniform Resource Locators*, referred to as URLs, identify web servers that have content on the Internet. A URL is often referred to as a *web address*. Just as you need a specific mailing address in order to identify your location to the post office, a web server has a unique web address that identifies its location to the Internet.

Project

Dennis Chun, the location director for Marquee Productions is gathering information for a new movie project. He has asked you to browse the websites for Yosemite National Park and Glacier National Park.

Note: Print instructions are not included in the project steps in this section. Check with your instructor to find out if you need to print the web pages that you visit.

(1) Make sure you are connected to the Internet and that the Windows desktop displays.

Check with your instructor to determine if you need to complete steps for accessing the Internet.

SNAP

Tutorial 1.1
Browsing the Internet

(2) Open Microsoft Internet Explorer by clicking the *Internet Explorer* icon 🌐 located on the Taskbar.

Figure 1.1 identifies the elements of the Internet Explorer, version 8, window. The web page that displays in your Internet Explorer window may vary from what you see in Figure 1.1. Refer to Figure 1.2 on the next page for descriptions of the tools available in Internet Explorer.

(3) At the Internet Explorer window, click in the Address bar (refer to Figure 1.1), type **www.nps.gov/yose**, and then press Enter.

For information on web addresses (URLs), please read the *In Addition* section at the bottom of the next page.

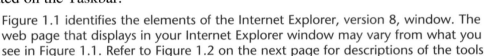

FIGURE 1.1 Internet Explorer Window

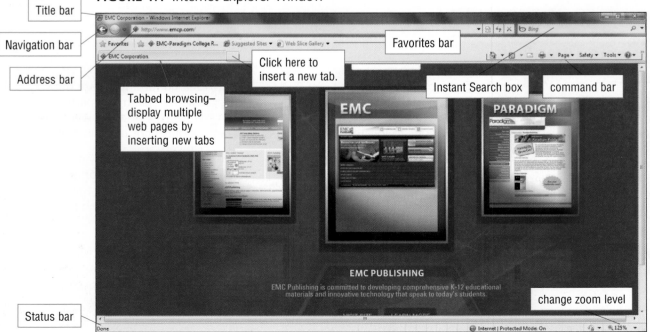

Title bar
Navigation bar
Address bar
Favorites bar
Click here to insert a new tab.
Instant Search box
command bar
Tabbed browsing— display multiple web pages by inserting new tabs
change zoom level
Status bar

4 Scroll down the home page for Yosemite National Park by pressing the Down Arrow key on the keyboard, or by clicking the down-pointing arrow on the vertical scroll bar located at the right side of the Internet Explorer window.

In Brief

Display Specific Website
1. At Windows desktop, click *Internet Explorer* icon in Taskbar.
2. Click in Address bar, type web address, press Enter.

The first web page that appears for a website is called the site's home page.

5 Display the home page for Glacier National Park by clicking in the Address bar, typing **www.nps.gov/glac**, and then pressing Enter.

As you begin to type the first few characters in the Address bar, a drop-down list appears below the Address bar with the names of websites that you have already visited that are spelled the same. Matched characters are displayed in blue for quick reference. If the web address you want displays in the drop-down list, you do not need to type the entire address—simply click the desired web address in the drop-down list.

6 Click the hyperlink to <u>HISTORY & CULTURE</u> displayed in the navigation area at the left side of the page.

Most web pages contain hyperlinks that you click to connect to another page within the website or to another site on the Internet. Hyperlinks display in a web page in a variety of ways such as underlined text, text in a navigation bar, buttons, images, or icons. To use a hyperlink, position the mouse pointer on the hyperlink until the mouse pointer turns into a hand and then click the left mouse button.

7 Scroll down and view the content on the History & Culture web page.

8 Click the Back button on the Navigation bar to return to the Glacier National Park home page.

9 Click the Forward button on the Navigation bar to return to the History & Culture page.

FIGURE 1.2 Browsing, Navigating, and Other Tools

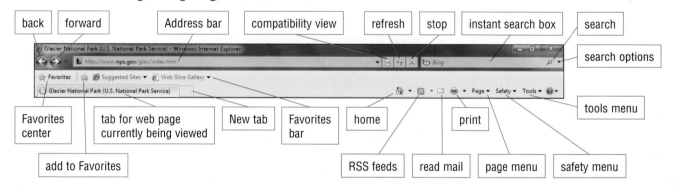

In Addition

Understanding URLs (Web Addresses)

URLs (Uniform Resource Locators) are used to identify locations on the Internet. The format of a URL is *http://server-name.domain*. The *http* stands for HyperText Transfer Protocol, the language used to transfer data within the World Wide Web. The colon and slashes separate the protocol from the server name. The server name in http://www.microsoft.com is *microsoft*. The last part of the URL is the domain to which the server belongs. For example, *.com* refers to "commercial," indicating that the URL is for a commercial company. Other domains include *.edu* for "educational," *.gov* for "government," and *.mil* for "military."

Activity 1.2

Finding Information Using Search Tools

If you do not know the web address for a specific site or you want to find information on the Internet but do not know what site to visit, complete a search with a search engine. A variety of search engines are available on the Internet, each offering the opportunity to search for specific information. One method for searching for information is to click in the Instant Search box, type a keyword or phrase related to your search, and then click the Search button or press Enter. Another method for completing a search is to go to the home page for a search engine and use options at the search engine's site.

Project

Tutorial 1.2
Searching for
Specific Sites

The research coordinator for Marquee Productions has asked you to locate sites with historical costumes for a new movie project. Specifically, she has asked you to locate information on Elizabethan and Renaissance costumes.

1. With the Internet Explorer window active, click in the Instant Search box (currently displays *Bing*) located at the right end of the Internet Explorer Navigation bar.

   Bing is Microsoft's online search portal and is the default search engine used. Bing organizes search results by topic category and provides related search suggestions.

2. Type **Renaissance costumes** and then click the Search button (or press Enter).

   As you begin to type, Bing displays search suggestions in a list below the Instant Search box. You can click a suggested phrase in the list instead of completing your typing. Characters in each suggested search phrase that match your typing are displayed in blue for quick reference.

3. Scroll down the search results list and click a hyperlink that interests you by positioning the mouse pointer on the hyperlink text until the pointer turns into a hand and then clicking the left mouse button.

4. Browse the content at the page you selected.

5. Use the Yahoo! search engine to find sites on Renaissance costumes by clicking in the Address bar, typing **www.yahoo.com**, and then pressing Enter.

6. At the Yahoo! website, type **Renaissance costumes** in the Search text box and then press Enter.

   As you begin to type, the Yahoo! search assist feature displays search suggestions in a list below the Search text box. Similar to Bing, you can click a suggested phrase in the list instead of completing your typing. Characters in each suggested search phrase that match your typing are displayed in another color for quick reference. Notice that Bing and Yahoo!'s suggested search phrases are different. Each search engine has its own way of cataloguing and indexing search terms.

7. Click a hyperlink to a site that interests you.

8. Use the Google search engine to find sites on Elizabethan costumes by clicking in the Address bar, typing **www.google.com**, and then pressing Enter.

9. At the Google website, type **Elizabethan costumes** in the Search text box and then press Enter.

Notice that Google also provides a drop-down list of suggested search phrases based on the characters you typed. Additionally, Google includes the number of results for each suggested search phrase. This information is useful as you can see at a glance which search phrase will produce the most or the least links.

In Brief

Search for Website
At Internet Explorer window, type search terms text in Instant Search box, then click Search button.

Step 9

Elizabethan costumes		Advanced Search Language Tools
elizabethan costumes shakespeare	295,000 results	
elizabethan costumes for women	162,000 results	
elizabethan costumes for men	167,000 results	
elizabethan costumes for romeo and juliet	55,700 results	
elizabethan costumes to buy	107,000 results	
elizabethan costumes romeo and juliet	30,600 results	
elizabethan costumes for actors	100,000 results	
elizabethan costumes for sale	126,000 results	
elizabethan costumes pictures	121,000 results	
elizabethan costumes hire	40,400 results	
		close

10. Click a hyperlink to a site that interests you.

11. Use the Dogpile search engine to find sites on Elizabethan costumes by clicking in the Address bar, typing **www.dogpile.com**, and then pressing Enter.

Dogpile is a *metasearch* search engine. A metasearch search engine sends your search phrase to other search engines and then compiles the results in one list. You benefit by typing the search phrase once but accessing results from a wider group of search engines that index web pages. Dogpile provides search results from Google, Yahoo!, Bing, and Ask.

12. At the Dogpile website, type **Elizabethan costumes** in the Search text box and then press Enter.

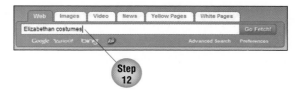

Step 12

13. Click a hyperlink to a site that interests you.

In Addition

Adding Frequently Used Web Pages to Favorites

If you visit a web page on a regular basis, add the page to the Favorites Center or add a button to the web page on the new Favorites bar. To add the web page to the Favorites bar, display the web page and then click the Add to Favorites bar button (displays as a yellow star with a green right-pointing arrow) located next to the Favorites button. If the Favorites bar is not visible, right-click in an unused section between the browsing tabs and the Command Bar and click *Favorites Bar* to turn the toolbar on. If you prefer, you can add

the website to the Favorites Center list. To do this, click the Favorites button and then click the Add to Favorites button at the Favorites Center. At the Add a Favorite dialog box that displays, make sure the information in the *Name* text box is the title by which you want to refer to the website (if not, type your own title for the page) and then click the Add button. The new website is added to the Favorites Center drop-down list. Jump quickly to the site by clicking the Favorites button and then clicking the site name at the drop-down list.

Activity 1.3

Refining Your Search Using Advanced Search Tools

The Internet contains an extraordinary amount of information. Depending on what you are searching for on the Internet and the search engine you use, some searches can result in several thousand "hits" (sites). Wading through a large number of sites can be very time-consuming. You can achieve a more targeted search results list if you hone your search technique by using the advanced search options offered by a search engine. Effective searching is a skill you obtain through practice. Look for an advanced search options link at your favorite search engine site the next time you need to locate information and experiment with various methods to limit the search results.

Project

The stunt coordinator at Marquee Productions has asked you to locate information on skydiving companies in the state of Oregon.

Tutorial 1.3
Researching Information

1. With the Internet Explorer window active, click in the Address bar, type **www.yahoo.com**, and then press Enter.

2. At the Yahoo! home page, click the Web Search button [Web Search] next to the Search text box.

3. Click the <u>More</u> link located above the Search text box and then click *Advanced Search* at the drop-down list.

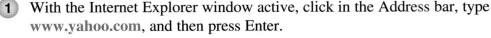

4. At the Advanced Web Search page, click in the *the exact phrase* text box and then type **skydiving in Oregon**.

   This limits the search to websites with the exact phrase "skydiving in Oregon."

5. Click the *Only .com domains* option.

   Clicking this option tells Yahoo! to only display websites with a .com extension and to ignore any other extension.

6. Click the Yahoo! Search button.

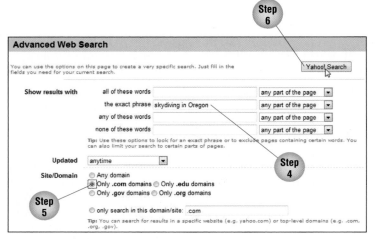

7 When the list of websites displays, click a hyperlink that interests you.

8 Click the Back button until the Yahoo! Advanced Web Search page displays.

9 Select and then delete the text *skydiving in Oregon* located in the *the exact phrase* text box.

10 Click in the *all of these words* text box and then type **skydiving Oregon tandem static line**.

> You want to focus on websites that offer tandem and static line skydiving in Oregon.

11 Click the *Any domain* option.

12 Click the Yahoo! Search button.

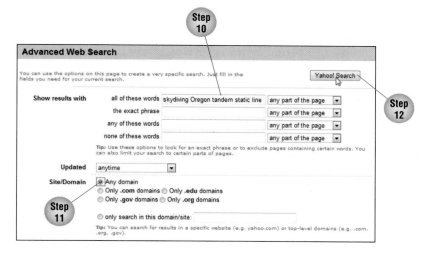

13 When the list of websites displays, click a hyperlink that interests you.

In Brief

Complete Advanced Search Using Yahoo!
1. At Internet Explorer window, click in Address bar, type **www.yahoo.com**, then press Enter.
2. Click Web Search button, click *more* link, click *Advanced Search*.
3. Click in desired search text box, type search criteria text.
4. Select search method and search options.
5. Click Yahoo! Search button.

In Addition

Displaying a List of Sites Visited

As you view various web pages, Internet Explorer keeps track of the websites visited. Display the History pane by clicking the Tools button on the Internet Explorer Command bar, pointing to Explorer Bars, and then clicking *History*. Click the timeframe for which the web page would have been viewed to expand the list and display the sites visited. For example, click *Last Week* to expand the list and view the pages that you visited within the past week. Click the desired hyperlink to revisit the page. At the top of the History pane, click the View button (currently displays View By Date) to change the order in which the history list is displayed. You can display websites in the History pane to *View By Date*, *View By Site*, *View By Most Visited*, or *View By Order Visited Today*. Click *Search History* at the View button drop-down list to search the websites in the History pane by keyword or phrase.

Activity 1.4

Downloading Content from a Web Page

Downloading content from a web page can involve saving to your hard disk or other storage medium images, text, video, audio, or the entire web page. Copyright laws protect much of the information on the Internet. Before using information or other media files you have downloaded from the Internet, check the source site for restrictions.

When in doubt, contact the website administrator or other contact person identified on the site and request permission to use the content. Finally, make sure to credit the source of any content you use that was obtained from a web page. Generally, you can use content from a website that is considered public domain such as government websites.

Project

SNAP

Tutorial 1.4
Downloading Images, Text, and Web Pages

The production manager of the new movie project at Marquee Productions has asked you to locate on the Internet a picture for Banff National Park and an image that shows a map of the park. She wants you to save the images as a separate file that she can insert into her presentation for the next production meeting.

1. With the Internet Explorer window active, click in the Address bar, type **www.google.com**, and then press Enter.

2. At the Google home page, click the hyperlink to <u>Images</u> at the top left of the home page.

3. At the Google images page, type **Banff National Park** in the Search text box and then press Enter or click the Search Images button.

4. Browse the images that display in the search results.

5. Position the mouse pointer over an image you want to download, right-click the mouse, and then click *Save Picture As* at the shortcut menu.

   The image that you choose may vary from the one shown here.

6. At the Save Picture dialog box, click *Desktop* in the *Favorites* section of the Navigation pane, select the current text in the *File name* text box, type **BanffPicture1**, and then click Save or press Enter.

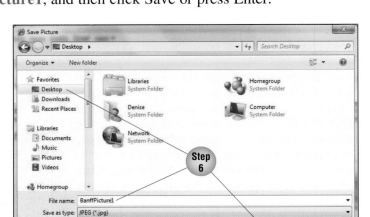

⑦ Click the Address bar, type **www.dogpile.com**, and then press Enter.

⑧ Click the Images tab at the Dogpile home page.

⑨ Click in the Search text box, type **Banff National Park Map**, and then press Enter or click the Go Fetch! button.

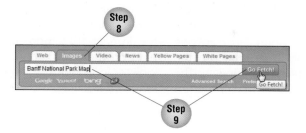

In Brief

Downloading Images from Web Page
1. Display desired web page in Internet Explorer window.
2. Right-click desired image.
3. Click *Save Picture As*.
4. Navigate to desired drive and/or folder.
5. Type file name in *File name* text box.
6. Click Save.

⑩ Browse the map images that display in the search results, right-click the mouse over one of the maps you want to download, and then click *Save Picture As* at the shortcut menu.

⑪ At the Save Picture dialog box, with *Desktop* already selected in the Address bar and with the current file name already selected in the *File name* text box, type **BanffMap1** and then click Save or press Enter.

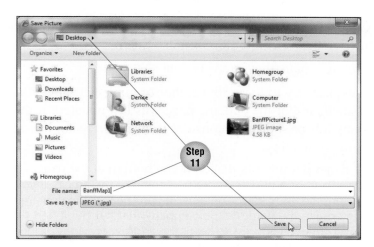

In Addition

Saving an Entire Web Page as a Separate File

You can save as a separate file all of the content that displays on a web page. The web page can be opened like any other file to view or print as needed. To do this, display the web page that you want to save a copy of, click the Page button on the Command bar, and click *Save As* at the drop-down list. At the Save Webpage dialog box, navigate to the drive and/or folder in which you want to save the web page, type a name for the web page in the *File name* text box, and then click Save or press Enter. By default, the web page is saved in the *Web Archive, single file (*.mht)* file format. To open the file at a later date, use Windows Explorer to locate the drive and folder in which you saved the file and then double-click the file name in the Content pane. The web page will open in an Internet Explorer window.

Activity 1.5

Evaluating Content on the Web

The Web is a vast repository of information that is easily accessible and constantly changing. Although there is a wealth of accurate and timely information available at your fingertips, there is also information that may be outdated, inaccurate, or of poor quality that should not be relied upon. Since anyone with an Internet connection and the right software can publish information on the Web, knowing the clues to recognizing accurate and current content is a worthwhile skill.

First, look for an author, publisher, or website owner name and consider if the source is credible. For example, is the author associated with a recognizable company, government, or news organization? Second, look for the date the information was published. Is the content outdated? If yes, consider the impact that more current information might have on the information you are evaluating. Third, look for indications that a bias may exist in the content. For example, is there a sponsor on the site that might indicate the information is one-sided? Can the information be validated by another source?

Project

The development manager at Marquee Productions is working on research for a new documentary about the Apollo space missions. She has asked you to locate information on the Web that she can add to her research. You want to be careful that the information you provide for the project is credible.

1 With the Internet Explorer window active, click in the Address bar, type **www.google.com**, and then press Enter.

2 At the Google home page, type **Apollo lunar missions** in the Search text box and then click the Search button or press Enter.

3 Click a link to a page that interests you.

4 At the web page, try to locate the author or publisher name, the date the article was published, and/or the date the page was last updated. If the web page contains any ads or sponsors, consider if this advertising has an impact on the content you are reading.

> Some pages put this information at the bottom of the page, while other pages place the author and date at the beginning of the article. If you cannot find an author or date, look for a Contacts link on the website you are viewing to see if you can determine the name of the company that has published the information. Also, look over the web address to see if the address provides a clue to the authorship. For example, a web address with a *.edu* domain is indicating the source is from a page connected with a university.

5 Click the New Tab tab to open a new browsing window.

6 Click in the Address bar, type **www.nasa.gov/ mission_pages/apollo**, and then press Enter.

Your tab name may vary.

Step 5

7 Scroll to the bottom of the page and read the information in the banner next to the NASA logo that provides information about the date the page was last updated, the page editor, and the NASA Official.

Step 7

8 Click the tab for the first web page that you visited about Apollo lunar missions and click the Back button to return to the search results list.

9 Click the link to another page that interests you and try to locate similar information about the date, author, and publisher that you viewed at NASA's website.

10 Compare the two pages shown side by side in Figure 1.3. Note that one page provides details about dates and authors while the other page does not have the same references.

> The page without the references may not necessarily have inaccurate data or be an otherwise poor quality source of information about the Apollo missions; however, the absence of an author or date of revision means that you would have difficulty citing this source for a research paper or other academic assignment.

11 Close Internet Explorer. Click the Close all tabs button at the Internet Explorer dialog box.

FIGURE 1.3

This page has source and date references.

This page has no author, publisher, or date reference.

Features Summary

Feature	Button	Keyboard Shortcut
go back to previous web page	←	Alt + Left Arrow
go forward to next web page	→	Alt + Right Arrow
History pane	Tools ▼	Ctrl + Shift + H
launch Internet Explorer		
print current web page	🖶 ▼	Ctrl + P
select Address bar	http://www.emcp.com/	Alt + D
select Instant Search box	Bing 🔍 ▼	Ctrl + E

Knowledge Check

Completion: In the space provided at the right, indicate the correct term, command, or option.

1. Type a URL in this bar at the Internet Explorer window. _____
2. The letters *URL* stand for this. _____
3. Click this button on the Internet Explorer toolbar to display the previous web page. _____
4. Click in this box located at the right end of the Internet Explorer Navigation bar to locate web pages using a keyword or phrase. _____
5. Reduce the number of search results by looking for these options at the search engine's website. _____
6. Download an image from a website to a file on your computer by right-clicking the image and selecting this option at the shortcut menu. _____

Skills Review

Note: Check with your instructor before completing the Skills Review activities to find out if you have to print the pages that you visit.

Review 1 Browsing the Internet and Navigating with Hyperlinks

1. Open Internet Explorer.
2. Click in the Address bar, type **www.si.edu**, and then press Enter. (This is the home page for the Smithsonian Institution.)
3. Click a link to a topic that interests you and read the page.
4. Click another link and read the page.
5. Click the Back button until the Smithsonian Institution home page displays.

Review 2 Searching for Specific Sites

1. At the Internet Explorer window, use the Instant Search box to look for websites on mountain climbing.
2. In the search results, click a link to a site that interests you.
3. Display the Yahoo! website and then use advanced options to search for websites with the *.com* domain on mountain climbing in British Columbia, Canada.
4. Visit at least two sites in the search results that interest you.

Review 3 Downloading Content from a Web Page

1. Using your favorite search engine, search for websites on parasailing in Hawaii. Find a site that contains a parasailing image that you like.
2. Download the parasailing image to the desktop, saving it as **ParasailImage1**.
3. Search for maps of Hawaii.
4. Browse the map images and then select one to download to the desktop, saving it as **HawaiiMap1**.
5. Close Internet Explorer.

Skills Assessment

Note: Check with your instructor before completing the Skills Assessment activities to find out if you have to print the pages that you visit.

Assessment 1 Visiting Web Pages for Current News Articles

1. Sam Vestering, a manager at Worldwide Enterprises, likes to keep up-to-date with current events by reading the daily headlines for various newspapers. He has asked you to scan the home pages for two online newspapers—the *New York Times* and *USA Today*—for articles of interest. To begin, open Internet Explorer.
2. Go to the website of the *New York Times* at www.nytimes.com. Scan the headlines for today's publication, click the link to an article that interests you, and then read the article.
3. Visit the website of *USA Today* at www.usatoday.com, click the link to an article that interests you, and then read the article.

Assessment 2 Navigating Websites for Theatre Programs

1. Cal Rubine, the chair of the Theatre Arts Division at Niagara Peninsula College, has asked you to visit the web pages for the theatre and/or drama departments at two universities to compare programs. Visit the home page for York University, Toronto, Canada, at www.yorku.ca.
2. Locate the web page for the Theatre Department and then read about the program.
3. Visit the home page for New York University at www.nyu.edu.
4. Using the NYU A–Z search in the ABOUT NYU section, locate the web page for the Department of Drama (undergraduate) and then read about the program. If necessary, click links to more pages to find program details.

Assessment 3 Downloading Content on Ski Resorts

1. You work for First Choice Travel and are preparing a brochure on snow skiing vacations. You need some information and images for the brochure. Search for information on snow skiing resorts in Utah.
2. Visit a website that interests you and contains an image of the resort or mountains.
3. Download an image from the web page to the desktop, saving it as **UtahResortImage1**.
4. Close Internet Explorer.

Assessment 4 Deleting Downloaded Content on the Desktop

1. At the Windows 7 desktop, right-click the *UtahResortImage1* file saved to the desktop and click *Delete* at the shortcut menu. Click *Yes* at the Delete File dialog box to move the file to the Recycle Bin.
2. Delete all of the other downloaded files saved to the desktop from this section.

Marquee Series

Microsoft®
Word
2010

Nita Rutkosky

Pierce College at Puyallup, Puyallup, Washington

Denise Seguin

Fanshawe College, London, Ontario

Audrey Rutkosky Roggenkamp

Pierce College at Puyallup, Puyallup, Washington

Paradigm
PUBLISHING

St. Paul • Los Angeles • Indianapolis

Managing Editor	Sonja Brown
Developmental Editor	Brenda Palo
Supplements Developmental Editor	Brenda Owens
Production Editor	Donna Mears
Cover and Text Designer	Leslie Anderson
Copy Editors	Susan Capecchi and Laura Nelson
Desktop Production	Ryan Hamner and Jack Ross
Proofreader	Laura Nelson
Testers	Carley Bomstad, Amy McGuire, Rob Neilly, and Lindsay Ryan
Indexers	Ina Gravitz and Sandi Schroeder

© 2011 by Paradigm Publishing, Inc.
875 Montreal Way
St. Paul, MN 55102
Email: educate@emcp.com
Website: www.emcp.com

Printed in the United States of America

19 18 17 16 15 14 13 12 11 10   1 2 3 4 5 6 7 8 9 10

Contents

Introducing

Word 2010

Microsoft Word 2010 is a word processing program used to create documents such as letters, reports, research papers, brochures, announcements, newsletters, envelopes, labels, and much more. Word is a full-featured program that provides a wide variety of editing and formatting features as well as sophisticated visual elements. While working in Word, you will produce business documents for the following six companies.

First Choice Travel is a travel center offering a full range of traveling services from booking flights, hotel reservations, and rental cars to offering travel seminars.

The Waterfront Bistro offers fine dining for lunch and dinner and also offers banquet facilities, a wine cellar, and catering services.

Worldwide Enterprises is a national and international distributor of products for a variety of companies and is the exclusive movie distribution agent for Marquee Productions.

Marquee Productions is involved in all aspects of creating movies from script writing and development to filming. The company produces documentaries, biographies, as well as historical and action movies.

Performance Threads maintains an inventory of rental costumes and also researches, designs, and sews special-order and custom-made costumes.

The mission of the Niagara Peninsula College Theatre Arts Division is to offer a curriculum designed to provide students with a thorough exposure to all aspects of the theater arts.

In Section 1 you will learn how to
Create and Edit Documents

Using Microsoft Word, you can create, edit, and format a variety of business documents and use Word's powerful editing and formatting features to produce well-written and visually appealing documents. Some powerful editing features include checking the spelling and grammar in a document and using Thesaurus to find appropriate synonyms for words; using AutoCorrect to improve the efficiency of entering information in a document; and creating a document using a predesigned template.

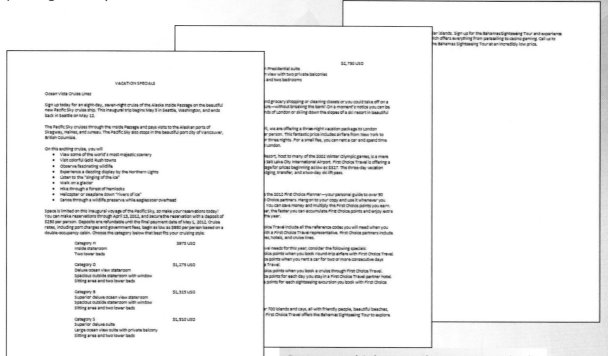

Prepare multiple-page documents and edit documents by completing a spelling and grammar check and using Thesaurus to find appropriate synonyms for words.

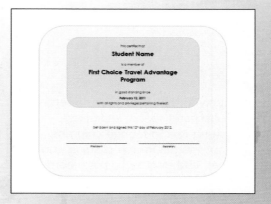

Download templates from Microsoft Office Online and create a variety of documents including letters, faxes, certificates, or awards.

In Section 2 you will learn how to
Format Characters and Paragraphs in Documents

Word contains a number of commands and procedures that affect how the document appears when printed. The appearance of a document in the document screen and how it looks when printed is called the *format*. Formatting can include such tasks as changing the font; aligning and indenting text; changing line and paragraph spacing; setting tabs; and inserting elements such as bullets, numbers, symbols, and special characters. You can also improve the readability of the document by setting text in tabbed columns and by formatting using styles.

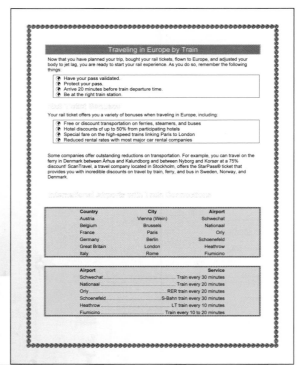

Use Quick Styles sets to apply predesigned formatting such as bolding and centering to text, changing fonts, and applying border lines to headings.

Apply formatting such as inserting bullets and special characters, setting text in tabbed columns, applying paragraph shading and lines, and inserting a page border.

In Section 3 you will learn how to
Enhance Documents

Improve the formatting of a document using features to rearrange text in a document, add special elements, or change the appearance of text. Use buttons on the Home tab to move, copy, and paste text in a document. Improve the appearance of documents by inserting page numbering, headers, and footers; changing margins and page orientation; and changing vertical alignment. Add visual appeal to documents by inserting and customizing clip art images and pictures.

Enhance the appearance of a document by applying a theme, which is a set of formatting choices that include a color, a font, and effects; inserting a cover page; inserting a watermark, which is a lightened image that displays behind text; and inserting a header and footer.

Enhance the visual appeal of a document by inserting a picture such as a company logo, a clip art image related to text in the document, and a page border and page background color.

Create envelopes and mailing labels quickly and automatically.

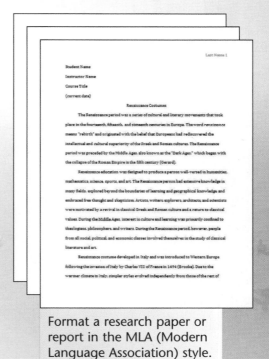

Format a research paper or report in the MLA (Modern Language Association) style.

Word SECTION 1
Creating and Editing a Document

Skills

- Complete the word processing cycle
- Move the insertion point
- Insert, replace, and delete text
- Scroll and navigate in a document
- Select and delete text
- Use Undo and Redo
- Check the spelling and grammar in a document
- Use AutoCorrect
- Use Thesaurus
- Change document views
- Find specific text
- Find and replace text
- Use the Help feature
- Print a document
- Close a document
- Create a document using a template
- Create and rename a folder
- Save a document in a different format

Student Resources

Before beginning the activities in Word, copy to your storage medium the Word folder on the Student Resources CD. This folder contains the data files you need to complete the projects in each Word section.

Projects Overview

Prepare a document describing a special vacation package and edit and format two documents describing various vacation specials offered by First Choice Travel.

Prepare a letter to First Choice Travel regarding a movie site using a letter template and to the manager of The Waterfront Bistro requesting catering information.

Customize a sample employee incentive agreement and prepare a fax cover page for the agreement.

Edit a letter to Marquee Productions regarding costuming for a film.

Write a letter to Josh Hart at Marquee Productions explaining the catering services offered by The Waterfront Bistro and then prepare a fax sheet for the letter.

1

Model Answers for Projects

These model answers for the projects that you complete in Section 1 provide a preview of the finished projects before you begin working and also allow you to compare your own results with these models to ensure you have created the materials accurately.

WS1-FCTTravelPkg.docx is the project in Activity 1.1.

First Choice Travel
Los Angeles Office
Travel Package

Are you spontaneous and enjoy doing something on a moment's notice? If this describes you, then you will be interested in First Choice Travel Moment's Notice Travel Package. For the low price of $599 you can fly from New York to London for a four-day stay. The catch to this incredible deal is that you must make your reservation within the next week and complete your London stay within thirty days.

WS1-FCTVacSpecials.docx (a three-page document) is the project in Activities 1.2 to 1.9.

VACATION SPECIALS

Ocean Vista Cruise Lines

Sign up today for an eight-day, seven-night cruise of the Alaska Inside Passage on the beautiful new Pacific Sky cruise ship. This inaugural trip begins May 5 in Seattle, Washington, and ends back in Seattle on May 12.

The Pacific Sky cruises through the Inside Passage and pays visits to the Alaskan ports of Skagway, Haines, and Juneau. The Pacific Sky also stops in the beautiful port city of Vancouver, British Columbia.

On this exciting cruise, you will
- View some of the world's most majestic scenery
- Visit colorful Gold Rush towns
- Observe fascinating wildlife
- Experience a dazzling display by the Northern Lights
- Listen to the "singing of the ice"
- Walk on a glacier
- Hike through a forest of hemlocks
- Helicopter or seaplane down "rivers of ice"
- Canoe through a wildlife preserve while eagles soar overhead

Space is limited on this inaugural voyage of the Pacific Sky, so make your reservations today! You can make reservations through April 15, 2012, and secure the reservation with a deposit of $250 per person. Deposits are refundable until the final payment date of May 1, 2012. Cruise rates, including port charges and government fees, begin as low as $950 per person based on a double-occupancy cabin. Choose the category below that best fits your cruising style:

Category H Inside stateroom Two lower beds	$975 USD
Category D Deluxe ocean view stateroom Spacious outside stateroom with window Sitting area and two lower beds	$1,275 USD
Category B Superior deluxe ocean view stateroom Spacious outside stateroom with window Sitting area and two lower beds	$1,315 USD
Category S Superior deluxe suite Large ocean view suite with private balcony Sitting area and two lower beds	$1,510 USD

these exciting and spectacular islands. Sign up for the Bahamas Sightseeing Tour and experience the lively city of Nassau, which offers everything from parasailing to casino gaming. Call us to discover how you can join the Bahamas Sightseeing Tour at an incredibly low price.

Category P $2,750 USD
Three-room Presidential suite
Large ocean view with two private balconies
Sitting area and two bedrooms

Getaway Weekends

You could spend the weekend grocery shopping or cleaning closets or you could take off on a romantic three-day adventure—without breaking the bank! On a moment's notice you can be taking in the sights and sounds of London or skiing down the slopes of a ski resort in beautiful Utah.

From February through April, we are offering a three-night vacation package to London beginning as low as $449 per person. This fantastic price includes airfare from New York to London and hotel lodging for three nights. For a small fee, you can rent a car and spend time visiting sights in and around London.

Scenic Park City Mountain Resort, host to many of the 2002 Winter Olympic games, is a mere half-hour drive from Utah's Salt Lake City International Airport. First Choice Travel is offering a three-day ski vacation package for prices beginning as low as $327. The three-day vacation package includes airfare, lodging, transfer, and a two-day ski lift pass.

First Choice Planner

First Choice Travel presents the 2012 First Choice Planner—your personal guide to over 50 special offers from our First Choice partners. Hang on to your copy and use it whenever you travel this summer and fall. You can save money and multiply the First Choice points you earn. The more you travel this year, the faster you can accumulate First Choice points and enjoy extra travel benefits throughout the year.

Specials offered by First Choice Travel include all the reference codes you will need when you make your arrangements with a First Choice Travel representative. First Choice partners include airlines, car rental companies, hotels, and cruise lines.

As you think about your travel needs for this year, consider the following specials:
- Earn 1,000 First Choice points when you book round-trip airfare with First Choice Travel.
- Earn 500 First Choice points when you rent a car for two or more consecutive days through First Choice Travel.
- Earn 5,000 First Choice points when you book a cruise through First Choice Travel.
- Earn 100 First Choice points for each day you stay in a First Choice Travel partner hotel.
- Earn 50 First Choice points for each sightseeing excursion you book with First Choice Travel.

Bahamas Sightseeing Tour

The Bahamas consist of over 700 islands and cays, all with friendly people, beautiful beaches, and magnificent dive spots. First Choice Travel offers the Bahamas Sightseeing Tour to explore

WS1-MPLtrtoFCT.docx is the project in Activity 1.10.

11/23/2012

Student Name
Marquee Productions
955 South Alameda Street
Los Angeles, CA 90037

Ms. Melissa Gehring
First Choice Travel
3588 Ventura Boulevard
Los Angeles, CA 90102

Dear Ms. Gehring:

Marquee Productions will be filming a movie in and around the Toronto area from July 5 through August 27. I would like scheduling and pricing information for flights from Los Angeles to Toronto as well as information on lodging.

Approximately 45 people from our company will need flight reservations and hotel rooms. Please locate the best group rates and let me know the approximate costs. I would like to finalize all preparations by the end of the month.

Sincerely,

Student Name
Projects Coordinator
Marquee Productions

Activity 1.1

Completing the Word Processing Cycle

The process of creating a document in Microsoft Word generally follows a word processing cycle. The steps in the cycle vary but typically include: opening Word; creating and editing the document; saving, printing, and closing the document; and then exiting Word.

Project As an employee of First Choice Travel, you have been asked to create a short document containing information on a travel package offered by First Choice Travel.

Tutorial 1.1
Creating, Saving, and Printing a Document

1 At the Windows desktop, click the Start button 🟦 on the Taskbar, point to *All Programs* at the pop-up menu, click *Microsoft Office*, and then click *Microsoft Word 2010*.

> Depending on your system configuration, these steps may vary.

2 At the Word blank document, identify the various features by comparing your screen with the one shown in Figure 1.1.

> Refer to Table 1.1 for a description of the screen features.

3 Type **First Choice Travel** as shown in Figure 1.2 and then hold down the Shift key, press the Enter key, and then release the Shift key.

> Shift + Enter is the New Line command. Use this command to keep lines of text within the same paragraph, which creates less space between one line and the next.

4 Type **Los Angeles Office** and then press Shift + Enter.

FIGURE 1.1 Word Document Screen

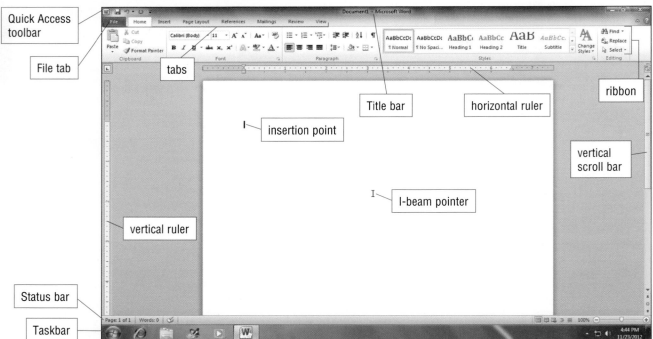

TABLE 1.1 Screen Features and Descriptions

Feature	Description
File tab	when clicked, displays Backstage view that contains buttons and tabs for working with and managing documents
horizontal ruler	used to set margins, indents, and tabs
I-beam pointer	used to move the insertion point or to select text
insertion point	indicates location of next character entered at the keyboard
Quick Access toolbar	contains buttons for commonly used commands
ribbon	area containing the tabs and commands divided into groups
Status bar	displays number of pages and words, view buttons, and Zoom slider bar
tabs	contains commands and features organized into groups
Taskbar	divided into three sections—the Start button, the task buttons area, and the notification area
Title bar	displays document name followed by program name
vertical ruler	used to set top and bottom margins
vertical scroll bar	used to view various parts of the document

5 Type **Travel Package** and then press Enter.

Pressing the Enter key begins a new paragraph in the document.

6 Type the remainder of the text shown in Figure 1.2.

Type the text as shown. When you type *adn* and then press the spacebar, the AutoCorrect feature will automatically correct it to *and*. When you type *teh* and then press the spacebar, AutoCorrect corrects it to *the*. Do not press the Enter key to end a line of text. Word will automatically wrap text to the next line.

FIGURE 1.2 Steps 3–6

First Choice Travel
Los Angeles Office
Travel Package

Are you spontaneous adn enjoy doing something on a moment's notice? If this describes you, then you will be interested in First Choice Travel Moment's Notice Travel Package. For teh low price of $599 you can fly from New York to London for a four-day stay. The catch to this incredible deal is that you must make your reservation within the next week and complete your London stay within thirty days.

continues

7 Save the document by clicking the Save button 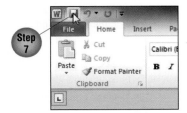 on the Quick Access toolbar.

8 At the Save As dialog box, make sure the WordS1 folder on your storage medium is the active folder, type **WS1-FCTTravelPkg** in the *File name* text box, and then press Enter (or click the Save button).

> Word automatically adds the file extension *.docx* to the end of a document name. The Address bar at the Save As dialog box displays the active folder. If you need to make the WordS1 folder active, click the drive in the *Folders* list box in the Navigation pane that contains your storage medium and then double-click the WordS1 folder in the Content pane.

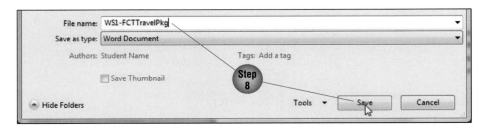

9 Print the document by clicking the File tab, clicking the Print tab at the Backstage view, and then clicking the Print button.

> The File tab is located in the upper left corner of the screen at the left side of the Home tab. When you click the File tab, the Backstage view displays with tabs and buttons for working with and managing documents. The Quick Commands area of the Backstage view contains four buttons for working with documents—Save, Save As, Open, and Close. Tabs at the Backstage view include Info, Recent, New, Print, Save & Send, and Help. Refer to Table 1.2 for descriptions of the options and information you will find in the tabs. Two buttons display below the Help tab—the Options button and the Exit button.

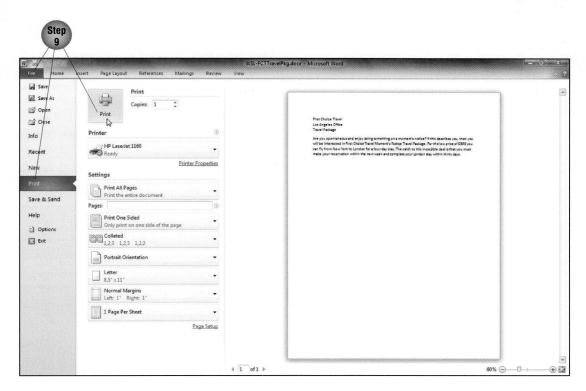

10 Close the document by clicking the File tab and then clicking the Close button.

TABLE 1.2 Tabs in Backstage View

Tab	Options and Information
Info	permissions, possible issues with sharing the document, document versions, properties (for example, number of pages, number of words), date created, date last modified, date last printed, author
Recent	recent documents
New	available templates (for example, blank document, blog post, sample templates, recent templates), templates from Office.com
Print	number of copies, printer, settings (for example, one-sided pages, letter size, normal margins, one page per sheet)
Save & Send	send the document using email, save it to the Web, save it to SharePoint, publish it as a blog post, change the file type, create a PDF
Help	Microsoft Office Help, Getting Started, Contact Us, Tools for Working with Office (for example, customizing the language and display, checking for updates)

In Addition

Default Document Formatting

A Word document is based on a template that applies default formatting. Default formatting refers to formatting automatically applied by Word. Some of the default formats include 11-point Calibri as the font, line spacing of 1.15, and 10 points of spacing after each paragraph (a press of the Enter key). You will learn more about fonts and paragraph spacing in Section 2.

Correcting Errors

Word contains a spelling feature that inserts a wavy red line below words that are not contained in the Spelling dictionary. You can edit the word or leave it as written. The wavy red line does not print.

Activity 1.2

Moving the Insertion Point; Inserting and Deleting Text

Many documents you create will need to have changes made to them. These changes may include adding text, called *inserting*, or removing text, called *deleting*. To insert or delete text, move the insertion point to certain locations without erasing the text through which it passes. To insert text, position the insertion point in the desired location and then type the text. Delete text in a document by pressing the Backspace key or Delete key.

Project

First Choice Travel marketing staff members have reviewed your document on vacation specials and have recommended a few changes. You need to create a revised version.

Tutorial 1.2
Editing a Document

1 At the Word document screen, click the File tab and then click the Open button.

You can add to the Quick Access toolbar buttons that represent commonly used features. For example, you might want to add the Open button to save steps when opening a document or the Quick Print button to save steps when printing a document. To add a button to the Quick Access toolbar, click the Customize Quick Access Toolbar button ⬇ that displays at the right side of the toolbar and then click the desired button name at the drop-down list.

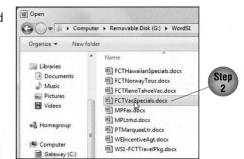

2 At the Open dialog box, make sure the WordS1 folder on your storage medium is the active folder and then double-click *FCTVacSpecials.docx* in the list box.

3 Click the File tab and then click Save As.

Need Help?

If the **FCTVacSpecials.docx** document does not display in the Open dialog box, check with your instructor.

4 At the Save As dialog box, press the Home key to move the insertion point to the beginning of the file name, type **WS1-** in the *File name* text box, and then press the Enter key. (The document name in the *File name* text box should display as **WS1-FCTVacSpecials.docx**.)

Pressing the Home key saves you from having to type the entire document name. If you open an existing document, make changes to it, and then want to save it with the same name, click the Save button on the Quick Access toolbar. If you want to keep the original document and save the document with the changes with a new name, click the File tab and then click the Save As button.

5 Position the mouse pointer at the beginning of the second paragraph and then click the left mouse button.

This moves the insertion point to the location of the mouse pointer.

6 Press the Up, Down, Left, and Right arrow keys located to the right of the regular keys on the keyboard.

Use the information shown in Table 1.3 to practice moving the insertion point in the document.

(7) Press Ctrl + Home to move the insertion point to the beginning of the document.

(8) Click at the beginning of the paragraph that begins *Sign up today for...* and then type **Ocean Vista Cruise Lines announces the inaugural voyage of the Pacific Sky ocean liner.** Press the spacebar once after typing the period.

> By default (automatically determined by Word), text you type in a document is inserted in the document and existing text is moved to the right.

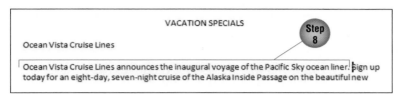

(9) Press Ctrl + End to move the insertion point to the end of the document and then click on any character in the last sentence in the document (the sentence that begins *Let First Choice Travel take...*).

(10) Press the Backspace key until the insertion point is positioned at the left margin and then press the Delete key until you have deleted the remainder of the sentence.

> Pressing the Backspace key deletes any characters to the left of the insertion point. Press the Delete key to delete any characters to the right of the insertion point.

(11) Click the Save button on the Quick Access toolbar.

> Clicking the Save button saves the document with the same name (**WS1-FCTVacSpecials.docx**).

In Brief

Open Document
1. Click File tab.
2. Click Open button.
3. Double-click document name.

Save Document
1. Click Save button on Quick Access toolbar.
2. Type document name.
3. Click Save or press Enter.

TABLE 1.3 Insertion Point Keyboard Control

Press	To move insertion point
End key	to end of line
Home key	to beginning of line
Page Up key	up one screen
Page Down key	down one screen
Ctrl + Home	to beginning of document
Ctrl + End	to end of document

In Addition

Using Overtype Mode

By default, text you type in a document is inserted in the document and existing text is moved to the right. If you want to type over something, you need to turn on the Overtype mode. With the Overtype mode on, anything you type will replace existing text. To turn on the Overtype mode, click the File tab and then click the Options button below the Help tab. At the Word Options dialog box, click *Advanced* in the left panel. In the *Editing options* section, insert a check mark in the *Use* *overtype mode* check box if you want the Overtype mode always on in the document. Or, insert a check mark in the *Use the Insert key to control overtype mode* check box if you want to use the Insert key to turn Overtype mode on and off. After making your selection, click the OK button located in the lower right corner of the dialog box.

Activity 1.3

Scrolling and Navigating in a Document

In addition to moving the insertion point to a specific location, you can use the mouse to move the display of text in the document screen. Use the mouse with the vertical scroll bar to scroll through text in a document. The vertical scroll bar displays toward the right side of the screen. Scrolling in a document changes the text displayed but does not move the insertion point. The Select Browse Object button located at the bottom of the vertical scroll bar contains options for browsing through a document. Scrolling in a document changes the text displayed, while browsing in a document moves the insertion point.

Project To minimize the need for additional editing, you have decided to review carefully the First Choice Travel Vacation Specials document on the screen.

Tutorial 1.2
Editing a Document

1 With **WS1-FCTVacSpecials.docx** open, press Ctrl + Home to move the insertion point to the beginning of the document.

2 Position the mouse pointer on the down scroll arrow on the vertical scroll bar and then click the left mouse button several times.

> This scrolls down the lines of text in the document. Scrolling changes the display of text but does not move the insertion point.

3 Position the mouse pointer on the vertical scroll bar below the scroll box and then click the left mouse button a couple of times.

> The scroll box on the vertical scroll bar indicates the location of the text in the document screen in relation to the remainder of the document. Clicking on the vertical scroll bar below the scroll box scrolls down one screen of text at a time.

4 Position the mouse pointer on the scroll box on the vertical scroll bar, hold down the left mouse button, drag the scroll box to the top of the vertical scroll bar, and then release the mouse button.

> Dragging the scroll box to the top of the vertical scroll bar displays text at the beginning of the document.

5 Click the Select Browse Object button located in the lower right corner of the screen and then click the *Go To* option.

> The location of the *Go To* option may vary. It may be the first option from the left in the top row. Position the arrow pointer on the option and the name of the option displays at the top of the palette. Use other options at the palette to browse to document features such as a field, endnote, footnote, comment, section, heading, graphic, table, or edit.

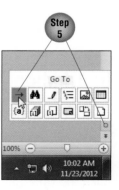

6 At the Find and Replace dialog box with the Go To tab selected, type **2** in the *Enter page number* text box, press the Enter key, and then click Close.

With options at the Find and Replace dialog box with the Go To tab selected, you can move the insertion point to various locations in a document such as a specific page, section, line, bookmark, and so on.

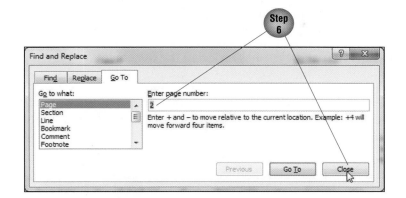
In Brief

Display Find and Replace Dialog Box with Go To Tab Selected
1. Click Select Browse Object button.
2. Click *Go To* option.

7 Click the Previous Page button located above the Select Browse Object button.

Clicking the Previous Page button moves the insertion point to the beginning of the previous page. The full names of and the tasks completed by the Previous and Next buttons vary depending on the last navigation completed.

8 Click the Next Page button located below the Select Browse Object button.

9 Press Ctrl + Home to move the insertion point to the beginning of the document.

10 Save the document by clicking the Save button on the Quick Access toolbar.

In Addition

Option Buttons

As you insert and edit text in a document, you may notice an option button popping up in your text. The name and appearance of this option button varies depending on the action. If a word you type is corrected by AutoCorrect, if you create an automatic list, or if autoformatting is applied to text, the AutoCorrect Options button appears.

Click this button to undo the specific automatic action. If you paste text in a document, the Paste Options button appears near the text. Click this button to display options for controlling the formatting of pasted text.

Activity 1.4

Selecting and Deleting Text; Using Undo and Redo

Previously, you learned to delete text by pressing the Backspace key or Delete key. You can also select text and then delete it, replace it with other text, or apply formatting to the selected text. If you make a change to text, such as deleting selected text, and then change your mind, use the Undo and/or Redo buttons on the Quick Access toolbar.

Project

The assistant manager, Jordan Keyes, has reviewed the document and asked you to make a few changes.

Tutorial 1.2
Editing a Document

1 With **WS1-FCTVacSpecials.docx** open, position the mouse pointer on the word *Behold* (located immediately after the first bullet) and then double-click the left mouse button.

Selected text displays with a blue background. You can also drag through text with the mouse to select the text. When you select text, a dimmed Mini toolbar displays. You will learn more about the Mini toolbar in Activity 2.1.

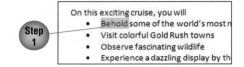

Step 1

On this exciting cruise, you will
• Behold some of the world's most n
• Visit colorful Gold Rush towns
• Observe fascinating wildlife
• Experience a dazzling display by th

Need Help?

If you select the wrong text and want to deselect it, click in the document.

2 Type **View**.

When you type *View*, it takes the place of *Behold*.

3 Move the insertion point to the beginning of the word *Glacier* (located in the second paragraph) and then press the F8 function key on the keyboard. Press the Right Arrow key until the words *Glacier Bay and* are selected.

Step 3

Pressing the F8 function key turns on the Extend mode. Use the insertion point movement keys to select text in Extend mode.

The Pacific Skye cruises through Glacier Bay and the Ins ports of Skagway, Haines, and Juneau. The Pacific Skye Vancouver, British Columbia.

4 Press the Delete key.

Pressing the Delete key deletes the selected text. If you want to cancel a selection, press the Esc key and then press any arrow key.

5 Position the mouse pointer on any character in the first sentence (which begins *Ocean Vista Cruise Lines announces...*), hold down the Ctrl key, click the mouse button, and then release the Ctrl key.

Holding down the Ctrl key while clicking the mouse button selects the entire sentence.

6 Press the Delete key to delete the selected sentence.

7 Click the Undo button  on the Quick Access toolbar.

When you click the Undo button, the deleted sentence reappears. Clicking the Undo button reverses the last command or deletes the last entry you typed. Click the down-pointing arrow at the right side of the Undo button and a drop-down list displays the changes made to the document since it was opened. Click an action and the action, along with any actions listed above it in the drop-down list, is undone.

8 Click the Redo button on the Quick Access toolbar.

Clicking the Redo button deletes the selected sentence. If you click the Undo button and then decide you do not want to reverse the original action, click the Redo button.

9 Position the mouse pointer between the left edge of the page and the first line of text in the second paragraph until the pointer turns into an arrow pointing up and to the right (instead of the left) and then click the left mouse button.

The space between the left edge of the page and the text is referred to as the **selection bar**. Use the selection bar to select specific amounts of text. Refer to Table 1.4 for more information on selecting text.

The Pacific Skye cruises through the Skagway, Haines, and Juneau. The P British Columbia.

10 Deselect the text by clicking in the document.

Deselecting cancels the selection of text.

11 Save the document by clicking the Save button on the Quick Access toolbar.

TABLE 1.4 Selecting with the Mouse

To select	Complete these steps using the mouse
a word	Double-click the word.
a line of text	Click in the selection bar to the left of the line.
multiple lines of text	Drag in the selection bar to the left of the lines.
a sentence	Hold down the Ctrl key and then click anywhere in the sentence.
a paragraph	Double-click in the selection bar next to the paragraph or triple-click anywhere in the paragraph.
multiple paragraphs	Drag in the selection bar.
an entire document	Triple-click in the selection bar.

In Addition

Undoing Multiple Actions

Word maintains actions in temporary memory. If you want to undo an action performed earlier, click the Undo button arrow. This causes a drop-down list to display. To make a selection from this drop-down list, click the desired action. Any actions listed above the selection in the drop-down list are also undone. Multiple actions must be undone in sequence.

Activity 1.5

Checking the Spelling and Grammar in a Document

Use Word's spelling checker to find and correct misspelled words and find duplicated words (such as *and and*). The spelling checker compares words in your document with words in its dictionary. If a match is found, the word is passed over. If no match is found for the word, the spelling checker stops, selects the word, and offers replacements. The grammar checker will search a document for errors in grammar, punctuation, and word usage. The spelling checker and the grammar checker can help you create a well-written document but do not replace the need for proofreading.

Project

Continuing with the editing process, you are ready to check the spelling and grammar in the First Choice Travel Vacation Specials document.

Tutorial 1.3
Using the Spelling and Grammar Feature

1. With **WS1-FCTVacSpecials.docx** open, press Ctrl + Home to move the insertion point to the beginning of the document.

2. Click the Review tab and then click the Spelling & Grammar button in the Proofing group.

3. When the word *inagural* is selected in the document and *inaugural* is selected in the *Suggestions* list box, click the Change button in the Spelling and Grammar dialog box.

   Refer to Table 1.5 for an explanation of the buttons in the Spelling and Grammar dialog box.

4. When the sentence that begins *Space are limited...* is selected, click the Explain button, read the information on subject-verb agreement that displays in the Word Help window, and then click the Close button.

5. Make sure *Space is* is selected in the *Suggestions* list box and then click the Change button.

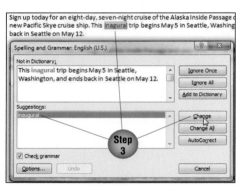

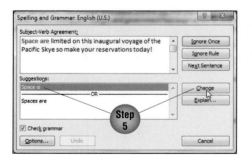

Need Help?

If you accidentally click outside the Spelling and Grammar dialog box, click the Resume button to continue checking.

TABLE 1.5 Spelling and Grammar Dialog Box Buttons

Button	Function
Ignore Once	during spell checking, skips that occurrence of the word; in grammar checking, leaves currently selected text as written
Ignore All	during spell checking, skips that occurrence and all other occurrences of the word in the document
Ignore Rule	during grammar checking, leaves currently selected text as written and ignores the current rule for remainder of the grammar check
Add to Dictionary	adds selected word to the main spelling check dictionary
Delete	deletes the currently selected word(s)
Change	replaces selected word in sentence with selected word in *Suggestions* list box
Change All	replaces selected word in sentence with selected word in *Suggestions* list box and all other occurrences of the word
Explain	during grammar checking, displays information about the grammar rule
AutoCorrect	inserts selected word and correct spelling of word in AutoCorrect dialog box
Undo	reverses most recent spelling and grammar action
Next Sentence	accepts manual changes made to sentence and then continues grammar checking
Options	displays a dialog box with options for customizing a spelling and grammar check

In Brief

Check Spelling and Grammar
1. Click Review tab.
2. Click Spelling & Grammar button in Proofing group.
3. Ignore or change as needed.
4. Click OK.

⑥ When the word *the* is selected (this word occurs twice), click the Delete button in the Spelling and Grammar dialog box.

⑦ When the sentence that begins *You could spent the weekend...* is selected, click the Explain button, read the information on verb form, and then close the Word Help window.

⑧ Make sure *spend* is selected in the *Suggestions* list box and then click the Change button.

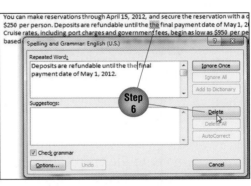

⑨ When the word *utah* is selected, click the Change button.

⑩ Click OK at the message box telling you the spelling and grammar check is complete.

⑪ Click the Save button on the Quick Access toolbar to save the changes made to the document.

In Addition

Changing Spelling Options

Control spelling and grammar checking options at the Word Options dialog box with the *Proofing* option selected. Display this dialog box by clicking the File tab and then clicking the Options button. At the Word Options dialog box, click *Proofing* in the left panel in the dialog box. With options in the dialog box, you can tell the spelling checker to ignore certain types of text, create custom dictionaries, show readability statistics, and hide spelling and/or grammar errors in the document.

Editing While Checking Spelling and Grammar

When checking a document, you can temporarily leave the Spelling and Grammar dialog box by clicking in the document. To resume the spelling and grammar check, click the Resume button.

Activity 1.6

Using AutoCorrect and Thesaurus

The AutoCorrect feature automatically detects and corrects some typographical errors, misspelled words, and incorrect capitalization. In addition to correcting errors, you can use the AutoCorrect feature to insert frequently used text. Use Thesaurus to find synonyms, antonyms, and related words for a particular word.

Project

Tutorial 1.4
Using the AutoCorrect Feature

Tutorial 1.5
Using the Thesaurus

You need to insert additional text in the First Choice Travel vacation specials document. To speed up the process, you will add an entry to AutoCorrect. You will also use Thesaurus to find synonyms for specific words in the document.

1. With **WS1-FCTVacSpecials.docx** open, click the File tab and then click the Options button located below the Help tab.

2. At the Word Options dialog box, click *Proofing* in the left panel and then click the AutoCorrect Options button in the *AutoCorrect options* section.

3. At the AutoCorrect dialog box, type **bst** in the *Replace* text box and then press the Tab key.

4. Type **Bahamas Sightseeing Tour** in the *With* text box and then click the Add button.

5. Click OK to close the AutoCorrect dialog box.

6. Click OK to close the Word Options dialog box.

7. Press Ctrl + End to move the insertion point to the end of the document, make sure the insertion point is positioned a double space below the last bulleted item, and then type the text shown in Figure 1.3. (Type the text exactly as shown. AutoCorrect will correct *bst* to *Bahamas Sightseeing Tour* when you press the Enter key or the spacebar.)

FIGURE 1.3 Step 7

bst

The Bahamas consist of over 700 islands and cays, all with friendly people, beautiful beaches, and magnificent dive spots. First Choice Travel offers the bst to explore these exciting and breathtaking islands. Sign up for the bst and experience the bustling city of Nassau, which offers everything from parasailing to casino gaming. Call us to discover how you can join the bst at an incredibly low price.

8 Click anywhere in the word *breathtaking* (located in the second sentence in the paragraph you just typed), click the Review tab, and then click the Thesaurus button in the Proofing group.

9 At the Research task pane, position the mouse pointer on the word *spectacular* in the task pane list box, click the down-pointing arrow, and then click *Insert* at the drop-down list.

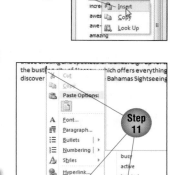

10 Close the Research task pane by clicking the Close button located in the upper right corner of the task pane.

11 Position the mouse pointer on the word *bustling* (located in the third sentence in the paragraph you just typed) and then click the *right* mouse button. At the shortcut menu that displays, point to *Synonyms* and then click *lively* at the side menu.

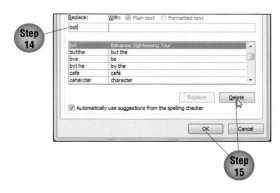

Need Help?
If the shortcut menu does not display, check to make sure you clicked the right mouse button.

12 Click the Save button to save the document with the same name.

13 Click the File tab and then click the Options button located below the Help tab. Click *Proofing* in the left panel in the dialog box and then click the AutoCorrect Options button.

14 At the AutoCorrect dialog box, type **bst** in the *Replace* text box.

> This selects *bst* and *Bahamas Sightseeing Tour* in the list box.

15 Click the Delete button and then click OK to close the dialog box.

16 Click OK to close the Word Options dialog box.

In Brief

Add AutoCorrect Entry
1. Click File tab, then click Options button.
2. Click *Proofing*.
3. Click AutoCorrect Options button.
4. Type text in *Replace* text box.
5. Type text in *With* text box.
6. Click Add button.
7. Click OK.
8. Click OK.

Use Thesaurus
1. Click in desired word.
2. Click Review tab.
3. Click Thesaurus button.
4. Click down-pointing arrow at right of desired word.
5. Click *Insert*.

In Addition

Using the Research Task Pane

Depending on the word you are looking up, the words in the Research task pane list box may display followed by *(n.)* for *noun*, *(adj.)* for *adjective*, or *(adv.)* for *adverb*. As you look up synonyms for various words, click the Previous search button or click the Next search button to display the next search in the sequence. You can also click the down-pointing arrow at the right side of the Next search button to display a list of words for which you have looked up synonyms.

Activity 1.7

Changing Document Views

By default, a document generally displays in Print Layout view. You can change this default to Full Screen Reading, Web Layout, Outline, or Draft. You can also change the zoom percentage for viewing a document. In Print Layout view, you can show and/or hide white space at the top and bottom of each page. With the Zoom button in the View tab and the Zoom slider bar on the Status bar, you can change the percentage of display. Use the Navigation pane to browse in a document, search for specific text or items in the document, and re-arrange the content of your document.

Project

Several people will be reviewing the First Choice Travel document on the screen so you decide to experiment with various views to determine the best view for reviewing on the screen.

Tutorial 1.6
Organizing the Document View

1 With **WS1-FCTVacSpecials.docx** open, press Ctrl + Home to move the insertion point to the beginning of the document and then change to Draft view by clicking the View tab and then clicking the Draft button in the Document Views group.

> You can also change to the Draft view by clicking the Draft button located in the view area near the right side of the Status bar.

2 Click the Print Layout button in the Document Views group.

3 Change the zoom by clicking the Zoom button in the Zoom group in the View tab. At the Zoom dialog box, click *75%* in the *Zoom to* section and then click OK.

> You can also display the Zoom dialog box by clicking the percentage that displays at the left side of the Zoom slider bar. The Zoom slider bar displays at the right side of the Status bar located toward the bottom of the screen.

Step 3

4 Return the view percentage to 100% by positioning the mouse pointer on the button on the Zoom slider bar and then dragging the button to the right until *100%* displays at the left side of the bar.

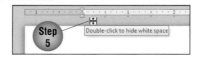

Step 4

In Brief

Display Draft View
1. Click View tab.
2. Click Draft button in Document Views group.
OR
Click Draft button in view area on Status bar.

Display Full Screen Reading View
1. Click View tab.
2. Click Full Screen Reading button in Document Views group.
OR
Click Full Screen Reading button in view area on Status bar.

Display Navigation Pane
1. Click View tab.
2. Click *Navigation Pane* check box.

5 To save space on the screen, you decide to remove the white and gray space that displays at the top and bottom of each page. To do this, position the mouse pointer on the gray space at the top of the page until the pointer turns into the hide white space icon and then double-click the left mouse button.

Step 5

Double-click to hide white space

6 Scroll through the document and then redisplay the white and gray space at the top and bottom of each page. To do this, position the mouse pointer on the gray line at the top of the page until the pointer turns into a show white space icon and then double-click the left mouse button.

Step 6

Double-click to show white space

Ocean Vista Cruise Lines

7 Click the Full Screen Reading button in the Document Views group and then navigate in the document using the commands shown in Table 1.6.

> Full Screen Reading view displays a document for easy viewing and reading. You can also display the document in Full Screen Reading view by clicking the Full Screen Reading button located in the view area on the Status bar.

8 Return to Print Layout view by clicking the Close button located in the upper right corner of the screen.

9 Click the *Navigation Pane* check box in the Show group in the View tab.

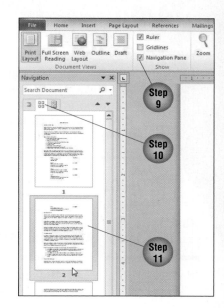

The Navigation pane displays at the left side of the screen and includes a Search text box and a pane with three tabs. Click the first tab to browse headings in a document (heading styles must be applied to text in the document for headings to display in the pane), click the second tab to browse pages in the document, and click the third tab to browse the current search results in the document.

10 Click the middle tab in the Navigation pane.

Clicking the middle tab displays miniatures of each page in the document in the Navigation pane.

11 Click the page 2 thumbnail in the Navigation pane.

This moves the insertion point to the beginning of page 2.

12 Click in the Search text box in the Navigation pane (contains the text *Search Document*) and then type **Pacific Skye**.

When you type *Pacific Skye*, each occurrence of the text is highlighted in the document.

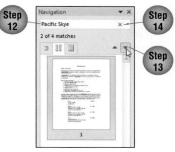

13 Click the Next Search Result button in the Navigation pane (displays as a down-pointing arrow) to select the next occurrence of *Pacific Skye*. Click the button again to select the next occurrence.

You can click the Previous Search Result button to display the previous occurrence of the search text.

14 Click the button containing a blue X that displays at the right side of the Search text box.

Clicking this button ends the current search, removes the search text in the Navigation pane, and selects the current search result in the document.

15 Close the Navigation pane by clicking the Close button that displays in the upper right corner of the pane or by clicking the *Navigation Pane* check box in the Show group in the View tab.

16 Click the Two Pages button 🔲 in the Zoom group to display two pages on the screen and then click the One Page button 🔳 in the Zoom group.

17 Drag the button on the Zoom slider bar or click the Zoom Out button ⊖ or Zoom In button ⊕ until *100%* displays at the left side of the bar.

TABLE 1.6 Navigating in Full Screen Reading View

Press this key	To complete this action
Page Down or spacebar	Move to next page or section.
Page Up or Backspace key	Move to previous page or section.
Right Arrow	Move to next page.
Left Arrow	Move to previous page.
Home	Move to first page in document.
End	Move to last page in document.
Esc	Return to Print Layout view.

In Addition

Hiding the Ribbon

If you want to view more of your document on the screen, you can hide the ribbon by clicking the Minimize the Ribbon button that displays at the right side of the ribbon immediately left of the Help button or by double-clicking the active tab. You can also hide the ribbon with the keyboard shortcut Ctrl + F1. The tabs remain on the screen but the groups and commands are removed. Redisplay the ribbon by clicking the Expand the Ribbon button (previously the Minimize the Ribbon button), by double-clicking any tab, or with the keyboard shortcut Ctrl + F1.

Activity
1.8

Finding and Replacing Text

In the previous activity you displayed the Navigation pane by clicking the *Navigation Pane* check box in the Show group in the View tab. You can also display this pane by clicking the Find button in the Editing group in the Home tab. You can use the Navigation pane to find specific text in a document. If you want to find text and then replace the text with other text, use options at the Find and Replace dialog box with the Replace tab selected. Display this dialog box by clicking the Replace button in the Editing group in the Home tab.

Project

Tutorial 1.7
Finding and
Replacing Text

As you review the vacation specials document, you discover that the name of the ship is spelled incorrectly and that the ship's cabins are divided into categories rather than classes. You decide to use the Find and Replace feature to makes these changes.

1. With **WS1-FCTVacSpecials.docx** open, press Ctrl + Home to move the insertion point to the beginning of the document. You realize that the name of the ship is the *Pacific Sky*, not the *Pacific Skye*. To change the name, click the Home tab and then click the Replace button in the Editing group.

2. At the Find and Replace dialog box with the Replace tab selected, type **Skye** in the *Find what* text box and then press the Tab key.

   Pressing the Tab key moves the insertion point to the *Replace with* text box.

3. Type **Sky** in the *Replace with* text box.

4. Click the Replace All button located toward the bottom of the dialog box.

   Clicking the Replace All button replaces all occurrences of the text in the document. If you want control over what is replaced in a document, click the Replace button to replace text or click the Find Next button to move to the next occurrence of the text.

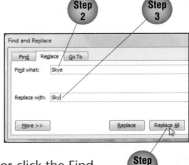

5. At the message telling you that four replacements were made, click the OK button.

6. Click the Close button to close the Find and Replace dialog box.

7. Looking at the document, you realize that the word "class" is used to designate cabins and the word should instead be "category." To make this change, click the Replace button in the Editing group in the Home tab.

8. At the Find and Replace dialog box with the Replace tab selected, type **class**.

   When you open the Replace dialog box, *Skye* is automatically selected in the *Find what* text box. When you begin typing *class*, the selected text is automatically deleted.

9. Press the Tab key and then type **category** in the *Replace with* text box.

   When you type the find text and the replace text in all lowercase letters, Word will find and replace all occurrences regardless of the capitalization. For example, Word will find *Class* in the document and replace it with *Category*.

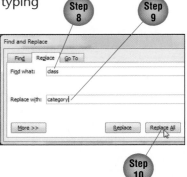

10 Click the Replace All button.

11 At the message telling you that six replacements were made, click the OK button.

12 Click the Close button to close the Find and Replace dialog box.

13 Click the Save button on the Quick Access toolbar to save the document.

In Brief

Find and Replace Text
1. Click Replace button in Editing group.
2. Type find text.
3. Press Tab key.
4. Type replace text.
5. Click Replace All button.

In Addition

Options at the Expanded Find and Replace Dialog Box

The Find and Replace dialog box contains a variety of check boxes with options you can choose for completing a find and replace. To display these options, click the More button located at the bottom of the dialog box. This causes the Find and Replace dialog box to expand as shown at the right. The options are described below.

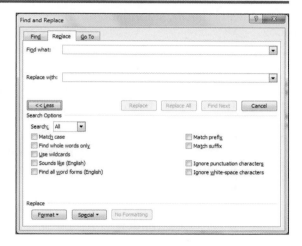

Option	Action
Match case	Exactly match the case of the search text. For example, if you search for *Book*, Word will stop at *Book* but not *book* or *BOOK*.
Find whole words only	Find a whole word, not a part of a word. For example, if you search for *her* and did not select *Find whole words only*, Word would stop at t*her*e, *her*e, *her*s, and so on.
Use wildcards	Search for wildcards, special characters, or special search operators.
Sounds like	Match words that sound alike but are spelled differently such as *know* and *no*.
Find all word forms	Find all forms of the word entered in the *Find what* text box. For example, if you enter *hold*, Word will stop at *held* and *holding*.
Match prefix	Find only those words that begin with the letters in the *Find what* text box. For example, if you enter *per*, Word will stop at words such as *perform* and *perfect* but will skip over words such as *super* and *hyperlink*.
Match suffix	Find only those words that end with the letters in the *Find what* text box. For example, if you enter *ly*, Word will stop at words such as *accurately* and *quietly* but skip over words such as *catalyst* and *lyre*.
Ignore punctuation characters	Ignore punctuation within characters. For example, if you enter *US* in the *Find what* text box, Word will stop at *U.S.*
Ignore white space characters	Ignore spaces between letters. For example, if you enter *F B I* in the *Find what* text box, Word will stop at *FBI*.

Activity 1.9

Using the Help Feature; Printing a Document

Microsoft Word includes a Help feature that contains information on Word features and commands. To access Help, click the Microsoft Word Help button located in the upper right corner of the screen to display the Word Help window. You can also get help within a dialog box or at the Backstage view. Display a dialog box and then click the Help button that displays in the upper right corner of the dialog box and the Word Help window displays with specific information about the dialog box.

To get information about the Backstage view click the File tab and then click the Help button that displays in the upper right corner of the screen. Click a tab and the Backstage view displays with options pertaining to the tab. For example, click the Print tab and the Print tab Backstage view displays with options for previewing and printing a document. With options in this tab you can preview your document, specify the number of copies to print, and choose specific pages for printing. To remove the Backstage view, click the File tab, click any other tab in the ribbon, or press the Esc key.

Project

You are ready to print certain sections of the First Choice Travel vacation specials document. But first you want to learn more about printing a document in the Backstage view. You decide to use the Help feature to learn about printing.

Tutorial 1.8
Using the Help Feature

Tutorial 1.9
Previewing and Printing Documents

1. With **WS1-FCTVacSpecials.docx** open, press Ctrl + Home to move the insertion point to the beginning of the document and then click the Microsoft Word Help button ❓ located in the upper right corner of the screen.

   You can also press the F1 function key to display the Word Help window.

2. At the Word Help window, type **print a document** and then press Enter.

   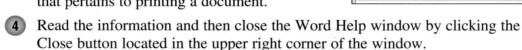

3. At the Word Help window, click a hyperlink that pertains to printing a document.

4. Read the information and then close the Word Help window by clicking the Close button located in the upper right corner of the window.

5. Click the File tab to display the Backstage view and then click the Help button located in the upper right corner of the screen.

6. Click a hyperlink in the Word Help dialog box related to the Backstage view, read the information, and then close the box.

7. Click the Print tab to display the Print tab Backstage view.

   At the Print tab Backstage view, your document displays at the right side of the screen as it will appear when printed. The left side of the Print tab Backstage view displays three categories—Print, Printer, and Settings. Click the Print button in the Print category to send the document to the printer. Specify the number of copies you want printed with the *Copies* option in the Print category. Use the gallery in the Printer category to specify the desired printer. The Settings category contains a number of galleries, each with options for specifying how you want your document printed, such as whether or not you want the pages collated when printed; the orientation, page size, and margins of your document; and how many pages of your document you want to print on a page.

8 Click the Next Page button located below and to the left of the preview page to display the next page in the document.

9 Click twice on the Zoom In button (containing a plus symbol) that displays at the right side of the Zoom slider bar.

> Click the Zoom In button to increase the size of the page or click the Zoom Out button (containing a minus symbol) to decrease the size of the page.

10 Click the Zoom to Page button located at the right side of the Zoom slider bar.

11 Print only page 2 of the document by clicking in the *Pages* text box (located in the Settings category), typing **2**, and then clicking the Print button.

12 Move the insertion point to any character in page 3 and then print page 3. Begin by clicking the File tab and then clicking the Print tab.

13 Click the top gallery in the Settings category and then click *Print Current Page* at the drop-down list.

14 Click the Print button.

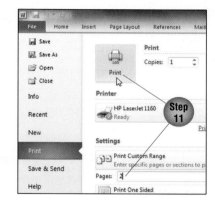

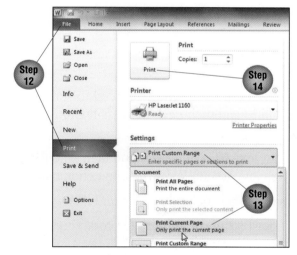

15 Save and then close **WS1-FCTVacSpecials.docx**.

In Brief

Use Help
1. Click Microsoft Word Help button.
2. Click desired option in Word Help window.

Print a Document
1. Click File tab.
2. Click Print tab.
3. Click Print button.

Print a Specific Page
1. Click File tab.
2. Click Print tab.
3. Click in *Pages* text box.
4. Type desired page number.
5. Click Print button.

Print Current Page
1. Position insertion point in desired page.
2. Click File tab.
3. Click Print tab.
4. Click top gallery in Settings category.
5. Click *Print Current Page* at drop-down list.

In Addition

Printing a Range of Pages

At the Print tab Backstage view, you can identify a specific page, multiple pages, and/or a range of pages for printing. To print specific pages, click in the *Pages* text box and then type the page numbers of the specific pages you want to print. If you want specific multiple pages printed, use a comma to indicate *and* and use a hyphen to indicate *through*. For example, to print pages 2 and 5, you would type **2,5** in the *Pages* text box. To print pages 6 through 10, you would type **6-10**. You can also enter both commas and hyphens when specifying page numbers. For example, to print pages 2 through 6 and pages 8 and 11, you would type **2-6,8,11** in the *Pages* text box.

Activity 1.10

Creating a Document Using a Template

Word includes a number of template documents formatted for specific uses. Each Word document is based on a template document with the *Normal* template the default. With Word templates (and Microsoft online templates), you can easily create a variety of documents, such as letters, faxes, and awards, with specialized formatting. Display available templates by clicking the *Sample templates* option at the New tab Backstage view. You can also choose from a variety of Microsoft online templates by clicking the desired category in the *Office.com Templates* section of the New tab Backstage view. You must be connected to the Internet to download the online templates.

Project

Tutorial 1.10
Creating Documents Using a Word Template

You are the projects coordinator for Marquee Productions, a movie production company. The company's travel agency is First Choice Travel, and you need the agency to make flight and hotel reservations for personnel involved in filming a movie in and around Toronto. You decide to use a letter template to help you format the letter.

1. Click the File tab and then click the New tab.

2. At the New tab Backstage view, click the *Sample templates* option.

3. Click the Equity Letter template (you will need to scroll down list to display the Equity Letter template) and then click the Create button that displays below the letter in the preview section.

4. Click the placeholder text *[Pick the date]* and then type the current date. (Your date will automatically change to numbers when you click outside the placeholder.)

5. Select the name that displays below the date and then type your first and last names.

6. Click the placeholder text *[Type the sender company name]* and then type **Marquee Productions**.

7. Click the placeholder text *[Type the sender company address]*, type **955 South Alameda Street**, press the Enter key, and then type **Los Angeles, CA 90037**.

8. Click the placeholder text *[Type the recipient name]* and then type **Ms. Melissa Gehring**.

9. Press the Enter key and then type **First Choice Travel**.

10. Click the placeholder text *[Type the recipient address]*, type **3588 Ventura Boulevard**, press the Enter key, and then type **Los Angeles, CA 90102**.

11. Click the placeholder text *[Type the salutation]* and then type **Dear Ms. Gehring:**.

12. Click on any character in the two paragraphs of text in the body of the letter and then type the text shown in Figure 1.4.

11/23/2012

Student Name
Marquee Productions
955 South Alameda Street
Los Angeles, CA 90037

Ms. Melissa Gehring
First Choice Travel
3588 Ventura Boulevard
Los Angeles, CA 90102

Dear Ms. Gehring:

Marquee Productions will be filming a movie in and around the Toronto area from July 5 through August 27. I would like scheduling and pricing information for flights from Los Angeles to Toronto as well as information on lodging.

Approximately 45 people from our company will need flight reservations and hotel rooms. Please locate the best group rates and let me know the approximate costs. I would like to finalize all preparations by the end of the month.

Step 12

In Brief

**Create Document
Using Template**
1. Click File tab.
2. Click New Tab.
3. Click desired
   template.
4. Click Create button.

13. Click the placeholder text *[Type the closing]* and then type **Sincerely,**.

14. Select the current name below *Sincerely* and then type your first and last names.

15. Click the placeholder text *[Type the sender title]* and then type **Projects Coordinator**.

16. Click the Save button on the Quick Access toolbar.

17. At the Save As dialog box, type **WS1-MPLtrtoFCT** and then press Enter.

18. Print the letter by clicking the File tab, clicking the Print tab, and then clicking the Print button (or you can click the Quick Print button on the Quick Access toolbar if it is visible on the toolbar).

19. Close the document by clicking the File tab and then clicking the Close button.

FIGURE 1.4 Step 12

Marquee Productions will be filming a movie in and around the Toronto area from July 5 through August 27. I would like scheduling and pricing information for flights from Los Angeles to Toronto as well as information on lodging.

Approximately 45 people from our company will need flight reservations and hotel rooms. Please locate the best group rates and let me know the approximate costs. I would like to finalize all preparations by the end of the month.

In Addition

Using Online Templates

If you are connected to the Internet, Microsoft offers a number of predesigned templates you can download. Templates are grouped into folders and the folders display in the *Office.com Templates* section of the New tab Backstage view. Click the desired template folder to display available templates. Click the desired template and then click the Create button.

Activity 1.11

Creating and Renaming Folders; Saving a Document in a Different Format

As you continue working with documents, consider document management tasks such as creating a folder and copying, moving, and deleting documents. You can complete many document management tasks at the Open dialog box on one document or selected documents. By default, Word saves a file as a Word document and adds the extension *.docx* to the name. With the *Save as type* option at the Save As dialog box, you can save a document in a different format such as rich text or an earlier version of Word, or as a web page or plain text file.

Project Since First Choice Travel will be communicating with Marquee Productions, you decide to create a folder into which you will insert Marquee Productions documents. You will also save a document in an older version of Word and as a plain text document.

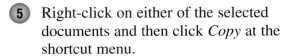

Tutorial 1.11
Managing Folders

Tutorial 1.12
Managing Documents

1. Click the File tab and then click the Open button.

2. At the Open dialog box with WordS1 the active folder, click the New folder button on the toolbar.

3. Type **Marquee** and then press Enter.

4. Click the document **MPFax.docx** in the *Open dialog box* list box, hold down the Ctrl key, click **WS1-FCTVacSpecials.docx**, and then release the Ctrl key.

    Use the Ctrl key to select nonadjacent documents. Use the Shift key to select adjacent documents.

5. Right-click on either of the selected documents and then click *Copy* at the shortcut menu.

6. Double-click the *Marquee* file folder.

    File folders display in the *Open dialog box* list box before documents. File folders display preceded by a file folder icon and documents display preceded by a document icon.

7. Position the mouse pointer in a white portion of the *Open dialog box* list box, click the *right* mouse button, and then click *Paste* at the shortcut menu.

    The copied documents are inserted in the Marquee folder.

8. You need to send the **WS1-FCTVacSpecials.docx** document to a colleague who uses Word 2003, so you need to save the document in that format. At the Open dialog box with the Marquee folder active, double-click **WS1-FCTVacSpecials.docx**.

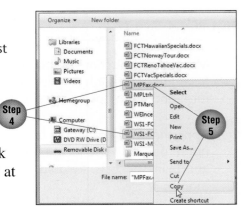

9 Click the File tab and then click the Save As button. At the Save As dialog box, type **WS1-FCTVacSpecialsWd2003** in the *File name* text box.

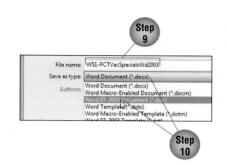

Step 9

10 Click the *Save as type* option box and then click *Word 97-2003 Document (*.doc)* at the drop-down list.

Step 10

11 Click the Save button located in the lower right corner of the dialog box and then close the document.

> If a compatibility checker message displays, click the Continue button.

12 Display the Open dialog box and then click *WordS1* in the Address bar.

13 Rename the Marquee folder. To do this, right-click on the folder name and then click *Rename* at the shortcut menu. Type **MarqueeProductions** and then press Enter.

> The new folder name replaces the original folder name. You can also rename a folder by clicking the Organize button, clicking *Rename*, and then typing the new folder name.

14 Delete the MarqueeProductions folder. To do this, click once on the folder to select it, click the Organize button on the toolbar, and then click *Delete* at the drop-down list. At the message asking if you are sure you want to delete the folder and all of its contents, click the Yes button.

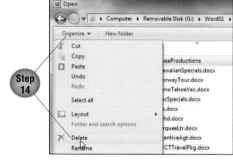

Step 14

15 Close the Open dialog box.

16 Exit Word by clicking the Close button located in the upper right corner of the screen.

> You can also exit Word by clicking the File tab and then clicking the Exit button located below the Help tab.

In Brief

Create Folder
1. Click File tab, then click Open button.
2. Click New Folder button.
3. Type folder name.
4. Press Enter.

Save Document in Different Format
1. Open document.
2. Click File tab, then click Save As button.
3. Type document name.
4. Change *Save as type* option to desired format.
5. Click Save button.

In Addition

Saving a Document for Viewing but Not Editing

If you want to send a document to someone so they can view it but not edit it, consider saving the document in the PDF or XPS file format or as a web page. Documents saved in the PDF and XPS file formats can be viewed in a variety of software and these formats preserve the page layout of the document. Save a document as a web page and the document can be viewed in a web browser. This format, however, does not preserve the page layout of the document.

Features Summary

Feature	Ribbon Tab, Group	Button	Quick Access Toolbar	File tab	Keyboard Shortcut
AutoCorrect dialog box				Options, Proofing, AutoCorrect Options	
close		X		Close	Ctrl + F4
Draft view	View, Document Views	📄			
exit Word				Exit	
Full Screen Reading view	View, Document Views	📖			
Help		❓			F1
Navigation pane	View, Show				Ctrl + F
New tab Backstage view				New	
Open dialog box				Open	Ctrl + O
Print tab Backstage view				Print	Ctrl + P
Print Layout view	View, Document Views	📄			
redo an action			↻		Ctrl + Y
Save As dialog box				Save As	F12
save document			💾	Save	Ctrl + S
Spelling & Grammar	Review, Proofing	ABC			F7
Thesaurus	Review, Proofing	📖			Shift + F7
undo an action			↺ ▾		Ctrl + Z
Word Options dialog box				Options	

Knowledge Check

Completion: In the space provided at the right, indicate the correct term, command, or option.

1. This area on the screen contains tabs and commands divided into groups.
2. Click this tab to display the Backstage view.
3. Use this keyboard command to move the insertion point to the beginning of the document.

4. To select a sentence, hold down this key and then click anywhere in the sentence.

        _____

5. This toolbar contains the Undo and Redo buttons.

        _____

6. To begin checking the spelling and grammar in a document, click this tab and then click the Spelling & Grammar button in the Proofing group.

        _____

7. This feature automatically detects and corrects some typographical errors.

        _____

8. Use this feature to find synonyms for a word.

        _____

9. Display a document in this view for easy viewing and reading.

        _____

10. The *Navigation Pane* check box is located in this group in the View tab.

        _____

11. Click this button at the Find and Replace dialog box to replace all occurrences of text.

        _____

12. Click this option at the New tab Backstage view to display available templates.

        _____

13. Click this button on the Open dialog box toolbar to create a new folder.

        _____

14. Select nonadjacent documents at the Open dialog box by holding down this key while clicking each document name.

        _____

Skills Review

Review 1 Editing a Hawaiian Specials Document

1. Create a new folder on your storage medium and name it **WordEOS**.
2. Open **FCTHawaiianSpecials.docx** from the WordS1 folder and then save it in the WordEOS folder and name it **WS1-R1-FCTHawaiianSpecials**.
3. Insert the word *spectacular* between the words *the* and *Pacific* in the first sentence below the *White Sands Charters* heading.
4. Move the insertion point to the beginning of the paragraph below the *Air Adventures* heading and then type the sentence **Experience beautiful coastlines and magnificent waterfalls, and fly inside an active volcano.**
5. Select and then delete the words *Depending on weather, marine conditions, and access, your* located in the third sentence in the paragraph below the *White Sands Charters* heading.
6. Capitalize the *g* in *guides*. (This word now begins the sentence.)
7. Select and then delete the last sentence in the *Air Adventures* section (the sentence that begins *View untouched areas from...*).
8. Undo the deletion and then redo the deletion.
9. Select and then delete the fourth bulleted item in the *Bicycle Safari* section (the text that reads *Vista dining*).
10. Undo the deletion and then deselect the text.
11. Move the insertion point to the beginning of the document and then complete a spelling and grammar check on the document. (*Molokini* is spelled correctly. If the grammar checker stops at what it considers a sentence fragment, click the Ignore button.)

FIGURE 1.5 Review 1

Luau Legends

Enjoy a spectacular HA dinner show featuring lavish prime rib and authentic HA buffet. This uniquely HA experience includes a traditional lei greeting, exceptional food and beverages, magic music of the islands, and Hawaii's finest performers. Join us each evening beginning at 7:30 p.m. for an evening of delicious HA food and spectacular performances.

12. Display the AutoCorrect dialog box, insert *HA* in the *Replace* text box, insert *Hawaiian* in the *With* text box, click the Add button, and then close the dialog box. Close the Word Options dialog box.
13. Move the insertion point to the end of the document and then type the text shown in Figure 1.5.
14. After typing the text, use Thesaurus to change *lavish* to *sumptuous* and change *exceptional* to *extraordinary*.
15. Save, print, and then close **WS1-R1-FCTHawaiianSpecials.docx**.

Review 2 Editing an Agreement

1. Open **WEIncentiveAgt.docx** and then save the document in the WordEOS folder and name it **WS1-R2-WEIncentiveAgt**.
2. Complete a spelling and grammar check on the document. (Ignore the suggestion to revise the use of *between*.)
3. Search for all occurrences of *Employee* and replace with *Carol Shepard*.
4. Search for all occurrences of *Company* and replace with *Worldwide Enterprises*.
5. Save, print, and then close **WS1-R2-WEIncentiveAgt.docx**.

Review 3 Preparing a Fax Sheet

1. Click the File tab, click the New tab, click the *Sample templates* option, click the *Equity Fax* template, and then click the Create button.
2. Insert the following information in the specified location:
   • To: Scott Drysdale   • Phone: (213) 555-3400
   • From: (Type your first and last names)   • Date: (Insert current date)
   • Fax: (213) 555-3349   • Re: Incentive Agreement
   • Pages: 3   • CC: (Delete this placeholder)
   Then insert a capital *X* in the *Please Reply* check box. Click the *[Type comments]* placeholder and then type the following comment: **Please review the Incentive Agreement and then call me so we can schedule an appointment.**
3. Save the document in the WordEOS folder and name it **WS1-R3-WEAgtFax**.
4. Print and then close the document.

Skills Assessment

Assessment 1 Editing a Letter

1. Open **PTMarqueeLtr.docx** and then save the document in the WordEOS folder with the name **WS1-A1-PTMarqueeLtr**.
2. Move the insertion point a double space below the paragraph of text in the letter and then add the following information. (Write the information as a paragraph—do not use bullets.)
   - Costume research takes approximately two to three weeks.
   - If appropriate costumes cannot be found, costumes are sewn.
   - Anticipate five working days to sew a costume.
   - Include the number of costumes and approximate sizes.
   - A price estimate will be provided before costumes are purchased or sewn.
3. Use Thesaurus to replace *regarding* in the first sentence with an appropriate synonym.
4. Save, print, and then close **WS1-A1-PTMarqueeLtr.docx**.

Assessment 2 Writing a Letter

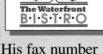

1. Open the Median Letter template from the New tab Backstage view and then use the following information to create the letter. (You determine the salutation and closing.)

   Sender's information:
   The Waterfront Bistro
   3104 Rivermist Drive
   Buffalo, NY 14280

   Recipient's information:
   Mr. Josh Hart, Locations Director
   Marquee Productions
   955 South Alameda Street
   Los Angeles, CA 90037

   Write a letter as Dana Hirsch that covers these points:
   Explain that The Waterfront Bistro is a full-service catering company with a number of menus for breakfast, lunch, dinner, and morning and afternoon snacks. Include the price ranges for breakfast, lunch, dinner, and snack menus. (You determine the ranges.) Offer a 5% discount if you cater for the duration of the filming. Tell Mr. Hart that you would like to fax a variety of menu options to him. Close the letter by telling him you are very interested in the business and say something positive about your catering service.
2. Save the completed letter document in the WordEOS folder and name it **WS1-A2-WBCateringLtr**. Print and then close the document.

Assessment 3 Preparing a Fax

1. Open the Equity Fax template from the New tab Backstage view and then insert the necessary information in the specified fields. You are Dana Hirsch and you are sending the fax to Josh Hart (see information in Assessment 2). His fax number is (612) 555-2009 and his telephone number is (612) 555-2005. Insert an *X* in the *Please Comment* check box and indicate that the fax contains 11 pages.
2. Save the fax document in the WordEOS folder and name it **WS1-A3-WBFax**.
3. Print and then close the document.

Assessment 4 Finding Information on Changing Grammar
Checking Options

1. Open **FCTNorwayTour.docx** and then save the document in the WordEOS folder with the name **WS1-A4-FCTNorwayTour**.
2. Use the Help feature to learn more about spelling and grammar checking. After reading the information, display the Word Options dialog box (click the File tab and then click the Options button) with the Proofing tab selected and then change the *Writing Style* option to *Grammar & Style* (this option is located in the *When correcting spelling and grammar in Word* section).
3. Complete a spelling and grammar check on the document. (*Myrdal* is spelled correctly.)
4. Change the *Writing style* option back to *Grammar Only*.
5. Save, print, and then close **WS1-A4-FCTNorwayTour.docx**.

Assessment 5 Individual Challenge
Creating a Certificate

1. Make sure you are connected to the Internet and then display the New tab Backstage view, click the Award certificates folder in the *Office.com Templates* list box, click the Other folder, and then double-click the Membership certificate template. (If the Membership certificate template is not available, choose a similar certificate.)
2. Identify yourself as a member in good standing in the *First Choice Travel Advantage Program*.
3. Save the completed document in the WordEOS folder and name it **WS1-A5-IC-Membership**.
4. Print and then close the document.

Marquee Challenge

Challenge 1 Preparing a Business Letter

1. Open **MPLtrhd.docx** and then save the document in the WordEOS folder with the name **WS1-C1-MPLtrtoWB**.
2. Create the letter shown in Figure 1.6.
3. Save, print, and then close **WS1-C1-MPLtrtoWB.docx**.

Challenge 2 Editing and Formatting a Travel Document

1. Open **FCTRenoTahoeVac.docx** and then save the document in the WordEOS folder with the name **WS1-C2-FCTRenoTahoeVac**.
2. Edit and format the document so it displays as shown in Figure 1.7. (Search for all occurrences of *Eldorado* and replace with *Sierra*. Expand the Find and Replace dialog box, insert a check mark in the *Match case* check box, and then search for all occurrences of *LT* and replace with *Lake Tahoe*. Complete a spelling and grammar check on the document.)
3. Save, print, and then close **WS1-C2-FCTRenoTahoeVac.docx**.

FIGURE 1.6 Challenge 1

V: 612 555 2005
F: 612 555 2009
info@emcp.net
www.emcp.net/marquee

(Current date) *(press Enter three times)*

Ms. Dana Hirsch *(press Shift + Enter)*
The Waterfront Bistro *(press Shift + Enter)*
3104 Rivermist Drive *(press Shift + Enter)*
Buffalo, NY 14280 *(press Enter)*

Dear Ms. Hirsch: *(press Enter)*

We will be filming a movie in and around Toronto and Buffalo from July 7 to August 30, 2012. During that time, we will require catering services for cast and crew members. The services we request include breakfast, mid-morning snack, lunch, and afternoon snack for each day of filming, including weekends. *(press Enter)*

Please send information on your breakfast and lunch catering menus and snack choices. We are interested in pricing for meals and snacks for approximately 45 people for the duration of the filming. If you have any questions about our catering needs, please contact me by telephone at (612) 555-2005 or e-mail at JoshH@emcp.net. *(press Enter)*

Sincerely, *(press Enter twice)*

Josh Hart *(press Shift + Enter)*
Locations Director *(press Enter)*

SN

955 South Alameda Street ◀ Los Angeles, CA 90037

FIGURE 1.7 Challenge 2

VACATIONING IN RENO AND LAKE TAHOE

Reno and Lake Tahoe are home to more snow, more ski resorts, and more nightlife than any other ski destination in North America. Come visit our area and experience a vast diversity of ski terrain, scenic beauty, and entertainment options. Getting to Reno and Lake Tahoe is as easy as taking one of over 250 flights that arrive daily at the Reno/Tahoe International Airport. Getting to your accommodations can be as quick as a ten-minute shuttle ride to a hotel casino in Reno or less than a scenic hour through the Sierra foothills to a variety of Lake Tahoe properties. All of the ski slopes are between 45 and 90 minutes from the Reno Airport. Getting around is easy with a variety of transportation options.

Destinations

Convenience and great locations make Incline Village and Crystal Bay desirable destinations at Lake Tahoe. Situated between Squaw Valley and Heavenly ski resorts, the two villages, along with other great resorts such as Mt. Rose and Diamond Peak, are just minutes away. Just 30 miles from Reno/Tahoe International Airport, the villages are central to all of the Lake Tahoe ski resorts. Diamond Peak offers 2,000 acres of classic Nordic terrain, over 35 kilometers of groomed tracks and skating lanes with incredible views of Lake Tahoe. The resort also boasts a 6.2 million dollar complex including an eight-lane indoor swimming pool, cardiovascular and strength-training center, aerobic studio, and gym. Additional recreational offerings include sledding, sleigh rides, snowshoeing, bowling, and a movie theater.

North Lake Tahoe is a favored destination for discriminating vacationers. Visit this beautiful area for the epic powder, seven resorts, downhill and cross-country skiing, and unlimited dining choices—all for affordable prices. Consider trying ice skating at the world's highest ice rink, snowmobiling and snowshoeing in the backcountry, or touring Lake Tahoe on an authentic paddle-wheeler. Visit one of 80 restaurants boasting award-winning cuisine in lakeshore and alpine settings. Visit the historic town of Truckee, an old railroad and logging community with quaint shops and sights.

Lake Tahoe South Shore is the ideal destination for variety with an amazing selection of skiing for all skill levels. Almost endless lodging possibilities await you with over 95 luxurious hotels and casinos, all-suite resorts, motels, condominiums, cabins, and homes. Tour the Sierra backcountry on a snowmobile, take a paddle-wheeler cruise to Emerald Bay, try a peaceful sleigh ride, or see the sights from a dogsled.

Word SECTION 2
Formatting Characters and Paragraphs

Skills

- Apply fonts and font effects
- Use Format Painter
- Repeat a command
- Align text in paragraphs
- Indent text
- Change line and paragraph spacing
- Reveal formatting
- Find and replace formatting
- Insert bullets and numbering
- Insert symbols and special characters
- Set tabs and tabs with leaders
- Add borders and shading to text
- Insert a page border
- Apply styles
- Change the document default formatting

Projects Overview

Edit and format documents on Oslo, Norway, and Petersburg, Alaska; format a document on traveling by train in Europe; and format documents on vacation packages in Oregon and Nevada and cross-country skiing vacation packages.

Prepare a letter to the chair of the Theatre Arts Division at Niagara Peninsula College requesting 20 theatre interns.

Prepare a movie distribution schedule.

Model Answers for Projects

These model answers for the projects that you complete in Section 2 provide a preview of the finished projects before you begin working and also allow you to compare your own results with these models to ensure you have created the materials accurately.

WS2-FCTOslo.docx (a two-page document) is the project in Activities 2.1 to 2.5.

OSLO, NORWAY

History

The founding of Oslo took place in the turbulent period between the *Viking Age* and Norway's *Catholic Middle Ages*. Many remnants and ruins from ancient Oslo can be found in Memorial Park. The city has a fascinating, interesting, and dramatic history.

Oslo's population was substantially reduced during the time of the Black Death in 1348, which claimed over fifty percent of the inhabitants. This epidemic also had political consequences for Norway, which was reduced to a province of Denmark. During this period, Copenhagen was the actual capital of Norway. Oslo was also greatly affected by the Lutheran Protestant Reformation of 1537, with religious conflicts, political separation from the Catholic Church, and the foundation of a Protestant National Church. Many ruins of churches and monasteries bear witness to this process.

Oslo was completely destroyed by fire in 1624. Following intense renewal and advanced city planning in the spirit of the Renaissance, a completely new city was created and named Christiania. In 1814 Norway was united with Sweden, and Christiania experienced strong economic and political growth. In 1905 the union with Sweden was dissolved and Norway gained its independence. The original name of Oslo was reinstated in 1924.

Population

Oslo is the capital of Norway and has more than 500,000 inhabitants. Approximately 900,000 people live in the Greater Oslo area, representing twenty percent of the total population of Norway.

Commerce and Industry

The working population of Oslo distributed according to occupation includes: industry, 16%; building and construction, 6%; transport, 9%; trade, services, and tourism, 69%.

Climate

Oslo's climate is temperate in the autumn and warm in spring and summer. Snow falls three to five months in the winter. Skiing conditions are good in the hills around Oslo between December and April. From May to July, the weather can be quite warm with long periods of sunshine. Drought can also occur from time to time. Statistically speaking, Oslo is Scandinavia's sunniest capital.

Holiday, Sport, and Leisure

Oslo is surrounded by forest and fjord. Preserving the fjord and the area surrounding the city for leisure and outdoor pursuits is an important part of Oslo's political tradition. Some of the major sports events in Oslo include the Grete Waitz Race, Holmenkollen Relay, Oslo Marathon, and the Holmenkollen Ski Festival. Oslo includes over 2,000 kilometers of prepared ski trails for cross-country skiing and a number of ski lifts for alpine skiing.

Sightseeing Tours

TOUR 1: MINI CRUISE
Fifty-minute cruise that departs on the hour

TOUR 2: FJORD CRUISE
Two-hour cruise that departs on the half hour

TOUR 3: FJORD CRUISE WITH DINNER
Two-hour cruise followed by dinner at Restaurant Lanternen

TOUR 4: SELECTED OSLO SIGHTSEEING
Three-hour tour of Vigeland Sculpture Park, the Holmenkollen Ski Jump, the Viking Ships, and the Kon-Tiki Raft

ALL TOURS BY BOAT AND COACH DEPART FROM PIER 3 IN FRONT OF THE OSLO CITY HALL.

Student Name
Date: 2/5/2012
Time: 9:24 AM

WS2-FCTRailTravel.docx is the project in Activities 2.6 to 2.11.

Traveling in Europe by Train

Now that you have planned your trip, bought your rail tickets, flown to Europe, and adjusted your body to jet lag, you are ready to start your rail experience. As you do so, remember the following things:

- Have your pass validated.
- Protect your pass.
- Arrive 20 minutes before train departure time.
- Be at the right train station.

Rail Ticket Bonuses

Your rail ticket offers you a variety of bonuses when traveling in Europe, including:

- Free or discount transportation on ferries, steamers, and buses
- Hotel discounts of up to 50% from participating hotels
- Special fare on the high-speed trains linking Paris to London
- Reduced rental rates with most major car rental companies

Some companies offer outstanding reductions on transportation. For example, you can travel on the ferry in Denmark between Århus and Kalundborg and between Nyborg and Korsør at a 75% discount! ScanTravel, a travel company located in Stockholm, offers the StarPass® ticket that provides you with incredible discounts on travel by train, ferry, and bus in Sweden, Norway, and Denmark.

International Airports with Train Connections

Country	City	Airport
Austria	Vienna (Wein)	Schwechat
Belgium	Brussels	Nationaal
France	Paris	Orly
Germany	Berlin	Schoenefeld
Great Britain	London	Heathrow
Italy	Rome	Fiumicino

Airport	Service
Schwechat	Train every 30 minutes
Nationaal	Train every 20 minutes
Orly	RER train every 20 minutes
Schoenefeld	S-Bahn train every 30 minutes
Heathrow	LT train every 10 minutes
Fiumicino	Train every 10 to 20 minutes

WS2-FCTMiddleton.docx is the project in Activity 2.12.

MIDDLETON VALLEY

JEFFERSON BASIN

RECREATIONAL OPPORTUNITIES

The Middleton Valley region is home to one of the state's largest natural freshwater lakes, the unique and beautiful Jefferson Basin, and numerous parks and recreational campgrounds. Middleton Valley has many convenient, quality visitor attractions and facilities, including a variety of lodging options to fit any budget. The Middleton Valley area is renowned for its beautiful scenery, wildlife, and outdoor recreational opportunities. If you are an outdoor enthusiast, you can enjoy a variety of recreational activities in and around the valley.

FISHING

With over 189,000 surface acres of water on or near Middleton Lake, fishing is a favorite activity. The lake is open all year for fishing where you can enjoy the thrill of catching walleye, trout, bass, perch, crappie, and catfish.

GEOLOGY

The geology of the Jefferson Basin accounts for its compatibility with both agriculture and outdoor recreation. The granite found in the Basin is approximately 60 million years old, but became exposed after 30 million years of adjustments in the earth's crust and erosion. Floods, fire, ice, and volcanoes all played into the historical shaping of the area. A complex system of reservoirs and waterways services the croplands in the Jefferson Basin and takes advantage of the unusual geologic features of the area.

SAND DUNES AND OFF-ROAD VEHICLES

Enjoy the fun and excitement of "conquering" a sand dune and more! The Jefferson County off-road vehicle area is one of the largest and is located just two miles from Lake Middleton. The Jefferson County off-road vehicle area and Lake Middleton boast rolling sand dunes, great fishing, and excellent waterskiing opportunities.

CONTACT INFORMATION

Jefferson Basin Chamber of Commerce
(320) 555-3022

Department of Fisheries
(320) 555-8886

Lake Middleton Resort
(320) 555-1255

Activity 2.1

Applying Formatting with the Font Group and the Mini Toolbar

Use buttons in the Font group in the Home tab to apply character formatting to text. Formatting a document changes how the document appears. The top row contains buttons for changing the font and font size and increasing and decreasing the size of the font. The bottom row contains buttons for applying formatting such as bold, italics, underlining, superscript, subscript, and text effects. The default font used by Word is Calibri. Change this default with the Font button in the Font group. Click the Clear Formatting button to remove all formatting from selected text. Microsoft Word has taken some commonly used commands and placed them on the Mini toolbar. The Mini toolbar displays in a faded manner when you select text and then becomes solid when you point to it.

Project

You have been asked to improve the appearance of a document on Oslo, Norway, by applying different font and font effects to the text.

Tutorial 2.1
Modifying the Font Using the Font Group

Tutorial 2.2
Formatting with the Mini Toolbar

1 Open **FCTOslo.docx** and then save the document and name it **WS2-FCTOslo**.

2 Select *Oslo, Norway* and then click the Bold button **B** in the Font group in the Home tab.

3 With *Oslo, Norway* still selected, click the Change Case button **Aa** in the Font group and then click *UPPERCASE* at the drop-down list.

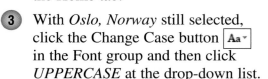

> Use options at the Change Case drop-down list to specify the case of selected text.

4 With *Oslo, Norway* still selected, click the Text Effects button and then click the *Fill - White, Outline - Accent 1* option at the drop-down gallery (fourth option from the left in the top row).

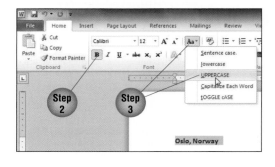

> This feature is referred to as *live preview* and provides you with an opportunity to see how the document will appear with text effect formatting before making a final choice.

5 Select *History* and then click the Underline button **U** in the Font group.

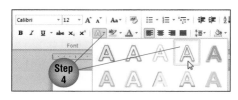

6 Select and then underline the remaining headings: *Population*; *Commerce and Industry*; *Climate*; *Holiday, Sport, and Leisure*; and *Sightseeing Tours*.

7 Select the words *Viking Age* located in the first paragraph below the *History* heading, point to the Mini toolbar that displays above the selected text, and then click the Italic button **I** on the Mini toolbar.

> The Mini toolbar displays in a faded manner until you point to it and then it becomes solid. The toolbar disappears when you move the mouse pointer away from it and when you click a button on the Mini toolbar.

8 Select the words *Catholic Middle Ages* that display in the first paragraph and then click the Italic button on the Mini toolbar.

9 Select the entire document by clicking the Select button in the Editing group in the Home tab and then clicking *Select All* at the drop-down list.

10 Click the Font button arrow in the Font group. Hover the mouse pointer over various typefaces in the Font drop-down gallery and notice how the text in the document reflects the selected font.

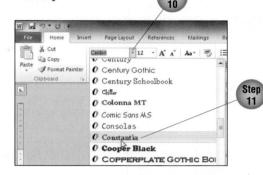

> This is another example of the Live Preview feature that provides you with an opportunity to see how the document will appear with font formatting before making a final choice.

11 Scroll down the gallery and then click *Constantia*.

12 Click the Font Size button arrow and then click *11* in the drop-down gallery.

13 Click the Font Color button arrow and then click *Dark Red* in the color gallery (first color from the left in the *Standard Colors* row).

14 Deselect the text by clicking anywhere in the document.

> Deselecting cancels the selection of text.

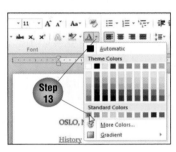

15 You want to identify specific text for review by colleagues so you decide to highlight the text. To do this, click the Text Highlight Color button arrow in the Font group and then click the yellow color at the drop-down list. Select the first sentence in the second paragraph (the sentence that begins *Oslo's population was substantially...*).

> When you click the Text Highlight Color button, the mouse pointer displays with a highlighter pen attached. Highlighting stays on until you click the Text Highlight Color button again.

16 Select the first sentence in the *Population* paragraph to highlight it and then click the Text Highlight Color button to turn it off.

17 Remove the text highlighting by pressing Ctrl + A (this selects the entire document), clicking the Text Highlight Color button arrow, and then clicking *No Color* at the drop-down list.

18 Save **WS2-FCTOslo.docx**.

In Addition

Using Typefaces

A typeface is a set of characters with a common design and shape and can be decorative or plain and either monospaced or proportional. Word refers to typeface as *font*. A monospaced typeface allots the same amount of horizontal space for each character while a proportional typeface allots a varying amount of space for each character. Proportional typefaces are divided into two main categories: *serif* and *sans serif*. A serif is a small line at the end of a character stroke. Consider using a serif typeface for text-intensive documents because the serifs help move the reader's eyes across the page. Use a sans serif typeface for headings, headlines, and advertisements.

Activity 2.2

Using the Font Dialog Box and Format Painter; Repeating a Command

In addition to buttons in the Font group, you can apply font formatting with options at the Font dialog box. With options at this dialog box, you can change the font, font size, and font style; change the font color; choose an underlining style; and apply formatting effects. Once you apply font formatting to text, you can copy that formatting to different locations in the document using the Format Painter. If you apply formatting to text in a document and then want to apply the same formatting to other text, use the Repeat command. Repeat a command by pressing the F4 function key.

Project

The changes you made to the Oslo document have enhanced the readability and visual appeal of the text. Now you will turn your attention to the headings.

Tutorial 2.3
Modifying the Font Using the Font Dialog Box

Tutorial 2.4
Using the Format Painter

1. With **WS2-FCTOslo.docx** open, press Ctrl + Home to move the insertion point to the beginning of the page and then select the entire document by pressing Ctrl + A.

    Ctrl + A is the keyboard shortcut to select the entire document.

2. Click the Font group dialog box launcher [⌐].

    The dialog box launcher displays as a small button containing a diagonal arrow.

3. At the Font dialog box, click *Cambria* in the *Font* list box (you will need to scroll up the list box to display this option) and then click *12* in the *Size* list box.

4. Click the down-pointing arrow at the right side of the *Font color* option and then click *Dark Blue* (second choice from the right in the Standard Colors row).

5. Click OK to close the dialog box.

6. Select the heading *History* and then click the Font group dialog box launcher.

7. Click *Candara* in the *Font* list box (you will need to scroll down the list box to display this option), click *Bold* in the *Font style* list box, and then click *14* in the *Size* list box (you will need to scroll down this list box to display *14*).

8. Click the down-pointing arrow at the right side of the *Underline style* option and then click *(none)* at the drop-down list.

9. Click OK to close the dialog box and then deselect the heading.

10. Click once on any character in the heading *History* and then double-click the Format Painter button [🖌] in the Clipboard group in the Home tab.

    When Format Painter is active, the mouse pointer displays with a paintbrush attached. Click the Format Painter button once to

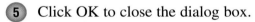

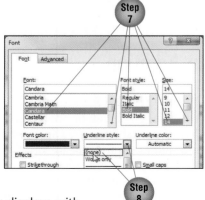

apply formatting to one location only. Double-click the Format Painter button if you want to apply formatting in more than one location.

11. Select the title *OSLO, NORWAY*.

    With Format Painter active, selecting text applies formatting. Selecting the title removed the text effect and applied the same formatting that you applied to the *History* heading.

12. Scroll down the document and then click on any character in the word *Population*.

    When using Format Painter, apply formatting to a single word by clicking on any character in the word. To apply formatting to more than one word at a time, select the text.

13. Select the heading *Commerce and Industry*, select the heading *Climate*, select the heading *Holiday, Sport, and Leisure*, and then select the heading *Sightseeing Tours*.

14. Click once on the Format Painter button in the Clipboard group to turn off Format Painter.

15. Select the last sentence in the document (the sentence that begins *All tours by boat...*) and then click the Font group dialog box launcher.

16. At the Font dialog box, click *Small caps* in the *Effects* section.

17. Click OK to close the dialog box.

18. Select the text *Tour 1: Mini Cruise* and then press F4.

    Pressing F4 repeats the previous command and applies the small caps effect to selected text.

19. Select the text *Tour 2: Fjord Cruise* and then press F4. Select the text *Tour 3: Fjord Cruise with Dinner* and then press F4. Select the text *Tour 4: Selected Oslo Sightseeing* and then press F4.

20. Press Ctrl + Home to move the insertion point to the beginning of the document, select the heading *OSLO, NORWAY,* and then change the font size to 16.

21. Save **WS2-FCTOslo.docx**.

In Brief

Change Font at Font Dialog Box
1. Click Font group dialog box launcher.
2. Choose desired font.
3. Click OK.

Apply Formatting with Format Painter
1. Apply formatting.
2. Double-click Format Painter button.
3. Select text.
4. Click Format Painter button to turn off.

Apply Font Effects
1. Select text.
2. Click Font group dialog box launcher.
3. Click desired effect check box.
4. Click OK.

In Addition

Font Keyboard Shortcuts

Along with buttons in the Font group and the Font dialog box, you can apply character formatting with the following keyboard shortcuts.

Font Group Button	Keyboard Shortcut		Font Group Button	Keyboard Shortcut
Font	Ctrl + Shift + F		Italic	Ctrl + I
Font Size	Ctrl + Shift + P		Underline	Ctrl + U
Grow Font	Ctrl + >		Subscript	Ctrl + =
Shrink Font	Ctrl + <		Superscript	Ctrl + Shift + +
Bold	Ctrl + B		Change Case	Shift + F3

Activity 2.3

Aligning and Indenting Text

Paragraphs of text in a document are aligned at the left margin by default. This default alignment can be changed to center, right, or justified. Change paragraph alignment with buttons in the Paragraph group in the Home tab or with keyboard shortcuts. You can indent the first line of text in a paragraph, indent all lines of text in a paragraph, and indent the second and subsequent lines of a paragraph (called a hanging indent). Several methods are available for indenting text, including buttons in the Paragraph group in the Home tab and the Page Layout tab, markers on the Ruler, options at the Paragraph dialog box with the Indents and Spacing tab selected, and keyboard shortcuts. With the keyboard shortcut Alt + Shift + D you can insert the current date in a document. Use the keyboard short Alt + Shift + T to insert the current time.

Project

You will improve the appearance of the Oslo document by changing text alignment and changing the alignment of specific paragraphs in the document.

Tutorial 2.5
Aligning Text in Paragraphs

Tutorial 2.6
Changing Text Indentation

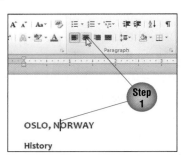

1. With **WS2-FCTOslo.docx** open, position the insertion point on any character in the title *OSLO, NORWAY* and then click the Center button in the Paragraph group in the Home tab.

2. Select from the middle of the first paragraph of text below the *History* heading to somewhere in the middle of the third paragraph of text and then click the Justify button in the Paragraph group.

   Entire paragraphs do not have to be selected, only a portion of each paragraph.

3. Press Ctrl + End to move the insertion point to the end of the document. Click the Align Text Right button in the Paragraph group, type your first and last names, and then press the Enter key.

4. Type **Date:**, press the spacebar once, press Alt + Shift + D, and then press the Enter key.

   Alt + Shift + D is the keyboard shortcut to insert the current date.

5. Type **Time:**, press the spacebar once, and then press Alt + Shift + T.

   Alt + Shift + T is the keyboard shortcut to insert the current time. You can also insert the date and time with options at the Date and Time dialog box. Display this dialog box by clicking the Insert tab and then clicking the Date & Time button in the Text group.

6. Press the Enter key and then click the Align Text Left button in the Paragraph group.

7. You decide to return the alignment to left for the paragraphs below the *History* heading and indent the text instead. To begin, select the three paragraphs below the *History* heading and then click the Align Text Left button in the Paragraph group.

8. With the text still selected, position the mouse pointer on the Left Indent marker on the Ruler, hold down the left mouse button, drag the marker to the 0.5-inch mark on the Ruler, and then release the mouse button.

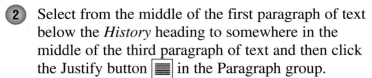

   If the Ruler is not visible, click the View Ruler button located above the vertical scroll bar. The ruler indent markers are shown in Figure 2.1. To precisely position a marker on the Ruler, hold down the Alt key while dragging the marker.

FIGURE 2.1 Ruler Indent Markers

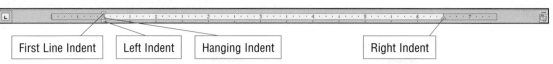

First Line Indent | Left Indent | Hanging Indent | Right Indent

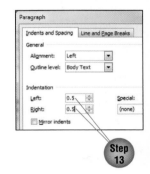

Step 9

History

The founding of
Norway's Cathol

9 Position the mouse pointer on the First Line Indent marker on the Ruler, hold down the left mouse button, and then drag the marker to the 1-inch mark on the Ruler.

Step 10

between the *Viking*
ins from ancient Oslo

10 Position the mouse pointer on the Right Indent marker on the Ruler, hold down the left mouse button, and then drag the marker to the 6-inch mark on the Ruler.

11 Click anywhere in the paragraph below the *Population* heading and then click the Page Layout tab. In the *Indent* section in the Paragraph group, click in the *Left* text box and then type **0.5**. Click the up-pointing arrow at the right side of the *Right* text box until 0.5" displays.

Step 11

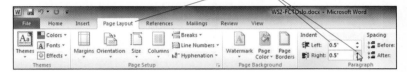

12 Click anywhere in the paragraph below the *Commerce and Industry* heading and then click the Paragraph group dialog box launcher.

13 At the Paragraph dialog box, select the measurement in the *Left* measurement box in the *Indentation* section and then type **0.5**. Select the measurement in the *Right* measurement box in the *Indentation* section, type **0.5**, and then click the OK button.

14 Click anywhere in the paragraph below the *Climate* heading and then press F4. Click anywhere in the paragraph below the *Holiday, Sport, and Leisure* heading and then press F4.

Step 13

15 Select the text below the *Sightseeing Tours* heading except the right-aligned text and then press F4.

16 Select the three paragraphs below the *History* heading and then click the Paragraph group dialog box launcher.

17 At the Paragraph dialog box, click the down-pointing arrow at the right side of the *Special* list box in the *Indentation* section and then click *Hanging* at the drop-down list.

Step 17

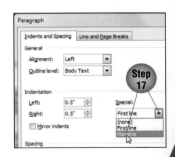

18 Click OK to close the Paragraph dialog box.

19 Save **WS2-FCTOslo.docx**.

In Addition

Aligning Text

Change text alignment with the following keyboard shortcuts:

Alignment	Keyboard Shortcut
Left	Ctrl + L
Center	Ctrl + E
Right	Ctrl + R
Justified	Ctrl + J

Indenting Text

Indent text with the following keyboard shortcuts:

Indentation	Keyboard Shortcut
Indent text from left margin	Ctrl + M
Decrease indent from left margin	Ctrl + Shift + M
Create a hanging indent	Ctrl + T
Remove hanging indent	Ctrl + Shift + T

Activity 2.4

Changing Line and Paragraph Spacing

By default, line spacing is set at 1.15. This default line spacing can be changed with the Line and Paragraph Spacing button in the Paragraph group in the Home tab, keyboard shortcuts, or with the *Line spacing* and *At* options at the Paragraph dialog box. Control spacing above and below paragraphs with options at the Line and Paragraph Spacing button drop-down list, the *Before* and *After* text boxes in the *Spacing* section in the Paragraph group in the Page Layout tab, or with the *Before* and *After* options in the *Spacing* section of the Paragraph dialog box with the Indents and Spacing tab selected.

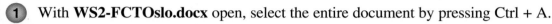

Project The Oslo document project deadline is at hand. However, you have time to make a few spacing changes in the document before printing the final version.

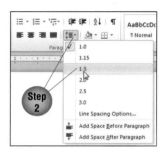

First Choice TRAVEL

SNAP

Tutorial 2.7
Setting Line and Paragraph Spacing

1 With **WS2-FCTOslo.docx** open, select the entire document by pressing Ctrl + A.

2 Click the Home tab, click the Line and Paragraph Spacing button in the Paragraph group, and then click *1.5* at the drop-down list.

3 Deselect the text and then scroll through the document. After viewing the document in 1.5 line spacing, you decide to decrease the line spacing to 1.2 (which is not an option available at the Line and Paragraph Spacing button drop-down list). To begin, press Ctrl + A to select the entire document, click the Line and Paragraph Spacing button, and then click *Line Spacing Options* at the drop-down list.

4 Type **1.2** in the *At* text box in the *Spacing* section of the Paragraph dialog box.

> The Paragraph dialog box also contains a *Line spacing* option. Click the down-pointing arrow at the right side of the option and a drop-down list displays with spacing choices.

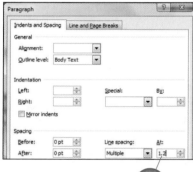

5 Click OK to close the dialog box and then deselect the text.

Need Help?

If line spacing seems too spread out, make sure you typed the period in *1.2* in the *At* text box at the Paragraph dialog box.

6 Select from the line of text beginning *TOUR 1: MINI CRUISE* through *TOUR 4: SELECTED OSLO SIGHTSEEING* and the two lines that follow.

7 Click the Line and Paragraph Spacing button and then click *1.0* at the drop-down list.

> Choosing this option changes the line spacing to single for the selected paragraphs of text. You can also change line spacing with keyboard shortcuts. Press Ctrl + 1 to change to single spacing, Ctrl + 2 to change to double spacing, and Ctrl + 5 to change to 1.5 line spacing.

8 Click anywhere in the last sentence (the sentence that begins *ALL TOURS BY BOAT...*).

9 Click the Line and Paragraph Spacing button and then click *Add Space Before Paragraph*.

> This inserts 12 points of space above the heading.

10 Press Ctrl + Home to move the insertion point to the beginning of the document, click anywhere in the *History* heading, and then click the Paragraph group dialog box launcher.

11 At the Paragraph dialog box, click once on the up-pointing arrow at the right side of the *After* text box and then click OK to close the dialog box.

> Clicking the up-pointing arrow at the right side of the *After* text box inserts *6 pt* in the text box.

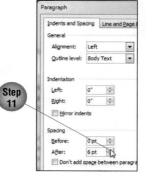

Step 11

12 Click anywhere in the *Population* heading, click the Page Layout tab, and then click once on the up-pointing arrow at the right side of the *After* text box in the *Spacing* section of the Paragraph group.

Step 12

> Clicking once on the up arrow changes the point measurement to *6 pt*.

13 Click anywhere in the *Commerce and Industry* heading and then press F4.

> Pressing F4 repeats the paragraph spacing command.

14 Click individually on any character in each of the remaining headings (*Climate*; *Holiday, Sport, and Leisure*; and *Sightseeing Tours*) and then press F4.

15 You also decide that you want to remove the hanging indent on the paragraphs in the *History* section. To do this, select the three paragraphs of text below the *History* heading and then press Ctrl + Shift + T.

> Ctrl + Shift + T is the keyboard shortcut to remove hanging indent formatting.

16 Scroll down the page and notice that the heading *Climate* displays at the bottom of the first page while the paragraph that follows the heading displays at the top of the second page. You want to keep the heading with the paragraph of text. Begin by clicking on any character in the heading *Climate* and then clicking the Paragraph group dialog box launcher.

Step 17

17 At the Paragraph dialog box, click the Line and Page Breaks tab, click the *Keep with next* check box, and then click OK.

18 Save **WS2-FCTOslo.docx**.

In Addition

Spacing Above or Below Paragraphs

Spacing above or below paragraphs is added in points. A vertical inch contains approximately 72 points and a half inch contains approximately 36 points. For example, to add 9 points of spacing below selected paragraphs, click the Page Layout tab or display the Paragraph dialog box with the Indents and Spacing tab selected. Select the current measurement in the *After* text box and then type 9. You can also click the up-pointing or down-pointing arrows to increase or decrease the amount of spacing before or after paragraphs.

Activity 2.5

Revealing Formatting; Finding and Replacing Formatting

Display formatting applied to specific text in a document at the Reveal Formatting task pane. The Reveal Formatting task pane displays font, paragraph, and section formatting applied to text where the insertion point is positioned or to selected text. With options at the Find and Replace dialog box with the Replace tab selected, you can search for specific formatting or characters containing specific formatting and replace it with other formatting or characters.

Project

Tutorial 2.8
Finding and Replacing Formatting

After reviewing the Oslo document, you decide that the headings would look better set in a different font and font color. To display the formatting applied to specific text, you will use the Reveal Formatting task pane and then find and replace font formatting.

1. With **WS2-FCTOslo.docx** open, press Ctrl + Home to move the insertion point to the beginning of the document and then press Shift + F1.

    Pressing Shift + F1 displays the Reveal Formatting task pane with information on the formatting applied to the title. Generally, a minus symbol precedes *Font* and *Paragraph* and a plus symbol precedes *Section* in the *Formatting of selected text* section. Click the minus symbol to hide any items below a heading and click the plus symbol to reveal items. Some items in the Reveal Formatting task pane are hyperlinks. For example, click the <u>Font</u> hyperlink and the Font dialog box displays. Use these hyperlinks to make changes to the document formatting.

2. Click anywhere in the heading *History* and look at the Reveal Formatting task pane to determine the formatting.

3. Click anywhere in the paragraph of text below the heading *History* and look at the Reveal Formatting task pane to determine the formatting.

4. Close the Reveal Formatting task pane by clicking the Close button located in the upper right corner of the task pane.

5. Find text set in 14-point Candara bold and dark blue color and replace it with text set in 14-point Arial bold italic and red color. To begin, position the insertion point at the beginning of the document and then click the Replace button in the Editing group in the Home tab.

6. At the Find and Replace dialog box, press the Delete key. (This deletes any text that displays in the *Find what* text box.)

7. Click the More button. (If a check mark displays in the *Find all word forms* check box, click the option to remove the mark.)

8. Click the Format button located at the bottom of the dialog box and then click *Font* at the drop-down list.

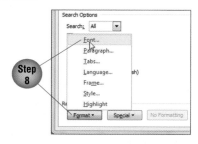

Step 8

In Brief
Reveal Formatting
1. Click in desired text.
2. Press Shift + F1.

(9) At the Find Font dialog box, change the font to Candara, the font style to bold, the size to 14, the font color to Dark Blue, and then click OK to close the dialog box.

(10) At the Find and Replace dialog box, select and then delete any text that displays in the *Replace with* text box.

(11) With the insertion point positioned in the *Replace with* text box, click the Format button located at the bottom of the dialog box and then click *Font* at the drop-down list.

(12) At the Replace Font dialog box, change the font to Arial, the font style to bold italic, the size to 14, and the font color to *Red, Accent 2, Darker 50%* (last option in the sixth column in the *Theme Colors* section).

(13) Click OK to close the dialog box.

(14) At the Find and Replace dialog box, click the Replace All button. At the message telling you that the search of the document is complete and six replacements were made, click OK.

(15) With the Find and Replace dialog box open and the insertion point positioned in the *Find what* text box, click the No Formatting button that displays at the bottom of the dialog box. Click in the *Replace with* text box and then click the No Formatting button.

(16) Click the Less button to reduce the size of the Find and Replace dialog box and then close the dialog box.

(17) Save, print, and then close **WS2-FCTOslo.docx**.

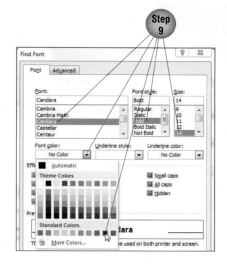

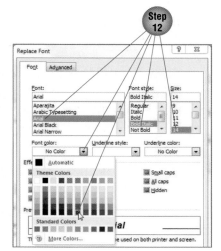

In Addition

Comparing Formatting

Along with displaying formatting applied to text, you can use the Reveal Formatting task pane to compare formatting of two text selections to determine what formatting is different. To compare formatting, display the Reveal Formatting task pane and then select the first instance of formatting to be compared. Click the *Compare to another* *selection* check box to insert a check mark and then select the second instance of formatting to compare. Any differences between the two selections will display in the *Formatting differences* list box.

Activity 2.6

Inserting Bullets and Numbering

If you want to draw the reader's attention to a list of items, consider inserting a bullet before each item. Click the Bullets button in the Paragraph group in the Home tab to insert a bullet before items in a list. If a list of items is in a sequence, consider inserting numbers before each item with the Numbering button in the Paragraph group. Create multiple-level bulleted or numbered paragraphs with options from the Multilevel List button in the Paragraph group.

Project

First Choice Travel has a new document on traveling in Europe by train. After reviewing the document, you decide to insert numbers and bullets before selected paragraphs to make the information easier to read.

Tutorial 2.9
Creating Bulleted and Numbered Lists

1. Open **FCTRailTravel.docx** and then save the document and name it **WS2-FCTRailTravel**.

2. Select text from the paragraph *Have your pass validated.* through the paragraph *Be at the right train station.* and then click the Numbering button in the Paragraph group in the Home tab.

Need Help?
If you click the wrong button, immediately click the Undo button.

3. Position the insertion point at the end of the second numbered paragraph (the paragraph that displays as *2. Protect your pass.*) and then press the Enter key once.

   Pressing the Enter key automatically inserts the number *3.* and renumbers the third paragraph to *4*.

4. Type **Arrive 20 minutes before train departure time.**

   Numbering before paragraphs is changed automatically when paragraphs of text are inserted and/or deleted.

5. Select text from the paragraph that begins *Free or discount transportation...* through the paragraph that begins *Reduced rental rates with...* and then click the Bullets button in the Paragraph group.

   Clicking the Bullets button inserts a round bullet before each paragraph. Other bullet options are available by clicking the Bullets button arrow.

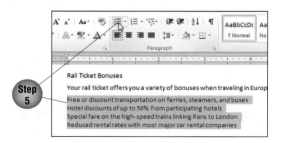

6. With the text still selected, you decide to replace the round bullet with a custom bullet. To begin, click the Bullets button arrow and then click *Define New Bullet* at the drop-down list.

7. At the Define New Bullet dialog box, click the Symbol button in the *Bullet character* section.

8. At the Symbol dialog box, click the down-pointing arrow at the right side of the *Font* list box, scroll down the drop-down list, and then click *Webdings*.

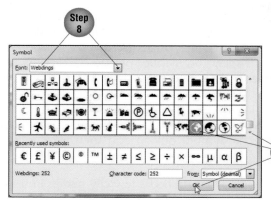

9. Scroll to the end of the symbol list, click the earth symbol that is the fourth symbol from the right in the bottom row, and then click OK to close the Symbol dialog box.

10. Click OK to close the Define New Bullet dialog box.

11. Select the text from *Rail Passes* through *Greece-Italy*, click the Multilevel List button in the Paragraph group, and then click the middle option in the top row in the *List Library* section.

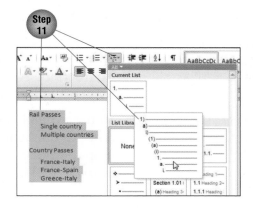

> This applies multiple-level numbering to the selected text.

12. With the text still selected, you decide to change to bullets instead of numbers. To do this, click the Multilevel List button and then click the first option from the left in the middle row in the *List Library* section.

13. Deselect the text.

14. Save **WS2-FCTRailTravel.docx**.

In Addition

Creating Numbered and/or Bulleted Text

If you type *1.*, press the spacebar, type a paragraph of text, and then press the Enter key, Word indents the number approximately 0.25 inch and then hang indents the text in the paragraph approximately 0.5 inch from the left margin. Additionally, *2.* is inserted 0.25 inch from the left margin at the beginning of the next paragraph. Continue typing items and Word inserts the next number in the list. Press Enter to turn off numbering or click the Numbering button in the Paragraph group. Bulleted lists with hanging indents are automatically created when you begin a paragraph with the symbol *, > , or -. Type one of the symbols, press the spacebar, type text, and then press Enter. The type of bullet inserted depends on the type of character entered. For example, if you use the asterisk (*) symbol, a round bullet is inserted, and an arrow bullet is inserted if you type the greater than symbol (>).

Turning Off Automatic Numbering and/or Bulleting

If you do not want automatic numbering or bulleting in a document, turn off the features at the AutoCorrect dialog box with the AutoFormat As You Type tab selected. To display this dialog box, click the File tab and then click the Options button located below the Help tab. At the Word Options dialog box, click the *Proofing* option and then click the AutoCorrect Options button. At the AutoCorrect dialog box, click the AutoFormat As You Type tab. Click the *Automatic numbered lists* check box and/or *Automatic bulleted lists* check box to remove the check mark.

Activity 2.7

Inserting Symbols and Special Characters

You can insert special symbols such as é, ö, and Å with options at the Symbol palette or at the Symbol dialog box. Display the Symbol palette by clicking the Insert tab and then clicking the Symbol button in the Symbols group. Click the desired symbol to insert it in the document. To display additional symbols, display the Symbol dialog box by clicking the Symbol button and then clicking

the *More Symbols* option. Click the desired symbol at the dialog box, click the Insert button, and then click the Close button. At the Symbol dialog box with the Symbols tab selected, you can change the font and display different symbols. Click the Special Characters tab at the dialog box and a list displays containing special characters and the keyboard shortcuts to insert the characters.

Project You have identified a few city names in the train travel document that need special letters in their spellings as well as a special character you need to insert in the document.

Tutorial 2.10
Inserting Symbols and Special Characters

1. With **WS2-FCTRailTravel.docx** open, move the insertion point to the end of the document and then select and delete the multiple-level bulleted text.

2. With the insertion point positioned at the end of the document a double space below the bulleted text, type the text shown in Figure 2.2 up to the Å in Århus. To insert the Å symbol, click the Insert tab, click the Symbol button Ω in the Symbols group, and then click *More Symbols* at the bottom of the palette.

3. At the Symbol dialog box with the Symbols tab selected, click the down-pointing arrow at the right side of the *Font* list box and then click *(normal text)* at the drop-down list. (You may need to scroll up to see this option. Skip this step if *(normal text)* is already selected.)

4. Scroll down the list box somewhere between the seventh and ninth rows and then click the Å symbol.

Need Help?

If you do not see the Å symbol, make sure *(normal text)* is selected at the *Font* list box.

5. Click the Insert button and then click the Close button.

6. Type text up to the ø symbol. To insert the ø symbol, click the Symbol button and then click *More Symbols*.

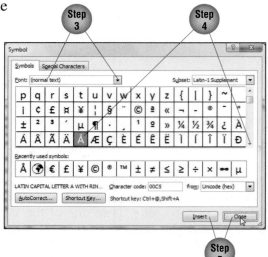

FIGURE 2.2 Steps 2–13

Some companies offer outstanding reductions on transportation. For example, you can travel on the ferry in Denmark between Århus and Kalundborg and between Nyborg and Korsør at a 75% discount! ScanTravel, a travel company located in Stockholm, offers the StarPass® ticket that provides you with incredible discounts on travel by train, ferry, and bus in Sweden, Norway, and Denmark.

In Brief

Insert Symbol
1. Click Insert tab.
2. Click Symbol button.
3. Click *More Symbols*.
4. Click desired symbol.
5. Click Insert button.
6. Click Close button.

Insert Special Character
1. Click Insert tab.
2. Click Symbol button.
3. Click *More Symbols*.
4. Click Special Characters tab.
5. Click desired character.
6. Click Insert button.
7. Click Close button.

7 At the Symbol dialog box, click the ø symbol (somewhere between the tenth and twelfth rows).

8 Click the Insert button and then click the Close button.

9 Type the text up to the ® character. To insert the ® character, click the Symbol button and then click *More Symbols*.

10 At the Symbol dialog box, click the Special Characters tab.

11 Click the ® character in the dialog box list box.

12 Click the Insert button and then click the Close button.

13 Type the remaining text in Figure 2.2.

14 Save **WS2-FCTRailTravel.docx**.

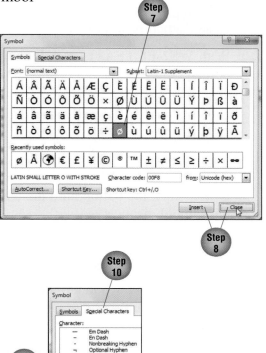

In Addition

Inserting Symbols with Keyboard Shortcuts

Another method for inserting symbols in a document is to use a keyboard shortcut. Click a symbol at the Symbol dialog box and the keyboard shortcut displays toward the bottom of the dialog box. For example, click the ø symbol and the keyboard shortcut *Ctrl+/,O* displays toward the bottom of the dialog box. To insert the ø symbol in a document using the keyboard shortcut, hold down the Ctrl key and then press the / key. Release the Ctrl key and then press the o key. Not all symbols contain a keyboard shortcut.

Inserting Symbols Using the Palette

When you click the Symbol button in the Symbols group, a drop-down palette displays with symbol choices. The palette displays the most recently used symbols. If the palette contains the desired symbol, click the symbol and it is inserted in the document.

Activity
2.8

Setting Tabs

Word offers a variety of default settings including left tabs set every 0.5 inch. You can set your own tabs using the Ruler or at the Tabs dialog box. Use the Ruler to set, move, and delete tabs. The default tabs display as tiny vertical lines along the bottom of the Ruler. With a left tab, text aligns at the left edge of the tab. The other types of tabs that can be set on the Ruler are center, right, decimal, and bar. The small button at the left side of the Ruler is called the Alignment button. Each time you click the Alignment button, a different tab or paragraph alignment symbol displays. To set a tab, display the desired alignment button on the Ruler and then click on the Ruler at the desired position.

Project

You have completed some additional research on train travel in Europe with train connections. You will add airport names to the train travel document.

Tutorial 2.11
Setting Tabs Using the Ruler

1. With **WS2-FCTRailTravel.docx** open, press Ctrl + End to move the insertion point a double space below the last paragraph of text in the document.

2. Type **International Airports with Train Connections** and then press the Enter key twice. (If tabs display on the Ruler, clear the tabs by clicking the Clear Formatting button in the Font group in the Home tab.)

3. Make sure the left tab symbol ⌐ displays in the Alignment button at the left side of the Ruler. (If the left tab symbol does not display in the Alignment button, click the button until the left tab symbol displays.)

   If the Ruler is not visible, click the View tab and then click the *Ruler* check box in the Show group.

4. Position the arrow pointer below the 1-inch mark on the Ruler and then click the left mouse button.

5. Click once on the Alignment button located at the left side of the Ruler to display the center tab symbol ⊥.

6. Position the arrow pointer below the 3.25-inch mark on the Ruler and then click the left mouse button.

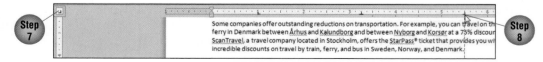

7. Click once on the Alignment button located at the left side of the Ruler to display the right tab symbol ⌐.

8. Position the arrow pointer below the 5.5-inch mark on the Ruler and then click the left mouse button.

9 Type the text shown in Figure 2.3, pressing the Tab key before typing each tabbed entry. Make sure you press the Tab key before typing the entry in the first column and that you bold the text in the first row.

 Need Help?

If your columns of text do not look similar to those in Figure 2.3, check to make sure you inserted the tab symbols at the correct locations on the Ruler and that you pressed the Tab key before typing each entry in the first column.

10 After typing the last entry in the third column (*Fiumicino*), press the Enter key twice and then click the Clear Formatting button in the Font group in the Home tab.

Clicking the Clear Formatting button removes paragraph and character formatting. You can also remove paragraph formatting by pressing the keyboard shortcut Ctrl + Q and remove character formatting by pressing the keyboard shortcut Ctrl + spacebar.

11 Save **WS2-FCTRailTravel.docx**.

FIGURE 2.3 Step 9

Country	City	Airport
Austria	Vienna (Wein)	Schwechat
Belgium	Brussels	Nationaal
France	Paris	Orly
Germany	Berlin	Schoenefeld
Great Britain	London	Heathrow
Italy	Rome	Fiumicino

In Addition

Moving a Tab

Move a tab on the Ruler by positioning the mouse pointer on the tab symbol on the Ruler. Hold down the left mouse button, drag the symbol to the new location on the Ruler, and then release the mouse button.

Deleting a Tab

Delete a tab from the Ruler by positioning the arrow pointer on the tab symbol, holding down the left mouse button, dragging the symbol down into the document screen, and then releasing the mouse button.

Setting a Decimal Tab

Set a decimal tab for column entries you want aligned at the decimal point. To set a decimal tab, click the Alignment button located at the left side of the Ruler until the decimal tab symbol displays and then click on the desired position on the Ruler.

Activity 2.9

Setting Tabs with Leaders

The four types of tabs can be set with leaders. Leaders are useful for material where you want to direct the reader's eyes across the page. Leaders can be periods, hyphens, or underlines. Tabs with leaders are set with options at the Tabs dialog box. To display this dialog box, click the Paragraph group dialog box launcher and then click the Tabs button at the Paragraph dialog box. At the Tabs dialog box, choose the type of tab, the type of leader, and then enter a tab position measurement.

Project

The information you found listing airports with train connections also includes schedule times. You will add this data to the train travel document.

Tutorial 2.12
Setting Tabs Using
the Tabs Dialog Box

1. With **WS2-FCTRailTravel.docx** open, move the insertion point to the end of the document.

2. Click the Alignment button at the left side of the Ruler until the left tab symbol displays.

3. Position the arrow pointer below the 1-inch mark on the Ruler and then click the left mouse button.

4. Click the Alignment button at the left side of the Ruler until the right tab symbol displays.

5. Position the arrow pointer below the 5.5-inch mark on the Ruler and then click the left mouse button.

6. Type the headings shown in Figure 2.4 by pressing the Tab key, clicking the Bold button in the Font group, and then typing **Airport**.

7. Press the Tab key and then type **Service**.

8. Press the Enter key once and then click the Clear Formatting button to remove the bold formatting and the paragraph tab formatting.

9. Set a left tab and a right tab with leaders at the Tabs dialog box. To begin, click the Paragraph group dialog box launcher and then click the Tabs button located in the lower left corner of the Paragraph dialog box.

    You can also display the Tabs dialog box by double-clicking on any tab symbol on the Ruler.

10. At the Tabs dialog box, make sure *Left* is selected in the *Alignment* section of the dialog box. (If it is not, click *Left*.) With the insertion point positioned in the *Tab stop position* text box, type **1** and then click the Set button.

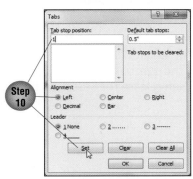

FIGURE 2.4 Step 6 and Step 13

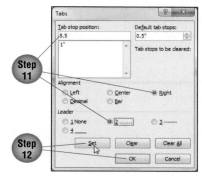

Airport	Service
Schwechat	Train every 30 minutes
Nationaal	Train every 20 minutes
Orly	RER train every 20 minutes
Schoenefeld	S-Bahn train every 30 minutes
Heathrow	LT train every 10 minutes
Fiumicino	Train every 10 to 20 minutes

In Brief

Set Tab with Leaders
1. Click Paragraph group dialog box launcher.
2. Click Tabs button.
3. Type tab measurement.
4. Click desired alignment.
5. Click desired leader.
6. Click Set.
7. Click OK.

11 Type **5.5** in the *Tab stop position* text box, click *Right* in the *Alignment* section of the dialog box, and click *2.....* in the *Leader* section of the dialog box.

12 Click the Set button and then click OK to close the dialog box.

13 Type the remaining text shown in Figure 2.4, making sure you press the Tab key before typing the first text entry.

Need Help?

If your columns of text do not look similar to those in Figure 2.4, check to make sure you inserted the tab symbols at the correct measurements and that you pressed Tab before typing each entry in the first column.

14 Press Ctrl + Home to move the insertion point to the beginning of the document and then select the four numbered paragraphs.

15 With the paragraphs selected, click the Bullets button arrow and then click the globe bullet in the *Bullet Library* section (this is the bullet you identified in Activity 2.6). If the globe bullet is not available at the drop-down list, complete steps similar to those in Activity 2.6, Steps 6 through 10, to select and apply the globe bullet.

16 Save **WS2-FCTRailTravel.docx**.

In Addition

Clearing Tabs at the Tabs Dialog Box

At the Tabs dialog box, you can clear an individual tab or all tabs. To clear all tabs, click the Clear All button. To clear an individual tab, specify the tab position and then click the Clear button.

Activity 2.10

Adding Borders and Shading

Insert a border around text and/or apply shading to text in a paragraph or selected text with the Border button and Shading button in the Paragraph group in the Home tab or at the Borders and Shading dialog box. At the Borders and Shading dialog box with the Borders tab selected, you can specify the border type, style, color, and width. Click the Shading tab and the dialog box contains options for choosing a fill color and pattern style. Click the Page Border tab and the dialog box contains options for applying a page border.

Project

To highlight certain information in First Choice Travel's train travel document, you will apply a border to selected text and apply border and shading formatting to the column text. You will also apply a page border to add visual appeal.

Tutorial 2.13
Adding a Border and Shading to Selected Text

1 With **WS2-FCTRailTravel.docx** open, select the first four bulleted paragraphs of text, click the Border button arrow in the Paragraph group in the Home tab, and then click *Outside Borders* at the drop-down list.

> The name of the button changes when you choose a border option at the drop-down list.

2 Select the second four bulleted paragraphs of text and then click the Border button in the Paragraph group.

> This applies the outside border since that is the last border option you selected.

3 Select from the column headings *Country*, *City*, and *Airport* through the line of text containing the column entries *Italy*, *Rome*, and *Fiumicino*.

4 Click the Border button arrow and then click *Borders and Shading* at the drop-down list.

5 At the Borders and Shading dialog box with the Borders tab selected, click the *Box* option in the *Setting* section.

6 Click the down-pointing arrow at the right side of the *Style* list box until the first double-line option displays and then click the double-line option.

7 Click the down-pointing arrow at the right side of the *Color* list box and then click *Blue, Accent 1, Darker 50%* at the color palette (bottom color in the fifth column in the *Theme Colors* section).

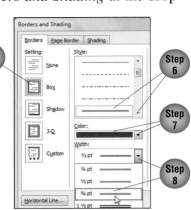

8 Click the down-pointing arrow at the right side of the *Width* list box and then click *¾ pt* at the drop-down list.

9 Click the Shading tab, click the down-pointing arrow at the right side of the *Fill* option, and then click *Blue, Accent 1, Lighter 80%* at the color palette (second color in the fifth column in the *Theme Colors* section).

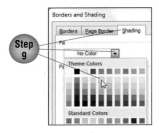

10 Click OK to close the dialog box.

11 Add the same border and shading to the other columns of text by selecting from the column headings *Airport* and *Service* through the line of text containing the column entries *Fiumicino* and *Train every 10 to 20 minutes* and then pressing F4.

12 Apply shading to the title by positioning the insertion point on the title *Traveling in Europe by Train*, clicking the Shading button arrow 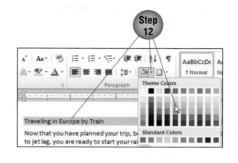, and then clicking the *Blue, Accent 1, Lighter 60%* color.

13 Apply a page border to the document. To begin, click the Border button arrow and then click *Borders and Shading* at the drop-down list.

14 At the Borders and Shading dialog box, click the Page Border tab, click the *Shadow* option in the *Setting* section, click the down-pointing arrow at the right side of the *Width* option, and then click *2¼ pt* at the drop-down list.

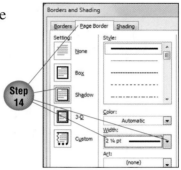

> You can also display the Borders and Shading dialog box with the Page Border tab selected by clicking the Page Layout tab and then clicking the Page Borders button in the Page Background group.

15 Click OK to close the dialog box.

16 Change the page border to an art image. To begin, click the Border button arrow and then click Borders and Shading. At the Borders and Shading dialog box, click the Page Border tab.

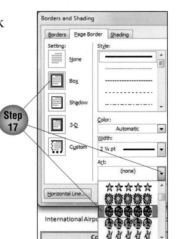

17 Click the *Box* option in the *Setting* section, click the down-pointing arrow at the right side of the *Art* option box, scroll down the list until the globe art images display, and then click the first set of globe images.

18 Select the measurement in the *Width* text box, type **10**, and then click OK to close the dialog box.

19 Save **WS2-FCTRailTravel.docx**.

In Brief

Insert Borders and Shading
1. Select text.
2. Click Border button arrow.
3. Click *Borders and Shading*.
4. Choose desired border(s).
5. Click Shading tab.
6. Choose desired shading and/or pattern.
7. Click OK.

Insert Page Border
1. Click Border button arrow.
2. Click *Borders and Shading*.
3. Click Page Border tab.
4. Choose desired options.
5. Click OK.

In Addition

Inserting Horizontal Lines

Word includes a horizontal line feature that inserts a graphic horizontal line in a document. To display the Horizontal Line dialog box, display the Borders and Shading dialog box with any tab selected and then click the Horizontal Line button [Horizontal Line...] located toward the bottom of the dialog box. Click the desired horizontal line in the list box and then click OK and the line is inserted in the document.

Activity
2.11

Applying Styles

A style is a set of formatting instructions you can apply to text. Word provides a number of predesigned styles and groups those that apply similar formatting into sets called Quick Styles sets. The Styles group in the Home tab displays a number of style thumbnails. Click the More button at the right side of the style thumbnails to display a drop-down list of additional styles. The styles in the Styles group change to reflect the currently selected Quick Styles set. To change the Quick Styles set, click the Change Styles button in the Home tab, point to Style Set, and then click the desired set at the side menu. Use options at the Change Styles button drop-down list to change the Quick Styles set colors and fonts. Click the Change Styles button and point to *Paragraph Spacing* and a side menu displays with predesigned paragraph spacing styles you can apply to the document. Hover the mouse pointer over a style in the side menu and a ScreenTip displays describing what formatting is applied by the style.

Project To further enhance the train travel document, you decide to apply styles and a Quick Styles set to text in the document.

SNAP

Tutorial 2.14
Applying Styles and Using the Quick Styles Gallery

① With **WS2-FCTRailTravel.docx** open, press Ctrl + Home to move the insertion point to the beginning of the document.

② Click on any character in the title *Traveling in Europe by Train* and then click the Heading 1 style thumbnail in the Styles group in the Home tab.

> The Heading 1 style in the default Quick Styles set changes the font, font size, and font color and adds 24 points of spacing above. The heading style also removes the shading you inserted in the previous activity.

③ Click on any character in the heading *Rail Ticket Bonuses* and then click the Heading 2 style thumbnail in the Styles group.

④ Click on any character in the heading *International Airports with Train Connections* and then click the Heading 2 style.

⑤ Apply a different Quick Styles set by clicking the Change Styles button in the Styles group in the Home tab, pointing to *Style Set*, and then clicking *Thatch* at the drop-down gallery.

> Applying the *Thatch* Quick Styles set changes the formatting of the title, headings, and text in the document.

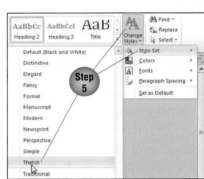

⑥ Change the font colors for the *Thatch* Quick Styles set by clicking the Change Styles button in the Styles group, pointing to *Colors*, and then clicking *Foundry* at the drop-down gallery.

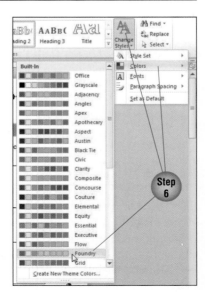

7. Change the fonts applied by the *Thatch* Quick Styles set by clicking the Change Styles button, pointing to *Fonts*, and then clicking *Clarity* at the drop-down gallery. (You will need to scroll down the gallery to display *Clarity*.)

8. Reduce the paragraph spacing so the text fits on one page by clicking the Change Styles button, pointing to *Paragraph Spacing*, and then clicking *Compact* at the side menu.

> The Change Styles button Paragraph Spacing side menu contains predesigned styles that will change the paragraph spacing and line spacing to text in a document. Hover the mouse over a style in the side menu and a ScreenTip displays describing what formatting is applied by the style.

In Brief

Change Quick Styles Set
1. Click Change Styles button.
2. Point to *Style Set*.
3. Click desired set.

Apply Quick Style
1. Position insertion point at desired location.
2. Click style in Styles group or click More button and then click desired style.

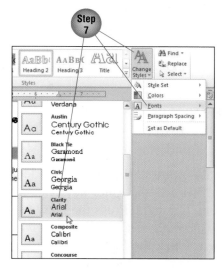
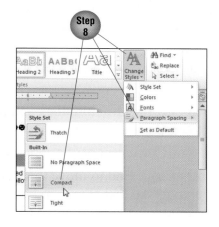

9. Select the title *Traveling in Europe by Train*, change the font size to 16, and change the paragraph alignment to center.

10. Save, print, and then close **WS2-FCTRailTravel.docx**.

In Addition

Printing Page Borders

By default, a page border displays and prints 24 points from the top, left, right, and bottom edges of the page. Some printers, particularly inkjet printers, have a nonprinting area around the outside edges of the page that can interfere with the printing of a border. Before printing a document with a page border, click the File tab and then click the Print tab. Look at the preview of the page at the right side of the Print tab Backstage view and determine whether or not the entire border is visible. If a portion of the border is not visible in the preview page (generally the bottom and right sides of the page), consider changing measurements at the Border and Shading Options dialog box. Display this dialog box by clicking the Border button arrow and then clicking *Borders and Shading*. At the Borders and Shading dialog box, click the Page Border tab and then click the Options button

that displays in the lower right corner of the dialog box. If you insert a page border and then display the document in the Print tab Backstage view and notice that not all of the bottom and right borders will print, increase the measurement in the *Right* measurement box and the *Bottom* measurement box at the Border and Shading Options dialog box. The *Measure from* option box at the Border and Shading Options dialog box has the default setting of *Edge of page*. You can change this option to *Text*, which changes the top and bottom measurements to *1 pt* and the left and right measurements to *4 pt* and moves the page border into the page. Use the measurement boxes to specify the distance you want the page border displayed and printed from the text in the document.

Activity 2.12

Changing Default Document Formatting

A Word document is based on a template that applies default formatting. Some of the default formats include 11-point Calibri, line spacing of 1.15, and 10 points of spacing after each paragraph. Many of the documents you have opened from your student CD have had changes made to them including changes to the font, line spacing, and paragraph spacing. If you create a document with the default formatting, you may need to use the New Line command, Shift + Enter, to keep lines of text within the same paragraph, creating less space between one line and the next. If you turn on the display of nonprinting characters by clicking the Show/Hide ¶ button in the Paragraph group in the Home tab, a line that ends with Shift + Enter displays as a curved arrow pointing left. This symbol can help you identify whether or not a line begins a new paragraph. You can modify the default formatting by manually changing individual features, change formatting by applying styles, or change formatting by applying a Quick Styles set.

Project

Your supervisor at First Choice Travel has asked you to complete a document on Middleton Valley. You need to type additional information and then apply formatting to improve the visual appeal of the document.

Tutorial 2.15
Changing Default Document Formatting

1 Open **FCTMiddleton.docx** and then save the document and name it **WS2-FCTMiddleton**.

This document has been prepared with default formatting.

2 Press Ctrl + End to move the insertion point to the end of the document and then type the text shown in Figure 2.5. Press the Enter key once after *Contact Information* and each of the telephone numbers. Press the New Line command, Shift + Enter, after *Jefferson Basin Chamber of Commerce*, *Department of Fisheries*, and *Lake Middleton Resort*. Click the Show/Hide button ¶ in the Paragraph group in the Home tab, notice the symbols identifying nonprinting characters including the New Line symbol, and then click the Show/Hide button to turn off the feature.

3 You decide to determine the current line spacing and then change it to single spacing. To do this, press Ctrl + A to select the entire document, click the Line and Paragraph Spacing button (notice the current setting is *1.15*), and then click *1.0*.

4 As you view the document, you decide to remove some of the spacing between the first three lines of text. To do this, select the first two lines of text *Middleton Valley* and *Jefferson Basin* and then click the Paragraph group dialog box launcher. At the Paragraph dialog box with the Indents and Spacing tab selected, select *10 pt* in the *After* text box in the *Spacing* section, type **0**, and then click OK.

Make sure you type a zero and not a capital O.

5 To improve the visual appeal of the document you decide to apply styles and a Quick Styles set. Begin by selecting the first three lines of text and then clicking the Heading 2 style in the Styles group.

6 Position the insertion point on any character in the heading *Fishing* and then click the More button ⬇ at the right side of the thumbnails in the Styles group.

FIGURE 2.5 Step 2

Contact Information

Jefferson Basin Chamber of Commerce
(320) 555-3022

Department of Fisheries
(320) 555-8886

Lake Middleton Resort
(320) 555-1255

(7) Click *Heading 3* at the drop-down gallery.

(8) Apply the Heading 3 style to the remaining headings: *Geology*, *Sand Dunes and Off-Road Vehicles*, and *Contact Information*.

(9) Apply a Quick Styles set by clicking the Change Styles button, pointing to *Style Set*, and then clicking *Thatch* at the drop-down gallery.

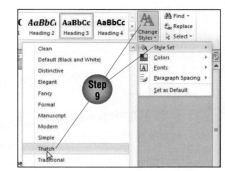

(10) Change the style set color by clicking the Change Styles button, pointing to *Colors*, and then clicking *Concourse* at the drop-down gallery.

(11) Save and then print **WS2-FCTMiddleton.docx**.

(12) You decide to experiment with another Quick Styles set. To do this, click the Change Styles button, point to *Style Set*, and then click *Formal*.

(13) Notice how the Formal style set increased the spacing above and below the first three lines of text. Remove some of the spacing by selecting the first three lines of text, clicking the Page Layout tab, clicking in the *Before* measurement text box in the Paragraph group, typing **0** (type a zero, not an O), and then pressing Enter.

(14) Deselect the text.

(15) Save, print, and then close **WS2-FCTMiddleton.docx**.

In Addition

Applying Styles

The Styles window provides additional styles you can apply to text in a document. Display this window by clicking the Styles group dialog box launcher. The styles in the currently selected Quick Styles set display in the window followed by a paragraph symbol (¶), indicating that the style applies paragraph formatting, or a character symbol (a), indicating that the style applies character formatting. If both characters display to the right of a style, the style applies both paragraph and character formatting. In addition to displaying styles that apply formatting, the Styles window also includes a *Clear All* style that clears all formatting from selected text.

Features Summary

Feature	Ribbon Tab, Group	Button, File Tab	Keyboard Shortcut
1.5 line spacing	Home, Paragraph		Ctrl + 5
align text left	Home, Paragraph		Ctrl + L
align text right	Home, Paragraph		Ctrl + R
bold	Home, Font		Ctrl + B
border	Home, Paragraph		
bullets	Home, Paragraph		
center	Home, Paragraph		Ctrl + E
change case	Home, Font		Shift + F3
change styles	Home, Styles		
clear formatting	Home, Font		
date	Insert, Text		Alt + Shift + D
decrease indent	Home, Paragraph		Ctrl + Shift + M
double line spacing	Home, Paragraph		Ctrl + 2
Find and Replace dialog box with Replace tab selected	Home, Editing		Ctrl + H
font	Home, Font		
font color	Home, Font		
Font dialog box	Home, Font		Ctrl + D
font size	Home, Font		Ctrl + Shift + P
Format Painter	Home, Clipboard		Ctrl + Shift + C
hanging indent	Home, Paragraph		Ctrl + T
highlight	Home, Font		
increase indent	Home, Paragraph		Ctrl + M
insert symbol	Insert, Symbols		
italics	Home, Font		Ctrl + I
justify	Home, Paragraph		Ctrl + J
line and paragraph spacing	Home, Paragraph		

Feature	Ribbon Tab, Group	Button, File Tab	Keyboard Shortcut
multilevel list	Home, Paragraph		
numbering	Home, Paragraph		
Paragraph dialog box	Home, Paragraph		
Quick Styles	Home, Styles		
remove hanging indent	Home, Paragraph		Ctrl + Shift + T
shading	Home, Paragraph		
single line spacing	Home, Paragraph		Ctrl + 1
spacing after	Page Layout, Paragraph	After: 0 pt	
spacing before	Page Layout, Paragraph	Before: 0 pt	
styles	Home, Styles		
Tabs dialog box	Home, Paragraph	, Tabs	
time	Insert, Text		Alt + Shift + T
underline	Home, Font	U	Ctrl + U

Knowledge Check

Completion: In the space provided at the right, indicate the correct term, command, or option.

1. The Bold button is located in this group in the Home tab
2. Click this button in the Font group and then click the *UPPERCASE* option to change selected text to uppercase letters.
3. Press these keys on the keyboard to italicize selected text.
4. The *Small caps* option is located in this section of the Font dialog box.
5. Click this button in the Paragraph group in the Home tab to align text at the right margin.
6. Indent text from the left margin by dragging the Left Indent marker on this.
7. The Line and Paragraph Spacing button displays in this group in the Home tab.
8. This is the keyboard shortcut to display the Reveal Formatting task pane.
9. Click this button at the Find and Replace dialog box to display additional options.
10. Click this button in the Paragraph group in the Home tab to number selected paragraphs.

11. Create multiple-level bulleted or numbered paragraphs with options from this button.

12. Display the Symbol palette by clicking this tab and then clicking the Symbol button in the Symbols group. _____

13. This is the name of the button that displays at the left side of the Ruler. _____

14. Set tabs at the Tabs dialog box or using this. _____

15. Click this button in the Font group in the Home tab to remove paragraph formatting from selected text. _____

16. These can be added to a tab to help guide the reader's eyes across the page. _____

17. Insert a page border with options at this dialog box with the Page Border tab selected. _____

18. A document contains a number of predesigned formats grouped into sets called this. _____

19. To change the Quick Styles set, click this button in the Styles group in the Home tab, point to *Style Set*, and then click the desired Quick Styles at the side menu. _____

20. At a new document, this is the default line spacing. _____

Skills Review

Review 1 Formatting a Petersburg, Alaska, Document

1. Open **FCTPetersburg.docx** from your WordS2 folder and then save it in the WordEOS folder on your storage medium and name it **WS2-R1-FCTPetersburg**.

2. Select the entire document, change the font to Cambria, the font size to 11, and the font color to *Purple, Accent 4, Darker 50%* (last option in the eighth column in the *Theme Colors* section).

3. Set the title *PETERSBURG, ALASKA* in 16-point Corbel bold.

4. Set the heading *Services* in 14-point Corbel bold and then use Format Painter to apply the same formatting to the remaining headings (*Visitor Attractions*, *Walking Tours*, *Accommodations*, and *Transportation*).

5. Apply small caps to the last sentence in the document (the sentence that begins *If you would like more...*). **Hint: Apply small caps formatting at the Font dialog box.**

6. Apply the *Gradient Fill - Purple, Accent 4, Reflection* text effect to the title *PETERSBURG, ALASKA* and then center the title.

7. Change the paragraph alignment to Justify for the paragraph below the title *PETERSBURG, ALASKA*.

8. Change the paragraph alignment to Center for the last sentence in the document (the sentence that begins *If you would like more...*).

9. Change the paragraph alignment to Justify and indent text 0.5 inch from the left margin for the two paragraphs below the *Services* heading. Apply the same formatting to the four paragraphs below the *Visitor Attractions* heading, the one paragraph below the *Walking Tours* heading, the two paragraphs below the *Accommodations* heading, and the two paragraphs below the *Transportation* heading.

10. Move the insertion point to the end of the document, press the Enter key twice, and then change the paragraph alignment to Right. Type your first and last names, press Shift + Enter, insert the current date, press Shift + Enter, and then insert the current time.

11. Select the entire document, change the line spacing to 1.15, and then deselect the document.

12. Click anywhere in the *Services* heading and then change the paragraph spacing after to 6 points.

13. Use the Repeat command (F4) to insert 6 points of spacing after the remaining headings (*Visitor Attractions*, *Walking Tours*, *Accommodations*, and *Transportation*).

14. Insert a double-line purple page border. ***Note: Check the document in the Print tab Backstage view. If the entire page border is not visible, display the Border and Shading Options dialog box [see the In Addition on page 63] and then increase the measurements in the measurements boxes.***

15. Save, print, and then close **WS2-R1-FCTPetersburg.docx**.

Review 2 Formatting a Vacation Package Document

1. Open **FCTVacPackages.docx** from your WordS2 folder on your storage medium and then save the document in the WordEOS folder and name it **WS2-R2-FCTVacPackages**.

2. Select the entire document and then change the line spacing to 1 and remove the 10 points of spacing after paragraphs.

3. Select the four paragraphs of text below *Fast Facts* in the *OREGON* section, click the Decrease Indent button to remove the indent, and then insert bullets.

4. Select the four paragraphs of text below *Fast Facts* in the *NEVADA* section, click the Decrease Indent button to remove the indent, and then insert bullets.

5. Use the Find and Replace dialog box to search for all occurrences of 12-point Corbel italic and replace with 14-point Candara bold.

6. Use the Find and Replace dialog box to search for all occurrences of 11-point Constantia and replace with 12-point Cambria.

7. Move the insertion point to the end of the document and then type the text shown in Figure 2.6. ***Hint: Insert the é, è, and ñ symbols with options at the Symbol dialog box with the Symbols tab selected and the (normal text) font selected.***

FIGURE 2.6 Review 2, Step 7

Additional accommodations are available at the Ste. Thérèse Chateau and Silver Creek Resort. For information, please contact Carlos Nuñez.

8. Move the insertion point to the line below the heading *Rates and Packages* in the *OREGON* section and then create the tabbed text shown in Figure 2.7. Set a left tab at the 1-inch mark on the Ruler, a center tab at the 3.5-inch mark, and a right tab at the 5.5-inch mark on the Ruler.
9. Move the insertion point to the line below the heading *Rates and Packages* in the *NEVADA* section and then create the tabbed text shown in Figure 2.8 using the measurements from Step 8.
10. Select the tabbed text below the *Rates and Packages* heading in the *OREGON* section, insert a border and shading of your choosing, and then deselect the text.
11. Select the tabbed text below the *Rates and Packages* heading in the *NEVADA* section, insert the same border and shading you chose in Step 10, and then deselect the text.
12. Apply the Heading 1 style to *OREGON* and *NEVADA*.
13. Apply the Heading 2 style to the headings *Fast Facts* and *Rates and Packages* in the *OREGON* section and the *NEVADA* section.
14. Change the Quick Styles set to *Distinctive* and apply the *Compact* paragraph spacing style.
15. Save, print, and then close **WS2-R2-FCTVacPackages.docx**.

FIGURE 2.7 Review 2, Step 8

Accommodations	No. Persons	Daily Price
Studio/one bedroom	2 to 4	$75 to $125
Two bedrooms	4 to 6	$95 to $225
Three bedrooms	6 to 8	$135 to $300
Four bedrooms	8 to 12	$160 to $400
Five/six bedrooms	10 to 16	$250 to $500

FIGURE 2.8 Review 2, Step 9

Package	Length	Price
Tuck 'n' Roll	3 days/2 nights	$269
Ski Sneak	4 days/3 nights	$409
Take a Break	6 days/5 nights	$649
Ultimate	8 days/7 nights	$1,009

Skills Assessment

Assessment 1 Formatting a Cross Country Skiing Document

1. Open **FCTLakeTahoeSkiing.docx** and then save the document in the WordEOS folder and name it **WS2-A1-FCTLakeTahoeSkiing**.
2. Make the following changes to the document:
   a. Set the entire document in 12-point Constantia.
   b. Set the title in 14-point Calibri bold.
   c. Set the names of the cross-country skiing resorts in 14-point Calibri bold.
   d. Change the line spacing for the entire document to 1.3.
   e. Change the paragraph spacing after the title to 0 pt.
   f. Change the paragraph spacing after each heading to 6 pt.
   g. Indent one-half inch from the left margin and change the alignment to Justify for the paragraph of text below each cross-country skiing resort name.
   h. Center the title and apply *Blue, Accent 1, Darker 50%* paragraph shading.
   i. Apply *Blue, Accent 1, Lighter 80%* paragraph shading and insert a single line bottom border to each cross-country skiing resort name.
   j. Insert a shadow page border in dark blue that is 3 points in width. ***Note: Check the document in the Print tab Backstage view. If the entire page border is not visible, display the Borders and Shading Options dialog box [see the In Addition on page 63] and then increase the measurements in the measurements boxes.***
3. Save, print, and then close **WS2-A1-FCTLakeTahoeSkiing.docx**.

Assessment 2 Preparing and Formatting a Letter

1. Open **MPLtrhd.docx** and then save the document in the WordEOS folder and name it **WS2-A2-MPLtrtoNPC**.
2. You are Neva Smith-Wilder, Educational Liaison for Marquee Productions. Write a letter using the date April 16, 2012, to Cal Rubine, Chair, Theatre Arts Division, Niagara Peninsula College, 2199 Victoria Street, Niagara-on-the-Lake, ON L0S 1J0 and include the following information (refer to page 35 for information on formatting a business letter):
   * Marquee Productions will be filming in and around the city of Toronto during the summer of 2012.
   * Marquee Productions would like to use approximately 20 theatre interns to assist in the shoot.
   * Interns will perform a variety of tasks including acting as extras, assisting the camera crew, working with set designers on set construction, and providing support to the production team.
   * Interns can work approximately 15 to 30 hours per week and will be compensated at minimum wage.
   * Close your letter by asking Mr. Rubine to screen interested students and then send approximately 20 names to you.
   * If Mr. Rubine has any questions, he may contact you at (612) 555-2005 or send the names to you by email at NevaSW@emcp.net. (Word will automatically convert the email address to a hyperlink.)

3. After typing the letter, apply the following formatting:
   a. Select the letter text and then change the font to Candara.
   b. Change the paragraph alignment to Justify for the paragraph(s) in the body of the letter.
4. Save, print, and then close **WS2-A2-MPLtrtoNPC.docx**.

Assessment 3 Setting Leader Tabs

1. At a blank document, type the text shown in Figure 2.9 with the following specifications:
   a. Center, bold, and italicize the text as shown.
   b. Set the tabbed text as shown using a left tab for the first column and a right tab with leaders for the second column.
   c. After typing the text, select the entire document, change to a font of your choosing (other than Calibri), and then change the spacing after paragraphs to 0 points.
2. Save the document in the Word EOS folder and name it **WS2-A3-WEDistSch**.
3. Print and then close **WS2-A3-WEDistSch.docx**.

FIGURE 2.9 Assessment 3

WORLDWIDE ENTERPRISES

Distribution Schedule

Two by Two

United States	May 10
Canada	June 7
Japan	July 26
Australia/New Zealand	August 2
Mexico	September 20

Assessment 4 Finding Information on Controlling Page Breaks

1. Use Word's Help feature to learn how to prevent page breaks between paragraphs and how to place at least two lines of a paragraph at the top or bottom of a page to prevent a widow (last line of a paragraph by itself at the top of a page) or orphan (first line of a paragraph by itself at the bottom of a page).
2. Create a document containing the following information:
   a. Create a title for the document.
   b. Write a paragraph discussing how to prevent page breaks between paragraphs and list the steps required to complete the task.
   c. Write a paragraph discussing how to keep selected paragraphs together on a single page and list the steps required to complete the task.
   d. Write a paragraph discussing how to prevent a widow or orphan on a page in a document and list the steps required to complete the task.
3. Apply formatting to enhance the visual appeal of the document.
4. Save the completed document in the WordEOS folder and name it **WS2-A4-PageBreaks**.
5. Print and then close **WS2-A4-PageBreaks.docx**.
6. Open **FCTVacSpecials.docx**.
7. Save the document in the WordEOS folder and name it **WS2-A4-FCTVacSpecials**.
8. Select the entire document and then change the font to 12-point Cambria.
9. Search for all occurrences of *Skye* and replace with *Sky*.
10. Search for all occurrences of *Class* and replace with *Category*.
11. Complete a spelling and grammar check on the document.
12. Select the heading *Category S* (located toward the bottom of the first page) and the three lines of text below it and then insert a command to keep all lines of text together with the next line.
13. Save the document and then print only page 2.
14. Close **WS2-A4-FCTVacSpecials.docx**.

Assessment 5 Individual Challenge
Creating a Document with Tabbed Text

1. Determine a city outside of your state or province that you would like to visit. Using the Internet, identify four or more airlines that will fly from the airport nearest you to the city you would like to visit and determine the round-trip airfare.
2. Using the information you find, create a document with two tabbed columns. Set the first column as a left tab and type the name of the airline in this column. Set the second column as a right tab with leaders and type the airfare price in this column.
3. Create an appropriate heading for the tabbed text. Apply a paragraph border and/or shading to enhance the visual appeal of the tabbed text.
4. Apply a page border to the document.
5. Save the completed document in the WordEOS folder and name it **WS2-A5-IC-Airfare**.
6. Print and then close **WS2-A5-IC-Airfare.docx**.

Marquee Challenge

Challenge 1 Editing and Formatting a Document on Juneau, Alaska

1. Open **FCTJuneau.docx** and then save the document in the WordEOS folder and name it **WS2-C1-FCTJuneau**.
2. Apply the Heading 1 style to the title and the Heading 2 style to the headings and then apply the *Modern* Quick Styles set. Change the Quick Styles color to *Equity* and change the Quick Styles font to *Module*.
3. Apply the paragraph formatting and make changes so your document appears as shown in Figure 2.10.
4. Save, print, and then close **WS2-C1-FCTJuneau.docx**.

Challenge 2 Creating and Formatting a Flyer about a Skiing Vacation Package

1. Create the document shown in Figure 2.11. Set the text in the Cambria font and apply the page, border, shading, and bullet formatting as shown in the figure.
2. Save the completed document in the WordEOS folder and name it **WS2-C2-FCTSkiTahoe**.
3. Print and then close **WS2-C2-FCTSkiTahoe.docx**.

FIGURE 2.10 Challenge 1

JUNEAU, ALASKA

Juneau, Alaska's capital since 1900, sits at the base of Mt. Juneau. This capital blends its history as a mining town containing old storefronts and saloons with the modern architecture of government and Native corporations.

HISTORY

In the late 1800s, gold became the foundation of Juneau. The town contained a variety of gold mines with the Alaska-Juneau, or A-J, mine the most successful. The A-J mine buildings are still visible above town. Other gold mines include the Treadwill Mine complex at Douglas and the Alaska-Gastineau mine south of town. A massive cave-in occurred at Treadwill in 1917 and the mine closed. When gold content dropped below profitable margins in 1921, the Alaska-Gastineau mine closed. The A-J mine continued operations until World War II, when labor shortages and high costs forced its closure.

VISITOR ATTRACTIONS

Walking, hiking, and biking trails abound in and around the Juneau area. Scenic flights take visitors over the spectacular ice fields and the Glacier Bay National Monument. Take an exciting boat ride along Juneau's wilderness waterways. Tour buses take visitors to Mendanhall Glacier where they can climb moraines left by receding glaciers, hike nearby trails, and visit the U.S. Forest Service observatory where guides and exhibits explain glacier features. Visitors also can reach the glacier by driving or taking a charter flight. Reminders of Juneau's past abound in the city. The Davis Log Cabin, built in 1881, was the community's first church and is now the visitor information center. Consider a visit to the St. Nicholas Russian Orthodox Church, which was built in 1894 and is considered the oldest original Orthodox Church in Southeast Alaska. Other city attractions include the Juneau Douglas City Museum, the pioneer cemetery, and the Wickersham House.

MUSEUMS

Juneau is the proud home to the Alaska State Museum, featuring permanent displays of Eskimo and Southeast Indian artifacts. The museum also offers changing displays of Alaska's political and natural history. Visit the Juneau Douglas City Museum and learn about Juneau's history. Exhibits include features on gold mining and Juneau's historic past. A small admission fee is charged to adults. Children under the age of 18 are admitted free of charge. The Alaska Maritime Heritage Foundation, a nonprofit group, is planning to build a tall ship for Alaska. It will be used to train sailors and people with disabilities in seamanship, environmental studies, goodwill trips, and charter work.

FIGURE 2.11 Challenge 2

Ski Lake Tahoe

Super Value Ski Package®

Our exciting new Super Value Ski Package features special rates on a full line of top-quality resort and hotel rentals for three days or more. Ask for the Super Value Ski Package and receive a blizzard of valuable savings for one low, inclusive price. Whatever resort or hotel you choose, you will receive the following items for free or at a considerable discount.

- Receive one free adult day lift ticket and ski all day.

- If you would like to travel throughout the Lake Tahoe area, rent any vehicle and receive a 25% discount coupon.

- For your comfort and convenience, we will include a coupon for a free ski rack rental.

- Book a Super Value Ski Package by October 31 and receive four $25 gift certificates you can use at any of the fine dining restaurants in the area.

Accommodations

Resort	3 to 5 Nights	7+ Nights
Ambassador Inn	$699	$959
Hanover's at Lake Tahoe	$679	$929
Moore Creek Lodge	$629	$879
Evergreen Suites	$619	$859
St. Rémi Resort	$607	$837
Cedar Ridge Lodge	$547	$757
Mountain Lodge	$539	$729
River Creek Resort	$525	$715
Alpine Lodge	$477	$677

Word SECTION 3

Formatting and Enhancing a Document

Skills

- Cut, copy, and paste text
- Use the Clipboard task pane to copy and paste items
- Change page margins, orientation, and size
- Apply a theme
- Insert a watermark, page color, and page border
- Insert page numbering
- Insert a header and footer
- Format a document in MLA style
- Insert citations
- Create a works cited page
- Edit a source
- Use the Click and Type feature
- Vertically align text
- Insert, size, and move images
- Prepare an envelope and mailing labels

Projects Overview

Edit and format documents on Thailand and Juneau, Alaska; prepare an announcement about a workshop on traveling on a budget; format a report on the Middleton Valley in MLA style; prepare envelopes and labels for mailing fact sheets and announcements.

Format reports in MLA style and a costume rental agreement.

Prepare an announcement about a workshop on employment opportunities in the movie industry; add a picture watermark.

Create an announcement for weekend work; prepare labels.

Prepare an announcement about internship positions available at Marquee Productions; prepare labels for the college.

Model Answers for Projects

These model answers for the projects that you complete in Section 3 provide a preview of the finished projects before you begin working and also allow you to compare your own results with these models to ensure you have created the materials accurately.

WS3-FCTThailand.docx (a three-page document) is the project in Activities 3.1 to 3.5.

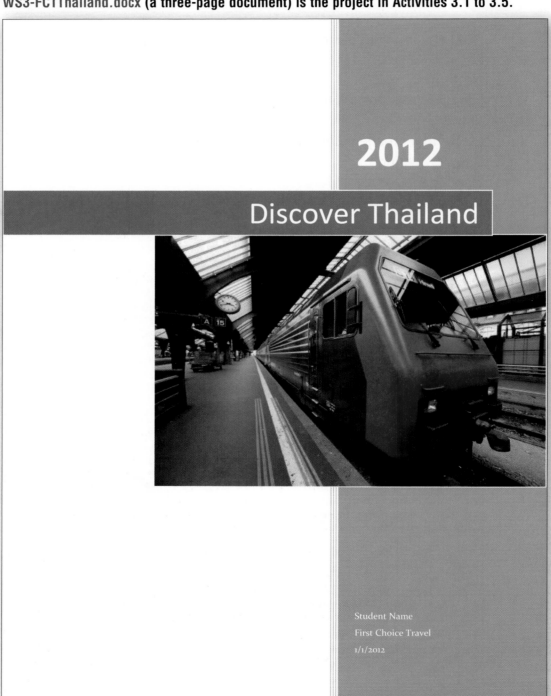

teahouses, cocktail lounges, amusement parks, museums, theaters, art galleries, and cinemas. Thailand's English-language newspapers carry daily listings of current attractions.

Accommodations

Thailand offers accommodations ranging from opulent hotels to simple beachside dwellings on remote islands. Major tourism destinations such as Bangkok, Pattaya, Chiang Mai, and Phuket boast modern

THAILAND

Thailand is a Southeast Asian country bordered to the north by Laos and Burma, to the east by Laos and Cambodia, to the south by the Gulf of Thailand and Malaysia, and to the west by the Andaman Sea. Bangkok, the capital of Thailand, is the country's largest city and the center of political, commercial, industrial, and cultural activities.

Transportation

Most visitors to Thailand enter through Bangkok's Don Muang International Airport, which is served by the world's major airlines. International flights also arrive from Malaysia and Singapore at Hat Yai and Phuket in southern Thailand, and from Hong Kong at Chiang Mai in northern Thailand.

Traveling In Thailand

Thai Airways, Thailand's domestic airline, offers tourism destinations such as Phuket and Chiang Mai with feeder routes to thriving commercial centers and provincial capitals with airfields. An efficient rail system links northern and northeastern towns with the capital and a southern route enables visitors to travel by rail into Malaysia and Singapore. Domestic express trains provide first-, second-, and third-class cars while slower trains may have only third-class seats. A modern highway system reaches into all corners of the country. If you possess a valid international driving license, you can rent an automobile. Thai automobile rental rates compare favorably with those found in other Asian countries.

Attractions

Thailand is a beautiful country with majestic mountains, national marine parks, sparkling beach resorts, ruined cities, archaeological wonders, and year-round festivals and events. Bangkok and the surrounding area boast Thailand's major attractions. While touring the capital city, visit the Emerald Buddha Temple and the Grand Palace complex. The Temple of the Dawn, the Temple of the Reclining Buddha, the Golden Mount, and the Marble Temple are popular attractions that were featured during Bangkok's Bicentennial Celebration in 1982. Take a trip to the Susan Pakkad Palace lacquer pavilion, which is decorated with seventeenth century gold leaf murals, or visit the Jim Thompson house, which contains a superb collection of Asian art and artifacts. One hour west of Bangkok is the Rose Garden, a riverside tropical park and country club that offers an 18-hole championship golf course. Just one-half hour from Bangkok is the Phra Pathom Chedi, the world's tallest Buddhist monument, which marks the spot where Buddhism was introduced to the region over 2,300 years ago.

Entertainment

Thailand offers a variety of entertainment options for visitors, such as boxing stadiums, race and golf courses, tennis and squash courts, billiard halls, nightclubs, gourmet restaurants, concert halls,

WORD SECTION 3
Project Model Answers

Last Name 2

Although the development of the Middleton Valley has come far, modern planners

today use the ancient wisdom of the Native people when building in the area. Realizing the

need to preserve the valley's beauty in the face of progress, the state formed the Middleton

Valley Regional Planning Department in 1965 to oversee environmentally responsible

Last Name 1

Student Name

Instructor Name

Course Title

(current date)

Middleton Valley

The Middleton Valley is home to one of the state's largest natural freshwater lakes,

the unique and beautiful Jefferson Basin, and numerous parks and recreational

campgrounds. Middleton Valley has many convenient and quality visitor attractions and

facilities, including a variety of lodging options to fit any budget. The Middleton Valley and

surrounding area is renowned for its beautiful scenery, wildlife, and outdoor recreational

opportunities.

In the 1860s, silver was discovered in the Middleton Valley area and fortune

seekers flocked to the area hoping to strike it rich at the massive Milestone Lode

discovered in 1860. Would-be miners rushed to the Middleton Valley over Culver Pass from

the north and Myers Pass and Gulliver Pass from the south. The influx of pioneers to the

valley was so great that Northridge Road was forged across the mountains. Silver wasn't

the only valuable commodity early settlers found in the area. Middleton Valley's timber-

rich forests became a necessary resource for the increasing number of people needing fuel

and to support the labyrinth of mines being constructed (Henderson). The easy availability

of timber soon led to the devastation of the valley forests, which were heavily logged

between 1860 and 1890. The decline of the Milestone Lode probably rescued the valley's

diminishing forests.

biking, skiing, golf, and tennis. The valley boasts over 20 lodges and resorts and offers a full range of services for visitors, from those interested in camping to those preferring first-class amenities.

Works Cited

Henderson, Joanne. "Natural Resources of Middleton Valley." Planet Earth's Resources

(2010): 7-9.

Marcello, Daniel. Middleton Valley Regional Planning Department. 5 January 2010. 30

November 2012 <www.emcp.org/middleton>.

WORD SECTION 3
Project Model Answers

WS3-FCTTravelIntl.docx is the project in Activity 3.8.

TRAVELING INTERNATIONALLY

Traveling on a Budget

Thursday, April 19, 2012

7:00 to 8:30 p.m.

Sponsored by

WS3-FCTEnvtoMP.docx is the project in Activity 3.9.

First Choice Travel
(Student Name)
3588 Ventura Boulevard
Los Angeles, CA 90102

Camille Matsui
Marquee Productions
955 South Alameda Street
Los Angeles, CA 90037

WS3-FCTLALabels.docx is part of the project in Activity 3.10.

First Choice Travel
(Student Name)
3588 Ventura Boulevard
Los Angeles, CA 90102

First Choice Travel
(Student Name)
3588 Ventura Boulevard
Los Angeles, CA 90102

First Choice Travel
(Student Name)
3588 Ventura Boulevard
Los Angeles, CA 90102

First Choice Travel
(Student Name)
3588 Ventura Boulevard
Los Angeles, CA 90102

First Choice Travel
(Student Name)
3588 Ventura Boulevard
Los Angeles, CA 90102

First Choice Travel
(Student Name)
3588 Ventura Boulevard
Los Angeles, CA 90102

First Choice Travel
(Student Name)
3588 Ventura Boulevard
Los Angeles, CA 90102

First Choice Travel
(Student Name)
3588 Ventura Boulevard
Los Angeles, CA 90102

First Choice Travel
(Student Name)
3588 Ventura Boulevard
Los Angeles, CA 90102

First Choice Travel
(Student Name)
3588 Ventura Boulevard
Los Angeles, CA 90102

First Choice Travel
(Student Name)
3588 Ventura Boulevard
Los Angeles, CA 90102

First Choice Travel
(Student Name)
3588 Ventura Boulevard
Los Angeles, CA 90102

First Choice Travel
(Student Name)
3588 Ventura Boulevard
Los Angeles, CA 90102

First Choice Travel
(Student Name)
3588 Ventura Boulevard
Los Angeles, CA 90102

First Choice Travel
(Student Name)
3588 Ventura Boulevard
Los Angeles, CA 90102

First Choice Travel
(Student Name)
3588 Ventura Boulevard
Los Angeles, CA 90102

First Choice Travel
(Student Name)
3588 Ventura Boulevard
Los Angeles, CA 90102

First Choice Travel
(Student Name)
3588 Ventura Boulevard
Los Angeles, CA 90102

First Choice Travel
(Student Name)
3588 Ventura Boulevard
Los Angeles, CA 90102

First Choice Travel
(Student Name)
3588 Ventura Boulevard
Los Angeles, CA 90102

First Choice Travel
(Student Name)
3588 Ventura Boulevard
Los Angeles, CA 90102

First Choice Travel
(Student Name)
3588 Ventura Boulevard
Los Angeles, CA 90102

First Choice Travel
(Student Name)
3588 Ventura Boulevard
Los Angeles, CA 90102

First Choice Travel
(Student Name)
3588 Ventura Boulevard
Los Angeles, CA 90102

First Choice Travel
(Student Name)
3588 Ventura Boulevard
Los Angeles, CA 90102

First Choice Travel
(Student Name)
3588 Ventura Boulevard
Los Angeles, CA 90102

First Choice Travel
(Student Name)
3588 Ventura Boulevard
Los Angeles, CA 90102

First Choice Travel
(Student Name)
3588 Ventura Boulevard
Los Angeles, CA 90102

First Choice Travel
(Student Name)
3588 Ventura Boulevard
Los Angeles, CA 90102

First Choice Travel
(Student Name)
3588 Ventura Boulevard
Los Angeles, CA 90102

WS3-FCTCustLabels.docx is part of the project in Activity 3.10.

Moreno Products
350 Mission Boulevard
Pomona, CA 91767

Mr. Miguel Santos
12120 Barranca Parkway
Irvine, CA 92612

Mr. and Mrs. Jack Lipinski
5534 Southeast 32nd Street
Los Angeles, CA 90092

Dr. Esther Riggins
9077 Walnut Street
Los Angeles, CA 90097

Automated Services, Inc.
4394 Seventh Street,
Long Beach, CA 92602

Ms. Samantha Schwartz
103-B Pacific Palms
Los Angeles, CA 90068

WS3-FCTTorontoLabels.docx is part of the project in Activity 3.10.

4277 Yonge Street
Toronto, ON M4P 2E6

4277 Yonge Street
Toronto, ON M4P 2E6

4277 Yonge Street
Toronto, ON M4P 2E6

4277 Yonge Street
Toronto, ON M4P 2E6

4277 Yonge Street
Toronto, ON M4P 2E6

4277 Yonge Street
Toronto, ON M4P 2E6

4277 Yonge Street
Toronto, ON M4P 2E6

4277 Yonge Street
Toronto, ON M4P 2E6

4277 Yonge Street
Toronto, ON M4P 2E6

4277 Yonge Street
Toronto, ON M4P 2E6

4277 Yonge Street
Toronto, ON M4P 2E6

4277 Yonge Street
Toronto, ON M4P 2E6

4277 Yonge Street
Toronto, ON M4P 2E6

4277 Yonge Street
Toronto, ON M4P 2E6

4277 Yonge Street
Toronto, ON M4P 2E6

4277 Yonge Street
Toronto, ON M4P 2E6

4277 Yonge Street
Toronto, ON M4P 2E6

4277 Yonge Street
Toronto, ON M4P 2E6

4277 Yonge Street
Toronto, ON M4P 2E6

4277 Yonge Street
Toronto, ON M4P 2E6

4277 Yonge Street
Toronto, ON M4P 2E6

4277 Yonge Street
Toronto, ON M4P 2E6

4277 Yonge Street
Toronto, ON M4P 2E6

4277 Yonge Street
Toronto, ON M4P 2E6

4277 Yonge Street
Toronto, ON M4P 2E6

4277 Yonge Street
Toronto, ON M4P 2E6

4277 Yonge Street
Toronto, ON M4P 2E6

4277 Yonge Street
Toronto, ON M4P 2E6

4277 Yonge Street
Toronto, ON M4P 2E6

4277 Yonge Street
Toronto, ON M4P 2E6

Activity 3.1

Cutting, Copying, and Pasting Text; Using Paste Special

With the Cut, Copy, and Paste buttons in the Clipboard group in the Home tab, you can move and/or copy words, sentences, or entire sections of text to other locations in a document. You can cut and paste text or copy and paste text within the same document or between documents. Specify the formatting of pasted text with options at the Paste Special dialog box.

Project You are working on a First Choice Travel document containing information on Thailand. You decide that some of the text in the document should be reorganized and you also decide to add additional information to the document.

Tutorial 3.1
Cutting, Copying, and Pasting Text

1. Open **FCTThailand.docx** and then save the document and name it **WS3-FCTThailand**.

2. Move the *Attractions* section below the *Traveling in Thailand* section. Begin by selecting the *Attractions* heading and the paragraph of text that follows the heading.

3. Click the Cut button 🔏 in the Clipboard group in the Home tab.

   Clicking the Cut button places the text in a special location within Word called the *clipboard*.

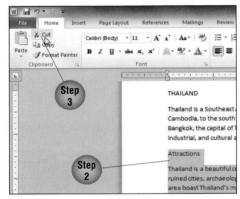

Need Help?

If you click the wrong button, immediately click the Undo button.

4. Move the insertion point to the beginning of the *Accommodations* heading and then click the Paste button 📋 in the Clipboard group in the Home tab.

   A Paste Options button 📋 (Ctrl) ▾ displays below the pasted text. Click this button and a drop-down list of buttons displays. Use these buttons to specify the formatting of the pasted text. By default, the Keep Source Formatting button (first button from the left) is selected. With this button selected, text is pasted with the formatting from the source document. You can also click the Merge Formatting button (middle button) to merge formatting with the destination formatting or click the Keep Text Only button (third button) to keep only the text and not the formatting.

5. Open **FCTThaiStats.docx**.

   You will copy text from this document and paste it in the Thailand information document.

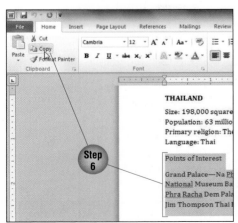

6. Select the *Points of Interest* heading and the four lines of text below the heading and then click the Copy button 📋 in the Clipboard group.

(7) Click the Word button on the Taskbar and then click the **WS3-FCTThailand.docx** thumbnail.

(8) Position the insertion point at the beginning of the heading *Passports/Visas* and then click the Paste button in the Clipboard group.

(9) Click the Paste Options button and then click the Merge Formatting button (middle button) at the Paste Options button drop-down list.

(10) Click the Word button on the Taskbar and then click the **FCTThaiStats.docx** thumbnail.

(11) Select the text *Resources:* and the three lines below it and then click the Copy button.

(12) Click the Word button on the Taskbar and then click the **WS3-FCTThailand.docx** thumbnail.

(13) Move the insertion point to the end of the document and then press the Enter key once. Paste the copied text into the document without the formatting by clicking the Paste button arrow and then clicking *Paste Special* at the drop-down list.

(14) At the Paste Special dialog box, click *Unformatted Text* in the *As* list box and then click OK.

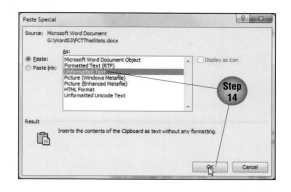

(15) Select the four lines of text you just pasted in the document and then remove the spacing after the paragraphs by clicking the Page Layout tab and then clicking twice on the down-pointing arrow at the right side of the After measurement box in the Paragraph group.

(16) Save **WS3-FCTThailand.docx**.

(17) Click the Word button on the Taskbar, click the **FCTThaiStats.docx** thumbnail, and then close the document.

> Closing the **FCTThaiStats.docx** document displays the **WS3-FCTThailand.docx** document.

In Brief

Cut and Paste Text
1. Select text.
2. Click Cut button in Clipboard group.
3. Move insertion point to desired position.
4. Click Paste button in Clipboard group.

Copy and Paste Text
1. Select text.
2. Click Copy button in Clipboard group.
3. Move insertion point to desired position.
4. Click Paste button in Clipboard group.

Display Paste Special Dialog Box
1. Cut or copy text.
2. Click Paste button arrow.
3. Click *Paste Special*.
4. Click desired format in *As* list box.
5. Click OK.

In Addition

Moving and Copying Text with the Mouse

You can move selected text using the mouse. To do this, select the text with the mouse and then move the I-beam pointer inside the selected text until the I-beam pointer turns into an arrow pointer. Hold down the left mouse button, drag the arrow pointer (displays with a gray box attached) to the location where you want the selected text inserted, and then release the button. You can copy and move selected text by following similar steps. The difference is that you need to hold down the Ctrl key while dragging with the mouse. With the Ctrl key down, a box containing a plus symbol displays near the gray box by the arrow pointer.

Activity 3.2

Using the Clipboard Task Pane

Using the Clipboard task pane, you can collect up to 24 different items and then paste them in various locations in a document. Display the Clipboard task pane by clicking the Clipboard group dialog box launcher. Cut or copy an item and the item displays in the Clipboard task pane. If the item is text, the first 50 characters display. Paste an item by positioning the insertion point at the desired location and then clicking the item in the Clipboard task pane. When all desired items are inserted, click the Clear All button located in the upper right corner of the task pane.

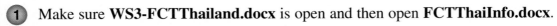

Project

You will open another document with information on Thailand, copy items in the document, and then paste the items into the Thailand document.

Tutorial 3.2
Using the Office
Clipboard

1 Make sure **WS3-FCTThailand.docx** is open and then open **FCTThaiInfo.docx**.

2 In the **FCTThaiInfo.docx** document, display the Clipboard task pane by clicking the Clipboard group dialog box launcher [image]. If any items display in the Clipboard task pane, click the Clear All button located in the upper right corner of the task pane.

3 Select the *Food and Beverages* heading and the paragraph of text below it and then click the Copy button in the Clipboard group.

   Notice how the copied item is represented in the Clipboard task pane.

4 Select the *Shopping* heading and the paragraph below it and then click the Copy button in the Clipboard group.

5 Select the *Entertainment* heading and the paragraph of text below it and then click the Copy button in the Clipboard group.

6 Click the Word button on the Taskbar and then click the **WS3-FCTThailand.docx** thumbnail.

7 Display the Clipboard task pane by clicking the Home tab and then clicking the Clipboard group dialog box launcher.

8 Move the insertion point to the beginning of the *Accommodations* heading.

9 Click the item in the Clipboard task pane representing *Entertainment*.

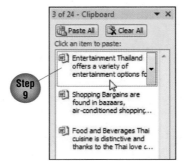

10 Move the insertion point to the beginning of the *Points of Interest* heading.

⑪ Click the item in the Clipboard task pane representing *Shopping*.

Use Clipboard Task Pane
1. Click Clipboard group dialog box launcher.
2. Select text.
3. Click Copy button.
4. Select and copy any additional items.
5. Move insertion point to desired position.
6. Click item in Clipboard task pane representing desired item.
7. Paste any other desired items from Clipboard task pane.
8. Click Clear All button.

⑫ Click the Clear All button located toward the upper right corner of the Clipboard task pane.

⑬ Close the Clipboard task pane by clicking the Close button ✖ located in the upper right corner of the task pane.

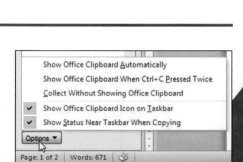

⑭ Click the Word button on the Taskbar, click the **FCTThaiInfo.docx** thumbnail, and then close the document.

> The **WS3-FCTThailand.docx** document displays when you close **FCTThaiInfo.docx**.

⑮ Press Ctrl + Home to move the insertion point to the beginning of the document, click on any character in the title *THAILAND*, and then click the Heading 1 style in the Styles group in the Home tab.

⑯ Select the heading *Transportation*, click the More button at the right side of the style thumbnails in the Styles group, and then click *Emphasis* at the drop-down gallery.

⑰ Select individually each of the remaining headings (*Traveling in Thailand*, *Attractions*, *Entertainment*, *Accommodations*, *Shopping*, *Points of Interest*, and *Passports/Visas*) and then apply the *Emphasis* style.

⑱ Click the Changes Styles button in the Styles group in the Home tab, point to *Style Set*, and then click *Thatch* at the side menu.

⑲ Press Ctrl + Home to move the insertion point to the beginning of the document and then center the title *THAILAND*.

⑳ Save **WS3-FCTThailand.docx**.

In Addition

Clipboard Task Pane Options

Click the Options button located toward the bottom of the Clipboard task pane and a pop-up menu displays with five options as shown at the right. Insert a check mark before those options that you want active. For example, you can choose to display the Clipboard task pane automatically when you cut or copy text, press Ctrl + C twice to display the Clipboard task pane, cut and copy text without displaying the Clipboard task pane, display the *Office Clipboard* icon on the Taskbar when the clipboard is active, or display the item message near the Taskbar when copying items to the Clipboard.

Activity 3.3

Customizing the Page Setup; Applying a Theme

In Word, a page contains a number of defaults such as a page size of 8.5 inches by 11 inches; top, bottom, left, and right margins of one inch; a portrait page orientation; and a page break after approximately nine inches of vertical text on a page. Use buttons in the Page Setup group in the Page Layout tab to customize pages in a document. Another method for customizing text on a page is to apply a theme. A theme applies formatting in much the same way as the Quick Styles sets discussed in Activity 2.11. A document theme is a set of formatting choices that include a color theme (a set of colors), a font theme (a set of heading and body text fonts), and an effects theme (a set of lines and fill effects). Apply a theme with buttons in the Themes group in the Page Layout tab.

Project To customize the Thailand document, you will change the document margins, orientation, and page size and then customize and add visual appeal by applying a theme.

Tutorial 3.3
Modifying Page Orientation and Changing Margins

Tutorial 3.4
Applying Themes

1. With **WS3-FCTThailand.docx** open, change the margins by clicking the Page Layout tab, clicking the Margins button in the Page Setup group, and then clicking the *Wide* option at the drop-down list.

    The *Wide* option changes the left and right margins to 2 inches.

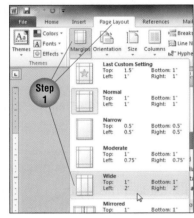

2. Change the page orientation by clicking the Orientation button in the Page Setup group in the Page Layout tab and then clicking *Landscape* at the drop-down list.

    Word considers a page in portrait orientation to be 8.5 inches wide and 11 inches tall. Word considers a page in landscape orientation to be 11 Inches wide and 8.5 inches tall. You can also change page orientation at the Page Setup dialog box with the Margins tab selected.

3. Change margins by clicking the Margins button in the Page Setup group in the Page Layout tab and then clicking the *Custom Margins* option that displays at the bottom of the drop-down list. (Make sure you click the very bottom *Custom Margins* option.)

4. At the Page Setup dialog box with the Margins tab selected and *2"* selected in the *Top* measurement box, type **0.8**.

5. Click the down-pointing arrow at the right side of the *Bottom* measurement box until *0.8"* displays.

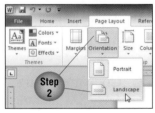

6. Click OK to close the Page Setup dialog box.

7. Change the paper size by clicking the Size button in the Page Setup group, and then clicking the *Legal* option at the drop-down list.

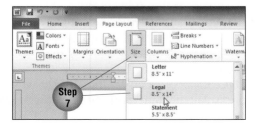

(8) Scroll through the document to view the pages in Legal size.

(9) Change the paper size back to *Letter* by clicking the Size button and then clicking the *Letter* option at the drop-down list.

(10) Save **WS3-FCTThailand.docx**. (Optional: Your instructor may want you to print the document at this point.)

(11) Change the page orientation by clicking the Orientation button in the Page Setup group and then clicking *Portrait* at the drop-down list.

(12) Change margins by clicking the Margins button in the Page Setup group and then clicking *Normal* at the drop-down list.

(13) Apply a theme to the document by clicking the Themes button in the Themes group and then clicking *Elemental* at the drop-down gallery.

> Apply formatting to an entire document using a theme. A document theme is formatting that includes a font theme, a color theme, and an effects theme.

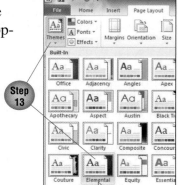

(14) Change the theme colors by clicking the Theme Colors button in the Themes group and then clicking *Apothecary* at the drop-down gallery.

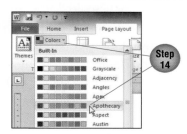

(15) Change the theme fonts by clicking the Theme Fonts button in the Themes group and then clicking *Flow*. (You will need to scroll down the list to display *Flow*.)

(16) Save **WS3-FCTThailand.docx**.

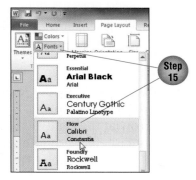

In Brief

Changing Margins
1. Click Page Layout tab.
2. Click Margins button.
3. Click desired option.

Changing Orientation
1. Click Page Layout tab.
2. Click Orientation button.
3. Click desired orientation option.

Changing Page Size
1. Click Page Layout tab.
2. Click Size button.
3. Click desired size option.

Apply a Theme
1. Click Page Layout tab.
2. Click Themes button.
3. Click desired theme.

In Addition

Applying Themes

Apply a predesigned theme with the Themes button in the Page Layout tab and use the three buttons that display at the right side of the Themes button to change the color and fonts of the theme. Click the Theme Colors button and a drop-down gallery displays with named color schemes. The names of the color schemes correspond to the names of the themes. Each theme applies specific fonts, which you can change with options from the Theme Fonts button. Click this button and a drop-down gallery displays with font choices. Each font group in the drop-down gallery contains two choices. The first choice in the group is the font that is applied to headings and the second choice is the font that is applied to body text in the document. If you are formatting a document containing graphics with lines and fills, you can apply a specific theme of effects with options at the Theme Effects button drop-down gallery.

Activity 3.4

Customizing the Page and Page Background

The Page Background group in the Page Layout tab contains buttons you can use to insert a watermark, change the page color, and insert a page border. A watermark is lightened text or image that displays behind text. Word provides a number of predesigned watermark images you can insert in a document. The Pages group in the Insert tab contains buttons for adding a cover page, a blank page, and a page break.

Project

To add visual appeal to the Thailand document, you will apply page color and a page border, and insert a cover page and blank page into the document. You will also identify the document as a draft by inserting a watermark.

Tutorial 3.5
Adding Borders, Shading, and Watermarks to Pages

1 With **WS3-FCTThailand.docx** open, press Ctrl + Home. Insert a watermark by clicking the Page Layout tab, clicking the Watermark button in the Page Background group, scrolling down the drop-down list, and then clicking the *DRAFT 1* option.

> A watermark is lightened text or image that displays behind text.

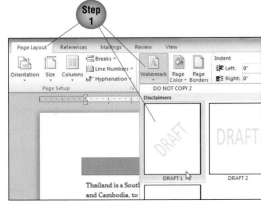

2 Apply a page color to the document by clicking the Page Color button in the Page Background group and then clicking the *Gray-50%, Accent 6, Lighter 60%* color (third choice in the last column).

> Page color is designed for viewing a document on screen and does not print.

3 Click the Page Borders button in the Page Background group.

4 At the Borders and Shading dialog box with the Page Border tab selected, click the down-pointing arrow at the right side of the *Art* option box. Scroll down the list of page borders and then click the art border option shown at the right. Click OK to close the dialog box.

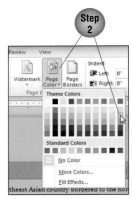

5 Press Ctrl + Home and then insert a cover page by clicking the Insert tab, clicking the Cover Page button in the Pages group, scrolling down the drop-down list, and then clicking *Motion*.

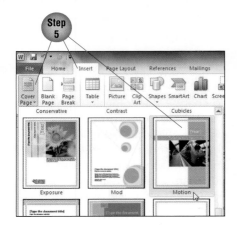

6 Click anywhere in the placeholder text *[Year]* and then type the current year.

7 Click anywhere in the placeholder text *[Type the document title]* and then type **Discover Thailand**.

8 Click anywhere in the placeholder text *[Type the company name]* and then type **First Choice Travel**.

9 You need a blank page at the end of the document for information that will be added later. Press Ctrl + End to move the insertion point to the end of the document and then click the Blank Page button 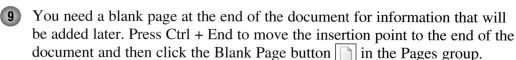 in the Pages group.

10 Move the insertion point to the beginning of the heading *Entertainment* and then insert a page break by clicking the Page Break button 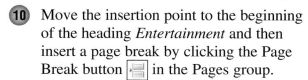 in the Pages group.

> You can also insert a hard page break with the keyboard shortcut, Ctrl + Enter.

11 Save **WS3-FCTThailand.docx** and then print only pages 1 and 2.

12 Remove the page border by clicking the Page Layout tab and then clicking the Page Borders button.

13 At the Borders and Shading dialog box click *None* in the *Setting* section and then click OK.

14 Position the insertion point on any character in page 2 and then remove page color by clicking the Page Color button in the Page Background group and then clicking *No Color* at the drop-down palette.

15 Delete the page break you inserted in Step 10 by positioning the insertion point at the end of the paragraph of text below the *Attractions* heading and then pressing the Delete key twice.

16 Remove the blank page by clicking the Home tab and then clicking the Show/Hide ¶ button ¶ in the Paragraph group. Position the insertion point at the beginning of the page break that displays on the third page and then press the Delete key twice. Click the Show/Hide ¶ button to turn off the display of nonprinting characters.

17 Save **WS3-FCTThailand.docx**.

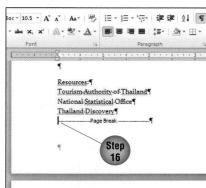

In Addition

Deleting a Cover Page

If you want to delete a cover page from a document use an option from the Cover Page button drop-down list. To do this, click the Insert tab, click the Cover Page button, and then click the *Remove Current Cover Page* option from the drop-down list.

Activity 3.5

Inserting Page Numbering, Headers, and Footers

Insert page numbering in a document with options from the Page Number button or in a header or footer. Click the Page Number button in the Header & Footer group in the Insert tab and a drop-down list displays with options for inserting page numbers at the top or bottom of the page or in the page margins, removing page numbers, and formatting page numbers. Text that appears at the top of every page is called a *header* and text that appears at the bottom of every page is referred to as a *footer*. Headers and footers are common in manuscripts, textbooks, reports, and other publications. Insert a predesigned header in a document with the Header button in the Header & Footer group in the Insert tab. Insert a predesigned footer in the same manner as a header. Predesigned headers and footers contain formatting that you can customize.

Project

Insert identifying information in the Thailand document using a header and footer and insert page numbering.

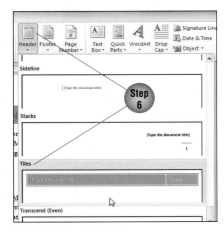

SNAP

Tutorial 3.6
Inserting Page Numbers and Page Breaks

Tutorial 3.7
Creating Headers and Footers

Tutorial 3.8
Modifying Headers and Footers

1. With **WS3-FCTThailand.docx** open, move the insertion point to the beginning of the title *THAILAND*.

2. Number pages at the bottom of each page by clicking the Insert tab, clicking the Page Number button in the Header & Footer group, and then pointing to *Bottom of Page*.

3. At the gallery of predesigned page numbers, click the *Accent Bar 1* option.

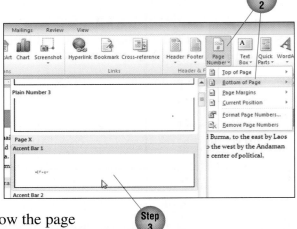

4. Double-click in the body of the document and then scroll through the document and notice how the page numbers display toward the bottom of each page except the cover page.

5. Remove page numbering by clicking the Insert tab, clicking the Page Number button in the Header & Footer group, and then clicking *Remove Page Numbers* at the drop-down list.

6. Insert a header in the document by clicking the Header button in the Header & Footer group, scrolling down the header list, and then clicking the *Tiles* header.

    Notice how the document title you entered in the cover page is inserted in the header along with the current year.

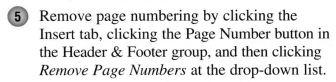

7. Double-click in the body of the document.

    This makes the document active and dims the header.

8. Insert a footer in the document by clicking the Insert tab, clicking the Footer button 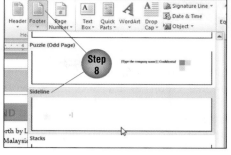 in the Header & Footer group, scrolling down the footer list, and then clicking the *Sideline* footer.

9. Double-click in the body of the document.

10. Scroll through the document and notice how the header and footer appear on each page except the cover page.

11. Remove the footer by clicking the Insert tab, clicking the Footer button in the Header & Footer group, and then clicking the *Remove Footer* option at the drop-down list.

12. Insert a new footer by clicking the Insert tab, clicking the Footer button in the Header & Footer group, scrolling through the footer list, and then clicking the *Tiles* footer.

13. With the placeholder text *[Type the company address]* selected, type your first and last names.

> You are using the placeholder text to insert your name rather than the company address.

14. Double-click in the body of the document.

15. Edit the header by clicking the Insert tab, clicking the Header button in the Header & Footer group, and then clicking *Edit Header* at the drop-down list.

16. Click on any character in the title *Discover Thailand* and then click the Title tab.

> Clicking the Title tab selects the title text.

17. Change the font size by clicking the Home tab, clicking the Font Size button arrow, and then clicking *16* at the drop-down list.

18. Double-click in the document.

19. Save, print, and then close **WS3-FCTThailand.docx**.

In Addition

Creating Your Own Header or Footer

You can create your own header or footer using the Edit Header or Edit Footer options from the drop-down list. For example, to create a header, click the Insert tab, click the Header button, and then click *Edit Header* at the drop-down list. This displays a Header pane in the document and also displays the Header & Footer Tools Design tab with buttons and options for editing the header. Make the desired edits to the header with options in the tab and then close the header window by clicking the Close Header and Footer button located in the Close group in the Header & Footer Tools Design tab.

Activity 3.6

Formatting a Document in MLA Style; Inserting Citations

When preparing a research paper or report, consider inserting citations and a bibliography to give credit to the sources of words, ideas, and any material borrowed or summarized. Word includes some common reference styles for citing and referencing research papers and reports including the Modern Language Association (MLA) style, which is generally used in the humanities and English. To create a citation, display the Create Source dialog box by clicking the References tab, clicking the Insert Citation button in the Citations & Bibliography group, and then clicking *Add New Source*. At the dialog box, insert bibliography information in the required fields. Once you insert source information in the Create Source dialog box, Word will automatically save the source information. To insert a citation in a document from a source that is already saved, click the Insert Citation button in the Citations & Bibliography group and then click the desired reference at the drop-down list. If you include a direct quote from another source, you will need to include the page number. To do this, click the citation in the document to select the citation placeholder, click the Citation Options arrow, and then click *Edit Citation* at the drop-down list. At the Edit Citation dialog box, type in the page or page numbers of the source from which the quote was borrowed.

Project

You are responsible for preparing and formatting a report on Middleton Valley for First Choice Travel. You have been asked to format the report in the MLA style.

Tutorial 3.9
Inserting and Modifying Sources and Citations

1. Open **FCTMiddletonRpt.docx** and then save the document and name it **WS3-FCTMiddletonRpt**.

2. Click the References tab and make sure *MLA Sixth Edition* displays in the *Style* option box in the Citations & Bibliography group.

   If *MLA Sixth Edition* does not display in the *Style* option box, click the down-pointing arrow located at the right side of the *Style* option box and then click *MLA Sixth Edition* at the drop-down list. Refer to Table 3.1 for general guidelines on formatting a research paper or report in the MLA style.

3. Press Ctrl + A to select the entire document and then change the font to 12-point Cambria.

4. With the text still selected, change the line spacing to 2 by clicking the Line and Paragraph Spacing button in the Paragraph group in the Home tab and then clicking *2.0* at the drop-down list.

5. With the text still selected, remove spacing after paragraphs by clicking the Page Layout tab, clicking in the *After* text box in the *Spacing* section, typing **0**, and then pressing Enter.

TABLE 3.1 MLA Style General Guidelines

Use standard-sized paper (8.5 × 11 inches).
Set one-inch top, bottom, left, and right margins.
Set text in a 12-point serif typeface (such as Cambria or Times New Roman).
Double-space text.
Indent the first line of each paragraph one-half inch.
Insert page numbers in the upper right corner of pages.

6 Press Ctrl + Home to position the insertion point at the beginning of the document, type your name, and then press the Enter key.

7 Type your instructor's name and then press the Enter key.

8 Type the title of your course and then press the Enter key.

9 Type the current date.

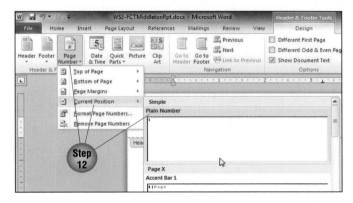

Steps 6-9

Student Name

Instructor Name

Course Title

(current date)

Middleto

The Middleton Valley is home to one of

10 Insert a header in the document by clicking the Insert tab, clicking the Header button in the Header & Footer group, and then clicking *Edit Header* at the drop-down list.

11 Press the Tab key twice to move the insertion point to the right margin in the Header pane, type your last name, and then press the spacebar.

12 Insert page numbers by clicking the Page Number button in the Header & Footer group in the Header & Footer Tools Design tab, pointing to *Current Position*, and then clicking the *Plain Number* option.

Step 12

13 Select the header text and then change the font to 12-point Cambria.

14 Double-click in the body of the document.

15 Insert a new citation in the document. Begin by positioning the insertion point immediately right of the word *constructed* (but before the period) that ends the fifth sentence in the second paragraph.

16 Click the References tab, click the Insert Citation button in the Citations & Bibliography group, and then click *Add New Source* at the drop-down list.

Step 16

surrounding area is renowned for

continues

17 At the Create Source dialog box, click the down-pointing arrow at the right of the *Type of Source* option and then click *Journal Article* at the drop-down list.

18 Click in the *Author* text box, type **Joanne Henderson**, and then press the Tab key three times.

19 Type **Natural Resources of Middleton Valley** in the *Title* text box and then press the Tab key.

20 Type **Planet Earth's Resources** in the *Journal Name* text box and then press the Tab key.

21 Type **2010** in the *Year* text box and then press the Tab key.

22 Type **7-9** in the *Pages* text box and then click OK.

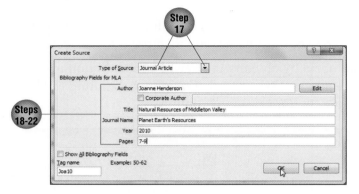

23 Position the insertion point immediately right of the word *century* that ends the third sentence in the third paragraph and then insert the following source information from a website (click the down-pointing arrow at the right of the *Type of Source* option and then click *Web site* at the drop-down list):

> *Author* = **Daniel Marcello**
> *Name of Web Page* = **Middleton Regional Planning Department**
> *Year* = **2010**
> *Month* = **January**
> *Day* = **5**
> *Year Accessed* = (type current year)
> *Month Accessed* = (type current month)
> *Day Accessed* = (type current day)
> *URL* = **www.emcp.org/middleton**

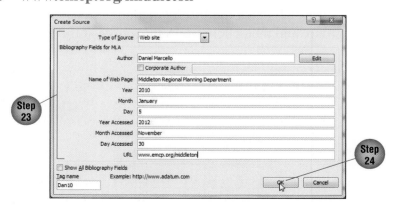

24 After entering the information from a website, click the OK button.

25 Insert a citation from an existing source. Begin by positioning the insertion point between the quotation mark after the word *erosion* and the period in the second sentence in the fourth paragraph.

26 Click the Insert Citation button in the Citations & Bibliography group and then click the *Joanne Henderson* reference in the drop-down list.

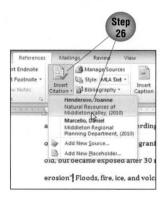

27 Because you are citing a direct quote, you need to include the page number of the journal article where you found the quote. Begin by clicking on any character in the Henderson citation you just inserted.

> This displays the citation placeholder.

28 Click the Citation Options arrow that displays at the right side of the citation placeholder and then click *Edit Citation* at the drop-down list.

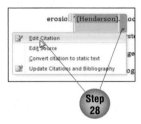

29 At the Edit Citation dialog box, type **8** in the *Pages* text box and then click OK.

30 Save **WS3-FCTMiddletonRpt.docx**.

In Addition

Formatting the First Page of an MLA-formatted Report

Your instructor may require you to omit the header from the first page of the document. To remove the header from the first page of a document that contains a previously created header, press Ctrl + Home to move the insertion point to the beginning of the document, click the Header button in the Header & Footer group in the Insert tab, and then click *Edit Header* at the drop-down list. Click the *Different First Page* check box in the Options group in the Header & Footer Tools Design tab. This inserts in the document a new header pane named *First Page Header*. Since you do not want a header on the first page, leave this header blank. Click the Next Section button in the Navigation group in the Header & Footer Tools Design tab and, if you previously created a header in the document, it displays in the Header pane. If the document did not include a header, type or insert the desired header text in the Header pane.

Activity 3.7

Creating a Works Cited Page; Editing Sources

Once you include citations in a report or research paper, you need to insert a works cited page on a separate page at the end of the document. A works cited page is an alphabetic list of the books, journal articles, web pages, or any other sources referenced in the document. To insert a works cited page, click the References tab and then click the Bibliography button in the Citations & Bibliography group. At the Bibliography drop-down list, click the *Format* option. If you edit a source, Word will not automatically update the works cited. To update the works cited, click anywhere in the works cited and then click the Update Citations and Bibliography tab. After inserting sources into a document, you may need to edit a citation to correct errors or change data. One method for editing a source is by clicking the desired citation in the document, clicking the Citation Options arrow, and then clicking *Edit Source* at the drop-down list. This displays the Edit Source dialog box with the information you originally typed. Make desired changes and then click OK to close the dialog box.

Project

To finish the Middleton Valley report, you need to add a works cited page, edit one of the sources, and apply MLA style formatting to the works cited page.

Tutorial 3.10
Inserting and
Modifying
Bibliographies

1 With **WS3-FCTMiddletonRpt.docx** open, insert a works cited page at the end of the document. Begin by pressing Ctrl + End to move the insertion point to the end of the document and then pressing Ctrl + Enter to insert a hard page break.

2 Click the References tab and then click the Bibliography button located in the Citations & Bibliography group.

3 Click the *Works Cited* option in the *Built-in* section of the drop-down list.

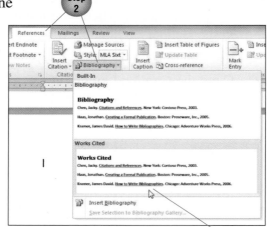

4 You realize that part of the web page title is missing and you need to edit the source. Begin by clicking on any character in the *Marcello* citation in the third paragraph.

This selects the citation placeholder.

5 Click the Citation Options arrow that displays at the right side of the citation placeholder and then click *Edit Source* at the drop-down list.

This displays the Edit Source dialog box, which contains the same options as the Create Source dialog box.

6 At the Edit Source dialog box, click in the *Name of Web Page* text box, edit the text so it displays as *Middleton Valley Regional Planning Department*, and then click OK to close the dialog box.

7 At the message telling you that the source exists in your master list and the current document and asking you if you want to update both, click the Yes button.

8 Update the works cited to include the edited source. Begin by pressing Ctrl + End to move the insertion point to the end of the document and then clicking on any character in the works cited text.

9 Click the Update Citations and Bibliography placeholder tab.

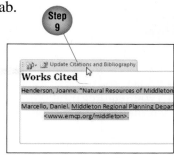

Step 9

The placeholder tab displays above the Works Cited title. Notice that the updated works cited includes the edited web page name.

10 Format the works cited page to MLA standards, which are listed in Table 3.2. Begin by selecting the *Works Cited* heading and the entries below the heading and then clicking the No Spacing style in the Styles group in the Home tab.

11 With the text still selected, change the font to *Cambria*, the font size to *12*, and the line spacing to *2.0*.

12 Click anywhere in the title *Works Cited* and then click the Center button in the Paragraph group.

13 Hang-indent the entries. Do this by selecting only the works cited entries, clicking the Paragraph group dialog box launcher, clicking the down-pointing arrow at the right side of the *Special* list box in the *Indentation* section, clicking *Hanging* at the drop-down list, and then clicking OK to close the Paragraph dialog box.

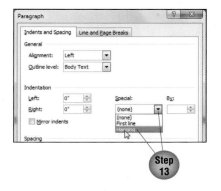

Step 13

You can also hang-indent text with the keyboard shortcut, Ctrl + T.

14 Press Ctrl + Home to move the insertion point to the beginning of the document.

15 Save, print, and then close **WS3-FCTMiddletonRpt.docx**.

TABLE 3.2 MLA Style Works Cited Page Formatting Guidelines

Begin works cited on a separate page at the end of the document.
Include the title "Works Cited" and center the title.
Double-space between and within entries.
Begin each entry at the left margin and hang-indent second and subsequent lines in each entry.
Alphabetize the entries.

In Addition

Modifying Sources at the Manage Sources Dialog Box

You can copy, delete, edit, and create new sources at the Manage Sources dialog box. Display this dialog box by clicking the References tab and then clicking the Manage Sources button in the Citations & Bibliography group. The *Master List* section of the dialog box displays all of the citations you have created in Word, and the *Current List* section displays all of the citations included in the currently open document.

Activity 3.8

Using Click and Type; Vertically Aligning Text; Inserting, Sizing, and Moving an Image

You can change paragraph alignment with the Click and Type feature. To use the Click and Type feature, position the mouse pointer at the left margin, in the center of the page, or at the right margin until the pointer displays with the desired alignment symbol and then double-click the mouse button. By default, text is aligned at the top of the page. You can change this alignment to Center, Justified, or Bottom with the *Vertical alignment* option at the Page Setup dialog box with the Layout tab selected. Microsoft Office includes a gallery of media images you can insert in a document such as clip art, photographs, and video files, as well as audio files. Use buttons in the Insert tab to insert a clip art image or insert a picture or image from a specific file location.

Project First Choice Travel is planning a workshop for people interested in traveling on a budget. You will create an announcement that contains center- and right-aligned text, vertically center the text on the page, and then add visual appeal by inserting a clip art image and the company logo.

Tutorial 3.11
Using Click and Type

Tutorial 3.12
Using Vertical Alignment

Tutorial 3.13
Inserting, Sizing, and Moving Images

1. Press Ctrl + N to display a blank document.

2. Position the I-beam pointer in the document between the left and right margins at about the 3.25-inch mark on the horizontal ruler and approximately one inch from the top of the page. When the center alignment lines display below the I-beam pointer, double-click the left mouse button.

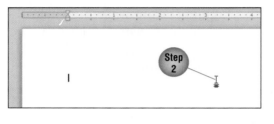

3. Type the centered text shown in Figure 3.1, pressing the Enter key once between each line of text.

4. Change to right alignment by positioning the I-beam pointer near the right margin at approximately the 6-inch mark on the vertical ruler until the right alignment lines display at the left side of the I-beam pointer and then double-clicking the left mouse button.

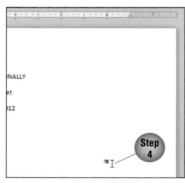

FIGURE 3.1 Steps 3 and 5

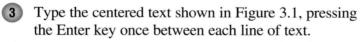

> TRAVELING INTERNATIONALLY
>
> Traveling on a Budget
>
> Thursday, April 19, 2012
>
> 7:00 to 8:30 p.m.
>
>
>
> Sponsored by
> First Choice Travel

5. Type the right-aligned text shown in Figure 3.1. After typing the first line of right-aligned text, press Shift + Enter to move the insertion point to the next line.

6. Select the centered text and then change the font to 14-point Candara bold. Select the right-aligned text, change the font to 10-point Candara bold, and then deselect the text.

7. Vertically center the text on the page. To do this, click the Page Layout tab and then click the Page Setup group dialog box launcher.

8. At the Page Setup dialog box, click the Layout tab, click the down-pointing arrow at the right side of the *Vertical alignment* option, and then click *Center* at the drop-down list.

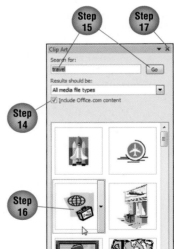

9. Click OK to close the Page Setup dialog box.

10. Save the document and name it **WS3-FCTTravelIntl**.

11. Print **WS3-FCTTravelIntl.docx**.

12. Return the vertical alignment to Top. To do this, click the Page Setup group dialog box launcher. At the Page Setup dialog box, click the Layout tab, click the down-pointing arrow at the right side of the *Vertical alignment* option, and then click *Top* at the drop-down list. Click OK to close the dialog box.

13. Click the Insert tab and then click the Clip Art button in the Illustrations group.

   This displays the Clip Art task pane at the right side of the screen.

14. If you are connected to the Internet, click in the *Include Office.com content* check box to insert a check mark.

   You can also access additional clip art images by clicking the Find more at Office.com hyperlink that displays at the bottom of the Clip Art task pane.

15. Type **travel** in the *Search for* text box and then click the Go button.

16. Click the image shown at the right. If this image is not available, choose another image related to travel.

   The image is inserted in the document, it is selected (sizing handles display around the image), and the Picture Tools Format tab displays as shown in Figure 3.2.

17. Close the Clip Art task pane by clicking the Close button located in the upper right corner of the task pane.

FIGURE 3.2 Picture Tools Format Tab Display

continues

18 With the image selected, click the Position button 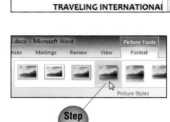 in the Arrange group and then click the first option from the left in the top row of the *With Text Wrapping* section (the option named *Position in Top Left with Square Text Wrapping*).

19 Add a shadow effect to the clip art image by clicking the fourth thumbnail style option in the Picture Styles group (*Drop Shadow Rectangle*).

20 Click the Corrections button in the Adjust group and then click the third option from the left in the fourth row (*Brightness: 0% (Normal) Contrast: +20%*).

21 Click the Picture Effects button in the Pictures Styles group, point to *Glow* and then click the first option from the left in the top row of the *Glow Variations* section (*Blue, 5 pt glow, Accent color 1*).

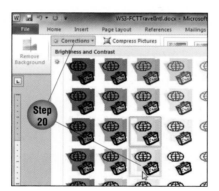

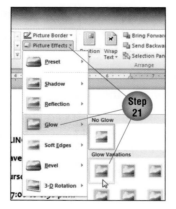

22 Click in the *Shape Height* measurement box in the Size group, type **1.7**, and then press Enter.

> When you change the height measurement, the width measurement is automatically changed to maintain the proportions of the image.

23 Select and then delete the text *First Choice Travel* that displays in small font size at the right side of the document.

24 Insert the First Choice Travel logo below *Sponsored by*. To begin, click the Insert tab and then click the Picture button in the Illustrations group.

25 At the Insert Picture dialog box, display the folder where your data documents are located and then double-click *FCTLogo.jpg*.

26 With the image selected in the document, click the Wrap Text button in the Arrange group and then click *Tight* at the drop-down list.

> With a wrapping style applied, you can move the image.

27 With the image still selected, hold down the Shift key and then drag one of the corner sizing handles (circles) to reduce the size of the logo so it displays as shown in Figure 3.3.

> Holding down the Shift key while increasing or decreasing the size of an image maintains the proportions of the image.

FIGURE 3.3

28 Drag the image so it is positioned as shown in Figure 3.3. To drag the image, position the insertion point inside the selected image until the arrow pointer displays with a four-headed arrow attached. Hold down the left mouse button, drag to the desired location, and then release the mouse button.

29 Click outside the logo to deselect it.

30 Save, print, and then close **WS3-FCTTravelIntl.docx**.

In Brief

Vertically Center Text
1. Click Page Layout tab.
2. Click Page Setup group dialog box launcher.
3. Click Layout tab.
4. Click *Vertical alignment* option.
5. Click *Center* at drop-down list.
6. Click OK.

Insert Clip Art Image
1. Click Insert tab.
2. Click Clip Art button.
3. Type category information in *Search for* text box.
4. Click Go button.
5. Click desired clip art image.

Insert Picture
1. Click Insert tab.
2. Click Picture button.
3. Navigate to desired folder.
4. Double-click desired picture file.

In Addition

Formatting an Image with Buttons in the Picture Tools Format Tab

Images inserted in a document can be formatted in a variety of ways, which might include adding fill color and border lines, increasing or decreasing the brightness or contrast, choosing a wrapping style, and cropping the image. Format an image with buttons in the Picture Tools Format tab as shown in Figure 3.2. With buttons in the Picture Tools group you can correct the brightness and contrast of the image; change the image color; change to a different image; reset the image to its original size, position, and color; and compress the picture. Compress a picture to reduce resolution or discard extra information to save room on the hard drive or to reduce download time. Use buttons in the Picture Styles group to apply a predesigned style, insert a picture border, or apply a picture effect. The Arrange group contains buttons for positioning the image, wrapping text around the image, and aligning and rotating the image. Use options in the Size group to crop the image and specify the height and width of the image.

Activity 3.9

Preparing an Envelope

Word automates the creation of envelopes with options at the Envelopes and Labels dialog box with the Envelopes tab selected. At this dialog box, type a delivery address and a return address. If you open the Envelopes and Labels dialog box in a document containing a name and address, the name and address are inserted automatically as the delivery address. If you enter a return address, Word will ask you before printing if you want to save the new return address as the default return address. Answer *yes* if you want to use the return address for future envelopes or answer *no* if you will use a different return address for future envelopes.

Project

You need to create an envelope for sending the information about Thailand to Camille Matsui at Marquee Productions.

SNAP

Tutorial 3.14
Creating and Printing Envelopes

1 Press Ctrl + N to display a blank document.

You can also display a blank document by clicking the File tab, clicking the New tab, and then clicking the Create button in the preview area in the New tab Backstage view. Another method is to insert a New button on the Quick Access toolbar and then click the button to display a blank document. To insert the button on the Quick Access toolbar, click the Customize Quick Access Toolbar button that displays at the right side of the toolbar and then click *New* at the drop-down list.

2 Click the Mailings tab and then click the Envelopes button in the Create group.

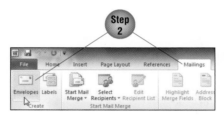

3 At the Envelopes and Labels dialog box with the Envelopes tab selected, type the following name and address in the *Delivery address* text box. (Press Enter at the end of each line, except the last line containing the city name, state, and zip code. Type your name where you see *(Student Name)*.)

> **Camille Matsui**
> **Marquee Productions**
> **955 South Alameda Street**
> **Los Angeles, CA 90037**

4 If any text displays in the *Return address* text box, delete it and then type the following name and address:

> **First Choice Travel**
> **(Student Name)**
> **3588 Ventura Boulevard**
> **Los Angeles, CA 90102**

5 Click the Add to Document button.

Clicking the Add to Document button inserts the envelope in the document. You can also send the envelope directly to the printer by clicking the Print button.

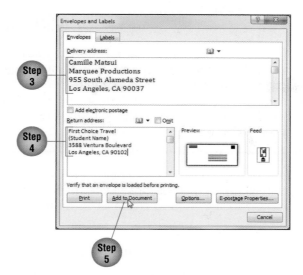

In Brief

Prepare Envelope
1. Click Mailings tab.
2. Click Envelopes button.
3. Type delivery address.
4. Type return address.
5. Click either Add to Document button or Print button.

6 At the message asking if you want to save the new return address as the default address, click the No button.

7 Save the document and name it **WS3-FCTEnvtoMP**.

8 Print and then close **WS3-FCTEnvtoMP.docx**. *Note: Manual feed of the envelope may be required. Please check with your instructor.*

In Addition

Customizing Envelopes

With options at the Envelope Options dialog box shown at the right, you can customize an envelope. Display this dialog box by clicking the Options button at the Envelopes and Labels dialog box. At the Envelope Options dialog box, you can change the envelope size, change the font for the delivery and return addresses, and specify the positioning of the addresses in relation to the left and top edges of the envelope.

Activity 3.10

Preparing Mailing Labels

Use Word's Labels feature to print text on mailing labels, file labels, disk labels, or other types of labels. You can create labels for printing on a variety of pre-defined labels, which you can purchase at an office supply store. With the Labels feature, you can create a sheet of mailing labels with the same name and address or image or enter a different name and address on each label. Create a label with options at the Envelopes and Labels dialog box with the Labels tab selected.

Project

Tutorial 3.15
Creating and Printing Labels

You decide to create a sheet of mailing labels containing the First Choice Travel name and address. You also need to create mailing labels for sending the Thailand document to several First Choice Travel customers. You also want to create labels for the First Choice Travel office in Toronto.

1. Press Ctrl + N to display a blank document.

2. Click the Mailings tab and then click the Labels button 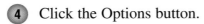 in the Create group.

3. Type the following information in the *Address* text box. (Press Enter at the end of each line, except the last line containing the city name, state, and zip code.)

   First Choice Travel
   (Student Name)
   3588 Ventura Boulevard
   Los Angeles, CA 90102

4. Click the Options button.

5. At the Label Options dialog box, click the down-pointing arrow at the right side of the *Label vendors* list box and then click *Avery US Letter*.

6. Scroll down the *Product number* list box, click *5160 Easy Peel Address Labels* in the list box, and then click OK to close the dialog box.

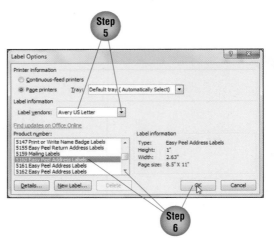

7. Click the New Document button at the Envelopes and Labels dialog box.

8. Save the document and name it **WS3-FCTLALabels**.

9. Print and then close **WS3-FCTLALabels.docx**.

   The number of labels printed on the page varies depending on the label selected at the Envelopes and Labels dialog box.

10. Click the Mailings tab and then click the Labels button in the Create group.

11. At the Envelopes and Labels dialog box, click the New Document button.

12. At the document, type the first name and address shown in Figure 3.4 in the first label. Press the Tab key twice to move the insertion point to the next label and then type the second name and address shown in Figure 3.4. Press the Tab key twice and then type the third name and address shown in the figure. Press the Tab key once and then type the fourth name and address. Continue in this manner until you have typed all of the names and addresses in Figure 3.4.

13 Save the document and name it **WS3-FCTCustLabels**.

14 Print and then close **WS3-FCTCustLabels.docx**.

15 At the blank document, create mailing labels for the Toronto office of First Choice Travel using an image. Begin by clicking the Insert tab and then clicking the Picture button in the Illustrations group.

16 At the Insert Picture dialog box, display the folder where your data documents are located and then double-click ***FCTTorontoLabel.jpg***.

17 With the label image selected, click the Mailings tab and then click the Labels button in the Create group.

18 At the Envelopes and Labels dialog box, make sure the Avery US Letter label number 5160 is selected and then click the New Document button.

> When you click the New Document button, the label image is inserted in each label in the page and inserted in a new document.

19 Save the document and name it **WS3-FCTTorontoLabels**.

20 Print and then close **WS3-FCTTorontoLabels.docx**.

21 Close the document containing the label image without saving it.

In Brief

Prepare Mailing Labels with Same Name and Address
1. Click Mailings tab.
2. Click Labels button.
3. Type name and address in *Address* text box.
4. Click either New Document button or Print button.

Prepare Mailing Labels with Different Names and Addresses
1. Click Mailings tab.
2. Click Labels button.
3. Click New Document button.
4. At document screen, type names and addresses.

Prepare Mailing Labels with Image
1. Click Insert.
2. Click Picture button.
3. Navigate to desired folder.
4. Double-click image.
5. Click Mailings tab.
6. Click Labels button.
7. Click New Document button.

FIGURE 3.4 Step 12

Moreno Products 350 Mission Boulevard Pomona, CA 91767	Mr. Miguel Santos 12120 Barranca Parkway Irvine, CA 92612	Mr. and Mrs. Jack Lipinski 5534 Southeast 32nd Street Los Angeles, CA 90092
Dr. Esther Riggins 9077 Walnut Street Los Angeles, CA 90097	Automated Services, Inc. 4394 Seventh Street Long Beach, CA 92602	Ms. Samantha Schwartz 103-B Pacific Palms Los Angeles, CA 90068

In Addition

Customizing Labels

Click the Options button at the Envelopes and Labels dialog box with the Labels tab selected and the Label Options dialog box displays as shown at the right. At this dialog box, choose the type of printer, the desired label vendor, and the product number. This dialog box also displays information about the selected label such as type, height, width, and paper size. When you select a label, Word automatically determines label margins. If, however, you want to customize these default settings, click the Details button at the Label Options dialog box.

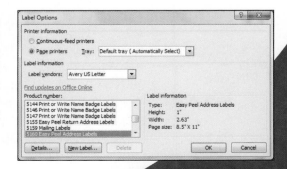

Features Summary

Feature	Ribbon Tab, Group	Button, File Tab	Keyboard Shortcut
blank page	Insert, Pages		
Clip Art task pane	Insert, Illustrations		
Clipboard task pane	Home, Clipboard		
copy selected text	Home, Clipboard		Ctrl + C
cover page	Insert, Pages		
Create Source dialog box	References, Citations & Bibliography	, Add New Source	
cut selected text	Home, Clipboard		Ctrl + X
Envelopes and Labels dialog box with Envelopes tab selected	Mailings, Create		
Envelopes and Labels dialog box with Labels tab selected	Mailings, Create		
footer	Insert, Header & Footer		
header	Insert, Header & Footer		
Insert Picture dialog box	Insert, Illustrations		
page border	Page Layout, Page Background		
page break	Insert, Pages		Ctrl + Enter
page color	Page Layout, Page Background		
page margins	Page Layout, Page Setup		
page number	Insert, Header & Footer		
page orientation	Page Layout, Page Setup		
Page Setup dialog box	Page Layout, Page Setup		
page size	Page Layout, Page Setup		
paste selected text	Home, Clipboard		Ctrl + V
Paste Special dialog box	Home, Clipboard	(Ctrl) ▾, Paste Special	
theme	Page Layout, Themes		
watermark	Page Layout, Page Background		
works cited page	References, Citations & Bibliography		

Knowledge Check

Completion: In the space provided at the right, indicate the correct term, command, or option.

1. The Cut button is located in this group in the Home tab. _____
2. Click this button to insert copied text in the document. _____
3. Click this to display the Clipboard task pane. _____
4. Click this tab to display the Margins button. _____
5. This is the default measurement for the top, bottom, left, and right margins. _____
6. This is the default page orientation. _____
7. This is the default page size. _____
8. A document theme is a set of formatting choices that includes a font theme, an effects theme, and this. _____
9. This term refers to lightened text or image that displays behind text. _____
10. The Cover Page button is located in the Pages group in this tab. _____
11. Insert a page break by clicking the Page Break button in the Pages group in the Insert tab or with this keyboard shortcut. _____
12. Insert a footer by clicking the Footer button in this group in the Insert tab. _____
13. The initials MLA refer to this type of report style generally used in the humanities and English. _____
14. General MLA style guidelines recommend this measurement for the top, bottom, left, and right margins. _____
15. General MLA style guidelines recommend this line spacing. _____
16. The Insert Citation button is located in this tab. _____
17. In an MLA report, this page is an alphabetic list of the books, journal articles, web pages, or other sources referenced in the document. _____
18. Use this feature to position the mouse pointer at the left margin, center of the page, or right margin. _____
19. This is the default page alignment. _____
20. Change page alignment with the *Vertical alignment* option at this dialog box. _____
21. The Clip Art button displays in this group in the Insert tab. _____
22. Click this button in the Picture Tools Format tab to choose a wrapping style. _____
23. When changing the size of an image, maintain the image proportions by holding down this key while dragging a corner sizing handle. _____
24. To display the Envelopes and Labels dialog box, click this tab and then click the Envelopes button or the Labels button. _____

Skills Review

Review 1 Formatting a Fact Sheet on Juneau, Alaska

1. Open **FCTJuneau.docx** and then save the document in the WordEOS folder and name it **WS3-R1-FCTJuneau**.
2. Select the entire document, click the No Spacing style in the Styles group, and then deselect the text.
3. Find every occurrence of *Mendanhall* and replace it with *Mendenhall*.
4. Find every occurrence of *Treadwill* and replace it with *Treadwell*.
5. Select the heading *Visitor Centers*, the three paragraphs of text below it, and the blank line below the three paragraphs and then move the selected text before the heading *Visitor Attractions*.
6. Select the heading *Museums*, the three paragraphs of text below it, and the blank line below the three paragraphs and then move the selected text before the heading *Visitor Attractions*.
7. With **WS3-R1-FCTJuneau.docx** open, open the document named **FCTJuneauInfo.docx**.
8. Display the Clipboard task pane and then make sure the task pane is empty.
9. In the **FCTJuneauInfo.docx** document, select and then copy from the heading *Visitor Services* through the two paragraphs of text below the heading and the blank line below the two paragraphs.
10. Select and then copy from the heading *Transportation* through the paragraph of text below the heading and the blank line below the paragraph.
11. Select and then copy from the heading *Points of Interest* through the columns of text below the heading and the blank line below the columns of text.
12. Make **WS3-R1-FCTJuneau.docx** the active document.
13. Display the Clipboard task pane.
14. Move the insertion point to the end of the document, press the Enter key once, and then paste the text that begins with the heading *Points of Interest*.
15. Move the insertion point to the beginning of the heading *Museums* and then paste the text that begins with the heading *Transportation*.
16. Move the insertion point to the beginning of the heading *Points of Interest* and then paste the text that begins with the heading *Visitor Services*.
17. Clear the contents of the Clipboard task pane and then close the task pane.
18. Make **FCTJuneauInfo.docx** the active document and then close it.
19. Change the top and bottom margins to 1.25 inches and the left and right margins to 1 inch.
20. Apply the Heading 1 style to the title *JUNEAU, ALASKA*.
21. Apply the Heading 2 style to the headings in the document including *History, Visitor Centers, Transportation, Museums, Visitor Attractions, Visitor Services,* and *Points of Interest*.
22. Change the Quick Styles set to *Traditional* and apply the *Compact* paragraph spacing style.
23. Apply the *Executive* theme. (To display the Themes button, click the Page Layout tab.)
24. Insert the *Plain Number 3* page numbering style that inserts the page number in the upper right corner of each page.

25. Insert the *Stacks* footer and type your first and last names in the *[Type the company name]* placeholder.
26. Insert a watermark that prints the word *Sample* across the page.
27. If the *Transportation* heading displays at the bottom of the first page, keep the heading together with the paragraph of text that follows it. (To do this, display the Paragraph dialog box with the Line and Page Breaks tab selected, click the *Keep with next* check box, and then click OK.)
28. Save, print, and then close **WS3-R1-FCTJuneau.docx**.

Review 2 Formatting a Document in MLA Style

1. Open **PTRenaissanceRpt.docx** and then save the document in the WordEOS folder and name it **WS3-R2-PTRenaissanceRpt**.
2. Make sure MLA style is selected in the Citations & Bibliography group in the References tab.
3. Select the entire document, change the font to 12-point Cambria, the line spacing to 2.0, and remove the spacing after paragraphs.
4. Move the insertion point to the beginning of the document, type your name, press Enter, type your instructor's name, press Enter, type the title of your course, press Enter, and then type the current date.
5. Insert a header that displays your last name and the page number at the right margin and changes the font to 12-point Cambria. (For help, refer to Steps 10 through 14 in Activity 3.6.)
6. Position the insertion point after the word *century* (but before the period) in the last sentence in the first paragraph and then insert the source information from a journal article using the following information:
   Author = **Marcus Gerard**
   Title = **History of the Renaissance Period**
   Journal Name = **European History: Early Modern Europe**
   Year = **2012**
   Pages = **13-17**
7. Position the insertion point after the text *1494* (but before the period) in the first sentence in the third paragraph and then insert the source information from a book using the following information:
   Author = **Iris Brooke**
   Title = **A History of Renaissance Costumes**
   Year = **2009**
   City = **New York**
   Publisher = **Hudson River Publishing House**
8. Insert a works cited page as a new page at the end of the document.
9. Edit the Gerard source so the journal name displays as *European History: Western European Civilization*.
10. Update the works cited page.
11. Format the works cited page to MLA standards, which includes selecting the *Works Cited* heading and all entries and then clicking the *No Spacing* style, changing the font to 12-point Cambria, changing the line spacing to *2.0*, centering the title *Works Cited*, and hang-indenting the entries. (For help, refer to Steps 9 through 12 in Activity 3.7.)
12. Save, print, and then close **WS3-R2-PTRenaissanceRpt.docx**.

Review 3 Preparing and Formatting an Announcement

1. At a blank document, use the Click and Type feature to type the text shown in Figure 3.5.
2. Select the centered text you just typed and then change the font to 14-point Candara bold.
3. Select the right-aligned text you just typed and then change the font to 10-point Candara bold.
4. Change the vertical alignment of the text on the page to Center.
5. Save the document in the WordEOS folder and name it **WS3-R3-MPEmpOpps01**.
6. Print **WS3-R3-MPEmpOpps01.docx**.
7. Save the document in the WordEOS folder with Save As and name it **WS3-R3-MPEmpOpps02**.
8. Change the vertical alignment of the text on the page back to Top.
9. Insert a clip art image of your choosing related to the announcement. (You determine the clip art image as well as the size and position of the image.) If you are connected to the Internet, insert a check mark in the *Include Office.com content* check box and search for clip art images related to movies. If you are limited to the clip art images provided with Office 2010, consider using the key word *business* to look for a clip art image.
10. Delete the text *Marquee Productions* from the document and then insert the Marquee Productions logo image named **MPLogo.jpg** below the text *Sponsored by*. ***Hint: Do this at the Insert Picture dialog box.*** Adjust the size and position of the image so it displays below *Sponsored by* and is approximately one and a half inches wide.
11. Save, print, and then close **WS3-R3-MPEmpOpps02.docx**.

FIGURE 3.5 Review 3

> EMPLOYMENT OPPORTUNITIES
>
> Working in the Movie Industry
>
> Wednesday, March 14, 2012
>
> 7:00 to 8:30 p.m.
>
> Sponsored by
> Marquee Productions

Review 4 Preparing an Envelope

1. At a blank document, prepare an envelope with the return address and delivery address shown below (type your name below *First Choice Travel* in the return address) and add the envelope to the document.
   Delivery address:
   > **Chris Greenbaum**
   > **Marquee Productions**
   > **955 South Alameda Street**
   > **Los Angeles, CA 90037**

Return address:
> **First Choice Travel**
> **(Student Name)**
> **3588 Ventura Boulevard**
> **Los Angeles, CA 90102**

2. Save the document in the WordEOS folder and name it **WS3-R4-FCTEnv**. Print and then close **WS3-R4-FCTEnv.docx**. (Manual feed of the envelope may be required.)

Review 5 Preparing Mailing Labels

1. At a blank document, prepare a sheet of mailing labels for the following name and address using the Avery US Letter 5160 labels option (type your name below *Worldwide Enterprises*).
> **Worldwide Enterprises**
> **(Student Name)**
> **1112-1583 Broadway**
> **New York, NY 10110**

2. Save the mailing label document in the WordEOS folder and name it **WS3-R5-WELabels**. Print and then close **WS3-R5-WELabels.docx**.

Skills Assessment

Assessment 1 Formatting a Costume Rental Agreement

1. Open **PTAgreement.docx** and then save the document in the WordEOS folder and name it **WS3-A1-PTAgreement**.
2. Search for all occurrences of *Customer* and replace with *Marquee Productions*.
3. Move the *4. Alterations* section above the *3. Marquee Productions Agrees* section. Renumber the two sections.
4. Select the entire document, change the font to 12-point Constantia, and then deselect the document.
5. Change the top margin to 1.5 inches.
6. Insert the *Alphabet* footer and type your first and last names in the *[Type text]* placeholder.
7. Save, print, and then close **WS3-A1-PTAgreement.docx**.

Assessment 2 Creating an Announcement

1. At a blank document, create an announcement for Niagara Peninsula College by typing the text shown in Figure 3.6.
2. Change the font for the entire document to a decorative font, size, and color of your choosing.
3. Change the line spacing to double for the entire document.
4. Insert, size, and move a clip art image of your choosing in the document. Choose a clip art image related to the subject of the announcement. If you have access to the Internet, insert a check mark in the *Include Office.com content* check box.

5. Save the document in the WordEOS folder and name it **WS3-A2-NPCInternship**.
6. Print and then close **WS3-A2-NPCInternship.docx**.

FIGURE 3.6 Assessment 2

NIAGARA PENINSULA COLLEGE

Internship Opportunities

June 18 through August 30, 2012

Marquee Productions, Toronto Office

Contact Cal Rubine, Theatre Arts Division

Assessment 3 Preparing Mailing Labels

1. Prepare return mailing labels with the following information (type your name below *Niagara Peninsula College*):
   Niagara Peninsula College
   (Student Name)
   2199 Victoria Street
   Niagara-on-the-Lake, ON L0S 1J0
2. Save the labels document in the WordEOS folder and name it **WS3-A3-NPCLabels**. Print and then close **WordS3-A3-NPCLabels.docx**.

Assessment 4 Finding Information on Creating a Picture Watermark

1. Open **WS3-R3-MPEmpOpps01.docx** and then save the document in the WordEOS folder and name it **WS3-A4-MPEmpOpps-Wtrmark**.
2. Use Word's Help feature to learn how to insert a picture watermark.
3. Insert the **MPLogo.jpg** file located in the WordS3 folder as a watermark.
4. Save, print, and then close **WS3-A4-MPEmpOpps-Wtrmark.docx**.

Assessment 5 Individual Challenge
Creating a Personal Letterhead

1. At a blank document, create a letterhead that includes your first and last names, address, telephone number, and insert a clip art image in the letterhead that represents you or something in which you are interested. Apply font formatting to the text in the letterhead and size and position the clip art image. (For letterhead examples, refer to **FCTLtrhd. docx** in the WordS3 folder and **MPLtrhd.docx** in the WordS2 folder. The letterheads in these two documents were created as headers. If you want to create your letterhead in a header, click the Insert tab, click the Header button in the Header & Footer group and then click *Edit Header*.)
2. Save the document in the WordEOS folder and name it **WS3-A5-IC-Ltrhd**.
3. Print and then close **WS3-A5-IC-Ltrhd.docx**.

Marquee Challenge

Challenge 1 Formatting a Costume Document

1. Open **PTCostumes.docx** and then save the document in the WordEOS folder and name it **WS3-C1-PTCostumes**.
2. Format your document so it displays similar to the document in Figure 3.7. To do this, apply the Civic theme to the document; apply the Heading 2 style and yellow shading to the headings; change the top margin to 1.25 inches; insert, size, and position the **PTLogo.jpg** picture as shown; change paragraph alignment as shown; insert the art page border; insert, size, and position the book clip art; and apply any other formatting to make your document consistent with the document in the figure. (If the book clip art image is not available, choose another book image.) *Note: Check the document in the Print tab Backstage view. If the entire page border is not visible, refer to the In Addition at the bottom of page 63 in Word Section 2 for suggestions on how to print the entire page border.*
3. Save, print, and then close **WS3-C1-PTCostumes.docx**.

Challenge 2 Preparing an Announcement

1. At a blank document, create the document shown in Figure 3.8 with the following specifications:
   - Change the page orientation to landscape.
   - Use the Picture button to insert the **WELogo.jpg** image in the upper left corner of the document. Change the background of the logo image to transparent by clicking the Color button in the Picture Tools Format tab, clicking the *Set Transparent Color* option, and then clicking in a white area inside the company logo. This changes the white background of the image to a transparent background. Size and position the image as shown in the figure.
   - When typing the text in the document, press Shift + Enter to end each line (except press Enter after typing the title).
   - Insert the clip art image of the people at the Clip Art task pane with a check mark in the *Include Office.com content* check box. If this image is not available, choose a similar clip art image. Set the background color of the clip art image to transparent.
   - Insert the watermark, page border, and page color as shown in the figure. (The page color does not print.)
2. Save the document in the WordEOS folder and name it **WS3-C2-WENotice**.
3. Print and then close **WS3-C2-WENotice.docx**.

FIGURE 3.7 Challenge 1

Renaissance Period

The Renaissance period was a series of cultural and literary movements that took place in the fourteenth, fifteenth, and sixteenth centuries in Europe. The word *renaissance* means "rebirth" and originated with the belief that Europeans had rediscovered the intellectual and cultural superiority of the Greek and Roman cultures. The Renaissance period was preceded by the Middle Ages, also known as the "Dark Ages," which began with the collapse of the Roman Empire in the fifth century. The term *renaissance* was coined by Jacob Burckhardt in the eighteenth century in *The Civilization of the Renaissance in Italy*.

Renaissance education was designed to produce a person well-versed in humanities, mathematics, science, sports, and art. The Renaissance person had extensive knowledge in many fields, explored beyond the boundaries of learning and geographical knowledge, and embraced free thought and skepticism. Artists, writers, explorers, architects, and scientists were motivated by a revival in classical Greek and Roman culture and a return to classical values. During the Middle Ages, interest in culture and learning was primarily confined to theologians, philosophers, and writers. During the Renaissance period, however, people from all social, political, and economic classes involved themselves in the study of classical literature and art.

Renaissance Costume

Renaissance costume developed in Italy and was introduced to Western Europe following the invasion of Italy by Charles VIII of France in 1494. Due to the warmer climate in Italy, simpler styles evolved independently from the rest of Europe. Men's clothing consisted of low-necked tunics and chemises and women's clothing consisted of simple and low-necked gowns called "Juliet" gowns. During the middle of the fifteenth century, clothing assumed a more natural appearance. Women wore dresses with attached bodices and skirts. Men's doublets became shorter and hosiery became more prominent. Interest by women in gothic headdresses declined and instead they trimmed their hair with veils, ribbons, and jewels. Lace and perfume became more prevalent during the Renaissance period.

Early in the Renaissance period, women's dress included a long, rigid, cone-shaped corset reaching below the waist to a "V" in the front. Women's gowns expanded below the waistline and by the middle sixteenth century were supported by hoops made of wire that were held together with ribbons. This hoop skirt, called a *farthingale*, reached its maximum width around the early seventeenth century and then changed to a cartwheel or drum shape. Ballooned sleeves and circular lace collars also typified the early seventeenth century costume. Men's clothing had a similar look with puffed-out hose, balloon sleeves, padded doublets, and large ruff collars.

Costume Vocabulary

1. Basquine: A very large skirt that was open and stretched on circles.
2. Berne: A very large, fixed, and pleated scarf that rested on the shoulder.
3. Jupon: Long-sleeved camisole generally worn by men and women in Spain.
4. Mantilla: A kind of shawl worn by women to cover the head and shoulders.
5. Marlotte: A coat with pleats in the back and short, curved sleeves.

Costume Books

- Arnold, Janet, *Patterns of Fashion*
- Barton, Lucy, *Historic Costume for the Stage*
- Boucher, Francois, *20,000 Years of Fashion*
- Brooke, Iris, *A History of Costume*
- Evans, Mary, *Costume Throughout the Ages*
- LaMar, Virginia A., *English Dress in the Age of Shakespeare*

FIGURE 3.8 Challenge 2

IMPORTANT NOTICE!!

We need additional employees to work the next two weekends to complete a special distribution order. If you are interested in working any shift this weekend and/or next, please contact Rhonda Trask in Human Resources at extension 3360. We are offering overtime pay plus a bonus based on your hourly or salaried wage.

Marquee Series

Microsoft® Excel® 2010

Nita Rutkosky

Pierce College at Puyallup, Puyallup, Washington

Denise Seguin

Fanshawe College, London, Ontario

Audrey Rutkosky Roggenkamp

Pierce College at Puyallup, Puyallup, Washington

Paradigm
PUBLISHING

St. Paul • Los Angeles • Indianapolis

Managing Editor	Sonja Brown
Developmental Editor	Brenda Palo
Supplements Developmental Editor	Brenda Owens
Production Editor	Donna Mears
Cover and Text Designer	Leslie Anderson
Copy Editors	Susan Capecchi and Laura Nelson
Desktop Production	Ryan Hamner and Jack Ross
Proofreader	Laura Nelson
Testers	Carley Bomstad, Amy McGuire, Rob Neilly, and Lindsay Ryan
Indexers	Ina Gravitz and Sandi Schroeder

Care has been taken to verify the accuracy of information presented in this book. However, the authors, editors, and publisher cannot accept responsibility for Web, email, newsgroup, or chat room subject matter or content, or for consequences from application of the information in this book, and make no warranty, expressed or implied, with respect to its content.

Trademarks: Some of the product names and company names included in this book have been used for identification purposes only and may be trademarks or registered trade names of their respective manufacturers and sellers. The authors, editors, and publisher disclaim any affiliation, association, or connection with, or sponsorship or endorsement by, such owners.

We have made every effort to trace the ownership of all copyrighted material and to secure permission from copyright holders. In the event of any question arising as to the use of any material, we will be pleased to make the necessary corrections in future printings. Thanks are due to the aforementioned authors, publishers, and agents for permission to use the materials indicated.

© 2011 by Paradigm Publishing, Inc.
875 Montreal Way
St. Paul, MN 55102
Email: educate@emcp.com
Website: www.emcp.com

Printed in the United States of America

19 18 17 16 15 14 13 12 11 10   1 2 3 4 5 6 7 8 9 10

Contents

Introducing

Excel 2010

Microsoft Excel 2010 is a popular choice among individuals and companies to organize, analyze, and present data in columns and rows in a document called a *worksheet*. More than one worksheet can be created and saved in a file called a *workbook*. Entries are placed in a worksheet in a *cell*, which is the intersection of a column with a row. A cell is labeled with the column letter and row number, such as A1. Worksheets can be created to track, analyze, and chart any type of data that can be set up in a column and row format. Expenses, sales, assets, liabilities, grades, statistics, research study data, machine production records, weather records, and gas usage are just a few examples of the type of information that can be stored in an Excel workbook. While working in Excel, you will create and edit worksheets for the following six companies.

First Choice Travel is a travel center offering a full range of traveling services from booking flights, hotel reservations, and rental cars to offering travel seminars.

The Waterfront Bistro offers fine dining for lunch and dinner and also offers banquet facilities, a wine cellar, and catering services.

Worldwide Enterprises is a national and international distributor of products for a variety of companies and is the exclusive movie distribution agent for Marquee Productions.

Marquee Productions is involved in all aspects of creating movies from script writing and development to filming. The company produces documentaries, biographies, as well as historical and action movies.

Performance Threads maintains an inventory of rental costumes and also researches, designs, and sews special-order and custom-made costumes.

The mission of the Niagara Peninsula College Theatre Arts Division is to offer a curriculum designed to provide students with a thorough exposure to all aspects of the theater arts.

In Section 1 you will learn how to
Create Worksheets to Analyze Data

Begin your work in Excel by entering labels in columns or rows to create the worksheet layout. Next, add the values that correspond to the labels. Finally, create formulas to add, subtract, multiply, or divide to calculate the desired results. Once a worksheet has been created, the power and versatility of Excel is put to use by performing what-if analyses. What happens to net profit if sales increase by 4 percent? What happens to monthly cash flow if the wages of all employees are raised 3 percent? To answer these types of questions, you edit a value and then watch Excel's recalculation feature automatically update all other values dependent on the number you changed.

Start a new worksheet by entering labels to create the worksheet layout.

Next, add the values to record quantities, rates, or other numeric entries.

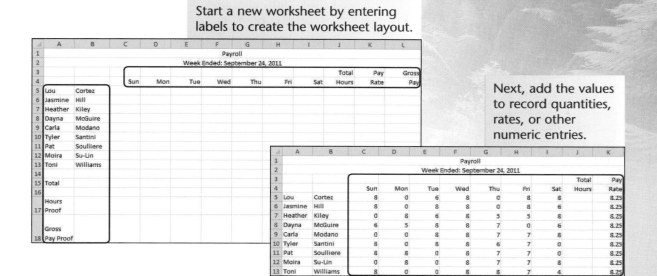

Create the formulas to add, subtract, multiply, or divide.

The desired results are shown in the finished worksheet

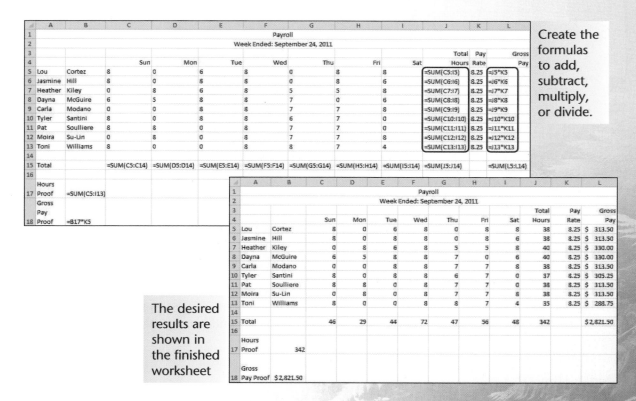

Edit and Format Worksheets

Excel allows you to apply formatting attributes and add color to enhance the appearance of the worksheet and draw a reader's attention to important titles, totals, or other results. A feature in Excel provides the ability to apply a theme which coordinates colors, fonts, and effects to provide a worksheet with a professional appearance in just a few mouse clicks. A variety of formats, grouped into categories, are available for numbers, dates, and times. Insert images such as clip art or a logo to enhance a worksheet or add a corporate identity.

The Waterfront Bistro

3104 Riverront Drive
Buffalo, NY 14280
716 555 3166

Quotation

TO: Marquee Productions
955 South Alameda Street
Los Angeles, CA 90037

DATE: 5-Nov-10

ATT: Camille Matsui

RE: Remote Location Filming
July 11 to August 31

Note: All prices include tax

Item	No. of Persons	Price per Person	No. of Days	Total
Buffet Lunch	56	8.34	52	$ 24,286.08
Soup and salad				
Vegetable tray with dip				
Seafood hors d'oeuvres				
Hot entrée				
Deli tray and rolls				
Dessert				
Beverages	56	3.91	52	11,385.92
Coffee and tea				
Assorted juice				
Mineral water				
Snacks	56	3.91	52	11,385.92
Muffins				
Donuts				
Fruit tray				
Vegetable tray with dip				
Transport		33.00	52	1,716.00
Total				$ 48,773.92

Terms: Due upon receipt of invoice payable in U.S. funds

Apply formatting enhancements including:

- adding borders
- adding fill color
- adjusting row height
- adjusting column width
- applying a cell style
- applying a theme
- changing text alignment within cells
- changing font, font size, font color
- changing font attributes to bold and/or italic
- indenting text within a cell
- formatting numbers

Niagara Peninsula College

Room: T1101			Period Covered: January 1 to April 30		
Time	Monday	Tuesday	Wednesday	Thursday	Friday
8:00 AM	SM100-01 Prasad	AC215-03 McLean (lab)		MG210-01 Spelberger	SM240-03 Prasad
9:00 AM			LE100-03 Das		
10:00 AM	LE253-03 Das			SM355-02 Prasad	SD350-04 Attea
11:00 AM					
12:00 PM	SD451-01 Attea	PD250-02 Kemper	**Common Period**	PD320-03 Kemper	
1:00 PM					LE310-02 Das
2:00 PM	PD340-02 Kemper	MG410-03 Spelberger	AC478-01 Simmons	AC480-01 Simmons (lab)	
3:00 PM					MG210-01 Spelberger
4:00 PM	MG150-02 Spelberger	SM165-01 Prasad	AC140-01 Chou		
5:00 PM					

Use features such as Format Painter, Cell Styles, and Themes to apply formats quickly and consistently.

In Section 3 you will learn how to

Use Function Formulas and Add Visual Elements

Excel's functions make the task of writing formulas easier. Functions are grouped by category such as statistical, financial, date, and logical. Excel provides over 300 prebuilt formulas to perform calculations. The Insert Function dialog box is available to assist with locating and creating a function. Create charts from data to emphasize trends or compare data sets. Add emphasis to worksheets or charts by drawing arrows and adding text boxes.

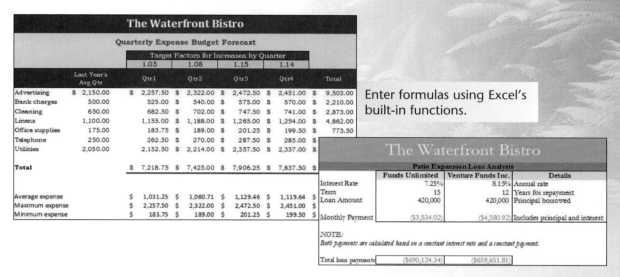

Enter formulas using Excel's built-in functions.

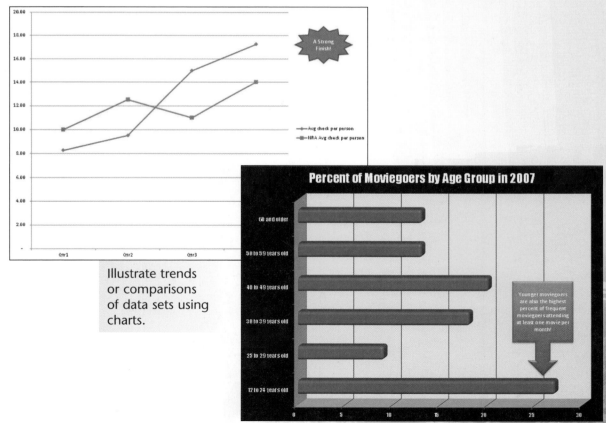

Illustrate trends or comparisons of data sets using charts.

Excel SECTION 1

Analyzing Data Using Excel

Skills

- Start Excel and identify features in the Excel window
- Save a workbook using Save and Save As
- Enter labels and values
- Use the fill handle to enter a series
- Enter formulas
- Create a formula using SUM
- Copy a formula
- Test a worksheet for accuracy
- Apply the Accounting Number format to values
- Right-align labels
- Sort a selection
- Use the Help feature
- Center a label across multiple columns
- Change the page orientation to landscape
- Preview and print a worksheet
- Display cell formulas in a worksheet
- Navigate a large worksheet using the mouse and the keyboard
- Jump to a specific cell using Go To

Student Resources

Before beginning the activities in Excel, copy to your storage medium the Excel folder on the Student Resources CD. This folder contains the data files you need to complete the projects in each Excel section.

Projects Overview

Edit a weekly sales report, create a payroll worksheet, create a condensed quarterly income statement, and sort a standard inventory list.

Complete an estimated travel costs worksheet.

Prepare a price quotation for costume alterations and rental.

Create a projected distribution revenue schedule for a new movie release.

Create an international student registration report and a target enrollment report.

1

Model Answers for Projects

These model answers for the projects that you complete in Section 1 provide a preview of the finished projects before you begin working and also allow you to compare your own results with these models to ensure you have created the materials accurately.

ES1-WBWeeklySales.xlsx is the project in Activity 1.1.

Weekly Sales Report

For the week ended:	24-Sep							
	Sunday	**Monday**	**Tuesday**	**Wednesday**	**Thursday**	**Friday**	**Saturday**	**Total**
Food - Dining Room	2,585.00	1,006.00	1,255.00	1,345.00	1,488.00	1,596.00	2,137.00	11,412.00
Food - Patio	1,154.00	312.00	488.00	578.00	1,065.00	1,147.00	1,549.00	6,293.00
Food - Catering	2,477.00	-	-	1,865.00	1,855.00	4,266.00	3,157.00	13,620.00
Total Food	**6,216.00**	**1,318.00**	**1,743.00**	**3,788.00**	**4,408.00**	**7,009.00**	**6,843.00**	**31,325.00**
Beverage - Dining Room	341.00	88.00	195.00	229.00	214.00	198.00	235.00	1,500.00
Beverage - Patio	244.00	49.00	88.00	97.00	96.00	84.00	128.00	786.00
Beverage - Catering	652.00	-	-	314.00	247.00	394.00	214.00	1,821.00
Total Beverage	**1,237.00**	**137.00**	**283.00**	**640.00**	**557.00**	**676.00**	**577.00**	**4,107.00**
Beer & Liquor - Dining Room	1,577.00	175.00	269.00	492.00	323.00	224.00	485.00	3,545.00
Beer & Liquor - Patio	652.00	56.00	96.00	78.00	184.00	168.00	227.00	1,461.00
Beer & Liquor - Catering	984.00	-	-	344.00	411.00	884.00	774.00	3,397.00
Total Beer & Liquor	**3,213.00**	**231.00**	**365.00**	**914.00**	**918.00**	**1,276.00**	**1,486.00**	**8,403.00**
TOTAL SALES	**10,666.00**	**1,686.00**	**2,391.00**	**5,342.00**	**5,883.00**	**8,961.00**	**8,906.00**	**43,835.00**
Gross Profit Factor	32%							
Estimated Gross Profit	3,413.12	539.52	765.12	1,709.44	1,882.56	2,867.52	2,849.92	14,027.20

ES1-WBPayroll.xlsx is the project in Activities 1.2 to 1.8.

Payroll
Week Ended: September 24, 2011

		Sun	Mon	Tue	Wed	Thu	Fri	Sat	Total Hours	Pay Rate	Gross Pay
Lou	Cortez	8	0	6	8	0	8	8	38	8.25	$ 313.50
Jasmine	Hill	8	0	8	8	0	8	6	38	8.25	$ 313.50
Heather	Kiley	0	8	6	8	5	5	8	40	8.25	$ 330.00
Dayna	McGuire	6	5	8	8	7	0	6	40	8.25	$ 330.00
Carla	Modano	0	0	8	8	7	7	8	38	8.25	$ 313.50
Tyler	Santini	8	0	8	8	6	7	0	37	8.25	$ 305.25
Pat	Soulliere	8	8	0	8	7	7	0	38	8.25	$ 313.50
Moira	Su-Lin	0	8	0	8	7	7	8	38	8.25	$ 313.50
Toni	Williams	8	0	0	8	8	7	4	35	8.25	$ 288.75
Total		46	29	44	72	47	56	48	342		$ 2,821.50

Hours
Proof   342

Gross
Pay Proof $ 2,821.50

Student Name

ES1-WBPayroll.xlsx is the project in Activity 1.9.

			Sun	Mon	Tue	Wed
						Payroll
						Week Ended: September 24, 2011
Lou	Cortez	8	0	6	8	0
Jasmine	Hill	8	0	8	8	0
Heather	Kiley	0	8	6	8	5
Dayna	McGuire	6	5	8	8	7
Carla	Modano	0	0	8	8	7
Tyler	Santini	8	0	8	8	6
Pat	Soulliere	8	8	0	8	7
Moira	Su-Lin	0	8	0	8	7
Toni	Williams	8	0	0	8	8
Total		=SUM(C5:C14)	=SUM(D5:D14)	=SUM(E5:E14)	=SUM(F5:F14)	=SUM(G5:G14)
Hours Proof	=SUM(C5:I13)					
Gross Pay Proof	=B17*K5					
Student Name						

Thu	Fri	Sat	Total Hours	Pay Rate	Gross Pay
8	8	=SUM(C5:I5)	8.25	=J5*K5	
8	6	=SUM(C6:I6)	8.25	=J6*K6	
5	8	=SUM(C7:I7)	8.25	=J7*K7	
0	6	=SUM(C8:I8)	8.25	=J8*K8	
7	8	=SUM(C9:I9)	8.25	=J9*K9	
7	0	=SUM(C10:I10)	8.25	=J10*K10	
7	0	=SUM(C11:I11)	8.25	=J11*K11	
7	8	=SUM(C12:I12)	8.25	=J12*K12	
7	4	=SUM(C13:I13)	8.25	=J13*K13	
=SUM(H5:H14)	=SUM(I5:I14)	=SUM(J5:J14)		=SUM(L5:L14)	

Activity 1.1

Completing the Excel Worksheet Cycle

Information is created in Excel in a *worksheet* and is saved in a file called a *workbook*. A workbook can contain several worksheets. Imagine a worksheet as a page with horizontal and vertical lines drawn in a grid representing columns and rows. Data is entered into a *cell*, which is the intersection of a column with a row. Columns are lettered A to Z, AA to AZ, BA to BZ, and so on. The last column in the worksheet is labeled *XFD*. Rows are numbered 1, 2, 3, and so on. A column letter and a row number identify each cell. For example, A1 is the cell address for the intersection of column A with row 1. Each worksheet in Excel contains 16,384 columns and 1,048,576 rows. By default, an Excel workbook contains three worksheets labeled *Sheet1, Sheet2,* and *Sheet3*. Additional sheets can be inserted as needed.

Project

You have been asked to update a weekly sales report for The Waterfront Bistro by adding data and viewing the impact of changing a cell used to calculate gross margin.

1. At the Windows desktop, click the Start button on the Taskbar.

2. Point to *All Programs.*

3. Click *Microsoft Office.*

Tutorial 1.1
Creating and Saving a Worksheet

4. Click *Microsoft Excel 2010.*

> Depending on your operating system and/or system configuration, the steps you complete to open Excel may vary.

5. At the Excel screen, identify the various features by comparing your screen with the one shown in Figure 1.1. If necessary, maximize the Excel window. Depending on your screen resolution, your screen may vary slightly. Refer to Table 1.1 for a description of the screen features.

FIGURE 1.1 The Excel Screen

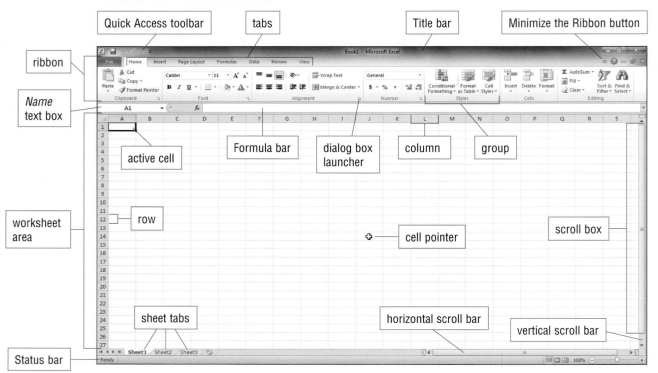

TABLE 1.1 Excel Screen Features

Feature	Description
active cell	location in the worksheet that will display typed data or that will be affected by a command
cell pointer	select cells when you see this icon by clicking or dragging the mouse
dialog box launcher	click the downward-pointing diagonal arrow at the bottom right in a group to open the dialog box with more options for that group
File tab	displays the Backstage view with document management actions, such as save or print, and a list of recently opened workbooks
Formula bar	displays the contents stored in the active cell
Minimize the Ribbon button	click to show or hide the ribbon
Name text box	displays the active cell address or name assigned to active cell
Quick Access toolbar	contains buttons for commonly used commands which can be executed with a single mouse click
ribbon	area from which commands and features for performing actions on a cell or worksheet are accessed; begin by selecting a tab and then choosing the command or feature
sheet tabs	identifies the worksheets in the workbook; use these tabs to change the active worksheet
Status bar	displays current mode, action messages, View buttons, and Zoom slider
tabs	commands and features in the ribbon are organized into related groups which are accessed by clicking a tab name
Title bar	displays workbook name followed by Microsoft Excel
vertical and horizontal scroll bars	used to view various parts of the worksheet beyond the current screen
worksheet area	contains cells used to create the worksheet

6 Click the File tab and then click the Open button in the Backstage view.

> The Backstage view organizes document management tasks into tabs. Quick Command buttons such as Save, Save As, Open, and Close are located at the top of the left pane in Backstage view. Below the Quick Command buttons the view is organized into tabs. You will learn more about these tabs in later activities. You can also open a workbook by clicking the Open button on the Quick Access toolbar. If the Open button does not display on the Quick Access toolbar, click the Customize Quick Access Toolbar button that displays at the right side of the toolbar and then click *Open* at the drop-down list.

7 At the Open dialog box, navigate to the ExcelS1 folder on your storage medium.

> To change to a different drive, click the drive letter in the *Computer* section in the Navigation pane. (You may need to scroll down the Navigation pane to see the *Computer* section.) Change to a different folder by double-clicking the folder name in the Content pane.

8 Double-click *WBWeeklySales.xlsx*.

> This workbook contains one worksheet with sales for The Waterfront Bistro for the week ended September 24, 2011. The formulas to sum the sales have already been created. Notice some of the cells in the column labeled *Saturday* are empty. You will enter these values in Steps 11 through 14.

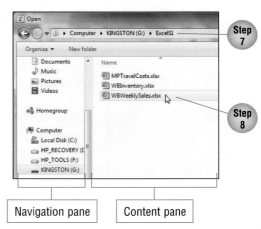

continues

9 Click the File tab and then click the Save As button in the Backstage view.

Use the *Save* option to save a file using the same name. If you want to keep the original workbook and save the workbook with the changes under a new name, use *Save As*.

10 At the Save As dialog box, with ExcelS1 the active folder on your storage medium, press the Home key, type **ES1-** at the beginning of the current file name in the *File name* text box, and then press Enter or click Save.

Excel files have the file extension .xlsx at the end of a workbook name. When naming a file do not change or delete this file extension because the operating system recognizes files ending with *.xlsx* are Microsoft Excel workbooks. If you change or delete the extension, the operating system will not know which program is associated with the data.

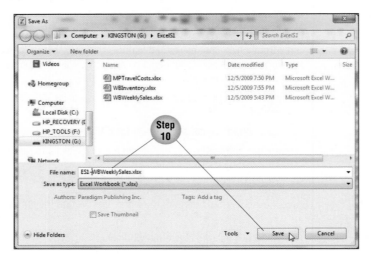

11 Move the cell pointer over the intersection of column H with row 6 (H6) and then click to make H6 the active cell.

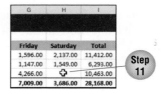

12 Type **3157** and then press Enter.

Notice that the entry in H7 has changed. This is because the formula created in H7 was dependent on H6. As soon as you enter a value in H6, any other dependent cells are automatically updated. Can you identify other cells that changed as a result of the new value in H6?

Need Help?

Typing mistake? Make corrections as you type by pressing the Backspace key to delete characters to the left of the insertion point; or, if you notice the mistake after you have left the cell, make the cell active and double-click the cell to open the cell for editing.

13 Click H10 to make the cell active and then type **214**.

14 Click H14 to make the cell active, type **774**, and then press Enter.

15 Look at the entry in B19. This percentage is used to calculate the Estimated Gross Profit in row 20 (Total Sales times the Gross Profit Factor). Next, you will change the entry in B19 to see the effect on the estimated gross profit values.

16 Click B19 to make the cell active, type **32%**, and then press Enter.

> Notice the new estimated gross profit values in cells B20 through I20.

G	H	I
Friday	Saturday	Total
1,596.00	2,137.00	11,412.00
1,147.00	1,549.00	6,293.00
4,266.00	3,157.00	13,620.00
7,009.00	6,843.00	31,325.00
198.00	235.00	1,500.00
84.00	128.00	786.00
394.00	214.00	1,821.00
676.00	577.00	4,107.00
224.00	485.00	3,545.00
168.00	227.00	1,461.00
884.00	774.00	3,397.00
1,276.00	1,486.00	8,403.00
8,961.00	8,906.00	43,835.00

Step 12
Step 13
Step 14

Step 16

17	TOTAL SALES	10,666.00	1,686.00	2,391.00	5,342.00	5,883.00	8,961.00	8,906.00	43,835.00
18									
19	Gross Profit Factor	32%							
20	Estimated Gross Profit	3,413.12	539.52	765.12	1,709.44	1,882.56	2,867.52	2,849.92	14,027.20

17 Click the File tab and then click the Save button, or click the Save button 💾 on the Quick Access toolbar.

18 Click the File tab, click the Print tab in the left pane of Backstage view, and then click the Print button, or click the Quick Print button 🖨 on the Quick Access toolbar.

> If the Quick Print button does not display on the Quick Access toolbar, click the Customize Quick Access Toolbar button that displays at the right side of the toolbar and then click *Quick Print* at the drop-down list. The worksheet's page layout options have been set to print the worksheet in landscape orientation and centered horizontally between the left and right margins. You will learn how to set these options in a later activity.

19 Click the File tab and then click the Close button in the Backstage view.

> When no workbooks are currently open, Excel displays a blank grey screen.

In Brief

Start Excel
1. Click Start.
2. Point to *All Programs.*
3. Point to *Microsoft Office.*
4. Click *Microsoft Excel 2010.*

Open Workbook
1. Click File tab.
2. Click Open button.
3. Navigate to storage medium and folder.
4. Double-click workbook name.

Save Workbook with New Name
1. Click File tab.
2. Click Save As button.
3. Type new workbook name.
4. Click Save or press Enter.

In Addition

AutoComplete

The AutoComplete feature in Excel will complete text entries for you as you start to type a new entry in a cell. If the first few letters that you type match another entry in the column, Excel automatically fills in the remaining text. Press Tab, Enter, or one of the arrow keys to accept the text Excel suggests, or continue typing the correct text. You can turn off AutoComplete by clicking the File tab and then clicking the Options button near the bottom of the left pane in the Backstage view. Click *Advanced* in the left pane of the Excel Options dialog box, click the *Enable AutoComplete for cell values* check box to clear the box, and then click OK.

Activity 1.2

Entering Labels and Values; Using Fill Options

A *label* is an entry in a cell that helps the reader relate to the values in the corresponding column or row. Labels are generally entered first when creating a new worksheet since they define the layout of the data in the columns and rows. By default, Excel aligns labels at the left edge of the column. A *value* is a number, formula, or function that can be used to perform calculations in the worksheet. By default, Excel aligns values at the right edge of the column. Take a few moments to plan or sketch out the layout of a new worksheet before entering labels and values. Decide the calculations you will need to execute and how to display the data so that it will be easily understood and interpreted.

Project

You need to calculate gross pay in a new payroll worksheet for the hourly paid staff at The Waterfront Bistro. Begin by entering labels and values.

Tutorial 1.2
Performing
Calculations
Using Formulas

1 At the blank Excel screen, click the File tab, click the New tab in the Backstage view, and then click the Create button with Blank Workbook already selected in the *Available Templates* section of the view.

> You can also start a new blank workbook by clicking the New button on the Quick Access toolbar. If the New button does not display on the Quick Access toolbar, click the Customize Quick Access Toolbar button that displays at the right side of the toolbar and then click *New* at the drop-down list. Also consider using the shortcut key Ctrl + N to begin a new blank workbook.

2 Type **Payroll** as the title for the new worksheet in A1.

> When you type a new entry in a cell, the entry appears in the Formula bar as well as within the active cell in the worksheet area. To end a cell entry, press Enter, move to another cell in the worksheet, or click the Enter button on the Formula bar.

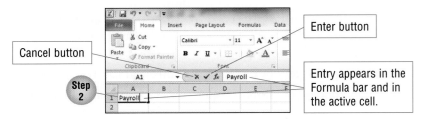

3 Press Enter.

4 With A2 the active cell, type **Week Ended: September 24, 2011** and then press Enter.

> Notice the entry in A2 is overflowing into columns B, C, and D. You can allow a label to spill over into adjacent columns as long as you do not plan to enter other data in the overflow cells. In a later section, you will learn how to adjust column widths.

5 Enter the remaining labels as shown on the next page by making the appropriate cell active, typing the label, and then pressing Enter or clicking another cell. (Do not complete the labels for the days of the week beyond *Sun*, as this will be done in Steps 6–8.)

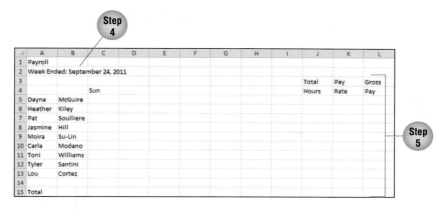

6 Click C4 to make the cell active.

A thick black border surrounds the active cell. A small black square displays at the bottom right corner of the active cell. This black square is called the **fill handle**. The fill handle is used to fill adjacent cells with the same data or consecutive data. The entries that are automatically inserted in the adjacent cells are dependent on the contents of the active cell. You will use the fill handle in C4 to automatically enter the remaining days of the week in D4 through I4.

7 Point at the fill handle in C4. The cell pointer changes from the large white cross ✛ to a thin black cross ✚.

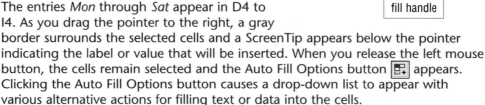

8 Hold down the left mouse button, drag the pointer to I4, and then release the mouse.

The entries *Mon* through *Sat* appear in D4 to I4. As you drag the pointer to the right, a gray border surrounds the selected cells and a ScreenTip appears below the pointer indicating the label or value that will be inserted. When you release the left mouse button, the cells remain selected and the Auto Fill Options button 🔲 appears. Clicking the Auto Fill Options button causes a drop-down list to appear with various alternative actions for filling text or data into the cells.

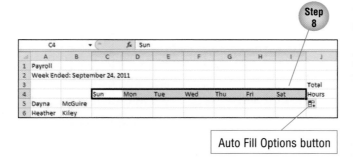

Auto Fill Options button

Need Help?

Mon through Sat does not appear? You probably dragged the mouse using the cell pointer instead of the fill handle. This action selects cells instead of filling them. Go back to Step 6 and try again, making sure you drag when you see the thin black cross.

continues

9 Click C5 to make the cell active.

10 Type **6** and then press the Right Arrow key.

11 Type **5** in D5 and then press the Right Arrow key.

12 Type the following values in the cells indicated:

E5	**8**
F5	**8**
G5	**7**
H5	**0**
I5	**6**

13 Make F5 the active cell.

14 Point at the fill handle in F5 and then drag the pointer down to F13.

This time the active cell contained a value. The value *8* is copied to the adjacent cells.

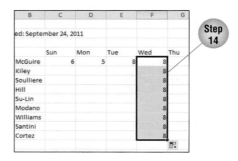

15 Enter the remaining values for employee hours as shown below. Use the fill handle where there are duplicate values in adjacent cells to enter the data as efficiently as possible.

	A	B	C	D	E	F	G	H	I	J
1	Payroll									
2	Week Ended: September 24, 2011									
3										Total
4			Sun	Mon	Tue	Wed	Thu	Fri	Sat	Hours
5	Dayna	McGuire	6	5	8	8	7	0	6	
6	Heather	Kiley	0	8	6	8	5	5	8	
7	Pat	Soulliere	8	8	0	8	7	7	0	
8	Jasmine	Hill	8	0	8	8	0	8	6	
9	Moira	Su-Lin	0	8	0	8	7	7	8	
10	Carla	Modano	0	0	8	8	7	7	8	
11	Toni	Williams	8	0	0	8	8	7	4	
12	Tyler	Santini	8	0	8	8	6	7	0	
13	Lou	Cortez	8	0	6	8	0	8	8	

Step 15

16 Click K5 to make the cell active, type **8.25**, and then press Enter.

17 Position the cell pointer over cell K5, hold down the left mouse button, drag down to K13, and then release the mouse.

A group of adjacent cells is referred to as a *range* (a range is two or more cells). Select a range of cells when you want to perform an action on a group of cells.

18 With Home the active tab in the ribbon, click the Fill button 🔽 Fill ▾ in the Editing group and then click *Down* at the drop-down list.

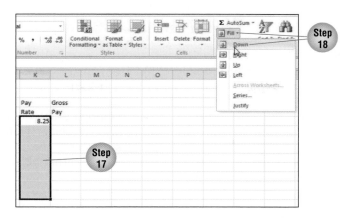

19 Click in any cell in the worksheet to deselect the range of cells in column K.

20 Click the Save button on the Quick Access toolbar.

21 At the Save As dialog box with ExcelS1 the active folder, type **ES1-WBPayroll** in the *File name* text box and then press Enter.

In Addition

More about the Fill Command

The fill handle is versatile and can be used to enter a series of values, dates, times, or other labels as a pattern. The pattern is established based on the cells you select before dragging the fill handle. In the worksheet shown below, the cells in columns C through J were all populated using the fill handle. In each row, the first two cells in columns A and B were selected and then the fill handle dragged right to column J. Notice the variety of patterns used to extend a series.

Use the Auto Fill Options button drop-down list to control how the series is entered. After dragging the fill handle, the Auto Fill Options button is displayed at the end of the series. Pointing at the button causes the button to expand and display a down-pointing arrow. Click the down-pointing arrow and then select the desired fill action from the options in the drop-down list. By default, *Fill Series* is active.

	A	B	C	D	E	F	G	H	I	J	K	L	M
1	**Examples using the fill handle to continue a series in adjacent cells**												
2	In each row below, the first two cells were selected and then the fill handle dragged right.												
3	1	2	3	4	5	6	7	8	9	10			
4	10	20	30	40	50	60	70	80	90	100			
5	9:00	10:00	11:00	12:00	13:00	14:00	15:00	16:00	17:00	18:00			
6	2011	2012	2013	2014	2015	2016	2017	2018	2019	2020			
7	Quarter 1	Quarter 2	Quarter 3	Quarter 4	Quarter 1	Quarter 2	Quarter 3	Quarter 4	Quarter 1	Quarter 2			
8	Period 1	Period 2	Period 3	Period 4	Period 5	Period 6	Period 7	Period 8	Period 9	Period 10			
9	Year 1	Year 2	Year 3	Year 4	Year 5	Year 6	Year 7	Year 8	Year 9	Year 10			
10													
11											○ Copy Cells		
12											⊙ Fill Series		
13											○ Fill Formatting Only		
14											○ Fill Without Formatting		
15													

Activity 1.3

Performing Calculations Using Formulas

A *formula* is entered into a cell to perform mathematical calculations in a worksheet. All formulas in Excel begin with the equals sign (=) as the first character. After the equals sign, the cell addresses that contain the values you want to calculate are entered between mathematical operators. The mathematical operators are + (addition), − (subtraction), * (multiplication), / (division), and ^ (exponentiation). An example of a valid formula is =A3*B3. The value in A3 is multiplied by the value in B3 and the result is placed in the formula cell. By including the cell address in the formula rather than typing the actual value, you can utilize the powerful recalculation feature in Excel. If you change a cell's content, the worksheet is automatically recalculated so that all values are current.

Project

SNAP

Tutorial 1.3
Copying and Testing a Formula

You will use two methods to enter formulas to calculate total hours and gross pay for the first two employees listed in the Payroll worksheet for The Waterfront Bistro.

1. With **ES1-WBPayroll.xlsx** open, make J5 the active cell.

   Begin a formula by activating the cell in which you want the result placed.

2. Type **=c5+d5+e5+f5+g5+h5+i5** and then press Enter.

   The values in C5 through I5 are added and the result, *40*, is displayed in J5.

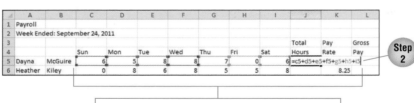

Cell references are color-coded to the originating cell for quick reference and error checking.

3. Press the Up Arrow key to move the active cell back to J5.

   Notice that the result of the formula is displayed in the worksheet area and the formula used to calculate the result is shown in the Formula bar. Notice also that the column letters in cell addresses are automatically converted to uppercase.

4. Make J6 the active cell, type the formula **=c6+d6+e6+f6+g6+h6+i6**, and then press Enter.

   Seem like too much typing? A more efficient way to add a series of cells is available. This method will be introduced in the next activity after you learn the pointing method for entering formulas.

5. Make L5 the active cell.

   To calculate gross pay, you need to multiply the total hours times the pay rate. In Steps 6–10, you will enter this formula using the pointing method.

6. Type the equals sign (=).

7. Click J5.

   A moving dashed border (called a *marquee*) displays around J5, indicating it is the cell included in the formula, and the cell address is added to the formula cell (J5) with a blinking insertion point after the reference. Notice also that the Status bar displays the action *Point*.

Need Help?
Click the wrong cell by mistake? Simply click the correct cell, or press Esc to start the formula over again.

In Brief

Enter Formula
1. Activate formula cell.
2. Type =.
3. Type first cell address.
4. Type operator symbol.
5. Type second cell address.
6. Continue Steps 3–5 until finished.
7. Press Enter or click Enter button.

Enter a Formula Using Pointing Method
1. Activate formula cell.
2. Type =.
3. Click first cell.
4. Type operator symbol.
5. Click second cell.
6. Repeat Steps 3–5 until finished.
7. Press Enter or click Enter button.

8 Type an asterisk (*), which is the multiplication symbol.

> The marquee surrounding cell J5 disappears and J5 is color-coded with the cell reference J5 within the formula cell.

9 Click K5.

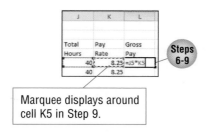

Marquee displays around cell K5 in Step 9.

10 Click the Enter button on the Formula bar.

> The result *330* is displayed in L5. In Activity 1.6 you will learn how to display two decimal places for cells containing dollar values.

11 Use the pointing method or type the formula **=j6*k6** to calculate the gross pay for Heather Kiley in L6.

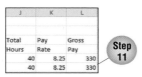

12 Click the Save button on the Quick Access toolbar.

In Addition

Order of Operations

If you include several operators in a formula, Excel calculates the result using the order of operations as follows: negations (e.g., –1) first, then percents (%), then exponentiations (^), then multiplication and division (* and /), and finally addition and subtraction (+ and –). If a formula contains more than one operator at the same level of precedence—for example, both an addition and a subtraction operation—Excel calculates the equation from left to right. To change the order of operations, use parentheses around the part of the formula you want calculated first.

Formula	Calculation
=B5*C5/D5	Both operators are at the same level of precedence—Excel would multiply the value in B5 times the value in C5 and then divide the result by the value in D5.
=B5+B6+B7*C10	Multiplication takes precedence over addition, so Excel would first multiply the value in B7 times the value in C10. Excel would then take the value in B5, add to it the value in B6, and then add the result of the multiplication.
=(B5+B6+B7)*C10	Because of the parentheses, Excel would first add the values in B5 through B7, then multiply this sum times the value in C10.

Activity 1.4

Using the SUM Function

The formulas to calculate the hours worked by the first two employees were lengthy. A more efficient way to calculate the total hours for Dayna McGuire in J5 would be to enter the formula =SUM(C5:I5). This formula includes one of Excel's built-in functions called SUM. A *function* is a preprogrammed formula. The structure of a formula utilizing a function begins with the equals sign (=), followed by the name of the function, and then the *argument*. Argument is the term given to the values identified within parentheses. In the example provided, the argument C5:I5 contains the starting cell and the ending cell separated by a colon (:). The colon is used to indicate a range is to be summed; a *range* is a rectangular-shaped block of cells. Since the SUM function is used frequently, an AutoSum button is available in the Home tab.

Project

Tutorial 1.3
Copying and Testing a Formula

You decide to use a more efficient method of payroll calculation, so you will use the SUM function to complete the hours worked for the Payroll worksheet.

1. With **ES1-WBPayroll.xlsx** open, make J5 the active cell and then press the Delete key.

    This deletes the cell contents. There was nothing wrong with the formula already entered in J5. You are deleting it so that the formulas in the completed worksheet will be consistent.

2. Click the AutoSum button Σ in the Editing group in the Home tab. (Do not click the down-pointing arrow to the right of the AutoSum button.)

    A moving marquee surrounds cells C5 through I5 and a ScreenTip appears below the formula cell indicating the correct format for the SUM function. Excel enters the formula *=SUM(C5:I5)* in J5. The suggested range C5:I5 is selected within the formula so that you can highlight a different range with the mouse if the suggested range is not correct.

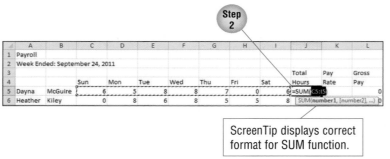

3. Press Enter.

    Since the range Excel suggests is the correct range, you can finish the formula by pressing Enter or by clicking the Enter button on the Formula bar.

4. With J6 the active cell, press the Delete key to delete the existing formula in the cell.

5. Click the AutoSum button. When Excel displays the formula *=SUM(C6:I6)*, click the Enter button in the Formula bar.

6. Make J7 the active cell and then click the AutoSum button.

    Notice this time the range of cells Excel is suggesting to add *(J5:J6)* is the wrong range. When you click the AutoSum button, Excel looks for multiple values in the cells immediately above the active cell. In this case, there are multiple values above J7 so Excel inserts J5:J6 as the range in the SUM formula. You need to correct the range of cells that you want to add.

(7) Position the cell pointer over C7, hold down the left mouse button, drag the pointer to the right to I7, and then release the mouse button.

	A	B	C	D	E	F	G	H	I		K	L
1	Payroll											
2	Week Ended: September 24, 2011											
3										Total	Pay	Gross
4			Sun	Mon	Tue	Wed	Thu	Fri	Sat	Hours	Rate	Pay
5	Dayna	McGuire	6	5	8	8	7	0	6	40	8.25	330
6	Heather	Kiley	0	8	6	8	5	5	8	40	8.25	330
7	Pat	Soulliere	8	8	0	8	7	7	0	=SUM(C7:I7)		
8	Jasmine	Hill	8	0	8	8	0	8	6	SUM(number1, [number2], ...)		

In Brief

Enter SUM Function
1. Activate formula cell.
2. Click AutoSum button.
3. Press Enter, or drag to select correct range and press Enter.

OR
1. Drag to select range of cells to be summed including result cell.
2. Click AutoSum button.

(8) Press Enter.

Now that you have seen how the AutoSum button operates, you already know that the suggested range for the next employee's total hours will be incorrect. In Step 9, you will select the range of cells *first* to avoid the incorrect suggestion.

(9) Position the cell pointer over C8, hold down the left mouse button, drag the pointer right to J8, and then release the mouse button.

Notice you are including J8, the cell that will display the result, in the range of cells.

(10) Click the AutoSum button.

The result, *38*, appears in cell J8.

	A	B	C	D	E	F	G	H	I	J
1	Payroll									
2	Week Ended: September 24, 2011									
3										Total
4			Sun	Mon	Tue	Wed	Thu	Fri	Sat	Hours
5	Dayna	McGuire	6	5	8	8	7	0	6	40
6	Heather	Kiley	0	8	6	8	5	5	8	40
7	Pat	Soulliere	8	8	0	8	7	7	0	38
8	Jasmine	Hill	8	0	8	8	0	8	6	38

Steps
9-10

(11) Click J8 and look in the Formula bar at the formula the SUM function created: *=SUM(C8:I8)*.

Since Excel created the correct SUM formula from a range of selected cells, you decide to try calculating total hours for more than one employee in one step using the method employed in Steps 9 and 10 but with an expanded range.

(12) Position the cell pointer over C9, hold down the left mouse button, drag the pointer down and right to J13, and then release the mouse button.

(13) Click the AutoSum button.

C	D	E	F	G	H	I	J
mber 24, 2011							
							Total
Sun	Mon	Tue	Wed	Thu	Fri	Sat	Hours
6	5	8	8	7	0	6	40
0	8	6	8	5	5	8	40
8	8	0	8	7	7	0	38
8	0	8	8	0	8	6	38
0	8	0	8	7	7	8	38
0	0	8	8	7	7	8	38
8	0	0	8	8	7	4	35
8	0	8	8	6	7	0	37
8	0	6	8	0	8	8	38

Steps
12-13

(14) Click cells J9, J10, J11, J12, and J13 to confirm that the correct formulas appear in the Formula bar.

(15) Click the Save button on the Quick Access toolbar.

Activity 1.5

Copying Formulas

Many times you may create a worksheet in which several formulas are basically the same. For example, in the payroll worksheet, the formula to total the hours for Dayna McGuire is =SUM(C5:I5), for Heather Kiley =SUM(C6:I6), and so on. The only difference between the two formulas is the row number. Whenever formulas are this similar, you can use the Copy and Paste feature to copy the formula from one cell to another. The cell containing the original formula is called the **source**, and the cell(s) to which the formula is copied is called the **destination**. When the formula is pasted, Excel automatically changes column letters or row numbers to reflect the destination location. By default, Excel assumes **relative addressing**—cell addresses update relative to the destination.

Project

To simplify your completion of the Payroll worksheet, you will copy formulas using two methods: Copy and Paste and the fill handle.

Tutorial 1.3
Copying and Testing a Formula

1. With **ES1-WBPayroll.xlsx** open, make L6 the active cell.

   This cell contains the formula =J6*K6 to calculate the gross pay for Heather Kiley. You will copy this formula to the remaining cells in column L to finish the Gross Pay column.

2. Click the Copy button 📋 in the Clipboard group in the Home tab. (Do not click the down-pointing arrow to the right of the Copy button.)

   A moving marquee surrounds the active cell indicating the source contents are copied to the Clipboard, which is a temporary storage location. The source being copied is the formula =J6*K6, not the value *330*.

3. Select the range L7:L13. To do this, position the cell pointer over L7, hold down the left mouse button, drag the pointer down to L13, and then release the mouse button.

marquee indicating source range

Step 3

4. Click the Paste button 📋 in the Clipboard group in the Home tab. (Do not click the down-pointing arrow on the button.)

   Excel copies the formula to the selected cells, displays the results, and the Paste Options (Ctrl) button appears. Clicking the Paste Options (Ctrl) button will display a drop-down list with various alternatives for pasting the data. The moving marquee remains around the source cell and the destination cells remain highlighted. The moving marquee disappears as soon as you start another activity or press the Esc key.

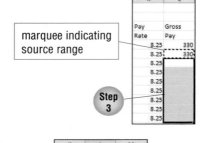

Step 4

Paste Options button

5. Press the Esc key to remove the marquee and the Paste Options (Ctrl) button, click L7, and then look at the entry in the Formula bar: =J7*K7.

   The row number in the source formula was increased by one to reflect the destination. The actions you completed in Steps 1 through 4 are called **relative copying**.

6. Use the Down Arrow key to check the remaining formulas in column L.

7. Make C15 the active cell.

8 Click the AutoSum button and then click the Enter button in the Formula bar.

> The SUM function inserts the formula =SUM(C5:C14). Next, you will copy the formula using the fill handle.

9 Drag the fill handle in C15 right to L15.

> When the active cell contains a formula, dragging the fill handle causes Excel to copy the formula and change cell references relative to each destination location.

	A	B	C	D	E	F	G	H	I	J	K	L
1	Payroll											
2	Week Ended: September 24, 2011											
3										Total	Pay	Gross
4			Sun	Mon	Tue	Wed	Thu	Fri	Sat	Hours	Rate	Pay
5	Dayna	McGuire	6	5	8	8	7	0	6	40	8.25	330
6	Heather	Kiley	0	8	6	8	5	5	8	40	8.25	330
7	Pat	Soulliere	8	8	0	8	7	7	0	38	8.25	313.5
8	Jasmine	Hill	8	0	8	8	0	8	6	38	8.25	313.5
9	Moira	Su-Lin	0	8	0	8	7	7	8	38	8.25	313.5
10	Carla	Modano	0	0	8	8	7	7	8	38	8.25	313.5
11	Toni	Williams	8	0	0	8	8	7	4	35	8.25	288.75
12	Tyler	Santini	8	0	8	8	6	7	0	37	8.25	305.25
13	Lou	Cortez	8	0	6	8	0	8	8	38	8.25	313.5
14												
15	Total		46	29	44	72	47	56	48	342	74.25	2821.5

Step 9

Need Help?

If the results do not appear in D15 through L15, you probably dragged the cell pointer instead of the fill handle. Click C15 and try again, making sure you drag using the thin black cross.

10 Make K15 the active cell and then press the Delete key.

> The sum of the *Pay Rate* column is not useful information.

11 Make D15 the active cell and look at the entry in the Formula bar: =SUM(D5:D14).

> The column letter in the source formula was changed to reflect the destination.

12 Use the Right Arrow key to check the formulas in the remaining columns.

13 Click the Save button on the Quick Access toolbar.

In Addition

Copy and Paste versus Fill

What is the difference between Copy and Paste and the fill handle? When you use Copy, the contents of the source cell(s) are placed in the Clipboard. The data will remain in the Clipboard and can be pasted several times in the current worksheet, into any other worksheet that is open, or into an open document in another program. Use Copy and Paste when the formula is to be inserted more than once or into nonadjacent cells. Use the fill handle when the formula is only being copied to adjacent cells.

Activity 1.6

Testing the Worksheet; Improving the Worksheet Appearance; Sorting

When you have finished building the worksheet, verifying that the formulas you entered are accurate is a good idea. The worksheet could contain formulas that are correct in structure but not mathematically correct for the situation. For example, the wrong range may be included in a SUM formula, or parentheses missing from a multioperator formula may cause an incorrect result. Various methods can be employed to verify a worksheet's accuracy. One method is to create a proof formula in a cell beside or below the worksheet that will verify the totals. For example, in the payroll worksheet the *Total Hours* column can be verified by creating a formula that adds all of the hours for all of the employees.

Data in Excel can be rearranged by sorting rows in either ascending order or descending order. You can select a single column or define a custom sort to specify multiple columns that determine the sort order.

Project

To confirm the accuracy of your calculations in the Payroll worksheet, you will enter proof formulas to test the worksheet and then use two formatting options to improve the worksheet's appearance.

SNAP

Tutorial 1.3
Copying and Testing a Formula

Tutorial 1.4
Sorting Data and Using Help

1. With **ES1-WBPayroll.xlsx** open, make A17 the active cell.

2. Type **Hours**, press Alt + Enter, type **Proof**, and then press Enter.

   Alt + Enter is the command to insert a line break in a cell. This command is used when you want multiple lines within the same cell. The height of the row is automatically expanded to accommodate the multiple lines.

3. Make B17 the active cell.

4. Click in the Formula bar, type **=sum(c5:i13)**, and then click the Enter button or press Enter. (Alternatively, you could click the AutoSum button and then drag the pointer across the range C5 through I13.)

   Excel displays the result, *342*, which verifies that your total hours in J15 is correct. Can you think of another formula that would have accomplished the same objective? *Hint: Think of the direction you added to arrive at the total hours in J15.*

Typed range is color-coded for easy referencing and error checking.

Step 4

	A	B	C	D	E	F	G	H	I	J
1	Payroll									
2	Week Ended: September 24, 2011									
3										Total
4			Sun	Mon	Tue	Wed	Thu	Fri	Sat	Hours
5	Dayna	McGuire	6	5	8	8	7	0	6	40
6	Heather	Kiley	0	8	6	8	5	5	8	40
7	Pat	Soulliere	8	8	0	8	7	7	0	38
8	Jasmine	Hill	8	0	8	8	0	8	6	38
9	Moira	Su-Lin	0	8	0	8	7	7	8	38
10	Carla	Modano	0	0	8	8	7	7	8	38
11	Toni	Williams	8	0	0	8	8	7	4	35
12	Tyler	Santini	8	0	8	8	6	7	0	37
13	Lou	Cortez	8	0	6	8	0	8	8	38
14										
15	Total		46	29	44	72	47	56	48	342
16										
17	Hours Proof	m(c5:i13)								

Need Help?

Didn't get 342? Then one of the cell entries is incorrect. Look through previous pages to see if the difference between 342 and your result equals a cell entry that you missed.

5 Make A18 the active cell.

6 Type **Gross**, press Alt + Enter, type **Pay Proof**, and then press Enter.

7 Make B18 the active cell.

Since all of the employees are paid the same rate of pay, you can verify the *Gross Pay* column by multiplying the total hours times the pay rate.

8 Type **=b17*k5** and then press the Right Arrow key.

The result, *2821.5*, confirms that the value in L15 is correct. The importance of testing a worksheet cannot be emphasized enough. Worksheets often contain important financial or statistical data that can form the basis for strategic business decisions.

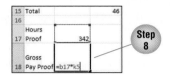

9 Look at the completed worksheet shown below. Notice that some of the values in column L show no decimals, while others show 1 or 2 decimal places. Also notice the labels do not align directly over the values below them.

Labels do not align directly over values.

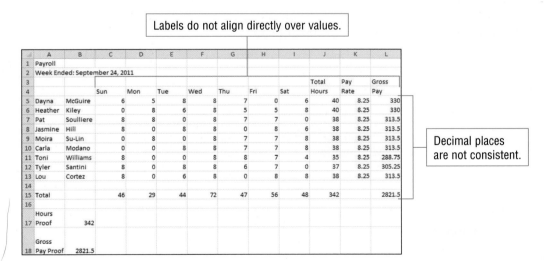

Decimal places are not consistent.

continues

10 Select the range L5:L15.

These final steps in building a worksheet are meant to improve the appearance of cells. In column L, Excel uses up to 15 decimal places for precision when calculating values. Since the *Gross Pay* column represents a sum of money, you will format these cells to display a dollar sign and show two decimal places.

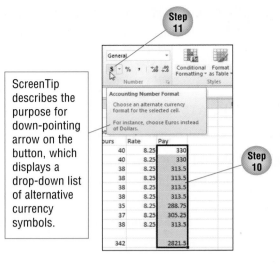

ScreenTip describes the purpose for down-pointing arrow on the button, which displays a drop-down list of alternative currency symbols.

11 Click the Accounting Number Format button $ in the Number group in the Home tab. (Do not click the down-pointing arrow to the right of the button.)

The Accounting Number format adds a dollar sign, a comma in the thousands place, and two decimal places to each value in the selection.

12 Make B18 the active cell and then click the Accounting Number Format button.

13 Select the range C3:L4.

As previously mentioned, labels are aligned at the left edge of a column while values are aligned at the right edge. In the next step, you will align the labels at the right edge of the column so they appear directly over the values they represent.

14 Click the Align Text Right button ≡ in the Alignment group in the Home tab.

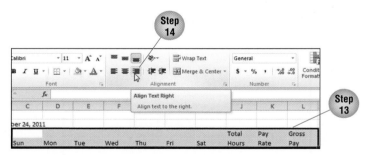

15 Click in any cell to deselect the range.

In the next steps, you will rearrange the names in the payroll worksheet so that they are in alphabetical order by last name. Since the last name is not the first column in the worksheet, you will need to define a custom sort.

16 Select the range A5:L13.

You are selecting the range before executing the sort command since you do not want to include the cells above and below the list of names in the sort action.

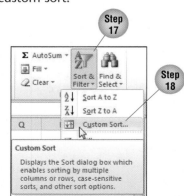

17 Click the Sort & Filter button ![AZ] in the Editing group in the Home tab.

18 Click *Custom Sort* at the drop-down list.

19 At the Sort dialog box, click the down-pointing arrow at the right of *Sort by* in the *Column* section and then click *Column B* at the drop-down list.

> The default entries of *Values* for *Sort On* and *A to Z* for *Order* are correct since you want the cells sorted by the text entries in column B in ascending order.

20 Click OK.

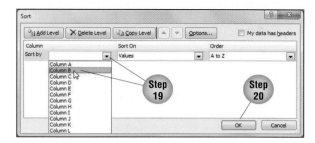

21 Click in any cell to deselect the range. Compare your sorted worksheet to the one shown below.

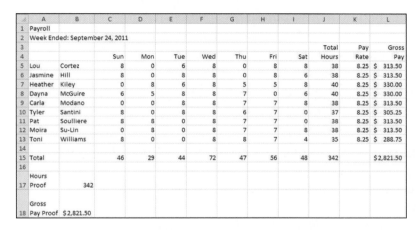

22 Click the Save button on the Quick Access toolbar.

In Addition

Rotating Text in Cells

The Alignment group in the Home tab contains an Orientation button, which can be used to rotate text within cells. Text can be rotated counterclockwise, clockwise, changed to a vertical alignment, rotated up vertically, or rotated down vertically. Often, text set in narrow columns is angled to improve the label appearance. In the screen shown at the right, the cells containing the days of the week in the payroll worksheet are angled counterclockwise.

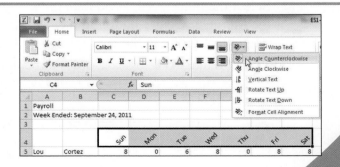

Activity 1.7

Using Help

An extensive online Help resource is available that contains information on Excel features and commands. Click the Microsoft Excel Help button located near the upper right corner of the screen (below the Minimize button on the Title bar) to open the Excel Help window. By default, the Help feature searches for an Internet connection. A message at the bottom right corner of the window will indicate whether Help will display information in Excel resources at Office Online or in the Offline Help file.

Another method to use Help resources is to point to a button in the tab and then press function key F1.

Project

Tutorial 1.4
Sorting Data and Using Help

After reviewing the Payroll worksheet, you think the first two title rows would look better if the text was centered over the columns in the worksheet. You will use the Help feature to look up the steps to do this.

1. With **ES1-WBPayroll.xlsx** open, make A1 the active cell.

   To center the title rows above the columns in the worksheet, you decide to browse the buttons in the Alignment group in the Home tab. The Merge & Center button in the group seems appropriate but you are not sure of the steps to work with this feature.

2. Point to the Merge & Center button in the Alignment group in the Home tab and read the information that displays in the ScreenTip.

3. With the pointer still resting on the Merge & Center button, press function key F1 and then read the paragraphs below the title *Merge cells or split merged cells* in the Excel Help window.

4. Scroll down the Help window, click <u>Merge and center adjacent cells</u> below the subtitle *What do you want to do?* and then read the information describing the steps to merge cells.

5. Close the Excel Help window.

6. Select the range A1:L1 and then click the Merge & Center button in the Alignment group in the Home tab.

   A1 is merged across columns A through L and the text *Payroll* is automatically centered within the merged cell.

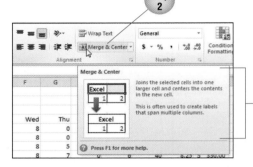

ScreenTip describes what the feature will do and when it might be useful.

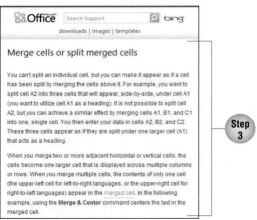

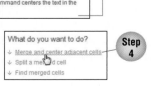

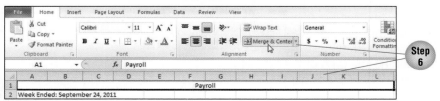

7 Select the range A2:L2 and then click the Merge & Center button.

The two titles in the payroll worksheet are now centered over the cells below them.

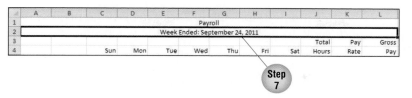

Step 7

8 Click the Microsoft Excel Help button located near the upper right corner of the screen (below the Minimize button on the Title bar).

You can also access Help resources by typing a search phrase and browsing related topics in the Help window.

9 Type **preview worksheet** in the Search text box and then click the Search button or press Enter.

Step 9

10 Click the <u>Preview worksheet pages before printing</u> hyperlink and then read the information that displays in the window.

Step 10

Since Microsoft Office Online is updated frequently, your search results list may vary for this hyperlink, including its title or position in the list.

11 Close the Excel Help window.

12 Click the Save button on the Quick Access toolbar.

In Addition

Using Offline Help

By default Excel checks for a live Internet connection when the Help feature is activated. If no connection is found, Excel displays the Help window shown at the right. Office Online provides additional resources such as online training and templates along with the most up-to-date information. You can disable online Help searches if you want to turn off the online access for reasons similar to the following:

- You are currently experiencing a slow Internet connection.
- You are in a location where you have to pay hourly for Internet access.
- You are away from your normal site and are concerned about privacy.

   Click the down-pointing arrow to the right of the Search button and then click *Excel Help* in the *Content from this computer* section at the drop-down list to temporarily suspend online searches.

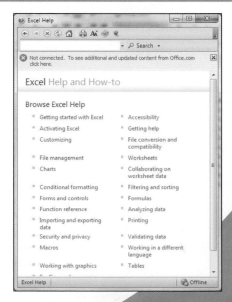

Activity 1.8

Previewing; Changing Page Orientation; Printing a Worksheet

Many times a worksheet is printed to have a paper copy, or **hard copy**, to file or to attach to a report. Large, complex worksheets are often easier to proofread and check from a paper copy. The Quick Print button on the Quick Access toolbar will print the active worksheet using default print options. Display the Print tab in Backstage view to preview the worksheet and modify print options. For example, to change the page orientation while previewing how the worksheet will print, click the File tab and then click the Print tab in Backstage view. A preview of how the worksheet will look when printed displays at the right side of Backstage view. The center of Backstage view is divided into three categories: *Print, Printer,* and *Settings*. Use the galleries available in each category to modify print options. Use Backstage view to preview the worksheet before printing to avoid wasted paper by checking in advance whether the entire worksheet will fit on one page, or to preview and/or change other print options.

Project The Payroll worksheet is finished. You want to preview the worksheet and then print a copy for the office manager.

Tutorial 1.5
Formatting and Printing Options

Tutorial 1.6
Previewing and Printing a Workbook

1 With **ES1-WBPayroll.xlsx** open, make A20 the active cell and then type the student information your instructor has directed for printouts. For example, type your first and last names and then press Enter.

Make sure you have checked if other identifying information such as your program or class number should be included.

2 Click the File tab and then click the Print tab to display the worksheet in Backstage view as shown in Figure 1.2.

FIGURE 1.2 Print Preview Window

Pages indicator shows the worksheet is two pages long.

3 The right side of the view displays the first page of the worksheet as it will print with the current print options. Notice the pages indicator at the bottom left of the preview shows that you are viewing page *1 of 2* pages. Click the Next Page button 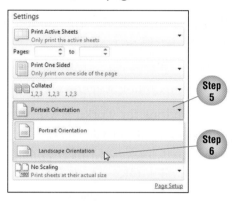 located at the right of the current page number to display page 2.

4 The second page of the printout appears showing the columns that could not fit on page 1.

5 Click the *Page Orientation* gallery (currently displays *Portrait Orientation*) in the *Settings* category of the Print tab.

> One method to reduce the printout to one page is to change the orientation of the paper from portrait to landscape. In **portrait** orientation, the page is printed on paper taller than it is wide. In **landscape** orientation, the data is rotated to print on paper that is wider than it is tall.

6 Click *Landscape Orientation* at the drop-down list.

> The preview updates to show the worksheet in landscape orientation. Notice that all of the columns now fit on one page.

7 Click the Print button located at the top left of the Print tab in the *Print* category.

> Backstage view closes and the worksheet prints on the default printer. The default settings in the Print tab of Backstage view are to print one copy of all pages in the active worksheet. You will learn how to adjust page layout and print settings in a later section.

Your printer name will vary.

8 At the worksheet, scroll right if necessary until you see the vertical dashed line between columns located to the right of the *Gross Pay* column.

> The dashed vertical line is a page break. Page breaks appear after you have previewed or printed a worksheet. A worksheet that spans many rows will display a horizontal dashed line below the last row that can fit on the page. The dashed lines do not print.

9 Click the Save button on the Quick Access toolbar.

In Brief

Preview Worksheet
1. Click File tab.
2. Click Print tab.

Change to Landscape Orientation
1. Click File tab.
2. Click Print tab.
3. Click *Page Orientation* gallery.
4. Click *Landscape Orientation*.

Activity 1.9

Displaying Formulas; Navigating a Worksheet

Sometimes you may want to print a worksheet with the cell formulas displayed rather than the formula results. Printing a second copy of a worksheet with the cell formulas is a good idea when complicated formulas that would take you a long time to redo exist in the worksheet. To display cell formulas, open the Excel Options dialog box from the Backstage view, click the Advanced tab and click the *Show formulas in cells instead of their calculated results* check box in the *Display options for this worksheet* section.

Once a worksheet becomes larger, you will need to scroll to the right or scroll down to locate cells with which you need to work. The horizontal and vertical scroll bars are used to scroll with the mouse. Scrolling using the scroll bars does not move the position of the active cell. You can also scroll using the arrow keys or with keyboard commands. Scrolling using the keyboard moves the active cell.

Project You will print a second copy of the payroll worksheet with the cell formulas displayed and practice navigating the worksheet using the scroll bars and keyboard shortcuts.

1. With **ES1-WBPayroll.xlsx** open, click the File tab to open Backstage view.

2. Click the Options button [Options] located near the bottom of the left pane just above the Exit button.

3. At the Excel Options dialog box, click *Advanced* in the left pane.

4. Scroll down the Advanced options for working with Excel pane until you see the section titled *Display options for this worksheet*.

5. Click the *Show formulas in cells instead of their calculated results* check box to insert a check mark and then click OK.

    The cells in the worksheet are automatically expanded and cells that contain formulas now display the formula in the worksheet area.

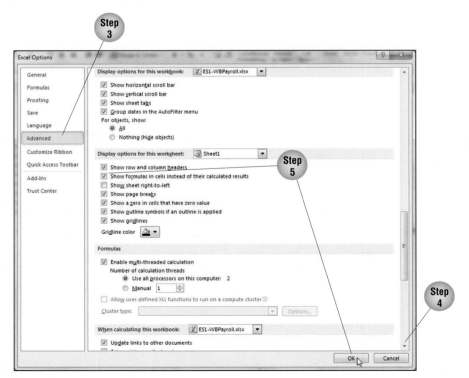

6 Click the File tab, click the Print tab, and then click the Print button to print the worksheet with the cell formulas, or click the Quick Print button on the Quick Access toolbar.

> The worksheet will print on two pages in the expanded cell formulas view. In a later section you will learn how to adjust column widths and scale a worksheet to reduce the number of pages for a wide printout.

7 Position the mouse pointer on the right scroll arrow at the right edge of the horizontal scroll bar and then click the left mouse button a few times to scroll to the right edge of the worksheet.

8 Position the mouse pointer on the horizontal scroll box, hold down the left mouse button, drag the scroll box to the left edge of the horizontal scroll bar, and then release the mouse button.

> The width or height of the scroll box indicates the proportional amount of the used cells in the worksheet that is visible in the current window. The position of the scroll box within the scroll bar indicates the relative location of the visible cells within the remainder of the worksheet.

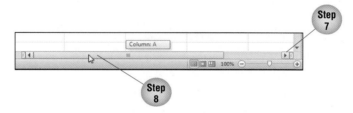

9 Press Ctrl + Home.

> Ctrl + Home makes A1 the active cell.

10 Press the Page Down key once.

> Each time you press the Page Down key you move the active cell down one screen.

11 Press the Page Up key once.

> Each time you press the Page Up key, you move the active cell up one screen.

12 Click the Find & Select button 🔍 in the Editing group in the Home tab and click *Go To* at the drop-down list.

continues

In Brief

Go to Specific Cell
1. Click Find & Select button.
2. Click *Go To.*
3. Type cell address.
4. Click OK.

13 At the Go To dialog box, type **L15** in the *Reference* text box and then click OK or press Enter.

> The active cell is positioned in L15. Notice that using Go To moved the position of the active cell.

14 Use the Up, Down, Left, and Right Arrow keys to practice moving around the worksheet.

> Holding down a directional arrow key causes the screen to scroll very quickly. Table 1.2 illustrates more keyboard scrolling techniques.

15 Click the Save button on the Quick Access toolbar.

16 Click the File tab and then click the Close button in the Backstage view.

TABLE 1.2 Keyboard Movement Commands

Press	To move to
Arrow keys	one cell up, down, left, or right
Ctrl + Home	A1
Ctrl + End	last cell in worksheet
Home	beginning of row
Page Down	down one screen
Page Up	up one screen
Alt + Page Down	one screen to the right
Alt + Page Up	one screen to the left

In Addition

Viewing a Large Worksheet by Splitting the Window

You can split a worksheet into more than one window to facilitate viewing different sections of a large worksheet at the same time. For example, to view the employee names at the left edge of the window and see the formulas to calculate each person's gross pay in column L while the worksheet is displayed with the wide columns in cell formulas, you could split the window vertically as shown below. Each window contains a set of scroll bars to allow you to scroll to different areas within each split section of the worksheet. To split a worksheet into two vertical windows, drag the split box located at the bottom right of the Excel window immediately right of the right scroll arrow in the horizontal scroll bar to the position you want the split to occur. When you rest the pointer on the split box, the pointer changes to a double vertical line with a left- and right-pointing arrow. Drag the split bar back to the right edge of the screen to remove the split. The split box at the top of the vertical scroll bar can be used to create a horizontal split in a worksheet.

	A	B	C	D	E	I	J	K	L
1									
2					Split bar				
3							Total	Pay	Gross
4			Sun	Mon	Tue	Sat	Hours	Rate	Pay
5	Lou	Cortez	8	0	6	8	=SUM(C5:I5)	8.25	=J5*K5
6	Jasmine	Hill	8	0	8	6	=SUM(C6:I6)	8.25	=J6*K6
7	Heather	Kiley	0	8	6	8	=SUM(C7:I7)	8.25	=J7*K7
8	Dayna	McGuire	6	5	8	6	=SUM(C8:I8)	8.25	=J8*K8
9	Carla	Modano	0	0	8	8	=SUM(C9:I9)	8.25	=J9*K9
10	Tyler	Santini	8	0	8	0	=SUM(C10:I10)	8.25	=J10*K10
11	Pat	Soulliere	8	8	0	0	=SUM(C11:I11)	8.25	=J11*K11
12	Moira	Su-Lin	0	8	0	8	=SUM(C12:I12)	8.25	=J12*K12
13	Toni	Williams	8	0	0	4	=SUM(C13:I13)	8.25	=J13*K13
14									
15	Total		=SUM(C5:C14)	=SUM(D5:D14)	=SUM(E5:E14)	=SUM(I5:I14)	=SUM(J5:J14)		=SUM(L5:L14)

Features Summary

Feature	Ribbon Tab, Group	Button	Quick Access Toolbar	File tab	Keyboard Shortcut
Accounting Number format	Home, Number	$			
align text right	Home, Alignment				
cell formulas		Options		Options	Ctrl + ~
close a workbook				Close	Ctrl + F4
copy	Home, Clipboard				Ctrl + C
custom sort	Home, Editing				
fill down	Home, Editing	Fill ▾			Ctrl + D
fill left	Home, Editing	Fill ▾			
fill right	Home, Editing	Fill ▾			Ctrl + R
fill up	Home, Editing	Fill ▾			
Go To	Home, Editing				Ctrl + G
Help		?			F1
merge and center	Home, Alignment				
new workbook				New	Ctrl + N
open				Open	Ctrl + O
paste	Home, Clipboard				Ctrl + V
Print Preview				Print	Ctrl + P
print				Print	Ctrl + P or Ctrl + F2
save			💾	Save	Ctrl + S
save with a new name				Save As	F12
SUM function	Home, Editing	Σ			Alt + =

Knowledge Check

Completion: In the space provided at the right, indicate the correct term, command, or option.

1. This area contains commands and features for performing actions divided into tabs and groups. _____

2. This area displays the formula stored within the cell (not the result). _____

3. The cell pointer changes to this when pointing at the small black square at the bottom right corner of the active cell. _____

4. This would be the formula entry to divide the contents of cell C6 by the contents in cell C12. _____

5. This is the term for the method used to create a formula by typing the equals sign and operator symbols while clicking reference cells between the typed symbols. _____

6. This term is used to refer to the values identified within parentheses in the SUM function. _____

7. The AutoSum button is located in this group in the Home tab. _____

8. Do this action if Excel suggests the wrong range after clicking the AutoSum button. _____

9. This button appears after copied cells are pasted into the destination range. _____

10. This is the term for the formulas entered beside or below a worksheet that are designed to verify the worksheet's accuracy. _____

11. This format adds a dollar sign, a comma in the thousands place, and two decimal places to each value in the selected range. _____

12. Click the Sort & Filter button in the Editing group in the Home tab and then click this option at the drop-down list to display the Sort dialog box. _____

13. This keyboard shortcut will open the Excel Help window when pointing to a button. _____

14. Display this tab in Backstage view to change the page orientation. _____

15. Open this dialog box to type a cell reference to which you want to move the active cell. _____

Skills Review

Note: If you submit your work in hard copy, check with your instructor before completing these reviews to find out if you need to print two copies of each worksheet with one of the copies showing the cell formulas instead of the calculated results.

Review 1 Creating Labels, Values, and Formulas

1. Create a new folder on your storage medium and name it **ExcelEOS**.
2. Create the worksheet shown in Figure 1.3. Use the fill handle whenever possible to facilitate data entry. In rows 8, 13, and 17, press the spacebar twice before typing the cell entry to indent the text.
3. Format E6:H17 to the Accounting Number format.
4. Create the following formulas by typing the entry, using the pointing method, or using the AutoSum button:
   a. In cell E8, subtract Cost of Goods Sold from Sales by entering **=e6-e7**.
   b. In cell E13, add the three expenses by entering **=sum(e10:e12)**.
   c. In cell E15, subtract Total Expenses from Gross Margin by entering **=e8-e13**.
   d. In cell E16, multiply Net Income Before Taxes by 22% by entering **=e15*22%**.
   e. In cell E17, subtract Taxes from Net Income Before Taxes by entering **=e15-e16**.
5. Copy and paste formulas in column E to columns F and G as follows:
   a. Copy the formula in E8 and then paste the formula to the range F8:G8.
   b. Copy the formula in E13 and then paste the formula to the range F13:G13.
   c. Select and copy the range E15:E17 and then paste the formulas to the range F15:G17.
6. Click in cell H6 and then use the AutoSum button to enter the formula to add E6:G6.
7. Copy the formula in H6 to the remaining cells in column H.
8. Save the workbook in the ExcelEOS folder and name it **ES1-R1-WBQtrlyIncome.xlsx**.

FIGURE 1.3 Review 1 Worksheet

	A	B	C	D	E	F	G	H
1	The Waterfront Bistro							
2	Condensed Quarterly Statement of Income							
3	For the Quarter Ended September 30, 2011							
4	In Thousands							
5					Jul	Aug	Sep	Total
6	Sales				51.2	53.7	55.6	
7	Cost of Goods Sold				35.2	44.8	45.7	
8	Gross Margin							
9								
10	Advertising Expense				2.1	2.1	2.1	
11	Wages and Benefits Expense				10.2	9.4	10.6	
12	Miscellaneous and Overhead Expense				1.3	1.3	1.3	
13	Total Expenses							
14								
15	Net Income Before Taxes							
16	Taxes							
17	Net Income After Taxes							

Review 2 Improving the Appearance of the Worksheet; Previewing and Printing

1. With **ES1-R1-WBQtrlyIncome.xlsx** open, merge and center the title in row 1 across columns A through H.
2. Merge and center A2, A3, and A4 across columns A through H.
3. Change the alignment of the range E5:H5 to Align Text Right.
4. Use the Help feature to find out how to display fewer decimal places.
5. Select the range E6:H17 and then decrease the number of decimal places to one decimal place.
6. Deselect the range E6:H17 and then display the worksheet in Backstage view to preview how the worksheet will look when printed.
7. Print the worksheet.
8. Display the worksheet with cell formulas displayed and then print another copy of the worksheet.
9. Clear the option to show formulas in cells.
10. Save and then close **ES1-R1-WBQtrlyIncome.xlsx**.

Skills Assessment

Note: If you submit your work in hard copy, check with your instructor before completing these assessments to find out if you need to print two copies of each worksheet with one of the copies showing the cell formulas instead of the calculated results.

Assessment 1 Adding Values and Formulas to a Worksheet

1. Open **MPTravelCosts.xlsx** and then save the workbook in the ExcelEOS folder and name it **ES1-A1-MPTravelCosts**.
2. This worksheet was started to calculate the travel costs for a remote location film shoot for July 11 to August 31, 2011. Melissa Gehring of First Choice Travel has just confirmed the following costs that you were waiting for to finish the worksheet. All costs are tax included.
   • Airfare to the location and back to Los Angeles airport is $588.15 per person.
   • The hotel is booked for two people per room and will cost $76.20 per room per night.
   • Each person travelling to the location will receive a daily expense allowance of $27.
3. Enter the appropriate values provided above in the *Unit Cost* column in the worksheet.
4. Enter formulas in the required cells in column G to calculate the extended cost. For example, the airfare formula is the quantity times the unit cost, the hotel and daily expense allowance formulas are the quantity times the unit cost times the number of days.
5. Enter the formula in G10 to add the three expense results.
6. Apply alignment and formatting options you learned in this section to any cells that you consider would improve the appearance of the worksheet.
7. Save, print, and then close **ES1-A1-MPTravelCosts.xlsx**.

Assessment 2 Creating a New Workbook

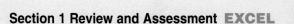

1. You work with Bobbie Sinclair, business manager at Performance Threads. You are preparing a contract quotation for costume rental and alteration fees for costumes needed by Marquee Productions for its remote location film shoot July 11 to August 31, 2011. Create a new workbook that will calculate the contract price using the following information.
   * Seventeen Renaissance period costumes will be provided at a rental cost of $88.50 per day, tax included, for a total of 50 days.
   * A fee of $110.00 per costume, tax included, is charged for alterations provided on site.
2. Make sure the total contract price is summed below the rental and alteration fee calculations.
3. Apply alignment and formatting options you learned in this section to any cells that you consider would improve the appearance of the worksheet.
4. Save the workbook in the ExcelEOS folder and name it **ES1-A2-PTCostumeCont**.
5. Print and then close **ES1-A2-PTCostumeCont.xlsx**.

Assessment 3 Creating a New Workbook

1. You work with Sam Vestering, manager of North American Distribution for Worldwide Enterprises. You are preparing a projected distribution revenue schedule for Marquee Productions' latest film *Going Global*, to be released September 2, 2011. Create a new workbook that will estimate Worldwide's projected revenue using the following information (see Table 1.3 on the next page):
   * Preview cities receive the film on the Friday before the general release date and pay Worldwide Enterprises 15% of projected box office revenues.
   * General release cities pay Worldwide Enterprises 10% of projected box office revenues.
   * All distribution fees and projected revenues are in U.S. dollars.
   * Include a total of the projected revenue for Worldwide Enterprises. *Hint: Consider creating this worksheet by grouping the preview cities and the general release cities separately.*
2. Apply alignment and formatting options you learned in this section to any cells that you consider would improve the appearance of the worksheet.
3. Use the Sort feature to rearrange the order of the cities in ascending order.
4. Save the workbook in the ExcelEOS folder and name it **ES1-A3-WEGGProjRev**.
5. Print and then close **ES1-A3-WEGGProjRev.xlsx**.

TABLE 1.3 Assessment 3

City	Release Category	Projected Box Office Sales in Thousands
New York	Preview	41.9
Tucson	General	15.3
Los Angeles	Preview	47.1
Denver	Preview	19.6
Orlando	General	29.6
Des Moines	General	10.4
Wichita	Preview	11.2
Boston	General	26.9
Philadelphia	General	21.4
Dallas	General	18.7
Milwaukee	General	12.6
Atlanta	Preview	33.1
Vancouver	General	31.7
Calgary	General	15.8
Toronto	Preview	29.2
Montreal	Preview	17.3

Assessment 4 Finding Information on Sorting

1. In Activity 1.6 you learned how to sort the employee names in the payroll worksheet using the Sort dialog box. There are other methods with which you can sort a worksheet. Use Excel Help to find out more ways you can sort data in Excel.
2. Open **WBInventory.xlsx** and then save the workbook with Save As in the ExcelEOS folder and name it **ES1-A4-WBInventory**.
3. Sort the worksheet in ascending order by the *Item* column.
4. Print the worksheet.
5. Sort the worksheet in ascending order by the *Supplier Name* column.
6. Print the worksheet.
7. Save and then close **ES1-A4-WBInventory.xlsx**.

Assessment 5 Individual Challenge
Creating a School Budget

1. Create a worksheet to calculate the estimated total cost of completing your diploma or certificate. You determine the items that need to be included in the worksheet such as tuition, fees, textbooks, supplies, accommodation costs, transportation, telephone, food, and entertainment. If necessary, use the Internet to find reasonable cost estimates if you want to include an item such as cell phone charges and want to research competitive rates for your area. Arrange the labels and values by quarter, semester, or academic year according to your preference. Make sure to include a total that shows the total cost of your education.
2. Save the worksheet in the ExcelEOS folder and name it **ES1-A5-SchoolBudget**.

3. Apply alignment and formatting options you learned in this section to any cells that you consider would improve the appearance of the worksheet.
4. If necessary, change the page orientation to landscape and then print the worksheet.
5. Save and then close **ES1-A5-SchoolBudget.xlsx**.

Marquee Challenge

Challenge 1 Preparing an International Student Registration Report

1. You work at Niagara Peninsula College in the Registrar's Office. The Registrar has asked you to create the annual report for international student registrations. Create the worksheet shown in Figure 1.4.
2. Calculate the tuition fees in column I by multiplying the credit hours times the fee per hour and then use the SUM function to calculate the total international student fees.
3. Apply format options as shown and format the values in column I to an appropriate number format.
4. Add the current date and your name in rows 4 and 19, respectively.
5. Change the page orientation to landscape.
6. Save the workbook in the ExcelEOS folder and name it **ES1-C1-NPCIntlRegRpt**.
7. Print and then close **ES1-C1-NPCIntlRegRpt.xlsx**.

FIGURE 1.4 Challenge 1

	A	B	C	D	E	F	G	H	I
1				Niagara Peninsula College					
2				International Student Registrations					
3				for the 2011/2012 Academic Year					
4				Report Date: (Current Date)					
5		Last	First	Home			Credit	Fee per	Tuition
6	ID #	Name	Name	Country	Program	Semester	Hours	Hour	Fee
7	241588	Cano	Sergio	Spain	BIS11	1	45	432	
8	241578	Flannigan	Maren	Ireland	BIS11	1	60	432	
9	241856	Chou	Terry	China	BMK12	1	45	432	
10	286953	Zhang	Joseph	China	BIN32	2	45	432	
11	274586	Alivero	Maria	Mexico	CMP12	2	45	432	
12	268451	Torres	Phillip	Ecuador	CTN14	2	60	432	
13	234851	Davis	Caitlyn	Australia	OAM24	3	60	432	
14	299635	Muir	Christa	Australia	GRD13	4	30	432	
15	247523	North	Marlo	Bahamas	HTC24	2	30	432	
16	277458	Cervinka	Mary	Croatia	TTM14	4	30	432	
17									
18					TOTAL INTERNATIONAL STUDENT FEES:				
19	Prepared by: (Student Name)								

Challenge 2 Preparing a Theatre Arts Target Enrollment Report

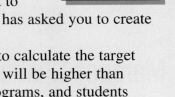

1. You work with Cal Rubine, chair of the Theatre Arts division at Niagara Peninsula College. Cal needs the target student enrollment report to assist with the revenue projections for the upcoming budget. Cal has asked you to create the worksheet shown in Figure 1.5.
2. Cal uses the actual enrollments from the prior year (2010/2011) to calculate the target for the next year. In some programs, Cal expects that enrollment will be higher than the previous year due to new registrants, transfers from other programs, and students returning to pick up missed credits. In other programs, Cal expects that enrollment will decline from the previous year due to students dropping the program, transfers to other colleges, and students failing to meet the minimum GPA for progression. Cal has provided the percentages in Table 1.4 for you to use to create the formulas in the *Target* column.
3. Use the SUM function to calculate the total target estimated enrollments.
4. Apply alignment options as shown and add the current date and your name in rows 8 and 9, respectively.
5. If necessary, format the values in the *Target* column to zero decimal places and then change the page orientation to landscape.
6. Save the workbook in the ExcelEOS folder and name it **ES1-C2-NPCTargetEnrolRpt**.
7. Print and then close **ES1-C2-NPCTargetEnrolRpt.xlsx**.

FIGURE 1.5 Challenge 2

	A	B	C	D	E	F	G	H	I	J
1					Niagara Peninsula College					
2					Target Student Enrollments					
3					For the 2012/2013 Academic Year					
4					Theatre Arts Division					
5										
6	Academic chair: Cal Rubine									
7										
8	Report date: (current date)									
9	Prepared by: (student name)						Actual			
10					Program	Semester		Enrollment		
11	Program Name				Code	Offering		2010/2011		Target
12	Theatre Arts: Acting				TAA12	1 2 3 4		210		
13	Theatre Arts: Stage Management				TAM23	1 2		55		
14	Theatre Arts: Lighting & Effects				TAL42	1 2		67		
15	Theatre Arts: Production				TAP32	1 2 3 4		221		
16	Theatre Arts: Sound				TAS14	1 2		38		
17	Theatre Arts: Business Management				TAB25	1 2 3 4		64		
18										
19					ESTIMATED ENROLLMENTS FOR 2012/2013:					

TABLE 1.4 Challenge 2

Program Name	Target Percent
Theatre Arts: Acting	95%
Theatre Arts: Stage Management	106%
Theatre Arts: Lighting & Effects	112%
Theatre Arts: Production	85%
Theatre Arts: Sound	103%
Theatre Arts: Business Management	75%

Excel SECTION 2

Editing and Formatting Worksheets

Skills

- Edit the content of cells
- Clear cells and cell formats
- Use proofing tools
- Insert and delete columns and rows
- Move and copy cells
- Use Paste Options to link cells
- Adjust column width and row height
- Change the font, size, style, and color of cells
- Apply numeric formats and adjust the number of decimal places
- Use Undo, Redo, and Repeat
- Change cell alignment and indentation
- Add borders and shading
- Copy formats using Format Painter
- Apply cell styles
- Apply a theme
- Find and replace cell entries and formats
- Freeze and unfreeze panes
- Change the zoom percentage
- Insert, move, and resize pictures and clip art

Projects Overview

Edit and format a quotation and invoice for catering services. View and edit a special events booking worksheet.

Create a direct wages budget for a remote film shoot.

Complete and format a costume cost report and an invoice for costume production.

Create a room timetable.

Edit and format a revenue summary report for movie distribution.

Model Answers for Projects

These model answers for the projects that you complete in Section 2 provide a preview of the finished projects before you begin working and also allow you to compare your own results with these models to ensure you have created the materials accurately.

ES2-WBQuoteToMP.xlsx is the project in Activities 2.1 to 2.9.

The Waterfront Bistro

3104 Rivermist Drive
Buffalo, NY 14280
716 555 3166

Quotation

TO: Marquee Productions
955 South Alameda Street
Los Angeles, CA 90037

DATE: 5-Nov-10

ATT: Camille Matsui

RE: Remote Location Filming
July 11 to August 31

Note: All prices include tax.

Item	No. of Persons	Price per Person	No. of Days	Total
Buffet Lunch	56	8.34	52	$ 24,286.08
Soup and salad				
Vegetable tray with dip				
Seafood hors d'oeuvres				
Hot entrée				
Deli tray and rolls				
Dessert				
Beverages	56	3.91	52	11,385.92
Coffee and tea				
Assorted juice				
Mineral water				
Snacks	56	3.91	52	11,385.92
Muffins				
Donuts				
Fruit tray				
Vegetable tray with dip				
Transport		33.00	52	1,716.00
Total				$ 48,773.92

Terms: Due upon receipt of invoice payable in U.S. funds

ES2-WBSpecEvents.xlsx is the project in Activities 2.10 to 2.12.

The Waterfront Bistro
2011 Special Event Bookings

Contact Name	Contact Phone	Event	Date	Room	Guests	Special Menu	Price Per Person
Cecily Hillmore	716 555 6598	Business Meeting	1/15/2011	Starlake	42	No	23.95
Frances Corriveau	716 555 3256	Birthday Party	1/23/2011	Westview	82	Yes	29.95
Orlando Fagan	716 555 3694	25th Wedding Anniversary	3/10/2011	Westview	95	Yes	29.95
Kim Pockovic	905 555 3698	Birthday Party	3/18/2011	Westview	65	Yes	36.95
Lane Gill	416 555 3264	Business Meeting	3/29/2011	Starlake	55	No	22.95
Percy Bresque	716 555 1248	50th Wedding Anniversary	4/12/2011	Westview	102	Yes	35.95
Max Santore	905 555 3264	Wedding	4/28/2011	Sunset	188	Yes	27.95
Omar Hamid	716 555 8796	Engagement Party	5/8/2011	Sunset	67	Yes	29.95
Jack Torrance	716 555 1469	Business Meeting	5/15/2011	Westview	34	No	24.95
Dana Russell	716 555 4965	Birthday Party	5/30/2011	Starlake	54	No	28.95
Walter Szucs	905 555 6998	Birthday Party	6/10/2011	Starlake	84	No	34.95
Nicole Griffin	905 555 4166	25th Wedding Anniversary	6/17/2011	Starlake	78	Yes	34.95
Zack Doucet	716 555 3488	Wedding	6/20/2011	Sunset	215	Yes	29.95
Jesse Golinsky	716 555 4218	Business Meeting	6/26/2011	Westview	60	No	25.95
Cora Jin Ping	716 555 7774	Baby Shower	7/10/2011	Sunset	75	Yes	22.95
Elizabeth McMaster	716 555 9442	Engagement Party	7/11/2011	Sunset	94	Yes	28.95
Reed Pavelich	716 555 2286	Wedding	7/25/2011	Starlake	145	Yes	34.95
Alfredo Juanitez	716 555 4668	Business Meeting	7/31/2011	Westview	37	No	24.95
Yanfang Guo	716 555 4856	50th Wedding Anniversary	8/10/2011	Starlake	62	No	34.95
Jelena Boskovic	716 555 3456	Business Meeting	8/18/2011	Westview	27	Yes	29.95
Priscilla Melo	716 555 3145	Business Meeting	8/25/2011	Westview	34	Yes	25.95
Tracie McIntyre	716 555 3496	Birthday Party	9/2/2011	Sunset	26	No	22.95
Krista Pressey	716 555 7469	50th Wedding Anniversary	9/5/2011	Sunset	95	No	28.95
Langford Hill	716 555 8798	Wedding	9/25/2011	Starlake	185	No	34.95
Naomi Sayers	905 555 3486	Wedding	10/15/2011	Starlake	245	Yes	24.95
Lesley Reedman	716 555 4123	Wedding	10/22/2011	Westview	110	Yes	34.95
Mitchell Langley	905 555 4637	Wedding	11/19/2011	Sunset	85	Yes	29.95
Sally Ramirez	716 555 9648	Engagement Party	12/5/2011	Starlake	34	No	25.95
Paulina Ordonez	905 555 1435	25th Wedding Anniversary	12/10/2011	Westview	45	No	22.95
Arietta Teneqja	905 555 1345	Business Meeting	12/15/2011	Sunset	67	Yes	28.95
Subrein El-Keri	416 555 9765	Engagement Party	12/18/2011	Westview	47	Yes	34.95
Edwina Blakely	716 555 3477	Birthday Party	12/20/2011	Westview	65	No	24.95
Laura Fernandez	416 555 1345	Shareholders Meeting	12/28/2011	Westview	194	No	39.95

Activity 2.1

Editing and Clearing Cells; Using Proofing Tools

The contents of a cell can be edited directly within the cell or in the Formula bar. Clearing a cell can involve removing the cell contents, format, or both. The Spelling feature is a useful tool to assist with correcting typing errors within a worksheet. After completing a spelling check, you will still need to proofread the worksheet since the spelling checker will not highlight all errors and cannot check the accuracy of values. Other Proofing tools available include a Research feature to search for external information, a Thesaurus to find a word with similar meaning, and a Translate tool to translate a selected word into a different language.

Project

Dana Hirsch, manager of The Waterfront Bistro, has begun a catering services quotation for Marquee Productions. Dana has asked you to finish the quotation by correcting spelling, following up on costs, and improving the appearance. You will be working on this quotation through most of this section.

SNAP

Tutorial 2.1
Editing Cells and Using Proofing Tools

1. Open **WBQuoteToMP.xlsx**. *Note: This worksheet contains intentional spelling errors that will be corrected in this activity.*

2. Save the workbook with Save As in the ExcelS2 folder and name it **ES2-WBQuoteToMP**.

3. Double-click D18.

   Double-clicking a cell inserts a blinking insertion point in the cell; Edit appears in the Status bar. The insertion point position varies depending on the location of the cell pointer when Edit mode is activated.

4. Press the Right or Left Arrow key as needed to move the insertion point between the decimal point and *7* and then press the Delete key.

5. Type **3** and then press Enter.

6. Make D30 the active cell.

7. Move the pointer after *7* in the Formula bar and then click the left mouse button.

   The cell pointer changes to an I-beam pointer I when positioned in the Formula bar.

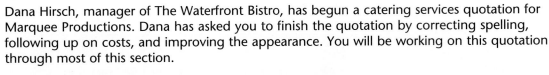

8. Press Backspace to delete *7*, type **4**, and then click the Enter button on the Formula bar.

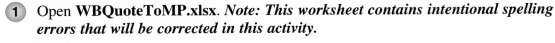

9. Make A7 the active cell and then press Delete.

   Delete or Backspace clears only the contents of the cell; formats or comments applied to the cell remain in effect.

10. Make A1 the active cell and then press Delete.

    Notice the text is deleted from the cell but the color in the background of the cell remains.

11. Select the range A1:C1. Click the Clear button in the Editing group in the Home tab and then click *Clear All* at the drop-down list.

    Clear All removes everything from a cell, including formats or comments.

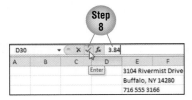

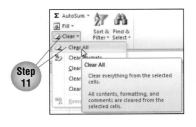

12 Click A1, click the Review tab, and then click the Spelling button .

Spell check begins at the active cell. Words within the worksheet that are not found in the dictionary are highlighted as potential errors. Use buttons in the Spelling dialog box to skip the word (Ignore Once or Ignore All), replace the word with the highlighted word in the *Suggestions* list box (Change), or add the word to the dictionary (Add to Dictionary) if spelled correctly.

13 Click the Ignore All button in the Spelling dialog box to skip all occurrences of *Rivermist* in the worksheet since the street name is spelled correctly.

14 Click the Change button in the Spelling dialog box to replace *Remoat* with *Remote*.

15 Click the Change button in the Spelling dialog box to replace *Persns* with *Persons*.

16 Complete the spell check, changing words as required. Click OK at the message that the spelling check is complete for the entire sheet.

Double-click the correct spelling in the *Suggestions* list box if the correct word is not initially selected. Click in the *Not in Dictionary* text box if the correct spelling is not in the list, edit as required, and then click Change. You can drag the Spelling dialog box out of the way if you need to see the selected word within the worksheet.

17 Make A36 the active cell.

18 Click the Thesaurus button in the Proofing group in the Review tab.

Use the Thesaurus to replace a word in the worksheet with another word of similar meaning. Thesaurus is a feature within the Research task pane.

19 Point to the word *Transport* in the task pane word list, click the down-pointing arrow that appears, and then click *Insert* at the drop-down list.

The word *Delivery* is replaced with *Transport* in A36.

20 Click the Close button at the top right of the Research task pane.

21 Save **ES2-WBQuoteToMP.xlsx**.

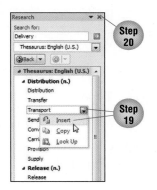

In Brief

Edit Cell
1. Double-click cell.
2. Insert and/or delete text.
3. Press Enter or click another cell.

Clear Cell
1. Click Clear button in Home tab.
2. Click *Clear All, Clear Formats, Clear Contents,* or *Clear Comments.*

Spell Check
1. Click Review tab.
2. Click Spelling button.
3. Click Ignore Once, Ignore All, Change, or Add to Dictionary as required.

In Addition

Research Task Pane

You can use the Research task pane to search for information online without leaving the worksheet. For example, you can conduct an Internet search, look up information in online encyclopedias or business reference sites, or find a current stock quote using MSN Money Stock Quote. Choose the online source by clicking the down-pointing arrow at the right of the *Resources* list box (located below the *Search for* text box).

Activity 2.2

Inserting and Deleting Columns and Rows

Insert rows or columns using options from the Insert button in the Home tab or from the context-sensitive shortcut menu that displays when you right-click a selected area. Inserted rows are placed above the active cell or selected rows and existing rows are shifted down. Columns are inserted left of the active cell or selected columns and existing columns are shifted right. When rows or columns are deleted, data automatically is shifted up or left to fill space and relative references in formulas are updated.

Project You will add items to and delete items from the quotation by inserting and deleting rows and columns.

Tutorial 2.2
Inserting, Adjusting, and Deleting Rows and Columns

1 With **ES2-WBQuoteToMP.xlsx** open, position the cell pointer (displays as a right-pointing black arrow ➡) over row indicator *21*, hold down the left mouse button, drag the mouse down over *22*, and then release the mouse.

> This selects rows 21 and 22. Inserted rows are placed *above* the selected rows and columns are inserted to the *left*.

2 Click the Home tab, click the Insert button arrow in the Cells group, and then click *Insert Sheet Rows* at the drop-down list.

> Two blank rows are inserted. All rows below the inserted rows are shifted down.

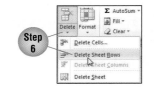

3 Click A21, type **Vegetable tray with dip**, and then press Enter.

4 Type **Seafood hors d'oeuvres** and then press Enter.

5 Make active any cell in row 29.

6 Click the Delete button arrow in the Cells group and then click *Delete Sheet Rows* at the drop-down list.

> The data in row *29* is removed from the worksheet. All rows below the deleted row shift up to fill in the space.

7 Right-click row 19 to display the shortcut menu and Mini toolbar and then click *Delete*.

Mini toolbar

8 Right-click row 26 to display the shortcut menu and Mini toolbar and then click *Delete*.

9 Delete row 30 from the worksheet.

10 Position the cell pointer over column indicator letter *F* (displays as a down-pointing black arrow ↓), right-click the mouse, and then click *Delete* at the shortcut menu.

> Data in columns to the right of the deleted column are shifted left to fill in the space.

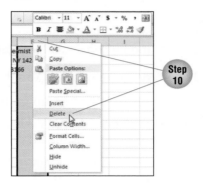

In Brief

Insert Rows or Columns
1. Select required number of rows or columns.
2. Click Insert button arrow.
3. Click *Insert Sheet Rows* or *Insert Sheet Columns*.

Delete Rows or Columns
1. Select rows or columns to be deleted.
2. Click Delete button arrow.
3. Click *Delete Sheet Rows* or *Delete Sheet Columns*.

11 Click in any cell to deselect the column.

12 Make F8 the active cell, type **November 5, 2010**, and then press Enter.

> By default, Excel displays dates in the format *dd-mmm-yy* (5-Nov-10).

13 Save **ES2-WBQuoteToMP.xlsx**.

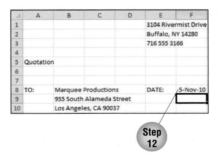

In Addition

Inserting and Deleting Cells

In this activity, you selected entire rows and columns before inserting or deleting. This practice is the more common method when you need to add to or delete data from a worksheet. Another method used less frequently is to insert new blank cells or delete a range of cells within the worksheet area. To insert new blank cells, select the range of cells you need to add and then click the Insert button in the Cells group, or click the Insert button arrow and then click *Insert Cells* at the drop-down list to display the dialog box shown at the right. Using the

dialog box, you can choose to shift existing cells right or down. Click the Delete button in the Cells group to delete a selected range of cells and shift up the cells below the deleted range. Click the Delete button arrow and then click *Delete Cells* to open the Delete dialog box with options similar to those for Insert.

Activity 2.3

Moving and Copying Cells

You learned how to use copy and paste to copy formulas in the payroll worksheet for The Waterfront Bistro. You can also use cut and paste to move the contents of a cell or range of cells to another location in the worksheet. The selected cells being cut or copied are called the *source*. The cell or range of cells that is receiving the source data is called the *destination*. If data already exists in the destination cells, Excel replaces the contents. Cells cut or copied to the Clipboard can be pasted more than once in the active workbook, in another workbook, or in another Office application.

Project

Continue to work on the catering quotation by moving text in the quotation, duplicating a price, linking cells containing prices, and by copying a food item description.

Tutorial 2.3
Moving and Copying Cells

1. With **ES2-WBQuoteToMP.xlsx** open, make A38 the active cell.

2. Click the Cut button in the Clipboard group in the Home tab.

   A moving marquee surrounds the source after you use Cut or Copy, indicating the cell contents have been placed in the Clipboard.

3. Make E15 the active cell and then click the Paste button in the Clipboard group. (Do not click the down-pointing arrow on the Paste button because this displays a drop-down list of Paste options.)

   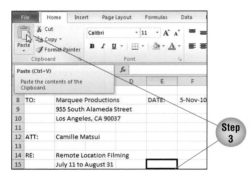

   The text *Note: All prices include tax.* is removed from A38 and placed in E15. In the next step, you will move a range of cells using a method called *drag and drop*.

4. Select the range A14:B15.

   You are only selecting to column B since the entries *Remote Location Filming* and *July 11 to August 31* are stored in B14 and B15, respectively.

5. Point at any one of the four borders surrounding the selected range.

   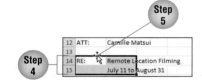

   When you point at a border, the pointer changes from the thick white cross to a white arrow with the move icon attached to it (four-headed arrow).

6. Hold down the left mouse button, drag the top left corner of the range to E12, and then release the mouse.

   A gray border will appear as you drag, indicating the placement of the range when you release the mouse. The destination range displays in a ScreenTip below the gray border.

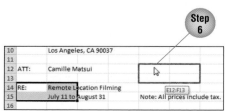

7 Make D25 the active cell.

8 Click the Copy button 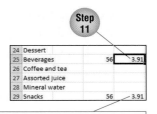 in the Clipboard group.

9 Make D29 the active cell, click the Paste button arrow in the Clipboard group, and then click the Paste Link button in the *Other Paste Options* section of the Paste gallery.

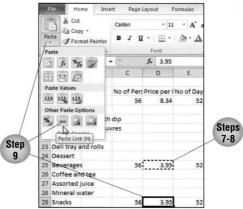

> The existing data in D29 is replaced with the value copied from D25 and the source and destination cells are now linked.
> Linking the cells means that any change made to the source cell (D25) will automatically be applied to the destination cell (D29). A Paste Options button appears next to the destination cell (D29). Click the button to return to the Paste Options gallery if you want to choose another paste option. See the In Addition section at the bottom of the page for more information on paste options.

10 Press Esc to remove the moving marquee from D25 and the Paste Options button near D29.

11 Make D25 the active cell and edit the value to *3.91*.

> Notice the value in D29 is also changed to 3.91 automatically.

D29 changes automatically since the two cells are linked.

12 Make A20 the active cell. Point at any one of the four borders surrounding A20 until the pointer displays as a white arrow with the move icon attached to it, hold down the Ctrl key, and then drag the mouse to A33.

13 Release the mouse button first and then release the Ctrl key.

> A plus sign attached to the pointer indicates the source contents are being *copied* when you drag and drop using the Ctrl key.

14 Save **ES2-WBQuoteToMP.xlsx**.

In Brief

Move or Copy Cells
1. Select source cells.
2. Click Cut or Copy button.
3. Select starting destination cell.
4. Click Paste button.

Copy and Link Cells
1. Select source cells.
2. Click Copy button.
3. Select destination cell.
4. Click Paste button arrow.
5. Click Paste Link button.

In Addition

Paste Options Gallery

The Paste Options gallery (shown at the right) appears in three places: the Paste button arrow in the Clipboard group, the Paste Options button that appears after an entry has been pasted into a cell, or the right-click shortcut menu. The gallery is divided into three sections: *Paste*, *Paste Values*, and *Other Paste Options*. Within each section buttons are included for various paste options. Hover the mouse over a button in the gallery to view a ScreenTip that describes the button's purpose as well as to see a preview of the paste option applied to the cell in the worksheet. The Paste Options gallery is context sensitive, meaning the buttons that appear are dependent on the type of content that has been copied and the location in which the content is being pasted.

Activity 2.4

Adjusting Column Width and Row Height; Using AutoFit

By default, columns are all the same width and rows are all the same height with columns set by default to a width of 8.43 characters (64 pixels) and rows to a height of 15 points (20 pixels). In some cases you do not have to increase the width when the text is too wide for the column, since labels "spill over" into the next cell if it is empty. Some column headings in the quotation are truncated because an entry exists in the column immediately to the right. Excel automatically adjusts the height of rows to accommodate the size of the text within the cells. Manually increasing the row height adds more space between rows, which can be used to improve readability or as a design technique to draw attention to a series of cells.

Project

Tutorial 2.2
Inserting, Adjusting, and Deleting Rows and Columns

You will widen the columns in which labels are truncated to make sure each entry is entirely visible to readers and increase the height of the row containing the column headings to make them stand out from the text below.

1. With **ES2-WBQuoteToMP.xlsx** open, make any cell in column A the active cell.

2. Click the Format button in the Cells group in the Home tab and then click *Column Width* at the drop-down list.

3. At the Column Width dialog box, type **14** and then click OK or press Enter.

   In the next step, you will adjust the width of column D using the mouse.

4. Position the mouse pointer on the boundary line in the column indicator row between columns D and E until the pointer changes to a vertical line with a left- and right-pointing arrow ↔.

5. Hold down the left mouse button, drag the boundary line to the right until *Width: 15.00 (110 pixels)* displays in the ScreenTip, and then release the mouse button.

   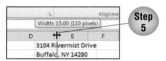

   As you drag the boundary line to the right or left, a dotted line appears in the column in the worksheet area, indicating the new width. If, after decreasing a column's width, cells that previously had values in them now display as a series of pound symbols (######), the column is now too narrow. Widen the column to redisplay the values.

6. Position the mouse pointer on the boundary line in the column indicator row between columns C and D until the pointer changes to a vertical line with a left- and right-pointing arrow and then double-click the left mouse button.

   Double-clicking the boundary line sets the width to fit the length of the longest entry within the column, referred to as *AutoFit*.

7. Make E17 the active cell, click the Format button in the Cells group, and then click *AutoFit Column Width* at the drop-down list.

   AutoFit Column Width adjusts the width of the column to accommodate the amount of text in the active cell. After reviewing the worksheet, you decide all of the columns with numeric values should be the same width. In the next steps, you will learn how to set the width of multiple columns in one operation.

8 Position the mouse pointer on column indicator letter *C*, hold down the left mouse button, and then drag the mouse right to column F.

> This selects columns C through F.

9 Position the mouse pointer on the right boundary line for column E within the selected range of columns until the pointer changes to a vertical line with a left- and right-pointing arrow.

> Any changes made to the width of one column boundary will affect all of the selected columns.

10 Drag the boundary line right until *Width: 15.00 (110 pixels)* displays in the ScreenTip and then release the mouse button.

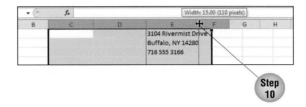

Step 10

11 Click in any cell to deselect the columns.

> Do not be concerned that the columns are now too wide after this step—you have many formatting tasks to complete that will improve the layout as you work through the next few activities.

12 Move E12:F13 to A14:B15 and then click in any cell to deselect the range. Refer to Activity 2.3 if you need assistance with this step.

> In the next steps, you will adjust row height using the mouse.

13 Position the mouse pointer on the boundary line below row 17 until the pointer changes to a horizontal line with an up- and down-pointing arrow ✛ .

14 Drag the boundary line down until *Height: 21.00 (28 pixels)* displays in the ScreenTip and then release the mouse button.

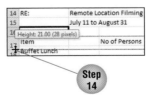

Step 14

15 Save **ES2-WBQuoteToMP.xlsx**.

In Addition

Row Height Dialog Box

A sequence of steps similar to the one used for adjusting column width using the Column Width dialog box can be used to increase or decrease the height of a row with the Row Height dialog box, shown at the right. Click any cell within the row, click the Format button in the Cells group in  the Home tab, and then click *Row Height* at the drop-down list. Type the desired height and press Enter or click OK.

In Brief

Increase or Decrease Column Width
1. Select column(s).
2. Click Format button in Cells group.
3. Click *Column Width*.
4. Type desired width.
5. Click OK.

Increase or Decrease Row Height
1. Select row(s).
2. Click Format button in Cells group.
3. Click *Row Height*.
4. Type desired height.
5. Click OK.

Adjust Width or Height Using Mouse
Drag boundary to right of column or below row, or double-click boundary to AutoFit.

Activity 2.5

Changing the Font, Size, Style, and Color of Cells

The *font* is the typeface used to display and print data. The default font in Excel is Calibri, but several other fonts are available. The size of the font is measured in units called *points*. A point is approximately 1/72 of an inch measured vertically. The default font size used by Excel is 11-point. The larger the point size, the larger the type. Each font's style can be enhanced to **bold**, *italic*, or ***bold italic***. Cell entries display in black with a white background. Changing the color of the font and/or the color of the background (called *fill*) adds interest or emphasis to the cell entry.

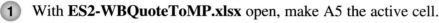

Project To add to the visual appeal of the quotation, you will change the font and font size and apply attributes such as font and fill color to the title *Quotation*.

Tutorial 2.4
Applying Formatting to Cell Contents; Using Undo and Redo; Changing Alignment

① With **ES2-WBQuoteToMP.xlsx** open, make A5 the active cell.

② Click the Font button arrow in the Font group in the Home tab, scroll down the list of fonts, and then point to *Book Antiqua* at the drop-down gallery. Notice that Excel applies the font you are pointing at to the active cell so that you can preview the result. This feature is called ***Live Preview***. Click *Book Antiqua* at the drop-down gallery.

Live Preview shows you how the cell will look before you choose the font so you can try different font options before making your selection.

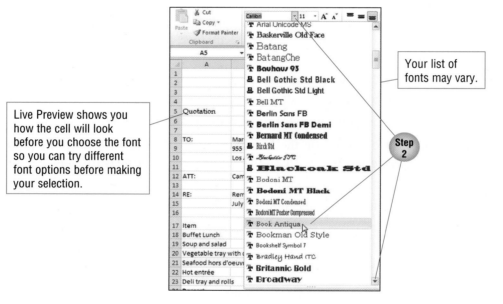

Your list of fonts may vary.

Step 2

③ Click the Font Size button arrow in the Font group and then click *18* at the drop-down list.

The row height is automatically increased to accommodate the larger type size.

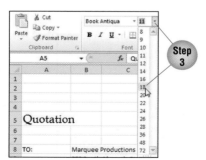

Step 3

4 With A5 still the active cell, click the Font Color button arrow in the Font group and then click the Blue color box (third from right) in the *Standard Colors* section of the color gallery.

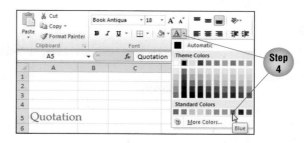

5 Select A5:F5 and then click the Merge & Center button in the Alignment group.

> The cells in the range A5:F5 have now been merged into one large cell that spans across the six columns. The text within A5, *Quotation*, is now centered within this large cell. As you learned in Section 1, Merge & Center centers titles over multiple columns.

6 With merged cell A5 still selected, click the Fill Color button arrow in the Font group and then click the *Aqua, Accent 5, Lighter 80%* color box (second from right in second row) in the *Theme Colors* section of the color gallery.

> *Fill* is the color of the background in the cell. Changing the fill color is sometimes referred to as *shading* a cell.

7 Make F36 the active cell.

8 Click the Bold button **B** and the Italic button *I* in the Font group.

9 Save **ES2-WBQuoteToMP.xlsx**.

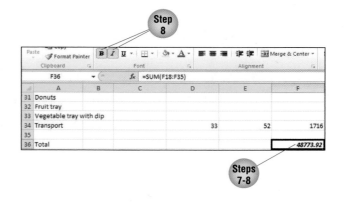

In Brief

Change Font
1. Select cells.
2. Click Font button arrow.
3. Click desired font.
4. Deselect cells.

Change Font Size
1. Select cells.
2. Click Font Size button arrow.
3. Click desired size.
4. Deselect cells.

Change Font Attributes
1. Select cells.
2. Click desired attribute button.
3. Deselect cells.

In Addition

Format Cells Dialog Box

You can use the Format Cells dialog box with the Font tab selected (shown at the right) to change the font, font size, font style, and color of text. Additional Underline style options such as *Single, Double, Single Accounting,* and *Double Accounting* are available, as well as special effects options *Strikethrough, Superscript,* and *Subscript.* Select the cells you want to change and then click the Font group dialog box launcher button to open the Format Cells dialog box with the Font tab active.

Activity 2.6

Formatting Numeric Cells; Adjusting Decimal Places; Using Undo and Redo

In the payroll worksheet for The Waterfront Bistro, you learned how to format numeric cells to the Accounting Number Format which adds a dollar symbol ($), comma in the thousands, and two decimal places and displays negative values in brackets. Other numeric formats include Comma, Percent, and Currency. By default, cells are initially set to the General format which has no specific numeric style. The number of decimal places in a selected range of cells can be increased or decreased using the Increase Decimal and Decrease Decimal buttons in the Number group of the Home tab.

Use the Undo button on the Quick Access toolbar to reverse the last action. Excel stores up to 100 actions that can be undone or redone and you can repeat actions as many times as you need. Some actions (such as Save) cannot be reversed with Undo.

Project
To display a consistent number of characters for the numeric values, you will apply the Accounting Number and Comma formats to selected ranges within the quotation.

Tutorial 2.4
Applying Formatting to Cell Contents; Using Undo and Redo; Changing Alignment

1. With **ES2-WBQuoteToMP.xlsx** open, make F18 the active cell.

2. Hold down the Ctrl key and click F36.

3. Click the Accounting Number Format button $ in the Number group in the Home tab.

4. Click in any cell to deselect the cells.

5. Select F25:F34.

6. Click the Comma Style button , in the Number group.

   Comma Style formats cells the same as the Accounting Number format with the exception of the dollar or alternative currency symbol.

7. Click in any cell to deselect the range and review the numeric values in the worksheet. Notice that column D could be improved by applying a format option to the cell that is not showing the same number of decimal places as other values in the column.

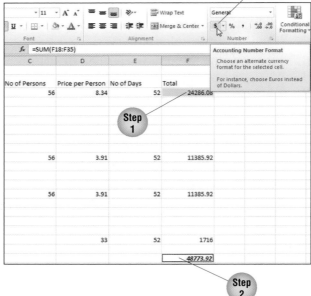

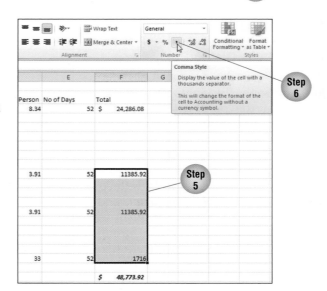

8 Make D34 the active cell.

9 Click the Increase Decimal button in the Number group.

> One decimal place is added to or removed from the cells in the selected range each time you click Increase Decimal or Decrease Decimal.

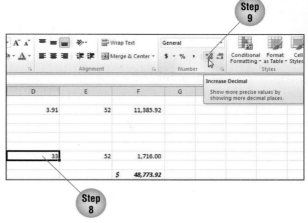

Step 9

Increase Decimal
Show more precise values by showing more decimal places.

Step 8

10 With D34 still selected, click the Increase Decimal button again.

> The value now displays as *33.00* which is consistent with the number of decimal places for the other values in column D.

11 Select F18:F36 and then click the Decrease Decimal button twice in the Number group.

12 Click in any cell to deselect the range.

13 Click the Undo button on the Quick Access toolbar.

> Excel reselects the range and restores one decimal place.

14 Click the Undo button a second time.

> Both decimal places are now restored. With the Undo button arrow, you can display a drop-down list of actions from which you can undo multiple actions in one step.

15 Click the Redo button on the Quick Access toolbar two times.

> Both decimal places are removed again from the selected range.

16 Restore the two decimal places by either clicking the Undo button twice or clicking the Increase Decimal button twice.

17 Click in any cell to deselect the range.

18 Save **ES2-WBQuoteToMP.xlsx**.

In Brief

Change Numeric Format
1. Select cells.
2. Click desired format style button in Number group.
3. Deselect cells.

Undo Action
Click Undo button on Quick Access toolbar or press Ctrl + Z.

Redo Action
Click Redo button on Quick Access toolbar or press Ctrl + Y.

In Addition

Additional Number Format Options

Click the Number Format button arrow in the Number group to display a drop-down list (shown at the right) with additional numeric format options including date, time, fraction, and scientific options. Click *More Number Formats* at the bottom of the list to open the Format Cells dialog box with the Number tab selected. Using this dialog box, you can access further customization options for a format, such as displaying negative values in red, or create your own custom format code.

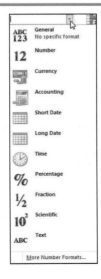

General — No specific format
Number
Currency
Accounting
Short Date
Long Date
Time
Percentage
Fraction
Scientific
Text
More Number Formats...

Data in a cell can be left-aligned, right-aligned, or centered within the column. Cells that have had Merge & Center applied can be formatted to align the text in the merged cell at the left or right. Use the Increase Indent and Decrease Indent buttons to indent text from the left edge of the cell approximately one character width each time the button is clicked. Using buttons along the top row in the Alignment group in the Home tab you can change vertical alignment, rotate text, or wrap text. Use the Repeat keyboard shortcut Ctrl + Y to replicate the last action on another cell. This is useful if you need to perform the same action several times in a row.

Project

To improve the appearance of the quotation, you will change the alignment of column headings and values and indent labels from the left edge of column A.

Tutorial 2.4
Applying Formatting to Cell Contents; Using Undo and Redo; Changing Alignment

1 With **ES2-WBQuotetoMP.xlsx** open, edit the column headings in C17 and E17 to include a period (.) after the abbreviation for number. For example, the edited column heading in C17 will be *No. of Persons*.

2 Select C17:F17.

3 Click the Center button in the Alignment group in the Home tab.

4 Select C18:C29 and then change the alignment to center.

5 Center the entries in E18:E34.

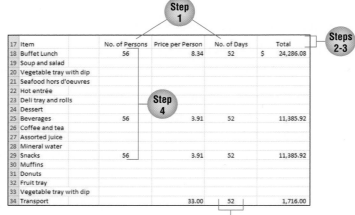

6 Select A19:A24.

7 Click the Increase Indent button in the Alignment group.

> Each time you click Increase Indent, the contents of the selected cells are indented by approximately one character width. If you click Increase Indent one too many times, click the Decrease Indent button to return the text to the previous indent position.

8 Select A26:A28 and then click the Increase Indent button.

9 Select A30:A33 and then click the Increase Indent button.

10 Select A17:F17 and then bold the cells.

11 Make F8 the active cell and then click the Align Text Left button in the Alignment group.

> By default, Excel aligns date entries at the right edge of a column since dates are converted to a serial number and treated in a similar manner to values. You will learn more about using dates in Excel in Section 3.

12 Select A17:F17.

In Activity 2.4, you increased the height of row 17 to 21.00. The Alignment group contains buttons that also allow you to control the alignment of the text between the top and bottom of the cell boundaries. In the next step, you will center the text vertically within the cells.

13 Click the Middle Align button ≡ in the Alignment group.

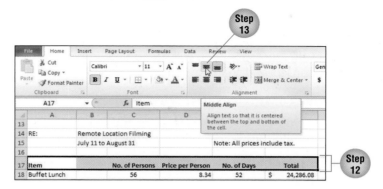

14 Deselect the range.

15 Select E1:F1 and then click *Merge & Center* in the Alignment group.

16 Select E2:F2 and then press Ctrl + Y (the Repeat command).

You can add a Repeat button to the Quick Access toolbar. To do this, click the Customize Quick Access Toolbar button ⤓ that displays at the right side of the toolbar and then click *More Commands* at the drop-down list. At the Excel Options dialog box with Quick Access Toolbar selected in the left pane, scroll down the left list box, click Repeat, click the Add button, and then click OK.

17 Select E3:F3 and then press Ctrl + Y.

You can merge and center in only one row at a time in this situation because data already exists in all three rows.

18 Select E1:E3 and then click the Align Text Right button ≡ in the Alignment group.

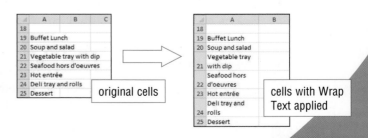

19 Deselect the range.

20 Save **ES2-WBQuoteToMP.xlsx**.

In Brief

Change Horizontal or Vertical Alignment
1. Select cells.
2. Click desired alignment button.
3. Deselect cells.

Indent Text within Cells
1. Select cells.
2. Click Increase Indent button.
3. Deselect cells.

Repeat Command
Press Ctrl + Y.

In Addition

Wrapping Text within a Cell

A Wrap Text button ⊞ is available in the Alignment group which you can use to wrap text within a cell if you do not want to widen the column width. Text too wide for the column is displayed on multiple lines and the height of the row is automatically increased. In the example shown at the right, the original cells are shown on the left and the wrapped cells in column A (which has also been made wider) displayed on the right.

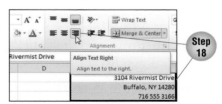

Activity 2.8

Adding Borders and Shading; Copying Formats with Format Painter

Borders in various styles and colors can be applied to display and print in selected cells within the worksheet. Borders can be added to the top, left, bottom, or right edge of a cell. Use borders to underscore headings or totals or to emphasize other cells. Shading adds color and/or a pattern to the background of a cell. Format Painter copies formats from a selected cell to another cell. Use this feature to apply multiple format options from one cell to another cell.

Project

Tutorial 2.5
Adding Borders and Shading to Cells and Using Format Painter

As you near completion of the quotation, you will spend time improving the presentation of the worksheet by adding borders and shading.

1. With **ES2-WBQuoteToMP.xlsx** open, select A17:F17.

   In the next steps, you will add a border to the top and bottom of the column headings using the Bottom Border button in the Font group of the Home tab.

2. Click the Bottom Border button arrow in the Font group in the Home tab.

   A drop-down list of border style options displays. The *More Borders* option at the bottom of the list opens the Format Cells dialog box with the Border tab selected in which you can create a custom border.

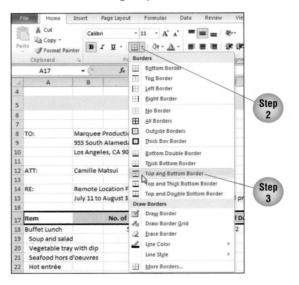

3. Click *Top and Bottom Border* at the drop-down list.

4. Click in any cell to deselect the range and view the border.

5. Select A18:B18, click the Top and Bottom Border button arrow, and then click *Outside Borders* at the drop-down list.

6. Select A25:B25 and then click the Outside Borders button. (Do not click the arrow.)

   Since the Borders button updates to the most recently selected border style, you can apply the *Outside Borders* option to the active cell without displaying the drop-down list.

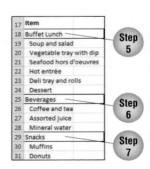

7. Select A29:B29 and then click the Outside Borders button.

8. Deselect the range.

9. Make F36 the active cell, click the Outside Borders button arrow, and then click *Top and Double Bottom Border* at the drop-down list.

10. Make A8 the active cell, apply bold, and right-align the cell.

    In the next steps, you will copy the formats from A8 to two other cells.

11 With A8 still the active cell, double-click the Format Painter button 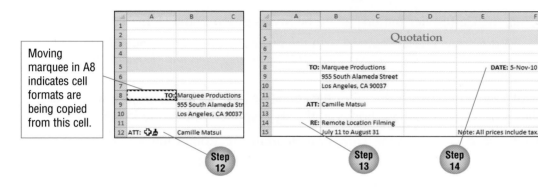 in the Clipboard group.

> A moving marquee surrounds the source cell and a paintbrush displays attached to the cell pointer. This icon means that the formats are copied from the source cell and can be pasted to multiple cells or ranges. Single-clicking Format Painter allows you to copy formats to the next cell or range that you click. Double-click the Format Painter button to toggle the feature on until you turn it off by clicking Format Painter again.

12 Click A12.

13 Click A14.

14 Click E8 and then click the Format Painter button to turn off the feature.

15 Save **ES2-WBQuoteToMP.xlsx.**

In Brief

Add Borders
1. Select cells.
2. Click Borders button arrow in Font group.
3. Click desired border style.
4. Deselect cells.

Copy Formats
1. Make active cell containing source formats.
2. Single-click (copy once) or double-click (multiple copy) the Format Painter button in Clipboard group.
3. Click destination cell(s).
4. If necessary, click Format Painter button to turn off feature.

Moving marquee in A8 indicates cell formats are being copied from this cell.

Step 12

Step 13

Step 14

In Addition

Creating a Custom Border

If none of the borders available in the drop-down list suit your needs, you can create a custom border. Click the *More Borders* option at the bottom of the Borders list to open the Format Cells dialog box with the Border tab selected shown below. At this dialog box, you can change to a different line style by clicking another line option in the *Style* box, and/or change the line color by clicking the *Color* box arrow and then choosing the desired color at the drop-down gallery. Next, specify the outside and/or inside border you want by clicking one of the buttons in the *Presets* section, clicking one or more of the Border buttons along the perimeter of the preview box, or by clicking inside the preview box at the edge of the cell along which you want the border to appear. When you are finished creating the border, click OK.

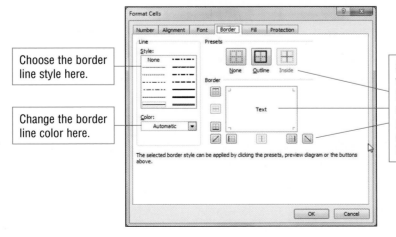

Choose the border line style here.

Change the border line color here.

Specify the border you want by clicking a button in *Presets*, a border button, or by clicking inside the preview box along the edge at which you want the border to appear.

Activity 2.9

Using Cell Styles and Themes

Cell Styles contain a group of pre-defined formatting options stored in a name. Styles are an efficient method to consistently apply formats, creating a professional, consistent worksheet appearance. Excel includes several predefined styles which you can apply or modify; you also can choose to create your own cell style. A theme is a set of formatting choices that include a set of colors, a set of heading and body text fonts, and a set of lines and fill effects. Excel provides a variety of themes you can use to format text and cells in a worksheet.

The Waterfront
B·I·S·T·R·O

SNAP

Tutorial 2.6
Using Cell Styles
and Themes

Project Your final steps in improving the presentation of the worksheet will involve applying cell styles and a theme.

1. With **ES2-WBQuoteToMP.xlsx** open, make A5 the active cell.

   You decide to change the formatting of the *Quotation* title to one of the predefined cell styles that Excel provides.

2. Click the Cell Styles button in the Styles group in the Home tab.

   A drop-down gallery appears with the predefined cell styles grouped into five sections: *Good, Bad and Neutral, Data and Model, Titles and Headings, Themed Cell Styles,* and *Number Format.*

3. Move the mouse over several of the cell style designs in the drop-down gallery and watch Live Preview show you the style applied to the title in A5.

4. Click the *Title* style in the *Titles and Headings* section of the gallery.

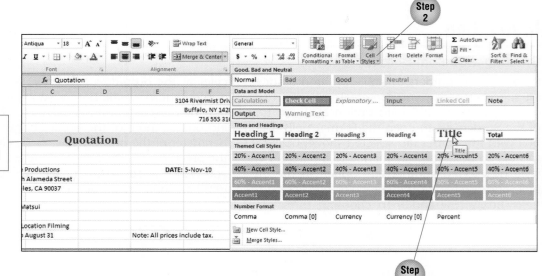

5 Select A17:F17, click the Cell Styles button in the Styles group, and then click the *Accent2* style in the *Themed Cell Styles* section.

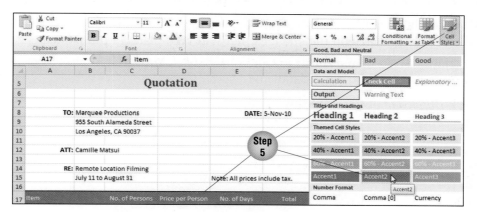

6 Select A18:B18, hold down Ctrl, select A25:B25 and A29:B29, and then release the Ctrl key.

7 Click the Cell Styles button and then click the *Accent1* style in the *Themed Cell Styles* section at the drop-down gallery.

In the next steps you will apply a theme to the quotation. Changing the theme will cause the fonts, colors, and effects to change for the cells. As with styles, you will be able to view a live preview of the changes before you choose a theme.

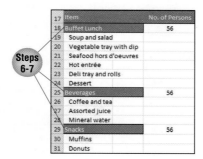

8 Deselect the cells.

continues

9 Click the Page Layout tab.

10 Click the Themes button in the Themes group.

11 Move the mouse over several of the themes in the drop-down gallery and watch Live Preview show you the changes that will take place in the worksheet.

> Notice that a theme affects the entire worksheet. You did not select a cell or range of cells before you applied a theme.

12 Click *Black Tie* at the drop-down gallery.

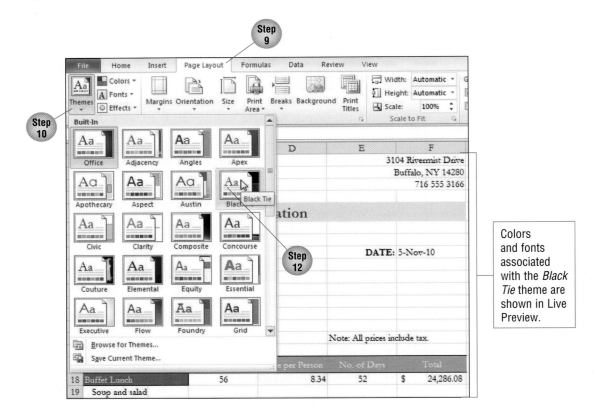

Step 9

Step 10

Step 12

Colors and fonts associated with the *Black Tie* theme are shown in Live Preview.

Need Help?

Apply the wrong theme? Since themes are applied to the entire worksheet, go back to the Themes gallery and select the correct theme. The existing theme will be replaced.

13. Make A1 the active cell, type **The Waterfront Bistro** and press Enter.

14. Select A1:D3, click the Home tab, click the Merge and Center button and the Middle Align button in the Alignment group.

15. With A1 still the active cell, click the Cell Styles button and then click *Accent2* in the *Themed Cell Styles* section of the drop-down gallery.

16. With A1 still the active cell, change the font size to *28*.

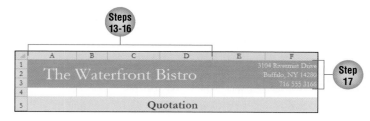

17. Select E1:E3 and apply the *Accent2* cell style.

18. Click in any cell to deselect the range.

19. Click the File tab, click the Print tab, and then click the Print button to print the finished quotation.

20. Save and then close **ES2-WBQuoteToMP.xlsx**.

In Addition

Creating a New Style

You can create your own style using the *New Cell Style* option at the bottom of the Cell Styles drop-down gallery. First, select a cell in the current worksheet and apply all of the formatting to the cell that you want saved in the style. Second, with the cell active to which you have applied the desired formats, click the Cell Styles button and then click *New Cell Style* at the drop-down gallery. At the Style dialog box shown at the right, type a name for the style in the *Style name* text box and then click OK. The new style will appear at the top of the Cell Styles gallery in a new section titled *Custom*. Custom styles are saved in the workbook in which they are created. You will not see the new style when you open a new workbook; however, you can copy styles from one workbook to another.

Activity 2.10

Using Find and Replace

Use the Find command to search for specific labels or values that you want to verify or edit. The Find command will move to each cell containing the text you specify. The Replace command will search for a label, value, or format and automatically replace it with another label, value, or format. Use Find and Replace to ensure that all occurrences of the specified label or value are verified or edited.

Project

Tutorial 2.7
Using Find and Replace

Dana Hirsch wants to know how many weddings are booked in 2011. You will use Find to review the wedding bookings in the special events workbook. Dana has also advised you that the prices that were input at 32.95 should be 34.95. You will use the Replace command to correct these errors.

1. Open **WBSpecEvents.xlsx**. Save the workbook with Save As in the ExcelS2 folder and name it **ES2-WBSpecEvents**.

2. Press Ctrl + Home to make A1 the active cell.

3. Click the Find & Select button in the Editing group in the Home tab and then click *Find* at the drop-down list.

4. Type **wedding** in the *Find what* text box and then click the Find Next button.

   Notice that Excel has moved to C6 which has the entry *25th Wedding Anniversary*. This cell contains the search text *wedding* but you do not want to review wedding anniversary events. In the next step you will specify that you want only cells that match the search text exactly.

5. Click the Options>> button in the Find and Replace dialog box, click the *Match entire cell contents* check box to insert a check mark and then click the Find Next button.

   The dialog box expands when you click the Options>> button to reveal find and replace options. Notice this time, Excel bypassed the entry *50th Wedding Anniversary* in C9 and moved directly to C10 which contains the text *Wedding*.

6. Click Find Next.

   Excel moves the active cell to C16.

7. Click Find Next.

   Excel moves the active cell to C20.

8. Continue clicking Find Next until the active cell returns to C10 near the top of the worksheet.

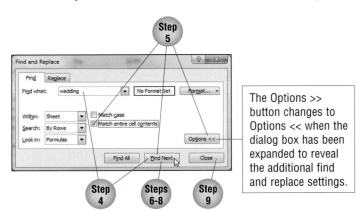

The Options >> button changes to Options << when the dialog box has been expanded to reveal the additional find and replace settings.

Your review has determined seven weddings are booked in 2011. Although in this small worksheet you could easily have done this calculation by quickly scanning the contents of column C, in a large worksheet with many rows and columns, the Find command is an efficient method of moving to a specific cell. Typing a specific value into the *Find what* text box could move you to a section title or label very quickly.

9 Click the Close button to close the Find and Replace dialog box.

10 Click the Find & Select button in the Editing group and then click *Replace* at the drop-down list.

11 With *Match entire cell contents* still selected in the Find and Replace dialog box with the Replace tab selected, drag to select *wedding* in the *Find what* text box and then type **32.95**.

12 Press Tab to move the insertion point to the *Replace with* text box and then type **34.95**.

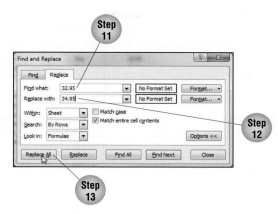

13 Click the Replace All button.

> Excel searches through the entire worksheet and automatically changes all occurrences of *32.95* to *34.95*.

14 Click OK at the message that Excel has completed the search and has made four replacements.

15 Click the *Match entire cell contents* check box to clear the check mark, click the Options<< button to remove the expanded find and replace options, and then click the Close button to close the Find and Replace dialog box.

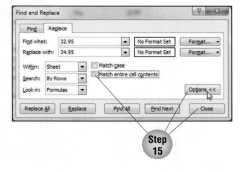

16 Review the entries in column H and note that no prices exist at 32.95.

17 Save **ES2-WBSpecEvents.xlsx**.

In Brief

Find Label or Value
1. Click Find & Select button in Editing group.
2. Click *Find*.
3. Type label or value in *Find what* text box.
4. Click Find Next.

Replace Label or Value
1. Click Find & Select button.
2. Click *Replace*.
3. Type label or value in *Find what* text box.
4. Type replacement label or value in *Replace with* text box.
5. Click Find Next or Replace All.

In Addition

Replacing Formats

You can use the Replace feature to find formats and replace them with other formats or no formatting. For example, you could use Excel to find all occurrences of bold and blue font color applied to a cell and replace with bold and green font color. At the Find and Replace dialog box with the Replace tab selected, click the Options>> button to expand the dialog box and display Format buttons to the right of the *Find what* and *Replace with* text boxes (shown at the right). Use these buttons to specify the required format options. The Preview box to the left (initially displays *No Format Set*) displays the formats Excel will find and replace.

Activity 2.11

Freezing Panes; Changing the Zoom

When you scroll to the right or down to view parts of a worksheet that do not fit in the current window, some column or row headings may scroll off the screen making it difficult to relate text or values. The Freeze Panes option causes rows and columns to remain fixed when scrolling. Magnify or reduce the worksheet display by dragging the Zoom slider bar button, clicking the Zoom In or Zoom Out buttons, or by specifying a percentage to zoom to at the Zoom dialog box. Changing the magnification does not affect printing since worksheets print at 100% unless scaling options are changed.

Project

You will freeze column and row headings in the special events worksheet to facilitate scrolling and practice with various Zoom settings to view more cells within the current window.

Tutorial 2.8
Freezing Panes and Changing the Zoom

1. With **ES2-WBSpecEvents.xlsx** open, make A4 the active cell.

2. Click the View tab.

3. Click the Freeze Panes button in the Window group.

4. Click *Freeze Panes* at the drop-down list.

   The position of the active cell before you freeze panes is important since all rows above and all columns left of the active cell are frozen. Notice you made the active cell A4 so that rows 1 to 3 are now frozen. A horizontal black line appears indicating which rows remain fixed when scrolling.

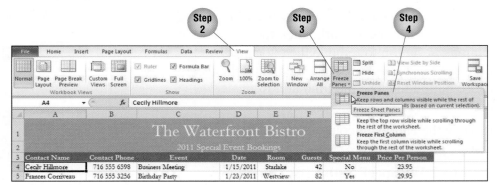

5. Press the Page Down key a few times to scroll down the worksheet.

   Notice rows 1 through 3 do not scroll off the screen.

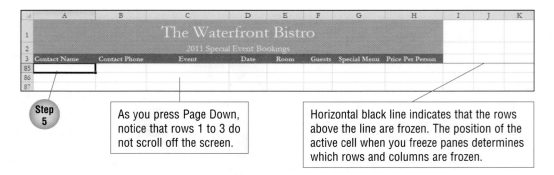

As you press Page Down, notice that rows 1 to 3 do not scroll off the screen.

Horizontal black line indicates that the rows above the line are frozen. The position of the active cell when you freeze panes determines which rows and columns are frozen.

6 Press Ctrl + Home. Notice that Excel returns to A4 instead of A1 since A1 is frozen.

7 Click the Freeze Panes button in the Window group and then click *Unfreeze Panes*.

> The Freeze Panes option changes to Unfreeze Panes when rows or columns have been frozen.

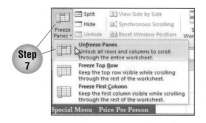

Step 8

8 Practice dragging the button on the Zoom slider bar (located at the right end of the Status bar above the system time) and watch the cells magnify and shrink as you drag right and left.

9 Drag the slider bar button to the halfway mark on the slider bar to redisplay the worksheet at 100%.

10 Click over *100%* at the left edge of the slider bar to open the Zoom dialog box.

11 At the Zoom dialog box, click *75%* and then click OK.

12 Click the Zoom In button at the right side of the Zoom slider bar (displays as a plus symbol inside a circle).

13 Continue to click the Zoom In button until the zoom percentage returns to 100%.

> When the worksheet is set to 100% magnification, clicking the Zoom In or Zoom Out buttons at either side of the slider bar magnifies or shrinks the display of the worksheet by 10% each time the button is clicked.

14 Save **ES2-WBSpecEvents.xlsx**.

In Brief

Freeze Panes
1. Make cell active below and right of row or column headings you want to freeze.
2. Click View tab.
3. Click Freeze Panes button.
4. Click *Freeze Panes*.

Change Zoom Setting
Drag Zoom slider bar.
OR
Click Zoom In or Zoom Out buttons.
OR
Click zoom percentage value and choose magnification option at Zoom dialog box.

In Addition

Zoom to Selection

The View tab contains a Zoom group with three buttons to change zoom settings. Click the Zoom button in the Zoom group to open the Zoom dialog box. This is the same dialog box that you displayed in Step 10. Click the 100% button to return the view to 100%. Select a range of cells and then click the Zoom to Selection button to cause Excel to scale the zoom setting so that the selected range fills the worksheet area.

Activity 2.12

Inserting, Moving, and Resizing Pictures and Clip Art

When connected to Office Online, the Microsoft Office suite includes a clip art gallery containing thousands of images. Once a clip art image has been inserted, it can be moved, resized, or deleted. The Clip Art task pane allows you to view images in the gallery and insert them into the worksheet with a single click. By default, Excel searches Office Online if you are connected to the Internet. A company logo or other digital picture can also be inserted into a worksheet using the Picture button in the Illustrations group of the Insert tab.

Project

Before printing the special events list, you decide to add a clip art image to the top right and the bistro's logo to the top left of the worksheet. After inserting the images, you will resize and move them.

Tutorial 2.9
Inserting Pictures and Clip Art

1 With **ES2-WBSpecEvents.xlsx** open, make A1 the active cell.

2 Click the Insert tab and then click the Clip Art button in the Illustrations group.

The Clip Art task pane opens at the right side of the worksheet area.

3 Click in the *Search for* text box at the top of the Clip Art task pane. Delete existing text if necessary and then type **seafood**.

4 If necessary, click the *Include Office.com content* check box to insert a check mark and then click the Go button.

Available images associated with the keyword *seafood* display in the *Results* section of the Clip Art task pane. By default, Excel searches all media file types (clip art, photographs, movies, and sounds) in all categories of the Office gallery, in Office Online, and in all favorites, unclassified clips, and downloaded clips that have been added to the computer you are using.

Step 4

Step 3

Images shown may vary.

5 Scroll the images in the *Results* section until you see the clip art shown at the right. Position the mouse pointer over the picture and then click the mouse once. ***Note: Substitute a similar image if the one shown is not available.***

The picture is inserted in the worksheet starting at A1.

Step 5

6 Position the pointer on the round white sizing handle at the bottom right corner of the image, hold down the left mouse button, and drag the pointer up and left until the image fits within the first two rows as shown.

Step 6

7 Move the pointer over the image until the four-headed arrow move icon appears attached to the pointer, hold down the left mouse button, and then drag the image until the right edge of the picture is aligned at the right edge of the worksheet.

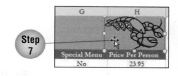

Step 7

8 Click the Close button in the upper right corner of the Clip Art task pane.

9 Click A1, click the Insert tab, and then click the Picture button in the Illustrations group.

10 At the Insert Picture dialog box, navigate to the ExcelS2 folder on your storage medium. If necessary, change the view to *Large Icons* and then double-click the file named *TWBLogo.jpg*.

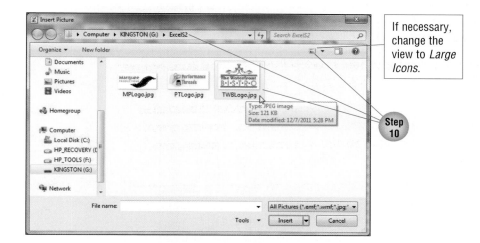

If necessary, change the view to *Large Icons*.

Step 10

11 Use the sizing handles to resize the picture until the logo image fits above the top left edge of the worksheet as shown below.

12 Click in any cell to deselect the logo image.

Steps 11-12

13 Select A1:A2 and add *Outside Borders*. Select A3:H36 and add *All Borders*.

14 Deselect the range, save, print, and then close **ES2-WBSpecEvents.xlsx**.

In Addition

Picture Tools

When a clip art image or picture inserted from a file is selected, the contextual Picture Tools Format tab becomes available. Customize the image using picture tools or picture styles. For example, use the crop button to cut an unwanted area from the image, or set a specific height or width measurement for the image. Buttons in the Arrange group allow you to group multiple images together, control the alignment, rotation, or order of the image within the worksheet. Buttons in the Adjust group allow you to control the brightness, contrast, and color of the image.

Features Summary

Feature	Ribbon Tab, Group	Button	Quick Access Toolbar	Keyboard Shortcut
Accounting Number format	Home, Number	$		
align text left	Home, Alignment			
align text right	Home, Alignment			
bold	Home, Font	B		Ctrl + B
borders	Home, Font			Ctrl + Shift + &
cell styles	Home, Styles			
center	Home, Alignment			
clear cell	Home, Editing			
clip art	Insert, Illustrations			
column width	Home, Cells			
Comma style	Home, Number			
copy	Home, Clipboard			Ctrl + C
cut	Home, Clipboard			Ctrl + X
decrease decimal	Home, Number			
decrease indent	Home, Alignment			
delete cell, column, or row	Home, Cells			
fill color	Home, Font			
find	Home, Editing			Ctrl + F
font	Home, Font	Calibri		Ctrl + 1
font color	Home, Font	A		Ctrl + 1
font size	Home, Font	11		Ctrl + 1
Format Painter	Home, Clipboard			
freeze panes	View, Window			
increase decimal	Home, Number			
increase indent	Home, Alignment			

Feature	Ribbon Tab, Group	Button	Quick Access Toolbar	Keyboard Shortcut
insert cell, column, or row	Home, Cells			
italic	Home, Font			Ctrl + I
merge and center	Home, Alignment			
middle-align	Home, Alignment			
paste	Home, Clipboard			Ctrl + V
picture from file	Insert, Illustrations			
redo an action				Ctrl + Y
repeat				Ctrl + Y
replace	Home, Editing			Ctrl + H
row height	Home, Cells			
Spelling	Review, Proofing			F7
theme	Page Layout, Themes			
Thesaurus	Review, Proofing			Shift + F7
undo an action				Ctrl + Z
zoom	View, Zoom			

Knowledge Check

Completion: In the space provided at the right, indicate the correct term, command, or option.

1. Use this feature to remove everything from a cell including text and formats. _____
2. Make a cell active anywhere in this row to insert a new row between 11 and 12. _____
3. Make a cell active anywhere in this column to insert a new column between E and F. _____
4. This is the term for adjusting a column width to the length of the longest entry. _____
5. This term refers to the feature where Excel shows the results of a format option while pointing to the option in a drop-down list or gallery. _____
6. By default, cells are initially set to this numeric style format. _____
7. Click this button in the Alignment group of the Home tab to center cells vertically between the top and bottom cell boundaries. _____
8. Click this button in the Clipboard group of the Home tab to copy the formats of the active cell. _____
9. This feature stores predefined format options. _____
10. This feature stores a set of colors, fonts, and effects that can be applied to the entire worksheet. _____
11. Make this cell active to freeze rows 1 through 5. _____
12. List two methods for changing the zoom magnification to view more cells in the current window. _____
13. Click this tab and button to search for art on Office Online. _____
14. Click this button in the Illustrations group to insert an image stored in a file. _____

Skills Review

Review 1 Editing, Moving, Copying, and Clearing Cells; Performing a Spell Check; Inserting and Deleting Rows

1. Open **WBInvToNPC.xlsx** and then save the workbook in the ExcelEOS folder and name it **ES2-R1-WBInvToNPC**.
2. Change the amount in D20 from *13.73* to *15.23* and then clear the contents of A8.
3. Change the label in A21 from *Soup* to *French Onion Soup*.
4. Type new data in the cells indicated.
   E14   **PO No.**   F14   **TA-11-643**
5. Delete rows 7, 8, and 9.
6. Complete a spelling check of the worksheet. (All names are spelled correctly.)
7. Move E7:F7 to E10:F10.
8. Copy A24 to A30.

9. Delete those rows that contain the labels *Milk* and *Donuts*.

10. Insert a new row between *Prime Rib* and *Mixed Vegetables* and then type **Seafood Pasta** in column A of the new row.

11. Save **ES2-R1-WBInvToNPC.xlsx**.

Review 2   Adjusting Column Widths; Replacing Data; Moving Cells; Applying Formatting Features; Inserting a Picture

1. With **ES2-R1-WBInvToNPC.xlsx** open, adjust the width of column A to *10.00 (75 pixels)*.

2. Change the width of column C to the length of the longest entry (AutoFit).

3. Change the width of column D to *15.00 (110 pixels)* and column E to *7.00 (54 pixels)*.

4. Use the Replace feature to replace the value *32* with *36* for all occurrences.

5. Create a SUM formula in F33 to total the cells in the column.

6. Apply numeric formats as follows:
   a. Format F17 and F33 to Accounting Number Format.
   b. Format F28 and F31 to Comma Style.

7. Indent once A18:A27 and A29:A30.

8. Select D1:D3 and change the font to 10-point Bookman Old Style bold. (Substitute another font of your choosing if Bookman Old Style is not available.)

9. Move D1:D3 to F1:F3 and then align the text at the right edge of the cells.

10. Merge and center and then apply the Input cell style (*Data and Model* section) to the ranges A17:B17 and A28:B28.

11. Merge and center A5 across columns A–F and then apply the Title cell style to A5.

12. Center the values in columns C and D and the label in F16.

13. Add a top and bottom border to A16:F16 and turn on bold.

14. Add a top and double bottom border to F33 and turn on bold.

15. Add an outside border to A1:F36.

16. Add the fill color Olive Green, Accent 3, Lighter 80% from the Fill Color palette to A5.

17. Add the fill color Olive Green, Accent 3, Lighter 60% from the Fill Color palette to A16:F16.

18. Apply the Clarity theme to the worksheet.

19. Make A1 the active cell, insert the picture file named *TWBLogo.jpg* and resize the picture as necessary so that the logo fits in the first four rows at the top left of the worksheet.

20. Save, print, and then close **ES2-R1-WBInvToNPC.xlsx**. *Note: Check with your Instructor if you submit your work in hard copy to see if you need to print two copies of this worksheet with one of the copies showing the cell formulas instead of the calculated results.*

Skills Assessment

Note: If you submit your work in hard copy, check with your instructor before completing these Assessments to find out if you need to print two copies of each worksheet, with one of the copies showing the cell formulas instead of the calculated results.

Assessment 1 Editing Cells; Inserting Columns; Copying Formulas; Inserting Pictures; Applying Formatting Features

1. Bobbie Sinclair of Performance Threads has started preparing a workbook that tracks the costs of costume research, design, and production for a Marquee Productions project. You have been asked to complete the workbook. Open **PTMarqCost.xlsx** and spend a few moments reviewing the worksheet Bobbie has started.
2. Save the workbook in the ExcelEOS folder and name it **ES2-A1-PTMarqCost.**
3. Complete the worksheet using the following information:
   a. Design costs for all costumes should be *122.50* instead of *22*.
   b. Insert a new column between *Fabric* and *Total Cost* and type the column heading Notions in J9. Type the values in J10:J16 as follows:

Henry II	101.50	John	47.85
Queen Eleanor	88.23	Geoffrey	47.85
Alias	58.40	Philip	47.85
Richard	47.85		

   c. The formula to calculate total cost for each costume is incorrect. Enter the correct formula for the first costume (K10) and then copy the formula to K11:K16. ***Hint: The current formula does not include the fabric and notions costs.***
   d. Create a formula in L10 to calculate the costume fee that will multiply the total cost in K10 by *2* and then copy the formula to L11:L16.
   e. Create a formula in M10 to calculate the profit as costume fee minus total cost and then copy the formula to M11:M16.
   f. Format the numeric cells in an appropriate style.
   g. Change the alignment of any headings that could be improved in appearance.
   h. Merge and center the titles in A6 and A7 over the columns.
   i. Insert the picture file named **PTLogo.jpg** and resize it to fit in the five rows at the top left of the worksheet.
   j. Insert a clip art image of your choosing after searching using the word *sewing* and resize the image to fit in the five rows at the top right of the worksheet.
   k. Apply font, border, and color changes to enhance the appearance of the worksheet. Adjust column widths as needed.
4. Change the page layout to landscape orientation and change the *Width* in the Scale to Fit group of the Page Layout tab to *1 page*.
5. Save, print, and then close **ES2-A1-PTMarqCost.xlsx**.

Assessment 2 Completing and Formatting a Worksheet

1. Camille Matsui, production assistant for Marquee Productions, has requested the invoice in advance for the custom-made costumes so that she can make sure the budget funds are allocated. Bobbie Sinclair has started the invoice and has asked you to finish it. Open **PTMarqCostInv.xlsx** and spend a few moments reviewing the invoice Bobbie has started. *Note: Completion of Assessment 1 is required to finish the invoice for this assessment.*
2. Save the workbook in the ExcelEOS folder and name it **ES2-A2-PTMarqCostInv**.
3. Complete the invoice using the following information:
   a. Type the current date in G6.
   b. Refer to your electronic copy or your printout of the costumes in Assessment 1, Step 5. Type the values from the *Costume Fee* column (L10:L16) into the appropriate cells in F15:F21.
   c. Create a formula to total the costume fees in F22. *Hint: Make sure the total agrees with the total costume fee on your printout from Assessment 1.*
   d. A transportation and storage container for each of the seven costumes is *$75.00*. Enter the appropriate formula in F24 that will calculate the fee for seven containers.
   e. Enter in F25 the delivery for all seven costumes as *$250.00*.
   f. Enter in F26 a formula that will add the total for the costume fees with the additional charges.
   g. Enter in F27 a formula that will calculate 13% Canadian Harmonized Sales Tax on the total in F26.
   h. Enter in F28 a formula to calculate the total invoice as the sum of F26 and F27.
4. Insert the picture file named **PTLogo.jpg** in A1 and resize it to fit in the three rows at the top left of the worksheet.
5. Improve the appearance of the worksheet by adjusting column widths, deleting blank rows, moving cells, and/or applying formatting features that you learned in this section.
6. Save, print, and then close **ES2-A2-PTMarqCostInv.xlsx**.

Assessment 3 Performing a Spelling Check; Adjusting Column Width; Using Find and Replace; Inserting Clip Art; Applying Formatting Features

1. Sam Vestering, manager of North American Distribution for Worldwide Enterprises, has created a workbook to summarize revenues from distribution of Marquee Productions' documentary film *The Endangered Monarch Butterfly*. You have been asked to review the worksheet and make enhancements to the appearance. Begin by opening **WEMBRev.xlsx** and reviewing the worksheet's layout, data, and formulas.
2. Save the workbook in the ExcelEOS folder and name it **ES2-A3-WEMBRev**.
3. Make the following corrections:
   a. Perform a spelling check.
   b. Adjust column widths so all data is completely visible.
   c. Change all of the venues named *Cinema House* to *Cinema Magic*.
   d. In A3, type **Date:** and then enter today's date in B3.
   e. Search for a clip art image of a monarch butterfly and then insert the image at the top right of the worksheet.
   f. Improve the appearance of the worksheet by applying formatting features that you learned in this section.
4. Print the worksheet in portrait orientation with the width scaled to fit 1 page.
5. Save and then close **ES2-A3-WEMBRev.xlsx**.

Assessment 4 Finding the Select All Button

1. Use the Help feature to find out where the Select All button is located in the Excel window.
2. Open **WBInventory.xlsx** and save the workbook in the ExcelEOS folder, naming it **ES2-A4-WBInventory**.
3. Click the Select All button and then apply italic formatting.
4. Deselect the cells and then scroll the worksheet to view the change.
5. Save, print, and then close **ES2-A4-WBInventory.xlsx**.

Assessment 5 Individual Challenge
Locating Information on Theatre Arts Programs

1. You are considering enrolling in a drama/theatre arts program at a college or university. Search the Internet for available programs in postsecondary schools in the United States and Canada. Choose three schools that interest you the most and find out as much as you can about the costs of attending these schools. Try to find information on costs beyond tuition and books, such as transportation and room and board.
2. Create a workbook that compares the costs for each of the three schools. For example, create the cost categories in column A and include three columns next to each cost category where you will enter the costs you found for each school. Total the costs for each of the schools.
3. Apply formatting features that you learned in this section to the worksheet.
4. Save the workbook in the ExcelEOS folder and name it **ES2-A5-TheatreArts**.
5. Print and then close **ES2-A5-TheatreArts.xlsx**.

Marquee Challenge

Challenge 1 Creating a Direct Wages Budget Report for a Film Shoot

1. You work with Chris Greenbaum, production manager at Marquee Productions. Chris has asked you to create the direct wages budget for the company's remote location film shoot. Create the worksheet shown in Figure 2.1. *Note: The logo is a file named MPLogo.jpg.*
2. Link the values in the *Estimated Daily Rates* table (columns I and J) to the *Daily Rate* column (column F) in the budget section.
3. Calculate the extended cost by summing the number of days for site prep, shoot, and cleanup and then multiplying by the daily rate.
4. Calculate the total in G16.
5. Apply formatting options as shown and format the values in column G to an appropriate number format. Use your best judgment to determine the font, font size, column widths, borders, and fill colors.
6. Although not visible in the figure, a border should also be applied along the top (columns A–G) and left edges (rows 1–14) of the budget cells so that when printed, the entire budget has a perimeter border.
7. Print the worksheet in landscape orientation and then save the workbook in the ExcelEOS folder naming it **ES2-C1-MPLocBudg**.
8. Close **ES2-C1-MPLocBudg.xlsx**.

FIGURE 2.1 Challenge 1

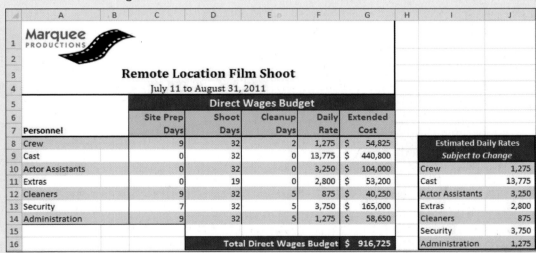

1. You are an assistant to the person who schedules classroom space in the Theatre Arts Division at Niagara Peninsula College. You have been given the room schedule for the auditorium for next semester. The division posts a printed copy of the timetable outside the auditorium door so that students know when the room is available to work on projects and rehearse for upcoming plays. You want to use Excel to create and format the timetable so that the printed copy is easy to read and has a more professional appearance.
2. Refer to the data in Figure 2.2 and then create the timetable in a new workbook. Apply formatting features learned in this section to create a colorful, easy-to-read room timetable.
3. Save the workbook in the ExcelEOS folder and name it **ES2-C2-NPCRoomSch**.
4. Print and then close **ES2-C2-NPCRoomSch.xlsx**.

FIGURE 2.2 Challenge 2

Niagara Peninsula College					
Room:	T1101		Period Covered: January 1 to April 30		
Time	Monday	Tuesday	Wednesday	Thursday	Friday
8:00 AM	SM100-01	AC215-03		MG210-01	SM240-03
9:00 AM	Prasad	McLean	LE100-03	Spelberger	Prasad
10:00 AM	LE253-03	(lab)	Das	SM355-02	SD350-04
11:00 AM	Das			Prasad	Attea
12:00 PM	SD451-01	PD250-02	Common	PD320-03	
1:00 PM	Attea	Kemper	Period	Kemper	LE310-02
2:00 PM	PD340-02	MG410-03	AC478-01	AC480-01	Das
3:00 PM	Kemper	Spelberger	Simmons	Simmons	MG210-01
4:00 PM	MG150-02	SM165-01	AC140-01	(lab)	Spelberger
5:00 PM	Spelberger	Prasad	Chou		
Use of this facility is restricted to staff and registered students only of Niagara Peninsula College. Failure to abide by this policy is considered a serious violation of the college's code of conduct.					
Note 1:	Monday through Thursday evenings, room is booked for Continuing Education department.				
Note 2:	Room is booked 8:00 AM to 5:00 PM the second Saturday of each month for the local community theatre group.				

Excel SECTION 3

Using Functions, Setting Print Options, and Adding Visual Elements

Skills

- Create formulas with absolute addresses
- Create AVERAGE, COUNT, MAX, and MIN formulas to perform statistical analysis
- Create TODAY, NOW, and DATE formulas
- Create PMT formulas to calculate loan payments
- Create and use range names
- Create an IF formula to return a result based on a logical test
- Create, edit, and format a column, pie, and line chart
- Draw shapes and text boxes
- Modify and format charts
- Change page layout options for printing such as margins, horizontal and vertical centering, and scaling
- Manipulate a worksheet in Page Layout view
- Insert headers and footers

Projects Overview

Add functions, create charts, and change page layout options for a quarterly expense and revenue budget forecast; finish an invoice by entering dates and changing page layout options; calculate loan payment amounts for a patio expansion loan; calculate year-end bonuses; create charts for performance benchmarks.

Create and format charts for a grades analysis report; create a chart and apply formatting enhancements to an international student registration report.

Calculate and analyze sales commissions; create charts, apply formatting enhancements, and change page layout options to a European Destinations report.

Calculate payments for an office expansion loan for two finance companies.

Create two charts that depict movie attendance statistics for a staff development workshop.

Model Answers for Projects

These model answers for the projects that you complete in Section 3 provide a preview of the finished projects before you begin working and also allow you to compare your own results with these models to ensure you have created the materials accurately.

ES3-WBQtrExpBudg.xlsx is the project in Activities 3.1 and 3.2 and part of the project in Activities 3.7, 3.8, and 3.10.

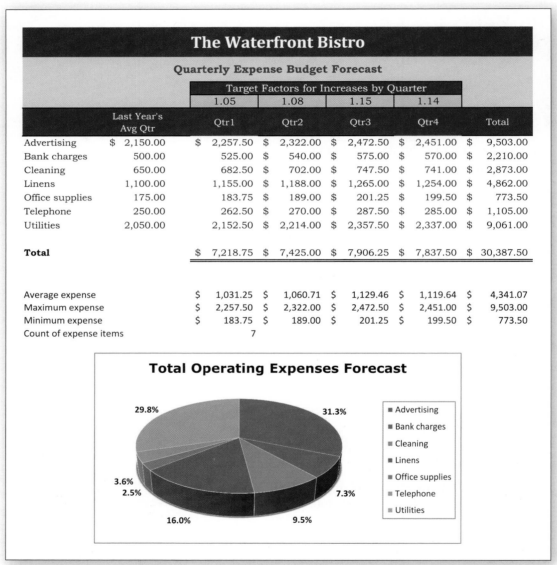

The Waterfront Bistro

Quarterly Expense Budget Forecast

	Last Year's Avg Qtr	Target Factors for Increases by Quarter				
		1.05	1.08	1.15	1.14	
		Qtr1	Qtr2	Qtr3	Qtr4	Total
Advertising	$ 2,150.00	$ 2,257.50	$ 2,322.00	$ 2,472.50	$ 2,451.00	$ 9,503.00
Bank charges	500.00	525.00	$ 540.00	$ 575.00	$ 570.00	$ 2,210.00
Cleaning	650.00	682.50	$ 702.00	$ 747.50	$ 741.00	$ 2,873.00
Linens	1,100.00	1,155.00	$ 1,188.00	$ 1,265.00	$ 1,254.00	$ 4,862.00
Office supplies	175.00	183.75	$ 189.00	$ 201.25	$ 199.50	$ 773.50
Telephone	250.00	262.50	$ 270.00	$ 287.50	$ 285.00	$ 1,105.00
Utilities	2,050.00	2,152.50	$ 2,214.00	$ 2,357.50	$ 2,337.00	$ 9,061.00
Total		$ 7,218.75	$ 7,425.00	$ 7,906.25	$ 7,837.50	$ 30,387.50
Average expense		$ 1,031.25	$ 1,060.71	$ 1,129.46	$ 1,119.64	$ 4,341.07
Maximum expense		$ 2,257.50	$ 2,322.00	$ 2,472.50	$ 2,451.00	$ 9,503.00
Minimum expense		$ 183.75	$ 189.00	$ 201.25	$ 199.50	$ 773.50
Count of expense items		7				

Total Operating Expenses Forecast

- 29.8%
- 31.3%
- 3.6%
- 2.5%
- 7.3%
- 16.0%
- 9.5%

Legend:
- Advertising
- Bank charges
- Cleaning
- Linens
- Office supplies
- Telephone
- Utilities

ES3-WBInvPTDirMtg.xlsx is the project in Activity 3.3 and part of the project in Activity 3.11.

The Waterfront Bistro

3104 Rivermist Drive
Buffalo, NY 14280
716 555 3166

Proudly serving you since June-77

Invoice

To: Performance Threads
4011 Bridgewater Street
Niagara Falls, ON L2E 2T6

Date: 3-Jun-2010

Due Date: 3-Jul-2010

Attention: Bobbie Sinclair
Re: Director's Meeting

Item		No. of Persons	Price per Person	Total	
1	Appetizer trays	15	5.15	$	77.25
2	Prime rib dinner	15	32.99		494.85
3	Dessert trays	15	5.95		89.25
4	Coffee and tea	15	1.85		27.75
	Meeting room charge	15	2.50		37.50
	Total			$	726.60

Note: All prices include tax and gratuity.
Terms: Due upon receipt of invoice payable in U.S. funds

Thank you for your business! Visit us at our website at www.emcp.net/wfbistro

ES3-WBPatioLoan.xlsx is the project in Activity 3.4 and part of the project in Activity 3.11.

The Waterfront Bistro

Patio Expansion Loan Analysis			
	Funds Unlimited	**Venture Funds Inc.**	**Details**
Interest Rate	7.25%	8.15%	Annual rate
Term	15	12	Years for repayment
Loan Amount	420,000	420,000	Principal borrowed
Monthly Payment	($3,834.02)	($4,580.92)	Includes principal and interest

NOTE:
Both payments are calculated based on a constant interest rate and a constant payment.

Total loan payments	($690,124.34)	($659,651.81)

ES3-WBEmpBonus.xlsx is the project in Activities 3.5, 3.6, and 3.12.

The Waterfront Bistro
Employee Profit Sharing Bonus
January 1, 2011 to December 31, 2011

Employee	Years of Service	Profit Sharing Bonus	Year End Profit	Bonus for 5+ years	Bonus for less than 5 years
Lou Cortez	2	7,177.35	$ 574,188	2.5%	1.25%
Jasmine Hill	5	14,354.70			
Heather Kiley	8	14,354.70			
Dayna McGuire	4	7,177.35			
Carla Modano	5	14,354.70			
Tyler Santini	12	14,354.70			
Pat Soulliere	7	14,354.70			
Moira Su-Lin	1	7,177.35			
Toni Williams	3	7,177.35			
Total		100,482.90			
Average service	5.2				

ES3-WBQtrExpBudg.xlsx is part of the project in Activities 3.7 and 3.10.

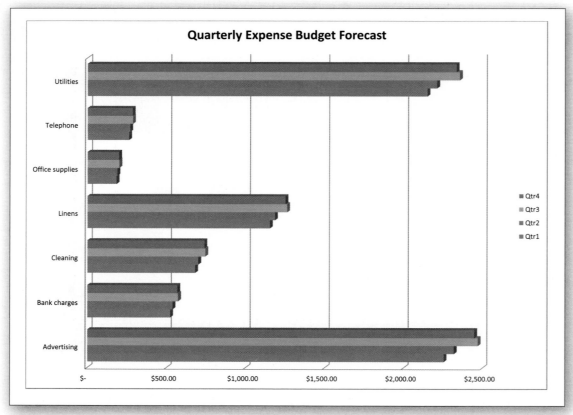

The Waterfront Bistro

Quarterly Performance Benchmarks

	Qtr1	Qtr2	Qtr3	Qtr4
Avg check per person	8.25	9.50	15.00	17.25
Avg seat turnover	2.0	1.0	1.5	2.6

National Restaurant Association Statistics

NRA Avg check per person	10.00	12.50	11.00	14.00
NRA Avg seat turnover	1.3	1.1	1.8	2.0

Activity 3.1

Creating Formulas with Absolute Addressing

In the previous two sections, when you copied and pasted formulas in worksheets, the cell addresses in the destination cells changed automatically *relative* to the destination row or column. The formulas in these worksheets used *relative addressing*. Sometimes you need a cell address to remain fixed when it is copied to another location in the worksheet. To do this, the formulas must include *absolute addressing* for those cell addresses that you do not want changed. Make a cell address absolute by typing a dollar symbol ($) in front of the column letter or row number that cannot be changed. You can also use function key F4 to toggle through variations of the address as relative, absolute, or mixed in which either the row is absolute and the column is relative or vice versa.

Project

Tutorial 3.1
Creating Formulas and Absolute Addressing

Dana has started a worksheet to forecast next year's expenses by quarter. Dana uses a model where next year's expenses are estimated based on last year's average quarter values multiplied by a factor that represents the expected increase for this year. For example, a factor of 1.05 means Dana is expecting the expense to increase by 5%. You will calculate each quarter's expense using the factors in the model Dana has started.

1. Open **WBQtrExpBudg.xlsx** and then save the workbook in the ExcelS3 folder naming it **ES3-WBQtrExpBudg**.

2. Review the layout of the worksheet. Notice the values in D4:G4 are factors that represent the increases by quarter for next year's expenses. For example, *Advertising* in *Qtr1* is expected to increase by a factor of *1.05* (an increase of five percent.)

3. Make D6 the active cell. All of the Qtr1 values in column D will be created by multiplying *Last Year's Avg Qtr* amount by the factor in D4. The formula will include an address that should not change when the formula is copied (D4). To create a formula with an absolute address, type **=b6*d4** and then press function key F4.

   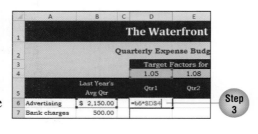

   Pressing F4 causes Excel to insert dollar symbols in front of the row number and column letter immediately left of the insertion point — *d4* becomes D4, an absolute address.

4. Press Enter.

   The result *$2,257.50* is entered in D6. In the D6 formula, the first cell reference (B6) is relative and the second cell reference (D4) is absolute. This is an example of *mixed referencing* with some addresses relative and some absolute. When the formula is copied in a later step, only D4 remains the same.

5. With D7 the active cell, type **=b7*d4** and press Enter.

   You can also type the dollar symbol in front of the column letter or row number to make an address absolute.

   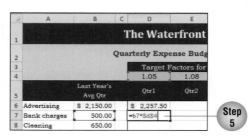

6. Make D7 the active cell and then drag the fill handle down to D12.

7 Click D8 and look at the formula in the Formula bar. Notice that the first cell address (B8) was changed relative to the current row number but the second cell address (D4) remained the same as the original when the formula was copied.

8 Make E6 the active cell, type **=b6*e4**, press function key F4, and then press Enter.

9 Make F6 the active cell and then create the formula *=B6*F4* by either typing **=b6*f4** and pressing function key F4 or by typing the dollar symbols before *f* and *4*.

10 Make G6 the active cell and then create the formula *=B6*G4* by either typing **=b6*g4** and pressing function key F4 or by typing the dollar symbols before *g* and *4*.

11 Select E6:G6 and then drag the fill handle down to row 12.

12 Click a few cells in the copied range and verify that in each case, the cell reference with the dollar symbols remained the same when the formula was copied.

13 Make D14 the active cell and click the AutoSum button to calculate the total for column D. Click the AutoSum button a second time to accept the suggested formula *=SUM(D6:D13)*.

14 Make H6 the active cell, click the AutoSum button, and then press Enter to accept the suggested formula *=SUM(D6:G6)*.

15 Complete the formulas in E14:H14 and H7:H12 by copying the appropriate SUM functions.

16 Save **ES3-WBQtrExpBudg.xlsx**.

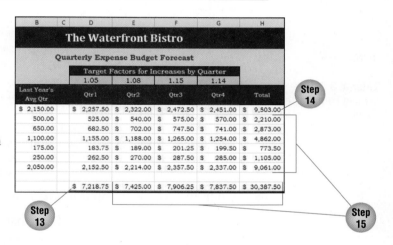

In Brief

Make Cell Address Absolute

With insertion point positioned just after cell address or with cell address selected in Formula bar, press F4.

OR

Type dollar symbol immediately preceding column letter and/or row number.

In Addition

More about Mixed Addressing

Excel can be instructed to fix only the row number or the column letter of a cell that is copied and pasted to another location. This table shows more ways that a cell address can use absolute referencing. Pressing F4 repeatedly causes Excel to scroll through each of these variations for the selected cell address.

Example	Action
=A12*.01	Neither the column nor the row will change.
=$A12*.01	The column will remain fixed at column A, but the row will change.
=A$12*.01	The column will change, but the row remains fixed at row 12.
=A12*.01	Both the column and row will change.

Activity 3.2

Using Statistical Functions
AVERAGE, COUNT, MAX, and MIN

Until now, you have only used the SUM function when you clicked the AutoSum button in the Editing group of the Home tab. Excel includes numerous other built-in formulas that are grouped into function categories. The Statistical category contains several functions that can be used to perform statistical analysis on data, such as calculating medians, variances, frequencies, and so on. The structure of a function formula begins with the equals sign (=), followed by the name of the function, and then the argument within parentheses. *Argument* is the term given to the values to be included in the calculation. The structure of the argument is dependent on the function being used and can include a single range of cells, multiple ranges, single cell references, or a combination thereof.

Project

SNAP

Tutorial 3.2
Writing Formulas in Excel

Dana has asked you to add statistics below the quarterly expenses budget forecast. Specifically, you will calculate the average, maximum, and minimum expenses as well as a count of the number of expense items.

1 With **ES3-WBQtrExpBudg.xlsx** open, type the following labels in the cells indicated.

A17	**Average expense**
A18	**Maximum expense**
A19	**Minimum expense**
A20	**Count of expense items**

2 Make D17 the active cell.

In the next steps, you will insert the AVERAGE function to determine the arithmetic mean of the expenses in column D. If an empty cell or a cell containing text is included in the argument, Excel ignores the cell when determining the result. If, however, the cell contains a zero value, it is included in the average calculation.

3 Click the AutoSum button arrow in the Editing group in the Home tab.

4 Click *Average* at the drop-down list.

Excel inserts the formula =AVERAGE(D14:D16) in the active cell with the suggested range highlighted. In the next step, you will drag to select the correct range and then complete the formula.

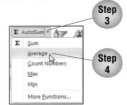

Step 3

Step 4

5 Position the cell pointer over D6, hold down the left mouse button, drag down to D12, and then release the left mouse button.

Excel inserts the range *D6:D12* in the formula and the moving marquee expands to display the selected cells.

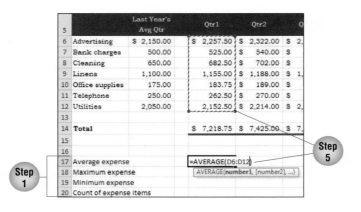

6 Press Enter or click the Enter button on the Formula bar.

Excel returns the result *$1,031.25* in D17.

7 Make D18 the active cell, click the AutoSum button arrow, and then click *Max* at the drop-down list.

The MAX function returns the largest value in the argument.

8 Type **d6:d12** and then press Enter.

Excel returns the result *$2,257.50* in D18. Typing the range into the formula is sometimes faster if you are sure of the starting and ending cell references.

In Brief

AVERAGE, MAX, MIN, COUNT Functions
1. Make desired cell active.
2. Click AutoSum button arrow.
3. Click desired function.
4. Type or select argument range.
5. Press Enter or click Enter button.

17	Average expense	$ 1,031.25
18	Maximum expense	=MAX(d6:d12)
19	Minimum expense	MAX(**number1**, [number2], ...)
20	Count of expense items	

Steps 7-8

9 With D19 the active cell, type the function **=min(d6:d12)** and then press Enter.

MIN returns the smallest value in the argument. As soon as you type the letter m after the equals sign, the Formula AutoComplete feature displays a drop-down list of functions that begin with the letter typed. Formula AutoComplete helps you to write formulas by displaying function names, descriptions, and argument syntax. You can scroll the list and point to a function name to display in a ScreenTip the function's purpose. Double-click a function name in the list to enter the function into the cell.

10 With D20 the active cell, type the function **=count(d6:d12)** and then press Enter.

COUNT returns the number of cells that contain numbers or numbers that have been formatted as text and dates. Empty cells, text labels, or error values in the range are ignored.

11 Select D17:D19 and then drag the fill handle right to column H. (You are not including the Count formula in D20 since the count value (7) does not change.

This copies the AVERAGE, MAX, and MIN formulas to columns E through H.

5		Last Year's Avg Qtr	Qtr1	Qtr2	Qtr3	Qtr4	Total
6	Advertising	$ 2,150.00	$ 2,257.50	$ 2,322.00	$ 2,472.50	$ 2,451.00	$ 9,503.00
7	Bank charges	500.00	525.00	$ 540.00	$ 575.00	$ 570.00	$ 2,210.00
8	Cleaning	650.00	682.50	$ 702.00	$ 747.50	$ 741.00	$ 2,873.00
9	Linens	1,100.00	1,155.00	$ 1,188.00	$ 1,265.00	$ 1,254.00	$ 4,862.00
10	Office supplies	175.00	183.75	$ 189.00	$ 201.25	$ 199.50	$ 773.50
11	Telephone	250.00	262.50	$ 270.00	$ 287.50	$ 285.00	$ 1,105.00
12	Utilities	2,050.00	2,152.50	$ 2,214.00	$ 2,357.50	$ 2,337.00	$ 9,061.00
13							
14	Total		$ 7,218.75	$ 7,425.00	$ 7,906.25	$ 7,837.50	$ 30,387.50
15							
16							
17	Average expense		$ 1,031.25	$ 1,060.71	$ 1,129.46	$ 1,119.64	4,341.07
18	Maximum expense		$ 2,257.50	$ 2,322.00	$ 2,472.50	$ 2,451.00	$ 9,503.00
19	Minimum expense		$ 183.75	$ 189.00	$ 201.25	$ 199.50	773.50
20	Count of expense items		7				

Step 11

12 Click in any cell to deselect D17:H19.

13 Save and then close **ES3-WBQtrExpBudg.xlsx**.

Activity 3.3

Using Date Functions TODAY, NOW, and DATE

Dates are stored as serial numbers, beginning with the number 1 for January 1, 1900, and increasing sequentially. Times are stored as decimal fractions representing portions of a day. Storing these entries as numbers enables calculations to be performed on cells containing a date or a time. The Date & Time category in the Insert Function dialog box contains functions that can be used to write formulas for cells containing dates. Cells containing dates and times can be formatted using the Number Format drop-down list in the Number group in the Home tab or using the Format Cells dialog box. Various combinations of year, month, day, hour, minutes, and seconds are available for displaying dates and times.

Project

Tutorial 3.2
Writing Formulas in Excel

An invoice to Performance Threads needs to be completed by entering the invoice date and the due date. You will open the invoice and experiment with the TODAY and NOW functions to enter the invoice date and then create a formula to calculate the due date. Finally, you will use a DATE function to enter the date The Waterfront Bistro opened in the invoice header.

1 Open **WBInvPTDirMtg.xlsx**.

2 Save the workbook in the ExcelS3 folder and name it **ES3-WBInvPTDirMtg**.

3 Make F6 the active cell, type **=now()**, and then press Enter.

> The current date and time are inserted in F6. In the next step, you will try the TODAY function to see the difference between the two date functions.

4 Make F6 the active cell, press Delete to clear the cell, type **=today()**, and then press Enter.

> The current date is inserted in the cell with the time displayed as 0:00. Normally, the time does not display when TODAY is used; however, since we first entered the NOW function, Excel retained the time format for the cell. In a later step, you will format the cell to display the month, day, and year only.

5 Make F8 the active cell, type **=f6+30**, and then press Enter to calculate the due date as 30 days from the invoice date.

6 Make F4 the active cell.

7 Click the Formulas tab in the ribbon and then click the Date & Time button 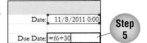 in the Function Library group.

8 Click *DATE* at the drop-down list of Date & Time functions.

> The Function Arguments dialog box opens with a text box for each section of the function argument.

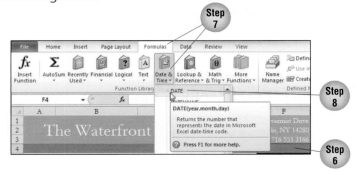

9 Type **1977** in the *Year* text box.

10 Press Tab to move the insertion point to the *Month* text box and then type **06**.

11 Press Tab to move the insertion point to the *Day* text box, type **15**, and then click OK.

> The Function Arguments dialog box displays the serial number for June 15, 1977, as 28291 which is the value Excel stores in the cell. Notice the formula in the Formula bar is *=DATE(1977,6,15)*.

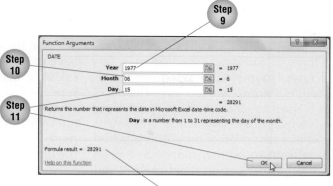

Step 9

Step 10

Step 11

This is the serial number representing June 15, 1977.

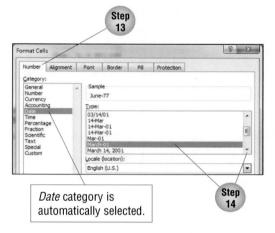

Step 13

Step 14

Date category is automatically selected.

Steps 12-15

Steps 16-18

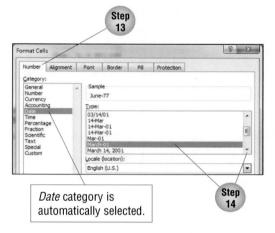

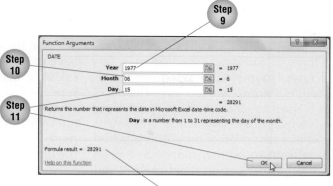

In Brief

Date Functions
1. Make desired cell active.
2. Click Formulas tab.
3. Click Date & Time button.
4. Click desired function at drop-down list.
5. If necessary, enter references in Function Arguments dialog box.
6. Click OK.

12 Right-click F4 and then click *Format Cells* at the shortcut menu.

13 If necessary, click the Number tab in the Format Cells dialog box.

> Since the active cell contains a date function, the *Date* category will be automatically selected in the *Category* list box.

14 Scroll down the list of formats in the *Type* list box; click *March-01*, the format that will display the date as the full month followed by two digits for the year; and then click OK.

15 Format F4 to 10-point Candara italic.

16 Select F6:F8 and then display the Format Cells dialog box with the Number tab selected.

17 Click *Date* in the *Category* list box. Scroll down the *Type* list box; click *14-Mar-2001*, the format that displays the date as dd-mmm-yyyy; and then click OK.

18 Click in any cell to deselect F6:F8.

19 Save and then close **ES3-WBInvPTDirMtg.xlsx**.

In Addition

TIME Function

Time values are stored as decimal numbers that represent the portion of a day starting at 0 (12:00:00 AM) and continuing up to 0.999988426, representing (23:59:59 PM). The format of the TIME function using the 24-hour clock is *=TIME(hour,minute,second)*. In the worksheet shown at the right, the formula *=(C2-B2)*24* is used to calculate how many hours the employee worked.

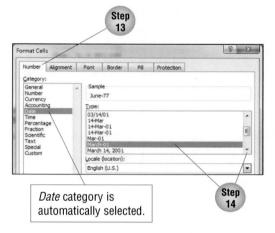

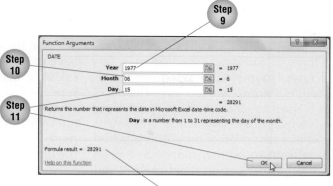

Activity 3.4

Using the Financial Function PMT

You can use Excel's financial functions to calculate depreciation, interest rates, payments, terms, present values, future values, and so on. The PMT function is used to calculate a payment for a loan based on constant payments, a constant interest rate, and a set period of time. This function is useful if you want to borrow money and need to estimate the payment you would make given a specified interest rate and length of time to pay back the loan. To use the PMT function correctly, the time periods for the interest rate and the term have to be consistent. For example, if you want to calculate the monthly payment on a loan, make sure the interest rate and the number of periods are expressed in months, or convert the interest rate and time period to months within the formula. The PMT function requires three arguments: the interest rate for the loan *(Rate)*, the number of payments to be made *(Nper)*, and the amount of money that is borrowed *(Pv)*.

Project

Tutorial 3.3
Using Financial
Functions

The Waterfront Bistro is planning a patio expansion next year. Dana Hirsch has received pre-approval from two finance companies and wants you to estimate monthly loan payments for each to help decide from which company to borrow funds.

1. Open **WBPatioLoan.xlsx**.

2. Save the workbook in the ExcelS3 folder and name it **ES3-WBPatioLoan**.

3. Make B10 the active cell.

4. Click the Formulas tab and then click the Financial button in the Function Library group.

5. Scroll down the *Financial* drop-down list and then click *PMT*.

6. If necessary, drag the Function Arguments dialog box Title bar to the right of column B.

7. With the insertion point positioned in the *Rate* text box, click the mouse in B6 and then type **/12**.

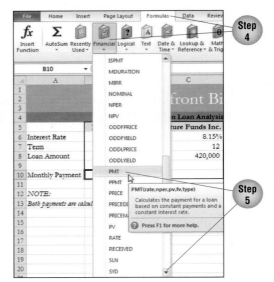

The interest rate in B6 is 7.25% which is the annual interest rate. Typing */12* divides the annual interest rate by 12 to obtain a monthly interest rate. Since you want to calculate a payment per month you need to ensure the time periods for all input values are the same.

8. Click in the *Nper* text box, click B7, and then type ***12**.

The term in B7 represents the number of years that loan payments will be made. Multiplying this value times 12 payments per year represents the total number of payments to be made for the loan. Note that you have converted both the interest rate and the number of payments within the function arguments to months.

9. Click in the *Pv* text box, click B8, and then click OK.

Pv stands for ***present value*** and represents the principal amount that is being borrowed. Excel returns the payment amount *$3,834.02* for the Funds Unlimited loan in B10. Payments are displayed as negative values; in this spreadsheet file, negative values are displayed in red and within parentheses. Consider loan payments as money that is subtracted from your cash balance, which helps you relate to the negative value returned in the formula cell. If you prefer, you can enter a negative value in B8 (-420,000) and the calculated payment displays as a positive number.

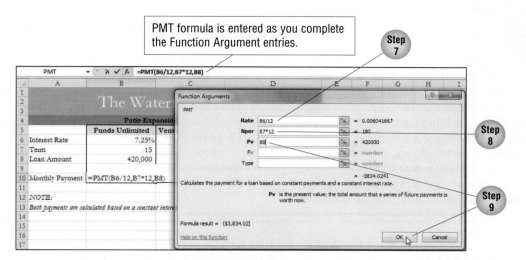

PMT formula is entered as you complete the Function Argument entries.

Step 7

Step 8

Step 9

In Brief

Financial Functions
1. Make desired cell active.
2. Click Formulas tab.
3. Click Financial button.
4. Click desired function name.
5. Enter references in Function Arguments dialog box.
6. Click OK.

⑩ Make C10 the active cell.

⑪ Click the Insert Function button 𝑓𝑥 on the Formula bar.

> The Insert Function dialog box can be used to find an Excel function. This is useful if you do not know the category for which a function is associated. You can locate a function by typing a description of the formula and then clicking the Go button.

⑫ At the Insert Function dialog box, type **loan payments** in the *Search for a function* text box and then click Go.

⑬ With *PMT* already selected in the *Select a function* list box, click OK.

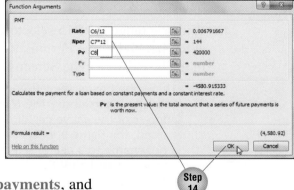

⑭ At the Function Arguments dialog box, enter the parameters as indicated and then click OK.

Rate	**C6/12**
Nper	**C7*12**
Pv	**C8**

Step 14

⑮ Make A15 the active cell, type **Total loan payments**, and press Enter.

⑯ Make B15 the active cell, type **=b10*12*b7**, and then press Enter.

> This calculates the total amount that will have to be paid back for the loan from Funds Unlimited.

⑰ Use the fill handle in B15 to copy the formula to C15.

⑱ Use the Format Painter feature to copy the formats from B10 to B15:C15 and then apply the *All Borders* option to B15:C15.

> Notice that the loan from Venture Funds Inc. is a better choice for The Waterfront Bistro provided the bistro can afford the higher monthly payments. Although the interest rate is higher than Funds Unlimited's loan, the shorter term means the loan is repaid faster with a lower total cost.

Steps 15-18

⑲ Save and then close **ES3-WBPatioLoan.xlsx**.

Activity 3.5

Creating and Using Range Names

Assigning a name to a cell or a range of cells allows you to reference the cell(s) by a descriptive label rather than the cell address or range address when creating formulas, printing, or when navigating a large worksheet. Referencing by name makes a formula easier to understand. For example, a formula such as =*Sales-Expenses* is readily understood. A standard formula such as =*D3-D13* requires the reader to look at the labels next to the values in the formula cells in order to grasp the formula's purpose. A range name can be a combination of letters, numbers, underscore characters, or periods up to 255 characters. The first character in a range name must be a letter, an underscore, or a backslash (\). Spaces are not valid in a range name. To create a range name, select the desired cells and then type the name in the *Name* text box at the left of the Formula bar.

Tutorial 3.4
Naming and Using a Range

Project

The profit-sharing bonus for the employees needs to be calculated. Dana has started the worksheet and asked you to finish it. Since the bonus amount varies depending on the employee's years of service, you decide to begin by naming cells so that you can use names in the function to help you build the correct formula.

1. Open **WBEmpBonus.xlsx**.

2. Save the workbook in the ExcelS3 folder and name it **ES3-WBEmpBonus**.

   To begin, you want to name the cells in column B *Years*. The first step in naming a range is to select the cell or group of cells to which the name will be associated.

3. Select B7:B15.

4. With the range B7:B15 selected, point at the white box at the left end of the Formula bar (currently displays *B7* in the box). Notice the ScreenTip displays *Name Box*.

   The white box at the left end of the Formula bar is called the *Name* box. The *Name* box displays the cell address of the active cell. If the active cell has been named, the name appears in the *Name* box. To assign a new name to a cell or selected range, click in the *Name* box and type the desired name.

5. Click in the *Name* box (white box at left end of Formula bar), type **Years**, and press Enter.

   Notice the range name now appears in the *Name* box. You want to assign a name to each cell that will be referenced when you create the profit-sharing formula in the next project. In the next steps you will assign a range name to individual cells that will be needed to calculate the profit-sharing bonus.

6. Make E7 the active cell.

7. Click in the *Name* box, type **Profit**, and press Enter.

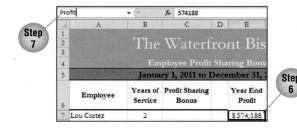

8 Make F7 the active cell, click in the *Name* box, type **FiveAndOver**, and then press Enter.

9 Make G7 the active cell, click in the *Name* box, type **LessThanFive**, and then press Enter.

10 Click the down-pointing arrow at the right of the *Name* box.

A drop-down list of range names in the current workbook appears. To move the active cell to a named cell or range, click the range name in the drop-down list.

11 Click *Years* at the drop-down list.

The range B7:B15 is selected since this is the group of cells associated with the name *Years*.

12 Make A19 the active cell, type **Average service**, and then press Enter.

13 Make B19 the active cell, type **=average(years)**, and then press Enter.

Notice that range names are not case sensitive when you use the name in a formula. When you type the range name *years* in the formula, notice that Excel color-codes B7:B15 to show you the cells that are being referenced in the formula.

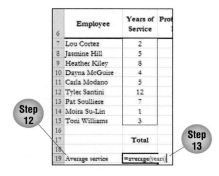

14 Format B19 to display only one decimal place.

15 Save **ES3-WBEmpBonus.xlsx**.

In Addition

Managing Range Names

To edit or delete a range name, display the Name Manager dialog box shown at the right. To do this, click the Formulas tab and then click the Name Manager button in the Defined Names group. The Name Manager dialog box displays the range names in the active workbook and provides buttons to edit or delete the name.

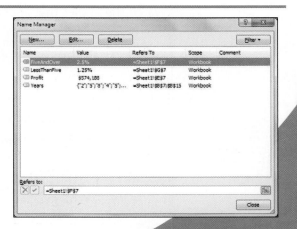

Activity 3.6

Using the Logical IF Function

The IF function returns one of two values in a cell based on a true or false answer to a question called a logical test. The format of an IF function is *=IF(logical_test,value_if_true,value_if_false)*. For example, assume a salesperson earns a 3 percent commission if sales are greater than or equal to $100,000, or a 2 percent commission for sales less than $100,000. Assume the sales value resides in B4. The logical_test in this example would be B4>=100000. Excel can only return a true or false answer when this test is performed. The commission will be calculated at either B4*3% *(value_if_true)* or B4*2% *(value_if_false)*. In this example, the IF function formula would be *=IF(B4>=100000,B4*3%,B4*2%)*.

Project

Tutorial 3.5
Using the Logical IF Function

The catering staff participate in a profit-sharing bonus at the end of a year. The bonus amount is based on the year-end profit and the employee's years of service—2.5% for those with 5 years of service and more, and 1.25% for those employees with less than 5 years of service. Since the percentage bonus can be either one of two values, you need an IF function to calculate the bonus.

1. With **ES3-WBEmpBonus.xlsx** open, make C7 the active cell.
2. Click the Formulas tab.
3. Click the Logical button ⬚ in the Function Library group.
4. Click *IF* at the drop-down list.

The Function Arguments dialog box for the IF statement opens. Notice the three arguments: *Logical_test, Value_if_true,* and *Value_if_false.* To begin, you want Excel to test whether the value in the years of service column (column B) is less than 5. This test determines whether Excel calculates the bonus using the lower percent paid to employees with fewer than five years of

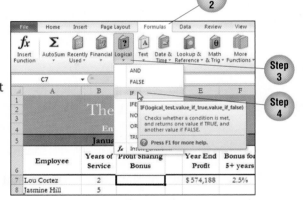

service or the higher percent paid to employees with five or more years of service. Recall that in the last project you created range names. In the next steps, you will see how using range names will make the IF statement much easier to create and understand.

5. With the insertion point positioned in the *Logical_test* text box, type **years<5** and then press Tab.

Watch the entries that appear at the right of each argument text box as you build the formula. Excel updates these entries to show you how the formula is working as you build each argument. Notice that next to the *Logical_test* text box you now see the TRUE and FALSE results Excel is calculating for each entry in the Years range.

6. With the insertion point positioned in the *Value_if_true* text box, type **profit*lessthanfive** and then press Tab.

If the value in B7 is less than 5, Excel calculates the bonus as the profit (E7) times 1.25% (G7). Another advantage to using range names is that by default, range names refer to the named cell using absolute references. Since the formula will be copied to rows 8–15, absolute references are required for those cells that reference the profit and the percents.

7 With the insertion point positioned in the *Value_if_false* text box, type **profit*fiveandover**.

> If the value in B7 is greater than or equal to 5, the formula calculates the profit (E7) times 2.5% (F7). Notice that below the text boxes, Excel shows the result that will be placed in the active cell *Formula result = 7177.35*. Looking at B7 you will note that Lou Cortez has 2 years of service so Excel is calculating Lou's bonus as $574,188 times 1.25%.

In Brief

IF Function
1. Make desired cell active.
2. Click Formulas tab.
3. Click Logical button.
4. Click IF.
5. Type formula in *Logical_test* text box.
6. Type value or formula in *Value_if_true* text box.
7. Type value or formula in *Value_if_false* text box.
8. Click OK.

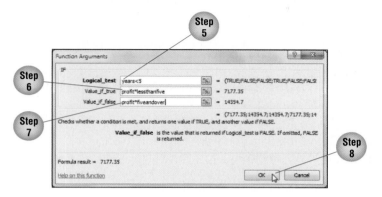

8 Click OK.

9 Drag the fill handle in C7 down to row 15 and then click in any cell to deselect the range.

10 Make C17 the active cell, click the AutoSum button in the Function Library group, and then press Enter to calculate the total bonuses to be paid.

11 Format the values in column C to Comma Style.

12 Click C7 and review the formula in the Formula bar that was created using the IF Function Arguments dialog box *=IF(Years<5, Profit*LessThanFive,Profit*FiveAndOver)*.

> The formula may be easier to comprehend if you include the range names when reading it to yourself.

13 Save and then close **ES3-WBEmpBonus.xlsx**.

In Addition

More about IF Function Arguments

One advantage to creating an IF function using the Function Arguments dialog box is that the correct syntax is added automatically to the formula. For example, you did not need to worry about typing commas between arguments or the opening and closing brackets in this project. These elements are automatically added to the formula. Notice also that the range names in the completed formula are displayed in the case used when the range name is created. For example, you typed profit*lessthanfive but the formula you reviewed at Step 12 displayed this entry as Profit*LessThanFive. When creating your range names consider the readability of the formula and use upper- and lowercase letters to facilitate comprehension. Another alternative is to use underscores between words in a range name.

Activity 3.7

Creating a Column Chart

Numerical values are often more easily understood when presented visually in a chart. Excel includes several chart types such as column, line, pie, bar, area, scatter, and others with which you can graphically portray data. The chart can be placed in the same worksheet as the data or it can be inserted into its own sheet. To create a chart, first select the cells containing the data you want to graph and then choose the chart type. Excel graphs the data in a separate object which can be moved, resized, and formatted.

Project

Dana Hirsch has asked you to create a chart to compare the quarterly expenses in the budget forecast you completed earlier in this section.

Tutorial 3.6
Creating Charts in Excel

1. Open **ES3-WBQtrExpBudg.xlsx**, select A5:A12, hold down the Ctrl key, and then select D5:G12.

    The first step in creating a chart is to select the range of cells containing the data you want to graph. Notice in the range that you are including the row labels in column A. Labels are included to provide the frame of reference for each bar, column, or other chart series. If you select multiple ranges, ensure that the data in each range has a consistent number of cells in the range.

2. Click the Insert tab.

3. Click the Column button in the Charts group.

4. Click *3-D Clustered Column* at the drop-down list (first from left in *3-D Column* section).

    Excel graphs the data in a 3-D column chart and places the chart inside an object box in the center of the worksheet.

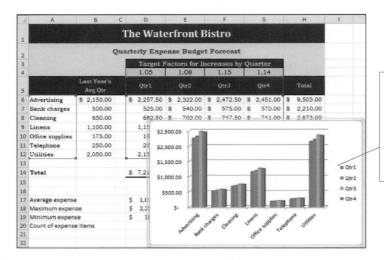

3-D column chart created at Step 4 is placed in an object box, which can be moved, resized, and formatted as needed.

5. Click the Move Chart button in the Location group in the Chart Tools Design tab.

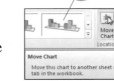

Need Help?

Can't see the Chart Tools Design tab? You probably clicked outside the chart to deselect the object and the contextual tab disappeared. Click over the chart to select the object and the contextual Chart Tools Design tab reappears.

6 At the Move Chart dialog box, click *New sheet*.

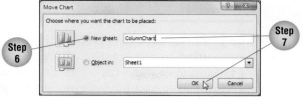

7 With *Chart1* selected in the *New sheet* text box, type **ColumnChart** and then click OK.

> The chart object is moved to a new sheet in the workbook with a tab labeled *ColumnChart*. The chart is automatically scaled to fill the entire page in landscape orientation.

8 Click *Layout 3* in the Chart Layouts group.

> This layout adds a title to the top center of the chart and moves the legend to the bottom center.

9 Click once over *Chart Title* to select the title object, click a second time at the beginning of the text to place an insertion point inside the chart title box, delete *Chart Title*, and then type **Quarterly Expense Budget Forecast**.

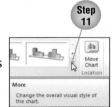

10 Click inside the chart area to deselect the title text.

11 Click the More arrow button ⟱ in the Chart Styles group in the Chart Tools Design tab.

12 Click *Style 26* in the drop-down gallery (second option in the fourth row).

13 Save **ES3-WBQtrExpBudg.xlsx**.

In Addition

Changing the Data in a Chart

Click the Select Data button in the Data group in the Chart Tools Design tab to add cells to, or delete cells from, the source range that was selected to generate the chart. At the Select Data Source dialog box shown at the right, you can add, edit, or delete a data series or edit the category axis labels.

In Brief

Create Column Chart
1. Select cells.
2. Click Insert tab.
3. Click Column button.
4. Click desired chart type.
5. Move and/or resize chart as required.
6. Apply design options.

Activity 3.8

Creating a Pie Chart

Pie charts illustrate each data point's size in proportion to the total of all items in the data source range. Each slice in the pie chart is displayed as a percentage of the whole pie. You can choose to display the percent values, the actual values used to gener- ate the chart, or both values as data labels inside or outside the pie slices. Use a pie chart when you have only one data series you want to graph and there are no negative or zero values within the data range.

Project

Dana Hirsch has requested a second chart from the quarterly expense budget forecast worksheet that displays each expense as a proportion of the total expenses.

The Waterfront
B·I·S·T·R·O

SNAP

Tutorial 3.6
Creating Charts in Excel

1. With **ES3-WBQtrExpBudg.xlsx** open, click the tab labeled *Sheet1* near the bottom left corner of the window above the Status bar.

Step 1

2. If necessary, click in any cell to deselect the range that was used to generate the column chart in the previous activity.

3. Select the range A5:A12, hold down the Ctrl key, and then select the range H5:H12.

4. Click the Insert tab.

5. Click the Pie button 🥧 in the Charts group.

6. Click *Pie in 3-D*, the first pie chart in the *3-D Pie* section in the drop-down list.

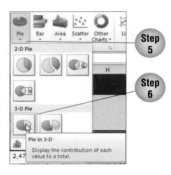
Step 5
Step 6

7. Point to the border of the chart object until the pointer displays with the four-headed arrow move icon, hold down the left mouse button, and then drag the chart below the worksheet. Position the chart approximately centered below columns A–H with the top edge in row 22.

Need Help?

You may find it helpful to scroll the worksheet until you see several blank rows below row 22 before moving the chart.

8. With the chart object still selected, click the Chart Tools Layout tab.

9. Click the Data Labels button 📊 in the Labels group and then click *More Data Label Options* at the drop-down list.

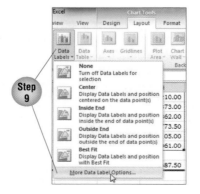

Step 9

10 At the Format Data Labels dialog box with *Label Options* selected in the left pane, click the *Value* check box in the *Label Contains* section to clear the box and then click the *Percentage* check box to add a check mark.

11 Click *Outside End* in the *Label Position* section.

12 Click *Number* in the left pane, click *Percentage* in the *Category* list box, select the number in the *Decimal places* text box, and then type **1**.

13 Close the Format Data Labels dialog box.

14 Click the Chart Tools Design tab.

15 Click the More arrow button in the Chart Styles group and then click *Style 10* at the drop-down list (second option in second row).

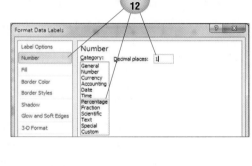

16 Change the chart title to **Total Operating Expenses Forecast**. Refer to Activity 3.7, Steps 9–10, if you need assistance with this step.

17 Click in the worksheet area outside the chart to deselect the chart.

18 Save and then close **ES3-WBQtrExpBudg.xlsx**.

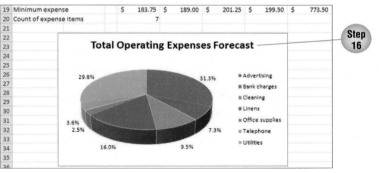

In Addition

Sparklines

A new Sparklines group was added to the Insert tab in Excel 2010. Sparklines are miniature charts that you can add to a cell. These miniature charts illustrate changes from a specified row or column of data. For example, in the worksheet shown, the sparkline chart was created in F4 based on the range of values in B4:E4. Click the Insert tab and then click Line, Column, or Win/Loss in the Sparklines group. At the Create Sparklines dialog box, select the data range that contains the values you want to base the chart upon (B4:E4), select the cell in which to draw the chart (F4), and then click OK.

Activity 3.9

Creating a Line Chart; Drawing Shapes

A line chart shows trends and change over time at even intervals. Line charts emphasize the rate of change over time rather than the magnitude of the change. You can easily spot a trend in a line chart, look for unusual points in the data series, or even predict future values based on the line's shape and direc-tion. The Shapes button in the Insert tab includes buttons with which you can draw lines, rectangles, basic shapes, block arrows, equation shapes, flow-chart symbols, stars and banners, and callouts. Enclosed shapes can also contain text. Draw shapes, arrows, or add text boxes to add emphasis or insert explanatory notes in a worksheet.

Project

The Waterfront BISTRO

Dana has created a worksheet with the bistro's performance statistics by quarter along with the National Restaurant Association's statistics. Dana would like you to create charts in order to compare the data visually.

1. Open **WBPerfStats.xlsx**. Save the workbook in the ExcelS3 folder and name it **ES3-WBPerfStats**.

2. Select A3:E4, hold down the Ctrl key, and then select A8:E8.

SNAP

Tutorial 3.6
Creating Charts in Excel

3. Click the Insert tab, click the Line button  in the Charts group, and then click *Line with Markers* in the *2-D Line* section at the drop-down list (first option in second row).

> Notice the line chart clearly shows that the bistro performed below the association's average check per person for the first half of the year but finished the year well above the association's statistics.

4. Point to the border of the chart object until the pointer displays with the four-headed arrow move icon and then drag the chart below the worksheet approximately centered below columns A–E and with the top edge in row 11.

5. Select A3:E3, A5:E5, and A9:E9 and then create a Line chart similar to the line chart created at Step 3.

6. Move the new line chart below the first one, leaving one blank row between the two charts.

> In the next steps you will draw shapes and add text to the shapes to add emphasis in the two line charts.

7. If necessary, click the Insert tab. Click the Shapes button in the Illustrations group.

> The Shapes drop-down list contains shape buttons grouped by category.

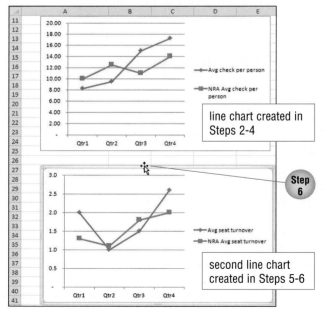

8 Click the *12-Point Star* button in the *Stars and Banners* group (fourth from right in first row).

> When a shape object tool has been selected, the pointer changes to a crosshairs.

In Brief

Create Line Chart
1. Select cells.
2. Click Insert tab.
3. Click Line button.
4. Click desired line type.
5. Move and/or resize chart as required.
6. Apply design options.

Draw Shape
1. Click Insert tab.
2. Click Shapes button.
3. Click desired shape.
4. Drag to create shape.
5. Move, resize, or format shape as required.

Add Text to Shape
1. Right-click shape.
2. Click *Edit Text*.
3. Type text.
4. Click outside shape.

9 Position the crosshairs in the white space above the legend in the first line chart near the top of the chart just right of the 20.00 grid line, drag the crosshairs down and right as shown, and then release the mouse. If you are not happy with the shape, press Delete to remove the star and then try again.

> When you release the mouse, the shape is positioned with eight white sizing handles around the perimeter of the shape as well as a green rotation handle and a yellow diamond center point. The Drawing Tools Format tab becomes active with options to customize the shape.

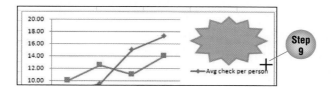

10 Right-click the shape and then click *Edit Text* at the shortcut menu.

> An insertion point appears inside the shape indicating you can begin typing.

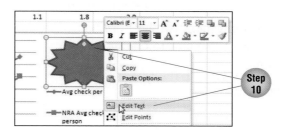

11 Type **A Strong Finish!**, press Ctrl + E to center the text, and then click in the worksheet outside the chart.

12 If necessary, click the Insert tab. Click the Shapes button and then click the *Wave* button 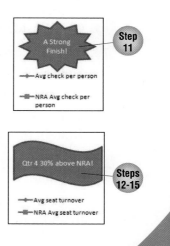 in the *Stars and Banners* group (second from right in second row).

13 Draw a wave shape in the white space above the legend in the second line chart similar to the one shown.

14 Right-click the shape and then click *Edit Text* at the shortcut menu.

15 Type **Qtr 4 30% above NRA!**, click the Home tab, click the Middle Align button in the Alignment group, and then click in the worksheet outside the chart.

16 Print the worksheet.

17 Save and then close **ES3-WBPerfStats.xlsx**.

Activity 3.10

Modifying and Formatting Charts

To make changes to an existing chart, click inside a chart or chart element to display the translucent border around the perimeter of the chart object. Point to the border to move the chart or point to one of the eight sizing handles to resize the chart. When the chart is selected, the Chart Tools Design, Layout, and Format tabs become available. Use these tabs to add, delete, or modify the chart or chart elements.

Project

Tutorial 3.7
Changing a Chart Type

You will modify the charts created for the quarterly expense budget forecast worksheet by formatting the legend, changing the font in the chart title, and changing the chart type.

1 Open **ES3-WBQtrExpBudg.xlsx** and then click anywhere inside the pie chart to select the chart object.

> Once a chart is selected, the three contextual Chart Tools tabs become available—Design, Layout, and Format.

2 Click inside the pie chart legend.

> Eight sizing handles appear around the legend indicating the object is selected. You can drag the legend to another location or resize the legend using one of the handles.

3 Click the Chart Tools Format tab.

4 Click the Shape Outline button in the Shape Styles group and then click the *Light Blue* color box in the color palette (fourth from right in *Standard Colors* section).

> This adds a thin, light blue border around the legend.

5 Right-click the chart title and then use the Font and Font Size buttons in the Mini toolbar to change the title to 14-point Verdana.

6 Click inside the chart area to deselect the chart title.

7 Click inside any one of the percent values around the edge of the pie.

> This selects all seven data labels.

8 Click the Home tab and then click the Bold button in the Font group.

9 Click in the worksheet area outside the pie chart.

10 Click the ColumnChart tab located near the bottom left corner of the window above the Status bar and then click inside the column chart to select the chart.

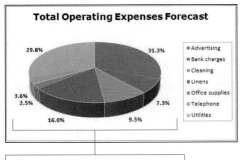

percent values bolded in Steps 7-8

11 Click the Chart Tools Design tab and then click the Change Chart Type button in the Type group.

12 At the Change Chart Type dialog box, click *Bar* in the left pane and then click *Clustered Bar in 3-D* in the *Bar* section in the right pane (fourth option in first row).

13 Click OK.

14 Click *Layout 1* in the Chart Layouts group.

> This layout moves the legend to the right side of the chart where there is more room.

15 Click the More arrow button in the Chart Styles group and then click *Style 2* in the drop-down list (second option in first row).

16 Print the chart.

17 Click the Sheet1 tab, click the File tab, and then click Print.

18 Click the Scaling gallery in the *Settings* group (last gallery that displays *No Scaling*), click *Fit Sheet on One Page* at the drop-down list, and then click the Print button.

> Scaling a worksheet means Excel will decrease the size of print proportionately in order to fit a worksheet to the specified number of pages (in this case one page).

19 Save and then close **ES3-WBQtrExpBudg.xlsx**.

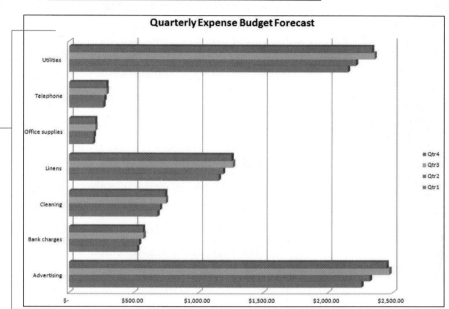

Step 12

Layout 1 and Style 2 applied to bar chart in Steps 14-15

Quarterly Expense Budget Forecast

In Addition

Chart Elements

Another method to edit a chart is to right-click a chart element to display a context-sensitive shortcut menu. For example, right-clicking the axis labels in the bar chart displays the shortcut menu shown at the right. The bottom section of the shortcut menu changes depending on the element you clicked.

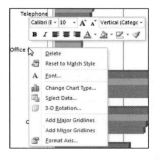

Activity 3.11

Changing Page Layout Options

The Page Layout tab contains buttons to modify the page setup and scaling options for printing purposes. You can also change print options while previewing the worksheet in the Print tab Backstage view. The margin on a worksheet is the blank space at the top, bottom, left, and right edges of the page and the beginning of the printed text. The default margins are 0.75 inch top and bottom and 0.7 inch left and right. Smaller worksheets can be centered horizontally and/or vertically to improve the printed appearance. For larger worksheets, you can choose to shrink the text by scaling the size of printed text to force the printout to a maximum number of pages such as the quarterly expense budget forecast printed in the last activity which you scaled to fit one page.

Project

Tutorial 3.8
Changing Page Margins and Layout Options

You need to print the invoice to Performance Threads completed in an earlier activity. Prior to printing you will adjust the margins to improve the worksheet's appearance using the Print tab Backstage view. Dana would also like the worksheet printed with the loan analysis for the patio expansion. You will center the worksheet horizontally before printing.

1. Open **ES3-WBInvPTDirMtg.xlsx**.

2. Click the File tab and then click Print to open the Print tab Backstage view.

   Notice the invoice is not balanced on the page. In the next steps you will change the margins to improve the page layout.

3. Click the Margins gallery in the *Settings* category (currently displays *Normal Margins*).

4. Click *Custom Margins* at the drop-down list.

   The Page Setup dialog box opens with the Margins tab active.

The worksheet is unbalanced on the page.

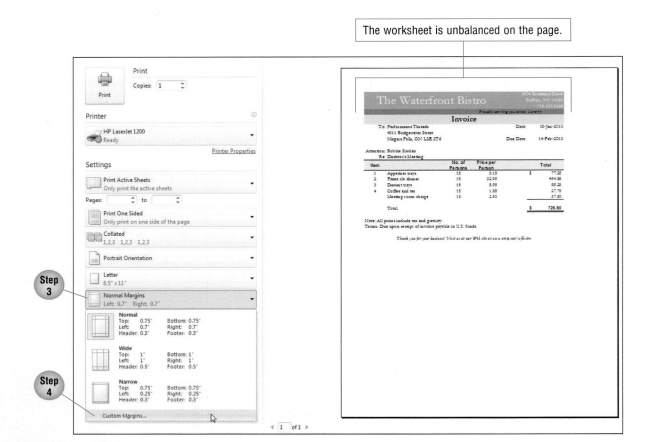

(5) Select the current entry in the *Top* text box, type **1.25**, select the current entry in the *Left* text box, type **1.25**, and then click OK.

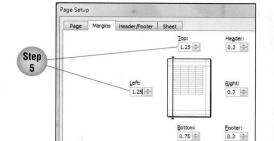

Step 5

> The preview pane in Backstage view shows the worksheet with the new margins applied. The page layout is improved for printing.

(6) Click the Print button.

(7) Save and then close **ES3-WBInvPTDirMtg.xlsx**.

(8) Open **ES3-WBPatioLoan.xlsx**.

(9) Click the Page Layout tab, click the Orientation button in the Page Setup group, and then click *Landscape*.

Step 9

(10) Click the Margins button in the Page Setup group and then click *Custom Margins* at the drop-down list.

> The Page Setup dialog box opens with the Margins tab active. This is another way to open the same Page Setup dialog box you accessed using the Margins gallery in Print tab Backstage view.

(11) Change the *Top* margin to *1.25*.

(12) Click the *Horizontally* check box in the *Center on page* section and then click OK.

Step 11

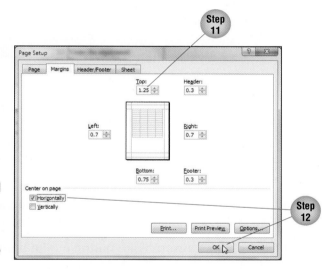

Step 12

> Centering the worksheet horizontally is another method that can be used to ensure the worksheet prints balanced between the left and right edges of the page. You can choose both the *Horizontally* and *Vertically* check boxes to print a worksheet that is centered between both the left and right edges (horizontally), and the top and bottom edges (vertically) of the page.

(13) Print the worksheet.

(14) Save and then close **ES3-WBPatioLoan.xlsx**.

In Addition

Printing Column or Row Headings on Multiple Pages

Use the Print Titles button in the Page Setup group in the Page Layout tab to define column or row headings that you want repeated at the top or left edge of each page to make the data in rows and columns in a multipage printout easier to identify.

Activity 3.12

Using Page Layout View; Inserting Headers and Footers

Page Layout view allows you to view the worksheet along with the print settings. Page Layout view also displays horizontal and vertical rulers to assist with measurements. A header is text that prints at the top of each work-sheet and a footer is text that prints at the bottom of each worksheet. Excel includes pre-defined headers and footers that can be selected from a drop-down list or you can create your own custom header or footer text.

Project

Before printing the profit-sharing bonus worksheet completed earlier, you want to add identifying information in a custom header and footer and check other print options using Page Layout view.

The Waterfront B·I·S·T·R·O

Tutorial 3.9
Adding Headers and Footers

1 Open **ES3-WBEmpBonus.xlsx**.

2 Click the Page Layout button [image] located at the right side of the Status bar near the Zoom slider bar.

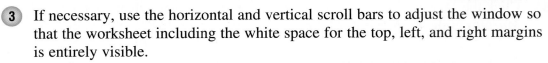
Step 2

3 If necessary, use the horizontal and vertical scroll bars to adjust the window so that the worksheet including the white space for the top, left, and right margins is entirely visible.

4 Click over the text *Click to add header* near the top center of the page.

Step 4

A header and footer are divided into three sections. Click at the left or right side of the header area to open the left or right section text box in which you can type or insert header and footer elements. By default, text in the left section is left-aligned, text in the center section is centered, and text in the right section is right-aligned.

5 Click at the left edge of the Header area to open the left section text box and then type your first and last names.

Step 5

6 Click at the right edge of the Header area to open the right section text box, type **Date Printed:**, and then press the spacebar once.

7 Click the Current Date button [image] in the Header & Footer Elements group in the Header & Footer Tools Design tab.

Excel inserts the code *&[Date]*, which causes the current date to be inserted at the location of the code when the worksheet is printed.

In Brief

Insert Header or Footer
1. Switch to Page Layout view.
2. Click over *Click to add header* or *Click to add footer*.
3. Insert desired header and footer elements and/or type text in left, center, or right section.
4. Click in the worksheet area to end header or footer editing.

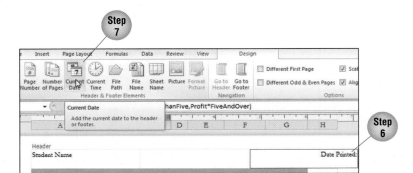
Step 7
Step 6

8 Click the Go to Footer button  in the Navigation group in the Header & Footer Tools Design tab.

> The right footer section at the bottom of the page opens for editing.

9 Click in the center of the Footer area to open the center section for editing.

10 Click the File Name button in the Header & Footer Elements group.

> Excel inserts the code *&[File]*, which causes the workbook file name to be inserted at the location of the code when the worksheet is printed.

11 Click anywhere in the worksheet area outside the footer to close the footer section.

12 Scroll to the top of the worksheet to view the header. Notice that Excel now displays the current date in place of the *&[Date]* code.

13 Look at the bottom of the worksheet and notice that the *&[File]* code now displays the workbook file name.

14 Click the Page Layout tab.

> By default, the header and footer margin is 0.3 inch. In the next step you will adjust the header and footer margin to provide more white space at the top and bottom of the page.

15 Click the Margins button in the Page Setup group, click *Custom Margins* at the drop-down list, and then change the margin settings as indicated below at the Page Setup dialog box with the Margins tab active:

Top	**1**	Header	**0.5**
Bottom	**1**	Footer	**0.5**
Left	**1**		

16 Click OK to close the Page Setup dialog box.

17 Review the new margin settings in Page Layout view.

18 Print the worksheet.

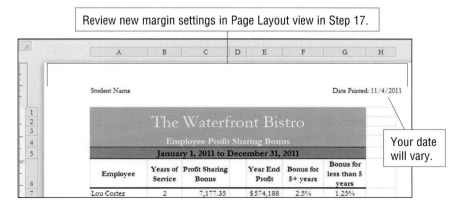

Review new margin settings in Page Layout view in Step 17.

Your date will vary.

19 Click the Normal button located at the right side of the Status bar near the Zoom slider bar (immediately left of the Page Layout View button).

20 Save and then close **ES3-WBEmpBonus.xlsx**.

Features Summary

Feature	Ribbon Tab, Group	Button
change margins	Page Layout, Page Setup OR File, Print	
create a column chart	Insert, Charts	
create a line chart	Insert, Charts	
create a pie chart	Insert, Charts	
Date & Time functions	Formulas, Function Library	
draw a shape	Insert, Illustrations	
Financial functions	Formulas, Function Library	
insert function	Formulas, Function Library	
insert header or footer	Insert, Text OR Page Layout View	
Logical functions	Formulas, Function Library	
Page Layout view	View, Workbook Views	OR
scale page width and/or height	Page Layout, Scale to Fit OR File, Print	
Statistical functions	Formulas, Function Library	

Knowledge Check

Completion: In the space provided at the right, indicate the correct term, command, or option.

1. This symbol next to a column or row number means the reference is absolute.
2. AVERAGE and COUNT are two of the functions grouped in this function category.
3. This Date and Time function inserts the current date (without the time) in the active cell.
4. This financial function returns the payment for a loan based on a constant interest rate and period of time for repayment.
5. A range name is typed in this box at the left end of the Formula bar.
6. The IF function is found in this category of functions in the Function Library.
7. This type of chart is used to illustrate each data point as a proportion of the total.
8. When a chart is selected, these three contextual Chart Tools tabs appear.

9. This button in the Illustrations group is used when you want to draw a star. _____

10. Page Setup options such as custom margins can be changed using the Page Layout tab or while viewing a preview of how the worksheet will print in this view. _____

11. You can type header or footer text directly in the worksheet while viewing the worksheet in this view. _____

12. This code is inserted in the header or footer when you click the File Name button in the Header & Footer Elements group. _____

Skills Review

Review 1 Creating Range Names; Inserting Statistical, Date, and IF Functions; Changing Page Layout Options

1. Open **WBQtrRev.xlsx** and then save the workbook in the ExcelEOS folder and name it **ES3-R1-WBQtrRev**.

2. Select and name the ranges indicated.

   | B4:B8 | *Quarter1* | C4:C8 | *Quarter2* | D4:D8 | *Quarter3* |
   | E4:E8 | *Quarter4* | F4:F8 | *TotalRev* | | |

3. Type labels in the cells indicated.

   A14   Average revenue   A15   Maximum revenue   A16   Minimum revenue

4. In B14, B15, and B16, enter the functions that will calculate the average, maximum, and minimum revenue values using the Quarter1 range name in each function.

5. Insert average, maximum, and minimum functions in C14:F16 using the Quarter2, Quarter3, Quarter4, and TotalRev range names, respectively, in each column's functions.

6. Make A18 the active cell and then type **Date created**.

7. Enter in B18 a DATE function that will insert the current date. ***Note: You do not want to use TODAY or NOW functions, because the date will update each time you open the file***.

8. Format B18 to display the date in the format *14-Mar-2001*.

9. Type the label **Next revision date** in A19 and then enter a formula in B19 that will add 350 days to the date in B18.

10. Type the label **Quarterly minimum target** in A21 and the value **350000** in B21.

11. Format B21 to Comma Style with no decimals and name the cell *MinTarget*.

12. Type the label **Revenue target not met by** in A22.

13. Dana Hirsch set the minimum target of $350,000 for each quarter's revenue. Calculate in B22 the amount under target the quarter's total revenue is by entering the IF formula: **=if(b10<mintarget,b10-mintarget,0)**.

14. Drag the fill handle from B22 to C22:E22.

15. Change the page orientation to landscape, change the top margin to 1.5 inches, and center the worksheet horizontally.

16. Create a header that will print your first and last names at the left margin and the current date and time separated by one space at the right margin.

17. Create a footer that will print the file name at the right margin.

18. Save and print **ES3-R1-WBQtrRev.xlsx**. ***Note: If you submit your work in hard copy, check with your instructor to see if you need to print two copies of this worksheet with one of the copies showing the cell formulas instead of the calculated results***.

Review 2 Creating Charts; Drawing Shapes

1. With **ES3-R1-WBQtrRev.xlsx** open, select the range A3:E8 and then create a column chart with the following options:
   a. Choose the *Clustered Column* in the *2-D Column* section (first chart option).
   b. Move the chart to a new sheet with the sheet label *ColumnChart*.
   c. Apply the Layout 1 chart layout.
   d. Apply the Style 34 chart style.
   e. Change the chart title to *Quarterly Revenue Budget Forecast*.
2. Print the ColumnChart sheet.
3. Make Sheet1 the active sheet, select the ranges A3:A8 and F3:F8, and then create a Pie chart with the following options.
   a. Choose the *Exploded Pie in 3-D* in the *3-D Pie* section (second chart option).
   b. Move the chart to a new sheet with the sheet label *PieChart*.
   c. Apply the Layout 6 chart layout.
   d. Apply the Style 34 chart style.
   e. Change the chart title to *Total Revenue Budget Forecast*.
4. With PieChart the active sheet, draw an *Up Arrow Callout* shape (last shape in second row in the *Block Arrows* group) in the white space below the pie chart. Draw the shape approximately 1 inch wide and 1.5 inches high with the top of the arrow pointing up towards 55% in the Dining room pie slice.
5. Add the text **This is a 10% increase over last year!** inside the up arrow callout shape.
6. Select the shape, click the Home tab, and click the Center button and the Middle Align button in the Alignment group.
7. Print the PieChart sheet.
8. Save and then close **ES3-R1-WBQtrRev.xlsx**.

Skills Assessment

Note: If you submit your work in hard copy, check with your instructor before completing these Assessments to find out if you need to print two copies of each worksheet with one of the copies showing the cell formulas instead of the calculated results.

Assessment 1 Creating Statistical and IF Functions; Using Absolute References

1. Alex Torres, manager of the Toronto office for First Choice Travel, has started a workbook to calculate sales commission for the Toronto sales agents. First Choice Travel has implemented a new bonus commission based upon the number of cruises booked. Alex has asked for your help in writing the correct formulas to calculate the commission owed to the agents and analyze the results. To begin, open **FCTSalesComm.xlsx** and then save the workbook in the ExcelEOS folder naming it **ES3-A1-FCTSalesComm**.

2. Create an IF function to calculate the commission for Lopez in D4 using the information in the Commission Parameters table in F2:G5 and in the box below the table. When writing your IF statement, use references to the percent values in G4 and G5 so that when Alex revises the percents the worksheet will automatically recalculate commissions correctly. *Hint: The formula will be copied in the next step, so G4 and G5 need to be absolute references*.
3. Copy the IF function in D4 to the remaining rows in column D.
4. Format the values in column D to an appropriate number style.
5. Enter Average commission in B20 and create a function in D20 to calculate the average commission paid. Enter Maximum commission in B21 and create a function in D21 to show the highest commission paid. Enter Minimum commission in B22 and create a function to show the lowest commission paid.
6. Change the top margin to 1.25 inches and the left margin to 1.5 inches.
7. Save, print, and then close **ES3-A1-FCTSalesComm.xlsx**.

Assessment 2 Applying the PMT Function

1. You are the assistant to Sam Vestering, manager of North American Distribution for Worldwide Enterprises. Sam has entered in a workbook details on financing from two companies for an office expansion loan. Sam would like you to enter the formulas to calculate the estimated monthly loan payments and the total cost of each loan. To begin, open **WELoan.xlsx** and then save the workbook in the ExcelEOS folder naming it **ES3-A2-WELoan**.
2. Calculate the monthly payments on the loan in B7 and D7.
3. Calculate the total payments required for each loan in B11 and D11.
4. Save, print, and then close **ES3-A2-WELoan.xlsx**.

Assessment 3 Creating Charts; Drawing Shapes

1. Cal Rubine, chair of the Theatre Arts Division at Niagara Peninsula College, has asked you to create charts from the grades analysis report to present at a divisional meeting. After reviewing the grades, you decide to create a line chart depicting the grades for all of the courses and a pie chart summarizing the total grades. To begin, open **NPCGrades.xlsx** and then save the workbook in the ExcelEOS folder naming it **ES3-A3-NPCGrades**.
2. Create a line chart in a new sheet labeled *LineChart* that displays the A+ through F grades for all five courses. Include an appropriate chart title. You determine the line chart style, layout, and any other chart elements and formats that will make the chart easy to interpret.
3. Create a 3-D pie chart that displays the total of each grade as a percentage of 100. *Hint: Select the ranges B4:G4 and B11:G11 to create the chart*. Include an appropriate chart title and display percents around the outside of the pie slices as well as the Category names. Position the pie chart below the grades worksheet starting in row 14.
4. In the white space at the top left of the chart draw a right-pointing block arrow pointing to the percent value above the pie slice for the F grade. Inside the block arrow type the text Lowest failure rate since 2008! If necessary, format the text to a smaller font to fit the text within the available space.
5. Print the worksheet centered horizontally and print the line chart.
6. Save and then close **ES3-A3-NPCGrades.xlsx**.

Assessment 4 Creating Charts; Changing Page Layout; Inserting a Footer

1. Melissa Gehring, manager of the Los Angeles office for First Choice Travel, has prepared a workbook with European destinations and current package pricing options. Melissa wants you to create two charts and improve the appearance of the worksheet before she presents it at the next staff meeting. To begin, open **FCTEurope.xlsx** and then save the workbook in the ExcelEOS folder naming it **ES3-A4-FCTEurope**.
2. Insert a new row above the worksheet and add the title *European Packages* merged and centered over the worksheet.
3. Increase the height of row 1 to *27.00 (36 pixels)*.
4. Apply the Opulent theme to the worksheet.
5. Apply the Title style to A1, the Accent2 style to the range A2:G2, and the Accent1 cell style to the range A3:G3.
6. Format the values in B4:G13 to Comma Style with zero decimals.
7. Create a *Clustered bar in 3-D* bar chart in a new sheet labeled *14NightsChart* that graphs the standard and deluxe rates for all of the destinations for 14 nights. Add an appropriate title to the chart and make any other formatting choices you think would enhance the chart.
8. Print the 14NightsChart sheet.
9. Create a *Clustered bar in 3-D* bar chart in a new sheet labeled *21NightsChart* that graphs the standard and deluxe rates for all of the destinations for 21 nights. Add an appropriate title to the chart and make any other formatting choices you think would enhance the chart.
10. Print the 21NightsChart sheet.
11. Make Sheet1 the active sheet, change the page orientation to landscape, change the top margin to 1.5 inches, and center the worksheet horizontally.
12. Create a custom footer that prints your name at the left margin and the file name at the right margin.
13. Print Sheet1.
14. Save and then close **ES3-A4-FCTEurope.xlsx**.

Assessment 5 Finding Information on Chart Axis Options

1. Use the Help feature to find information on changing the vertical axis scale options in a chart.
2. Open **ES3-A4-FCTEurope.xlsx**.
3. Save the workbook in the ExcelEOS folder and name it **ES3-A5-FCTEurope**.
4. Make the 14NightsChart sheet active.
5. Using the information you learned in Help, change the value axis options so that the minimum value is fixed at 1000 and the major unit is fixed at 500. This means the value axis will start at $1,000 instead of zero and gridlines will show at every $500 interval.
6. Print the 14NightsChart sheet.
7. Save and then close **ES3-A5-FCTEurope.xlsx**.

Assessment 6 Individual Challenge
Social Networking Survey

1. You want to know which social networking tool and which social activity is the most popular among your friends, family, and classmates. Ask 10 to 20 friends, family, or classmates the following two questions and collect the responses in an Excel worksheet.
   a. Which of the following social networking sites do you use?

Facebook	LinkedIn
MySpace	Flixster
Twitter	HI5

   b. Which social networking activities do you do at these sites?

Share photos	Share updates about me or my family
Write a blog	Write reviews
Connect with people	

2. Create a chart in a new sheet labeled *SocialNetSites* that displays the total users for each of the social networking sites in the first survey question. You determine the most appropriate chart type to display the survey results. Add an appropriate chart title and any other chart formatting options to enhance the chart's appearance.
3. Print the SocialNetSites sheet.
4. Create a chart in a new sheet labeled *SocialNetAct* that displays the total participants for each type of social networking activity in the second survey question. You determine the appropriate chart type to display the survey results. Add an appropriate chart title and any other chart formatting options to enhance the chart's appearance.
5. Print the SocialNetAct sheet.
6. Save the workbook and name it **ES3-A6-SocialNetSurvey**.
7. Print the worksheet with the source data for the two charts and then close **ES3-A6-SocialNetSurvey.xlsx**.

Marquee Challenge

Challenge 1 Creating Charts on Movie Attendance Statistics

1. You are working with Shannon Grey, president of Marquee Productions, on presentation materials for an upcoming staff development workshop on producing and marketing movies. As part of Shannon's research for the workshop, she compiled a workbook with statistics related to movie attendance by age group and by household income. Shannon has asked you to create two charts for the workshop based on this source data. To begin, open **MPMovieStats.xlsx** and then save the workbook in the ExcelEOS folder naming it **ES3-C1-MPMovieStats**.
2. Using the data in the workbook, create the two charts shown in Figure 3.1.
3. The font for the title and axis text is Impact. Use your best judgment to determine chart style, layout, and other formatting options. Explore the various formatting options for elements such as the chart area, walls, axes, and gridlines.
4. Position the bar chart in a new sheet with the label *AgeChart*.
5. Position the doughnut chart in a new sheet with the label *IncomeChart*.
6. Save the revised workbook.
7. Print each chart and then close **ES3-C1-MPMovieStats.xlsx**.

FIGURE 3.1 Challenge 1

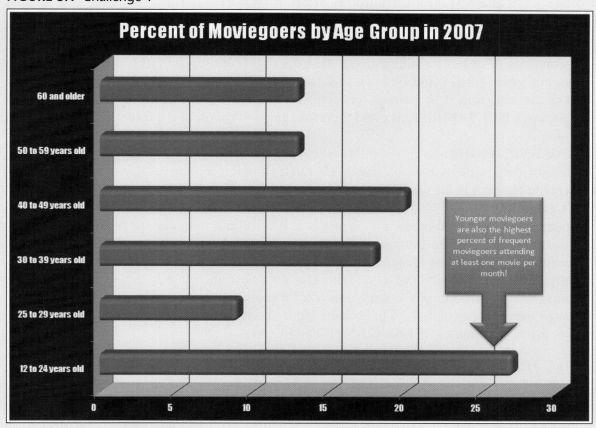

Percent of Moviegoers by Age Group in 2007

Younger moviegoers are also the highest percent of frequent moviegoers attending at least one movie per month!

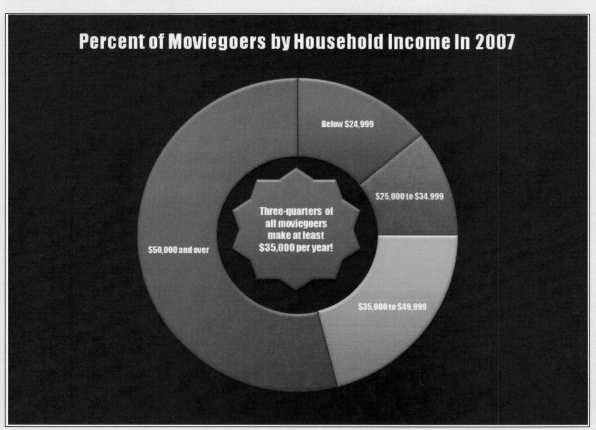

Percent of Moviegoers by Household Income In 2007

Below $24,999

$25,000 to $34,999

$35,000 to $49,999

$50,000 and over

Three-quarters of all moviegoers make at least $35,000 per year!

Challenge 2 Preparing an International Student Report

1. You work in the Registrar's Office at Niagara Peninsula College. Terri VanDaele, the registrar, has sent you a workbook with the top ten countries of origin for international students registered for the 2011 academic year. Terri would like you to format the workbook to improve the appearance and create a chart next to the data for inclusion with the annual report to the board. To begin, open **NPCTop10Int.xlsx** and then save the workbook in the ExcelEOS folder naming it **ES3-C2-NPCTop10Int**.
2. Using the data in the workbook, create the chart shown in Figure 3.2.
3. Insert the Niagara Peninsula College logo as shown in Figure 3.2 using the file named **NPCLogo.jpg**.
4. Format the worksheet as shown in Figure 3.2. If the clip art images are not available on the computer you are using, select an appropriate alternative image. *Hint: Use the keyword* **diversity** *when searching for the picture at the top right of the worksheet.* Apply the Verve theme to the worksheet. Use your best judgment to determine font size, column widths, row heights, colors, and other formatting elements.
5. Change the page orientation to landscape and make sure the workbook fits on one page.
6. Save, print, and then close **ES3-C2-NPCTop10.xlsx**.

FIGURE 3.2 Challenge 2

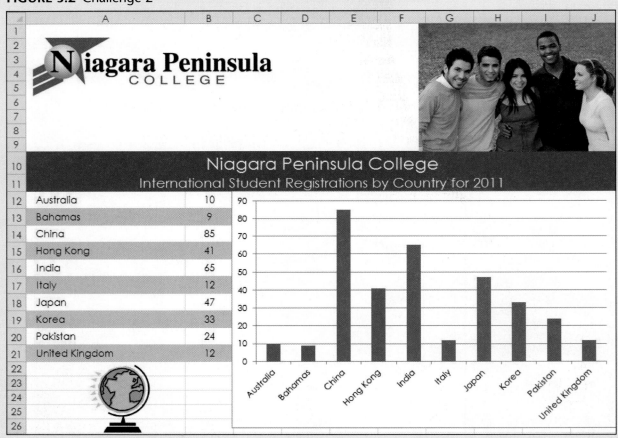

Marquee Series

Microsoft®
Access®
2010

Nita Rutkosky

Pierce College at Puyallup, Puyallup, Washington

Denise Seguin

Fanshawe College, London, Ontario

Audrey Rutkosky Roggenkamp

Pierce College at Puyallup, Puyallup, Washington

Paradigm
PUBLISHING

St. Paul • Los Angeles • Indianapolis

Managing Editor	Sonja Brown
Developmental Editor	Brenda Palo
Supplements Developmental Editor	Brenda Owens
Production Editor	Donna Mears
Cover and Text Designer	Leslie Anderson
Copy Editors	Susan Capecchi and Laura Nelson
Desktop Production	Ryan Hamner and Jack Ross
Proofreader	Laura Nelson
Testers	Carley Bomstad, Amy McGuire, Rob Neilly, and Lindsay Ryan
Indexers	Ina Gravitz and Sandi Schroeder

© 2011 by Paradigm Publishing, Inc.
875 Montreal Way
St. Paul, MN 55102
Email: educate@emcp.com
Website: www.emcp.com

Printed in the United States of America

19 18 17 16 15 14 13 12 11 10   1 2 3 4 5 6 7 8 9 10

Contents

Introducing
Access 2010

Microsoft Access 2010 is a *database management system (DBMS)* included with the Microsoft Office suite. Interacting with a DBMS occurs often as one performs daily routines such as withdrawing cash from the ATM, purchasing gas using a credit card, or looking up a telephone number in an online directory. In each of these activities a DBMS is accessed to retrieve information, and data is viewed, updated, and/or printed. Any application that involves storing and maintaining a large amount of data in an organized manner can be set up as an Access database. Examples include customers and invoices, suppliers and purchases, inventory and orders. While working in Access, you will create and maintain databases for the following six companies.

 First Choice Travel is a travel center offering a full range of traveling services from booking flights, hotel reservations, and rental cars to offering travel seminars.

 The Waterfront Bistro offers fine dining for lunch and dinner and also offers banquet facilities, a wine cellar, and catering services.

 Worldwide Enterprises is a national and international distributor of products for a variety of companies and is the exclusive movie distribution agent for Marquee Productions.

 Marquee Productions is involved in all aspects of creating movies from script writing and development to filming. The company produces documentaries, biographies, as well as historical and action movies.

 Performance Threads maintains an inventory of rental costumes and also researches, designs, and sews special-order and custom-made costumes.

 The mission of the Niagara Peninsula College Theatre Arts Division is to offer a curriculum designed to provide students with a thorough exposure to all aspects of the theater arts.

In Section 1 you will learn how to
Maintain Data in Tables

Access databases are comprised of a series of objects. A table is the first object that is created in a new Access database. Information in the database is organized by topic and a table stores data for one topic. For example, one table in a customer database might store customer names and addresses while another table stores the customer invoices and another table stores the customer payments. Table datasheets are organized like a spreadsheet with columns and rows. Each column in the table represents one *field*, which is a single unit of information about a person, place, item, or object. Each row in the table represents one *record*, which includes all of the related fields for one person, place, item, or object. Working in tables involves adding or deleting records, editing fields, sorting, filtering, or formatting datasheets. Access provides the Navigation pane for managing database objects.

Group objects in the database by various catagories and display them in the Navigation pane.

Data in tables display in a datasheet comprised of columns and rows similar to an Excel worksheet. Each column in a table datasheet represents one field. Each row in a table datasheet represents one record.

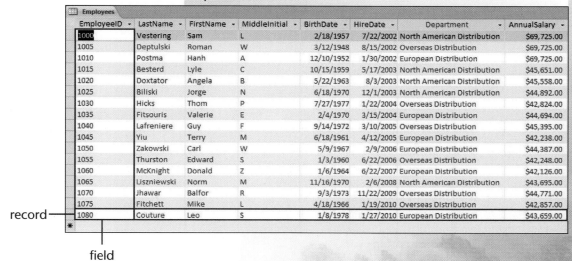

record —

field

Create New Tables and Establish Relationships

New tables can be created starting in a blank datasheet or by creating the table structure by defining fields in a view called *Design* view. Each field in a table has a set of *field properties*, which are a set of characteristics that control how the field interacts with data in objects such as tables, forms, queries, or reports. The ability to create a relationship between two tables allows one to maintain or extract data in multiple tables as if they were one large table.

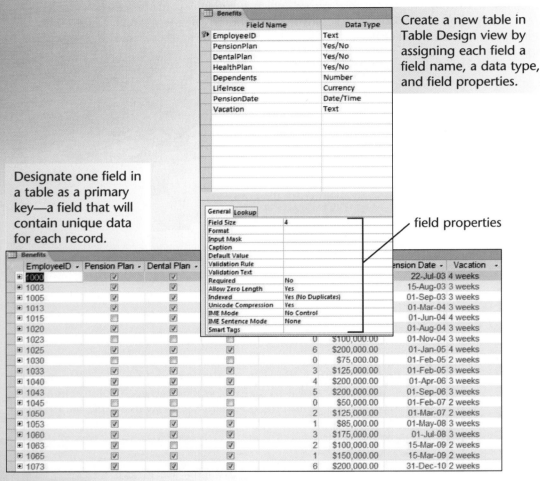

Create a new table in Table Design view by assigning each field a field name, a data type, and field properties.

field properties

Designate one field in a table as a primary key—a field that will contain unique data for each record.

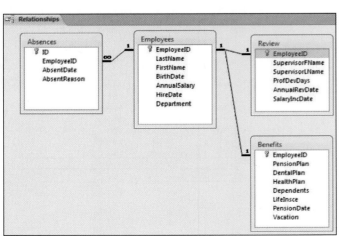

Create relationships between tables by joining one table to another on a common field. These relationships are displayed in the Relationships window by black join lines between table field list boxes.

In Section 3 you will learn how to
Create Queries, Forms, and Reports

Queries and forms are objects based on tables and are created to extract, view, and maintain data. Queries can be used to view specific fields from tables that meet a particular criterion. For example, create a query to view customers from a specific state or zip code. Forms provide a more user-friendly interface for entering, editing, deleting, and viewing records in tables. Create a report to generate professionally designed printouts of information from tables or queries.

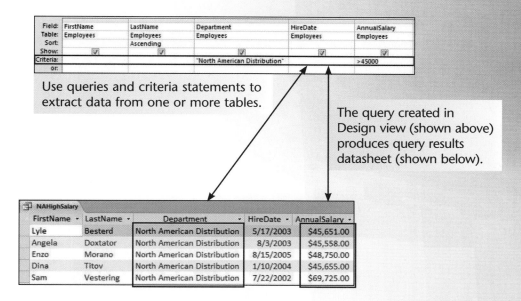

Use queries and criteria statements to extract data from one or more tables.

The query created in Design view (shown above) produces query results datasheet (shown below).

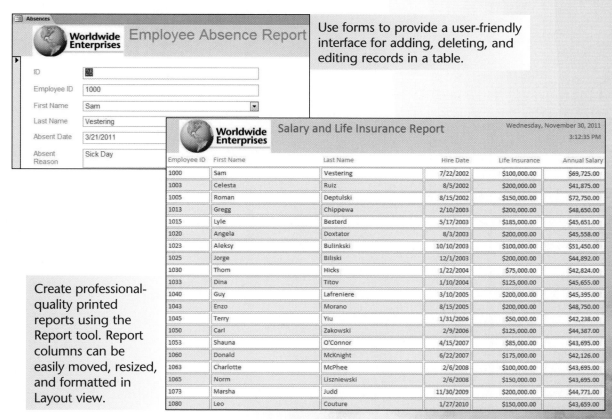

Use forms to provide a user-friendly interface for adding, deleting, and editing records in a table.

Create professional-quality printed reports using the Report tool. Report columns can be easily moved, resized, and formatted in Layout view.

Access SECTION 1

Maintaining Data in Access Tables

Skills

- Describe how data is organized in a database
- Define *field, record, table, datasheet,* and *database*
- Start Access
- Open, navigate, and close a database, table, and form
- Adjust column widths
- Find and edit records
- Add and delete records
- Sort and filter records
- Move columns in a datasheet
- Preview and print a table
- Change margins
- Change the page orientation
- Use the Help feature
- Change the font size for selected records
- Hide columns in a datasheet

Student Resources

Before beginning the activities in Access, copy to your storage medium the Access folder on the Student Resources CD. This folder contains the data files you need to complete the projects in each Access section.

Projects Overview

Worldwide Enterprises

Add, delete, find, sort, and filter records; preview and change page orientation and margins; format and hide columns in a datasheet in Distributors and Employees databases.

Niagara Peninsula COLLEGE

Find student records and enter grades into the Grades database.

The Waterfront B·I·S·T·R·O

Maintain the Inventory database by adding and deleting records. Add, delete, and modify records; sort, filter, and set print options for a catering event database.

Performance Threads

Delete records, sort and print a report from the Costume Inventory database. Create field names and table names for a new custom costume database.

Note: On some computer systems, a file copied from a CD to another storage medium retains the source file's read-only attribute. If this occurs, you will not be able to make changes to the database file. Complete the following steps to check and then remove a file's read-only status:

1. Open a Computer window.
2. Navigate to the drive representing your storage medium.
3. Navigate to the *AccessS1* folder.
4. Right-click a database file and then click *Properties* at the shortcut menu.
5. At the Properties dialog box with the General tab selected, look at the *Read-only* check box in the *Attributes* section. If a check mark is in the box, click the check box to clear it; if no check mark is in the box, the read-only attribute is not turned on (no action is required).
6. Click OK.

If the read-only attribute is not active for one file in the copied folder, then you can assume all files copied without an active read-only attribute. If you cleared the *Read-only* check box for one file, you will need to clear the attribute for all files after copying from the Student Resources CD. You can select multiple files and remove the read-only attribute in one operation.

Model Answers for Projects

These model answers for the projects that you complete in Section 1 provide a preview of the finished projects before you begin working and also allow you to compare your own results with these models to ensure you have created the materials accurately.

The US_Distributors table (a two-page document) within the WEDistributors1.accdb database is the project in Activities 1.1 to 1.10.

US_Distributors   11/30/2011

DistID	State	City	CompanyName	StreetAdd1	StreetAdd2	ZIPCode	Telephone	Fax
7	AZ	Phoenix	LaVista Cinemas	111 Vista Road		86355-6014	602-555-6231	602-555-6233
10	CA	Los Angeles	Marquee Movies	1011 South Alameda Street		90045	612-555-2398	612-555-2377
15	FL	Tampa	Sunfest Cinemas		341 South Fourth Avenue	33562	813-555-3185	813-555-3177
8	GA	Atlanta	Liberty Cinemas	P. O. Box 998	12011 Ruston Way	73125	404-555-8113	404-555-2349
13	IL	Oak Park	O'Shea Movies	59 Erie		60302	312-555-7719	312-555-7381
11	KS	Emporia	Midtown Moviehouse	1033 Commercial Street		66801	316-555-7013	316-555-7022
1	KY	Louisville	All Nite Cinemas	2188 3rd Street		40201	502-555-4238	502-555-4240
5	MA	Cambridge	Eastown Movie House	P. O. Box 429	1 Concourse Avenue	02142	413-555-0981	413-555-0226
20	MD	Baltimore	Dockside Movies	P. O. Box 224	155 S. Central Avenue	21203	301-555-7732	301-555-9836
21	MI	Detroit	Renaissance Cinemas	3599 Woodward Avenue		48211	313-555-1693	313-555-1699
6	NJ	Baking Ridge	Hillman Cinemas	55 Kemble Avenue		07920	201-555-1147	201-555-1143
17	NY	Buffalo	Waterfront Cinemas	P. O. Box 3255		14288	716-555-3845	716-555-4860
23	NY	New York	Cinema Festival	318 East 11th Street		10003	212-555-9715	212-555-9717
22	NY	New York	Movie Emporium	203 West Houston Street		10014	212-555-7278	212-555-7280
19	NY	New York	Westview Movies	1112 Broadway		10119	212-555-4875	212-555-4877
12	OH	Dublin	Mooretown Movies	P. O. Box 11	331 Metro Place	43107	614-555-8134	614-555-8339
14	OR	Portland	Redwood Cinemas	P. O. Box 112F	336 Ninth Street	97466-3359	503-555-8641	503-555-8633
18	PA	Philadelphia	Wellington 10	1203 Tenth Southwest		19178	215-555-9045	215-555-9048
4	SC	Columbia	Danforth Cinemas	P. O. Box 22	18 Pickens Street	29201	803-555-3487	803-555-3421
2	TX	Arlington	Century Cinemas	3687 Avenue K		76013	817-555-2116	817-555-2119
9	WA	Seattle	Mainstream Movies	P. O. Box 33	333 Evergreen Building	98220-2791	206-555-3269	206-555-3270

US_Distributors   11/30/2011

EmailAdd
lavista@emcp.net
marqueemovies@emcp.net
sunfest@emcp.net
libertycinemas@emcp.net
oshea@emcp.net
midtown@emcp.net
allnite@emcp.net
eastown@emcp.net
dockside@emcp.net
rencinemas@emcp.net
hillman@emcp.net
waterfrontcinemas@emcp.net
cinemafest@emcp.net
emporium@emcp.net
westview@emcp.net
mooretown@emcp.net
redwoodcinemas@emcp.net
wellington10@emcp.net
danforth@emcp.net
centurycinemas@emcp.net
mainstream@emcp.net

Page 2

The US_Distributors table within the WEDistributors1.accdb database is the project in Activity 1.11.

US_Distributors   11/30/2011

State	City	CompanyName	StreetAdd1	StreetAdd2	ZIPCode	Telephone	Fax
AZ	Phoenix	LaVista Cinemas	111 Vista Road		86355-6014	602-555-6231	602-555-6233
CA	Los Angeles	Marquee Movies	1011 South Alameda Street		90045	612-555-2398	612-555-2377
FL	Tampa	Sunfest Cinemas		341 South Fourth Avenue	33562	813-555-3185	813-555-3177
GA	Atlanta	Liberty Cinemas	P. O. Box 998	12011 Ruston Way	73125	404-555-8113	404-555-2349
IL	Oak Park	O'Shea Movies	59 Erie		60302	312-555-7719	312-555-7381
KS	Emporia	Midtown Moviehouse	1033 Commercial Street		66801	316-555-7013	316-555-7022
KY	Louisville	All Nite Cinemas	2188 3rd Street		40201	502-555-4238	502-555-4240
MA	Cambridge	Eastown Movie House	P. O. Box 429	1 Concourse Avenue	02142	413-555-0981	413-555-0226
MD	Baltimore	Dockside Movies	P. O. Box 224	155 S. Central Avenue	21203	301-555-7732	301-555-9836
MI	Detroit	Renaissance Cinemas	3599 Woodward Avenue		48211	313-555-1693	313-555-1699
NJ	Baking Ridge	Hillman Cinemas	55 Kemble Avenue		07920	201-555-1147	201-555-1143
NY	Buffalo	Waterfront Cinemas	P. O. Box 3255		14288	716-555-3845	716-555-4860
NY	New York	Cinema Festival	318 East 11th Street		10003	212-555-9715	212-555-9717
NY	New York	Movie Emporium	203 West Houston Street		10014	212-555-7278	212-555-7280
NY	New York	Westview Movies	1112 Broadway		10119	212-555-4875	212-555-4877
OH	Dublin	Mooretown Movies	P. O. Box 11	331 Metro Place	43107	614-555-8134	614-555-8339
OR	Portland	Redwood Cinemas	P. O. Box 112F	336 Ninth Street	97466-3359	503-555-8641	503-555-8633
PA	Philadelphia	Wellington 10	1203 Tenth Southwest		19178	215-555-9045	215-555-9048
SC	Columbia	Danforth Cinemas	P. O. Box 22	18 Pickens Street	29201	803-555-3487	803-555-3421
TX	Arlington	Century Cinemas	3687 Avenue K		76013	817-555-2116	817-555-2119
WA	Seattle	Mainstream Movies	P. O. Box 33	333 Evergreen Building	98220-2791	206-555-3269	206-555-3270

Page 1

Activity 1.1

Understanding Database Concepts and Terminology

Organizations use a database to keep track of customers, suppliers, employees, inventory, sales, orders, purchases, and more. A *database* can be defined as a collection of data that has been organized so that the data can be easily stored, sorted, extracted, and reported. A key concept for understanding databases is that the data has to be organized. Data is organized first into a series of *tables* within the database where one table contains all of the data that describe a person, place, object, event, or other subject. Within each table, the data is further broken down into small units of information about the subject called *fields*. All of the data about one subject in the table—for example, one customer—is called a *record*. Within the database a series of objects exist with which one can enter, manage, and view data. The first objects created are the tables. Once a table exists, other objects can be created that use the table structure to provide other means to enter and view the data.

Project You will open a database used by Worldwide Enterprises to keep track of distributors, orders, and movies and examine tables in order to gain an understanding of the key concepts and terminology.

Tutorial 1.1
Opening Access,
Navigating and
Printing a Table

Note: Make sure you have copied the files from the Student Resources CD to your storage medium. Open all database files from your removable storage device and NOT directly from the Student Resources CD since Access database files on the Student Resources CD are read-only. Please refer to the note on page 1 regarding checking and removing read-only attributes before proceeding with the projects in this section.

1 At the Windows desktop, click the Start button on the Taskbar.

2 Point to *All Programs*, click *Microsoft Office*, and then click *Microsoft Access 2010*.

Depending on your operating system and/or system configuration, the steps you complete to open Access may vary.

3 Click the Open Quick Command button at the New tab Backstage view.

Access 2010 opens with the New tab in Backstage view as your starting point. From this view you can open an existing database or create a new one. Backstage view (the view that is active from the File tab in the ribbon) organizes database management tasks into tabs. Quick Command buttons such as Save, Save Object As, Save Database As, Open, and Close Database are located at the top of the left pane in the view. Below the Quick Command buttons the view is organized into tabs such as Info, Recent, New, Print, Save & Publish, and Help. You will learn more about these tabs in later activities.

4 At the Open dialog box, navigate to the AccessS1 folder on your storage medium.

To change to a different drive, click the drive letter in the *Computer* section in the Navigation pane. (You may need to scroll down the Navigation pane to see the *Computer* section.) Change to a different folder by double-clicking the folder name in the Content pane.

5 Double-click *WEDistributors1.accdb*.

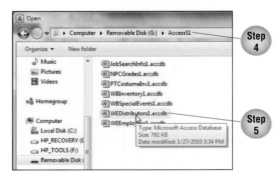

Access database file names end with the file name extension *accdb*. A security Warning message bar appears if Access determines the file you are opening did not originate from a trusted location on your computer and may have viruses or other security hazards. This often occurs when you copy a file from another medium (such as a CD or the Web). Active content in the file is disabled until you click the Enable Content button.

6 Click the Enable Content button if the Security Warning message bar appears. At the Access screen, identify the various features by comparing your screen with the one shown in Figure 1.1.

7 Position the mouse pointer on *US_Distributors* in the Tables group in the Navigation pane and then double-click to open the table.

> The table opens in Datasheet view in the work area. Datasheets display the contents of a table in a column and row format similar to an Excel worksheet.

8 Notice that each column in the datasheet contains only one unit of information. Each column represents one *field*. Identify the fields and field names at the top of each column by comparing your screen with the one shown in Figure 1.2 on page 6.

> The field names *DistID, CompanyName, StreetAdd1, StreetAdd2, City,* and so on are displayed in the header row at the top of the datasheet.

9 Identify the records in the US_Distributors table. Each record is one row in the table.

10 Position the mouse pointer on *Movies* in the Tables group in the Navigation pane and then double-click to open the table in a new tab in the work area.

11 Examine the fields and records in the Movies table.

FIGURE 1.1 The Access Screen

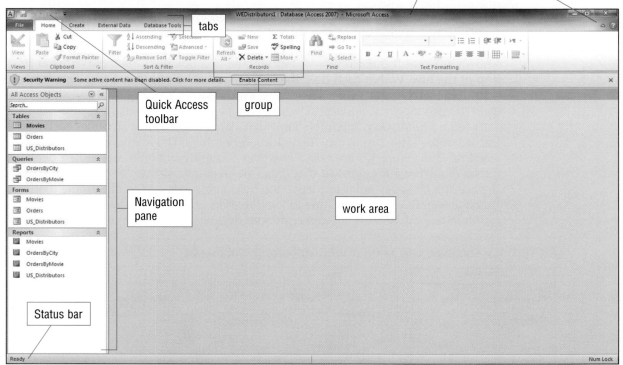

continues

FIGURE 1.2 US_Distributors Table in Datasheet View

Each object opens in a tab in the work area.

field names

DistID	CompanyName	StreetAdd1	StreetAdd2	City	State	ZIPCode	Telephone	Fax	EmailAdd	Click to
1	All Nite Cinemas	2188 3rd Street		Louisville	KY	40201	502-555-4238	502-555-4240	allnite@emcp.net	
2	Century Cinemas	3687 Avenue K		Arlington	TX	76013	817-555-2116	817-555-2119	centurycinemas@	
3	Countryside Cinem	22 Hillside Street		Bennington	VT	05201	802-555-1469	802-555-1470	countryside@emc	
4	Danforth Cinemas	P. O. Box 22	18 Pickens Stre	Columbia	SC	29201	803-555-3487	803-555-3421	danforth@emcp.r	
5	Eastown Movie Hou	P. O. Box 722	1 Concourse A	Cambridge	MA	02142	413-555-0981	413-555-0226	eastown@emcp.r	
6	Hillman Cinemas	55 Kemble Avenue		Baking Ridg	NJ	07920	201-555-1147	201-555-1143	hillman@emcp.ne	
7	LaVista Cinemas	111 Vista Road		Phoenix	AZ	86355-6014	602-555-6231	602-555-6233	lavista@emcp.net	
8	Liberty Cinemas	P. O. Box 998	12011 Ruston V	Atlanta	GA	73125	404-555-8113	404-555-2349	libertycinemas@e	
9	Mainstream Movies	P. O. Box 33	333 Evergreen	Seattle	WA	98220-2791	206-555-3265	206-555-3270	mainstream@emc	
10	Marquee Movies	1011 South Alameda S		Los Angeles	CA	90045	612-555-2398	612-555-2377	marqueemovies@	
11	Midtown Moviehou	1033 Commercial Stre		Emporia	KS	66801	316-555-7013	316-555-7022	midtown@emcp.i	
12	Mooretown Movies	P. O. Box 11	331 Metro Plac	Dublin	OH	43107	614-555-8134	614-555-8339	mooretown@emc	
13	O'Shea Movies	59 Erie		Oak Park	IL	60302	312-555-7719	312-555-7381	oshea@emcp.net	
14	Redwood Cinemas	P. O. Box 112F	336 Ninth Stree	Portland	OR	97466-3359	503-555-8641	503-555-8633	redwoodcinemas	
15	Sunfest Cinemas		341 South Four	Tampa	FL	33562	813-555-3185	813-555-3177	sunfest@emcp.ne	
16	Victory Cinemas	12119 South 23rd		San Diego	CA	97432-1567	619-555-8746	619-555-8748	victory@emcp.ne	
17	Waterfront Cinema	P. O. Box 3255		Buffalo	NY	14288	716-555-3845	716-555-3947	waterfrontcinema	
18	Wellington 10	1203 Tenth Southwes		Philadelphi	PA	19178	215-555-9045	215-555-9048	wellington10@en	
19	Westview Movies	1112 Broadway		New York	NY	10119	212-555-4875	212-555-4877	westview@emcp.	
(New)										

Each row is one record in the table.

Record Navigation bar

Each column represents a field in the table.

Record: 1 of 19   No Filter   Search

12 Position the mouse pointer on *Orders* in the Tables group in the Navigation pane and then double-click to open the table.

Three tabs are now open in the work area with one table datasheet in each tab. You can click a tab along the top of the work area to view a table in the background.

13 Examine the fields and records in the Orders table.

The basic elements of a database are described in Table 1.1 on page 7. Tables in Access are the first objects created in a new database since all other database objects rely on a table for the data source. Creating a new database involves planning the number of tables needed and the fields that will be included in each table. Notice that each table you examined in the WEDistributors1 database contains information about one subject only. Database designers often create a visual representation of the database's structure in a diagram similar to the one shown in Figure 1.3. Each table is represented in a box with the table name at the top of the box. Within each box, the fields that will be stored in the table are listed with the field names that will be used when the tables are created. Notice that one field in each table has an asterisk next to the field name. The field with the asterisk is called a *primary key.* A primary key holds data that uniquely identifies each record in the table (usually an identification number). The lines drawn between each table in Figure 1.3 are called *join lines* and represent links established between tables (called *relationships*) so that data can be extracted from two or more tables. Notice the join lines point to a common field name included in each table that is to be linked. (You will learn how to join tables in Section 2.) A database with one or more related tables is called a *relational database.*

FIGURE 1.3 Database Diagram for WEDistributors1 Database

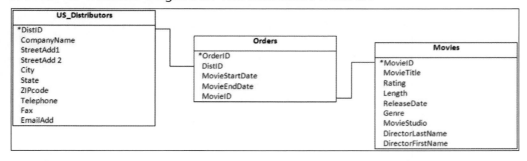

US_Distributors

*DistID
CompanyName
StreetAdd1
StreetAdd 2
City
State
ZIPcode
Telephone
Fax
EmailAdd

Orders

*OrderID
DistID
MovieStartDate
MovieEndDate
MovieID

Movies

*MovieID
MovieTitle
Rating
Length
ReleaseDate
Genre
MovieStudio
DirectorLastName
DirectorFirstName

14 Click the tab along the top of the work area with the label *US_Distributors*.

> The US_Distributors table datasheet is now in the foreground of the work area.

15 Click the Close button ![X] at the top right corner of the work area to close the table.

16 Click the Close button two more times to close the remaining two tables.

> In the next activity you will further explore the WEDistributors1 database by viewing the other objects in the database besides tables.

In Brief

Start Access
1. Click Start.
2. Point to *All Programs*.
3. Click *Microsoft Office*.
4. Click *Microsoft Access 2010*.

Open Table Datasheet
1. Open database file.
2. Double-click table name in Navigation pane.

TABLE 1.1 Basic Elements of a Database

Element	Description
Field	A single component of information about a person, place, item, or object.
Record	All of the fields related to one logical unit in the table such as a customer, supplier, contact, or inventory item.
Table	All of the related records for one logical group.
Database	A file containing related tables and objects.

In Addition

Planning and Designing a Table

Table 1.2 contains the steps involved in planning and designing a new database. The design process may seem time-consuming; however, the time expended to produce a well-designed database saves time later. A database that is poorly designed will likely have logic errors or structure errors that require redefining of data or objects after live data has been entered.

TABLE 1.2 Steps in the Database Design Process

Step	Description
1. Determine the purpose of the database.	Describe who will use the database and for what purpose. This helps to focus the efforts for the remaining steps on the mission the database is to fulfill.
2. Determine all of the data that will need to be tracked in the database.	Gather all of the data elements that you will need to store in the database. You can find this information by looking at records of invoices, inventory lists, purchase orders, and so on. You can also ask individuals what information they want to get out of the database to help you determine the required data.
3. Group the data elements into tables.	Divide the information into subjects (also referred to as entities) so that one table will be about one subject only.
4. Decide the fields and field names for each table.	Break down each data element into its smallest unit. For example, a person's name could be broken down into first name, middle name, and last name.
5. Make sure each table includes a field that will be used to uniquely identify each record in the table.	Access can create an ID field for you if you do not have an existing unique identification number such as a product number, student number, social security number, or similar field.
6. Decide which tables need to be linked by a relationship and include in the table the common field upon which to join the tables if necessary.	Identifying relationships at this stage helps you determine if you need to add a field to a related table to allow you to join the table. You will learn more about relationships in Section 2.

Activity 1.2

Exploring Access Objects and the User Interface

In Activity 1.1, you examined the table datasheets in the WEDistributors1 database and learned the terminology and basic concepts that apply to table structure. Once a table exists in a database, other objects that are based upon the table can be created. These other objects are used to enter, edit, and view data that reside in the table. The interface in Access is different from the other applications within the Microsoft Office suite. The Navigation pane at the left side of the screen displays the objects in the database organized into categories and is used to open an object. You can change the Navigation pane view to group the database objects in a different way.

Project

Explore further in the WEDistributors1 database by opening and viewing a query, form, and report. You will also experiment with changing the Navigation pane view before you begin to work with the US_Distributors table in the remainder of this section.

Tutorial 1.1
Opening Access, Navigating and Printing a Table

1 With the **WEDistributors1.accdb** database open, double-click *OrdersByCity* in the Queries group of the Navigation pane.

A query resembles a table datasheet in that the information is displayed in a column and row format. The purpose of a query is to view data from one or more related tables. You can also specify criteria to examine only certain records within the tables. You will learn how to create queries in Section 3.

OrderID	City	CompanyName	MovieID	MovieStartDate	MovieEndDate
	Arlington	Century Cinemas	Ring of Roses	3/23/2011	5/1/2011
5	Atlanta	Liberty Cinemas	The Life of Winston Churchill	3/20/2011	4/30/2011
8	Baking Ridge	Hillman Cinemas	Ring of Roses	3/22/2011	4/10/2011
2	Bennington	Countryside Cinemas	Ring of Roses	3/15/2011	4/1/2011
4	Cambridge	Eastown Movie House	Two by Two	3/15/2011	4/15/2011
1	Columbia	Danforth Cinemas	The Life of Winston Churchill	3/10/2011	4/29/2011
3	Emporia	Midtown Moviehouse	The Codebreakers of World War II	3/15/2011	4/20/2011
13	Los Angeles	Marquee Movies	Ring of Roses	3/28/2011	4/28/2011

A query displays data from one or more related tables. In this query, fields from all three tables are selected for viewing.

2 Double-click *Movies* in the Forms group of the Navigation pane. *Note:* **Movies appears in three of the four Navigation pane groups. Be sure to double-click Movies in the Forms group.**

A form is used to view and edit data in a table one record at a time. Forms can be created in Access that resemble paper-based forms used within the organization. A Record Navigation bar at the bottom of the form is used to scroll through the table records.

3 Click the Next record button ▶ in the Record Navigation bar to display the second record in the Movies form.

Record Navigation bar

4 Click the Previous record button ◀ in the Record Navigation bar to return the display to the first record in the Movies form.

5 Double-click *US_Distributors* in the Reports group of the Navigation pane.
Note: Be sure to double-click* US_Distributors *in the Reports group.

> Reports are used to display or print data from one or more tables in a specific layout. In a report, you can control how the data will be arranged, formatted, grouped, and sorted. You can add descriptive labels, insert a logo, or include calculations in a report.

6 Scroll down the Report View window and notice the US_Distributors report is displayed in one long, continuous screen.

continues

7 Click the down-pointing arrow on the View button  in the Views group of the Home tab and then click *Print Preview* at the drop-down list.

> The report now displays how it will look when printed. All database objects have more than one view. *Design* view or *Layout* view is used to make changes to the object's data elements or appearance. The available views are dependent on the active object. For example, *Print Preview* is available for a report object but not for a table, query, or form.

8 Click the Close button at the top right corner of the work area to close the report.

> You have now viewed one of each type of object included in the WEDistributors1 database. Table 1.3 further describes database objects.

9 Click the Close button two more times to close the remaining two objects.

10 Click the down-pointing arrow to the right of *All Access Objects* at the top of the Navigation pane and then click *Tables and Related Views* at the drop-down list.

> The current view for the Navigation pane was *Object Type*. In this view, objects are grouped by type such as all table objects, all query objects, all form objects, and all report objects. In *Tables and Related Views*, the Navigation pane groups objects by the table to which objects are associated.

11 Notice the Navigation pane has changed to show one group for each table name. Below each table name, all of the objects for which the table is associated are listed.

> In this view, one can determine that a query, form, or report is reliant upon more than one table since the same query, form, or report name appears in multiple table groups. Notice the query named OrdersByCity appears below each table name in the Navigation pane. This means the query uses fields from each of the three tables in the database.

(12) Click the down-pointing arrow to the right of *All Tables* at the top of the Navigation pane and then click *Object Type* at the drop-down list.

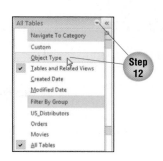

> In the remainder of this section you will work with the existing US_Distributors table datasheet and form to find, edit, add, delete, sort, and filter data. Once you are comfortable with the Access environment, you will create your own tables and relationships in Section 2 and queries, forms, and report objects in Section 3.

(13) Click the File tab and then click the Close Database Quick Command button.

In Brief

Open Database Object
1. Open database file.
2. Double-click object name in Navigation pane.

Change Navigation Pane View
1. Click down-pointing arrow to right of current view at top of Navigation pane.
2. Click desired view.

TABLE 1.3 Database Objects

Object	Description
Table	Organizes data in fields (columns) and records (rows); a database must contain at least one table. The table is the base upon which other objects are created.
Query	Used to display data from one or more tables that meets a conditional statement and/or to perform calculations; for example, display only those records in which the city is Toronto.
Form	Allows fields and records to be presented in a different layout than the datasheet; used to facilitate data entry and maintenance.
Report	Prints data from tables or queries.
Macro	Automates repetitive tasks.
Module	Advanced automation through programming using Visual Basic for Applications.

In Addition

More about the Access User Interface

Unlike other Microsoft Office applications, only one database can be open at a time. If you open a new database in the current Access window, the existing database is closed. In other Microsoft Office applications, you have to save your revisions after you edit text or values. In a database program, changes to the data are saved automatically when you move to the next record. For this reason, the Undo command is often not available to undo changes made to data. If you are prompted to save changes when you close an object in Access, the prompt is referring to changes made to the layout and/or format of the object.

Activity 1.3

Adjusting Column Width; Navigating in Datasheet View

As you have seen, a table opens in Datasheet view which displays data in a manner similar to a spreadsheet with a grid of columns and rows. Columns contain the field values, with the field names in the header row at the top of the datasheet, and records are represented as rows. A Record Navigation bar at the bottom contains buttons with which to navigate the datasheet.

Project

You will reopen the WEDistributors1 database, adjust column widths, and practice scrolling and navigating through records in the US_Distributors table.

Tutorial 1.2
Formatting a Datasheet

1 At the New tab Backstage view, click *WEDistributors1.accdb* located in the left pane between the Close Database button and Info tab. *Note: Use the Open button to locate the database if the file name does not appear in the left pane*.

Recently opened databases display in the left pane and in the Recent tab of the Backstage view. By default, the 4 most recently opened databases appear in the left pane and the 17 most recently opened databases appear in the Recent tab of the Backstage view. Use these options to quickly open a database if the database file name appears in either list.

Step 1

2 Double-click *US_Distributors* in the Tables group in the Navigation pane.

Notice that some columns contain data that is not entirely visible. In Steps 3–6, you will learn how to adjust the column widths using two methods.

3 Click the mouse over any character in the first row of the *CompanyName* column to open the field for editing.

4 Click the More button ▦ in the Records group in the Home tab and then click *Field Width* at the drop-down list.

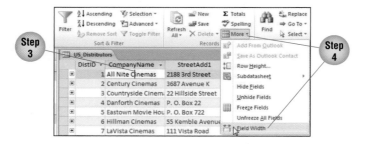

Step 3

Step 4

5 At the Column Width dialog box, with the current entry already selected in the *Column Width* text box, type **20** and then press Enter or click OK.

Type a value to increase or decrease the column width or use the Best Fit button to set the width to accommodate the length of the longest entry. In the next step, you will use the mouse to best fit a column.

Step 5

Best Fit adjusts the width to the length of the longest entry in the field.

6 Position the mouse pointer on the right column boundary line in the header row between columns three and four (*StreetAdd1* and *StreetAdd2*) until the pointer changes to a vertical line with a left- and right-pointing arrow and then double-click the left mouse button.

> Double-clicking the column boundary performs the Best Fit command, which automatically sets the width to the length of the longest entry within the field.

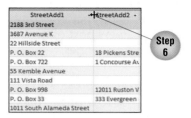

Step 6

7 Best Fit the remaining columns in the datasheet using either method learned in Steps 3–5 or Step 6. *Note: If necessary, click the right-pointing horizontal scroll arrow as many times as necessary to view the remaining columns.*

8 Drag the scroll box to the left edge of the horizontal scroll bar.

Step 8

9 Click the Last record button on the Record Navigation bar to move to the last row in the table.

10 Click the Previous record button on the Record Navigation bar to move up one row in the table and then click the Next record button to move down one row.

11 Click the First record button on the Record Navigation bar to move to the first row in the table.

12 Press Ctrl + End to move to the last field in the last record in the datasheet.

13 Press Ctrl + Home to move to the first field in the first record in the table.

14 Practice other scrolling techniques using the keyboard shortcuts described in Table 1.4.

15 Click the Save button on the Quick Access toolbar.

> The Save button is used in Step 15 to save the changes made to the column widths. Database programs save changes made to data automatically; however, changes made to the layout or appearance of a database object need to be saved manually.

TABLE 1.4 Scrolling Techniques Using the Keyboard

Press	To move to
Home	first field in the current record
End	last field in the current record
Tab	next field in the current record
Shift + Tab	previous field in the current record
Ctrl + Home	first field in the first record
Ctrl + End	last field in the last record

In Brief

Adjust Column Width
1. Position insertion point in desired column.
2. Click More button.
3. Click *Field Width*.
4. Type *Column Width* value or click Best Fit.
5. Click OK.
OR
Drag or double-click right column boundary line in header row.

Activity 1.4

Finding and Editing Records

The Find command can be used to quickly move the insertion point to a specific record in a table. This is a time-saving feature when the table contains several records that are not all visible in one screen. Once a record has been located, click the insertion point within a field and insert or delete text as required to edit the record.

Project You have received a note from Sam Vestering that Waterfront Cinemas has changed its fax number and Eastown Movie House has a new post office box number. You will use the Find feature to locate the records and make the changes.

Worldwide Enterprises

SNAP

Tutorial 1.3
Finding and Replacing Specific Data in Records

1 With the US_Distributors table open, press Tab or click the insertion point in the *CompanyName* column in the first row of the datasheet and then click the Find button in the Find group in the Home tab.

Clicking the Find button opens the Find and Replace dialog box.

2 Type **Waterfront Cinemas** in the *Find What* text box and then click the Find Next button.

The active record moves to record 17 and the text *Waterfront Cinemas* is selected in the *CompanyName* field. If necessary, drag the dialog box title bar to move the dialog box out of the way in order to view the datasheet.

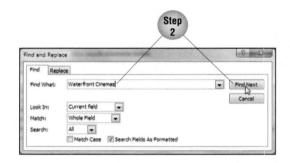
Step 2

Current record *DistID* is 17 and the search text is automatically selected in the field.

	16 Victory Cinemas	12119 South 23rd
	17 Waterfront Cinemas	P. O. Box 3255
	18 Wellington 10	1203 Tenth Southwest

3 Click the Close button on the Find and Replace dialog box Title bar.

4 Press Tab or Enter seven times to move to the *Fax* column.

The entire field value is selected when you move from column to column using Tab or Enter. If you need to edit only a few characters within the field, you will want to use *Edit* mode. As an alternative, you could scroll and click the insertion point within the field to avoid having to turn on *Edit* mode.

5 Press F2 to turn on Edit mode.

6 Press Backspace four times to delete 3947 and then type **4860**.

Step 6

619-555-8746	619-555-8748
716-555-3845	716-555-4860
215-555-9045	215-555-9048

7 Look at the record selector bar (blank column at the left edge of the datasheet) at record 17 and notice the pencil icon that is displayed.

The pencil icon indicates the current record is being edited and the changes have not yet been saved.

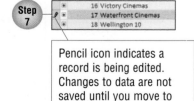

Step 7

	16 Victory Cinemas
	17 Waterfront Cinemas
	18 Wellington 10

Pencil icon indicates a record is being edited. Changes to data are not saved until you move to another record in the table.

8 Press Enter twice to move to the next record in the table.

    The pencil icon disappears, indicating the changes have now been saved.

9 Click in any record in the *StreetAdd1* column and then click the Find button.

10 Type **Box 722** in the *Find What* text box.

In Brief

Find a Record
1. Click in any row in field by which you want to search.
2. Click the Find button.
3. Type search text in *Find What* text box.
4. Click Find Next.

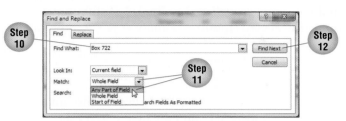

11 Click the down-pointing arrow next to the *Match* option box and then click *Any Part of Field* in the drop-down list.

    Using the options from the *Match* option box you can find records without specifying the entire field value. Specifically, you can instruct Access to stop at records where the entry typed in the *Find What* text box is the *Whole Field*, is *Any Part of Field*, or is the *Start of Field*.

12 Click Find Next.

13 Close the Find and Replace dialog box.

    The insertion point moved to record 5. You were able to correctly locate the record for Eastown Movie House using only a portion of the field value for *StreetAdd1*. Notice that Access has selected *Box 722* in the field—only the text specified in the *Find What* text box (not *P. O. Box 722,* which is the entire field value).

14 Press F2 to turn on Edit mode, press Backspace three times, type **429**, and then click in any other record to save the changes to record 5.

In Addition

Using the Replace Command

Use the Replace tab in the Find and Replace dialog box to automatically change a field entry to something else. For example, in Steps 9–12 you searched for *Box 722* and then edited the field to change the box number to *429*. The Replace command could have been used to change the text automatically. To do this, click the Replace button [ab/ac] in the Find group in the Home tab, type **Box 722** in the *Find* What text box, type **Box 429** in the *Replace With* text box, change the *Match* option box to *Any Part of Field*, and then click the Find Next button. Click the Replace button when the record is found. Use the Replace All button in the dialog box to change multiple occurrences of a field.

Activity 1.5

Adding Records to a Datasheet

New records can be added to a table in either Datasheet view or Form view. To add a record in Datasheet view, open the table and then click the New (blank) record button on the Record Navigation bar, or click the New button in the Records group in the Home tab. When you press Tab or Enter after typing the last field, the record is saved auto- matically. When a datasheet is opened, the records are sorted alphanumerically by the primary key. Recall that a **primary key** is a field that provides Access with a unique identifier for each record. In the US_Distributors table, the *DistID* field is the primary key. The In Addition section at the end of this activity provides more information about the functions of a primary key field.

Project Worldwide Enterprises has signed two new distributors in the United States. You will add the information in two records in the US_Distributors table using the datasheet.

Tutorial 1.4
Adding Records in
Datasheet View

1 With the US_Distributors table open, click the New (blank) record button ▶✳ in the Record Navigation bar.

> The insertion point moves to the first column in the blank row at the bottom of the datasheet and the *Current Record* box in the Record Navigation bar indicates you are editing record *20 of 20* records.

2 Press Tab to move past the *DistID* field (currently displays *(New)*) since Access automatically assigns the next sequential number to this field.

> You will learn more about the AutoNumber field data type in Section 2. The number will not appear in the field until you type an entry in the first field and move to another field.

3 Type **Dockside Movies** in the *CompanyName* field and then press Tab.

4 Type **P. O. Box 224** and then press Tab.

5 Type **155 S. Central Avenue** and then press Tab.

6 Type **Baltimore** and then press Tab.

7 Type **MD** and then press Tab.

8 Type **21203** and then press Tab.

> If you use the numeric keypad to type numbers, consider using the Enter key to move to the next field since it will be more comfortable.

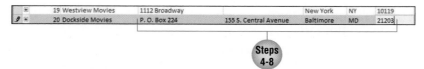

9 Type **301-555-7732** and then press Tab.

10 Type **301-555-9836** and then press Tab.

11 Type dockside@emcp.net and then press Tab.

> The insertion point moves to a new row when you press Tab or Enter after the last field in a new record to allow you to continue typing the next new record in the table. The record just entered is saved automatically.

12 Type the following information in the next row in the appropriate fields:

Renaissance Cinemas
3599 Woodward Avenue
Detroit, MI 48211
313-555-1693
313-555-1699
rencinemas@emcp.net

| | | 20 Dockside Movies | P. O. Box 224 | 155 S. Central Avenue | Baltimore | MD | 21203 |
| | | 21 Renaissance Cinemas | 3599 Woodward Avenue | | Detroit | MI | 48211 |

name and address fields of
new record added at Step 12

13 Close the US_Distributors table.

DistID	CompanyName	StreetAdd1	StreetAdd2	City	State	ZIPCode	Telephone	Fax	
1	All Nite Cinemas	2188 3rd Street		Louisville	KY	40201	502-555-4238	5...	
2	Century Cinemas	3687 Avenue K		Arlington	TX	76013	817-555-2116	817-555-2119	centu
3	Countryside Cinemas	22 Hillside Street		Bennington	VT	05201	802-555-1469	802-555-1470	count
4	Danforth Cinemas	P. O. Box 22	18 Pickens Street	Columbia	SC	29201	803-555-3487	803-555-3421	danfo
5	Eastown Movie House	P. O. Box 429	1 Concourse Avenue	Cambridge	MA	02142	413-555-0981	413-555-0226	easto
6	Hillman Cinemas	55 Kemble Avenue		Baking Ridge	NJ	07920	201-555-1147	201-555-1143	hillma
7	LaVista Cinemas	111 Vista Road		Phoenix	AZ	86355-6014	602-555-6231	602-555-6233	lavista
8	Liberty Cinemas	P. O. Box 998	12011 Ruston Way	Atlanta	GA	73125	404-555-8113	404-555-2349	liberty
9	Mainstream Movies	P. O. Box 33	333 Evergreen Building	Seattle	WA	98220-2791	206-555-3269	206-555-3270	mains
10	Marquee Movies	1011 South Alameda Street		Los Angeles	CA	90045	612-555-2398	612-555-2377	marqu
11	Midtown Moviehouse	1033 Commercial Street		Emporia	KS	66801	316-555-7013	316-555-7022	midto
12	Mooretown Movies	P. O. Box 11	331 Metro Place	Dublin	OH	43107	614-555-8134	614-555-8339	moore
13	O'Shea Movies	59 Erie		Oak Park	IL	60302	312-555-7719	312-555-7381	oshea
14	Redwood Cinemas	P. O. Box 112F	336 Ninth Street	Portland	OR	97466-3359	503-555-8641	503-555-8633	redwo
15	Sunfest Cinemas		341 South Fourth Avenue	Tampa	FL	33562	813-555-3185	813-555-3177	sunfes
16	Victory Cinemas	12119 South 23rd		San Diego	CA	97432-1567	619-555-8746	619-555-8748	victor
17	Waterfront Cinemas	P. O. Box 3255		Buffalo	NY	14288	716-555-3845	716-555-4860	water
18	Wellington 10	1203 Tenth Southwest		Philadelphia	PA	19178	215-555-9045	215-555-9048	wellin
19	Westview Movies	1112 Broadway		New York	NY	10119	212-555-4875	212-555-4877	westv
20	Dockside Movies	P. O. Box 224	155 S. Central Avenue	Baltimore	MD	21203	301-555-7732	301-555-9836	docks
21	Renaissance Cinemas	3599 Woodward Avenue		Detroit	MI	48211	313-555-1693	313-555-1699	rencin

Step 13
Close 'US_Distributors'

In Brief

Add Records to Datasheet
1. Open table.
2. Click New (blank) record button in Navigation bar OR click New button in Records group.
3. Type data in fields.

In Addition

Primary Key Field

Recall from Activity 1.1 that in each table one field is designated as the *primary key*. A primary key is the field by which the table is sorted whenever the table is opened. The primary key field must contain unique data for each record. When a new record is being added to the table, Access checks to ensure there is no existing record with the same data in the primary key. If there is, Access displays an error message indicating there are duplicate values and will not allow the record to be saved. The primary key field cannot be left blank when a new record is

being added, since it is the field that is used to sort and check for duplicates. Access includes a feature where a field named *ID* defined as the primary key is included automatically in a new table that is created in a blank datasheet. The *ID* field uses the AutoNumber data type which assigns the first record a field value of 1 and each new record is assigned the next sequential number.

Activity 1.6

Adding Records Using a Form

Forms are used to enter, edit, view, and print data. Forms provide a user-friendly interface between the user and the underlying table of data. Adding records in a form is easier than using a datasheet since all of the fields in the table are presented in a different layout which usually allows all fields to be visible in the current screen. Other records in the table do not distract the user since only one record displays at a time. Forms can be customized to present a variety of layouts. You will learn how to create and edit forms in Section 3.

Project

Worldwide Enterprises has just signed two new distributors in New York. You will add the information in two records in the US_Distributors table using a form.

Tutorial 1.5
Adding Records and Navigating in a Form

1 With the **WEDistributors1.accdb** database open, double-click *US_Distributors* in the Forms group of the Navigation pane.

> The US_Distributors form opens with the first record in the US_Distributors table displayed in the form.

2 Click the New button in the Records group in the Home tab.

> A blank form appears in Form view and the Record Navigation bar indicates you are editing record number 22. Notice the New (blank) record and Next record buttons on the Record Navigation bar are dimmed.

3 Press Tab to move to the *CompanyName* field since Access automatically assigns the next sequential number to the *DistID* field.

> The *DistID* field does not display a field value until you begin to type data in another field in the record.

4 Type **Movie Emporium** and then press Tab or Enter.

5 Type **203 West Houston Street** and then press Tab or Enter.

> Use the same navigation methods you learned in Activity 1.5 on adding records to a datasheet.

6 Type the remaining field values as shown at the right. Press Tab or Enter after typing the last field.

> When you press Tab or Enter after the *EmailAdd* field, a new form will appear in the work area.

7 Type the following information in the appropriate fields in a new form for record 23:

> **Cinema Festival**
> **318 East 11th Street**
> **New York, NY 10003**
> **212-555-9715**
> **212-555-9717**
> **cinemafest@emcp.net**

8 Click the First record button ⏮ in the Record Navigation bar.

This displays the information for All Nite Cinemas in Form view.

9 Click the Last record button ⏭ in the Record Navigation bar.

This displays the information for Cinema Festival in Form view.

10 Use the Previous record button ◀ to scroll the records one at a time back to the first record.

11 Click the insertion point within the *CompanyName* field and then click the Find button in the Find group in the Home tab.

You can use the Find feature to find a record that you need to view or edit in Form view using the same method as you learned in Activity 1.4 for finding and editing records in a datasheet.

In Brief

Add Record In Form View
1. Open form.
2. Click New (blank) record button in Navigation bar OR click New button in Records group.
3. Type data in fields.

12 With existing text already selected in the *Find What* text box, type **Dockside Movies** and then click Find Next.

Access scrolls the form to make the *DistID* record 20 active, which is the record in which the search string *Dockside Movies* exists in the *CompanyName* field.

13 Close the Find and Replace dialog box to view the record for Dockside Movies.

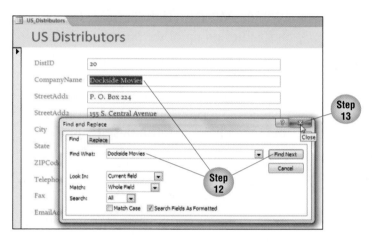

Need Help?

Record not found? Check your spelling in the *Find What* text box. A typing mistake will mean Access could not match the search string with a *CompanyName* field value.

14 Close the US_Distributors form.

15 Open the US_Distributors table and then view the two records added to the table using the form.

16 Close the US_Distributors table.

In Addition

Scrolling in Form View Using the Keyboard

Records can be scrolled in Form view using the following keyboard techniques:
- Page Down displays the next record.
- Page Up displays the previous record.
- Ctrl + End moves to the last field in the last record.
- Ctrl + Home moves to the first field in the first record.

Activity 1.7

Deleting Records in a Datasheet and Form

Records can be deleted in either Datasheet view or Form view. To delete a record, open the datasheet or form, activate any field in the record to be deleted, and then click the Delete button in the Records group in the Home tab. Access displays a message indicating the selected record will be permanently removed from the table. Click Yes to confirm the record deletion.

Project The Countryside Cinemas and Victory Cinemas distributor agreements have lapsed and you have just been informed that they have signed agreements with another movie distributing company. You will delete their records in the US_Distributors table using the datasheet and the form.

Tutorial 1.6
Deleting and Sorting Records

1. With the **WEDistributors1.accdb** database open, double-click *US_Distributors* in the Tables group of the Navigation pane.

2. Position the mouse pointer in the record selector bar (empty column to the left of *DistID*) for record 3 until the pointer changes to a right-pointing black arrow and then click the left mouse button.

    This action selects the entire record.

3. Click the Delete button ☒ in the Records group in the Home tab.

4. Access displays a message box indicating you are about to delete 1 record and that the undo operation is not available after this action. Click Yes to confirm the deletion.

Step 3

Step 2

Step 4

![laptop icon] **Need Help?**
Check that you are deleting the correct record before clicking Yes. Click No if you selected the wrong record by mistake.

5. Notice that Access does not renumber the remaining records in the *DistID* field once record 3 has been deleted from the table.

    The *DistID* field is defined as an AutoNumber field. For this field data type, once a number has been used, Access does not make the number available again for another record even after the record is deleted.

6. Close the US_Distributors table.

7. Open the US_Distributors form.

8. Click in the *CompanyName* field and then use the Find feature to locate the record for Victory Cinemas.

9. Close the Find and Replace dialog box when the record has been located.

10 Click the Delete button arrow in the Records group in the Home tab and then click *Delete Record* at the drop-down list.

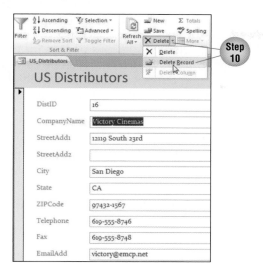

11 Click Yes to confirm the deletion.

12 Click the First record button in the Record Navigation bar to move the active record to All Nite Cinemas.

13 Click the Next record button in the Record Navigation bar twice to move the active record to Danforth Cinemas.

14 Notice the *DistID* field value for Danforth Cinemas is *4* while the Record Navigation bar displays *3 of 21* in the *Current Record* text box.

> Do not get confused between the record numbers in the Navigation bar and the *DistID* field values. They are separate identifiers. The *DistID* field values are assigned as new records are added to the table. Deleting a record does not make the number available for use again. In other words, the field values in *DistID* are not dynamic—they do not change once the number has been assigned in the field. The numbers in the Navigation bar are dynamic and update to reflect the current number of records that exist in the table.

15 Close the US_Distributors form.

In Addition

More about Deleting Records

In a multiuser environment, deleting records is a procedure that should be performed only by authorized personnel; once the record is deleted, crucial data can be lost. It is a good idea to back up the database file before deleting records. You can use the Windows Copy and Paste features to make a backup copy of a database. Access also includes a Backup utility which you will learn in Section 4.

Activity 1.8

Sorting Records; Moving Columns

Records in a table are displayed alphanumerically and sorted in ascending order by the primary key field values. To rearrange the order of the records, click in any record in the column you want to sort by and then click the Ascending or Descending buttons in the Sort & Filter group in the Home tab. To sort by more than one column, select the columns first and then click the Ascending or Descending button. Access sorts first by the leftmost column in the selection, then by the next column, and continues this pattern for the remainder of the sort keys. Columns can be moved in the datasheet if necessary to facilitate a multiple-column sort. Access saves the sort order when the table is closed.

Project

You will perform one sort routine using a single field and then perform a multiple-column sort. To do the multiple-column sort, you will have to move columns in the datasheet.

1. With the **WEDistributors1.accdb** database open, open the US_Distributors table.

2. Click in any record in the *City* column.

3. Click the Ascending button ![AZ] in the Sort & Filter group in the Home tab.

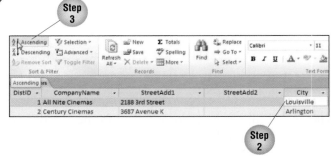

   The records are rearranged to display in order of the city names starting with *A* through *Z*.

4. Click the Descending button ![ZA] in the Sort & Filter group.

   The records are rearranged to display the cities starting with *Z* through *A*. Notice also that the *City* column heading displays with a downward pointing arrow to indicate the field that is being used to sort the datasheet in descending order. In Steps 5–9 you will move the *State* and *City* columns to the left of the *CompanyName* column to perform a multiple-column sort.

5. Position the mouse pointer in the *State* column heading until the pointer changes to a downward-pointing black arrow and then click the left mouse button.

   The selected *State* column can be moved by dragging the column heading to another position in the datasheet.

6. With the *State* column selected, move the pointer to the column heading *State* until the white arrow pointer appears.

7. Hold down the left mouse button, drag the column between *DistID* and *CompanyName*, and then release the mouse. *State* is now positioned before the *CompanyName* field in the datasheet.

   A thick black line appears between columns as you drag, indicating the position to which the column will be moved when you release the mouse. In addition, the pointer displays with the outline of a gray box attached to it, indicating you are performing a move operation.

8 Click in any field to deselect the *State* column.

9 Move the *City* column between *State* and *CompanyName* by completing steps similar to those in Steps 5–8.

10 Position the mouse pointer in the *State* column heading until the pointer changes to a downward-pointing black arrow; hold down the left mouse button; drag right until the *State*, *City*, and *CompanyName* columns are selected; and then release the left mouse button.

11 Click the Ascending button and then click in any cell to deselect the three columns.

> The records are sorted first by *State*, then by *City* within each State, and then by *CompanyName* within each City.

12 Look at the four records for the state of New York. Notice the order of the records is Waterfront Cinemas in Buffalo first, then Cinema Festival, Movie Emporium, and Westview Movies in New York City next.

Step 10

US_Distributors			
DistID	State	City	CompanyName
15	FL	Tampa	Sunfest Cinemas
9	WA	Seattle	Mainstream Movies
14	OR	Portland	Redwood Cinemas

Step 12

US_Distributors				
	DistID	State	City	CompanyName	StreetAdd1
	7	AZ	Phoenix	LaVista Cinemas	111 Vista Road
	10	CA	Los Angeles	Marquee Movies	1011 South Alameda Street
	15	FL	Tampa	Sunfest Cinemas	
	8	GA	Atlanta	Liberty Cinemas	P. O. Box 998
	13	IL	Oak Park	O'Shea Movies	59 Erie
	11	KS	Emporia	Midtown Moviehouse	1033 Commercial Street
	1	KY	Louisville	All Nite Cinemas	2188 3rd Street
	5	MA	Cambridge	Eastown Movie House	P. O. Box 429
	20	MD	Baltimore	Dockside Movies	P. O. Box 224
	21	MI	Detroit	Renaissance Cinemas	3599 Woodward Avenue
	6	NJ	Baking Ridge	Hillman Cinemas	55 Kemble Avenue
	17	NY	Buffalo	Waterfront Cinemas	P. O. Box 3255
	23	NY	New York	Cinema Festival	318 East 11th Street
	22	NY	New York	Movie Emporium	203 West Houston Street
	19	NY	New York	Westview Movies	1112 Broadway
	12	OH	Dublin	Mooretown Movies	P. O. Box 11
	14	OR	Portland	Redwood Cinemas	P. O. Box 112F
	18	PA	Philadelphia	Wellington 10	1203 Tenth Southwest
	4	SC	Columbia	Danforth Cinemas	P. O. Box 22
	2	TX	Arlington	Century Cinemas	3687 Avenue K
	9	WA	Seattle	Mainstream Movies	P. O. Box 33

13 Close the US_Distributors table. Click Yes when prompted to save the design changes.

In Brief

Sort Datasheet by Single Field
1. Open table.
2. Click in column by which to sort.
3. Click Ascending or Descending button.

Sort Datasheet by Multiple Fields
1. Open table.
2. If necessary, move columns to accommodate desired sort order.
3. Select columns from left to right in order of the sort.
4. Click Ascending or Descending button.

In Addition

More about Sorting

When you are ready to sort records, consider the following alphanumeric rules:
- Numbers stored in fields that are not defined as numeric (i.e., social security number or telephone number) are sorted as characters (not numeric values). To sort them as if they were numbers, all field values must be the same length.
- Records in which the selected field is empty are listed first.
- Numbers are sorted before letters.

Activity 1.9

Applying and Removing Filters

A *filter* is used to view only those records that meet specified criteria. The records that do not meet the filter criteria are hidden from view temporarily. Using a filter, you can view, edit, and/or print a subset of rows within the table. For example, you might want to view only those records of distributors in one state.

Project
You want to view a list of distributors in New York state and then further filter the list to display only those in the city of New York. In a second filter operation you will view the distributors located in California and Georgia.

Tutorial 1.7
Filtering Records

1 With the **WEDistributors1.accdb** database open, open the US_Distributors table.

2 Click the insertion point within any record in the *State* column.

3 Click the Filter button ⧩ in the Sort & Filter group of the Home tab.

A field is filtered by selecting criteria from a drop-down list. Access looks in the active column and includes in the filter list box each unique field value that exists within the column. Adjacent to each field value is a check box. Clear the check box for those states that you do not wish to view. When you click OK, only those records with a field value that matches the states with a check mark retained in the check box are displayed; all other records are temporarily hidden.

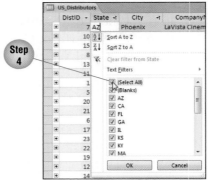

4 Click the *Select All* check box to clear the check marks from all of the check boxes.

5 Scroll down the filter list box, click the check box next to *NY*, and then click OK.

The filter list box closes and only four records remain, as shown below. Notice the two icons next to *State* indicating the field is both filtered and sorted. Notice also the message *Filtered* displays in the Record Navigation bar. In the next step, you will further filter the records to display only those in New York City.

Only those records that meet the filter criterion, *State* is *NY*, are displayed in Step 5.

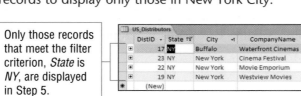

6 Click the filter arrow (displays as a down-pointing arrow) next to *City* to open the filter list box.

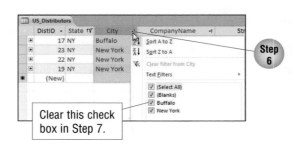

Clear this check box in Step 7.

7 Click the check box next to *Buffalo* to clear the check mark and then click OK.

This action removes the record from the datasheet for the company located in Buffalo. Now only three records remain, as shown below.

The filtered datasheet is filtered again to show only those distributors in New York City in Step 7.

In Brief

Filter Records
1. Open table.
2. Click in field by which to filter.
3. Click Filter button or click down-pointing arrow next to field name.
4. Clear check boxes for items you do not want to view.
5. Click OK.

Remove Filter
Click Toggle Filter button when datasheet is filtered.

Clear Filter Settings
1. Click Advanced button.
2. Click *Clear Grid*.

8 Click the Toggle Filter button [Y] in the Sort & Filter group.

When a filter has been applied to a datasheet, clicking Toggle Filter acts as the Remove Filter command. The Toggle Filter button switches between Apply Filter and Remove Filter, depending on the state of the datasheet. Notice all records are redisplayed in the datasheet. Notice also that the message in the Record Navigation bar has changed to *Unfiltered*.

Step 8

9 Click the Advanced button [▼] in the Sort & Filter group of the Home tab.

10 Click *Filter By Form* at the drop-down list.

All records are temporarily removed from the datasheet. Specify the field value in the field by which you want to filter by using the drop-down lists in the fields in the blank row. Access retains the most recent filter settings. In the next step, you will clear the previous settings so that you can begin a new filter.

Step 9

Step 10

11 Click the Advanced button and then click *Clear Grid* at the drop-down list.

This action clears all previous filter options.

12 Click in the *State* column, click the down-pointing arrow that appears, and then click *CA* at the drop-down list.

Step 12

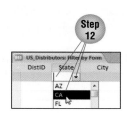

13 Click the Or tab located at the bottom of the datasheet.

Using the Or tab you can filter by more than one state. A new blank form appears in which you specify a second filter criteria.

Step 13

14 With *State* the active column, click the down-pointing arrow that appears and then click *GA*.

15 Click the Toggle Filter button (displays the ScreenTip *Apply Filter*) to apply the filter settings.

Two records display in the filtered datasheet: Marquee Movies in Los Angeles, CA and Liberty Cinemas in Atlanta, GA.

16 Click the Toggle Filter button (displays the ScreenTip *Remove Filter*) to redisplay the entire datasheet.

17 Close the US_Distributors table. Click Yes when prompted to save the design changes.

Activity 1.10

Previewing and Printing; Changing Margins and Page Orientation

Click the File tab, click the Print tab in Backstage view and then click the Quick Print or Print button to print a table in Datasheet view. To avoid wasting paper, use the Print Preview option at the Print tab Backstage view to see how the datasheet will appear on the page before you print. By default, Access prints a datasheet on letter size paper in portrait orientation. You can change the paper size, orientation, or margins using buttons in the Page Size and Page Layout groups of the Print Preview tab.

Project Sam Vestering has requested a list of the U.S. distributors. You will open the US_Distributors table, preview the printout, change the page orientation, change the left and right margins, and then print the datasheet.

Tutorial 1.1
Opening Access, Navigating and Printing a Table

1. With the **WEDistributors1.accdb** database open, open the US_Distributors table.

2. Click the File tab, click the Print tab, and then click Print Preview to display the datasheet in the Print Preview window shown in Figure 1.4.

3. Move the mouse pointer (displays as a magnifying glass) 🔍 over the top center of the table and click the left mouse button.

   The zoom changes to 100% magnification. Notice that Access prints the table name at the top center and the current date at the top right of the page. At the bottom center, Access prints the word *Page* followed by the current page number.

4. Click the left mouse button again to zoom the datasheet back to fit the current page within the window.

5. Click the Next Page button located on the Navigation bar at the bottom left of the Print Preview window two times.

FIGURE 1.4 Print Preview Window

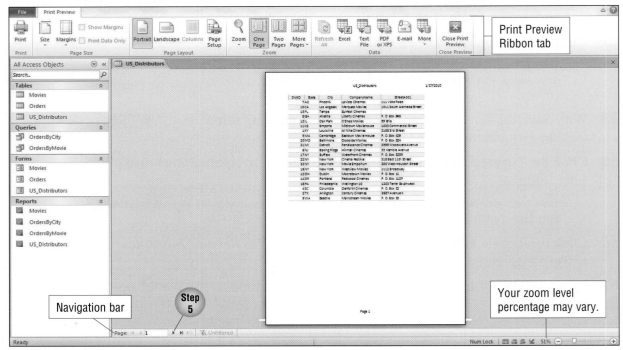

The US_Distributors table requires three pages to print with the default margins and orientation. In the next step, you will change the orientation to landscape to see if all of the columns will fit on one page.

6 Click the Landscape button 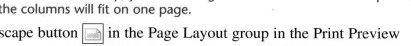 in the Page Layout group in the Print Preview tab.

> Landscape orientation rotates the printout to print wider than it is tall. Changing to landscape allows more columns to fit on a page.

7 Look at the page number in the Navigation bar at the bottom of the Print Preview window. Notice that the page number is now 2. In landscape orientation, the US_Distributors table still needs two pages to print.

> Another method to fit more text on a page is to reduce the margins. In the next step, you will try reducing the left and right margins to see the effect on the number of pages.

8 Click the Margins button in the Page Size group and then review the predefined margin options in the drop-down list.

> You decide you want to set your own custom margins since none of the predefined margin settings meet your needs.

9 Click outside the drop-down list to remove it and then click the Page Setup button in the Page Layout group.

10 At the Page Setup dialog box with the Print Options tab active, drag across *1* in the *Left* text box and then type **0.25**.

11 Press Tab, type **0.25** in the *Right* text box, and then click OK.

12 Click the Print button in the Print group and then click OK at the Print dialog box.

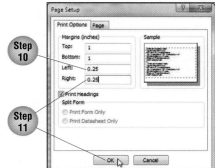

Step 10

Step 11

> In a few seconds the table will print on the default printer installed on your computer. Making the left and right margins smaller than 0.25 inch would still not allow the entire datasheet to fit on one page. In Section 3, titled "Creating Queries, Forms, and Reports," you will learn how to create a report for a table. Using a report you can control the data layout on the page and which columns are printed.

13 Click the Close Print Preview button in the Close Preview group.

14 Close the US_Distributors table.

In Addition

Previewing Multiple Pages

Use buttons in the Preview group of the Print Preview tab to view a datasheet that requires multiple pages all in one window. Click the Two Pages button to view the datasheet with two pages side-by-side. Click the More pages button and then choose from *Four Pages*, *Eight Pages*, or *Twelve Pages* at the drop-down list. The US_Distributors datasheet is shown with the Two Pages view at the right.

Activity
1.11

Using Help;
Hiding Columns in a Datasheet

An extensive online Help resource is available that contains information on Access features and commands. Click the Microsoft Access Help button located near the upper right corner of the screen (below the Close button on the Title bar) to open the Access Help window. By default, the Help feature searches for an Internet connection. A message at the bottom right corner of the window reads *Connected to Office.com* when an Internet connection is found. Help information is available without Internet access; however, fewer resources display for help topics when using the Offline Help file.

You can hide a column in a datasheet if a field exists in the table that you do not need for data entry or editing purposes. Hiding the column provides more space in the work area. Hidden columns do not print. To hide a column, right-click the field name in the header row of the datasheet and then click *Hide Fields* at the shortcut menu.

Project

You will explore topics in the Help feature and change the font size of the text in the datasheet. Finally, you will reprint the formatted datasheet with two columns hidden that you decide you do not need on the printout.

Note: The following steps assume you are connected to the Internet to access Office Online.

Tutorial 1.8
Using Help

1. With the **WEDistributors1.accdb** database open, open the US_Distributors table.

2. Click the Microsoft Access Help button located near the upper right corner of the screen (below the Close button on the Title bar).

> Find information in Help resources by clicking links to categories of Help topics in the main Access Help window or by typing a search word or phrase and then clicking the Search button.

3. At the opening Access Help window, click the hyperlink <u>Getting started with Access 2010</u>.

4. Click the hyperlink <u>What's new in Microsoft Access</u> in the table below the *Getting started with Access 2010* article title and paragraph.

5. Read the first few paragraphs in the next Help window that describe new features in Microsoft Access 2010 and then click the Home button in the Access Help window toolbar.

Step 3

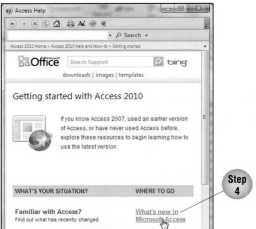

Step 4

Step 5

6 Click in the Search text box located at the top of the Access Help window below the toolbar, type **keyboard shortcuts**, and then click the Search button.

Keyboard shortcuts are helpful to know since frequently used commands can often be performed more quickly using a keyboard shortcut.

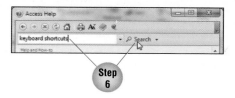

Step
6

7 Click *Keyboard shortcuts for Access* in the Results list.

8 At the Keyboard shortcuts for Access Help window, scroll down and then click Select text and data in the *Keys for working with text and data* section.

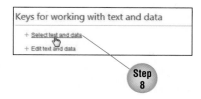

Step
8

9 Click Selecting a field or record in the expanded list of topics.

10 Read the descriptions and keyboard shortcuts in the table that is displayed. Notice the keyboard shortcut for the last option, *Select all records*, is *Ctrl + A* or *Ctrl + Shift + Spacebar*.

11 Close the Help window.

12 At the US_Distributors datasheet, press Ctrl + A to select all records.

13 Click the Font Size button `11` arrow in the Text Formatting group in the Home tab and then click *10* at the drop-down list.

14 Click in any field to deselect the records.

15 Right-click the *DistID* field name at the top of the column and then click *Hide Fields* at the shortcut menu.

16 If necessary, scroll the datasheet right, right-click the *EmailAdd* field name, and then click *Hide Fields* at the shortcut menu.

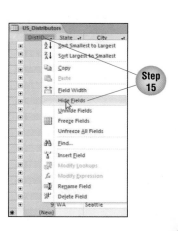

Step
15

17 Click the File tab, click the Print tab, and then click Print Preview.

18 Change the orientation to landscape and set the left and right margins to 0.5 inch.

19 Print the datasheet.

20 Close the Print Preview window and then close the US_Distributors table. Click Yes when prompted to save the layout changes.

21 Click the File tab and then click Close Database.

Features Summary

Feature	Ribbon Tab, Group	Button	Quick Access Toolbar	Keyboard Shortcut
add records	Home, Records	⬜ OR ▶		Ctrl + +
change font size	Home, Text Formatting	11 ▾		
change margins	Print Preview, Page Size OR Page Layout	⬜ OR ⬜ to open Page Setup		
column width	Home, Records	⬜		
delete records	Home, Records	✕		Delete
filter	Home, Sort & Filter	▽		
Find	Home, Find	🔍		Ctrl + F
Help		?		F1
landscape orientation	Print Preview, Page Layout	⬜		
print	Print Preview, Print	🖨		Ctrl + P
Print Preview	File, Print			
save			💾	Ctrl + S
select all records	Home, Find	↖		Ctrl + A
sort ascending order	Home, Sort & Filter	A↓Z		
sort descending order	Home, Sort & Filter	Z↓A		

Knowledge Check

Completion: In the space provided at the right, indicate the correct term, command, or option.

1. Access opens with this view displayed. _____
2. This term describes a single unit of information about a person place, item, or event. _____
3. This term describes all of the data about one subject in a table. _____
4. This object is created first before any other objects in a database. _____
5. This database object is used to display or print data from one or more tables in a specific layout or format. _____
6. Click this button at the Column Width dialog box to set the column width to the length of the longest entry in the column. _____
7. Press this key to turn on Edit mode in a datasheet. _____
8. This object provides a user-friendly interface with which you can edit, view, or print data by working with only one record at a time. _____
9. Access displays a message box requesting confirmation when a record is about to be deleted because this feature is not available for a Delete operation. _____
10. When more than one column is selected for a sort operation, Access sorts first by this column. _____
11. This feature temporarily hides records in the datasheet that do not meet the specified criteria. _____
12. This page layout orientation rotates the printout to print wider than it is tall. _____
13. Display this dialog box to set your own custom margins. _____
14. These are the steps to hide a column in a datasheet. _____
15. This keyboard command selects all records in the datasheet. _____

Skills Review

Review 1 Adjusting Column Widths; Finding and Editing Records; Adding and Deleting Records

1. Open the **WEEmployees1.accdb** database. If the Security Warning message bar appears below the ribbon, click the Enable Content button.
2. Open the Employees table.
3. Adjust all column widths to Best Fit.
4. Find the record for Carl Zakowski and then change the birth date from *5/9/1967* to *12/22/1987*.
5. Find the record for Roman Deptulski and then change the salary from *$69,725.00* to *$72,750.00*. ***Note: You do not need to type the dollar symbol, comma, and decimal***.
6. Find the record for Terry Yiu and then change the hire date from *4/12/2005* to *1/31/2006*.
7. Delete the record for Valerie Fitsouris.
8. Delete the record for Edward Thurston.

9. Add the following records to the table in the appropriate fields using the datasheet.
*Note: In this table **EmployeeID** is not an AutoNumber field; therefore, you will need to type the numbers in the first field.*

1085	1090	1095
Yousef J Armine	Maria D Quinte	Patrick J Kilarney
11/19/1990	4/16/1991	2/27/1985
3/14/2010	11/29/2010	12/12/2010
European Distribution	Overseas Distribution	North American Distribution
$42,177	$42,177	$42,177

10. Close the Employees table. Click Yes when prompted to save changes.

Review 2 Sorting; Previewing; Changing Page Orientation; Filtering; Hiding Columns; Printing

1. With **WEEmployees1.accdb** open, open the Employees table.
2. Sort the table in ascending order first by *Department* and then by *LastName*.
3. Preview the table in the Print Preview window.
4. Change the orientation to landscape and then print the datasheet.
5. Filter the table to display only those employees who work in the European Distribution department.
6. Hide the *EmployeeID* column.
7. Print the datasheet and then close the Employees table. Click Yes when prompted to save changes.
8. Close the **WEEmployees1.accdb** database.

Skills Assessment

Assessment 1 Adjusting Column Width; Finding and Editing Records; Previewing and Printing

1. Jai Prasad, instructor in the Theatre Arts Division, has been called out of town to attend a family matter. The grades for SM100-01 have to be entered into the database by the end of today. Jai has provided you with the following grades:

Terry Yiu	A+	Kevin Gibson	C
Maren Bastow	C	Ash Bhullar	A
Martine Gagne	B	Bruce Morgan	B
Armado Ennis	D	Russell Clements	A
Bentley Woollatt	B	Richard Loewen	F
Susan Retieffe	C		

To begin, open the **NPCGrades1.accdb** database. Click the Enable Content button if the Security Warning message bar appears below the ribbon.
2. Open the SM100-01Grades table.
3. Adjust column widths to Best Fit.
4. Enter the grades provided in Step 1 in the appropriate records.
5. Preview and then print the table.
6. Close the SM100-01Grades table. Click Yes when prompted to save changes.
7. Close the **NPCGrades1.accdb** database.

Assessment 2   Finding, Adding, and Deleting Records; Formatting Datasheet

1. Dana Hirsch, manager, has ordered three new inventory items and decided to discontinue three others. Dana has asked you to update the inventory database. To begin, open the **WBInventory1.accdb** database. Click the Enable Content button if the Security Warning message bar appears below the ribbon.
2. Open the InventoryList table and adjust all column widths to Best Fit.
3. Locate and then delete the inventory items *Pita Wraps*, *Tuna*, and *Lake Erie Perch*.
4. Add the following new records to the InventoryList table.

ItemNo	ItemDescription	Unit	SupplierCode
051	Atlantic Scallops	case	9
052	Lake Trout	case	9
053	Panini Rolls	flat	1

5. Change the font size for all records to 10.
6. Preview the table in Print Preview and adjust the top and/or bottom margin settings until all of the records will print on one page and then print the table.
7. Close the InventoryList table. Click Yes when prompted to save changes.
8. Close the **WBInventory1.accdb** database.

Assessment 3   Finding, Sorting, Filtering, and Deleting Records

1. You are the assistant to Bobbie Sinclair, business manager. Bobbie has just informed you that some costumes in the rental inventory have been destroyed in a fire at an offsite location. Bobbie has asked you to delete these costumes from the rental inventory database and then print updated reports. To begin, open the **PTCostumeInv1.accdb** database. Click the Enable Content button if the Security Warning message bar appears below the ribbon.
2. Open the CostumeInventory table and adjust all column widths to Best Fit.
3. Locate and then delete the records for the following costumes that were destroyed in a fire at a Shakespearean festival:

   Macbeth   Othello
   Lady Macbeth   King Lear
   Hamlet   Richard III

4. Sort the table in ascending order by *CostumeTitle*.
5. Preview the table, adjust margins so that all data fits on one page, and then print the table.
6. Sort the table in ascending order first by *Date Out*, then by *Date In*, and then by *CostumeTitle*.
7. Filter the table so that only those records that were rented out on *10/1/2011* are displayed.
8. Print the filtered list.
9. Redisplay all records.
10. Close the CostumeInventory table. Click Yes when prompted to save changes.
11. Close the **PTCostumeInv1.accdb** database.

Assessment 4 Finding Information on Designing a Database

1. Open an Access Help window and then use the following navigation guidelines to find information on dividing information into tables.
   a. Search for help using the keywords *database design*.
   b. Click the link to the article titled <u>Database design basics</u> in the results list.
   c. Scroll down and click the hyperlink to <u>Dividing the information into tables</u>.
2. The information in the section titled *Dividing the information into tables* describes the reasons why a table should be about one subject (also called entity) only. Read the information in this Help section.
3. Use Microsoft Word to create a memo addressed to your instructor as follows:
   • Use one of the memo templates.
   • Provide in a list format all of the reasons that were described in Help that explain why a table should contain information about one subject only. ***Note: Copying and pasting the text from the Help window is not acceptable—describe the reasons in your own words***.
4. Save the memo in Word and name it **AS1-A4-TableMemo**.
5. Print and close **AS1-A4-TableMemo.docx** and then exit Word.

Assessment 5 Individual Challenge
Creating a Job Search Company Database

1. You are starting to plan ahead for your job search after graduation. You decide to maintain a database of company information in Access. To begin, search the Internet for at least eight companies in your field of study (four out of state or out of province.) Include company name, address, telephone and fax numbers, and a contact person in the human resources department, if possible.
2. Open the **JobSearchInfo1.accdb** database. Click the Enable Content button if the Security Warning message bar appears below the ribbon.
3. Open the CompanyInfo table.
4. Enter at least eight records for the companies you researched on the Internet.
5. Adjust column widths as necessary.
6. Sort the records in ascending order by the *CompanyName* field.
7. Preview the table. Format all records to a smaller font size and change page layout options as necessary to minimize the paper used for printing.
8. Print and then close the CompanyInfo table.
9. Close the **JobSearchInfo1.accdb** database.

Marquee Challenge

Challenge 1   Updating and Printing a Catering Event Database

1. Dana Hirsch, manager, has given you information related to five new catering events that were recently booked at the bistro. Dana would like you to update the catering database and produce a report. To begin, open **WBSpecialEvents1.accdb**. Click the Enable Content button if the Security Warning message bar appears below the ribbon.
2. Open the CateringContracts table and then add the following information. Dana advises that deposits have been received for all of these events. The columns in the table that have check boxes displayed are defined as Yes/No fields. In these columns, click to insert a check mark in the box indicating "Yes"; otherwise leave the check box empty to indicate "No."

Name	Phone	Event	Date	Room	Guests	Charge	Special Menu
Cora Spriet	905-555-1623	Wedding	8/8/2010	Westview	150	26.95	Yes
Sean Vezina	716-555-3846	Business Meeting	8/12/2010	Starlake	24	23.75	No
William Graham	716-555-8694	25th Wedding Anniversary	8/15/2010	Sunset	80	24.95	No
Helena Kosjovic	716-555-3441	Engagement Brunch	8/16/2010	Sunset	56	22.95	No
Pieter Borman	716-555-6994	Business Meeting	8/22/2010	Starlake	41	24.95	Yes

3. Jack Torrance has called and cancelled his business meeting on May 15. Delete the record.
4. Dana has updated the charge for the Pavelich wedding to $33.50 per person.
5. Dana would like a report that is sorted by the room booked first and then by the last name. Make sure the data is entirely visible in all columns and that the printout is only 1 page. For this report Dana does not need to see the *ID* or the *ContactPhone* fields.
6. Close the CateringContracts table saving design changes.
7. Close the **WBSpecialEvents1.accdb** database.

Challenge 2 Determining Fields and Table Names for a New Database

1. Bobbie Sinclair, business manager, is considering having you create a new database to store the custom costume business at Performance Threads. Bobbie has jotted down rough notes regarding the information to be stored in the new database in Table 1.5. Using Microsoft Word, create a document that provides the proposed field names and table names for each table. Incorporate the information in the additional notes as you develop the tables. As you create this document, consider the following two database design practices:
   - The use of spaces in field names or table names is discouraged.
   - Within each table, one field must contain unique identifying information.
2. At this stage of the design process, you are only considering the breakdown of fields to accommodate the information in Table 1.5. Other elements of the table and database design such as data type, properties, and relationships will be added in a challenge project for Section 2.
3. Save the Word document and name it **AS1-C2-PTCostumes**.
4. Print and then close the document.

TABLE 1.5 Challenge 2

Customer Information	Order Information
Customer's name, address, contact telephone numbers	Description of costume
	Customer for whom costume is being made
	Contract price
	Date due
	Seamstress
	Estimated hours for each of the main cost centers: Research, Design, Production
	Deposit amount received in advance
Contract Seamstresses	**Ship To Information**
Name, address, and contact telephone numbers for seamstresses on contract with Performance Threads	Customer
	Costume
	Address for delivery of costume
	Shipping company
	Shipping charge

Additional notes:
Costumes are quoted a contract price which the customer accepts in advance by signing a contract document. The signed document must be on file before work begins.
The hours for the three cost centers are estimated at the time of the quote. Bobbie wants to use the database to also enter actual hours after the costume is complete to generate hours variance reports.

Access SECTION 2
Creating Tables and Relationships

Skills

- List guidelines for field names
- Choose an appropriate data type for a field
- Define primary key field
- Create a new database
- Create a table using a blank datasheet
- Create and modify a table in Design view
- Set the primary key for a table
- Limit the number of characters allowed in a field
- Display a descriptive title for fields by using a caption
- Display a default value in a field
- Verify data entry using a validation rule
- Restrict data entry using an input mask
- Set the format for displaying data
- Create a Lookup list in a field
- Insert, move, and delete fields
- Add a total row to a datasheet
- Describe why tables are joined in a relationship
- Create and edit a one-to-many relationship
- Define foreign key field
- Create and edit a one-to-one relationship
- Print a relationship report
- Delete a relationship

Projects Overview

Create and modify tables to store distributor contract information, employee benefit information, and employee review information; create relationships between tables. Review tables in an existing database and improve the table design.

Create a table to store student grades for a course in the Theatre Arts Division.

Create a new database to store local event information.

Create a new database to store employee expense claims.

Modify and correct field properties in a costume inventory table to improve the design. Continue design work on a new database for custom costumes and create the database.

Model Answers for Projects

These model answers for the projects that you complete in Section 2 provide a preview of the finished projects before you begin working and also allow you to compare your own results with these models to ensure you have created the materials accurately.

AS2-A2.1Contracts.docx is the project in Activity 2.1.

Contracts table

Fields needed in new table	Field name	Data Type
Contract number	*ContractNo	Text
Company Name	Company	Text
Contact First Name	ContactFN	Text
Contact Last Name	ContactLN	Text
Telephone	Phone	Text
Extension for telephone number	Ext	Text
Fax Number	Fax	Text
Is this a renewal contract?	Renewal	Yes/No
Start date of contract	StartDate	Date/Time
End date of contract	EndDate	Date/Time
Shipping fee per movie	ShipFee	Currency
Percentage of box office sales	Percentage	Number
Internal notes	Notes	Memo

The **Contracts** table (a two-page document) within the **WEContracts2.accdb** database is the project in Activity 2.2.

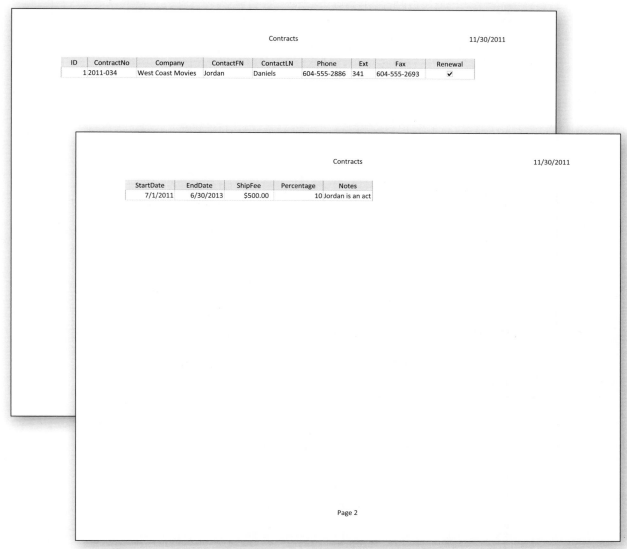

ID	ContractNo	Company	ContactFN	ContactLN	Phone	Ext	Fax	Renewal
1	2011-034	West Coast Movies	Jordan	Daniels	604-555-2886	341	604-555-2693	✔

Contracts   11/30/2011

StartDate	EndDate	ShipFee	Percentage	Notes
7/1/2011	6/30/2013	$500.00	10	Jordan is an act

Page 2

The Benefits table within the WEEmployees2.accdb database is the project in Activities 2.3 to 2.7.

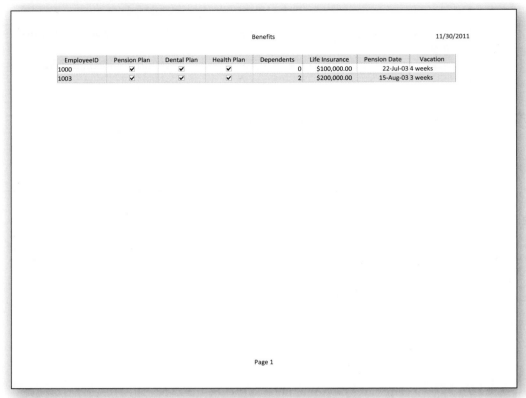

Benefits   11/30/2011

EmployeeID	Pension Plan	Dental Plan	Health Plan	Dependents	Life Insurance	Pension Date	Vacation
1000	✓	✓	✓	0	$100,000.00	22-Jul-03	4 weeks
1003	✓	✓	✓	2	$200,000.00	15-Aug-03	3 weeks

Page 1

The Employees table within the WEEmployees2.accdb database is the project in Activity 2.8.

Employees   11/30/2011

EmployeeID	LastName	FirstName	BirthDate	AnnualSalary	HireDate	Supervisor	Department
1000	Vestering	Sam	2/18/1957	$69,725.00	7/22/2002		North American Distribution
1003	Ruiz	Celesta	3/12/1975	$41,875.00	8/5/2002		North American Distribution
1005	Deptulski	Roman	3/12/1948	$72,750.00	8/15/2002		Overseas Distribution
1013	Chippewa	Gregg	6/15/1985	$48,650.00	2/10/2003		European Distribution
1015	Besterd	Lyle	10/15/1959	$45,651.00	5/17/2003		North American Distribution
1020	Doxtator	Angela	5/22/1963	$45,558.00	8/3/2003		North American Distribution
1023	Bulinkski	Aleksy	7/30/1986	$51,450.00	10/10/2003		European Distribution
1025	Biliski	Jorge	6/18/1970	$44,892.00	12/1/2003		North American Distribution
1030	Hicks	Thom	7/27/1977	$42,824.00	1/22/2004		Overseas Distribution
1033	Titov	Dina	8/15/1990	$45,655.00	1/10/2004		North American Distribution
1040	Lafreniere	Guy	9/14/1972	$45,395.00	3/10/2005		Overseas Distribution
1043	Morano	Enzo	10/22/1984	$48,750.00	8/15/2005		North American Distribution
1045	Yiu	Terry	6/18/1961	$42,238.00	1/31/2006		European Distribution
1050	Zakowski	Carl	12/22/1987	$44,387.00	2/9/2006		European Distribution
1053	O'Connor	Shauna	9/12/1987	$43,695.00	4/15/2007		North American Distribution
1060	McKnight	Donald	1/6/1964	$42,126.00	6/22/2007		European Distribution
1063	McPhee	Charlotte	4/16/1978	$43,695.00	2/6/2008		North American Distribution
1065	Liszniewski	Norm	11/16/1970	$43,695.00	2/6/2008		North American Distribution
1073	Judd	Marsha	5/4/982	$44,771.00	11/30/2009		North American Distribution
1080	Couture	Leo	1/8/1978	$43,659.00	1/27/2010		European Distribution
1083	Arnold	Drew	1/27/1969	$43,659.00	6/22/2010		North American Distribution
1085	Armine	Yousef	11/19/1990	$42,177.00	3/14/2010		European Distribution
1090	Quinte	Maria	4/16/1991	$42,177.00	11/29/2010		Overseas Distribution
1093	Vaquez	Luis	11/19/1976	$42,177.00	12/5/2010		North American Distribution
1095	Kilarney	Patrick	2/27/1985	$42,177.00	12/12/2010		North American Distribution
Total				$1,163,808.00			

Page 1

The Relationships report within the WEEmployees2Relshp.accdb database is the project in Activities 2.9 to 2.12.

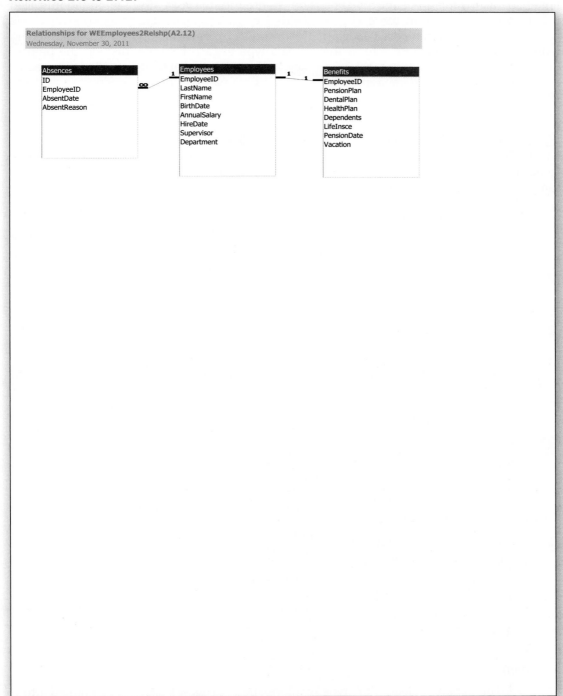

Activity 2.1

Understanding Table Design Principles and Primary Keys

In Section 1 you were introduced to database concepts, terminology, and how to maintain data in tables. An introduction to how a database operates from the end user perspective is a useful foundation before you learn how to create new tables. Since tables form the basis for all other database objects each table must be carefully planned to adhere to database design principles. Recall from Section 1, that each table should be about one subject only and that all of the data elements included in the table are broken down into the smallest units of information, called fields. Designing a new table generally involves the following steps: determining field names, assigning a data type to each field, designating the primary key, and naming the table object. All of the preceding steps are part of a process referred to as defining the table *structure*.

Project

Tutorial 2.1
Creating a New Database

Riya Singh, paralegal at Worldwide Enterprises, has asked you to create a new database in which distributor contracts can be maintained. Riya has provided the information that needs to be stored and asked you to determine how to set up the database. You will analyze the sample data and design a table that follows table design best practices.

1. Look at the information Riya has provided in Figure 2.1. This is a list of the data elements that Riya would like to keep track of in the new database. Example data from an existing record is supplied with each data element.

2. Start a new Microsoft Word document, type **Contracts table** at the top of the page as the document title and then press Enter twice.

3. Type a list of fields that would be needed for this new table. Break down each data element into its smallest unit.

    For example, the contact name ideally should be broken down into separate first name and last name fields. By breaking the name into two fields you will be able to properly sort and filter the data. Notice also that the sample data for the telephone number includes an extension number. Consider adding the extension number as a separate field.

4. Next to each field in the list, type a field name. Refer to Table 2.1 for a list of guidelines to help you create the field names.

5. Look at the sample data in Figure 2.1 for each field and locate an appropriate data type for the field from the list of data types provided in Table 2.2. Type the data type next to each field name.

FIGURE 2.1 Sample Data for New Contracts Table

Contract Number	2011-034
Company Name	West Coast Movies
Contact Name	Jordan Daniels
Telephone	604 555 2886 ext 341
Fax	604 555 2693
Renewal?	Yes
Start date of contract	July 1, 2011
End date of contract	June 30, 2013
Shipping fee per movie	$500
Percentage of box office sales	10%
Internal notes	Jordan is an active member of the Western Film Association.
(For some distributors these could be lengthy notes about the distributor or the negotiations.)	

The data type defines the type of information Access will allow to be entered into the field. For example, Access will not allow alphabetic characters to be entered into a field with a data type set to *Number*. Text fields can hold alphanumeric information, including letters, numbers, spaces and punctuation marks. Some fields, such as a telephone number, social security number or a zip code, contain numbers but you will still define the data type as *Text* because you will not be performing mathematical operations on the values stored in these columns.

6 Type an asterisk next to the field name in the table that will uniquely identify each contract record in the table. This denotes the field that will be defined as the primary key.

> Access creates a field named *ID* automatically in new tables. The field is designated as the primary key and is assigned the *AutoNumber* data type. You can use this field or create your own primary key. It is possible to create a table that does not have an assigned primary key; however, this is not common and can lead to duplicate records in a table. Recall from Section 1 that Access checks each new record as it is added to the table to make sure that another record with the same field value in the primary key field does not exist. Access also ensures that no primary key field is left blank. Primary keys help to maintain data integrity.

7 Save the Word document and name it **AS2-A2.1Contracts**. Check with your instructor to find out if he or she would like you to print the document.

8 Compare your document with Figure 2.2 on page 44 in the next Activity.

> Discuss with a classmate any differences between your list and the one shown in Figure 2.2, keeping in mind that differences are acceptable provided your field names conform to the field name guidelines and you selected appropriate data types for each field.

9 Exit Microsoft Word.

In Brief

Design New Table
1. Analyze required data elements.
2. Break down data into smallest unit.
3. Create a field name.
4. Assign each field an appropriate data type.
5. Identify field suitable for primary key.
6. Assign table a name.

TABLE 2.1 Field Name Guidelines

A field name can be up to 64 characters including a combination of letters and numbers. Some symbols are permitted but others are excluded, so it is best to avoid symbols other than the underscore character which is often used as a word separator.

Do not use a space in a field name. Although a space is an accepted character, most database designers avoid using spaces in field names and object names. This practice facilitates easier management of the data with scripting or other database programming tools. Use compound words for field names or the underscore character as a word separator. For example, a field to hold a person's last name would be named *LastName, Last_Name,* or *LName.*

Abbreviate field names so that the names are as short as possible while still able to be readily understood. For example, a field such as *ContactLastName* could be abbreviated to *ContactLN* or a field such as *Telephone* to *Phone.* Shorter names are easier to manage and type into expressions.

TABLE 2.2 Data Types

Data Type	Description
Text	Alphanumeric data up to 255 characters in length, such as a name, address, or value such as a telephone number or social security number that is used as an identifier and not for calculating.
Memo	Alphanumeric data up to 64,000 characters in length.
Number	Positive or negative values that can be used in calculations; do not use for values that will calculate monetary amounts (see Currency).
Date/Time	Use this type to ensure dates and times are entered and sorted properly.
Currency	Values that involve money; Access will not round off during calculations.
AutoNumber	Access automatically numbers each record sequentially (incrementing by 1) when you begin typing a new record.
Yes/No	Data in the field will be either Yes or No, True or False, On or Off.
OLE Object	Used to embed or link objects created in other Office applications.
Hyperlink	Field that will store a hyperlink such as a URL.
Attachment	Use this data type to add file attachments to a record such as a Word document or an Excel workbook.
Calculated	The contents of a calculated field are generated by Access from an expression you create; for example, a total cost could be calculated by adding a price plus a sales tax column.
Lookup Wizard	Can be used to enter data in the field from another existing table or display a list of values in a drop-down list for the user to choose from.

Activity 2.2

Creating a New Database; Creating a Table

As you learned in Section 1, Access saves data automatically as you enter records into a datasheet. For this reason, to begin a new database you start by assigning the database a file name and pointing Access to the storage location at the New tab in Backstage view. Once the file has been created, a new table is presented in Datasheet view. Create the table by assigning each column a data type and typing the field name. Once the columns have been defined you can begin entering data into records.

Project

Tutorial 2.1
Creating a New Database

You will create a new database file in which to store the contracts and then create the Contracts table. After the table is created you will look at the table in a view which allows you to make changes to the table's structure.

1. Start Microsoft Access 2010.

2. At the New tab Backstage view, click the Browse button located at the right of the *File Name* text box (currently displays *Database1.accdb*) in the *Blank database* section.

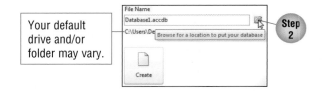

Your default drive and/or folder may vary.

Step 2

3. At the File New Database dialog box, navigate to the AccessS2 folder on your storage medium, select the current text in the *File Name* text box, type **WEContracts2**, and then click OK.

   One of the differences between Access and other programs is that the file name is assigned before any data is entered. Do not remove your storage medium while working in Access since the file will frequently have data written to it.

4. Click the Create button at the New tab Backstage view.

   A blank datasheet appears in the work area with the tab labeled *Table1*. Notice the column with the field name *ID* has been created automatically. Access creates *ID* as an AutoNumber field in which the field value is assigned automatically by Access as you enter each record. The heading *Click to Add* appears at the top of the first blank column.

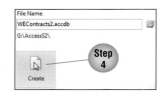

Step 4

5. Review the table design shown in Figure 2.2. This is the table you will create in Steps 6–22. Note that in this design the *ID* field that Access automatically creates will be used for the primary key.

   Assume that the contract number is not changed when a contract is renewed. You want to add a new record with the dates for each contract renewal so that you have a history of

FIGURE 2.2 Fields for Contracts Table

Contracts		
Field Name	**Data Type**	**Sample Data**
*ID	AutoNumber	
ContractNo	Text	2011-034
Company	Text	West Coast Movies
ContactFN	Text	Jordan
ContactLN	Text	Daniels
Phone	Text	604-555-2886
Ext	Text	341
Fax	Text	604-555-2693
Renewal	Yes/No	Yes
StartDate	Date/Time	July 1, 2011
EndDate	Date/Time	June 30, 2013
ShipFee	Currency	$500
Percentage	Number	10
Notes	Memo	Jordan is an active member of the Western Film Association.

how long the distributor has been signed with Worldwide Enterprises. For this reason, the *ContractNo* field cannot be the primary key since duplicate records would exist. Begin creating a new table by selecting the field's data type and then typing the field names into the header row of the blank datasheet.

6 Click the Text button **AB** in the Add & Delete group in the Table Tools Fields tab.

Access adds a new column to the datasheet with the Text data type assigned and selects the field name in the table header row in order for you to type the correct field name.

7 Type **ContractNo** and then press Enter.

Access moves to the *Click to Add* column and opens the data type drop-down list for the next new column.

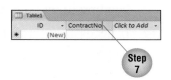

8 Click *Text* at the drop-down list.

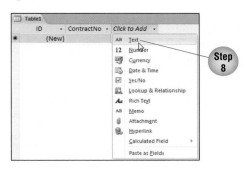

9 Type **Company** and then press Enter.

10 Click *Text* at the drop-down list, type **ContactFN**, and then press Enter.

11 Click *Text* at the drop-down list, type **ContactLN**, and then press Enter.

12 Click *Text* at the drop-down list, type **Phone**, and then press Enter.

13 Click *Text* at the drop-down list, type **Ext**, and then press Enter.

14 Click *Text* at the drop-down list, type **Fax**, and then press Enter.

15 Click *Yes/No* at the drop-down list.

The *Renewal* column will contain only one of two entries; *Yes* for those records that represent renewals of existing contracts or *No* if the record is a contract for a new distributor. Notice when you change the data type to *Yes/No* a check box is inserted in the column.

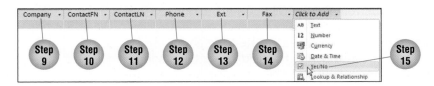

continues

16 Type **Renewal** and then press Enter.

17 Continue changing the data types and typing the field names for the remainder of the fields as shown in Figure 2.2 on page 44.

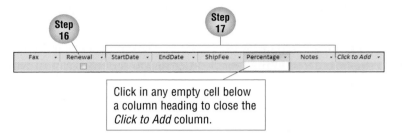

Click in any empty cell below a column heading to close the *Click to Add* column.

18 Press Enter after typing *Notes* as the last field name to close the drop-down list in the *Click to Add* column, and then click in any empty cell below a column heading to end the table.

19 If necessary, scroll to the left edge of the datasheet. Click in the empty cell below *ContractNo*, type **2011-034**, and then press Tab or Enter to move to the next field.

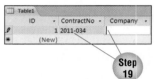

20 Continue typing the sample data for the remainder of the fields as shown in Figure 2.2. At the *Renewal* field, click to insert a check mark in the box to indicate the field entry is *Yes*.

Notice that Access converts dates that you enter into the format m/d/yyyy. When entering dates, be careful to use the proper punctuation and spacing between the month, day, and year so that Access recognizes the entry as a valid date.

21 Click the Save button 💾 on the Quick Access toolbar.

22 At the Save As dialog box with *Table1* selected in the *Table Name* text box, type **Contracts** and then press Enter or click OK.

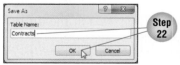

In the next steps you will review the table in a view called *Design view*. Every object created in Access can be opened in Design view in which you can create or edit the object's structure.

23 Click the View button in the Views group of the Home tab. (Do not click the down-pointing arrow on the button.)

The View button alternates between Design view and Datasheet view. In Design view, each row in the top section represents one field in the table and is used to define the field name, the field's data type, and an optional description. The *Field Properties* section in the lower half of the work area displays the properties for the active field. The properties will vary depending on the active field.

24 Notice the key icon in the field selector bar (blank column left of field names) next to the *ID* field. This indicates the field is the primary key.

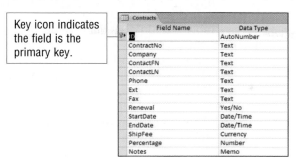

Key icon indicates the field is the primary key.

Contracts	
Field Name	Data Type
ID	AutoNumber
ContractNo	Text
Company	Text
ContactFN	Text
ContactLN	Text
Phone	Text
Ext	Text
Fax	Text
Renewal	Yes/No
StartDate	Date/Time
EndDate	Date/Time
ShipFee	Currency
Percentage	Number
Notes	Memo

25 Compare the entries in the *Field Name* and *Data Type* column for each field with those shown in Figure 2.2. If necessary, correct a typing error in a field name by positioning the insertion point over the existing field name, clicking to open the field and then inserting and deleting text as necessary. To change a data type, click in the *Data Type* column for the field, click the down-pointing arrow that appears, and then click the desired data type at the drop-down list.

26 Click the View button ▦ in the Views group of the Table Tools Design tab. If you made changes while in Design view, you will be prompted to save the table when you switch views. If necessary, click Yes at any prompts that appear.

> Since you were in Design view, the View button changed to the Datasheet view button to switch you back to looking at the table's datasheet.

27 Best Fit the *ID*, *Company*, and *Ext* columns.

28 Print the table in landscape orientation and then close the table saving the changes to the table layout.

29 Click the File tab and then click Close Database.

In Brief

Create New Database
1. Start Access.
2. Click Browse button.
3. Navigate to desired drive and/or folder.
4. Type file name in *File Name* text box.
5. Click OK.
6. Click Create button.

Create Table
1. Click desired data type in Add & Delete group of Table Tools Fields tab.
2. Type field name and press Enter.
3. Click desired field data type in drop-down list.
4. Type field name and press Enter.
5. Repeat Steps 3–4 for remaining columns.
6. Click Save button.
7. Type table name.
8. Press Enter or click OK.

In Addition

Add & Delete Group in the Table Tools Fields tab

Consider adding fields by using the buttons in the Add & Delete group of the Table Tools Fields tab as you did in Step 6. Buttons are included to add a Number, Currency, Date & Time, or Yes/No field. Click the More Fields button to choose from a list of other field data types and fields that have predefined field properties. Scroll down the More Fields drop-down list to the new *QuickStart* category. Options in this category allow you to add a group of related fields in one step. For example, click *Address* to add 5 new fields: Address, City, StateProvince, ZIPPostal, CountryRegion.

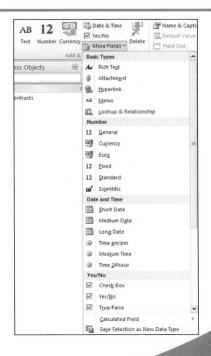

Activity 2.3

Creating a Table in Design View; Setting the Primary Key

As an alternative to creating a new table in a blank datasheet, you can create the table structure directly in Design view and add data later. In Design view, you can set the field's properties the way you need them right away. When you use Design view, Access does not add the *ID* field to the new table automatically. As mentioned previously, a table should have a field used to store a unique field value for each record. Examples of fields suitable for a primary key are fields that store an identification value such as an employee number, a part number, a vendor number, or a customer number. If, when you are working on a table's design you do not have any data suited to a primary key field, create a field labeled *ID* and set the data type to *AutoNumber*.

Project

Worldwide Enterprises

SNAP

Tutorial 2.2
Creating a Table and
Setting a Primary
Key

Rhonda Trask, human resources manager, has asked you to work in the employees database. Rhonda would like you to create a new table in the file in which to store the employee benefit plan information. You decide to create this table using Design view.

1. Open the **WEEmployees2.accdb** database. Click the Enable Content button if the Security Warning message bar appears.

2. Open the Employees table and review the datasheet.

    This database is similar to the database you worked with in the Skills Review for Section 1. This version of the database file has additional records added.

3. Close the Employees table.

4. Click the Create tab and then click the Table Design button in the Tables group.

5. With the insertion point positioned in the *Field Name* column in the first row, type **EmployeeID** and then press Enter or Tab to move to the next column.

6. With *Text* already entered in the *Data Type* column, press Enter or Tab to move to the next column.

    The *EmployeeID* field will contain numbers; however, leave the data type defined as *Text* since no calculations will be performed with employee numbers.

7. Type **Enter the four-digit employee number** in the *Description* column and then press Enter to move to the second row.

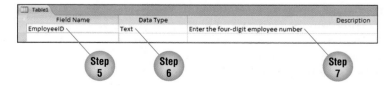

8. Type **PensionPlan** in the *Field Name* column in the second field row and then press Enter.

9 Click the down-pointing arrow at the right of the *Data Type* column, click *Yes/No* at the drop-down list, and then press Enter.

> In this field, the data is only one of two entries: *Yes* if the employee is enrolled in the pension plan or *No* if the employee is not.

Step 8

Step 9

10 Type **Click or press spacebar for Yes; leave empty for No** and then press Enter.

11 Enter the remaining field names, data types, and descriptions as shown in Figure 2.3 by completing steps similar to those in Steps 8–10.

> Descriptions are optional entries. The description text displays above the Status bar when adding records to a datasheet or form.

FIGURE 2.3 Design View Table Entries

Field Name	Data Type	Description
EmployeeID	Text	Enter the four-digit employee number
PensionPlan	Yes/No	Click or press spacebar for Yes; leave empty for No
DentalPlan	Yes/No	Click or press spacebar for Yes; leave empty for No
HealthPlan	Yes/No	Click or press spacebar for Yes; leave empty for No
Dependents	Number	Type the number of dependents related to this employee
LifeInsce	Currency	Type the amount of life insurance subscribed by this employee

12 Click the insertion point in any character in the *EmployeeID* field row.

13 Click the Primary Key button 🔑 in the Tools group in the Table Tools Design tab.

> A key icon appears in the field selector bar to the left of *EmployeeID* indicating the field is the primary key.

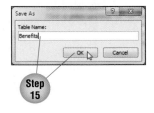

Step 13

Step 12

14 Click the Save button on the Quick Access toolbar.

15 At the Save As dialog box, type **Benefits** in the *Table Name* text box and then press Enter or click OK.

16 Close the Benefits table.

Step 15

In Brief

Create Table in Design View
1. Click Create tab.
2. Click Table Design button.
3. Type field names, change data types, add descriptions, or modify other field properties as desired.
4. Assign primary key.
5. Click Save button.
6. Type table name.
7. Click OK.

Assign Primary Key
1. Open table in Design view.
2. Make active desired primary key field.
3. Click Primary Key button.
4. Save table.

In Addition

Help Tips in Design View

Access displays information from Help about each entry in Design view in the bottom right of the work area. Look at this box for information or tips about each design parameter as you move around the Design window. The entry shown for the *Description* column is shown at the right.

> The field description is optional. It helps you describe the field and is also displayed in the Status bar when you select this field on a form. Press F1 for help on descriptions.

Activity 2.4

Modifying Field Size, Caption, and Default Value Properties

Each field has a set of characteristics associated with it that are called **field properties**. Field properties are used to control the behavior or interactivity of the field in database objects. The *Field Size* property can be used to limit the number of characters that are allowed in a field entry. A field size of 4 for an ID field would prevent ID numbers longer than four characters from being stored in a record. The *Caption* property stores descriptive titles for fields and is useful if you abbreviated a field name or want to show spaces between words in a compound field name. An entry in the *Default Value* property displays automatically in the field for all new records. If most records are likely to contain the same data, create a default entry to save typing and reduce errors.

Project

You will modify the *EmployeeID* Field Size property in the Benefits table to set the maximum number of characters to 4. Since most employees opt into the Pension Plan, you will set the default value for the *Pension Plan* field to *Yes*. You will also add captions to display spaces between words in field names in the datasheet.

Tutorial 2.3
Modifying Field Properties

Tutorial 2.4
Modifying Table Fields

1. With the **WEEmployees2.accdb** database open, right-click the *Benefits* table name in the Navigation pane and then click *Design View* at the shortcut menu.

2. With *EmployeeID* already selected in the *Field Name* column, double-click the value *255* that appears in the *Field Size* property box in the *Field Properties* section and then type **4**.

   Alternatively, click in the *Field Size* property box to activate the insertion point, delete *255*, and then type **4**.

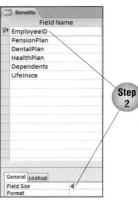

3. Click in the *PensionPlan* row in the *Field Name* column to display the *PensionPlan* properties in the *Field Properties* section.

   Notice the list of available properties has changed. The items displayed in the *Field Properties* section change to reflect the options for the active field's data type. Since *PensionPlan* is a Yes/No field, the list of properties shown is different than those for *EmployeeID,* which is a Text field.

4. Click in the *Caption* property box and type **Pension Plan**.

   If the *Caption* property box is blank, Access displays the field name as the column heading in the datasheet or as the label in forms and reports. Type an entry in the property box if you want to display a more descriptive heading in objects associated with the table or to show spaces between words in compound field names.

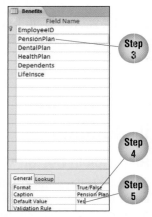

5. Select the current entry in the *Default Value* field property box and then type **Yes**.

6. Click in the *DentalPlan* field row in the *Field Name* column to display the *DentalPlan* properties in the *Field Properties* section.

7. Click in the *Caption* property box and type **Dental Plan**.

8. Click in the *HealthPlan* field row, click in the *Caption* property box, and then type **Health Plan**.

9 Click in the *LifeInsce* field row, click in the *Caption* property box, and then type **Life Insurance**.

10 Click the Save button.

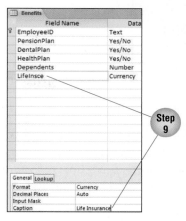

> If a field property is changed after data has been entered into records, Access displays warning messages when you save the table that some data could be lost if, for example, a field size is changed to a shorter size. You will be prompted to continue with the save in these situations. If a large amount of data was entered into a table before a property such as field size is changed, consider making a backup copy of the database before modifying the table design.

11 Click the View button in the Views group in the Table Tools Design tab to switch to Datasheet view. (Do not click the down-pointing arrow on the button.)

> Notice the column headings in the datasheet show the caption properties for those fields that have an entry in the *Caption* property box.

12 Type **1000111** in the *EmployeeID* field in the first blank row of the datasheet and then press Enter.

> A beep sounds if the computer's speakers are on and the volume is not muted each time you type a character that extends beyond the field size of 4. Access does not display any characters in the field after the fourth character typed.

13 At the *Pension Plan* field, notice a check mark already exists in the check box since the default value was set to *Yes*. Press Enter to accept the default value.

> When presented with a default value in a field, you have the option of accepting the default value by pressing Enter or Tab, or of overwriting the default value by typing another entry. In the case of a Yes/No field, you would press the spacebar or click to clear the check box.

14 Enter the following data in the remaining fields in the first row:

Dental Plan	**Yes**
Health Plan	**Yes**
Dependents	**0**
Life Insurance	**100000**

15 Adjust all column widths to Best Fit.

16 Close the Benefits table. Click Yes when prompted to save the changes to the layout.

In Addition

More about the Field Size Property

The default field size property varies depending on the data type. The default value for a Text field is 255. In an AutoNumber or Numeric field, the default field size is Long Integer. Long Integer stores whole numbers from –2,147,483,647 to 2,147,483,647 (negative to positive). The field size property is not available for fields with a data type set to Memo, Date/Time, Currency, Yes/No, OLE Object, Hyperlink, or Attachment.

Activity 2.5

Validating Field Entries

The **Validation Rule** property can be used to enter a statement that is checked each time data is entered into the field. When data is entered that fails to satisfy the statement, the entry is not accepted and an error message displays. For example, suppose a policy is in place that the company will not purchase life insurance for employees over $200,000 per employee. You could set up a validation rule on the field containing the life insurance amounts so that no number greater than $200,000 can be entered into the field. A statement such as *<=200000* (meaning less than or equal to 2 hundred thousand) in the Validation Rule property checks each entry against the acceptable range. Validation rules reduce errors and ensure business policies are enforced. Enter in the **Validation Text** property the content of the error message that you want the user to see if he or she enters an invalid amount.

Project

Tutorial 2.5
Validating Data in
a Table

Worldwide Enterprises offers life insurance up to a maximum of $200,000 per employee. You will add a validation rule and enter an error message in the Validation Text property for the *LifeInsce* field in the Benefits table to ensure no amount exceeds this maximum.

1 With the **WEEmployees2.accdb** database open, open the Benefits table in Design view.

2 Click in the *LifeInsce* field row to display the associated field properties.

3 Click in the *Validation Rule* property box, type **<=200000**, and then press Enter.

Pressing Enter after typing the validation rule moves the insertion point to the *Validation Text* property box.

Need Help?

Invalid syntax? Check your typing. Do not type a dollar symbol or comma in the validation rule statement. Also make sure you have the correct less than symbol (<) and equals symbol (=) and that the order is <=.

4 Type **Enter a value that is less than or equal to $200,000** and then press Enter.

5 Click the Save button.

Since a validation rule has been created *after* data has been entered into the table, Access displays a message warning that some data may not be valid.

6 At the Microsoft Access message box, click Yes to instruct Access to test the data with the new rules.

Step 6

In Brief

Create Validation Rule
1. Open table in Design view.
2. Click in desired field row.
3. Click in *Validation Rule* property box.
4. Type statement.
5. Click in *Validation Text* property box.
6. Type error message.
7. Click Save.

7 Click the View button in the Views group in the Table Tools Design tab to switch to Datasheet view.

8 Add the following record to the table:

EmployeeID	**1003**
Pension Plan	**Yes**
Dental Plan	**Yes**
Health Plan	**Yes**
Dependents	**2**
Life Insurance	**210000**

When you enter *210000* into the *Life Insurance* field and press Enter or Tab, Access displays an error message. The text in the error message is the text you entered in the *Validation Text* property box.

9 Click OK at the Microsoft Access error message.

Step 9

10 Backspace to delete *210000*, type **200000**, and then press Enter.

Step 10

11 Close the Benefits table.

In Addition

Other Validation Rule Examples

Validation rules should be created whenever possible to avoid data entry errors. The examples below illustrate various ways to use the validation rule to verify data.

Field Name	Validation Rule	Data Check
Customer_No	>1000 And <1100	Limits customer numbers to 1001 through 1099.
Credit_Limit	<=5000	Restricts credit limits to values of 5000 or less.
State	"CA"	Only the state of California is accepted.
Country	"CA" Or "US"	Only the United States or Canada is accepted.
Crder_Qty	>=25	Quantity ordered must be a minimum of 25.

Activity 2.6

Creating Input Masks; Formatting a Field

An *input mask* displays a pattern in the datasheet or form indicating how data is to be entered into the field. For example, an input mask in a telephone number field that displays (___)___-____ indicates to the user that the three-digit area code is to be entered in front of all telephone numbers. Input masks ensure that data is entered consistently in tables. In addition to specifying the position and amount of characters in a field you can create masks that restrict the data entered to digits, letters, or characters, and whether or not each digit, letter, or character is required or optional. The **Format** property controls how the data is *displayed* in the field *after* it has been entered.

Project

You will create a new field in the Benefits table for Pension Plan eligibility dates and include an input mask and format property in the field.

Worldwide Enterprises

SNAP

Tutorial 2.6
Using the Input Mask Wizard and the Lookup Wizard

1. With the **WEEmployees2.accdb** database open, open the Benefits table in Design view.

2. Click in the *Field Name* column in the blank row below *LifeInsce*, type **PensionDate**, and then press Enter.

3. Change the data type to *Date/Time* and then press Enter.

4. Type **Type date employee is eligible for pension plan in the format dd-mmm-yy (example: 31-Dec-11).**

5. Click Save.

6. With *PensionDate* the active field, click in the *Input Mask* property box in the *Field Properties* section and then click the Build button [...] at the right end of the box.

7. Click *Medium Date* at the first Input Mask Wizard dialog box and then click Next.

   The input masks that display in the list in the first dialog box are dependent on the data type for the field for which you are creating an input mask.

8. Click Next at the second Input Mask Wizard dialog box.

   This dialog box displays the input mask code in the *Input Mask* text box and sets the placeholder character that displays in the field. The default placeholder is the underscore character.

9. Click Finish at the last Input Mask Wizard dialog box to complete the entry in the *Input Mask* property box and then press Enter.

   The mask built by the wizard broken down into parts is: *00*\- two required digits for the day followed by a hyphen displayed in the field; *>L<LL*\- three required letters for the month, first letter uppercase and remaining two lowercase, followed by a hyphen displayed in the field; *00* two required digits for the year. Following the date

requirement *;0* instructs Access to store literal characters used in the field (hyphens between dates). The mask ends with *;_* which is the placeholder character.

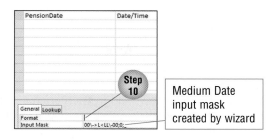

In Brief

Use Input Mask Wizard
1. Open table in Design view.
2. Click in desired field row.
3. Click in Input Mask property box.
4. Click Build button.
5. Click input mask you want to create.
6. Click Next.
7. Select placeholder character.
8. Click Next.
9. Click Finish at the last wizard dialog box.
10. Click Save button.

10 Click in the *Format* property box.

The input mask controls how a date is entered into the field; however, by default, Access displays dates in the format *m/dd/yyyy*. To avoid confusion, you will format the field to display the date in the same format that the input mask accepts the data.

11 Click the down-pointing arrow at the end of the property box and then click *Medium Date* at the drop-down list.

12 Click in the *Caption* property box and then type **Pension Date**.

13 Click the Save button and then switch to Datasheet view.

14 Click in the *Pension Date* column for the first row in the datasheet.

The input mask __-___-__ appears in the field.

15 Type **22jul03** and then press the Down Arrow key.

Notice the hyphens are not required to enter the date and the first character in the month is converted to uppercase. The greater than symbol (>) preceding *L* in the mask causes Access to convert the first character to uppercase.

16 Type **150803**.

A beep sounds as you type every character after *15*. The only characters allowed after the first hyphen are letters. Notice the insertion point remains in the month section of the field.

17 Type **aug03** and then press Enter.

18 Adjust the width of *Pension Date* to Best Fit.

19 Close the Benefits table. Click Yes when prompted to save changes to the layout.

In Addition

Input Mask Codes

The Input Mask Wizard is only available for fields with a data type set to Text or Date/Time. For fields such as Number or Currency or for an input mask for which the wizard does not provide an option, you can create your own by entering the codes directly into the property box. Following is a list of commonly used input mask codes.

Use	To restrict data entry to
0	digit, zero through nine, entry is required
9	digit or space, entry is not required
L	letter, A through Z, entry is required
?	letter, A through Z, entry is not required
>	all characters following are converted to uppercase
<	all characters following are converted to lowercase

Activity 2.7

Creating a Lookup List

Create a *Lookup* field when you want to restrict the data entered into the field to a list of values from an existing table, or a list of values that you create. The Lookup tab in the *Field Properties* section in Design view contains the options used to create a *Lookup* field. Access includes the Lookup Wizard to facilitate entering the lookup settings.

Project

You will create a new field in the Benefits table to store vacation entitlement for each employee. You want the field to display a drop-down list of vacation periods and restrict the field to accept only those entries that match items in the list.

Tutorial 2.6
Using the Input Mask Wizard and the Lookup Wizard

1. With the **WEEmployees2.accdb** database open, open the Benefits table in Design view.

2. Click in the *Field Name* column in the blank row below *PensionDate*, type **Vacation**, and then press Enter.

3. Change the data type to *Lookup Wizard*.

4. At the first Lookup Wizard dialog box, click *I will type in the values that I want.* and then click Next.

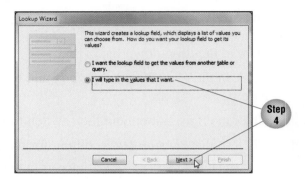

5. Click in the blank row below *Col1*, type **1 week**, and then press Tab or the Down Arrow key.

Need Help?

If you press Enter by mistake and find yourself at the next step in the Lookup Wizard, click the Back button to return to the previous dialog box.

6. Type **2 weeks** and then press Tab.

7. Type **3 weeks** and then press Tab.

8. Type **4 weeks** and then click Next.

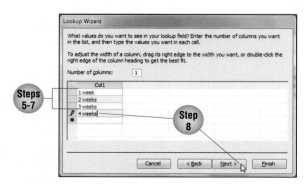

9. Click Finish in the last Lookup Wizard dialog box to accept the default label *Vacation*. No entry is required in the *Description* column.

10 Click the Lookup tab in the *Field Properties* section and view the entries made to each property by the Lookup Wizard.

11 Click in the *Limit To List* property box, click the down-pointing arrow that appears, and then click Yes.

> By changing the *Limit To List* property to *Yes* you are further restricting the field to only those items in the drop-down list. If someone attempts to type an entry other than *1 week, 2 weeks, 3 weeks,* or *4 weeks,* Access displays an error message and will not store the data.

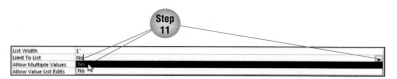

Step 10

General	Lookup	
Display Control	Combo Box
Row Source Type	Value List
Row Source	"1 week";"2 weeks";"3 weeks";"4 weeks"
Bound Column	1
Column Count	1
Column Heads	No
Column Widths	1"
List Rows	16
List Width	1"
Limit To List	No
Allow Multiple Values	No
Allow Value List Edits	Yes
List Items Edit Form	
Show Only Row Source V	No

Step 11

List Width	1"
Limit To List	No
Allow Multiple Values	Yes
Allow Value List Edits	No

12 Click in the *Allow Value List Edits* property box, click the down-pointing arrow that appears, and then click No.

> You want to make sure that changes to the list that you created are not allowed by someone using the datasheet or a form.

13 Click Save and then click View to switch to Datasheet view.

14 If necessary, scroll the datasheet right and then click in the *Vacation* column in the first row in the datasheet. Click the down-pointing arrow that appears and then click *4 weeks* in the drop-down list.

Step 14

15 Press the Down Arrow key to move to the *Vacation* column in the second row, type **6 weeks**, and then press Enter.

16 Click OK at the message that displays informing you that the text entered isn't an item in the list, click *3 weeks* at the drop-down list, and then press Enter.

17 Display the datasheet in Print Preview. Change the page orientation to landscape and then print the datasheet.

18 Close the Benefits table.

In Addition

Looking Up Data from Another Table

Items in a drop-down list can also be generated by specifying an existing field in another table or query. To do this, click Next at the first Lookup Wizard dialog box to accept the default setting *I want the lookup column to look up the values in a table or query.* In the remaining wizard dialog boxes, you choose the table or query and the field that you want to use, choose the sort order for displaying the field values, adjust the column width for the lookup list, select the value to store, and assign a label to the column. Creating field entries using this method ensures that data is consistent between tables and eliminates duplicate typing of information that can lead to data errors. For example, in a database used to store employee information, one table could be used to enter employee numbers and then the remaining tables look up the employee number by scrolling a list of employee names.

Activity 2.8

Inserting, Moving, and Deleting Fields; Inserting a Total

Fields can be inserted, moved, or deleted in either Datasheet or Design view. Exercise caution when deleting fields since data will be lost and the operation cannot be reversed with the Undo command. As a precaution, consider making a backup copy of the database before deleting a field. Use the Totals button in the Records group of the Home tab to add a total row to a datasheet and then choose from a list of functions to find the sum, average, maximum, minimum, count, standard deviation, or variance result in a numeric column.

Project

Tutorial 2.3
Modifying Field Properties

You will make changes to the structure of the Employees table by inserting a field, deleting a field, and repositioning a field in the table. In Datasheet view you decide to remove gridlines, change the font size, and add a total to the *AnnualSalary* column.

① With the **WEEmployees2.accdb** database open, open the Employees table in Design view.

② Click the insertion point in any text in the *MiddleInitial* field row.

③ Click the Delete Rows button in the Tools group in the Table Tools Design tab.

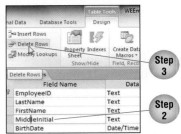

④ At the Microsoft Access message box asking you to confirm that you want to permanently delete the selected field(s) and all of the data in the field(s), click Yes.

> If you have more than one field to delete and they are adjacent, use the field selector bar to select the multiple fields and delete all of them in one operation.

⑤ Move the mouse pointer in the field selector bar beside *AnnualSalary* until the pointer changes to a right-pointing black arrow and then click the left mouse button to select the field.

⑥ With the pointer still positioned in the field selector bar beside *AnnualSalary* (pointer now displays as a white arrow), drag the pointer up between the *BirthDate* and *HireDate* fields and then release the left mouse button.

> As you drag the mouse, a black line appears between existing field names, indicating where the selected field will be repositioned when the mouse button is released, and the white arrow pointer displays with a gray-shaded box attached to it.

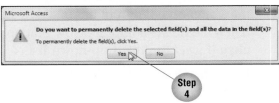

⑦ Click in any field to deselect the *AnnualSalary* row.

> In the next step you will insert a new field in the table. In previous activities, you added a field to the table by typing the field name in the first available blank row below existing fields. You can also position a new field between other fields using the Insert Rows button. New rows are inserted above the active field.

⑧ Click the insertion point in any text in the *Department* row.

9. Click the Insert Rows button in the Tools group in the Table Tools Design tab.

> A new blank row is inserted above the *Department* field row.

10. With the insertion point positioned in the *Field Name* column for the new row, type **Supervisor** and press Enter.

11. Click the Save button and then switch to Datasheet view.

> Review the changes in the datasheet with *MiddleInitial* deleted, *AnnualSalary* repositioned after *BirthDate,* and the new *Supervisor* column.

12. Click the Gridlines button in the Text Formatting group and then click *Gridlines: None* at the drop-down list.

13. Click the down-pointing arrow next to the Font Size button in the Text Formatting group and then click *12* at the drop-down list.

> Buttons in the Text Formatting group of the Home tab can be used to enhance the appearance of datasheets. Consider experimenting with formatting options when you create or edit tables.

14. Click the Totals button in the Records group in the Home tab.

> Access adds a row to the bottom of the datasheet with the label *Total* at the left.

15. Click in the *Total* row at the bottom of the *AnnualSalary* column, click the down-pointing arrow that appears, and then click *Sum* at the pop-up list. Click in any cell in the datasheet to view the result.

> The sum *$1,163,808.00* appears at the bottom of the *AnnualSalary* column.

16. Display the datasheet in Print Preview, change the page orientation to landscape, and then print the datasheet.

17. Close the Print Preview window and then close the Employees table. Click Yes when prompted to save changes to the layout of the table.

18. Click the File tab and then click Close Database.

In Brief

Insert Field in Design View
1. Open table in Design View.
2. Make desired field active.
3. Click Insert Row button.
4. Click in *Field Name* area of new row and type field name.
5. Change data type, description, or field properties as desired.
6. Click Save button.

Delete Field
1. Open table in Design view.
2. Make desired field active.
3. Click Delete Rows button.
4. Click Yes.
5. Save table.

Move Field
1. Open table in Design view.
2. Select field using field selector bar.
3. With pointer in field selector bar, drag field to desired position.
4. Save table.

Insert Total
1. Open table.
2. Click Totals button.
3. Click in *Total* row in desired field.
4. Click down-pointing arrow.
5. Click desired function.
6. Save table.

In Addition

Working with Wide Datasheets

When working in a datasheet with many columns, scrolling right can make it difficult to relate to the record in which you need to make a change since descriptor fields such as *EmployeeID* or *LastName* may have scrolled off the screen. To alleviate this problem, you can freeze columns so they do not disappear when the datasheet is scrolled right. To do this, select the columns that you want to freeze, click the More button in the Records group in the Home tab, and then click *Freeze Fields*.

Activity 2.9

Understanding Relationships; Using the Relationships Window

Access is referred to as a *relational database management system*. A relational database is one in which tables have been joined. When two or more tables have been joined to create a relationship, you can look up or create reports from multiple tables as if they were one table. In most cases, tables are joined by a common field that exists in both tables. When designing a new database, consider if two tables need to be joined and make sure to include a common field in each table so that you can create the relationship after the tables have been created. Relationships between tables allow you to avoid duplication by repeating the same data in multiple tables. For example, in an employee database, the employee's first and last names would only need to appear in one table. In the remaining tables, only the identification number is included. When the tables are joined on the common identification field, you can then look up someone's name by matching the identification field values.

Project You have been given a new employees database file that has additional records in the Benefits table and a new table that is used to store absence reports. You will use this database to explore the Relationships window.

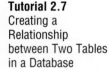

Tutorial 2.7
Creating a Relationship between Two Tables in a Database

1. Open the **WEEmployees2Relshp.accdb** database. Click the Enable Content button if the Security Warning message bar appears.

2. Open the Absences table and scan the entries in the datasheet.

   This table is used to record employee absence reports. Notice that some employees have more than one record in the table.

3. Open the Benefits table and review the datasheet.

4. Open the Employees table and review the datasheet.

5. The Employees table includes fields for the employee's name. Using the tabs along the top of the work area, look at the Absences table and the Benefits table and note that the names are not duplicated in either of these tables; however, all three tables contain an *EmployeeID* field.

   > Review the structure of each table and note that the employee's first and last names appear only in the Employees table; however, all three tables contain a common *EmployeeID* field.

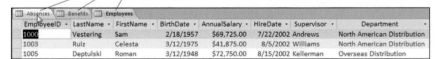

6. Close all three tables now that you have familiarized yourself with the data in the database.

   In the next steps you will open the Relationships window and arrange the tables in the window. Prior to working in the Relationships window, always make sure that the tables you want to join have a common field that exists in each table.

7. Click the Database Tools tab.

8. Click the Relationships button in the Relationships group.

   The Relationships window opens in the work area along with the Show Table dialog box in which you select the tables to add to the window.

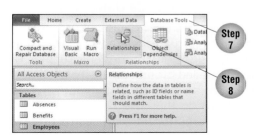

9 At the Show Table dialog box with *Absences* already selected in the *Tables* list box, click the Add button.

> A field list box for the Absences table is added to the Relationships window. The Show Table dialog box remains open for you to add the next table.

In Brief

Arrange Tables in Relationships Window
1. Click Database Tools tab.
2. Click Relationships button.
3. Add required tables to window at Show Table dialog box.
4. Close Show Table dialog box.
5. Resize field list boxes as necessary.
6. Move field list boxes as necessary.
7. Save layout.

10 Click *Benefits* in the *Tables* list box and then click the Add button.

> Depending on the position of the Show Table dialog box in the Relationships window, the *Benefits* field list box may be hidden behind the dialog box. If necessary, drag the Show Table dialog box title bar to move the dialog box out of the way.

Absences field list box added to Relationships window at Step 9

11 Double-click *Employees* in the *Tables* list box.

> Double-clicking a table name also adds a field list box to the Relationships window.

12 Click the Close button in the Show Table dialog box.

> The three field list boxes are side-by-side in the window. In the next steps you will arrange and resize the field list boxes.

13 Position the mouse pointer on the bottom border of the *Benefits* field list box until the pointer changes to an up- and down-pointing arrow and then drag the bottom border down until the vertical scroll bar disappears.

> This action expands the height of the field list box so that you can see all of the field names in the box.

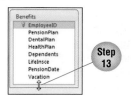

14 Expand the height of the *Employees* field list box to see all of the field names by completing a step similar to Step 13.

15 Position the mouse pointer on the *Employees* field list title bar and then drag the field list box below the *Benefits* field list box.

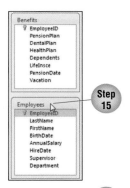

16 Move the *Benefits* field list box to the right and then move the *Employees* field list box up to fill in the space as shown below by dragging the field list box title bars.

> You have been arranging the field list boxes in the Relationships window to position the Employees table in the middle of the other two tables that will be joined. This layout will make it easier to create the relationship and understand the join lines that will appear. You will create the relationships in the next two activities.

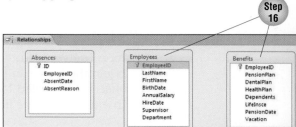

17 Click the Save button on the Quick Access toolbar to save the layout.

18 Click the Close button in the Relationships group of the Relationship Tools Design tab.

Activity 2.10

Creating and Editing a One-To-Many Relationship

When two tables are joined in a relationship, one table is called the *primary table* and the other table is called the *related table*. A one-to-many relationship means that one table in the relationship contains one unique record in the field used to join the tables (this table will be the primary table), while the other table can have several records with a matching field value in the joined field (this table will be the related table).

This is the most common type of relationship created between Access tables. In this type of relationship, the common field in the primary table is also the primary key field. In the related table the common field is not the primary key and is known as the *foreign key* field. A foreign key is a field added to a table that is a primary key in another table and the field is being added for the purpose of creating a relationship.

Project

SNAP

Tutorial 2.7
Creating a Relationship between Two Tables in a Database

You will create a one-to-many relationship between the Employees table and the Absences table using the common field *EmployeeID*.

1 With the **WEEmployees2Relshp.accdb** database open, click the Database Tools tab and then click the Relationships button in the Relationships group.

2 Review the field list boxes in the window that were added in the previous activity. Notice the *EmployeeID* field in the Employees table is the primary key but it is not the primary key in the Absences table. This is because an employee can be absent many times; therefore, *EmployeeID* could not be a primary key in the Absences table.

> Employees will be the primary table since the table contains only one record per employee and Absences will be the related table since the same employee can have many records detailing his or her absences.

3 Position the mouse pointer over *EmployeeID* in the *Employees* field list box, hold down the left mouse button, drag the pointer left to *EmployeeID* in the *Absences* field list box, and then release the mouse button.

> A relationship is created by dragging the common field name from the primary table's field list box to the related table's field list box. Always be careful to drag the common field starting from the *primary table*. The Edit Relationships dialog box appears when you release the mouse button.

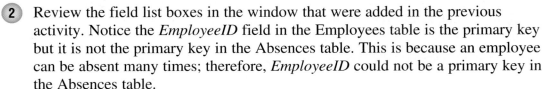

> Drag *EmployeeID* starting in the *Employees* field list box over to *EmployeeID* in the *Absences* field list box at Step 3.

4 Notice *One-To-Many* is in the *Relationship Type* section of the Edit Relationships dialog box.

> Access determined the relationship type based on the common field that was used to join the tables. In the primary table (Employees), *EmployeeID* is the primary key while in the related table (Absences) *EmployeeID* is not the primary key. In the Absences table, the field *EmployeeID* is referred to as the foreign key.

⑤ Click the *Enforce Referential Integrity* check box at the Edit Relationships dialog box and then click Create.

> *Referential integrity* means that Access will ensure that a record with the same employee number already exists in the primary table when a new record is being added to the related table. This prevents what is known as *orphan records*—a record in a related table for which no matching record is found in the primary table.

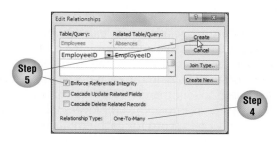

Step 5

Step 4

⑥ Click the Save button.

> A black line (referred to as a *join line*) joins the two tables at the common field. A *1* appears next to the primary table, indicating the *one* side of the relationship and the infinity symbol **∞** appears next to the related table, indicating the *many* side of the relationship.

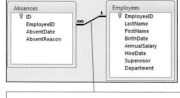

> Join line illustrating the relationship that links the tables at the common field in each table.

⑦ Close the Relationships window.

⑧ Open the Absences table.

> In Steps 9–11 you will test referential integrity by attempting to add an absence record for an employee who does not have a record in the primary table.

⑨ Click in the blank row at the bottom of the datasheet in the *EmployeeID* column, type **1099,** and then press Enter.

⑩ Type **March 3, 2011** in the *Absent Date* column and press Enter.

⑪ With *Sick Day* the default value in the *Absence Reason* column, press Enter to accept the entry.

> Access displays an error message indicating you cannot add or change a record because a related record is required in the Employees table.

⑫ Click OK at the Microsoft Access message box.

Microsoft Access

⚠ You cannot add or change a record because a related record is required in table 'Employees'.

OK   Help

⑬ Close the Absences table. Click OK at the Microsoft Access error message that appears for the second time.

Step 12

⑭ Click Yes at the second error message box to close the table and confirm that the data changes will be lost.

In Addition

Cascade Relationship Options

At the Edit Relationships dialog box, two additional options are dimmed until you turn on referential integrity: *Cascade Update Related Fields* and *Cascade Delete Related Records*. If you change the field value in the field used to join the tables, you can elect to have Access make the same change in the record in the related table. If you delete a record in the primary table you can also instruct Access to delete the records with the same field value in the joined field in the related table.

Activity 2.11

Creating and Editing a One-to-One Relationship

A one-to-one relationship exists when both the primary table and the related table contain only one record with a matching field value in the common field. In this relationship the common field used to join the tables is the primary key in each table. For example, the Employees table would contain only one record for each employee. The Benefits table would also contain only one record for each employee. If these tables are joined on the common *EmployeeID* field, a one-to-one relationship would be created. In this type of relationship, consider the primary table to be the table with the fields (such as the employee names) that describe the identity of each ID number (describe for whom the employee number was created).

Project You will create a one-to-one relationship between the Employees and the Benefits table and then edit the relationship after it has been created.

Tutorial 2.7
Creating a Relationship between Two Tables in a Database

1. With the **WEEmployees2Relshp.accdb** database open, open the Relationships window.

2. Notice the *EmployeeID* field is the primary key in both the *Employees* field list box and the *Benefits* field list box.

3. Position the mouse pointer over *EmployeeID* in the *Employees* field list box, hold down the left mouse button, drag the pointer to *EmployeeID* in the *Benefits* field list box, and then release the mouse button.

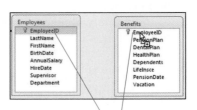

Drag *EmployeeID* starting in the *Employees* field list box over to *EmployeeID* in the *Benefits* field list box at Step 3.

4. Notice *One-To-One* displays in the *Relationship Type* section of the Edit Relationships dialog box.

   > Access determined the relationship type as one-to-one since the common field that was used to join the two tables is the primary key field in each table. In both tables, only one record can exist for each unique employee number.

   Need Help?
   Relationship Type not One-To-One? Check the field names that are displayed in the list box below each Table name. You probably released the mouse while pointing at a field other than *EmployeeID*. Click Cancel and try again.

5. Click Create.

   A black join line connecting the two *EmployeeID* fields appears between the two tables in the Relationships window. The join line does not show a *1* at each end similar to that shown in the previous activity because referential integrity was not turned on.

Step 5

Step 4

6. Click the Close button in the Relationships group of the Relationship Tools Design tab to close the Relationships window. Click Yes if prompted to save changes.

   > In the next steps you will add a record to the Benefits table to illustrate why referential integrity is a good idea to ensure primary tables are updated first.

7 Open the Benefits table and then add the following record to the table:

EmployeeID	**1100**
Pension Plan	**Yes**
Dental Plan	**Yes**
Health Plan	**Yes**
Dependents	**5**
Life Insurance	**200000**
Pension Date	**31-Dec-11**
Vacation	**1 week**

In Brief

Create One-to-One Relationship
1. Open Relationships window.
2. If necessary, add desired tables to window.
3. Close Show Table dialog box.
4. Drag common field from primary table field list box to related table field list box.
5. Turn on desired relationship options.
6. Click Create.
7. Click Save.

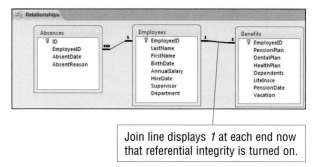

8 Open the Employees table. If necessary, scroll down to view the last record in the datasheet. Notice that no employee record exists in the table with an *EmployeeID* of *1100*.

> Since referential integrity was not turned on when the relationship was created between the Employees and the Benefits table, you were able to add a record to the related table for which no matching record is found in the primary table. Although you could easily add the matching record to the Employees table afterwards, it is generally considered good practice that the employee's record is established first in the primary table.

9 Close the Employees table.

10 Delete the record you added at Step 7 with *EmployeeID* 1100 in the Benefits table and then close the table.

11 Open the Relationships window.

12 Position the mouse pointer on the black join line between the *Employees* field list box and the *Benefits* field list box, right-click, and then click *Edit Relationship* at the shortcut menu.

> You can also double-click the join line to open the Edit Relationships dialog box, or single-click the join line and click the Edit Relationships button in the Tools group of the Relationship Tools Design tab.

Right-click the join line to display the Relationship shortcut menu.

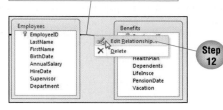

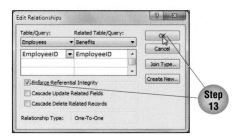

13 Click the *Enforce Referential Integrity* check box at the Edit Relationships dialog box and then click OK.

> With referential integrity turned on, the join line displays a *1* at each end.

Join line displays *1* at each end now that referential integrity is turned on.

14 Close the Relationships window.

Activity 2.12

Printing a Relationships Report; Deleting a Relationship

Once all relationships have been created in a database, printing a hard copy of the relationships report to file away for future reference is a good idea. This documentation is a quick reference that displays at a glance all of the table names, fields within each table, and relationships between the tables. Should you ever have to recreate a relationship, the documenta-tion would be of assistance to you. Relationships can be deleted if you redesign the database and the existing relationship no longer applies. You may also need to delete a relationship in order to make a structural change to a table. In this case the relationship can be deleted, the change made, and then the relationship recreated.

Project You will print a relationships report for the employees database to file away for safekeeping. Next, you will practice deleting a relationship.

Worldwide Enterprises

SNAP

Tutorial 2.7
Creating a Relationship between Two Tables in a Database

1   With the **WEEmployees2Relshp.accdb** database open, open the Relationships window.

2   Click the Relationship Report button 🔲 in the Tools group of the Relationship Tools Design tab.

> Access generates the report and displays it in Print Preview in a new tab in the work area.

3   Click the Print button in the Print group.

4   At the Print dialog box, click OK.

5   Click the Close Print Preview button in the Close Preview group.

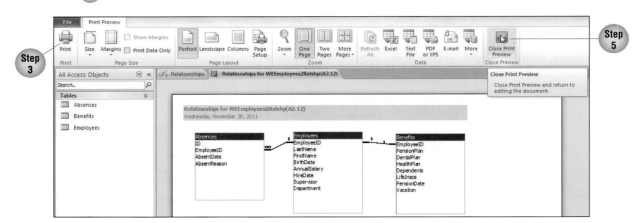

6   Access displays the report in a Design view window. Click the Close button at the top right of the work area to close the report.

7   Click Yes at the Microsoft Access message box asking if you want to save the report.

8   At the Save As dialog box with the existing report name already selected in the *Report Name* text box, type **Relationships** and click OK or press Enter.

> In the next steps you will delete a relationship and then recreate the relationship for more practice.

9 At the Relationships window, right-click the black join line between the Absences table and the Employees table, and then click *Delete* at the shortcut menu.

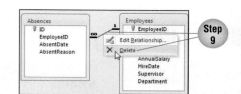

Step 9

10 Click Yes at the Microsoft Access message box asking if you are sure you want to permanently delete the relationship.

> The black join line is removed from the two tables.

Step 10

11 Recreate the relationship by positioning the mouse pointer over *EmployeeID* in the *Employees* field list box, holding down the left mouse button, dragging the pointer to *EmployeeID* in the *Absences* field list box, and then releasing the mouse.

12 Click the *Enforce Referential Integrity* check box at the Edit Relationships dialog box and then click Create.

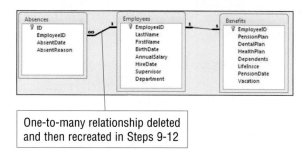

One-to-many relationship deleted and then recreated in Steps 9-12

13 Close the Relationships window.

14 Close the **WEEmployees2Relshp.accdb** database.

In Brief

Printing a Relationships Report
1. Open Relationships window.
2. Click Relationship Report button.
3. Click Print and then click OK.
4. Click Close Print Preview.
5. Close report in work area.
6. Click Yes to save report, or No to close without saving.
7. Type report name.
8. Click OK.
9. Close Relationships window.

Delete a Relationship
1. Open Relationships window.
2. Right-click join line between tables.
3. Click Delete.
4. Click Yes.

In Addition

Displaying Records in a Subdatasheet

When two tables are joined, you can view related records within a *subdatasheet*. A subdatasheet is a datasheet within a datasheet. When you open the primary table in Datasheet view, a column of plus symbols (referred to as *expand indicators*) displays between the record selector bar and the first column. Click the plus symbol next to the record for which you want to view related records. A subdatasheet opens similar to the one shown below. The plus symbol changes to a minus symbol when a record has been expanded. Click the minus symbol (referred to as a *collapse indicator*) to close the subdatasheet.

Click to collapse the record and remove the subdatasheet.

Click to expand the record and show the subdatasheet.

Subdatasheet

Features Summary

Feature	Ribbon Tab, Group	Button	Keyboard Shortcut
create table	Create, Tables	⊞	
create table in Design view	Create, Tables	⊞	
Datasheet view	Home, Views	⊞	
delete fields	Table Tools Design, Tools	⇥×	Delete
edit relationship	Relationship Tools Design, Tools	✎	
font size	Home, Text Formatting	11 ▾	
gridlines	Home, Text Formatting	⊞▾	
insert fields	Table Tools Design, Tools	⇥	
insert totals	Home, Records	Σ	
primary key	Table Tools Design, Tools	🔑	
relationship report	Relationship Tools Design, Tools	⊟	
relationships	Database Tools, Relationships	⊟	

Knowledge Check

Completion: In the space provided at the right, indicate the correct term, command, or option.

1. A field name can contain this number of characters.
2. Assign a field this data type if the field will contain dollar values that you do not want rounded off in calculations.
3. This is the term for the field in a table that must contain unique information for each record.
4. Enter a value in this field property if you want the value to appear automatically in the field whenever a new record is created.
5. Enter a statement in this field property to prevent data that does not meet the range or other criteria from being entered into the field.
6. This is the field property that controls data as it is being entered by ensuring data typed in the field conforms to the code entered in the property box.
7. This field property controls how data is displayed after it has been accepted for entry in the field.

8. This is the name of the wizard used to create a drop-down list in a field. _____

9. This button can be used to add a SUM function to the bottom of a numeric field in the datasheet. _____

10. One table in a relationship is referred to as the primary table. The other table is referred to as this. _____

11. In this type of relationship one table can have only one record with a matching field value in the common field while the other table can have several records with a matching field value. _____

12. This is the term for the black line that displays between the common field name in the two field list boxes after a relationship has been created. _____

13. This type of relationship is created when the field used to join the two tables is the primary key in both tables. _____

14. Turn this relationship option on to make sure new records are added first to the primary table before a record with a matching value in the common field can be added to the related table. _____

15. Click this button in the Relationships window to print a hard copy of the relationships. _____

Skills Review

Review 1 Creating and Modifying a Table in Design View

Worldwide Enterprises

1. Open the **WEEmployees2Relshp.accdb** database and enable content if the security warning message bar appears.

2. Create a table in Design view using the following field names and data types. You decide whether to add an appropriate description. Do *not* set any field properties since these will be changed later in this activity.

Field Name	Data Type
EmployeeID	Text
SupervisorLName	Text
SupervisorFName	Text
AnnualRevDate	Date/Time
SalaryIncDate	Date/Time
ProfDevDays	Number

3. Define *EmployeeID* as the primary key field.

4. Save the table and name it **Review**.

5. Switch to Datasheet view and then enter the following two records:

EmployeeID	1013	*EmployeeID*	1030
SupervisorLName	Vestering	*SupervisorLName*	Deptulski
SupervisorFName	Sam	*SupervisorFName*	Roman
AnnualRevDate	2/10/11	*AnnualRevDate*	1/22/12
SalaryIncDate	9/01/11	*SalaryIncDate*	7/22/12
ProfDevDays	5	*ProfDevDays*	10

6. Adjust all columns to Best Fit.
7. Save the changes to the datasheet layout.
8. Switch to Design view and then make the following changes to the field properties.
   a. Change the field size for the *EmployeeID* field to 4.
   b. Create a validation rule for the *ProfDevDays* field to ensure that no number greater than 10 is entered into the field. Enter an appropriate validation text error message.
   c. Save the table and click Yes at each message that indicates some data may be lost and to test the data with the new validation rule.
   d. Create an input mask for both date fields to set the pattern for entering dates to *Medium Date*. Use the default entry for the placeholder character. Click Yes if prompted to save the table before displaying the Input Mask Wizard.
   e. Change the Format property for both date fields to display the date in the *Medium Date* format.
9. Save the table.
10. Switch to Datasheet view and add the following two records:

EmployeeID	1040	*EmployeeID*	1043
SupervisorLName	**Ruiz**	*SupervisorLName*	**Deptulski**
SupervisorFName	**Celesta**	*SupervisorFName*	**Roman**
AnnualRevDate	**10-Mar-12**	*AnnualRevDate*	**15-Aug-11**
SalaryIncDate	**01-Sep-12**	*SalaryIncDate*	**01-Feb-12**
ProvDevDays	**8**	*ProfDevDays*	**6**

11. Display the datasheet in Print Preview.
12. Change the page orientation to landscape and then print the table.
13. Close Print Preview and then close the Review table.

Review 2 Modifying, Moving, and Deleting Fields; Creating Relationships

1. With the **WEEmployees2Relshp.accdb** database open, open the Review table in Design view.
2. Move the *ProvDevDays* field between *SupervisorFName* and *AnnualRevDate*.
3. Move *SupervisorFName* before *SupervisorLName*.
4. Add caption properties so that the fields display the following headings in Datasheet view:

   Supervisor First Name   Annual Review Date
   Supervisor Last Name   Salary Increase Date
   Professional Development Days

5. Save the table, switch to Datasheet view, adjust all column widths as necessary, and then print the datasheet in landscape orientation and with the left and right margin set to 0.5 inch.
6. Close the Review table saving changes to the layout.
7. Open the Employees table in Design view.
8. Delete the *Supervisor* field.

9. Save and then close the Employees table.
10. Open the Relationships window.
11. Click the Show Table button in the Relationships group of the Relationship Tools Design tab, add the Review table to the window, and then close the Show Table dialog box.
12. Create a one-to-one relationship between the Employees table (primary table) and the Review table (related table) using the *EmployeeID* field. Turn on referential integrity.
13. Save the changes to the relationships.
14. Generate a new relationship report and then print the report in landscape orientation.
15. Save the new report naming it **Relationships2** and then close the report.
16. Close the relationships window and then close **WEEmployees2Relshp.accdb**.

Skills Assessment

Assessment 1 Creating a Table in Design View; Creating a Lookup Field

1. Gina Simmons, instructor in the Theatre Arts Division, has asked you to create a new table to store the grades for the AC478-01 course she is currently teaching. Gina would prefer to enter grades by selecting from a drop-down list. To begin, open the **NPCGrades2.accdb** database and enable content if the security warning message bar appears.
2. Create a new table in Design view using the following field names: *StudentNo*; *LastName*; *FirstName*; *Grade*. Set the data type to *Text* for each field except *Grade*.
   At the *Grade* field, use the Lookup Wizard to create a drop-down list with the following grades: A+, A, B, C, D, F.
3. Restrict the *Grade* lookup properties to items within the list only and do not allow the values within the list to be edited from the datasheet.
4. Define *StudentNo* field as the primary key.
5. Save the table and name it **AC478-01Grades**.
6. Enter the following four records in the datasheet:

StudentNo	111-785-156	*StudentNo*	118-487-578
LastName	Bastow	*LastName*	Andre
FirstName	Maren	*FirstName*	Ian
Grade	A+	*Grade*	C
StudentNo	137-845-746	*StudentNo*	138-456-749
LastName	Knowlton	*LastName*	Yiu
FirstName	Sherri	*FirstName*	Terry
Grade	B	*Grade*	D

7. Adjust all column widths to Best Fit.
8. Print and then close the AC478-01Grades table saving changes.
9. Close the **NPCGrades2.accdb** database.

Assessment 2 Changing Field Size; Validating Entries; Creating an
Input Mask; Formatting Dates; Formatting a Datasheet

1. Bobbie Sinclair, business manager, has asked you to look at the design
of the CostumeInventory table and try to improve it with data restrictions and validation
rules. While reviewing the table design, you discover an error has been made in assigning
the data type for one of the fields. To begin, open the **PTCostumeInv2.accdb** database
and enable content if the security warning message bar appears.
2. Open the CostumeInventory table in Design view.
3. Notice the *DateIn* field is not the same data type as the *DateOut* field. Fields that will
contain dates should always be set to the Date/Time data type so that Access verifies each
entry as a valid date when records are added to the datasheet or form. Change *DateIn* to a
Date/Time field.
4. Change the field size for *CostumeNo* to 5 to limit the field to the number of characters
Performance Threads assigns to a costume inventory item.
5. Performance Threads has a minimum daily rental fee of $85.00. Create a validation rule
and validation text entry that will ensure no one enters a value less than $85.00 in the
DailyRentalFee field.
6. To ensure no one mixes the order of the month and day when entering the *DateOut* and
DateIn fields, create an input mask for these two fields to require that the date be entered
in the *Medium Date* format.
7. Since Performance Threads is open seven days a week, format the *DateOut* and *DateIn*
fields to display the dates in the *Long Date* format. This adds the day of the week to the
entry and spells the month in full.
8. Save the table and then switch to Datasheet view.
9. Adjust the column widths of the two date columns to Best Fit. (Access displays pound
symbols (#) across a column when the width is not wide enough to display the data.)
10. Change the font size of the datasheet to 10 and then adjust all column widths to Best Fit.
11. Preview the datasheet. Change the margins for the page as necessary so that the entire
datasheet fits on one page.
12. Save, print, and then close the CostumeInventory table.
13. Close the **PTCostumeInv2.accdb** database.

Assessment 3 Creating a New Database

1. Alex Torres, manager of the Toronto office, has asked you to help
the accounting staff by creating a database to track employee expense
claims information. To begin, create a new database on your storage medium named
FCTExpenses2.
2. Look at the sample expense form in Figure 2.4. On your own or with another student in
the class, make a list of the fields that would be needed to store the information from this
form in a table. Alex has advised that you do not need to include fields for the mailing
address for the employee. For each field on your list, determine the appropriate data type
and field properties that could be used.
3. Create a new table from a blank datasheet so that Access creates an *ID* field automatically
that you can use as the primary key. Use the design information you created in Step 2 to
enter the field names, data types, and field properties in the table.
4. Switch to Datasheet view and then enter the expense claim information shown in Figure 2.4
in a record.

FIGURE 2.4 Assessment 3

First Choice TRAVEL   **Expense Statement**

Employee Information

Name:	Terry Blessing	Emp ID:	LA-104
Address:	3341 Ventura Boulevard	Position:	President
City, State, ZIP:	Los Angeles, CA 90102	Manager:	Not required

Expense Claim Details

Date	Description	TOTAL CLAIMED
5/26/2011	Travel expenses to Toronto office for meeting	$2,344.10

NOTE: All expense claims must have original receipts attached.

Signature _____

5. Preview, print, and then close the Expenses table. Make sure all column headings and data are entirely visible and use formatting and/or page layout options as necessary to print using only one page if possible.
6. Close **FCTExpenses2.accdb**.

Assessment 4   Finding Information on Table Templates

HELP

1. Use the Help feature to find information on creating a new database using one of the sample templates provided with Access.
2. Create a new database from the Events sample template on your storage medium and name it **WBEvents2**. Enable content if the security warning message bar appears.
3. At the blank Event List form that appears, enter the following records.

Title	Start Time	End Time	Description	Location
Sailing Regatta	June 10, 2011	June 12, 2011	Daily races at yacht club	Buffalo Yacht Club
Sunfest Festival	July 29, 2011	July 31, 2011	Celebration of world cultures with music, crafts, and cuisine	Broderick Park

4. Close the Events List form and then expand the Navigation pane by clicking the right-pointing chevrons at the top of the minimized Navigation pane (displays the ScreenTip *Shutter Bar Open/Close Button*).
5. Change the Navigation pane view to *Object Type*.
6. Open the Events table in Design view and then delete the field named *Attachments*. Click Yes at all prompts that appear.
7. Rename the *ID* field *EventID*.
8. Delete the space between the words in the field names *Start Time* and *End Time* and create caption properties to display the space between the words in other database objects.

9. Save the design changes and switch to Datasheet view. Adjust all column widths to Best Fit.
10. Preview the datasheet. Change the page orientation to landscape and then print the datasheet.
11. Close Print Preview and then close the Events table saving changes.
12. Close the **WBEvents2.accdb** database.

Assessment 5 Individual Challenge

Investigating Social Media Websites

1. New social media websites are cropping up frequently. Beyond Facebook and Twitter are an abundance of websites in which you can participate in social interaction, wikis, or publish your own content. Launch Internet Explorer and go to the website www.go2web20.net. This website contains an extensive directory of social media (referred to as Web 2.0).
2. Browse the GO2WEB20 site and investigate at least five of the sites that are in the directory that you are not familiar with. Consider using the tags to sort and filter the list of sites by category. For example, click the Blogging tag to view a list of blogging websites.
3. Create a new database on your storage medium named **NewWeb20_2**.
4. Create a table named **SocialMedia** using Design view. Include fields to store the social media website name, the site's URL, the category (or tag) to which you would associate the site (for example, *Blog, Social, Video* and so on), and add a Memo field in which you can type a brief note about the site's purpose. Include an ID field as the primary key.
5. Save the table and then add records to the datasheet for the sites that you investigated in Step 2.
6. Preview and then print the SocialMedia table, adjusting page layout options as necessary to minimize paper.
7. Save and close the SocialMedia table.
8. Close the **NewWeb20_2** database.

Marquee Challenge

Challenge 1 Refining Tables in a Database; Creating Relationships

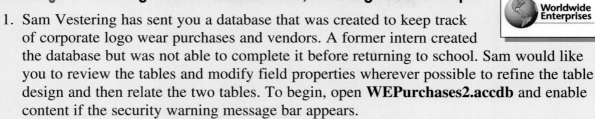

1. Sam Vestering has sent you a database that was created to keep track of corporate logo wear purchases and vendors. A former intern created the database but was not able to complete it before returning to school. Sam would like you to review the tables and modify field properties wherever possible to refine the table design and then relate the two tables. To begin, open **WEPurchases2.accdb** and enable content if the security warning message bar appears.

2. Open each table and look at the sample data entered in the datasheet and then, in Design view, modify field properties to maximize Access features that can control or otherwise validate data entered. Consider the following practices at Worldwide Enterprises as you complete this task:

   a. Worldwide uses a 4-character purchase order numbering system.

   b. All vendors are assigned a 3-character vendor number.

   c. Staff at Worldwide are used to entering dates in the format dd-mmm-yy.

   d. Telephone numbers must all include the area code with the area code in brackets, for example, (212) 555-6549.

   e. Worldwide will not issue a purchase order for corporate wear that has a value less than $300.00.

3. Sam asked that you set up a new field in the Purchases table to enter the shipment method. Worldwide will only receive shipments from the following carriers with whom credit accounts have been set up: *UPS, FedEx, Express Freight,* and *Global Transport.* After creating the new field, populate the existing records with one of the carrier companies to test the field.

4. Create a relationship between the Vendors table and the Purchases table.

5. Create and print a relationship report.

6. Print each datasheet making sure all data is visible and minimizing paper.

7. Create a memo using Microsoft Word to your instructor that documents the field properties in each table that you modified including the property box entry that you made. Save the memo and name it **AS2-C1-Memo**. Print and then close the memo. Exit Word.

8. Close **WEPurchases2.accdb**.

Challenge 2 Creating a New Database

1. Bobbie Sinclair, business manager, has approved the project to create the new database that will store the custom costume business at Performance Threads. Begin this challenge assessment by opening **AS1-C2-PTCostumes.docx**. (This document was created in Marquee Challenge 2 in Section 1.)
2. Use Save As and name the document **AS2-C2-PTCostumes**.
3. Continue your work on the table design for this database by documenting next to each field name the properties that you will set. For each field, consider applying properties learned in this section that will help maintain data integrity. Consider making assumptions about some business rules and then setting field properties that will conform to those rules. You may make any reasonable assumptions that you think would protect the data in a business setting similar to a custom costume manufacturer. For example, you may assume a minimum price for a custom costume. You determine any acceptable limits. Document all of your assumptions.
4. Consider the relationships in the new database. Document in **AS2-C2-PTCostumes.docx** on a separate page the tables that will be related and the type of relationship that will be created. Include the common field name upon which you will join each table.
5. Create a new blank database named **AS2-C2-PTCostumes**.
6. Create the tables as per your design document. Make sure that you change your design document if you change your mind about a field property once you create the table.
7. Populate each table with a few sample records to ensure your properties work as expected.
8. Create relationships between the tables as per your design document.
9. Create, save, and print the relationships report. (Accept the default report name.)
10. Print each datasheet making sure all data is entirely visible and that paper usage is minimized as much as possible.
11. Close **AS2-C2-PTCostumes.accdb**.
12. Save the revised Word document and then print **AS2-C2-PTCostumes.docx**.

Access SECTION 3
Creating Queries, Forms, and Reports

Skills

- Create a select query using the Simple Query Wizard
- Create a select query in Design view
- Add multiple tables to a query
- Add criteria statements to a query
- Prevent columns in the query design grid from displaying in the query results datasheet
- Select records using AND and OR statements
- Sort the query results
- Perform calculations in a query
- Create and edit a form using the Form tool
- Add a field to a form
- Add a logo image to a form
- Resize and format an object on a form
- Create, edit, and print a report using the Report tool
- Move and resize columns in a report

Projects Overview

Create queries to produce custom employee lists, add criteria, and calculate pension contributions and monthly salaries; create and modify forms to facilitate data entry and viewing of records; create and modify reports to produce custom printouts of data.

Create a query, and create and print a report that lists all costumes rented in a particular month; create and modify a form for browsing the costume inventory and entering new records; continue design work on a new database for custom costume activities by creating a form and a report.

Create and print a query to extract records of students who achieved A+ in all of their courses.

Create queries and design a report for the catering events database to extract event information for a banquet room, extract all events booked in a particular month, and calculate the estimated revenue from the catering events.

Model Answers for Projects

These model answers for the projects that you complete in Section 3 provide a preview of the finished projects before you begin working and also allow you to compare your own results with these models to ensure you have created the materials accurately.

The BenefitPlans query results datasheet within the WEEmployees3.accdb database is the project in Activity 3.1.

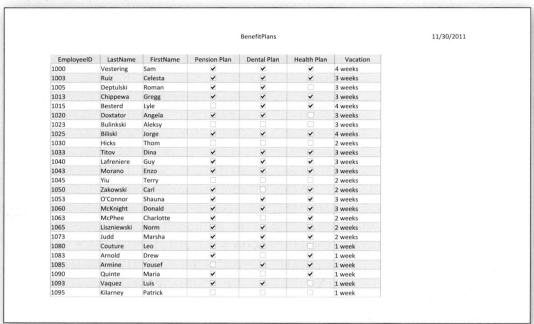

BenefitPlans   11/30/2011

EmployeeID	LastName	FirstName	Pension Plan	Dental Plan	Health Plan	Vacation
1000	Vestering	Sam	✔	✔	✔	4 weeks
1003	Ruiz	Celesta	✔	✔	✔	3 weeks
1005	Deptulski	Roman	✔	✔	☐	3 weeks
1013	Chippewa	Gregg	✔	✔	✔	3 weeks
1015	Besterd	Lyle	☐	✔	✔	4 weeks
1020	Doxtator	Angela	✔	✔	☐	3 weeks
1023	Bulinkski	Aleksy	☐	☐	☐	3 weeks
1025	Biliski	Jorge	✔	✔	✔	4 weeks
1030	Hicks	Thom	☐	☐	☐	2 weeks
1033	Titov	Dina	✔	✔	✔	3 weeks
1040	Lafreniere	Guy	✔	✔	✔	3 weeks
1043	Morano	Enzo	✔	✔	✔	3 weeks
1045	Yiu	Terry	☐	☐	☐	2 weeks
1050	Zakowski	Carl	✔	☐	✔	2 weeks
1053	O'Connor	Shauna	✔	✔	✔	3 weeks
1060	McKnight	Donald	✔	✔	✔	3 weeks
1063	McPhee	Charlotte	✔	☐	✔	2 weeks
1065	Liszniewski	Norm	✔	✔	✔	2 weeks
1073	Judd	Marsha	✔	✔	✔	2 weeks
1080	Couture	Leo	✔	✔	☐	1 week
1083	Arnold	Drew	✔	☐	✔	1 week
1085	Armine	Yousef	☐	✔	✔	1 week
1090	Quinte	Maria	✔	☐	✔	1 week
1093	Vaquez	Luis	✔	✔	☐	1 week
1095	Kilarney	Patrick	☐	☐	☐	1 week

The SalaryList query results datasheet within the WEEmployees3.accdb database is the project in Activity 3.2.

SalaryList   11/30/2011

EmployeeID	FirstName	LastName	AnnualSalary	HireDate
1000	Sam	Vestering	$69,725.00	7/22/2002
1003	Celesta	Ruiz	$41,875.00	8/5/2002
1005	Roman	Deptulski	$72,750.00	8/15/2002
1013	Gregg	Chippewa	$48,650.00	2/10/2003
1015	Lyle	Besterd	$45,651.00	5/17/2003
1020	Angela	Doxtator	$45,558.00	8/3/2003
1023	Aleksy	Bulinkski	$51,450.00	10/10/2003
1025	Jorge	Biliski	$44,892.00	12/1/2003
1030	Thom	Hicks	$42,824.00	1/22/2004
1033	Dina	Titov	$45,655.00	1/10/2004
1040	Guy	Lafreniere	$45,395.00	3/10/2005
1043	Enzo	Morano	$48,750.00	8/15/2005
1045	Terry	Yiu	$42,238.00	1/31/2006
1050	Carl	Zakowski	$44,387.00	2/9/2006
1053	Shauna	O'Connor	$43,695.00	4/15/2007
1060	Donald	McKnight	$42,126.00	6/22/2007
1063	Charlotte	McPhee	$43,695.00	2/6/2008
1065	Norm	Liszniewski	$43,695.00	2/6/2008
1073	Marsha	Judd	$44,771.00	11/30/2009
1080	Leo	Couture	$43,659.00	1/27/2010
1083	Drew	Arnold	$43,659.00	6/22/2010
1085	Yousef	Armine	$42,177.00	3/14/2010
1090	Maria	Quinte	$42,177.00	11/29/2010
1093	Luis	Vaquez	$42,177.00	12/5/2010
1095	Patrick	Kilarney	$42,177.00	12/12/2010

ACCESS SECTION 3
Project Model Answers

The ReviewList query results datasheet within the WEEmployees3.accdb database is the project in Activity 3.3.

ReviewList   11/30/2011

EmployeeID	FirstName	LastName	Supervisor First Name	Supervisor Last Name	HireDate	Annual Review Date
1013	Gregg	Chippewa	Sam	Vestering	2/10/2003	10-Feb-11
1015	Lyle	Besterd	Sam	Vestering	5/17/2003	17-May-11
1020	Angela	Doxtator	Celesta	Ruiz	8/3/2003	03-Aug-12
1023	Aleksy	Bulinkski	Sam	Vestering	10/10/2003	15-Oct-12
1025	Jorge	Biliski	Roman	Deptulski	12/1/2003	01-Dec-12
1030	Thom	Hicks	Roman	Deptulski	1/22/2004	22-Jan-12
1033	Dina	Titov	Roman	Deptulski	1/10/2004	01-Jan-12
1040	Guy	Lafreniere	Celesta	Ruiz	3/10/2005	10-Mar-12
1043	Enzo	Morano	Roman	Deptulski	8/15/2005	15-Aug-11
1045	Terry	Yiu	Celesta	Ruiz	1/31/2006	01-Jan-12
1050	Carl	Zakowski	Sam	Vestering	2/9/2006	09-Feb-11
1053	Shauna	O'Connor	Sam	Vestering	4/15/2007	15-Apr-11
1060	Donald	McKnight	Roman	Deptulski	6/22/2007	25-Jun-11
1063	Charlotte	McPhee	Celesta	Ruiz	2/6/2008	10-Feb-11
1065	Norm	Liszniewski	Sam	Vestering	2/6/2008	10-Feb-11
1073	Marsha	Judd	Roman	Deptulski	11/30/2009	30-Nov-11
1080	Leo	Couture	Roman	Deptulski	1/27/2010	27-Jan-11
1083	Drew	Arnold	Celesta	Ruiz	6/22/2010	22-Jun-11
1085	Yousef	Armine	Celesta	Ruiz	3/14/2010	14-Mar-11
1090	Maria	Quinte	Sam	Vestering	11/29/2010	30-Nov-11
1093	Luis	Vaquez	Sam	Vestering	12/5/2010	10-Dec-11
1095	Patrick	Kilarney	Celesta	Ruiz	12/12/2010	15-Dec-11

Page 1

The **4WksVac** query results datasheet within the **WEEmployees3.accdb** database is the project in Activity 3.4.

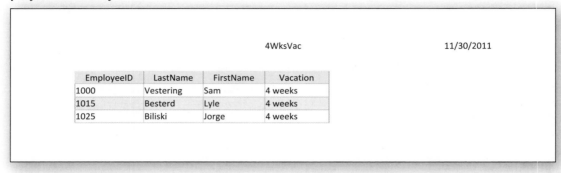

The **NAHighSalary** query results datasheet within the **WEEmployees3.accdb** database is the project in Activity 3.5.

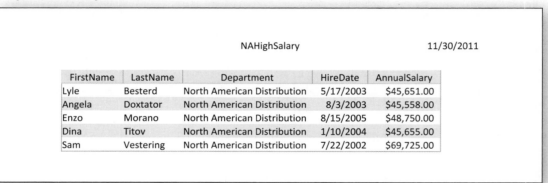

The **3or4WksVac** query results datasheet within the **WEEmployees3.accdb** database is the project in Activity 3.6.

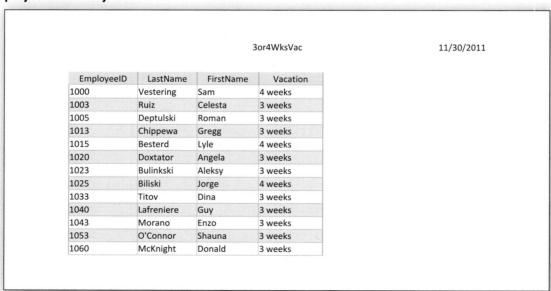

The **PensionCont** query results datasheet within the **WEEmployees3.accdb** database is the project in Activity 3.7.

PensionCont   11/30/2011

EmployeeID	FirstName	LastName	AnnualSalary	PensionContribution
1000	Sam	Vestering	$69,725.00	$2,091.75
1003	Celesta	Ruiz	$41,875.00	$1,256.25
1005	Roman	Deptulski	$72,750.00	$2,182.50
1013	Gregg	Chippewa	$48,650.00	$1,459.50
1015	Lyle	Besterd	$45,651.00	$1,369.53
1020	Angela	Doxtator	$45,558.00	$1,366.74
1023	Aleksy	Bulinkski	$51,450.00	$1,543.50
1025	Jorge	Biliski	$44,892.00	$1,346.76
1030	Thom	Hicks	$42,824.00	$1,284.72
1033	Dina	Titov	$45,655.00	$1,369.65
1040	Guy	Lafreniere	$45,395.00	$1,361.85
1043	Enzo	Morano	$48,750.00	$1,462.50
1045	Terry	Yiu	$42,238.00	$1,267.14
1050	Carl	Zakowski	$44,387.00	$1,331.61
1053	Shauna	O'Connor	$43,695.00	$1,310.85
1060	Donald	McKnight	$42,126.00	$1,263.78
1063	Charlotte	McPhee	$43,695.00	$1,310.85
1065	Norm	Liszniewski	$43,695.00	$1,310.85
1073	Marsha	Judd	$44,771.00	$1,343.13
1080	Leo	Couture	$43,659.00	$1,309.77
1083	Drew	Arnold	$43,659.00	$1,309.77
1085	Yousef	Armine	$42,177.00	$1,265.31
1090	Maria	Quinte	$42,177.00	$1,265.31
1093	Luis	Vaquez	$42,177.00	$1,265.31
1095	Patrick	Kilarney	$42,177.00	$1,265.31
Total			**$1,163,808.00**	**$34,914.24**

The **Absences** form within the **WEEmployees3.accdb** database is the project in
Activities 3.8 to 3.10.

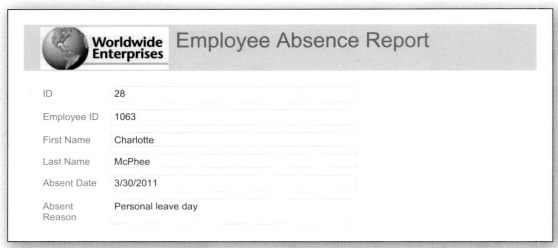

The **NAHighSalary** report within the **WEEmployees3.accdb** database is the project in
Activity 3.11.

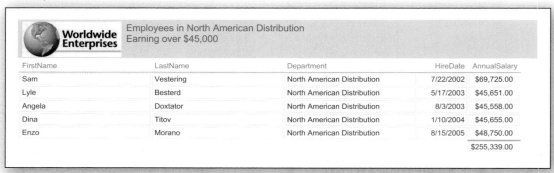

The ReviewList report within the WEEmployees3.accdb database is the project in Activity 3.12.

Employee Review List

EmployeeID	FirstName	LastName	HireDate	Supervisor First Name	Supervisor Last Name	Annual Review Date
1013	Gregg	Chippewa	2/10/2003	Sam	Vestering	10-Feb-11
1015	Lyle	Besterd	5/17/2003	Sam	Vestering	17-May-11
1020	Angela	Doxtator	8/3/2003	Celesta	Ruiz	03-Aug-12
1023	Aleksy	Bulinkski	10/10/2003	Sam	Vestering	15-Oct-12
1025	Jorge	Biliski	12/1/2003	Roman	Deptulski	01-Dec-12
1030	Thom	Hicks	1/22/2004	Roman	Deptulski	22-Jan-12
1033	Dina	Titov	1/10/2004	Roman	Deptulski	01-Jan-12
1040	Guy	Lafreniere	3/10/2005	Celesta	Ruiz	10-Mar-12
1043	Enzo	Morano	8/15/2005	Roman	Deptulski	15-Aug-11
1045	Terry	Yiu	1/31/2006	Celesta	Ruiz	01-Jan-12
1050	Carl	Zakowski	2/9/2006	Sam	Vestering	09-Feb-11
1053	Shauna	O'Connor	4/15/2007	Sam	Vestering	15-Apr-11
1060	Donald	McKnight	6/22/2007	Roman	Deptulski	25-Jun-11
1063	Charlotte	McPhee	2/6/2008	Celesta	Ruiz	10-Feb-11
1065	Norm	Liszniewski	2/6/2008	Sam	Vestering	10-Feb-11
1073	Marsha	Judd	11/30/2009	Roman	Deptulski	30-Nov-11
1080	Leo	Couture	1/27/2010	Roman	Deptulski	27-Jan-11
1083	Drew	Arnold	6/22/2010	Celesta	Ruiz	22-Jun-11
1085	Yousef	Armine	3/14/2010	Celesta	Ruiz	14-Mar-11
1090	Maria	Quinte	11/29/2010	Sam	Vestering	30-Nov-11
1093	Luis	Vaquez	12/5/2010	Sam	Vestering	10-Dec-11
1095	Patrick	Kilarney	12/12/2010	Celesta	Ruiz	15-Dec-11

22

Page 1 of 1

Activity 3.1

Creating a Query Using the Simple Query Wizard

A *query* is an Access object designed to extract data from one or more tables. Usually a query is created to select records that answer a question. For example, a question such as *Which employees are enrolled in the Pension Plan?* could be answered with a query. The query would be designed to select records for those employees with a *Yes* in the *PensionPlan* field. Query results display in a datasheet that pulls the data from existing tables. A query can be created to serve a variety of purposes, from very simple field selection to complex conditional statements or calculations. In its simplest form, a query may be used to display or print selected fields from two tables. Access includes the Simple Query Wizard to facilitate creating a query.

Project

Tutorial 3.1
Creating Queries
Using the Simple
Query Wizard

Using the Simple Query Wizard, you will generate a list of each employee's first and last names and benefit selections. This will allow you to print a list by selecting fields from two tables.

1. Open the **WEEmployees3.accdb** database. Click the Enable Content button if the Security Warning message bar appears.

2. Click the Employees table name in the Navigation pane and then click the Create tab.

3. Click the Query Wizard button in the Queries group.

4. At the New Query dialog box, with *Simple Query Wizard* already selected in the list box, click OK.

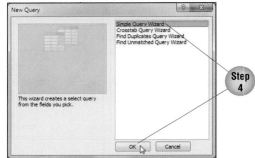

5. At the first Simple Query Wizard dialog box, with *Table: Employees* already selected in the *Tables/Queries* list box, and with *EmployeeID* already selected in the *Available Fields* list box, click the Add Field button **>** to move *EmployeeID* to the *Selected Fields* list box.

6. With *LastName* now selected in the *Available Fields* list box, click the Add Field button to move *LastName* to the *Selected Fields* list box.

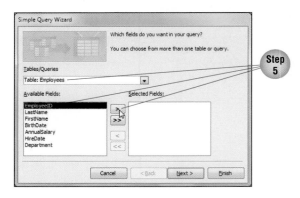

7. Click the Add Field button to move *FirstName* to the *Selected Fields* list box.

8. Click the down-pointing arrow at the right of the *Tables/Queries* list box and then click *Table: Benefits* at the drop-down list.

   The list of fields in the *Available Fields* list box changes to display the field names from the Benefits table.

9. Double-click *PensionPlan* in the *Available Fields* list box.

   Double-clicking a field name is another way to move a field to the *Selected Fields* list box.

10 Double-click the following fields in the *Available Fields* list box to move them to the *Selected Fields* list box:

> *DentalPlan*
> *HealthPlan*
> *Vacation*

11 Click Next.

12 Click Next at the second Simple Query Wizard dialog box to accept *Detail* (*shows every field of every record*) in the *Would you like a detail or summary query?* section.

13 At the third Simple Query Wizard dialog box, select the current text in the *What title do you want for your query?* text box, type **BenefitPlans**, and then click Finish.

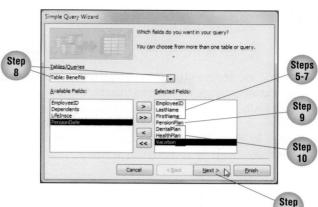

In Brief

Create Query Using Simple Query Wizard
1. Click Create tab.
2. Click Query Wizard.
3. Click OK.
4. Choose table(s) and field(s) to include in query.
5. Click Next.
6. Choose *Detail* or *Summary* query.
7. Click Next.
8. Type title for query.
9. Click Finish.

14 View the query results datasheet shown in Figure 3.1.

> The query results datasheet shown in Figure 3.1 can be sorted, edited, or formatted in a manner similar to a table datasheet. Data displayed in query results is not stored as a separate entity—the query is simply another interface for viewing and editing data in the associated table(s). When a saved query is opened, the query results are updated dynamically each time by running the query.

15 Display the datasheet in Print Preview, change the orientation to landscape, and then print the datasheet.

16 Close the Print Preview window and then close the BenefitPlans query.

FIGURE 3.1 Query Results Datasheet

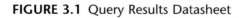

EmployeeID	LastName	FirstName	Pension Plan	Dental Plan	Health Plan	Vacation
1000	Vestering	Sam	✓	✓	✓	4 weeks
1003	Ruiz	Celesta	✓	✓	✓	3 weeks
1005	Deptulski	Roman	✓	✓	☐	3 weeks
1013	Chippewa	Gregg	✓	✓	✓	3 weeks
1015	Besterd	Lyle	☐	✓	✓	4 weeks
1020	Doxtator	Angela	✓	✓	☐	3 weeks
1023	Bulinkski	Aleksy	☐	☐	☐	3 weeks
1025	Biliski	Jorge	✓	✓	✓	4 weeks
1030	Hicks	Thom	☐	☐	☐	2 weeks
1033	Titov	Dina	✓	✓	✓	3 weeks
1040	Lafreniere	Guy	✓	✓	✓	3 weeks
1043	Morano	Enzo	✓	✓	✓	3 weeks
1045	Yiu	Terry	☐	☐	☐	2 weeks
1050	Zakowski	Carl	✓	☐	✓	2 weeks
1053	O'Connor	Shauna	✓	✓	✓	3 weeks
1060	McKnight	Donald	✓	✓	✓	3 weeks
1063	McPhee	Charlotte	✓	☐	✓	2 weeks
1065	Liszniewski	Norm	✓	✓	✓	2 weeks
1073	Judd	Marsha	✓	✓	✓	2 weeks
1080	Couture	Leo	✓	✓	☐	1 week
1083	Arnold	Drew	✓	☐	✓	1 week
1085	Armine	Yousef	☐	✓	✓	1 week
1090	Quinte	Maria	✓	☐	✓	1 week
1093	Vaquez	Luis	✓	✓	☐	1 week
1095	Kilarney	Patrick	☐	☐	☐	1 week

Activity 3.2

Creating a Query in Design View Using a Single Table

In Section 2 you learned to work with tables in Design view to define or modify the table structure. Similarly, a query can be created using Design view in which you define the structure of the query. In Design view, you begin by choosing the table you wish to select records from and then use the field list box to select the fields to display in the query results datasheet. When you have finished selecting fields, you instruct Access to display the records by switching to Datasheet view or by clicking the Run button.

Project

Rhonda Trask, human resources manager, has asked for a list of employees with their annual salary and hire date. You will produce the list by creating a query to obtain the required fields from the Employees table.

1 With the **WEEmployees3.accdb** database open and the Create tab active, click the Query Design button 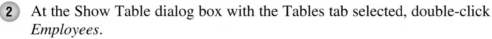 in the Queries group.

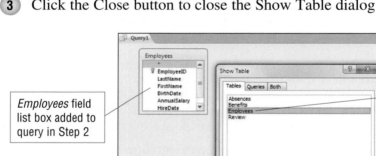

Tutorial 3.2
Creating Queries in
Design View

2 At the Show Table dialog box with the Tables tab selected, double-click *Employees*.

> A field list box for the Employees table is added to the query. The first step in building a query in Design view is to add a field list box for each table from which records will be selected.

3 Click the Close button to close the Show Table dialog box.

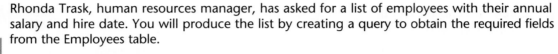

Employees field list box added to query in Step 2

Step 2

Step 3

4 Double-click *EmployeeID* in the *Employees* table field list box.

> The blank columns at the bottom represent the columns in the query results datasheet and are referred to as the *design grid*. You place the field names in the columns in the order in which you want the fields displayed in the query results datasheet. Double-clicking a field name adds the field to the next available column. In Steps 5 and 6, you will practice two other methods of adding fields to the design grid.

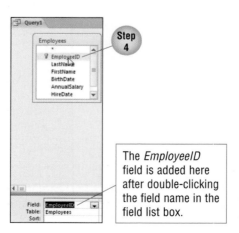

Step 4

The *EmployeeID* field is added here after double-clicking the field name in the field list box.

⑤ Position the mouse pointer on the *FirstName* field in the *Employees* table field list box, hold down the left mouse button, drag to the *Field* row in the second column of the design grid, and then release the mouse button.

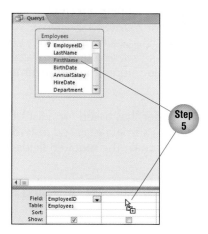

In Brief

Create Query in Design View with Single Table
1. Click Create tab.
2. Click Query Design button.
3. Double-click required table in Show Table dialog box.
4. Close Show Table dialog box.
5. Add required field names from field list box to columns in design grid.
6. Click Save button.
7. Type query name and click OK.
8. Click Run button.

⑥ Click in the *Field* row in the third column of the design grid, click the down-pointing arrow that appears, and then click *LastName* at the drop-down list.

⑦ Using any of the three methods learned in Steps 4–6, add the fields *AnnualSalary* and *HireDate* from the *Employees* table field list box to the design grid.

⑧ Click the Save button on the Quick Access toolbar.

⑨ At the Save As dialog box, type **SalaryList** in the *Query Name* text box and then press Enter or click OK.

⑩ Click the Run button in the Results group in the Query Tools Design tab.

> A query stores instructions on how to select data. The Run command instructs Access to carry out the instructions and display the results.

⑪ Print the datasheet.

⑫ Close the SalaryList query.

In Addition

Action Queries

In the last activity and in this activity, you created *select queries* that displayed selected fields from tables. Another type of query, called an *action query*, makes changes to a group of records. Four types of action queries are available in Access: delete, update, append, and make-table. A delete query deletes records. An update query makes global changes to a field. Append queries add a group of records from one table to the end of another table. A make-table query creates a new table from all or part of the data in existing tables.

Activity 3.3

Creating a Query in Design View Using Multiple Tables

Often a query is used to select records from more than one table. As you learned in the first activity, you were able to view records from the Employees table and the Benefits table in a query results datasheet. In Design view, multiple tables are added to the query at the Show Table dialog box. Once you have added a table field list box for each table, you can then add the fields to the design grid in the desired order using any one of the three methods learned in the last activity.

Project

Worldwide Enterprises

Tutorial 3.2
Creating Queries in Design View

Rhonda Trask, human resources manager, has asked for a list of employees along with each employee's hire date and review date. This data is stored in two different tables. You will produce the list by creating a query to obtain the required fields from each table to generate the list.

1. With the **WEEmployees3.accdb** database open and the Create tab active, click the Query Design button.

2. At the Show Table dialog box with the Tables tab selected, double-click *Employees*.

3. Double-click *Review* and then click the Close button to close the Show Table dialog box.

   A black join line with *1* at each end of the line between the Employees and the Review tables illustrates the one-to-one relationship that has been defined between the two tables.

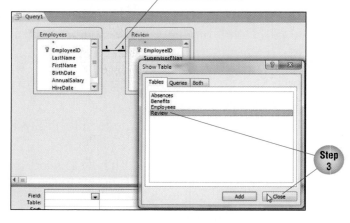

Join line indicates the relationship that has been defined between the two tables.

Step 3

4. Double-click *EmployeeID* in the *Employees* table field list box.

5. Double-click *FirstName* in the *Employees* table field list box.

6. Double-click *LastName* in the *Employees* table field list box.

7. Double-click *SupervisorFName* and *SupervisorLName* in the *Review* table field list box to add the fields from the second table to the design grid.

8. Double-click *HireDate* in the *Employees* table field list box.

   You can add fields in any order from either table to the design grid.

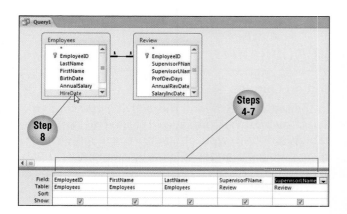

Step 8

Steps 4-7

9 Double-click *AnnualRevDate* in the *Review* table field list box.

10 Look at the table names in the *Table* row in the design grid. The table from which each field is associated is displayed so that you know in which table field list box the field originated.

Step 9

Step 10

11 Click the Save button on the Quick Access toolbar.

12 At the Save As dialog box, type **ReviewList** in the *Query Name* text box and then press Enter or click OK.

Step 12

13 Click the Run button in the Results group in the Query Tools Design tab.

Query results datasheet from Step 13

EmployeeID	FirstName	LastName	Supervisor First Name	Supervisor Last Name	HireDate	Annual Review Date
1013	Gregg	Chippewa	Sam	Vestering	2/10/2003	10-Feb-11
1015	Lyle	Besterd	Sam	Vestering	5/17/2003	17-May-11
1020	Angela	Doxtator	Celesta	Ruiz	8/3/2003	03-Aug-11
1023	Aleksy	Bulinkski	Sam	Vestering	10/10/2003	15-Oct-12
1025	Jorge	Biliski	Roman	Deptulski	12/1/2003	01-Dec-12
1030	Thom	Hicks	Roman	Deptulski	1/22/2004	22-Jan-12
1033	Dina	Titov	Roman	Deptulski	1/10/2004	01-Jan-12
1040	Guy	Lafreniere	Celesta	Ruiz	3/10/2005	10-Mar-12
1043	Enzo	Morano	Roman	Deptulski	8/15/2005	15-Aug-11
1045	Terry	Yiu	Celesta	Ruiz	1/31/2006	01-Jan-12
1050	Carl	Zakowski	Sam	Vestering	2/9/2006	09-Feb-11
1053	Shauna	O'Connor	Sam	Vestering	4/15/2007	15-Apr-11
1060	Donald	McKnight	Roman	Deptulski	6/22/2007	25-Jun-11
1063	Charlotte	McPhee	Celesta	Ruiz	2/6/2008	10-Feb-11
1065	Norm	Liszniewski	Sam	Vestering	2/6/2008	10-Feb-11
1073	Marsha	Judd	Roman	Deptulski	11/30/2009	30-Nov-11
1080	Leo	Couture	Roman	Deptulski	1/27/2010	27-Jan-11
1083	Drew	Arnold	Celesta	Ruiz	6/22/2010	22-Jun-11
1085	Yousef	Armine	Celesta	Ruiz	3/14/2010	14-Mar-11
1090	Maria	Quinte	Sam	Vestering	11/29/2010	30-Nov-11
1093	Luis	Vaquez	Sam	Vestering	12/5/2010	10-Dec-11
1095	Patrick	Kilarney	Celesta	Ruiz	12/12/2010	15-Dec-11

14 Display the datasheet in Print Preview, change the orientation to landscape, and then print the datasheet.

15 Close the Print Preview window and then close the ReviewList query.

In Brief

Create Query in Design View with Multiple Tables
1. Click Create tab.
2. Click Query Design button.
3. Double-click required tables in Show Table dialog box.
4. Close Show Table dialog box.
5. Add required field names from field list boxes to columns in design grid.
6. Click Save button.
7. Type query name and click OK.
8. Click Run button.

In Addition

More about Adding Tables to the Query Design Grid

If you have closed the Show Table dialog box and then realize that you need to add another table field list box to the query design grid, you do not need to start over again. The Show Table button in the Query Setup group of the Query Tools Design tab will redisplay the Show Table dialog box in which you can add more tables to the query design grid.

Click the Show Table button to add a table field list box to the query design grid.

Activity 3.4

Extracting Records Using Criteria Statements; Hiding Columns

In the previous queries, all records from the tables were displayed. Adding a criterion statement to the query design grid will cause Access to display only those records that meet the criterion. For example, you could generate a list of employees who are entitled to four weeks of vacation. Extracting specific records from the tables is where the true power in creating queries is found since you are able to separate out only those records that serve your purpose. By default, each check box in the *Show* row in the query design grid contains a check mark, meaning the column will be displayed in the query results datasheet. Clear the check mark from a field's *Show* box to hide the column in the query results datasheet.

Project

Worldwide Enterprises

Rhonda Trask has requested a list of employees who receive four weeks of vacation. Since you already have the employee names and vacation fields set up in an existing query, you decide to modify the query by adding the vacation criteria and then save the query using a new name.

SNAP

Tutorial 3.3
Using Criteria
Statements in
Queries

1 With the **WEEmployees3.accdb** database open, right-click the *BenefitPlans* query name in the Navigation pane and then click *Design View* at the shortcut menu.

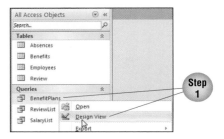

2 Click the File tab and then click the Save Object As Quick Command button 🔲 at the Backstage view.

3 Type **4WksVac** in the *Save 'BenefitPlans' to* text box at the Save As dialog box and then click OK.

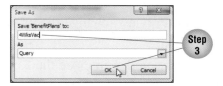

4 Click the Query Tools Design tab to return to the query design grid.

5 Click in the *Criteria* row in the *Vacation* column in the design grid (the blank row below the check box).

Before you type a criteria statement, make sure you have placed the insertion point in the *Criteria* box for the field by which you will be selecting records.

6 Type **4 weeks** and then press Enter.

The insertion point moves to the *Criteria* row in the next column and Access inserts quotation marks around *4 weeks* in the *Vacation* column. Since quotation marks are required in criteria statements for text fields, Access automatically inserts them if they are not typed into the *Criteria* text box.

7 Click the Run button in the Results group in the Query Tools Design tab.

8 View the query results in the datasheet and then click the View button in the Views group in the Home tab to switch to Design view. (Do *not* click the down-pointing arrow on the View button.)

In Brief

Add Criteria Statement to Query
1. Open query in Design view.
2. Click in *Criteria* row in column to attach criterion to.
3. Type criterion statement.
4. Save revised query.
5. Run query.

Since Rhonda Trask is interested only in the employee names and vacation weeks, you will instruct Access not to display the other fields in the query results datasheet.

9 Click the check box in the *Show* row in the *PensionPlan* column to clear the box.

Clearing the check box instructs Access to hide the column in the query results datasheet.

10 Clear the *Show* check box in the *DentalPlan* and *HealthPlan* columns in the design grid.

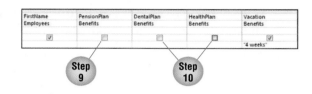

11 Click the View button to switch to Datasheet view.

The columns for which the *Show* check box was cleared do not display in the query results. Notice that you displayed the query results datasheet by switching views. Clicking the Run button or switching views accomplishes the same result for Select queries. For other types of queries, such as a delete query, the two buttons have different purposes.

12 Print the query results datasheet.

13 Close the 4WksVac query. Click Yes to save changes to the design of the query.

In Addition

Criteria Statement Examples

The following are examples of criteria statements for text, number, and date fields showing the proper syntax required by Access. Access inserts the quotation symbols (") automatically for text fields and the pound symbols (#) automatically for date fields when you type a valid entry in the Criteria box.

Criterion Statement	Records That Would Be Extracted
"Finance Department"	those with Finance Department in the field
Not "Finance Department"	all except those with Finance Department in the field
"Fan*"	those that begin Fan and end with any other characters in the field
>15000	those with a value greater than 15,000 in the field
#5/1/09#	those that contain the date May 1, 2009 in the field
>#5/1/09#	those that contain dates after May 1, 2009 in the field

Activity 3.5

Extracting Records Using AND Criteria; Sorting Query Results

You may need to select records by using more than one criterion. For example, you may wish to view records of those employees who have enrolled in more than one benefit plan. More than one column in the query design grid can have an entry in the *Criteria* box. Multiple criteria all entered in the same *Criteria* row becomes an *And* statement where each criterion must be met for the record to be selected. For example, the word Yes in both the *Criteria* box for the *PensionPlan* column and the *DentalPlan* column would mean a record would need to have a check mark in both check boxes in order for Access to display the record in the query results datasheet. Use the *Sort* row in the design grid to specify the field by which records should be sorted. Sort a query using the same principles as sorting a datasheet—columns are sorted from left to right for multiple sort keys.

Project

Tutorial 3.4
Using And/Or
Criteria in Queries

Rhonda Trask is reviewing salaries and has requested a list of employees who work in the North American Distribution department who earn over $45,000. You will create a new query in Design view to produce the list.

1. With the **WEEmployees3.accdb** database open, click the Create tab and then click the Query Design button.

2. At the Show Table dialog box, double-click the table named *Employees* and then click the Close button.

3. Double-click the following fields in order to add the fields to the design grid. *Note: You may have to scroll down the field list box to see all of the fields.*
   > FirstName
   > LastName
   > Department
   > HireDate
   > AnnualSalary

4. Click in the *Criteria* row in the *Department* column in the design grid, type **North American Distribution**, and then press Enter.

5. Position the mouse pointer on the right column boundary line for the *Department* field in the gray header row at the top of the design grid until the pointer changes to a black vertical line with a left- and right-pointing arrow and then double-click to best fit the column width.

6 Click in the *Criteria* row in the *AnnualSalary* column, type **>45000**, and then press Enter.

> Placing multiple criterion statements on the same row in the design grid means that each criterion must be satisfied in order for Access to select the record.

Department	HireDate	AnnualSalary	
Employees	Employees	Employees	Step 6
☑	☑	☑	
"North American Distribution"		>45000	

7 Click in the *Sort* row in the *LastName* column, click the down-pointing arrow that appears, and then click *Ascending* at the drop-down list.

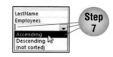

8 Click the Run button.

9 Review the records selected in the query results datasheet. Notice that the *Department* field value for each record is *North American Distribution* and the field values in the *AnnualSalary* column are all greater than $45,000. The list is also displayed sorted by the employee's last name.

FirstName ˅	LastName ˅	Department ˅	HireDate ˅	AnnualSalary ˅	
Lyle	Besterd	North American Distribution	5/17/2003	$45,651.00	
Angela	Doxtator	North American Distribution	8/3/2003	$45,558.00	Step 9
Enzo	Morano	North American Distribution	8/15/2005	$48,750.00	
Dina	Titov	North American Distribution	1/10/2004	$45,655.00	
Sam	Vestering	North American Distribution	7/22/2002	$69,725.00	

10 Click the Save button, type **NAHighSalary** in the *Query Name* text box, and then press Enter or click OK.

11 Print the query results datasheet.

12 Close the NAHighSalary query.

In Brief

Extracting Records Using AND Criteria
1. Start new query in Design view.
2. Add desired table(s) and field(s) to design grid.
3. Click in *Criteria* row in column in which to attach criterion.
4. Type criterion statement.
5. Repeat Steps 3–4 for the remaining criterion fields.
6. Save query.
7. Run query.

Sort Query Results
1. Open query in Design view.
2. Click in *Sort* row in field by which to sort.
3. Click down-pointing arrow.
4. Click *Ascending* or *Descending*.
5. Save query.
6. Run query.

In Addition

More AND Criteria Examples

The following are additional examples of AND criteria statements.

Criterion Statement in field named *PensionPlan*	Criterion Statement in field named *HireDate*	Criterion Statement in field named *AnnualSalary*	Records That Would Be Extracted
	>#1/1/2010#	>40000 And <50000	employees hired after January 1, 2010 who earn between 40 and 50 thousand
Yes	>#1/1/2004#	>45000	employees hired after January 1, 2004 who are enrolled in the Pension Plan and earn over 45 thousand
No	Between #1/1/2005# And #12/31/2010#	<50000	employees hired between January 1, 2005 and December 31, 2010 who are not enrolled in the Pension Plan and earn less than 50 thousand

Activity 3.6

Extracting Records Using OR Criteria

Multiple criterion statements on different rows in the query design grid becomes an OR statement in which any of the criterion can be met in order for Access to select the record. For example, in this activity you will generate a list of employees who are entitled to either three or four weeks of vacation. Creating select queries with OR statements is often done to generate mailing lists. Assume a business wants to create mailing labels for customers who live in Texas and Nevada. In this situation, the query to select the records needs to be an OR statement since the State field in a customer table would have Texas or Nevada in the field (it would not be possible to have both state names in the same record.)

Project

Worldwide Enterprises

SNAP

Tutorial 3.4
Using And/Or
Criteria in Queries

Rhonda Trask has requested a list of employees who receive either three or four weeks of vacation. Since you already have a query created that selected the records of employees with four weeks of vacation, you decide to modify the existing query by adding the second vacation criteria.

1. With the **WEEmployees3.accdb** database open, right-click the *4WksVac* query name in the Navigation pane and then click *Design View* at the shortcut menu.

2. Click the File tab and then click the Save Object As Quick Command button at the Backstage view.

3. Type **3or4WksVac** in the *Save '4WksVac' to* text box at the Save As dialog box and then click OK.

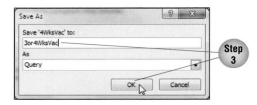

4. Click the Query Tools Design tab to return to the query design grid.

5. Click in the *or* row in the *Vacation* column in the design grid (blank row below *"4 weeks"*), type **3 weeks**, and then press Enter.

   Including a second criterion below the first one instructs Access to display records that meet either of the two criteria.

6. Click the Run button.

7 View the query results datasheet. Notice the records that have been selected contain either *4 weeks* or *3 weeks* in the *Vacation* column.

3or4WksVac			
EmployeeID	LastName	FirstName	Vacation
1000	Vestering	Sam	4 weeks
1003	Ruiz	Celesta	3 weeks
1005	Deptulski	Roman	3 weeks
1013	Chippewa	Gregg	3 weeks
1015	Besterd	Lyle	4 weeks
1020	Doxtator	Angela	3 weeks
1023	Bulinkski	Aleksy	3 weeks
1025	Biliski	Jorge	4 weeks
1033	Titov	Dina	3 weeks
1040	Lafreniere	Guy	3 weeks
1043	Morano	Enzo	3 weeks
1053	O'Connor	Shauna	3 weeks
1060	McKnight	Donald	3 weeks
*			

Step 7

8 Print the query results datasheet.

9 Click the Save button to save the revised query.

10 Close the 3or4WksVac query.

In Brief

Extracting Records Using OR Criteria
1. Start new query in Design view.
2. Add desired table(s) and field(s) to design grid.
3. Click in *Criteria* row in column in which to attach criterion.
4. Type criterion statement.
5. Click in the *or* row in column in which to attach next criterion.
6. Type criterion statement.
7. Repeat Steps 5–6 as necessary moving down one *Criteria* row for each new criterion.
8. Save query.
9. Run query.

In Addition

Combining AND and OR Criteria Statements

Assume that Rhonda Trask wants to further explore the vacation entitlements for the North American Distribution employees only. Rhonda wants a list of employees who work in the North American Distribution department *and* have four weeks of vacation *or* the North American Distribution department *and* have three weeks of vacation. To perform this query, you would use two rows in the design grid to enter the criteria as shown below. Note that the *Department* field has been added to the design grid.

Field:	EmployeeID	LastName	FirstName	Vacation	Department
Table:	Employees	Employees	Employees	Benefits	Employees
Sort:					
Show:	✓	✓	✓	✓	✓
Criteria:				"4 weeks"	"North American Distribution"
or:				"3 weeks"	"North American Distribution"

multiple AND/OR criteria

query results datasheet

EmployeeID	LastName	FirstName	Vacation	Department
1000	Vestering	Sam	4 weeks	North American Distribution
1003	Ruiz	Celesta	3 weeks	North American Distribution
1015	Besterd	Lyle	4 weeks	North American Distribution
1020	Doxtator	Angela	3 weeks	North American Distribution
1025	Biliski	Jorge	4 weeks	North American Distribution
1033	Titov	Dina	3 weeks	North American Distribution
1043	Morano	Enzo	3 weeks	North American Distribution
1053	O'Connor	Shauna	3 weeks	North American Distribution

Activity 3.7

Performing Calculations in a Query

Calculations involving mathematical operations such as adding or multiplying a field value can be included in a query. In a blank field text box in Query Design view, type the text that you want to appear as the column heading followed by a colon (:) and then the mathematical expression for the calculated values. Field names in the mathematical expression are encased in square brackets. For example, the entry *TotalSalary:[BaseSalary]+[Commission]* would add the value in the field named *BaseSalary* to the value in the field named *Commission*. The result would be placed in a new column in the query datasheet with the column heading *TotalSalary*. Calculated columns do not exist in the associated table; the values are calculated dynamically each time the query is run. Numeric format and decimal places for calculated columns are set using the property sheet in Design view.

Project

Tutorial 3.5
Performing Calculations in a Query

Worldwide Enterprises contributes 3% of each employee's annual salary to a registered pension plan. You will create a new query to calculate the employer's annual pension contributions.

1 With the **WEEmployees3.accdb** database open, click the Create tab and then click the Query Design button.

2 At the Show Table dialog box, double-click the table named *Employees* and then click the Close button.

3 Double-click the following fields in the order shown to add the fields to the design grid.
> *EmployeeID*
> *FirstName*
> *LastName*
> *AnnualSalary*

4 Click in the blank *Field* row next to the *AnnualSalary* column in the design grid.

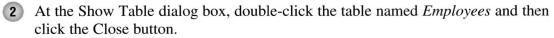

5 Type **PensionContribution:[AnnualSalary]*.03** and then press Enter.

Need Help?

Did a message appear stating that the expression contains invalid syntax? Check that you have used the correct type of brackets, typed a colon, and that there are no other typing errors.

6 Position the mouse pointer on the right vertical boundary line for the *PensionContribution* column in the gray field selector bar at the top of the design grid until the pointer changes to a black vertical line with a left- and right-pointing arrow and then double-click the left mouse button.

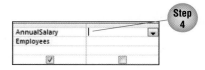

(7) Click the Save button. At the Save As dialog box, type **PensionCont** in the *Query Name* text box and then press Enter or click OK.

(8) Click the Run button.

(9) In the query results datasheet, adjust the column width for the *PensionContribution* column to Best Fit.

> The values in the calculated column need to be formatted to display a consistent number of decimal places. You will correct this in the next steps by changing the format option in the *PensionContribution* field's *Field Properties* sheet.

(10) Switch to Design view.

(11) Click the insertion point anywhere within the *PensionContribution* field row in the design grid.

(12) Click the Property Sheet button 📷 in the Show/Hide group of the Query Tools Design tab.

> Available properties for the active field display in the Property Sheet task pane at the right side of the work area.

(13) Click in the *Format* property box in the Property Sheet task pane, click the down-pointing arrow that appears, and then click *Currency* at the drop-down list.

(14) Click the Close button at the top right of the Property Sheet task pane.

(15) Click the Save button and then click the Run button.

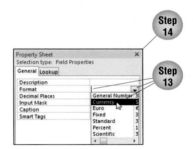

(16) Click the Totals button Σ in the Records group of the Home tab to add a total row to the bottom of the datasheet and then add a Sum function to the bottom of the *AnnualSalary* and *PensionContribution* columns. ***Note: Refer to Activity 2.8 if you need assistance with this step.***

PensionCont				
EmployeeID ▾	FirstName ▾	LastName ▾	AnnualSalary ▾	PensionContribution ▾
1000	Sam	Vestering	$69,725.00	$2,091.75
1003	Celesta	Ruiz	$41,875.00	$1,256.25
1005	Roman	Deptulski	$72,750.00	$2,182.50
1013	Gregg	Chippewa	$48,650.00	$1,459.50
1015	Lyle	Besterd	$45,651.00	$1,369.53
1020	Angela	Doxtator	$45,558.00	$1,366.74
1023	Aleksy	Bulinkski	$51,450.00	$1,543.50
1025	Jorge	Biliski	$44,892.00	$1,346.76
1030	Thom	Hicks	$42,824.00	$1,284.72
1033	Dina	Titov	$45,655.00	$1,369.65
1040	Guy	Lafreniere	$45,395.00	$1,361.85
1043	Enzo	Morano	$48,750.00	$1,462.50
1045	Terry	Yiu	$42,238.00	$1,267.14
1050	Carl	Zakowski	$44,387.00	$1,331.61
1053	Shauna	O'Connor	$43,695.00	$1,310.85
1060	Donald	McKnight	$42,126.00	$1,263.78
1063	Charlotte	McPhee	$43,695.00	$1,310.85
1065	Norm	Liszniewski	$43,695.00	$1,310.85
1073	Marsha	Judd	$44,771.00	$1,343.13
1080	Leo	Couture	$43,659.00	$1,309.77
1083	Drew	Arnold	$43,659.00	$1,309.77
1085	Yousef	Armine	$42,177.00	$1,265.31
1090	Maria	Quinte	$42,177.00	$1,265.31
1093	Luis	Vaquez	$42,177.00	$1,265.31
1095	Patrick	Kilarney	$42,177.00	$1,265.31
*				
	Total		$1,163,808.00	$34,914.24

(17) Print the query results datasheet.

(18) Close the PensionCont query. Click Yes when prompted to save changes to the query.

Step 14
Step 13
Step 16

> Property Sheet ✕
> Selection type: Field Properties
> General | Lookup
> Description
> Format
> Decimal Places — General Number
> Input Mask — Currency
> Caption — Euro
> Smart Tags — Fixed
> — Standard
> — Percent
> — Scientific

In Brief

Create Calculated Field in Query
1. Open query in Design view.
2. Click in first available blank field row in design grid.
3. Type column heading for calculated field.
4. Type a colon (:).
5. Type the mathematical expression.
6. Press Enter or click in another field.
7. Click Save button.
8. Click Run button.

Format Calculated Field
1. Open query in Design view.
2. Click in field containing calculated expression.
3. Click Query Tools Design tab.
4. Click Property Sheet button.
5. Click in *Format* property box.
6. Click down-pointing arrow.
7. Click desired format at drop-down list.
8. Close Property Sheet task pane.
9. Save query.
10. Run query.

Activity 3.8

Creating and Editing Forms Using Form Tools

Recall from Section 1 that forms provide a user-friendly interface for viewing, adding, editing, and deleting records. The Form button creates a new form with one mouse click. All fields in the selected table are added to the form in a columnar layout. The form appears in the work area in Layout view, which is used to make changes to the form. Three Form Layout Tools tabs become active when a form has been created. Use buttons in the Form Layout Tools Design tab to change the theme or add new objects to the form. The Form Layout Tools Arrange tab contains buttons to rearrange the fields from columnar to tabular or stacked or to otherwise modify the position of the objects on the form. To make changes to the form's font, font attributes, or other format characteristics, use the Form Layout Tools Format tab. In the Form Wizard, the user is guided through a series of dialog boxes to generate the form, including selecting the fields to be included and the form layout.

Project

Tutorial 3.6
Creating a Form

Tutorial 3.7
Modifying a Form

You decide to create two forms for the assistant who works with you since she prefers to see only one record at a time while entering data. One form will be used to record employee absences and the other form will be used to enter new employee records.

1. With the **WEEmployees3.accdb** database open, click once on the *Absences* table name in the Navigation pane.

   In order to create a form using the Form tool, you first select the table or query object upon which to base the new form.

2. Click the Create tab and then click the Form button in the Forms group.

   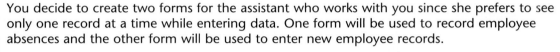

   Access creates the form using all fields in the table in a vertical layout and displays the form in Layout view with the Form Layout Tools Design tab active.

3. Click the View button in the Views group of the Form Layout Tools Design tab to switch to Form view.

   Similar to Tables and Queries, using the View button you can switch back and forth between the Form view where you view the data and Layout view where you make changes to the form's appearance and structure.

4. Click the Next record button on the Record Navigation bar a few times to scroll through a few records in Form view.

5. Click the View button in the Views group of the Home tab to return to Layout view.

   In the next few steps you will edit the form to change the theme and edit the form's title.

6. Click the Themes button in the Themes group of the Form Layout Tools Design tab and then click *Clarity* (second option in third row of *Built-In* section) at the drop-down gallery.

   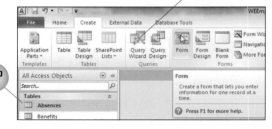

   Themes in the Microsoft Office suite are standardized across the applications. A business can apply a consistent look to documents, spreadsheets, presentations, and databases by using the same theme in each application.

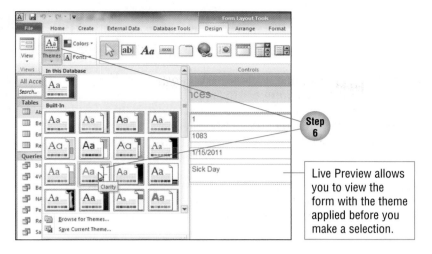

In Brief

Create Form Using Form Button
1. Click once to select table name in Navigation pane.
2. Click Create tab.
3. Click Form button.

Create Form Using Form Wizard
1. Click Create tab.
2. Click Form Wizard button.
3. Choose table for which to create form.
4. Select fields to include in form.
5. Click Next.
6. Choose form layout.
7. Click Next.
8. Type form title.
9. Click Finish.

Live Preview allows you to view the form with the theme applied before you make a selection.

(7) Click the Form Layout Tools Format tab.

(8) Position the mouse pointer over the form's title *Absences* and then click to select the title's control object.

> A form is comprised of a series of objects referred to as **controls**. To make changes to a form, you generally select the control object first for the form element that you want to change.

(9) Click the Font Size button 18 in the Font group of the Form Layout Tools Format tab and then click *24* at the drop-down list.

(10) Position the mouse pointer inside the selected title *Absences* and then click to position an insertion point inside the title control object. Use the left and right arrow keys and insert and delete text as necessary to change the form's title to *Employee Absence Report*.

(11) Close the Absences form. Click Yes to save the changes to the form's design and then click OK at the Save As dialog box to accept the default form name *Absences*.

(12) Click the Create tab and then click the Form Wizard button in the Forms group.

(13) At the first Form Wizard dialog box, click the down-pointing arrow at the right of the *Tables/Queries* list box and then click *Table: Employees* at the drop-down list.

(14) Click the Add All Fields button >> to move all of the fields in the *Available Fields* list box to the *Selected Fields* list box and then click Next.

(15) At the second Form Wizard dialog box with *Columnar* already selected as the form layout, click Next.

(16) Click Finish at the last Form Wizard dialog box to accept the default title of *Employees* and *Open the form to view or enter information*.

> The completed form appears in Form view in the work area.

(17) Click the Next record button on the Record Navigation bar a few times to scroll through a few records in Form view and then close the Employees form.

Activity 3.9

Adding Fields to a Form from Another Table

When two tables have been joined by a relationship, you can add fields from a related table to a form. For example, in the Absences form created in the previous activity, the names of the employees are not on the form because the first and last name fields are not in the Absences table. It would be helpful to be able to see the employee's name while entering an absence report so that the correct employee ID can be verified as a new record is being added. You can add fields from another table to a form using the Field List pane in Layout view.

Project You will edit the Absences form to add the employee's first and last names from the Employees table.

Tutorial 3.7
Modifying a Form

1. With the **WEEmployees3.accdb** database open, double-click the *Absences* form name in the Navigation pane to open the form.

2. Click the View button in the Views group of the Home tab to switch to Layout view.

3. With the Form Layout Tools Design tab active, click the Add Existing Fields button in the Tools group.

Step 3

The Field List pane opens at the right side of the work area in one of two states: with one section titled *Fields available for this view* and with a <u>Show all tables</u> link at the top of the Field List task pane; or, with three sections titled *Fields available for this view, Fields available in related tables,* and *Fields available in other tables.* A <u>Show only fields in the current record source</u> link is at the top of the Field List task pane when it displays three sections.

4. Click <u>Show all tables</u> located at the top of the Field List pane just above the Status bar. ***Note: Skip this step if the link at the top of the Field List task pane on your computer reads* Show only fields in the current record source.**

Step 4

Clicking *Show all tables* in the Field List task pane displays two new sections: *Fields available in related tables* and *Fields available in other tables*. Within each section box, each table name displays with an expand button (plus symbol) with which you can display the fields in the related table.

5. Click the expand button next to the *Employees* table name in the *Fields available in related tables* list box to expand the list.

Step 5

6. Click to select *FirstName* in the expanded *Employees* table field list.

In the next step, you will add the field by dragging and dropping the field name to the desired position on the form.

7. Position the mouse pointer over the selected *FirstName* field in the Field List pane, hold down the left mouse button, drag the field name to the form between the *EmployeeID* and *Absent Date* fields, and then release the mouse button.

As you drag the field over the form, a gold bar indicates where the field will be positioned between existing fields. When you release the mouse the field is added to the form. The Field List pane updates to move the Employees table to the *Fields available for this view* section. By adding a field from the related table, Employees is now associated with the Absences form.

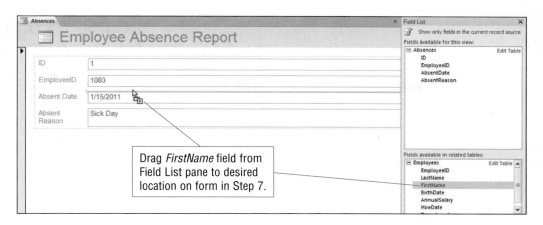

Drag *FirstName* field from Field List pane to desired location on form in Step 7.

(8) Position the mouse pointer over the *LastName* field in the *Fields available for this view* section of the Field List pane, hold down the left mouse button, drag the field name to the form between the *FirstName* and *Absent Date* fields and then release the mouse button.

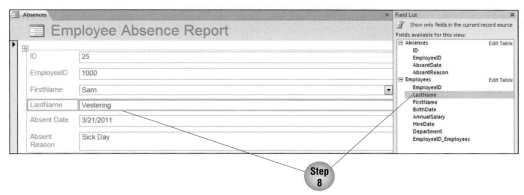

(9) Click the Close button located at the top right of the Field List pane to close the pane.

(10) Click the Save button to save the revised form design.

(11) Switch to Form view and scroll through a few records.

The addition of the employee's first and last names to the form makes the form easier to use. In the next step you will add a new record using the form to see how the employees' names will populate automatically once you enter a valid EmployeeID.

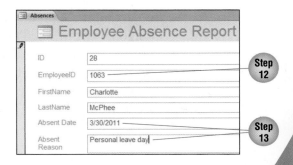

(12) Click the New button 🔳 in the Records group of the Home tab, press Tab to move past the *ID* AutoNumber field, type **1063** in the *EmployeeID* field, and then press Tab or Enter.

Access automatically displays *Charlotte* in the *FirstName* field and *McPhee* in the *LastName* field. Since the Employees and Absences tables are related, Access matched the *EmployeeID* field values and displayed the two field entries from the primary table.

(13) Press Tab twice to move to the *AbsentDate* field, type **3/30/2011**, press Tab, type **Personal leave day** in the *AbsentReason* field, and then press Enter.

(14) Close the Absences form.

Activity 3.10

Adding a Logo; Resizing and Editing Objects

As you learned in a previous activity, a form is comprised of a series of objects referred to as **controls**. Each field from the table has a **label control** and a **text box control** placed side-by-side, with the label control object placed first. The label control contains the field name or the caption property text if a caption has been added to the field's properties. The text box control is the field placeholder where data is entered or edited. The controls can be moved, resized, formatted, or deleted from the form. You can format label controls separately from the text box controls. Additional control objects such as a logo or date can be added to the form using buttons in the Form Layout Tools Design tab.

Project

Tutorial 3.8
Adding and Modifying Objects

You decide to further customize the Absences form by adding the Worldwide Enterprises logo and resizing the controls in which data is typed. To complete the form, you will edit the label control objects so they all show spaces between the words.

1 With the **WEEmployees3.accdb** database open, right-click the *Absences* form name in the Navigation pane and then click *Layout View* at the shortcut menu.

2 Click to select the logo container control object at the top left of the form next to the title, *Employee Absence Report*.

3 Click the Logo button in the Header/ Footer group in the Form Layout Tools Design tab.

4 At the Insert Picture dialog box, navigate to the AccessS3 folder on your storage medium if AccessS3 is not the current folder and then double-click *WELogo-Small.jpg*.

5 Position the mouse pointer on the bottom right corner of the selected logo control object until the pointer changes to a diagonal two-headed arrow, hold down the left mouse button, and drag the control to the approximate height and width shown. Resize the object as necessary until you can see the entire logo within the control object.

6 Click the *ID* text box control. This is the control object that displays the data next to the label *ID*.

The controls in which data is typed are much wider than necessary. In the next steps, you will shorten these controls.

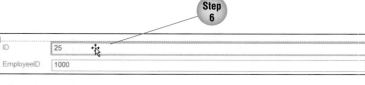

7 Hold down the Shift key and then click each of the text box controls below *ID* to *Absent Reason* (contains the text *Sick Day*).

Use the Shift key to select multiple control objects in a form or report.

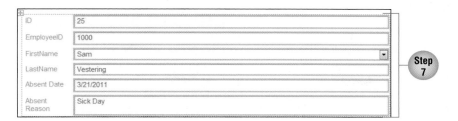

In Brief

Add Logo to Form
1. Open form in Layout view.
2. Click logo container object.
3. Click Logo button.
4. Navigate to location of graphic file.
5. Double-click graphic file name.

Resize Control Object
1. Open form in Layout view.
2. Select desired control object.
3. Point to left, right, top, or bottom edge, or to corner.
4. Drag height or width to desired size.

(8) Position the mouse pointer on the right edge of any of the selected control objects until the pointer changes to a left- and right-pointing arrow, drag the right border left to the approximate width shown below (align at the space between *Absence* and *Report* in the title), and then release the mouse.

(9) Click in a blank area of the form to deselect the control objects.

> In the next steps you will edit the field names in the label control objects that currently do not show a space between words, in order to improve the readability of the labels.

(10) Click to select the *EmployeeID* label control object. This is the control object to the left of the data.

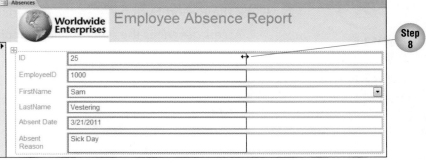

Step 8

(11) Click the *EmployeeID* label control object a second time to place an insertion point inside the selected control.

(12) Use the left and right arrow keys as needed to move the insertion point between *e* and *I* in *EmployeeID*, press the spacebar to insert a space, and then press Enter.

Steps 10-12

(13) Click to select the *FirstName* label control object. Click the *FirstName* label control object a second time, move the insertion point between *t* and *N*, press the spacebar, and then press Enter.

Step 13

(14) Insert a space in the *LastName* label control object between *t* and *N*.

(15) Switch to Form view.

(16) Scroll through the records in the form until you reach the absence report for *EmployeeID* 1063 (Charlotte McPhee).

(17) Click the File tab, click Print, and then click the Print button.

(18) At the Print dialog box, click the Setup button and then click the Columns tab. Select the current value in the *Width* text box in the *Column Size* section, type **8**, and then click OK. Click *Selected Record(s)* in the *Print Range* section of the Print dialog box and then click OK.

> Scroll through the records until you reach the absent report for *EmployeeID* 1063 (Charlotte McPhee) in Step 16.

(19) Close the Absences form. Click Yes when prompted to save changes to the form's design.

Activity 3.11

Creating and Editing a Report

Information from the database can be printed while viewing tables in Datasheet view, while viewing a query results datasheet, or while browsing through forms. In these printouts all of the fields are printed in a tabular layout for datasheets or in the designed layout for forms. Create a report when you want to specify which fields to print and to have more control over the report layout and format. Access includes a Report button similar to the Form button that can be used to generate a report with one mouse click. Reports are created for viewing and printing purposes only. You cannot add or edit data while viewing a report.

Project

Rhonda Trask, human resources manager, has requested a hard copy of the NAHighSalary query. You decide to experiment with the Report feature to print the data.

Worldwide Enterprises

1. With the **WEEmployees3.accdb** database open, click the *NAHighSalary* query name in the Navigation pane and then click the Create tab.

   As with the Form tool, a table or query is selected first before clicking the Report button.

SNAP

Tutorial 3.9
Creating a Report

Tutorial 3.10
Modifying a Report

2. Click the Report button in the Reports group.

   Access generates the report using a tabular layout with records displayed in rows. A title along with the current day, date, and time are placed automatically at the top of the report as well as a container for an image such as a logo placed at the left of the title text.

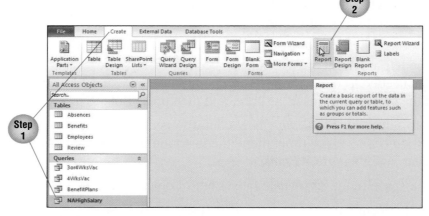

3. Double-click the title text to place an insertion point inside the label control object.

4. Delete the existing query name that was added as the title text, type **Employees in North American Distribution**, press Shift + Enter to insert a line break, type **Earning over $45,000**, and then press Enter.

5. With the title label control object still selected, click the Report Layout Tools Format tab, click the Font Size button arrow in the Font group, and then click *14* at the drop-down list.

6. Click in a blank area of the report to deselect the title label control object.

7. Click the Auto_Logo container control object located next to the report title.

8 Click the Report Layout Tools Design tab and then click the Logo button in the Header/Footer group.

9 At the Insert Picture dialog box, navigate to the AccessS3 folder on your storage medium if AccessS3 is not the current folder and then double-click *WELogo-Small.jpg*. Resize the logo object to the approximate height and width shown below.

In Brief
Create Report Using Report Tool
1. Click object name in Navigation pane.
2. Click Create tab.
3. Click Report button.

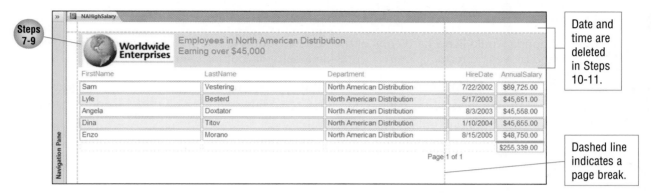

Steps 7-9

Date and time are deleted in Steps 10-11.

Dashed line indicates a page break.

10 Click the current date located at the top right of the report to select the object and then press Delete.

11 Click the current time located at the top right of the report to select the object and then press Delete.

12 Minimize the Navigation pane by clicking the Shutter Bar Open/Close button (displays as left-pointing chevrons) at the top of the Navigation pane.

13 Notice the dashed line between the *Department* and *HireDate* columns indicating a page break.

14 Click the Report Layout Tools Page Setup tab.

15 Click the Landscape button in the Page Layout group.

The page break disappears indicating all columns now fit on one page.

16 Click the Save button. At the Save As dialog box, click OK to accept the default report name *NAHighSalary*.

17 Print and then close the report.

18 Redisplay the Navigation pane.

Step 15

Step 14

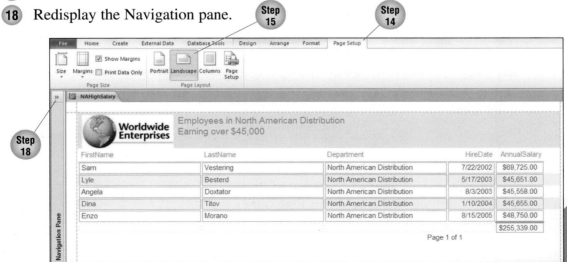

Step 18

Activity 3.12

Resizing and Moving Columns in a Report

Once a report has been created, the report can be modified by opening it in Layout view. A report is similar to a form in that it is comprised of a series of objects referred to as controls. A report can be modified using techniques similar to those learned in the activities related to form creation and editing.

Project

Rhonda would like a hard copy of the ReviewList query. You decide to create a new report and move and resize columns to provide a better layout for the report.

Worldwide Enterprises

SNAP

Tutorial 3.10
Modifying a Report

1. With the **WEEmployees3.accdb** database open, click the *ReviewList* query name in the Navigation pane, click the Create tab, and then click the Report button.

2. Minimize the Navigation pane.

3. With the report displayed in Layout view, click to select the *HireDate* column heading.

4. Hold down the Shift key and then click over the data below the *HireDate* column heading.

   This selects the entire column as indicated by the gold border around all of the entries in the column.

5. Position the pointer inside the selected *HireDate* column, until the pointer displays with the four-headed move icon attached.

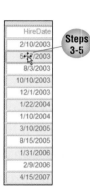

6. Drag the column left between the *LastName* and *Supervisor First Name* columns.

   A vertical gold bar indicates the location at which the column will be placed when you release the mouse.

Drag selected column left between *LastName* and *Supervisor First Name* columns in Step 6.

7. Click the *FirstName* column heading.

8. Position the mouse pointer on the right border of the selected column heading until the pointer displays as a left- and right-pointing arrow and then drag left to decrease the column width to the approximate width shown.

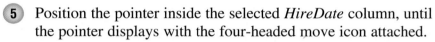
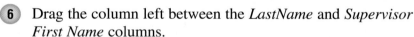

Steps 7-8

⑨ Decrease the width of the *LastName*, *Supervisor First Name*, and *Supervisor Last Name* columns to the approximate width shown below by completing steps similar to those in Steps 7–8.

⑩ Click the Report Layout Tools Page Setup tab and change the orientation to landscape.

⑪ Edit the title text to *Employee Review List*.

⑫ Click to select the *Auto_Logo* container object and then press Delete to remove the control object.

In Brief

Move Report Columns
1. Open report in Layout view.
2. Click column heading.
3. Shift + click over data below column heading.
4. Position mouse pointer inside selected column.
5. Drag column to desired location.
6. Save report.

Resize Report Columns
1. Open report in Layout view.
2. Click column heading.
3. Drag right or left border of selected column heading to desired width.
4. Save report.

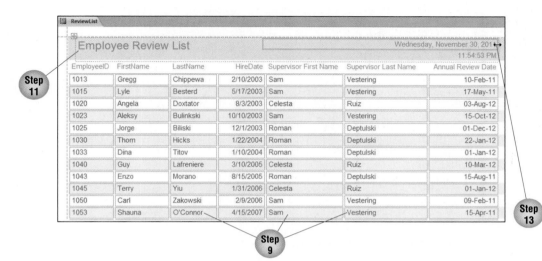

⑬ Click to select the control object that contains the current day and date. Position the mouse pointer on the right edge of the selected control until the pointer changes to a left- and right-pointing arrow and drag right until the right edge of the date aligns with the right edge of the last column.

> Access prints the current day, date, and time on all reports. In businesses with time-sensitive report needs, the inclusion of these controls is important.

⑭ Save the report accepting the default report name of *ReviewList*.

⑮ Print and then close the ReviewList report.

⑯ Redisplay the Navigation pane and then close **WEEmployees3.accdb**.

In Addition

Report Sections

A report is divided into five sections described below.

Report Section	Description
Report Header	Controls in this section are printed once at the beginning of the report, such as the report title.
Page Header	Controls in this section are printed at the top of each page, such as column headings.
Detail	Controls in this section make up the body of the report by printing the data from the associated table or query.
Page Footer	Controls in this section are printed at the bottom of each page, such as the report date and page numbers.
Report Footer	Controls in this section are printed once at the end of the report, such as column totals.

Features Summary

Feature	Ribbon Tab, Group	Button	Keyboard Shortcut
add fields to a form	Form Layout Tools Design, Tools		
create query in Design view	Create, Queries		
Design view	Home, Views		
Form tool	Create, Forms		
Form view	Home, Views		
Form Wizard	Create, Forms		
insert logo in form or report	Form Layout Tools Design, Header/Footer OR Report Layout Tools Design, Header/Footer		
Layout view	Home, Views		
minimize navigation pane			
property sheet in query	Query Tools Design, Show/Hide		Alt + Enter
redisplay navigation pane			
Report tool	Create, Reports		
run a query	Query Tools Design, Results		
Simple Query Wizard	Create, Queries		

Knowledge Check

Completion: In the space provided at the right, indicate the correct term, command, or option.

1. This is the name of the wizard used to facilitate creating a query to select records from a table. _____

2. Click this button to show the query results datasheet after creating a query using Design view. _____

3. Type this entry in the *AnnualSalary* criteria row in the query design grid to extract records of employees who earn more than $40,000. _____

4. Click the check box in this row in the query design grid to prevent a column from being displayed in the query results datasheet. _____

5. Multiple criteria typed in the same *Criteria* row in the query design grid become this type of statement. _____

6. Multiple criteria typed in different *Criteria* rows in the query design grid become this type of statement. _____

7. This entry in a blank field text box in the query design grid would add the values in a field named *RegHours* to the values in a field named *OTHours* and title the column in the query results datasheet *TotalHours*. _____

8. Click this button in the Query Tools Design tab to change a field's format to display in Currency. _____

9. These three tabs become active when the form is displayed in Layout view. _____

10. Create a form using this method if you want the ability to specify the form's layout before the form is generated. _____

11. A form or report is comprised of a series of objects referred to by this term. _____

12. This button opens the Field List pane to add fields from another table to the form. _____

13. A form created using the Form button adds this object next to the title so you can easily add an image such as a company logo. _____

14. List two items that are added to the top of a report automatically when the report is generated using the Report tool. _____

15. A report's page orientation can be changed from portrait to landscape at this Report Layout Tools tab. _____

Skills Review

Review 1 Creating a Query Using the Simple Query Wizard; Sorting a Query; Creating a Calculated Field; Extracting Records

1. Open the **WEEmployees3.accdb** database and click the Enable Content button if the Security Warning message bar appears.
2. Use the Simple Query Wizard to create a query that displays fields from the Employees and Benefits tables in order as follows:

Employees	**Benefits**
EmployeeID	*LifeInsce*
FirstName	
LastName	
HireDate	
AnnualSalary	

3. Accept the default Detail query and type LifeInsceList as the title for the query.
4. View the query results datasheet and then switch to Design view.
5. Sort the query results by the *LastName* field in ascending order.
6. Create a calculated field in the column after *LifeInsce* that divides *AnnualSalary* by 12 and label the new column *MonthlySalary*.
7. Format *MonthlySalary* to display the calculated values in the Currency format.
8. Save and run the query and then adjust the column width of *MonthlySalary* to Best Fit.
9. Print the query results datasheet with the left and right margins at 0.5 inch.
10. Use Save Object As to copy the query design and name it *HiresAfter2004*.
11. Switch to Design view and then type >December 31, 2004 in the *Criteria* row of the *HireDate* column. ***Note: Access will convert the text you type to >#12/31/2004# after you press Enter***.
12. Save and then run the query.
13. Print the query results datasheet with the left and right margins set to 0.5 inch and then close the HiresAfter2004 query.

Review 2 Creating and Modifying a Form

1. With the **WEEmployees3.accdb** database open, create a new form for the Review table using the Form button.
2. With the form open in Layout view, make the following changes to the form design.
    a. Add the logo named **WELogo-Small.jpg** to the top left of the form and resize the image until the entire logo image is visible.
    b. Change the title text to *Annual Review and Salary Increase Dates*.
    c. Change the font size of the title text to 20.
    d. Resize the text box control objects containing the data to align the right edge of the objects below the end of the word *Salary* in the title text.
3. Save the revised form, accepting the default name *Review*.
4. Switch to Form view and then display the Print dialog box. Click the Setup button, click the Columns tab, change the *Width* to **8**, and then click OK. Click *Selected Record(s)* in the *Print Range* section of the Print dialog box and then click OK.
5. Close the form. Click Yes if prompted to save changes to the form's design.

Review 3 Creating and Modifying a Report

1. With the **WEEmployees3.accdb** database open, use the Report button to create a report based on the LifeInsceList query.
2. With the report open in Layout view, make the following changes to the report design.
   a. Add the logo named **WELogo-Small.jpg** to the top of the report and resize the image as needed until the entire logo image is visible.
   b. Change the title text to *Salary and Life Insurance Report*.
   c. Change the font size of the title text to 20.
   d. Change the page orientation to landscape.
   e. Move the *LifeInsce* column between *HireDate* and *AnnualSalary*.
   f. Decrease the width of the *FirstName* and *LastName* columns approximately 0.25 inch.
   g. Increase the width of the *Life Insurance* and *AnnualSalary* columns approximately 0.25 inch.
   h. Edit column heading labels for those field names that do not have a space between compound words. For example, edit *FirstName* to *First Name*.
3. Change the report theme to *Composite* (third option in third row of *Built-In* section).
4. Scroll to the bottom of the report. Select and then delete any totals that appear below columns. *Note: You may also have to delete an underscore before a total. To do this, click the cell where the line appears and then press Delete.*
5. Display the report in Print Preview. Click the Columns button in the Page Layout group of the Print Preview tab. Select the current value in the *Width* text box, type **10**, and then press Enter.
6. Save the report accepting the default name *LifeInsceList*.
7. Print and then close the report.
8. Close **WEEmployees3.accdb**.

Skills Assessment

Assessment 1   Creating a Query in Design View; Sorting a Query; Extracting Records Using Multiple Criteria

1. The Bursary Selection Committee at Niagara Peninsula College would like you to provide them with the names of students who have achieved an A+ in all three of their courses. To begin, open **NPCGrades3.accdb** and click the Enable Content button if the Security Warning message bar appears.
2. Create a query in Design view that extracts the records of those students with an A+ grade in all three courses using the following specifications:
    a. Add all three tables to the query design grid and then drag the primary key field name from the first table field list box to the second table field list box. This creates a join line between the first two tables on the *StudentNo* field.
    b. Drag the primary key field from the second table field list box to the third table field list box to create a join line between the second and third tables on the *StudentNo* field.
    c. Include in the query results the student number, first name, last name, and grade from the first table field list box and sort in ascending order by last name.
    d. Add the grade field from the second and third tables to the design grid.
    e. Enter the required criteria statements to select the records of those students who achieved A+ in all three courses. ***Hint: Type A+ encased in quotation marks ("A+")*** *in the* **Criteria** *row to indicate the plus symbol is not part of a mathematical expression*.
3. Save the query and name it *A+Students*.
4. Run the query.
5. Best Fit the columns in the query results datasheet.
6. Print the query results datasheet in landscape orientation.
7. Close the A+Students query saving changes and then close **NPCGrades3.accdb**.

Assessment 2 Creating a Query and Report; Modifying a Report

1. Bobbie Sinclair, business manager, would like a report that lists the costumes that were rented in July and August 2011. To begin, open the **PTCostumeInv3.accdb** database and click the Enable Content button if the Security Warning message bar appears.
2. Create a new query in Design view using the CostumeInventory table that lists fields in the following order: *CostumeNo, DateOut, DateIn, CostumeTitle, DailyRentalFee.*
3. Type the following criterion statement in the *DateOut* column to extract records for costumes rented in the months of July and August 2011:

    Between July 1, 2011 and August 31, 2011
4. Expand the column width of the *DateOut* column to view the entire criterion statement. Notice Access converted the long dates to short dates and added pound symbols to the beginning and end of dates in the criterion statement.
5. Sort the query results in ascending order first by *DateOut*, then by *DateIn*, and then by *CostumeTitle*.
6. Save the query and name it *Summer2011Rentals*.
7. Run the query.
8. Close the query after viewing the query results datasheet.
9. Create a report based on the Summer2011Rentals query using the Report button.
10. Add the logo image **PTLogo-Small.jpg** to the top of the report and resize the image as needed so that the entire logo image is visible.
11. Change the title text to *Costume Rentals for July and August 2011* and change the font size to 16.
12. Adjust column widths in the report until all columns fit on the page in portrait orientation. Move and/or resize any other control objects as necessary so that the entire report fits on one page to print. ***Hint: Make sure you check the page numbering control objects at the bottom of the page***.
13. Adjust the page layout to fit the report on one page.
14. Save the report accepting the default name *Summer2011Rentals* and then print the report.
15. Close the report and then close **PTCostumeInv3.accdb**.

Assessment 3 Creating and Modifying a Form

1. Staff at Performance Threads have mentioned that working in the datasheet for CostumeInventory is useful for looking up information but they would prefer a form for entering new records. You decide to create a costume rental form for the staff. To begin, open the **PTCostumeInv3.accdb** database and click the Enable Content button if the Security Warning message bar appears.
2. Create a form for the CostumeInventory table.
3. Change the theme for the form. You choose the theme.
4. Add the logo image **PTLogo-Small.jpg** to the top of the form and resize the image as needed so that the entire logo image is visible.
5. Change the title of the form. You determine appropriate title text and format.
6. Decrease the width of the data control forms to improve the appearance and ensure the form will print on standard size paper width.
7. Make any other changes you think are necessary to improve the form.
8. Save the form accepting the default name *CostumeInventory*.
9. Display the first record in the table in Form view and then print the selected record making sure the form fits on one page.
10. Close the form saving changes and then close **PTCostumeInv3.accdb**.

Assessment 4 Finding Information on Creating a Form with a Subform

1. Use the Help feature to learn how Access creates a form when the table selected with the Form tool has a one-to-many relationship. *Hint: Find and read the article titled* **Create a form by using the Form tool**.
2. Open the **WEVendors3.accdb** database and click the Enable Content button if the Security Warning message bar appears.
3. Open the Relationships window and observe that there is a one-to-many relationship between the Vendors (primary) and the Purchases (related) tables.
4. Close the Relationships window.
5. Create a new form using the Form button based on the Vendors table.
6. Modify the form in Layout view to improve the appearance by applying the skills you have learned in this section.
7. Display the first vendor record in Form view. Print the first record only, making sure the record will require only one page to print.
8. Close the form. Click Yes to save the form and accept the default form name.
9. Close **WEVendors3.accdb**.

Assessment 5 Individual Challenge

Researching Movies on the Internet for a New Blog

1. You and your friends are thinking of starting a blog where you will write reviews for current movies playing in your area. You decide you want to create a database to store records for all of the movies you and your friends will review. Choose four to six movies that are currently playing in your vicinity that you would like to review on your blog. Find the movie websites on the Internet. Look for the information listed in Step 3 that you will be entering into the new database.
2. Create a new database on your storage medium and name it **AS3-Movies.accdb**.
3. Create a table named *MovieFacts* that will store the following information. You determine the field names and field properties:

Movie title	Lead Female Actor
Director's name	Supporting Female Actor
Producer's name	Movie category — drama, action, thriller, and so on
Lead Male Actor	Movie rating — R, PG, and so on
Supporting Male Actor	Website address

4. Create a form to enter the records for the movies you researched. Modify the form by applying the skills learned in this section.
5. Enter records for the movies you researched using the form created in Step 4.
6. Print only the first record displayed in Form view.
7. Create a report for the MovieFacts table. Modify the report by applying the skills learned in this section.
8. Print the MovieFacts report.
9. Close **AS3-Movies.accdb**.

Marquee Challenge

Challenge 1 Creating Queries and a Report for a Catering Events Database

1. Dana Hirsch, manager, has provided you with a copy of the database file used to track catering events at the bistro. Dana has been filtering records in the datasheet to obtain the lists needed for managing the events but is finding this process too time-consuming. Dana has asked you to figure out how to create queries that can provide the information more efficiently. To begin, open the **WBSpecialEvents3.accdb** database and click the Enable Content button if the Security Warning message bar appears.
2. Create the following queries.
   a. A query named WestviewEvents that displays all events booked in the Westview room. In the query results datasheet, Dana would like the first and last names, event description, date the event is booked, the number of guests, and the special menu detail. Print the query results datasheet using only one page with all column widths adjusted to Best Fit.
   b. A query named JuneEvents that displays all of the events booked in June, 2011. In the query results datasheet, show the first and last names, event description, date the event is booked, and the room in which the event will be held. Print the query results datasheet with all column widths adjusted to Best Fit.
   c. A query named EventRevenue that displays all records. In the query results datasheet, show the last name, event description, date the event is booked, the number of guests, and per person charge. Calculate in the query the estimated revenue by multiplying the guests by the per person charge. You determine an appropriate column label and format for the calculated column. In the query results datasheet, add a total at the bottom of the calculated column. Print the query results datasheet using only one page and with all column widths adjusted to Best Fit.
3. Create a report based on the EventRevenue query as shown in Figure 3.2. The company logo is stored in the file named **TWBLogo-Small.jpg**. Use your best judgment to determine the report formatting elements. The theme used is the default Office theme with individual formatting applied to headings. Totals can be inserted at the bottom of columns by right-clicking the column heading for which a total is desired and then using options at the shortcut menu. Save the report using the default name.
4. Print the report, making sure you use only one page.
5. Close **WBSpecialEvents3.accdb**.

FIGURE 3.2 Challenge 1

Catering Event Revenue

Wednesday, November 30, 2011
10:33:48 AM

Last Name	Event	Date of Event	Guests	Per Person Charge	Event Total
Hillmore	Business Meeting	1/15/2011	35	$21.95	$768.25
Fontaine	Engagement Party	1/20/2011	177	$28.95	$5,124.15
Corriveau	Birthday Party	1/23/2011	85	$25.95	$2,205.75
Kressman	Wedding	2/28/2011	266	$28.95	$7,700.70
Fagan	25th Wedding Anniversary	3/10/2011	88	$28.95	$2,547.60
Pockovic	Birthday Party	3/18/2011	62	$35.95	$2,228.90
Gill	Business Meeting	3/29/2011	71	$21.95	$1,558.45
Bresque	50th Wedding Anniversary	4/12/2011	62	$32.95	$2,042.90
Santore	Wedding	4/28/2011	157	$25.95	$4,074.15
Hamid	Engagement Party	5/8/2011	85	$28.95	$2,460.75
Torrance	Business Meeting	5/15/2011	26	$23.95	$622.70
Russell	Birthday Party	5/30/2011	36	$26.95	$970.20
Szucs	Birthday Party	6/10/2011	42	$28.95	$1,215.90
Griffin	25th Wedding Anniversary	6/17/2011	54	$31.95	$1,725.30
Doucet	Wedding	6/20/2011	168	$28.95	$4,863.60
Golinsky	Business Meeting	6/26/2011	57	$24.95	$1,422.15
Jin Ping	Baby Shower	7/10/2011	62	$21.95	$1,360.90
McMaster	Engagement Party	7/11/2011	75	$27.95	$2,096.25
Pavelich	Wedding	7/25/2011	110	$31.95	$3,514.50
Juanitez	Business Meeting	7/31/2011	49	$23.95	$1,173.55
				$552.00	$49,676.65

Challenge 2 Creating Forms and a Report for a Custom Costume Database

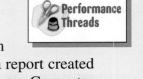

1. Bobbie Sinclair, business manager, is pleased with the way the custom costume database is taking shape. Bobbie would now like forms and a report created to facilitate data entry and printing of the custom orders. To begin, open a Computer window, navigate to your storage medium, and make a copy of the database **AS2-C2-PTCostumes.accdb** in the AccessS3 folder. (This database was created in Marquee Challenge 2 in Section 2.) Rename the copied file **AS3-C2-PTCostumes.accdb**.

2. Open **AS3-C2-PTCostumes.accdb** and click the Enable Content button if the Security Warning message bar appears.

3. Create a form for the costume orders table. You determine the layout and form design by applying skills learned in this section.

4. With the first record displayed in Form view, print the selected record, making sure you use only one page. Save and close the form, saving changes and accepting the default form name.

5. Create a report to print the costume orders table. You determine the layout and other elements of the report design by applying skills learned in this section. Consider the example shown in Figure 3.3. In this report, the layout is changed to a stacked arrangement that allows all fields to print on one page since there are numerous fields in the table. To create your report similar in layout to Figure 3.3, explore options in the Report Layout Tools Arrange tab. *Hint: To change a report's layout you need to select all of the control objects using the four-headed arrow selection icon at the top left of the report*.

6. Save the report accepting the default report name and then print the report making sure you minimize the paper used.

7. Close **AS3-C2-PTCostumes.accdb**.

FIGURE 3.3 Challenge 2

Performance Threads	**Custom Costume Orders**

Wednesday, November 30, 2011
11:05:03 AM

Costume ID	150
Description	Othello
Customer ID	100
Contract Price	$675.00
Signed Contract?	☑
Deposit	$100.00
Seamstress ID	201
Estimated Research Hours	10
Estimated Design Hours	10
Estimated Production Hours	25
Actual Research Hours	15
Actual Design Hours	8
Actual Production Hours	30

> Use this example as a guide for layout purposes only. Your report will vary depending on how you created your table structure in Marquee Challenge 2 in Access Section 2.

Marquee Series

Microsoft®
PowerPoint® 2010

Nita Rutkosky

Pierce College at Puyallup, Puyallup, Washington

Denise Seguin

Fanshawe College, London, Ontario

Audrey Rutkosky Roggenkamp

Pierce College at Puyallup, Puyallup, Washington

Paradigm
PUBLISHING

St. Paul • Los Angeles • Indianapolis

Managing Editor	Sonja Brown
Developmental Editor	Brenda Palo
Supplements Developmental Editor	Brenda Owens
Production Editor	Donna Mears
Cover and Text Designer	Leslie Anderson
Copy Editors	Susan Capecchi and Laura Nelson
Desktop Production	Ryan Hamner and Jack Ross
Proofreader	Laura Nelson
Testers	Carley Bomstad, Amy McGuire, Rob Neilly, and Lindsay Ryan
Indexers	Ina Gravitz and Sandi Schroeder

© 2011 by Paradigm Publishing, Inc.
875 Montreal Way
St. Paul, MN 55102
Email: educate@emcp.com
Website: www.emcp.com

Printed in the United States of America

19 18 17 16 15 14 13 12 11 10   1 2 3 4 5 6 7 8 9 10

Contents

Introducing

PowerPoint 2010

Create colorful and powerful presentations using PowerPoint, Microsoft's presentation program that is included in the Office 2010 suite. With PowerPoint, you can organize and present information and create visual aids for a presentation. PowerPoint is a full-featured presentation program that provides a wide variety of editing and formatting features as well as sophisticated visual elements such as clip art, pictures, SmartArt, WordArt, and drawn objects. While working in PowerPoint, you will produce presentations for the following six companies.

 First Choice Travel is a travel center offering a full range of traveling services from booking flights, hotel reservations, and rental cars to offering travel seminars.

 The Waterfront Bistro offers fine dining for lunch and dinner and also offers banquet facilities, a wine cellar, and catering services.

 Worldwide Enterprises is a national and international distributor of products for a variety of companies and is the exclusive movie distribution agent for Marquee Productions.

 Marquee Productions is involved in all aspects of creating movies from script writing and development to filming. The company produces documentaries, biographies, as well as historical and action movies.

 Performance Threads maintains an inventory of rental costumes and also researches, designs, and sews special-order and custom-made costumes.

 The mission of the Niagara Peninsula College Theatre Arts Division is to offer a curriculum designed to provide students with a thorough exposure to all aspects of the theater arts.

In Section 1 you will learn how to
Prepare a Presentation

Prepare a presentation using a template provided by PowerPoint or create your own presentation and apply formatting with a design theme. Preparing a presentation consists of general steps such as creating and editing slides; adding enhancements to slides; and saving, running, previewing, printing, and closing a presentation. When running a presentation, how one slide is removed from the screen and the next slide is displayed is referred to as the *transition.* You can add interesting transitions to slides as well as sound to a presentation.

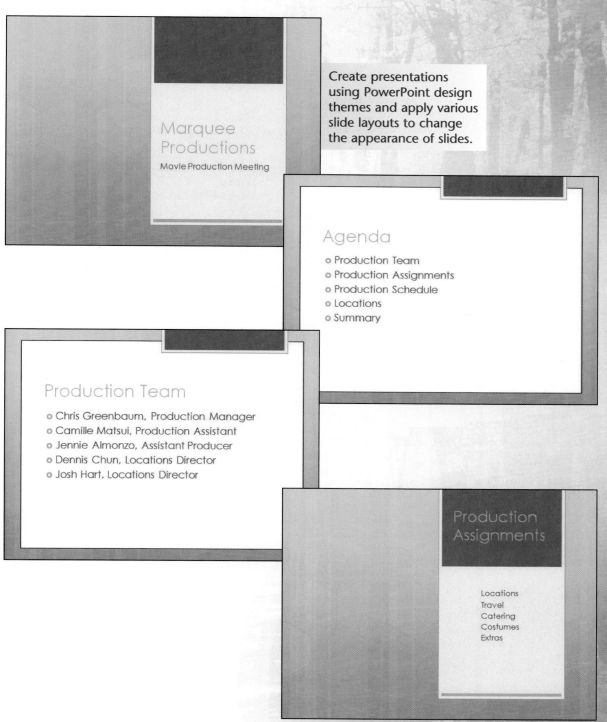

Create presentations using PowerPoint design themes and apply various slide layouts to change the appearance of slides.

In Section 2 you will learn how to
Edit and Enhance Slides

Edit slides and slide elements in a presentation to customize and personalize the presentation. Editing can include such functions as rearranging and deleting slides; cutting, copying, and pasting text; changing the font, paragraph alignment, and paragraph spacing; and changing the design theme, theme color, and theme font. Add visual appeal to a presentation by inserting clip art images, pictures, and SmartArt organizational charts and graphics.

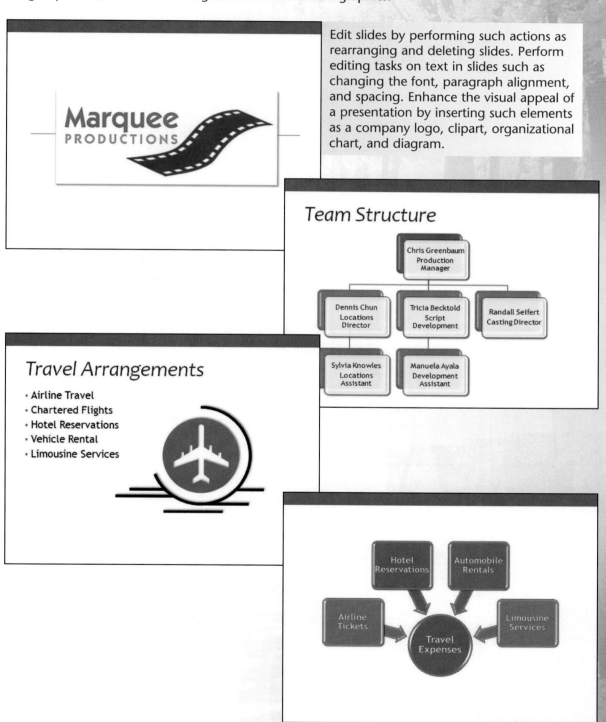

Edit slides by performing such actions as rearranging and deleting slides. Perform editing tasks on text in slides such as changing the font, paragraph alignment, and spacing. Enhance the visual appeal of a presentation by inserting such elements as a company logo, clipart, organizational chart, and diagram.

Performance Threads

Management Team

```
Kim Waverly
President
├── Camilla Yong
│   Design Manager
│   └── Scott Bercini
│       Supervisor
└── Bobbie Sinclair
    Business Manager
    └── Andy Newell
        Sales Director
```

Employee Benefits

- Health/Dental
- Disability Insurance
- Life Insurance
- Retirement

Costuming Process

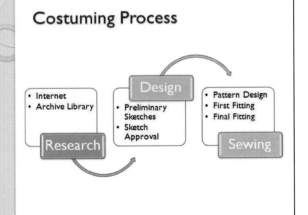

- Internet
- Archive Library

Research

Design

- Preliminary Sketches
- Sketch Approval

- Pattern Design
- First Fitting
- Final Fitting

Sewing

PowerPoint® SECTION 1
Preparing a Presentation

Skills

- Complete the presentation cycle
- Choose a design theme
- Add a new slide to a presentation
- Navigate in a presentation
- Insert a slide in a presentation
- Change the presentation view
- Change the slide layout
- Rearrange, delete, and hide slides
- Use the Help feature
- Check spelling in a presentation
- Use Thesaurus to display synonyms for words
- Run a presentation and use the pen during a presentation
- Add transitions and sound to a presentation
- Print and preview a presentation

Student Resources

Before beginning the activities in PowerPoint, copy to your storage medium the PowerPoint folder on the Student CD. This folder contains the data files you need to complete the projects in each PowerPoint section.

Projects Overview

Use an installed template to prepare a presentation about the new features in PowerPoint 2010; prepare a movie production meeting presentation and a location team meeting presentation.

Prepare an executive meeting presentation for Worldwide Enterprises.

Prepare a presentation containing information on the accommodations and services offered by The Waterfront Bistro.

Prepare a presentation on Toronto, Ontario, Canada.

Prepare a presentation for a costume meeting.

Model Answers for Projects

These model answers for the projects that you complete in Section 1 provide a preview of the finished projects before you begin working and also allow you to compare your own results with these models to ensure you have created the materials accurately.

PS1-MPPProj.pptx (a two-page document) is the project in Activities 1.2 to 1.10.

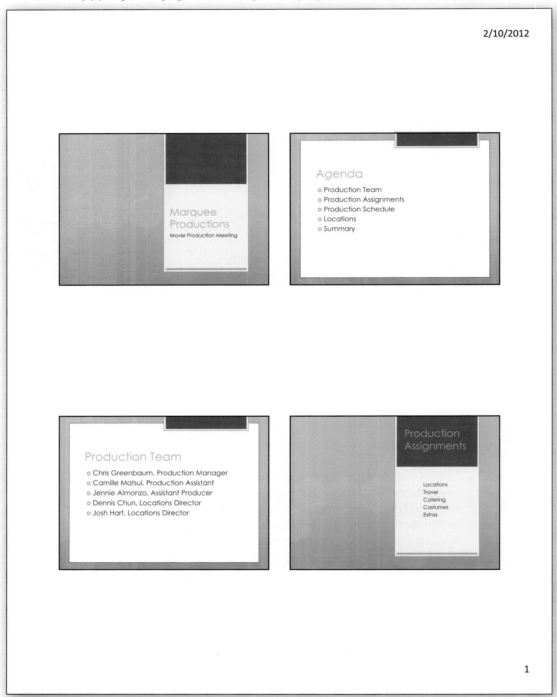

Activity 1.1

Completing the Presentation Cycle

PowerPoint is a presentation graphics program you can use to organize and present information. With PowerPoint, you can create visual aids for a presentation and then print copies of the aids as well as run the presentation. Preparing a presentation in PowerPoint generally follows a presentation cycle. The steps in the cycle vary but generally include opening PowerPoint; creating and editing slides; saving, printing, running, and closing the presentation; and then closing PowerPoint.

Project

Tutorial 1.1
Creating and Saving a Presentation

You are an employee of Marquee Productions and Office 2010 has just been installed on your computer. You need to prepare a presentation in the near future so you decide to open a presentation provided by PowerPoint and experiment with running the presentation.

1 Open PowerPoint by clicking the Start button 🪟 on the Windows Taskbar, pointing to *All Programs*, clicking *Microsoft Office*, and then clicking *Microsoft PowerPoint 2010*.

> Depending on your system configuration, the steps you complete to open PowerPoint may vary.

2 At the PowerPoint window, click the File tab and then click the New tab at the Backstage view. Click the *Sample templates* option in the *Available Templates and Themes* section of the New tab Backstage view.

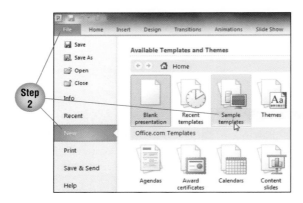

3 Double-click the *Introducing PowerPoint 2010* template.

> The *Introducing PowerPoint 2010* template opens in the PowerPoint window. What displays in the PowerPoint window will vary depending on what type of presentation you are creating. However, the PowerPoint window contains some consistent elements as identified in Figure 1.1. Refer to Table 1.1 for a description of the window elements.

In Brief

Create Presentation with Installed Template
1. Click File tab.
2. Click New tab.
3. Click *Sample templates* option.
4. Double-click desired template.

FIGURE 1.1 PowerPoint Window

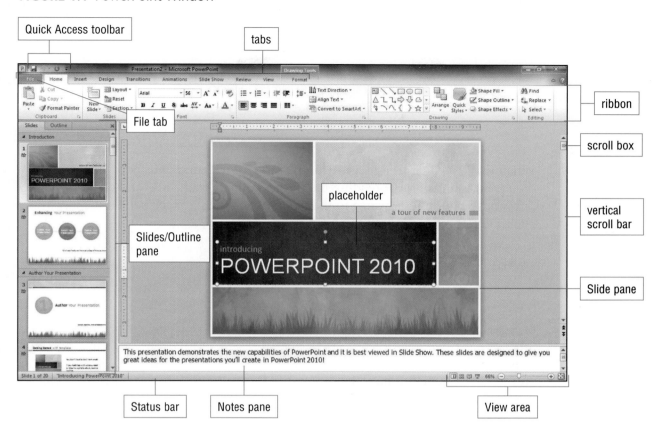

TABLE 1.1 PowerPoint Window Elements

Feature.	Description
File tab	when clicked, displays buttons and tabs for working with and managing files
horizontal scroll bar	shifts text left or right in the Slide pane
I-beam pointer	used to move the insertion point or to select text
insertion point	indicates location of next character entered at the keyboard
Notes pane	add notes to a presentation in this pane
placeholder	location on a slide with a dotted border that holds text or objects
Quick Access toolbar	contains buttons for commonly used commands
ribbon	area containing the tabs and commands divided into groups
Slide pane	displays the slide and slide contents
Slides/Outline pane	displays at the left side of the window with two tabs — Slides and Outline. With the Slides tab selected, slide miniatures display in the pane; with the Outline tab selected, presentation contents display in the pane.
Status bar	displays slide number, design theme, View buttons, and Zoom slider bar
tabs	contain commands and features organized into groups
Title bar	displays file name followed by program name
vertical scroll bar	display specific slides using this scroll bar
View area	located toward right side of Status bar; contains buttons for changing the presentation view

continues

④ Run the presentation by clicking the Slide Show tab and then clicking the From Beginning button  in the Start Slide Show group.

Step 4

⑤ When the first slide fills the screen, read the information and then click the left mouse button. Continue reading the information in each slide and clicking the left mouse button to advance to the next slide. When a black screen displays, click the left mouse button to end the slide show.

⑥ Save the presentation by clicking the Save button  on the Quick Access toolbar.

Step 6

⑦ At the Save As dialog box, make sure the PowerPointS1 folder on your storage medium is the active folder, type **PS1-MPPowerPoint2010** in the *File name* text box, and then press Enter.

The Address bar at the Save As dialog box displays the active folder and the folder path.

Step 7

⑧ At the PowerPoint window, print the presentation information in outline view by clicking the File tab and then clicking the Print tab.

The File tab is located in the upper left corner of the screen at the left side of the Home tab. When you click the File tab, the Backstage view displays with tabs and buttons for working with and managing files. The Quick Commands area of the Backstage view contains four buttons for working with files—Save, Save As, Open, and Close. Tabs at the Backstage view include Info, Recent, New, Print, Save & Send, and Help. Two buttons display below the Help tab—Options and Exit.

⑨ Click the second gallery in the *Settings* category (the gallery containing the text *Full Page Slides*) and then click *Outline* in the *Print Layout* section of the drop-down list.

10 Click the Print button. *Note: Always check with your instructor before printing.*

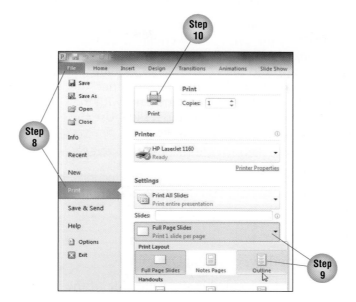

11 Close the presentation by clicking the File tab and then clicking the Close button.

If a message displays asking if you want to save the presentation, click *Yes*.

12 Close PowerPoint by clicking the File tab and then clicking the Exit button located below the Help tab.

You can also exit PowerPoint by clicking the Close button that displays in the upper right corner of the screen.

In Addition

Getting Started with PowerPoint 2010

Microsoft provides a number of tools to help you learn about and get started creating presentations in PowerPoint. One method for accessing helpful information is to click the File tab and then click the Help tab. The middle panel of the Help tab Backstage view contains two sections—*Support* and *Tools for Working With Office*. In the *Support* section, click the *Microsoft Office Help* option to display the PowerPoint Help window where you can search for specific information on PowerPoint features.

Click the *Getting Started* option and you are connected to the Microsoft website where information displays introducing PowerPoint 2010. Click the *Contact Us* option and the Microsoft support web page displays with options for support centers and customer service solution centers, and information on how to buy Microsoft Office products.

Activity 1.2

Choosing a Design Theme; Creating Slides; Closing a Presentation

Create a PowerPoint presentation using an installed template as you did in the previous activity or begin with a blank presentation and apply your own formatting or apply formatting with a slide design theme. To display a blank PowerPoint presentation, use the keyboard shortcut Ctrl + N or click the File tab, click the New tab, and then click the Create button in the *Blank presen-* *tation* section of the New tab Backstage view. A PowerPoint presentation screen displays in Normal view with three panes available for entering text—the Slides/Outline pane, Slide pane, and Notes pane. Use either the Slide pane or the Slides/Outline pane with the Outline tab selected to enter text in a slide. Use the Notes page to insert a note in a slide.

Project

Chris Greenbaum, production manager for Marquee Productions, has asked you to prepare slides for a movie production meeting. You decide to prepare the presentation using a design template offered by PowerPoint.

Tutorial 1.1
Creating and Saving
a Presentation

1 Open PowerPoint.

2 At the PowerPoint window, click the Design tab.

3 Click the More button ⊽ located at the right side of the themes thumbnails.

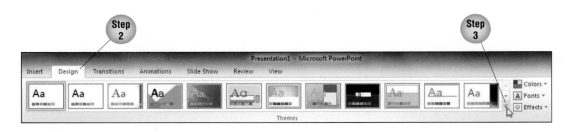

4 Click *Austin* in the *Built-In* section of the drop-down gallery. (Design thumbnails display in alphabetic order at the drop-down gallery.)

> When you click the More button, a drop-down gallery displays. This gallery is an example of the *live preview* feature. When you hover your mouse pointer over one of the design themes, the slide in the Slide pane displays with the design theme formatting applied. With the live preview feature, you can view a design theme before actually applying it to the presentation.

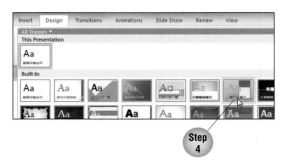

5 Click anywhere in the *Click to add title* placeholder that displays in the slide in the Slide pane and then type **Marquee Productions**.

> A placeholder is a location on a slide marked with a border that holds text or an object.

6 Click anywhere in the *Click to add subtitle* placeholder that displays in the slide and then type **Movie Production Meeting**.

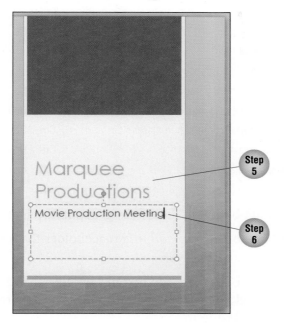

7 Click the Home tab and then click the New Slide button 🗖 in the Slides group.

> When you click this button, a new slide displays in the Slide pane with the Title and Content layout. You will learn more about layouts in Activity 1.4.

8 Click anywhere in the *Click to add title* placeholder that displays in the slide and then type **Agenda**.

9 Click anywhere in the *Click to add text* placeholder that displays in the slide and then type **Production Team**.

10 Press the Enter key and then type the following agenda items, pressing the Enter key after each item except the last: **Production Assignments**, **Production Schedule**, **Locations**, and **Summary**.

> You can use keys on the keyboard to move the insertion point to various locations within a placeholder in a slide. Refer to Table 1.2 for a list of insertion point movement commands.

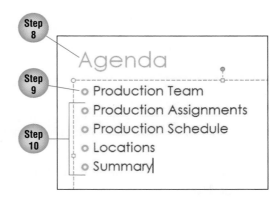

continues

TABLE 1.2 Insertion Point Movement Commands

To move insertion point	Press
One character left	Left Arrow
One character right	Right Arrow
One line up	Up Arrow
One line down	Down Arrow
One word to the left	Ctrl + Left Arrow
One word to the right	Ctrl + Right Arrow
To end of a line of text	End
To beginning of a line of text	Home
To beginning of current paragraph in placeholder	Ctrl + Up Arrow
To beginning of previous paragraph in placeholder	Ctrl + Up Arrow twice
To beginning of next paragraph in placeholder	Ctrl + Down Arrow
To beginning of text in placeholder	Ctrl + Home
To end of text in placeholder	Ctrl + End

11 Click the New Slide button in the Slides group in the Home tab.

12 Click anywhere in the *Click to add title* placeholder that displays in the slide and then type **Department Reports**.

13 Click anywhere in the *Click to add text* placeholder that displays in the slide and then type the bulleted text as shown in the slide below. Press the Enter key after each item except the last item.

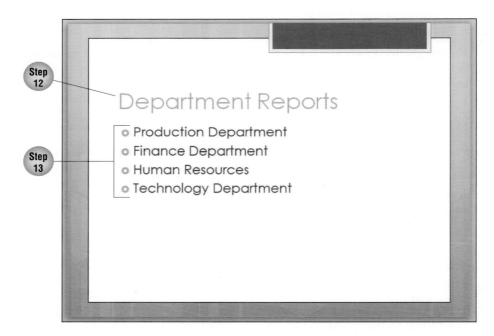

14 Click the New Slide button in the Slides group in the Home tab.

15 Click the Outline tab located toward the top of the Slides/Outline pane.

16 Click in the Slides/Outline pane immediately right of the slide icon after the number *4*, type **Locations**, and then press Enter.

17 Press the Tab key, type **Studio Shoots**, and then press the Enter key.

> Pressing the Tab key demotes the insertion point to the next level, while pressing Shift + Tab promotes the insertion point to the previous level.

18 Press the Tab key, type **Vancouver Studio**, and then press Enter.

19 Type **Los Angeles Studio** and then press Enter.

20 Press Shift + Tab, type **Location Shoots**, and then press Enter.

21 Press the Tab key, type **Stanley Park**, and then press Enter.

22 Type **Downtown Streets**.

23 Click anywhere in the text *Click to add notes* in the Notes pane and then type **Camille Matsui will report on the park location.**

24 Click the Slides tab located toward the top of the Slides/Outline pane.

25 Click the Save button on the Quick Access toolbar.

26 At the Save As dialog box, make sure the PowerPointS1 folder on your storage medium is the active folder, type **PS1-MPProdMtg** in the *File name* text box, and then press Enter.

27 Close the presentation by clicking the File tab and then clicking the Close button.

Steps 16–22

Slides	Outline

1 **Marquee Productions**
Movie Production Meeting
2 **Agenda**
  ○ Production Team
  ○ Production Assignments
  ○ Production Schedule
  ○ Locations
  ○ Summary
3 **Department Reports**
  ○ Production Department
  ○ Finance Department
  ○ Human Resources
  ○ Technology Department
4 **Locations**
  ○ Studio Shoots
    ○ Vancouver Studio
    ○ Los Angeles Studio
  ○ Location Shoots
    ○ Stanley Park
    ○ Downtown Streets

Step 23

Camille Matsui will report on the park location.

In Addition

Using Tabs

The ribbon area displays below the Quick Access toolbar. The buttons and options in the ribbon area vary depending on the tab selected and the width of the window displayed on the screen. PowerPoint commands and features are organized into command tabs that display in the ribbon area. Commands and features are organized into groups within a tab. For example, the Home tab, which is the default tab, contains the Clipboard, Slides, Font, Paragraph, Drawing, and Editing groups. When you hover the mouse over a button, a ScreenTip displays with the name of the button, a keyboard shortcut (if any), and a description of the purpose of the button.

Activity 1.3

Opening, Navigating, and Inserting Slides in a Presentation

Open a saved presentation by displaying the Open dialog box and then double-clicking the desired presentation. Display the Open dialog box by clicking the File tab and then clicking the Open button. Navigate through slides in a presentation with buttons on the vertical scroll bar, by clicking text in the desired slide in the Slides/Outline pane, or using keys on the keyboard. Insert a new slide with a specific layout by clicking the New Slide button arrow and then clicking the desired layout at the drop-down list.

Project

Tutorial 1.2
Opening, Organizing, and Viewing a Presentation

Chris Greenbaum has asked you to add more information to the movie production meeting presentation. You will insert a new slide between the second and third slides in the presentation.

1 Click the File tab and then click the Open button.

> You can also open a presentation by inserting an Open button on the Quick Access toolbar and then clicking the button. To insert the button, click the Customize Quick Access Toolbar button that displays at the right side of the toolbar and then click *Open* at the drop-down list.

2 At the Open dialog box, make sure the PowerPointS1 folder on your storage medium is the active folder and then double-click *PS1-MPProdMtg.pptx* in the Content pane.

3 With **PS1-MPProdMtg.pptx** open, click the Next Slide button ⬇ located at the bottom of the vertical scroll bar.

> Clicking this button displays the next slide, Slide 2, in the presentation. Notice that *Slide 2 of 4* displays at the left side of the Status bar.

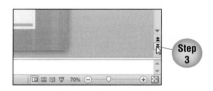

4 Click the Previous Slide button ⬆ located toward the bottom of the vertical scroll bar to display Slide 1.

> When you click the Previous Slide button, *Slide 1 of 4* displays at the left side of the Status bar.

5 Display Slide 2 in the Slide pane by clicking the Next Slide button located at the bottom of the vertical scroll bar.

6 Insert a new slide between Slides 2 and 3 by clicking the New Slide button in the Slides group in the Home tab.

7 Click anywhere in the *Click to add title* placeholder in the slide in the Slide pane and then type **Production Schedule**.

8 Click anywhere in the *Click to add text* placeholder located in the slide and then type the bulleted text as shown in the slide on the next page. Press the Enter key after each item except the last item.

Step 7
Step 8

Production Schedule

- Studio Shoots
- Location Shoots
- Dubbing
- Music

In Brief

Open Presentation
1. Click File tab.
2. Click Open button.
3. At Open dialog box, double-click desired presentation.

(9) Click the Outline tab located toward the top of the Slides/Outline pane.

(10) Click immediately right of the text *Music* located toward the middle of the Slides/Outline pane, press the Enter key, and then press Shift + Tab.

> This moves the insertion point back a level and inserts the number *4* followed by a slide icon.

(11) Type **Production Assignments**, press the Enter key, and then press the Tab key. Type the remaining text for Slide 4 as shown at the right. Do not press the Enter key after typing *Extras*.

> When you are finished typing the text, the presentation will contain six slides.

(12) Click the Save button on the Quick Access toolbar to save **PS1-MPProdMtg.pptx**.

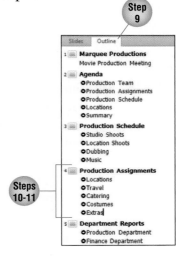

Step 9

Steps 10-11

In Addition

Planning a Presentation

Consider the following basic guidelines when preparing the content for a presentation:

- **Determine the main purpose of the presentation.** Do not try to cover too many topics. Identifying the main point of the presentation will help you stay focused and convey a clear message to the audience.
- **Determine the output.** To help decide the type of output needed, consider the availability of equipment, the size of the room where you will make the presentation, and the number of people who will be attending the presentation.
- **Show one idea per slide.** Each slide in a presentation should convey only one main idea. Too many ideas on a slide may confuse the audience and cause you to stray from the purpose of the slide.

- **Maintain a consistent design.** A consistent design and color scheme for slides in a presentation will create continuity and cohesiveness. Do not use too much color or too many pictures or other graphic elements.
- **Keep slides easy to read and uncluttered.** Keep slides simple and easy for the audience to read. Keep words and other items such as bullets to a minimum.
- **Determine printing needs.** Will you be providing audience members with handouts? If so, will these handouts consist of a printing of each slide? an outline of the presentation? a printing of each slide with space for taking notes?

Activity 1.4

Changing Views; Choosing a Slide Layout

PowerPoint provides viewing options for a presentation. Change the presentation view with buttons in the Presentation Views group in the View tab or with buttons in the View area on the Status bar. The Normal view is the default view and displays three panes—Slides/Outline, Slide, and Notes. You can change the view to Slide Sorter view or Notes Page view. Choose the view based on the type of activity you are performing in the presentation. You can also increase the size of the slide in the Slide pane by closing the Slides/Outline pane. Do this by clicking the Close button located in the upper right corner of the pane. Click the New Slide button arrow located in the Slides group in the Home tab and a drop-down list displays with layout choices. Choose the layout that matches the type of text or object you want to insert in the slide.

Project After reviewing the movie production presentation, Chris Greenbaum has asked you to edit a slide and add a new slide.

Tutorial 1.2
Opening, Organizing, and Viewing a Presentation

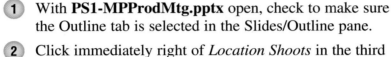

1. With **PS1-MPProdMtg.pptx** open, check to make sure the Outline tab is selected in the Slides/Outline pane.

2. Click immediately right of *Location Shoots* in the third slide.

3. Press the Enter key and then type **Editing**.

   This inserts *Editing* between *Location Shoots* and *Dubbing*.

4. Display the slides in Notes Page view by clicking the View tab and then clicking the Notes Page button in the Presentation Views group.

   In Notes Page view, an individual slide displays on a page with any added notes displayed below the slide.

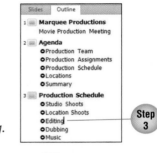

5. Click the Next Slide button on the vertical scroll bar until Slide 6 (the last slide) displays.

   Notice that the note you created about Camille Matsui displays below the slide in the page.

6. Increase the zoom by clicking the Zoom button in the Zoom group in the View tab, clicking *100%* at the Zoom dialog box, and then clicking OK.

7. You can also change the zoom using the Zoom slider bar. Change the zoom by positioning the mouse pointer on the Zoom slider bar button located at the right side of the Status bar. Hold down the left mouse button, drag to the right until the zoom percentage at the left side of the Zoom slider bar displays as approximately *136%*, and then release the mouse button.

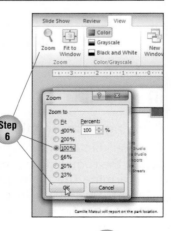

8. Click the Zoom Out button located at the left side of the Zoom slider bar until *70%* displays at the left side of the slider bar.

   Click the Zoom Out button to decrease the zoom display and click the Zoom In button to increase the display.

9 View all slides in the presentation in slide miniature by clicking the Slide Sorter button ⊞ in the Presentation Views group.

In Brief

Normal View
1. Click View tab.
2. Click Normal button.
OR
Click Normal button in View area on Status bar.

Slide Sorter View
1. Click View tab.
2. Click Slide Sorter button.
OR
Click Slide Sorter button in View area on Status bar.

Notes Page View
1. Click View tab.
2. Click Notes Page button.

10 View the presentation in Reading view by clicking the Reading View button 📖 in the Presentation Views group.

> Use Reading view to show the presentation to someone viewing the presentation on his or her own computer. You can also use the Reading view to view a presentation in a window with controls that make the presentation easy to view. In Reading view, navigation buttons display in the lower right corner of the screen immediately left of the View area on the Status bar.

11 Return the presentation to the Normal view by clicking the Normal button ⊞ in the View area on the Status bar (located in the lower right corner of the screen).

12 Click the Slides tab in the Slides/Outline pane.

> With the Slides tab selected, slide miniatures display in the Slides/Outline pane.

13 Scroll down the Slides/Outline pane until the Slide 6 miniature displays and then click below the slide miniature.

> When you click below the slide miniature, a blinking horizontal line displays below Slide 6.

14 Click the Home tab, click the New Slide button arrow, and then click the *Title Slide* layout that displays in the drop-down gallery.

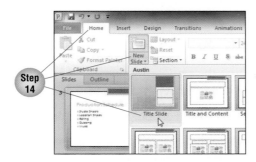

15 Click the *Click to add title* placeholder and then type **Production Leader**.

16 Click the *Click to add subtitle* placeholder and then type **Chris Greenbaum**.

17 Save **PS1-MPProdMtg.pptx**.

In Addition

Correcting Errors in PowerPoint

PowerPoint's AutoCorrect feature automatically corrects certain words as you type them. For example, type *teh* and press the spacebar, and AutoCorrect changes it to *the*. PowerPoint also contains a spelling feature that inserts a wavy red line below words that are not contained in the Spelling dictionary or not corrected by AutoCorrect. If the word containing a red wavy line is correct, you can leave it as written since the red wavy line does not print. If the word is incorrect, edit it.

Activity 1.5

Changing the Slide Layout; Selecting and Moving a Placeholder

The slides you have created have been based on a slide layout. You can change the slide layout by clicking the Layout button in the Slides group in the Home tab and then clicking the desired layout at the drop-down list. Objects in a slide such as text, a chart, a table, or other graphic element, are generally positioned in a placeholder. Click the text or object to select the placeholder and a dashed border surrounds the placeholder. You can move, size, and/or delete a selected placeholder.

Project You have decided to make a few changes to the layout of slides in the movie production presentation.

1. With **PS1-MPProdMtg.pptx** open, make sure Slide 7 displays in the Slide pane.

2. Click the Layout button 🔲 in the Slides group in the Home tab and then click the *Title and Content* layout at the drop-down gallery.

   Position the mouse pointer on a slide layout and the name of the layout displays in a box.

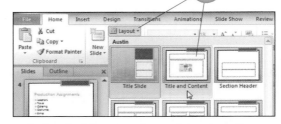

SNAP

Tutorial 1.2
Opening, Organizing, and Viewing a Presentation

Tutorial 1.3
Editing Text within Slides and Modifying Placeholders

3. Click immediately right of the *r* in *Leader* (this selects the placeholder), press the Backspace key until *Leader* is deleted, and then type **Team**.

   Sizing handles display around the selected placeholder. Use these sizing handles to increase and/or decrease the size of the placeholder.

4. Click immediately right of the *m* in *Greenbaum*.

5. Type a comma (,), press the spacebar, and then type **Production Manager**.

6. Press the Enter key and then type the remaining names and titles shown in the slide below. (Do not press the Enter key after typing *Josh Hart, Locations Director*.)

7. Click the Previous Slide button on the vertical scroll bar until Slide 4 displays.

8. Change the slide layout by clicking the Layout button in the Slides group and then clicking the *Title Slide* layout at the drop-down list.

9. Click anywhere in the title *Production Assignments*.

   This selects the placeholder.

10. Decrease the size of the placeholder by positioning the mouse pointer on the middle sizing handle that displays at the top of the placeholder until the pointer turns into a double-headed arrow pointing up and down. Hold down the left mouse button, drag down to the approximate location shown on the next page, and then release the mouse button.

11 Move the title placeholder so it positions the title as shown in Figure 1.2. To do this, position the mouse pointer on the placeholder border until the mouse pointer displays with a four-headed arrow attached, hold down the left mouse button, drag to the approximate location shown in the figure, and then release the mouse button.

12 Increase the size of the subtitle placeholder (and the size of the text). Begin by clicking on any character in the text *Locations*.

> This selects the placeholder containing the text.

13 Position the mouse pointer on the middle sizing handle that displays at the top of the placeholder until the pointer turns into a double-headed arrow pointing up and down. Hold down the left mouse button, drag up approximately one inch, and then release the mouse button.

> Increasing the size of the placeholder automatically increased the size of the text in the placeholder. This is because, by default, PowerPoint automatically sizes the contents to fit the placeholder. Read the In Addition at the bottom of this page for information on the AutoFit Options button.

14 Move the content placeholder so it positions the text as shown in Figure 1.2. To do this, position the mouse pointer on the placeholder border until the mouse pointer displays with a four-headed arrow attached, hold down the left mouse button, drag to the approximate location shown in the figure, and then release the mouse button.

15 Click outside the placeholder to deselect it.

> If you are not satisfied with the changes you make to a placeholder, click the Reset button 📑 in the Slides group in the Home tab. This resets the position, size, and formatting to the default settings.

16 Save **PS1-MPProdMtg.pptx**.

In Brief

Change Slide Layout
1. Make desired slide active.
2. Click Home tab.
3. Click Layout button.
4. Click desired layout at drop-down list.

Move Placeholder
1. Click inside placeholder.
2. Drag with mouse to desired position.

Size Placeholder
1. Click inside placeholder.
2. Drag sizing handles to increase/ decrease size.

FIGURE 1.2 Slide 4

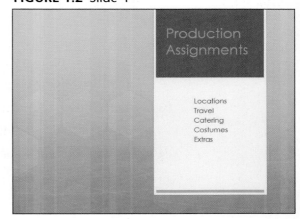

In Addition

Using the AutoFit Options Button

If you decrease the size of a placeholder so the existing text does not fit within it, PowerPoint will automatically decrease the size of the text so it fits in the placeholder. If you click on any character in the text that has been decreased in size, an AutoFit Options button displays at the left side of the placeholder. Click the AutoFit Options button and a list of choices displays as shown at the right for positioning objects in the placeholder. The *AutoFit Text to Placeholder* option is selected by default and tells PowerPoint to fit text within the boundaries of the placeholder. Click the middle choice, *Stop Fitting Text to This Placeholder*, and PowerPoint will not automatically fit the text or object within the placeholder. Choose the last option, *Control AutoCorrect Options*, to display the AutoCorrect dialog box with the AutoFormat As You Type tab selected. Additional options may display depending upon the placeholder and the type of data inserted in the placeholder.

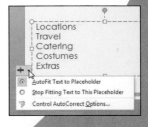

Activity 1.6

Rearranging, Deleting, and Hiding Slides

As you edit a presentation, you may need to rearrange slides, delete slides, or hide specific slides. PowerPoint provides various views for creating and managing a presentation. Manage slides in the Slides/ Outline pane or in Slide Sorter view. Switch to Slide Sorter view by clicking the Slide Sorter button in the view area on the Status bar or by clicking the View tab and then clicking the Slide Sorter button in the Presentation Views group.

Project

Chris Greenbaum has asked you to make some changes to the presentation including rearranging slides, deleting a slide, and hiding a slide.

Tutorial 1.4
Rearranging, Deleting, and Hiding Slides

1 With **PS1-MPProdMtg.pptx** open, right-click Slide 5 in the Slides/Outline pane and then click *Delete Slide* at the drop-down list.

You can also delete a selected slide by pressing the Delete key on the keyboard.

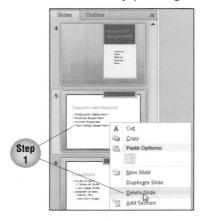

2 Click the Slide Sorter button ⊞ in the view area on the Status bar.

3 Click Slide 6 to make it active.

A selected slide displays with an orange border.

4 Position the mouse pointer on Slide 6, hold down the left mouse button, drag the arrow pointer (with a square attached) to the left of Slide 3 (a thin vertical line will display between Slides 2 and 3), and then release the mouse button.

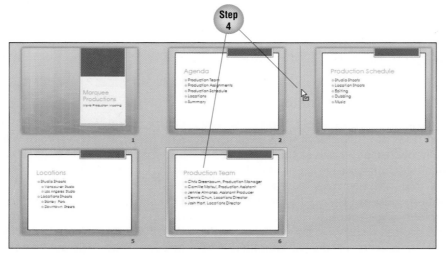

5 Click the Normal button located in the view area on the Status bar.

6 Click the Slides tab in the Slides/Outline pane. (Skip this step if the Slides tab is already selected.)

7 Position the mouse pointer on the Slide 5 miniature, hold down the left mouse button, drag up until a thin, horizontal line displays immediately below the Slide 3 miniature, and then release the mouse button.

8 With the Slide 4 miniature selected in the Slides/Outline pane (miniature displays with an orange background), hide the slide by clicking the Slide Show tab and then clicking the Hide Slide button in the Set Up group.

> When a slide is hidden, the slide miniature displays dimmed and the slide number displays with a diagonal line across the number.

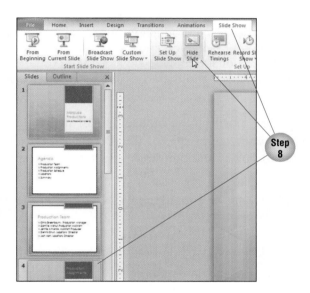

In Brief

Delete Slide
1. Right-click desired slide in Slides/Outline view.
2. Click *Delete Slide*.

Move Slide
1. Click Slide Sorter button in View area on Status bar.
2. Click desired slide.
3. Drag slide to desired position.

Hide Slide
1. Click desired slides in Slides/Outline pane.
2. Click Slide Show tab.
3. Click Hide Slide button.

9 Run the presentation by clicking the From Beginning button in the Start Slide Show group. Click the left mouse button to advance each slide.

10 After running the presentation, you decide to redisplay the hidden slide. To do this, make sure the Slide 4 miniature is selected in the Slides/Outline pane and then click the Hide Slide button in the Set Up group.

11 Save **PS1-MPProdMtg.pptx**.

In Addition

Copying Slides within a Presentation

Copying a slide within a presentation is similar to moving a slide. To copy a slide, position the arrow pointer on the desired slide, hold down the Ctrl key and the left mouse button. Drag to the location where you want the slide copied, release the left mouse button, and then release the Ctrl key. When you drag with the mouse, the mouse pointer displays with a square and a plus symbol next to the pointer.

Activity 1.7

Use the PowerPoint Help feature to display information on PowerPoint. To use the Help feature, click the Microsoft PowerPoint Help button (a circle with a question mark inside) located toward the upper right corner of the screen. At the PowerPoint Help window that displays, type the text for which you want information and then press Enter or click the Search button. A list of topics related to the search text displays in the results window. Click the desired topic and information displays in the PowerPoint Help window. Use PowerPoint's spelling checker to find and correct misspelled words and find duplicated words (such as *and and*). The spelling checker compares words in your slide with words in its dictionary. If a match is found, the word is passed over. If no match is found for the word, the spelling checker stops, selects the word, and offers replacements. Use Thesaurus to find synonyms, antonyms, and related words for a particular word. To use Thesaurus, click the word for which you want to display synonyms and antonyms, click the Review tab, and then click the Thesaurus button in the Proofing group. This displays the Research task pane with information about the word where the insertion point is positioned.

Project

Tutorial 1.5
Using Help

Tutorial 1.6
Using the Spelling and Thesaurus Feature

You have decided to create a new slide in the movie production presentation. Because several changes have been made to the presentation, you know that checking the spelling of all the slide text is important, but you are not sure how to do it. You will use the Help feature to learn how to complete a spelling check and then use Thesaurus to replace a couple of words with synonyms.

1. With **PS1-MPProdMtg.pptx** open, position the mouse pointer on the scroll box located on the vertical scroll bar at the right side of the screen. Hold down the left mouse button, drag the scroll box to the bottom of the scroll bar, and then release the mouse button.

    This displays Slide 6 in the Slide pane. As you drag the scroll box on the vertical scroll bar, a box displays indicating the slide number and slide title if the slide contains a title.

2. Click the Home tab and then click the New Slide button in the Slides group.

    This inserts a new slide at the end of the presentation.

3. Click the *Click to add title* placeholder and then type **Summary**.

4. Click the *Click to add text* placeholder and then type the text shown in the slide below.

    Type the words exactly as shown. You will check the spelling in a later step.

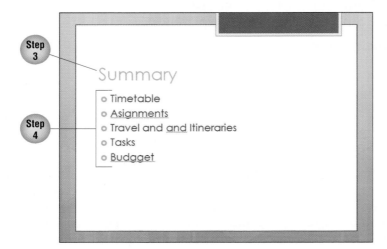

5 Learn how to complete a spelling check by clicking the Microsoft PowerPoint Help button ❓ located toward the upper right corner of the screen.

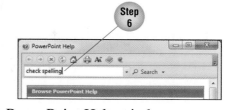

6 At the PowerPoint Help window, type **check spelling** and then press Enter.

7 Click a hyperlink in the PowerPoint Help window that will display information on checking spelling.

8 Read the information that displays about spell checking and then click the Close button ❌ located in the upper right corner of the PowerPoint Help window.

9 Complete a spelling check by moving the insertion point to the beginning of *Timetable*, clicking the Review tab, and then clicking the Spelling button 🔤 in the Proofing group.

10 When the spelling checker selects *Asignments* in Slide 7 and displays *Assignments* in the *Change to* text box in the Spelling dialog box, click the Change button.

Refer to Table 1.3 for a description of the Spelling dialog box options.

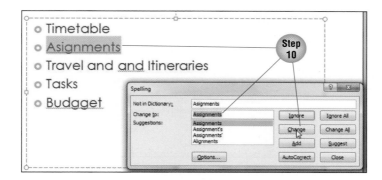

TABLE 1.3 Spelling Dialog Box Options

Button	Function
Ignore	skips that occurrence of the word and leaves currently selected text as written
Ignore All	skips that occurrence of the word and all other occurrences of the word in the presentation
Delete	deletes the currently selected word(s)
Change	replaces selected word in sentence with selected word in the *Suggestions* list box
Change All	replaces selected word with selected word in *Suggestions* list box and all other occurrences of the word in the presentation
Add	adds selected word to the main spelling check dictionary
Suggest	moves the insertion point to the *Suggestions* list box where you can scroll through the list of suggested spellings
AutoCorrect	inserts selected word and correct spelling of word in AutoCorrect dialog box
Options	displays a dialog box with options for customizing a spelling check

continues

11) When the spelling checker selects the second *and* in the slide, click the Delete button.

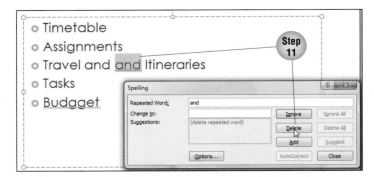

12) When the spelling checker selects *Budgget* in Slide 7 and displays *Budget* in the *Change to* text box in the Spelling dialog box, click the Change button.

13) When the spelling checker selects *Greenbaum* in Slide 6, click the Ignore button.

> Greenbaum is a proper name and is spelled correctly. Clicking the Ignore button tells the spelling checker to leave the name as spelled.

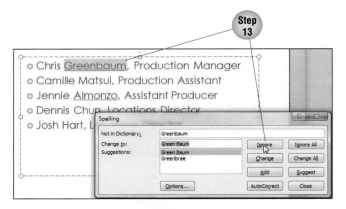

14) When the spelling checker selects *Almonzo* in Slide 6, click the Ignore button.

15) At the message telling you that the spelling check is complete, click the OK button.

16) Display Slide 7 in the Slide pane and then click the word *Timetable*.

17) Look up synonyms for *Timetable* by clicking the Thesaurus button in the Proofing group.

> This displays the Research task pane containing lists of synonyms for *Timetable*. Depending on the word you are looking up, the words in the Research task pane list box may display followed by *(n.)* for *noun*, *(adj.)* for *adjective*, or *(adv.)* for *adverb*. Antonyms may display in the list of related synonyms, generally at the end of the list of related synonyms, and are followed by *(Antonym)*.

18 Position the mouse pointer on the word *Schedule* in the Research task pane, click the down-pointing arrow at the right of the word, and then click *Insert* at the drop-down list.

> This replaces *Timetable* with *Schedule*.

19 Close the Research task pane by clicking the Close button located in the upper right corner of the task pane.

In Brief

Use Help
1. Click Microsoft PowerPoint Help button.
2. Type text for desired information.
3. Click Search button.

Complete Spelling Check
1. Click Review tab.
2. Click Spelling button.
3. Change or ignore highlighted words.
4. When spelling check is completed, click OK.

Use Thesaurus
1. Click desired word.
2. Click Review tab.
3. Click Thesaurus button.
4. Position mouse pointer on desired replacement word in Research task pane, click down-pointing arrow at right of word, and then click *Insert*.

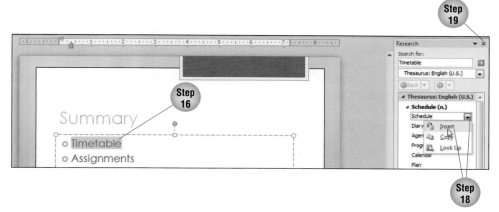

20 Right-click on the word *Tasks*, point to *Synonyms*, and then click *Responsibilities*.

> The shortcut menu offers another method for displaying synonyms for words.

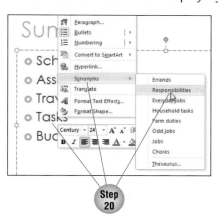

21 Save **PS1-MPProdMtg.pptx**.

In Addition

Changing Spelling Options

Control spelling options at the PowerPoint Options dialog box with the Proofing option selected. Display this dialog box by clicking the File tab and then clicking the Options button below the Help tab. At the PowerPoint Options dialog box, click *Proofing* at the left side of the dialog box. With options in the dialog box, you can tell the spelling checker to ignore certain types of text, create custom dictionaries, and hide spelling errors in the presentation.

Editing While Checking Spelling

When checking a presentation, you can temporarily leave the Spelling dialog box by clicking in the slide. To resume the spelling check, click the Resume button, which was formerly the Ignore button.

Activity 1.8

Running a Presentation; Using the Pen During a Presentation

You can run a presentation in PowerPoint manually, advance the slides automatically, or set up a slide show to run continuously for demonstration purposes. To run a slide show manually, click the Slide Show tab and then click the From Beginning button in the Start Slide Show group or click the Slide Show button in the View area on the Status bar. You can also run the presentation beginning with the currently active slide by clicking the From Current Slide button in the Start Slide Show group or clicking the Slide Show button in the View area. Use the mouse or keyboard to advance through the slides. You can also use buttons on the Slide Show toolbar that display when you move the mouse pointer while running a presentation. Emphasize major points or draw the attention of the audience to specific items in a slide during a presentation using the pen. To use the pen on a slide, run the presentation, and when the desired slide displays, move the mouse to display the Slide Show toolbar. Click the mouse pointer button on the toolbar and then click *Pen*. Use the mouse to draw in the slide to emphasize a point or specific text.

Project

You are now ready to run the movie production meeting presentation. You will use the mouse to perform various actions while running the presentation and use the pen to emphasize points in slides.

1. With **PS1-MPProdMtg.pptx** open, click the Slide Show tab and then click the From Beginning button in the Start Slide Show group.

   Clicking this button begins the presentation, and Slide 1 fills the entire screen.

SNAP

Tutorial 1.7
Completing the
Presentation Cycle

2. After viewing Slide 1, click the left mouse button to advance to the next slide.

3. At Slide 2, move the mouse pointer until the Slide Show toolbar displays in the lower left corner of the slide (appears in a dimmed manner) and then click the left arrow button on the toolbar to display the previous slide (Slide 1).

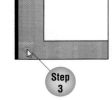

Step 3

   With buttons on the Slide Show toolbar you can display the next slide, the previous slide, display a specific slide, and use the pen and highlighter to emphasize text on the slide. You can also display the Slide Show Help window shown in Figure 1.3 that describes all the navigating options when running a presentation. Display this window by clicking the slide icon button on the Slide Show toolbar and then clicking Help.

4. Click the right arrow button on the Slide Show toolbar to display the next slide (Slide 2).

FIGURE 1.3 Slide Show Help Window

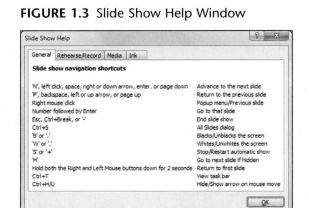

5. Display the previous slide (Slide 1) by clicking the right mouse button anywhere on the slide and then clicking *Previous* at the shortcut menu.

Clicking the right mouse button causes a shortcut menu to display with a variety of options including options to display the previous or next slide.

6. Display the next slide by clicking the slide icon button on the Slide Show toolbar and then clicking the *Next* option.

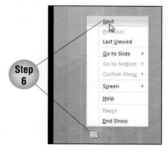

Step 6

7. Display Slide 5 by typing the number *5* on the keyboard and then pressing Enter.

Move to any slide in a presentation by typing the slide number and pressing Enter.

8. Change to a black screen by typing the letter *B* on the keyboard.

When you type the letter *B*, the slide is removed from the screen and the screen displays black. This might be useful in a situation where you want to discuss something with your audience unrelated to the slide.

9. Return to Slide 5 by typing the letter *B* on the keyboard.

Typing the letter *B* switches between the slide and a black screen. Type the letter *W* if you want to switch between the slide and a white screen.

10. Click the left mouse button to display Slide 6. Continue clicking the left mouse button until a black screen displays. At the black screen, click the left mouse button again.

This returns the presentation to the Normal view.

11. Make sure that Slide 1 is the active slide.

This displays Slide 1 in the Slide pane.

12. Display Slide 2 by clicking the Next Slide button located at the bottom of the vertical scroll bar.

13. Click the From Current Slide button ⊡ in the Start Slide Show group in the Slide Show tab.

Clicking this button begins the presentation with the active slide.

14. Run the presentation by clicking the left mouse button on each slide until Slide 5 is active (the slide that contains the title *Production Schedule*).

15. Move the mouse to display the Slide Show toolbar, click the Pen button, and then click *Pen*.

This turns the mouse pointer into a small circle.

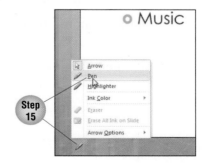

Step 15

continues

16. Using the mouse, draw a circle around the text *Location Shoots*.

17. Using the mouse, draw a line below *Dubbing*.

18. Erase the pen markings by clicking the Pen button on the Slide Show toolbar and then clicking *Erase All Ink on Slide*.

19. Change the color of the ink by clicking the Pen button, pointing to *Ink Color*, and then clicking *Blue* in the *Standard Colors* section (third option from the right).

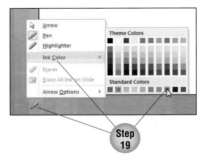

20. Draw a blue line below the word *Music*.

21. Return the mouse pointer back to an arrow by clicking the Pen button and then clicking *Arrow*.

22. Click the left mouse button to advance to Slide 6.

23 Click the Pen button and then click *Highlighter*.

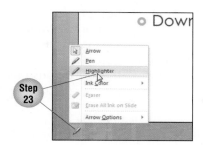

24 Using the mouse, drag through the words *Studio Shoots*.

25 Using the mouse, drag through the words *Location Shoots*.

26 Return the mouse pointer back to an arrow by clicking the Pen button and then clicking *Arrow*.

27 Press the Esc key on the keyboard to end the presentation without running the remaining slides. At the message asking if you want to keep your ink annotations, click the Discard button.

In Addition

Hiding/Displaying the Mouse Pointer

When running a presentation, the mouse pointer is set, by default, to be hidden automatically after three seconds of inactivity. The mouse pointer will appear again when you move the mouse. You can change this default setting by clicking the pen button on the Slide Show toolbar, pointing to *Arrow* *Options* and then clicking *Visible* if you want the mouse pointer always visible or *Hidden* if you do not want the mouse to display at all as you run the presentation. The *Automatic* option is the default setting.

Activity 1.9

Adding Transitions and Sound

You can apply interesting transitions and sounds to a presentation. A transition is how one slide is removed from the screen during a presentation and the next slide is displayed. Interesting transitions can be added such as fades, dissolves, push, cover, wipes, stripes, and bar. Add a sound to a presentation and the sound is heard when a slide is displayed on the screen during a presentation. Add transitions and sounds with options in the Transitions tab.

Project

You have decided to enhance the movie production meeting presentation by adding transitions and sound to the slides.

Tutorial 1.8
Adding Transition Effects and Sound

1. With **PS1-MPProdMtg.pptx** open, click the Transitions tab.

2. Click the More button located at the right side of the transition thumbnails that display in the Transition to This Slide group.

3. At the drop-down gallery, click the *Cube* option in the *Exciting* section of the drop-down gallery.

   A gallery contains the live preview feature that shows the transition in the slide in the Slide pane as you hover the mouse over a transition option in the drop-down gallery.

4. Click the Effect Options button in the Transition to This Slide group and then click *From Bottom* at the drop-down list.

   The effect options change depending on the transition selected.

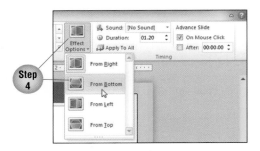

5. Click the down-pointing arrow at the right side of the Sound button in the Timing group.

6. At the drop-down gallery that displays, click the *Click* option.

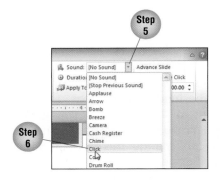

⑦ Apply three seconds to each slide transition by clicking in the *Duration* option box, typing **3**, and then pressing Enter.

⑧ Click the Apply To All button 🖼 in the Timing group.

> Notice that a play animations star icon displays below the slide numbers in the Slides/Outline pane.

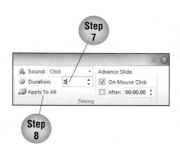

Step 7

Step 8

⑨ Click the Slide 1 miniature in the Slides/Outline pane.

⑩ Run the presentation by clicking the Slide Show button 🖳 in the View area on the Status bar.

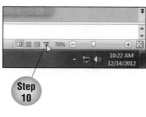

Step 10

⑪ Click the left mouse button to advance each slide.

⑫ At the black screen that displays after the last slide, click the left mouse button again to return the presentation to the Normal view.

⑬ Click the More button located at the right side of the transition thumbnails that display in the Transition to This Slide group.

⑭ Click the *Gallery* option in the *Exciting* section of the drop-down gallery.

⑮ Click the down-pointing arrow at the right side of the Sound button and then click *Push* at the drop-down gallery.

⑯ Click the down-pointing arrow at the right of the *Duration* option until *01.25* displays.

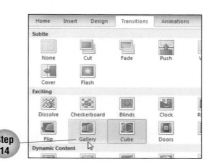

Step 14

⑰ Click the Apply To All button in the Timing group.

⑱ With Slide 1 active, run the presentation.

⑲ Save **PS1-MPProdMtg.pptx**.

In Brief

Add Transition to All Slides in Presentation
1. Click Transitions tab.
2. Click More button at right side of transition thumbnails.
3. Click desired transition at drop-down gallery.
4. Click Apply To All button.

Add Transition Sound to All Slides in Presentation
1. Click Transitions tab.
2. Click Sound button arrow.
3. Click desired option at drop-down gallery.
4. Click Apply To All button.

In Addition

Running a Slide Show Automatically

Slides in a slide show can be advanced automatically after a specific number of seconds by inserting a check mark in the *After* check box in the Timing group and removing the check mark from the *On Mouse Click* check box. Change the time in the *After* text box by clicking the up- or down-pointing arrow at the right side of the text box or by selecting any text in the text box and then typing the desired time. If you want the transition time to affect all slides in the presentation, click the Apply To All button. In Slide Sorter view, the transition time displays below each affected slide. Click the Slide Show button to run the presentation. The first slide displays for the specified amount of time and then the next slide automatically displays.

Activity 1.10

Printing and Previewing a Presentation

You can print each slide on a separate piece of paper; print each slide at the top of the page, leaving the bottom of the page for notes; print up to nine slides or a specific number of slides on a single piece of paper; or print the slide titles and topics in outline form. Before printing a presentation, consider previewing it. You can choose print options and display a preview of the presentation in the Print tab Backstage view. Display this view by clicking the File tab and then clicking the Print tab. Click the File tab again to remove the Backstage view without clicking a tab or button.

Project

Staff members need the movie production meeting slides printed as handouts and as an outline. You will preview and print the presentation in various formats.

Tutorial 1.9
Printing a Presentation

Tutorial 1.10
Previewing Slides

1. With **PS1-MPProdMtg.pptx** open, display Slide 1 in the Slide pane.

2. Click the File tab and then click the Print tab.

    Slide 1 of your presentation displays at the right side of the screen as it will when printed. Use the Next Page button (right-pointing arrow) located below and to the left of the slide to view the next slide in the presentation, click the Previous Page button (left-pointing arrow) to display the previous slide in the presentation, use the Zoom slider bar to increase/decrease the size of the slide, and click the Zoom to Page button to fit the slide in the viewing area in the Print tab Backstage view. The left side of the Print tab Backstage view displays three categories—Print, Printer, and Settings. Galleries display below each category name. For example, the Printer category has one gallery that displays the name of the currently selected printer. The Settings category has a number of galleries that describe how the slides will print.

3. Click the Next Page button located below and to the left of the preview slide to display the next slide in the presentation.

    This displays Slide 2 in the preview area of the Backstage view.

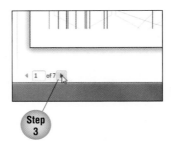

Step 3

4. Click twice on the Zoom In button that displays at the right side of the Zoom slider bar.

    Click the Zoom In button to increase the size of the slide or click the Zoom Out button (displays with a minus symbol) to decrease the size of the slide.

5. Click the Zoom to Page button located at the right side of the Zoom slider bar.

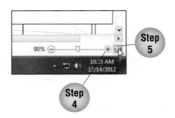

Step 5

Step 4

6 You decide to print the slides on two pages and you want to preview how the slides will appear on the page. To do this, click the second gallery in the *Settings* category (contains the text *Full Page Slides*) and then click *4 Slides Horizontal* in the *Handouts* section.

> Notice how four slides display on the preview page.

7 Click the Print button in the *Print* category.

8 You want to print all slide text on one page and use the printing as a reference. To do this, click the File tab and then click the Print tab.

9 At the Print tab Backstage view, click the second gallery in the *Settings* category (contains the text *4 Slides Horizontal*) and then click *Outline* in the *Print Layout* section.

10 Click the Print button in the *Print* category.

> With the *Outline* option selected, the presentation prints on one page with slide numbers, slide icons, and slide text in outline form.

11 You need a printing of Slide 6. To do this, click the File tab and then click the Print tab.

12 At the Print tab Backstage view, click the second gallery in the *Settings* category (contains the text *Outline*) and then click *Full Page Slides* in the *Print Layout* section.

13 Click in the *Slides* text box located below the first gallery in the *Settings* category, type **6**, and then click the Print button.

14 Save **PS1-MPProdMtg.pptx**.

15 Close the presentation by clicking the File tab and then clicking the Close button.

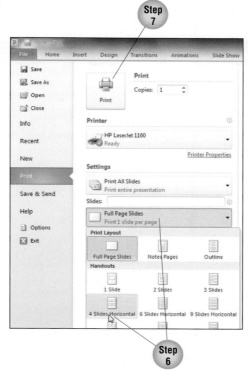

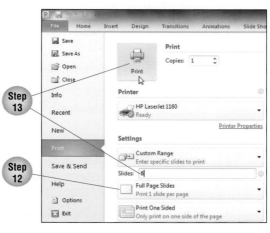

In Addition

Using Options at the Page Setup Dialog Box

You can change orientation with the Slide Orientation button located in the Page Setup group in the Design tab or with options at the Page Setup dialog box shown at the right. Display this dialog box by clicking the Design tab and then clicking the Page Setup button. With options at this dialog box you can specify how you want slides sized; page width and height; orientation for slides; and orientation for notes, handouts, and outline.

Features Summary

Feature	Ribbon Tab, Group	Button	File Tab	Keyboard Shortcut
apply transitions and sound to all slides	Transitions, Timing			
close		X	Close	Ctrl + F4
exit PowerPoint			Exit	
Help		?		F1
layout	Home, Slides			
new slide	Home, Slides			Ctrl + M
Normal view	View, Presentation Views			
Notes Page view	View, Presentation Views			
open blank presentation				Ctrl + N
Open dialog box			Open	Ctrl + O
Print tab Backstage view			Print	Ctrl + P
run presentation from current slide	Slide Show, Start Slide Show			Shift + F5
run presentation from Slide 1	Slide Show, Start Slide Show			F5
save			Save	Ctrl + S
save with a new name			Save As	F12
Slide Sorter view	View, Presentation Views			
Spelling	Review, Proofing	ABC		F7
themes	Design, Themes			
Thesaurus	Review, Proofing			Shift + F7
transitions	Transitions, Transition to This Slide			
transition sound	Transitions, Timing			
transition duration	Transitions, Timing			
Zoom dialog box	View, Zoom			

Knowledge Check

Completion: In the space provided at the right, indicate the correct term, command, or option.

1. To run a presentation beginning with Slide 1, click the Slide Show tab and then click this button.
2. The Save button is located on this toolbar.
3. The Normal view contains the Slides/Outline pane, the Slide pane, and this pane.
4. The New Slide button is located in this tab.
5. The Zoom slider bar is located at the right side of this bar.
6. Click the Microsoft PowerPoint Help button and this displays.
7. Use this feature to find synonyms, antonyms, and related words for a particular word.
8. The Spelling button is located in the Proofing group in this tab.
9. Move the mouse while running a presentation and this toolbar displays.
10. Press this key on the keyboard to change to a black screen while running a presentation.
11. Press this key on the keyboard to end a presentation without running all of the slides.
12. Add transitions and sound to a presentation with options in this tab.
13. Specify the length of a transition using the Duration option located in this group in the Transitions tab.
14. You can print up to this number of slides on a single piece of paper.

Skills Review

Review 1 Creating a Presentation for Marquee Productions

1. Create a new folder on your storage medium and name it **PowerPointEOS**.
2. With a blank presentation open in PowerPoint, click the Design tab, click the More button at the right side of the thumbnails in the Themes group, and then click *Pushpin* in the drop-down gallery (located in the *Built In* section).
3. Type the title and subtitle for Slide 1 as shown in Figure 1.4.
4. Click the Home tab and then click the New Slide button in the Slides group.
5. Type the text shown for Slide 2 in Figure 1.4.
6. Continue creating the slides for the presentation as shown in Figure 1.4.
7. Insert a new Slide 3 between the current Slides 2 and 3 with the text shown in Figure 1.5.
8. Display Slide 2 in the Slide pane and then change the slide layout to *Title Slide*.
9. Click in the text *Current Status* to select the placeholder and then move the placeholder up approximately one inch.
10. Click in the text *Overview of Project* to select the placeholder and then move the placeholder up approximately one-half inch.
11. Change to Slide Sorter view and then move Slide 3 (*Resources*) immediately after Slide 1 (*Marquee Productions*).
12. Change to the Normal view, click the Transitions tab, click the More button located at the right side of the transition thumbnails in the Transition to This Slide group, and then click the *Orbit* option in the *Dynamic Content* section.
13. Click the down-pointing arrow at the right of the Sound button and then click *Drum Roll* at the drop-down gallery.
14. Click the down-pointing arrow at the right side of the *Duration* text box until *00.75* displays in the text box.
15. Apply the transition, sound, and duration to all slides in the presentation.
16. Save the presentation in the PowerPointEOS folder and name it **PS1-R1-MPTeamMtg**.
17. Run the presentation beginning with Slide 1.
18. View the presentation as an outline in the Print tab Backstage view.
19. Print the presentation with all five slides positioned horizontally on the page.
20. Save and then close **PS1-R1-MPTeamMtg.pptx**.

FIGURE 1.4 Review 1

| Slide 1 | Title | Marquee Productions |
| | Subtitle | Location Team Meeting |

Slide 2   Title   Current Status
            Bullets
- Overview of Project
- Tasks on Schedule
- Tasks behind Schedule

Slide 3   Title   Filming Sites
            Bullets
- Gardiner Expressway
- Kings Mill Park
- Island Airport
- Royal Ontario Museum
- Black Creek Pioneer Village
- Additional Sites

Slide 4   Title   Key Issues
            Bullets
- Equipment Rental
- Budget Overruns
- Transportation Concerns
- Location Agreements

FIGURE 1.5 Review 1

Slide 3   Title   Resources
            Bullets
- Location Contacts
- Movie Extras
- Catering Company
- Lodging
- Transportation Rentals

Skills Assessment

Assessment 1 Preparing a Presentation for Worldwide Enterprises

1. Prepare a presentation for Worldwide Enterprises with the information shown in Figure 1.6. (You determine the design template.)
2. Add a transition, sound, and transition duration time of your choosing to all slides in the presentation.
3. Run the presentation.
4. Print the presentation with all five slides positioned horizontally on one page.
5. Save the presentation in the PowerPointEOS folder and name it **PS1-A1-WEExecMtg**.
6. Close **PS1-A1-WEExecMtg.pptx**.

FIGURE 1.6 Assessment 1

Slide 1	Title	Worldwide Enterprises
	Subtitle	Executive Meeting
Slide 2	Title	Accounting Policies
	Bullets	• Cash Equivalents
		• Short-term Investments
		• Inventory Valuation
		• Property and Equipment
		• Foreign Currency Translation
Slide 3	Title	Financial Instruments
	Bullets	• Investments
		• Derivative Instruments
		• Credit Risks
		• Fair Value of Instruments
Slide 4	Title	Inventories
	Bullets	• Products
		• Raw Material
		• Equipment
		• Buildings
Slide 5	Title	Employee Plans
	Bullets	• Stock Options
		• Bonus Plan
		• Savings and Retirement Plan
		• Defined Benefits Plan
		• Foreign Subsidiaries

Assessment 2 Preparing a Presentation for The Waterfront Bistro

1. Prepare a presentation for The Waterfront Bistro with the information shown in Figure 1.7. (You determine the design template.)
2. Add a transition, sound, and transition duration time of your choosing to all slides in the presentation.
3. Run the presentation.
4. Print the presentation with all five slides positioned horizontally on one page.
5. Save the presentation in the PowerPointEOS folder and name it **PS1-A2-WBServices**.
6. Close **PS1-A2-WBServices.pptx**.

FIGURE 1.7 Assessment 2

Slide 1	Title	The Waterfront Bistro
	Subtitle	3104 Rivermist Drive
		Buffalo, NY 14280
		(716) 555-3166
Slide 2	Title	Accommodations
	Bullets	• Dining Area
		• Salon
		• Two Banquet Rooms
		• Wine Cellar
Slide 3	Title	Menus
	Bullets	• Lunch
		• Dinner
		• Wines
		• Desserts
Slide 4	Title	Catering Services
	Bullets	• Lunch
		– Continental
		– Deli
		– Hot
		• Dinner
		– Vegetarian
		– Meat
		– Seafood
Slide 5	Title	Resource
	Subtitle	Dana Hirsch, Manager

Assessment 3 Finding Information on Setting Slide Show Timings

1. Open **MPProj.pptx** and then use the Help feature to learn how to save a presentation with Save As.
2. Save the presentation with Save As in the PowerPointEOS folder and name it **PS1-A3-MPProj**.
3. Use the Help feature or experiment with the options in the Transitions tab and learn how to set slide show timings manually.
4. Set up the presentation so that, when running the presentation, each slide advances automatically after three seconds.
5. Run the presentation.
6. Save and then close **PS1-A3-MPProj.pptx**.

Assessment 4 Individual Challenge
Preparing a Presentation on Cancun, Mexico

1. You are interested in planning a vacation to Cancun, Mexico. Connect to the Internet and search for information on Cancun. (One possible site for information is www.cancun.com.) Locate information on lodging (hotels), restaurants, activities, and transportation.
2. Using PowerPoint, create a presentation about Cancun that contains the following:
   - Title slide containing the title *Vacationing in Cancun*, and your name as the subtitle
   - Slide containing the names of at least three major airlines that travel to Cancun
   - Slide containing the names of at least four hotels or resorts in Cancun
   - Slide containing the names of at least four restaurants in Cancun
   - Slide containing at least four activities in Cancun
3. Run the presentation.
4. Print all of the slides on one page.
5. Save the presentation in the PowerPointEOS folder and name it **PS1-A4-IC-Cancun**.
6. Close **PS1-A4-IC-Cancun.pptx**.

Marquee Challenge

Challenge 1 Preparing a Presentation on Toronto, Ontario, Canada

1. Create the presentation shown in Figure 1.8. Apply the appropriate design theme and slide layouts, and size and move placeholders so your slides display as shown in the figure.
2. Apply a transition, sound, and transition duration time of your choosing to each slide in the presentation.
3. Save the completed presentation in the PowerPointEOS folder and name it **PS1-C1-FCTToronto**.
4. Print the presentation as a handout with all six slides on the same page.
5. Close the presentation.

Challenge 2 Preparing a Presentation for Performance Threads

1. Open **PTCostumeMtg.pptx** and then save the presentation in the PowerPointEOS folder and name it **PS1-C2-PTCostumeMtg**.
2. Apply the Hardcover design theme, add and rearrange slides, change slide layouts, and move a placeholder so the presentation displays as shown in Figure 1.9. (Read the slides in Figure 1.9 from left to right.)
3. Apply a transition, sound, and transition duration time of your choosing to each slide in the presentation.
4. Save and then print the presentation as a handout with all six slides on the same page.
5. Close the presentation.

FIGURE 1.8 Challenge 1

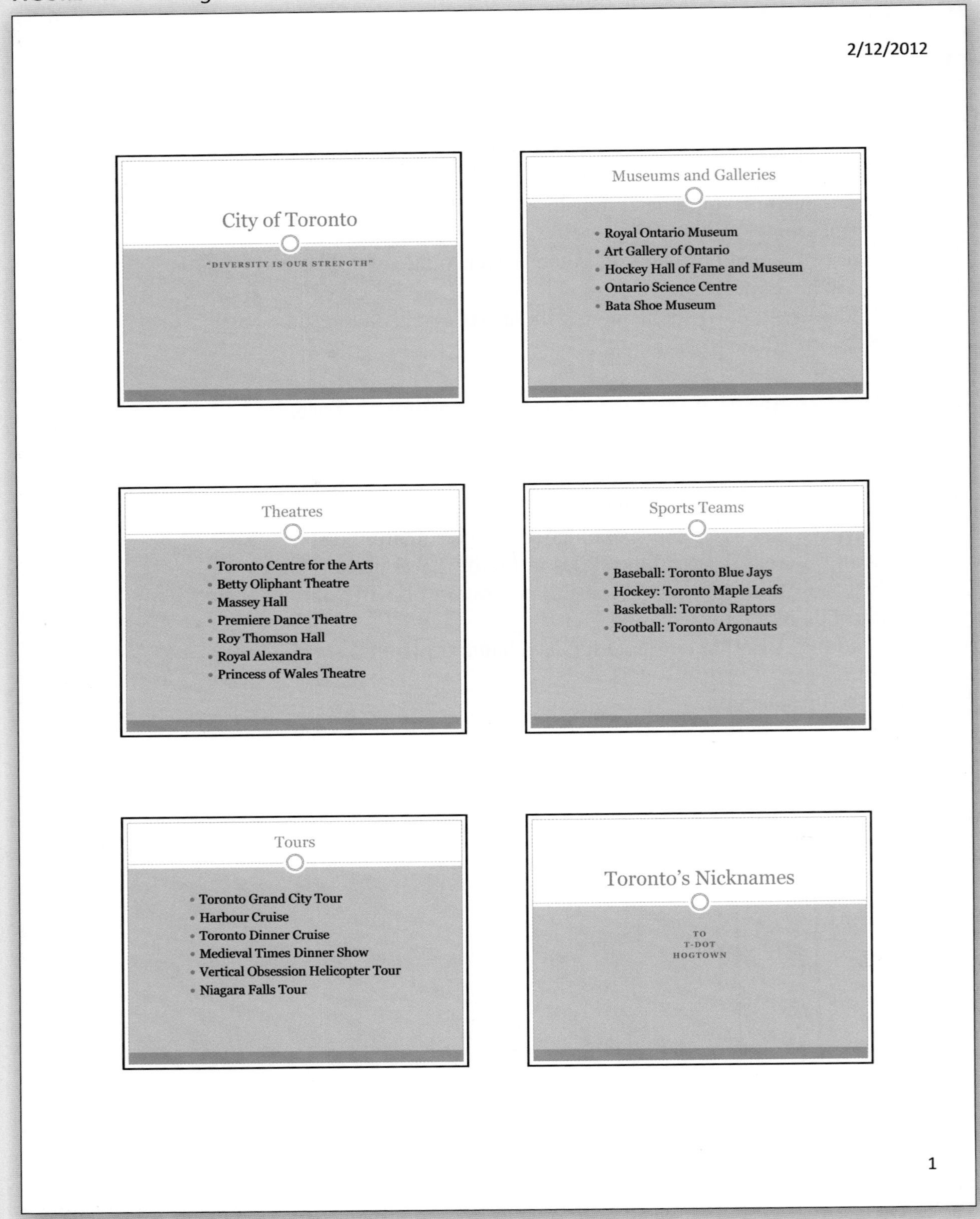

2/12/2012

City of Toronto

"DIVERSITY IS OUR STRENGTH"

Museums and Galleries

- Royal Ontario Museum
- Art Gallery of Ontario
- Hockey Hall of Fame and Museum
- Ontario Science Centre
- Bata Shoe Museum

Theatres

- Toronto Centre for the Arts
- Betty Oliphant Theatre
- Massey Hall
- Premiere Dance Theatre
- Roy Thomson Hall
- Royal Alexandra
- Princess of Wales Theatre

Sports Teams

- Baseball: Toronto Blue Jays
- Hockey: Toronto Maple Leafs
- Basketball: Toronto Raptors
- Football: Toronto Argonauts

Tours

- Toronto Grand City Tour
- Harbour Cruise
- Toronto Dinner Cruise
- Medieval Times Dinner Show
- Vertical Obsession Helicopter Tour
- Niagara Falls Tour

Toronto's Nicknames

TO
T-DOT
HOGTOWN

1

FIGURE 1.9 Challenge 2

2/18/2012

1

PowerPoint SECTION 2
Editing and Enhancing Slides

Skills

- Open a presentation and save it with a new name
- Increase and decrease the indent of text
- Select, cut, copy, and paste text
- Apply font and font effects
- Find and replace fonts
- Apply formatting with Format Painter
- Change alignment and line and paragraph spacing
- Change the design theme, theme color, and theme font
- Insert, size, and move images
- Insert and format clip art images
- Insert and format a SmartArt organizational chart
- Insert and format a SmartArt graphic
- Apply animation to an object in a slide

Projects Overview

Open an existing project presentation for Marquee Productions, save the presentation with a new name, and then edit and format the presentation. Open an existing annual meeting presentation for Marquee Productions and then save, edit, and format the presentation.

Open an existing presentation for the Theatre Arts Division of Niagara Peninsula College and then save, edit, and format the presentation.

Open an existing presentation containing information on vacation specials offered by First Choice Travel and then save, edit, and format the presentation.

Prepare and format a presentation on the services offered by the bistro.

Prepare and format a presentation on the company structure, policies, and benefits.

Prepare and format a presentation for a planning meeting of the distribution department.

Model Answers for Projects

These model answers for the projects that you complete in Section 2 provide a preview of the finished projects before you begin working and also allow you to compare your own results with these models to ensure you have created the materials accurately.

PS2-MPPProj.pptx **(a two-page document) is the project in Activities 2.1 to 2.11.**

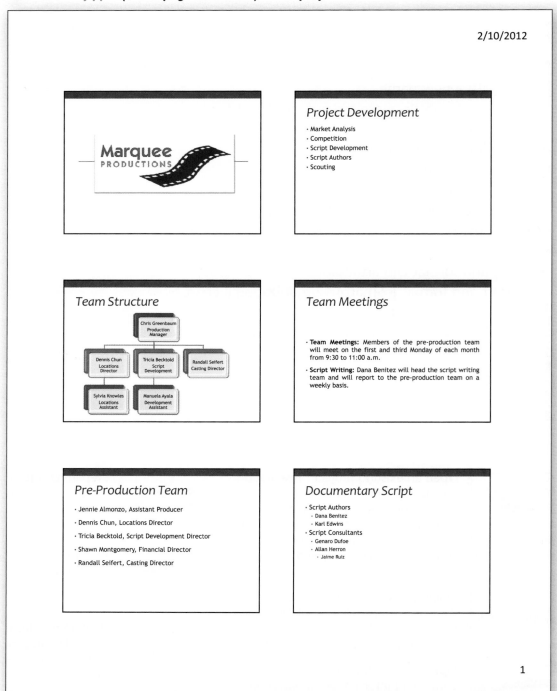

2/10/2012

Script Schedule

- **Phase 1**
  - Research
  - Script First Draft
- **Phase 2**
  - Documenting
  - Editing
  - Rewriting
- **Phase 3**
  - Final Draft
  - Script Approval

Marquee
PRODUCTIONS

Raising the Bar

SCRIPT

Dana Benitez
Karl Edwins

September, 2012

Pre-Production Assignments

- Researching: Jaime Ruiz, Allan Herron
- Documenting: Allan Herron, Genaro Dufoe
- Writing: Dana Benitez, Karl Edwins
- Scouting Sites: Josh Hart, Jaime Ruiz
- Casting: Randall Seifert, Jennie Almonzo, Tricia Becktold

Travel Arrangements

- Airline Travel
- Chartered Flights
- Hotel Reservations
- Vehicle Rental
- Limousine Services

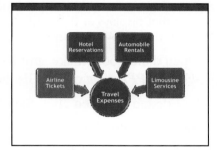

2

Activity 2.1

Increasing and Decreasing Indent; Cutting, Copying, and Pasting Text

If you open an existing presentation and make changes to it, you can then save it with the same name or a different name. Save an existing presentation with a new name at the Save As dialog box. In the Slides/Outline pane with the Outline tab selected, you can organize and develop the content of the presentation by rearranging points within a slide, moving slides, or increasing and decreasing text level indent. Click the Decrease List Level button in the Paragraph group in the Home tab or press Shift + Tab to decrease text to the previous level. Click the Increase List Level button or press the Tab key to increase text to the next level. You can also increase and/or decrease the indent of text in the slide in the Slide pane. You can select text in a slide and then delete the text from the slide, cut text from one location and paste into another, or copy and paste the text. Use buttons in the Clipboard group in the Home tab to cut, copy, and paste text.

Project

Tutorial 2.1
Cutting, Copying, Pasting, and Aligning Text

Chris Greenbaum has prepared a documentary project presentation and has asked you to edit the presentation by increasing and decreasing text level and selecting, deleting, moving, copying, and pasting text in slides.

1. With PowerPoint open, click the File tab and then click the Open button.

   You can add buttons to the Quick Access toolbar that represent commonly used features. For example, you can add the Open button to save steps when opening a presentation. To add the Open button, click the Customize Quick Access Toolbar button that displays at the right side of the Quick Access toolbar and then click Open at the drop-down list.

2. At the Open dialog box, make sure PowerPointS2 is the active folder and then double-click *MPProj.pptx* in the list box.

3. Click the File tab and then click Save As.

4. At the Save As dialog box, press the Home key to move the insertion point to the beginning of the file name, type **PS2-** in the *File Name* text box, and then press the Enter key. (The file name in the *File Name* text box should display as *PS2-MPProj.pptx*.)

   Pressing the Home key saves you from having to type the entire file name.

5. Display Slide 5 in the Slide pane.

6. You decide to promote the names below *Script Authors*. To do this, position the mouse pointer immediately left of the *D* in *Dana*, click the left mouse button, and then click the Decrease List Level button in the Paragraph group in the Home tab.

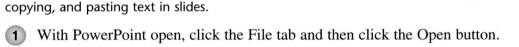

7. Position the insertion point immediately left of the *K* in *Karl* in Slide 5 and then promote the text to the previous level by pressing Shift + Tab.

8. Demote two of the names below *Script Consultants* by clicking immediately left of the *J* in *Jaime* and then clicking the Increase List Level button in the Paragraph group in the Home tab.

9 Position the insertion point immediately left of the *G* in *Genaro* and then press the Tab key.

10 Display Slide 6 in the Slide pane.

11 Position the mouse pointer on the bullet that displays before *Script Rewriting* until the mouse pointer turns into a four-headed arrow and then click the left mouse button.

> This selects the text *Script Rewriting*. Refer to Table 2.1 for additional information on selecting text.

12 Press the Delete key.

> This deletes the selected text.

13 Display Slide 5 in the Slide pane, position the mouse pointer on the bullet that displays before *Genaro Dufoe* until the mouse pointer turns into a four-headed arrow, and then click the left mouse button.

14 Click the Cut button ✂ in the Clipboard group in the Home tab.

> The keyboard shortcut to cut text is Ctrl + X.

15 Position the mouse pointer immediately left of the *A* in *Allan Herron*, click the left mouse button, and then click the Paste button 📋 in the Clipboard group.

16 Using the mouse, drag to select the text *Script Authors* and then click the Copy button 📑 in the Clipboard group.

> The keyboard shortcut to copy text is Ctrl + C.

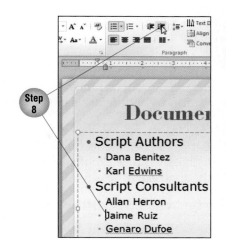

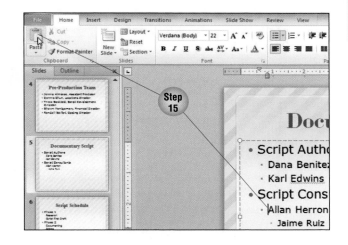

17 Make Slide 2 active, position the insertion point immediately left of the *S* in *Scouting*, and then click the Paste button in the Clipboard group.

> If *Script Authors* and *Scouting* display on the same line, press the Enter key. The keyboard shortcut to paste text is Ctrl + V.

18 Save **PS2-MPProj.pptx**.

In Brief

Save Presentation with New Name
1. Click File tab.
2. Click Save As button.
3. Type presentation name.
4. Click Save or press Enter.

Decrease Text Level Indent
Click Decrease List Level button or press Shift + Tab.

Increase Text Level Indent
Click Increase List Level button or press Tab.

Cut and Paste Text
1. Select text.
2. Click Cut button.
3. Position insertion point.
4. Click Paste button.

Copy and Paste Text
1. Select text.
2. Click Copy button.
3. Position insertion point.
4. Click Paste button.

TABLE 2.1 Selecting Text

To select	Perform this action
entire word	Double-click word.
entire paragraph	Triple-click anywhere in paragraph.
entire sentence	Ctrl + click anywhere in sentence.
text mouse pointer passes through	Click and drag with mouse.
all text in selected object box	Click Select button in Editing group and then click Select All; or press Ctrl + A.

Activity 2.2

Applying Fonts and Font Effects

The Font group in the Home tab contains two rows of buttons. The top row contains buttons for changing the font and font size and a button for clearing formatting.

The bottom row contains buttons for applying font effects such as bold, italic, underline, strikethrough, and character spacing as well as buttons for changing the case of selected text and font color.

Project

Tutorial 2.2
Changing Font
Attributes

Certain text elements on slides in the documentary project presentation need to be highlighted to make them stand out. You will apply font effects to specific text and change the font size of selected text.

1. With **PS2-MPProj.pptx** open, display Slide 1 in the Slide pane.

2. Select the title *Marquee Productions* and then click the Italic button I in the Font group in the Home tab.

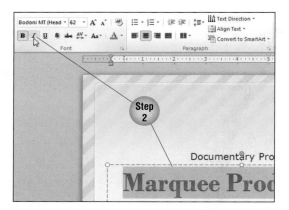

3. Select the subtitle *Documentary Project*, click the Increase Font Size button $A^{\cdot}$, and then click the Bold button B in the Font group.

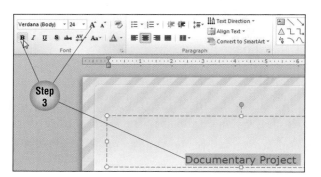

4. Make Slide 6 active in the Slide pane, select the text *Phase 1*, and then click the Underline button U in the Font group.

5. Select and then underline the text *Phase 2*.

6. Select and then underline the text *Phase 3*.

7. Make Slide 1 active.

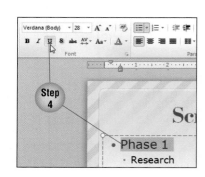

8 Select the title *Marquee Productions*, click the Font button arrow in the Font group, scroll down the drop-down gallery (fonts display in alphabetical order), and then click *Calibri*.

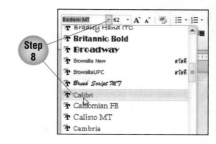

9 Select the subtitle *Documentary Project*, click the Font button arrow, and then click *Calibri* at the drop-down gallery.

> The drop-down gallery displays the most recently used fonts toward the beginning of the gallery.

10 Make Slide 6 active, select the text *Phase 1*, click the Underline button to remove underlining, and then click the Bold button to apply bold formatting.

11 With *Phase 1* still selected, click the Font button arrow and then click *Calibri* at the drop-down gallery.

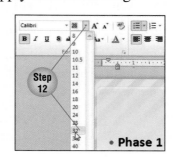

12 Click the Font Size button arrow, scroll down the drop-down gallery, and then click *32*.

13 Select the text *Phase 2*, remove the underlining, turn on bold, change the font to Calibri, and change the font size to 32.

14 Select the text *Phase 3*, remove the underlining, turn on bold, change the font to Calibri, and change the font size to 32.

15 Print Slides 1 and 6. Begin by clicking the File tab and then clicking the Print tab.

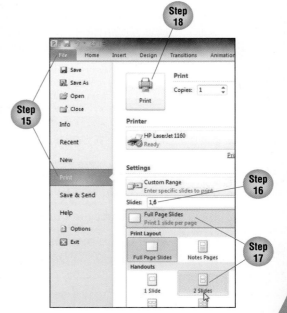

16 At the Print tab Backstage view, click in the *Slides* text box (located below the first gallery in the *Settings* category) and type **1,6**.

17 Click the second gallery in the *Settings* category (contains the text *Full Page Slides*) and then click *2 Slides* in the *Handouts* section at the drop-down list.

18 Click the Print button in the *Print* category.

> The two slides print in miniature on the same page.

19 Save **PS2-MPProj.pptx**.

In Brief

Apply Font Effects with Font Group
1. Select text.
2. Click button in Font group.

In Addition

Choosing Typefaces

A typeface is a set of characters with a common design and shape. PowerPoint refers to a typeface as a **font**. Typefaces can be decorative or plain and are either monospaced or proportional. A monospaced typeface allots the same amount of horizontal space for each character while a proportional typeface allots a varying amount of space for each character. Proportional typefaces are divided into two main categories: serif and sans serif. A serif is a small line at the end of a character stroke. Consider using a serif typeface for text-intensive slides because the serifs help move the reader's eyes across the text. Use a sans serif typeface for titles, subtitles, headings, and short text lines.

Activity 2.3

Changing the Font at the Font Dialog Box; Replacing Fonts

In addition to buttons in the Font group in the Home tab, you can apply font formatting with options at the Font dialog box. With options at this dialog box, you can change the font, font style, and size; change the font color; and apply formatting effects such as underline, strikethrough, superscript, subscript, and all caps. If you decide to change the font for all slides in a presentation, use the Replace Font dialog box to replace all occurrences of a specific font in the presentation.

Project Still not satisfied with the font choices in the documentary project presentation, you decide to change the font for the title and subtitle and replace the Verdana font on the remaining slides.

1. With **PS2-MPProj.pptx** open, make Slide 1 active.

2. Select the title *Marquee Productions*.

3. Display the Font dialog box by clicking the Font group dialog box launcher in the Home tab.

Tutorial 2.2
Changing Font
Attributes

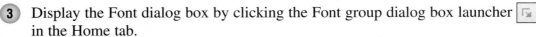
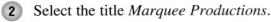

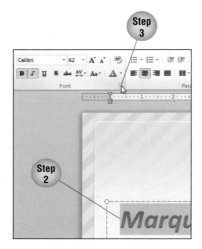

4. At the Font dialog box, click the down-pointing arrow at the right side of the *Latin text font* option box and then click *Candara* at the drop-down list.

5. Select the current measurement in the *Size* text box and then type **55**.

6. Click the Font color button in the *All text* section and then click the *Turquoise, Accent 3, Darker 25%* option.

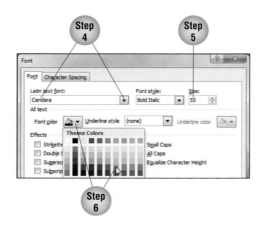

7. Click OK to close the Font dialog box.

8. Select the subtitle *Documentary Project*.

9. Click the Font group dialog box launcher.

10. At the Font dialog box, click the down-pointing arrow at the right side of the *Latin text font* option box and then click *Candara* at the drop-down list.

11. Click the down-pointing arrow at the right side of the *Font style* option box and then click *Bold Italic* at the drop-down list.

12. Select the current measurement in the *Size* text box and then type **30**.

13. Click the Font color button in the *All text* section and then click the *Dark Blue* color (second color option from the right in the *Standard Colors* section).

14. Click OK to close the Font dialog box.

15. Make Slide 2 active.

16. You decide to replace all occurrences of the Verdana font in the presentation with the Cambria font. To begin, click the Replace button arrow in the Editing group in the Home tab and then click *Replace Fonts* at the drop-down list.

17. At the Replace Font dialog box, click the down-pointing arrow at the right side of the *Replace* option box and then click *Verdana* at the drop-down list.

18. Click the down-pointing arrow at the right side of the *With* option box and then click *Cambria* at the drop-down list. (You will need to scroll down the list box to display *Cambria*.)

19. Click the Replace button and then click the Close button.

20. Save **PS2-MPProj.pptx**.

In Brief

Change Font at Font Dialog Box
1. Select text.
2. Click Font group dialog box launcher.
3. Click desired options at Font dialog box.
4. Click OK.

Change All Occurrences of Font
1. Click Replace button arrow, then click *Replace Fonts*.
2. At Replace Font dialog box, make sure desired font displays in *Replace* text box.
3. Press Tab.
4. Click down-pointing arrow at right of *With*, click desired font.
5. Click Replace button.
6. Click Close button.

In Addition

Choosing Presentation Typefaces

Choose a typeface for a presentation based on the tone and message you want the presentation to portray. For example, choose a more serious typeface such as Constantia or Times New Roman for a conservative audience and choose a less formal font such as Comic Sans MS, Lucida Handwriting, or Mistral for a more informal or lighthearted audience. For text-intensive slides, choose a serif typeface such as Cambria, Candara, Times New Roman, or Bookman Old Style. For titles, subtitles, headings, and short text items, consider a sans serif type-face such as Calibri, Arial, Tahoma, or Univers. Use no more than two or three different fonts in each presentation. To ensure text readability in a slide, choose a font color that contrasts with the slide background.

Activity 2.4

Formatting with Format Painter

Use the Format Painter feature to apply the same formatting in more than one location in a slide or slides. To use the Format Painter, apply the desired formatting to text, position the insertion point anywhere in the formatted text, and then double-click the Format Painter button in the Clipboard group in the Home tab. Using the mouse, select the additional text to which you want the formatting applied. After applying the formatting in the desired locations, click the Format Painter button to deactivate it. If you need to apply formatting in only one other location, click the Format Painter button once. The first time you select text, the formatting is applied and the Format Painter is deactivated.

Project

Tutorial 2.2
Changing Font
Attributes

Improve the appearance of slides in the documentary project presentation by applying a font and then using the Format Painter to apply the formatting to other text.

1. With **PS2-MPProj.pptx** open, make sure Slide 2 is the active slide.

2. Select the title *Project Development*.

3. Click the Font group dialog box launcher.

4. At the Font dialog box, click the down-pointing arrow in the *Latin text font* option box and then click *Candara* at the drop-down list.

    You will need to scroll down the list to display *Candara*.

5. Click the down-pointing arrow at the right side of the *Font style* option box and then click *Bold Italic* at the drop-down list.

6. Select the current measurement in the *Size* text box and then type **50**.

7. Click the Font color button in the *All text* section and then click the *Dark Blue* option (second option from the right in the *Standard Colors* section).

8. Click OK to close the Font dialog box.

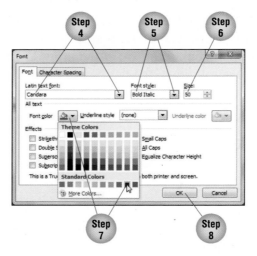

9. At the slide, deselect the text by clicking in the slide.

10. Click anywhere in the title *Project Development*.

11 Double-click the Format Painter button in the Clipboard group in the Home tab.

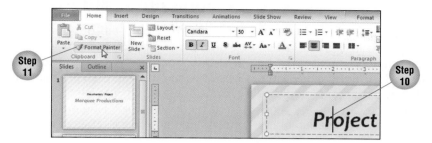

In Brief
Format with Format Painter
1. Position insertion point on text containing desired formatting.
2. Double-click Format Painter button.
3. Select text to which you want to apply formatting.
4. Click Format Painter button.

12 Click the Next Slide button to display Slide 3.

13 Using the mouse, click the word *Team* and then click the word *Meetings* in the title placeholder.

> The mouse pointer displays with a paintbrush attached. This indicates that the Format Painter feature is active. You can also apply the formatting by selecting the title.

14 Click the Next Slide button to display Slide 4.

15 Using the mouse, select the title *Pre-Production Team*.

Need Help?
If the paintbrush is no longer attached to the mouse pointer, Format Painter has been turned off. Turn it back on by clicking in a slide title with the desired formatting and then double-clicking the Format Painter button.

16 Apply formatting to the titles in the remaining three slides.

17 When formatting has been applied to all slide titles, click the Format Painter button in the Clipboard group in the Home tab.

> Clicking the Format Painter button turns off the feature.

18 Save **PS2-MPProj.pptx**.

In Addition

Choosing a Custom Color

Click the Font Color button at the Font dialog box and a palette of color choices displays. Click the *More Colors* option and the Colors dialog box with the Standard tab selected displays with a honeycomb of color options. Click the Custom tab and the dialog box displays as shown at the right. With options at this dialog box you can mix your own color. Click the desired color in the *Colors* palette or enter the values for the color in the *Red*, *Green*, and *Blue* text boxes. Adjust the luminosity of the current color by dragging the slider located at the right side of the color palette.

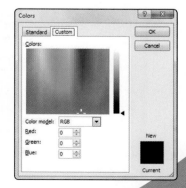

Activity 2.5

Changing Alignment and Line and Paragraph Spacing

The slide design template generally determines the horizontal and vertical alignment of text in placeholders. Text may be left-aligned, center-aligned, or right-aligned in a placeholder as well as aligned at the top, middle, or bottom of the placeholder. You can change alignment for specific text with buttons in the Paragraph group in the Home tab or with options from the Align Text button drop-down list. Use options at the Line Spacing button drop-down list or the *Line Spacing* option at the Paragraph dialog box to change line spacing. The Paragraph dialog box also contains options for changing text alignment and indentation and spacing before and after text.

Tutorial 2.3
Changing Paragraph Formatting

Project Change the alignment for specific text in slides and improve the appearance of text in slides by adjusting the vertical alignment and paragraph spacing of text.

1. With **PS2-MPProj.pptx** open, make Slide 1 active.

2. Click anywhere in the text *Documentary Project* and then click the Align Text Right button ▤ in the Paragraph group in the Home tab.

   You can also change text alignment with the keyboard shortcuts shown in Table 2.2.

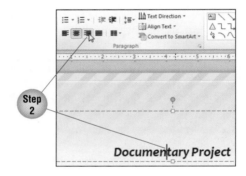

3. Click anywhere in the text *Marquee Productions* and then click the Align Text Right button.

4. Make Slide 3 active (this slide contains the title *Team Meetings*), click once in the bulleted text, and then press Ctrl + A to select all of the bulleted text.

   Ctrl + A is the keyboard shortcut for selecting all text in a placeholder.

5. Justify the text by clicking the Justify button ▤ in the Paragraph group.

6. Click the Align Text button ▤ in the Paragraph group and then click *Middle* at the drop-down list.

   This aligns the bulleted text in the middle of the placeholder.

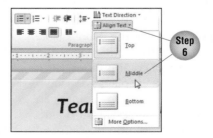

(7) With the bulleted text still selected, click the Line Spacing button ![=] and then click *Line Spacing Options* at the drop-down list.

(8) At the Paragraph dialog box, click twice on the up-pointing arrow at the right side of the *After* option in the *Spacing* section.

> This inserts *12 pt* in the *After* option box.

(9) Click OK to close the dialog box.

(10) Make Slide 4 active (contains the title *Pre-Production Team*).

(11) Click once in the bulleted text and then select all of the bulleted text by clicking the Select button ![cursor] in the Editing group in the Home tab and then clicking *Select All* at the drop-down list.

(12) Click the Line Spacing button and then click *1.5* at the drop-down list.

(13) Make Slide 7 active (contains the title *Pre-Production Assignments*).

(14) Click once in the bulleted text and then press Ctrl + A.

(15) Click the Line Spacing button in the Paragraph group and then click *Line Spacing Options* at the drop-down list.

(16) At the Paragraph dialog box, click twice on the up-pointing arrow at the right side of the *After* option in the *Spacing* section.

> This inserts *12 pt* in the *After* option box.

(17) Click OK to close the dialog box.

(18) Print only Slide 1 of the presentation as a handout.

(19) Save **PS2-MPProj.pptx**.

In Brief

Change Horizontal Text Alignment
1. Select text or click in text paragraph.
2. Click desired alignment button in bottom row of Paragraph group.

Change Vertical Text Alignment
1. Click Align Text button.
2. Click desired alignment at drop-down list.

Change Line Spacing
1. Click Line Spacing button.
2. Click desired spacing at drop-down list.
OR
1. Click Line Spacing button.
2. Click *Line Spacing Options* at drop-down list.
3. At Paragraph dialog box, specify desired spacing.
4. Click OK.

TABLE 2.2 Alignment Shortcut keys

Alignment	Keyboard Shortcut
left-align	Ctrl + L
center-align	Ctrl + E
right-align	Ctrl + R
justify-align	Ctrl + J

In Addition

Inserting a New Line

When creating bulleted text in a slide, pressing the Enter key causes the insertion point to move to the next line, inserting another bullet. Situations may occur where you want to create a blank line between bulleted items without creating another bullet. One method for doing this is to use the New Line command, Shift + Enter. Pressing Shift + Enter inserts a new line that is considered part of the previous paragraph.

Activity 2.6

Changing the Design Theme, Theme Color, and Theme Font

You can change the design theme applied to slides in a presentation or change the color, font, or effects of a theme. To change the design theme, click the Design tab and then click the desired theme in the Themes group or click the More button that displays at the right side of the themes thumbnails and then click the desired theme. You can customize a theme by changing the colors, fonts, and effects. Click the Colors button in the Themes group and then click the desired color scheme at the drop-down gallery. Click the Fonts button and then click the desired font at the drop-down gallery. Theme effects are sets of lines and fill effects. You can change theme effects with options from the Effects button drop-down gallery.

Tutorial 2.4
Changing the Design Theme, Theme Color, and Background Style

Project You are not pleased with the design theme for the documentary project presentation and decide to apply a different theme and then change the color and font for the theme.

1. With **PS2-MPProj.pptx** open, click the Design tab.

2. Click the More button that displays at the right side of the themes thumbnails.

3. At the Themes drop-down gallery, click the *Clarity* theme.

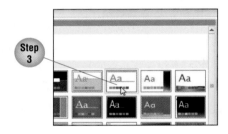

4. Run the presentation beginning with Slide 1 and notice how the theme change affected the slides.

5. Display the presentation in Normal view, make Slide 2 active, and then click the Design tab.

6. Click the Colors button in the Themes group and then click *Foundry* at the drop-down gallery.

7. Run the presentation beginning with Slide 1 and notice how the color change affected the slides.

8. Click the Design tab, click the Colors button, and then click *Urban* at the drop-down gallery.

> You may need to scroll down the drop-down gallery to display *Urban*.

9. Make Slide 2 active.

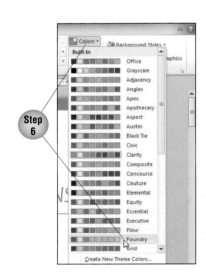

10 Click the Fonts button 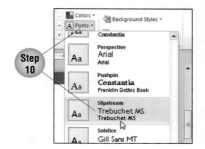 in the Themes group and then click *Slipstream* at the drop-down gallery.

> You may need to scroll down the drop-down gallery to display *Slipstream*.

11 Apply a background style by clicking the Background Styles button in the Background group and then clicking the *Style 10* option (second option from the left in the third row) at the drop-down gallery.

> Background styles display in slides in a presentation but do not print.

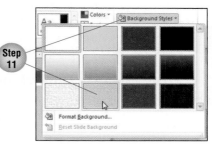

12 Run the presentation beginning with Slide 1.

13 After running the presentation, remove the background style by clicking the Design tab, clicking the Background Styles button in the Background group, and then clicking *Style 1* at the drop-down gallery (first option from the left in the top row).

14 Make Slide 1 active.

15 Delete the title and placeholder. To do this, click in the title text, position the mouse pointer on the placeholder border until the pointer displays with a four-headed arrow attached, and then click the left mouse button. With the placeholder selected (displays with a solid border line), press the Delete key.

> This deletes the title text and placeholder and then displays the title placeholder.

16 Position the mouse pointer on the CLICK TO ADD TITLE placeholder border until the pointer displays with a four-headed arrow attached, click the left mouse button, and then press the Delete key.

17 Complete steps similar to Steps 15 and 16 to delete the subtitle and placeholder.

> Slide 1 is now blank except for the formatting applied by the Clarity theme.

18 Save **PS2-MPProj.pptx**.

In Addition

Customizing Theme Colors

Design theme colors consist of four text colors, six accent colors, and two hyperlink colors. You can customize these theme colors with options at the Create New Theme Colors dialog box shown at the right. Display this dialog box by clicking the Colors button in the Themes group in the Design tab and then clicking *Create New Theme Colors* at the drop-down list. Change a color by clicking the desired color option in the *Theme colors* section and then clicking the desired color at the color palette. Changes made to colors display in the *Sample* section of the dialog box. You can name a custom color theme with the *Name* option in the dialog box. Click the Reset button to return the colors to the default theme colors.

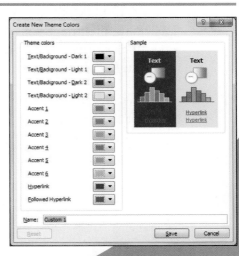

Activity 2.7

Inserting, Sizing, and Moving an Image

Add visual appeal to a presentation by inserting a graphic image such as a logo, picture, or clip art in a slide. Insert an image from a drive or folder with the Picture button in the Insert tab or by choosing a slide layout containing a Content placeholder. Click the Picture button in the Insert tab or click the picture image in the Content placeholder and the Insert Picture dialog box displays. At this dialog box, navigate to the desired drive or folder and then double-click the image. Use buttons on the Picture Tools Format tab to recolor the picture, apply a picture style, arrange the picture in the slide, and size the image. You can also size an image using the sizing handles that display around the selected image and move the image using the mouse.

Project

Chris Greenbaum has asked you to insert the company logo on the first slide of the presentation.

1. With **PS2-MPProj.pptx** open, make sure Slide 1 is active.

2. Insert the company logo in the new slide as shown in Figure 2.1. To begin, click the Insert tab and then click the Picture button 🖼 in the Images group.

Step 2

3. At the Insert Picture dialog box, navigate to the PowerPointS2 folder on your storage medium and then double-click the file named ***MPLogo.jpg***.

   The image is inserted in the slide, selection handles display around the image, and the Picture Tools Format tab is selected.

4. Increase the size of the logo by clicking in the *Width* measurement box in the Size group, typing **7**, and then pressing Enter.

   When you change the width of the logo, the height automatically changes to maintain the proportions of the logo. You can also size an image using the sizing handles that display around the selected image. Use the middle sizing handles to increase or decrease the width of an image. Use the top and bottom handles to increase or decrease the height and use the corner sizing handles to increase or decrease both the width and height of the image at the same time.

Step 4

5. Move the logo so it is positioned as shown in Figure 2.1. To do this, position the mouse pointer on the image until the pointer displays with a four-headed arrow attached, drag the image to the position shown in the figure, and then release the mouse button.

6. With the image selected, click the Color button 🖼 in the Adjust group and then click *Indigo, Accent color 1 Light* (second option from the left in the third row of the *Recolor* section).

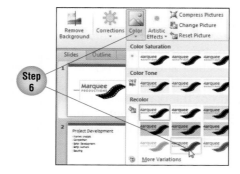

Step 6

FIGURE 2.1 Slide 1

7 Click the Corrections button ⚙ in the Adjust group and then click the *Sharpen: 50%* option in the *Sharpen and Soften* section.

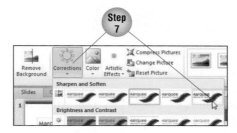

8 Click the *Simple Frame, White* option in the Picture Styles group.

9 Click the Picture Effects button ▭ in the Picture Styles group, point to *Shadow*, and then click the *Offset Diagonal Bottom Right* option (first option from the left in the top row of the *Outer* section).

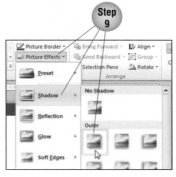

10 Click outside the logo to deselect it.

continues

11 Make Slide 6 the active slide.

12 Insert a screen capture image from a Word document into the slide. Begin by opening Word and then opening the document named **MPScript.docx**.

> Make sure PS2-MPProj.pptx and MPScript.docx are the only open programs on your desktop.

13 Click the button on the Taskbar representing the PowerPoint presentation **PS2-MPProj.pptx**.

14 Click the Insert tab, click the Screenshot button ▨ in the Images group, and then click *Screen Clipping* at the drop-down list.

> When clicking the Screen Clipping button, the Word document will automatically display dimmed and the insertion point will display as a + symbol.

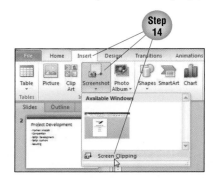

15 With the Word document displayed in a dimmed manner, position the insertion point in the top left corner of the Word document, and drag down and to the right to select the entire document.

> Once you have created a screen shot of the Word document, the image will automatically be inserted into Slide 6 of PS2-MPProj.pptx.

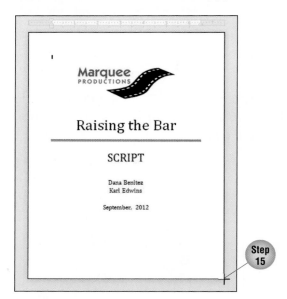

16 With the screen shot selected, click in the *Height* measurement box in the Size group in the Picture Tools Format tab, type **5**, and then press Enter.

17 Click the Picture Border button arrow in the Picture Styles group and then click *Indigo, Accent 1* at the drop-down list (fifth option from the left in the top row of the *Theme Colors* section).

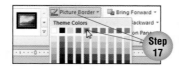

Step 17

In Brief

Insert Image
1. Click Insert tab.
2. Click Picture button.
3. At Insert Picture dialog box, navigate to desired folder.
4. Double-click desired picture file.

Insert Screenshot
1. Click Insert tab.
2. Click Screenshot button.
3. Click *Screen Clipping*.
4. Select desired image or text.

18 Position the screen shot in the slide as shown in Figure 2.2.

19 Click the Word button on the taskbar, close the document, and then exit Word.

If a message displays asking if you want to save changes made in the document, click the Don't Save button.

20 Save **PS2-MPProj.pptx**.

FIGURE 2.2 Slide 1

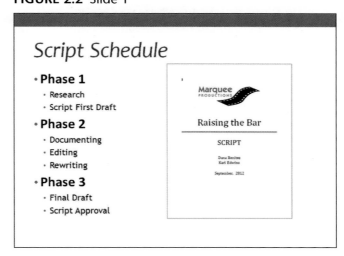

In Addition

Formatting with Buttons in the Picture Tools Format Tab

You can format images in a slide with buttons and options in the Picture Tools Format tab shown below. Use buttons in the Adjust group to correct the brightness and contrast of the image; change the image color, change to a different image, reset the image to its original size, position, and color; and compress the picture. Compress a picture to reduce the resolution or discard extra information to save room on a hard drive or to reduce download time. Use buttons in the Picture Styles group to apply a predesigned style, insert a picture border, or apply a picture effect. The Arrange group contains buttons for positioning the image and aligning and rotating the image. Use options in the Size group to crop the image and specify the height and width of the image.

Activity 2.8

Inserting and Formatting Clip Art Images

Microsoft Office includes a gallery of clip art images you can insert in an Office program such as PowerPoint. Insert a clip art image at the Clip Art task pane. Display this task pane by clicking the Clip Art button in the Images group in the Insert tab or clicking the Clip Art button in a Content place-holder. At the Clip Art task pane, type a category in the *Search for* text box and then press Enter. In the list of clip art images that displays, click the desired image. The image is inserted in the slide and the Picture Tools Format tab is selected. Use buttons and options in this tab to format and customize the clip art image.

Project

Chris Greenbaum has asked you to include an additional slide containing information on travel arrangements. You decide to enhance the visual appeal of the slide by inserting and formatting a clip art image.

Tutorial 2.5
Inserting and
Formatting Images

1. With **PS2-MPProj.pptx** open, make Slide 7 active.

    This is the last slide in the presentation.

2. Insert a new slide by clicking the New Slide button in the Slides group in the Home tab.

3. Click the *Click to add title* placeholder and then type **Travel Arrangements**.

4. Click the *Click to add text* placeholder and then type the bulleted text shown in the slide in Figure 2.3.

5. Click the Insert tab and then click the Clip Art button in the Images group.

6. At the Clip Art task pane, select any text that displays in the *Search for* text box, type **transportation**, and then press Enter.

7. Scroll down the list of clip art images and then click the image shown in Figure 2.3. (The clip art image displays with black and blue colors. You will change the colors in Step 9.)

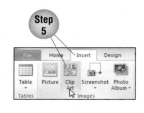

FIGURE 2.3 Slide 1

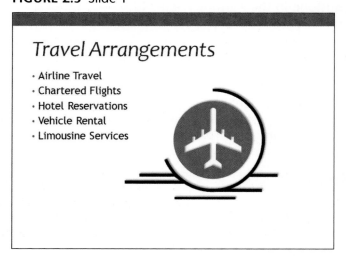

8 Close the Clip Art task pane by clicking the Close button (contains an X) that displays in the upper right corner of the task pane.

In Brief

Insert Clip Art Image
1. Click Insert tab.
2. Click Clip Art button.
3. At Clip Art task pane, type desired category, press Enter.
4. Click desired clip art image.

9 Recolor the image so it complements the slide design color scheme. To do this, click the Color button in the Adjust group in the Picture Tools Format tab and then click the *Indigo, Accent color 1 Light* option (second option from the left in the third row).

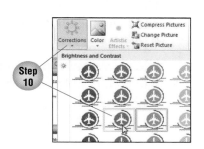

10 Click the Corrections button in the Adjust group and then click *Brightness: -20% Contrast: 0% (Normal)* at the drop-down gallery (second option from the left in the third row).

11 Click the Picture Effects button in the Picture Styles group, point to *Shadow*, and then click the *Offset Diagonal Top Right* option (first option from the left in the bottom row of the *Outer* section).

12 Click in the *Height* measurement box, type **3.5**, and then press Enter.

> When you change the height measurement, the width measurement changes automatically to maintain the proportion of the image.

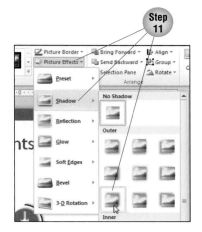

13 Using the mouse, drag the image so it is positioned as shown in Figure 2.3.

14 Make Slide 7 active and then click the Home tab.

15 Click on any character in the title *Pre-Production Assignments* and then click the Format Painter button in the Clipboard group.

16 Make Slide 8 active and then select the entire title *Travel Arrangements*.

> This applies 50-point Candara italic formatting.

17 Save **PS2-MPProj.pptx**.

In Addition

Downloading Clip Art Images

If you are connected to the Internet, click the *Include Office.com* content check box to insert a check mark and clip art images from Office.com display in the Clip Art task pane. You can view additional clip art images by visiting the Office.com website. To do this, click the <u>Find more at Office.com</u> hyperlink that displays towards the bottom of the Clip Art task pane.

Activity 2.9

Inserting and Formatting a SmartArt Organizational Chart

If you need to visually illustrate hierarchical data, consider creating an organizational chart with SmartArt. To display a menu of SmartArt choices, click the Insert tab and then click the SmartArt button in the Images group. This displays the Choose a SmartArt Graphic dialog box. At this dialog box, click *Hierarchy* in the left panel and then double-click the desired organizational chart in the middle panel. This inserts the organizational chart in the slide. Some SmartArt graphics are designed to include text. You can type text in a graphic by selecting the shape and then typing text in the shape or you can type text in the *Type your text here* window that displays at the left side of the SmartArt graphic.

Project Chris Greenbaum has asked you to create a slide of an organizational chart illustrating the hierarchy of the people involved in production.

Tutorial 2.6
Inserting and
Formatting SmartArt

1 With **PS2-MPProj.pptx** open, make Slide 2 active and then click the New Slide button in the Slides group in the Home tab.

2 Create the organizational chart shown in Figure 2.4. To begin, click the Insert tab and then click the SmartArt button in the Illustrations group.

3 At the Choose a SmartArt Graphic dialog box, click *Hierarchy* in the left panel of the dialog box and then double-click the *Hierarchy* option in the middle panel.

> This displays the organizational chart in the slide with the SmartArt Tools Design tab selected. Use buttons in this tab to add additional boxes, change the order of the shapes, choose a different layout, apply formatting with a SmartArt style, and reset the formatting of the organizational chart.

4 If a *Type your text here* window displays at the left side of the organizational chart, close it by clicking the Text Pane button in the Create Graphic group.

> You can also close the window by clicking the Close button that displays in the upper right corner of the window.

5 Delete one of the boxes in the organizational chart. Begin by clicking the border of the second text box from the top at the left side.

> Make sure *[Text]* displays in the box.

6 Press the Delete key.

7 Click the second box from the top at the right side to select it and then click the Add Shape button in the Create Graphic group.

> This inserts a box to the right of the selected box. Your organizational chart should contain the same boxes as shown in Figure 2.4. (The new text box does not contain a [Text] placeholder. Click in the box and type the text.)

8 Click *[Text]* in the top box, type **Chris Greenbaum**, press the Enter key, and then type **Production Manager**. Click in each of the remaining boxes and type the text as shown in Figure 2.4.

FIGURE 2.4 Organizational Chart

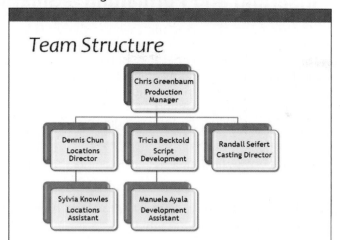

In Brief

Create Organizational Chart
1. Click Insert tab.
2. Click SmartArt button.
3. Click *Hierarchy* at Choose a SmartArt Graphic dialog box.
4. Double-click desired organizational chart.

9　Click the Change Colors button ⊞ in the SmartArt Styles group in the SmartArt Tools Design tab and then click the first color option from the left in the *Colorful* section (*Colorful - Accent Colors*).

10　Click the More button located at the right side of the SmartArt Styles group.

11　Click the *Inset* option located in the *3-D* section.

12　Click the SmartArt Tools Format tab.

13　Click inside the SmartArt graphic border but outside any shape.

14　Click in the *Shape Width* measurement box in the Size group, type **8.4**, and then press Enter.

15　Click the *Click to add title* placeholder and then type **Team Structure**.

16　Make Slide 2 active and then click the Home tab.

17　Click on any character in the title *Project Development* and then click the Format Painter button in the Clipboard group.

18　Make Slide 3 active and then select the entire title *Team Structure*.

This applies 50-point Candara italic formatting.

19　Save **PS2-MPProj.pptx**.

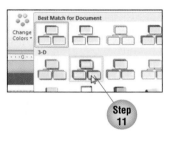

Step 9

Step 11

In Addition

Moving a SmartArt Graphic

Move a SmartArt graphic by positioning the arrow pointer on the graphic border until the pointer displays with a four-headed arrow attached, holding down the left mouse button, and then dragging the SmartArt graphic to the desired location. You can increase the size of the graphic with the *Height* and *Width* options or by dragging a corner of the graphic border. If you want to maintain the proportions of the graphic, hold down the Shift key while dragging the border to increase or decrease the size.

Activity 2.10

Inserting and Formatting a SmartArt Graphic

Use the SmartArt feature to create a variety of graphic diagrams including process, cycle, relationship, matrix, and pyramid diagrams. Click the Insert tab and then click the SmartArt button to display the Choose a SmartArt Graphic dialog box. Click the desired graphic type in the left panel of the dialog box and then use the scroll bar at the right side of the middle panel to scroll down the list of graphic choices. Double-click a graphic in the middle panel of the dialog box and the graphic is inserted in the slide. Use buttons in the SmartArt Tools Design tab and the SmartArt Tools Format tab to customize a graphic.

Project

The finance director has asked you to include a slide containing a SmartArt graphic diagram of travel expenses.

Tutorial 2.6
Inserting and
Formatting SmartArt

1. With **PS2-MPProj.pptx** open, make Slide 9 active and then click the New Slide button in the Slides group in the Home tab.

2. Click the Layout button in the Slides group and then click the *Blank* layout at the drop-down list.

3. Create the SmartArt graphic diagram shown in Figure 2.5. To begin, click the Insert tab and then click the SmartArt button in the Illustrations group.

4. At the Choose a SmartArt Graphic dialog box, click *Relationship* in the left panel of the dialog box and then double-click the *Converging Radial* option (this option may be the first option from the right in the sixth row or the first option from the left in the seventh row).

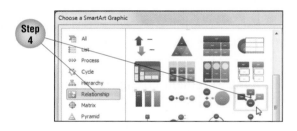

5. If necessary, close the *Type your text here* window by clicking the Close button that displays in the upper right corner of the window.

6. Click the Add Shape button in the Create Graphic group.

7. Click in each of the shapes and insert the text shown in Figure 2.5.

8. Click the Change Colors button in the SmartArt Styles group and then click the second color option from the left in the *Colorful* section (*Colorful Range - Accent Colors 2 to 3*).

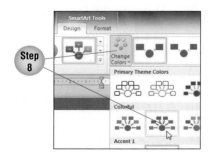

9. Click the More button located at the right side of the thumbnails in the SmartArt Styles group.

10 Click the *Cartoon* option located in the *3-D* section.

11 Click the SmartArt Tools Format tab.

12 Click inside the SmartArt graphic border but outside any shape.

> This deselects the shapes but keeps the graphic selected.

13 Click the More button located at the right side of the thumbnails in the WordArt Styles group and then click *Fill - Indigo, Accent 1, Inner Shadow - Accent 1* (fourth option from the left in the second row).

14 Click the *Width* measurement box in the Size group, type **7.5**, and then press Enter.

15 Click the Align button in the Arrange group and then click *Align Center* at the drop-down list.

16 Save **PS2-MPProj.pptx**

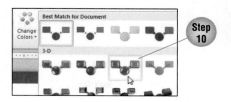

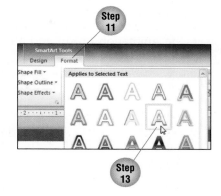

In Brief

Create SmartArt Graphic
1. Click Insert tab.
2. Click SmartArt button.
3. Click desired category in left panel of Choose a SmartArt Graphic dialog box.
4. Double-click desired graphic.

FIGURE 2.5 Diagram

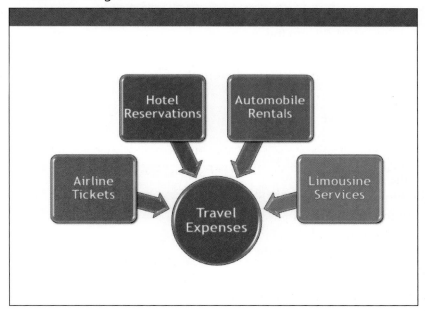

In Addition

Inserting Text in the Text Pane

You can enter text in a SmartArt shape by clicking in the shape and then typing the text. You can also insert text in a SmartArt shape by typing text in the Text pane. Display the Text pane by clicking the Text Pane button in the Create Graphic group in the SmartArt Tools Design tab.

Activity 2.11

Applying Animation to Objects and Text

You can animate an individual object and text in a slide with options in the Animations tab. Click the Animations tab and the ribbon displays with a variety of animation styles and options for customizing and applying times to animations in a presentation. Click the More button at the right side of the thumbnails in the Animation group and a gallery of animation styles displays that you can apply to objects and text as they enter a slide, exit a slide, and follow a motion path. You can also apply animations to emphasize objects in a slide. If you want the same animation applied to other objects in a presentation, use the Animation Painter button in the Advanced Animation group in the Animations tab.

Project

To finalize the presentation, Chris Greenbaum has asked you to apply animation to objects and text in the presentation.

Tutorial 2.7
Applying Animation to Objects and Text

1. With **PS2-MPProj.pptx** open, make sure Slide 10 is the active slide and the SmartArt graphic is selected.

2. Click the Animations tab and then click the *Fly In* option in the Animations group.

3. Click the Effect Options button 🔼 in the Animation group and then click *One by One* at the drop-down list.

4. Click twice on the up-pointing arrow to the right of the *Duration* option in the Timing group.

   This inserts *01.00* into the option box.

5. Click the Preview button ⭐ in the Preview group to view the animation applied to the SmartArt graphic.

6. Make Slide 3 active and then click the organizational chart to select it.

7. Click the More button located to the right of the thumbnails in the Animation group and then click the *Float In* option at the drop-down gallery.

8. Click the Effect Options button in the Animation group and then click *One by One* at the drop-down list.

9. Click Slide 2 to make it active and then click in the bulleted text to select the placeholder.

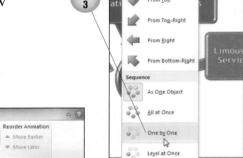

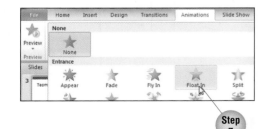

10 Click the *Fly In* option in the Animation group

> Applying this animation creates a **build** for the bulleted items. A build displays important points in a slide one point at a time and is useful for keeping the audience's attention focused on the point being presented rather than reading ahead.

11 Click twice on the up-pointing arrow to the right of the *Duration* option in the Timing group.

> This inserts *01.00* into the option box.

12 Apply the same animation to the bulleted text in Slides 4 through 9. To begin, click anywhere in the bulleted text to select the placeholder, and then double-click the Animation Painter button in the Advanced Animation group.

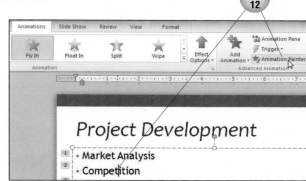

13 Make Slide 4 active and then click anywhere in the bulleted text. (This selects the placeholder and applies the *Fly In* animation and the duration time.)

14 Make Slide 5 active and then click anywhere in the bulleted text.

15 Make Slide 6 active and then click in the bulleted text. Make Slide 7 active and then click in the bulleted text. Make Slide 8 active and then click in the bulleted text. Make Slide 9 active and then click in the bulleted text.

16 Click the Animation Painter button to turn off the feature.

17 Make Slide 1 active and then run the presentation. Click the mouse button to advance slides and to display the individual organizational chart boxes, bulleted items, and SmartArt graphic boxes.

18 Print the presentation as handouts with six slides per page. To do this, click the File tab and then click the Print tab.

19 At the Print tab Backstage view, click the second gallery (contains the text *Full Page Slides*) in the *Settings* category and then click *6 Slides Horizontal* at the drop-down list.

20 Click the Print button.

21 Save and then close **PS2-MPProj.pptx**.

In Addition

Applying a Custom Animation

Apply custom animation to selected objects in a slide by clicking the Animation Pane button in the Advanced Animation group in the Animations tab. This displays the Animation task pane at the right side of the screen. Use options in this task pane to control the order in which objects appear on a slide, choose animation direction and speed, and specify how objects will appear in the slide.

Features Summary

Feature	Ribbon Tab, Group	Button	Keyboard Shortcut
align text left	Home, Paragraph		Ctrl + L
align text right	Home, Paragraph		Ctrl + R
align text vertically	Home, Paragraph		
animation effect options	Animations, Animation		
bold	Home, Font	**B**	Ctrl + B
center	Home, Paragraph		Ctrl + E
copy selected text	Home, Clipboard		Ctrl + C
cut selected text	Home, Clipboard		Ctrl + V
decrease font size	Home, Font		Ctrl + Shift + <
decrease list level	Home, Paragraph		Shift + Tab
design theme	Design, Themes		
font	Home, Font		
font color	Home, Font		
Font dialog box	Home, Font		Ctrl + Shift + F
font size	Home, Font		
Format Painter	Home, Clipboard		
increase font size	Home, Font		Ctrl + Shift + >
increase list level	Home, Paragraph		Tab
insert clip art image	Insert, Images		
insert picture	Insert, Images		
insert SmartArt	Insert, Illustrations		
italic	Home, Font	*I*	Ctrl + I
justify	Home, Paragraph		Ctrl + J
line spacing	Home, Paragraph		
paste selected text	Home, Clipboard		Ctrl + V
preview animation	Animations, Preview		
theme colors	Design, Themes		
theme effects	Design, Themes		

Feature	Ribbon Tab, Group	Button	Keyboard Shortcut
theme fonts	Design, Themes	**A**	
underline	Home, Font	**U**	Ctrl + U

Knowledge Check

Completion: In the space provided at the right, indicate the correct term, command, or option.

1. Save an existing presentation with a new name at this dialog box. _____
2. Increase the text level indent by clicking the Increase List Level button or by pressing this key on the keyboard. _____
3. Decrease the text level indent by clicking the Decrease List Level button or by pressing these keys on the keyboard. _____
4. The Cut button is located in this group in the Home tab. _____
5. This is the keyboard shortcut to copy selected text. _____
6. Press these keys on the keyboard to select all text in a placeholder. _____
7. Use this feature to apply the same formatting in more than one location in a slide or slides. _____
8. Click this button in the Paragraph group in the Home tab to change the text alignment to right. _____
9. Change the vertical alignment of text in a placeholder with options from this button drop-down list. _____
10. This dialog box contains options for changing line spacing and text alignment, indentation, and spacing. _____
11. Click this tab to display the Themes group. _____
12. Use buttons in this tab to change the color of the selected picture, apply a picture style, arrange the picture, and size the picture. _____
13. Display the Clip Art task pane by clicking the Insert tab and then clicking the Clip Art Pane button in this group. _____
14. Use this feature to create an organizational chart or a variety of graphic diagrams. _____
15. The Effect Options button is located in this tab. _____

Skills Review

Review 1 Editing and Formatting a Presentation for Marquee Productions

1. Open the presentation named **MPAnnualMtg.pptx** located in the PowerPointS2 folder.
2. Save the presentation with Save As in the PowerPointEOS folder on your storage medium and name it **PS2-R1-MPAnnualMtg**.
3. Apply the Apothecary design theme to the slides in the presentation, change the theme colors to Executive, and change the theme font to Aspect.
4. Delete Slide 5 (contains the title *Financial*) in the Slides/Outline pane.
5. Change to Slide Sorter view and move Slide 7 (*Expenses*) immediately after Slide 3 (*Review of Goals*).
6. Move Slide 6 (*Future Goals*) immediately after Slide 7 (*Technology*).
7. Change to the Normal view and then make Slide 4 (*Expenses*) the active slide.
8. Decrease the indent of *Payroll* so it displays aligned at the left with *Administration*.
9. Decrease the indent of *Benefits* so it displays aligned at the left with *Payroll* and *Administration*.
10. Make Slide 6 (*Technology*) active and then increase the indent of *Hardware* to the next level, the indent of *Software* to the next level, and the indent of *Technical Support* to the next level.
11. Make Slide 7 (*Future Goals*) active, select the name *Chris Greenbaum*, and then click the Copy button. (Make sure you select only the name and not the space following the name.)
12. Make Slide 3 (*Review of Goals*) active.
13. Move the insertion point immediately to the right of *Overview of Goals*, press the Enter key, press the Tab key, and then click the Paste button. (Clicking the Paste button inserts the name *Chris Greenbaum.*)
14. Move the insertion point immediately to the right of *Completed Goals*, press the Enter key, press the Tab key, and then click the Paste button.
15. Make Slide 7 (*Future Goals*) active, select the name *Shannon Grey* (do not include the space after the name), and then click the Copy button.
16. Make Slide 3 (*Review of Goals*) active and then paste the name *Shannon Grey* below *Goals Remaining* at the same tab location as *Chris Greenbaum*.
17. Paste the name *Shannon Grey* below *Analysis/Discussion* at the same tab location as *Chris Greenbaum*.
18. Make Slide 1 active, select the text *Marquee Productions*, change the font to Candara, the font size to 44, and turn on bold.
19. Select the text *Annual Meeting*, change the font to Candara, the font size to 32, and turn on bold.
20. Make Slide 2 (*Agenda*) active, select the title *Agenda*, change the font to Candara, the font size to 48, and turn on bold.
21. Using Format Painter, apply the same formatting to the title in each of the remaining slides.
22. Make Slide 6 active, select all of the bulleted text, and then change the line spacing to 1.5.
23. Make Slide 8 active, select all of the bulleted text, and then change the spacing before paragraphs to 24 pt.
24. Make Slide 2 active and then insert the clip art image shown in Figure 2.6 with the following specifications:

- At the Clip Art task pane, type **target** in the *Search for* text box and the insert the image shown in Figure 2.6.
- Change the color of the clip art image to *Indigo, Accent color 1 Dark.*
- Size and position the image as shown in the figure.

25. Make Slide 5 active and then insert the clip art image shown in Figure 2.7. Use the word *buildings* in the Clip Art task pane to find the clip art and change the color to the same color you used for the clip art image in Slide 2. Size and position the clip art image as shown in Figure 2.7.
26. Apply a transition, sound, and transition duration time to all slides in the presentation.
27. Run the presentation.
28. Print the presentation as handouts with all eight slides printed horizontally on one page.
29. Save and then close **PS2-R1-MPAnnualMtg.pptx**.

FIGURE 2.6 Slide 2

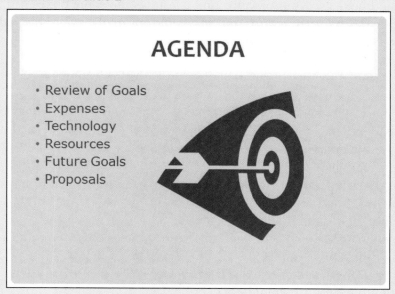

FIGURE 2.7 Slide 5

Review 2 Formatting a Presentation for Performance Threads

1. Open **PTPres.pptx** and then save the presentation in the PowerPointEOS folder and name it **PS2-R2-PTPres**.
2. Change the design theme colors (not the theme, just the colors) to *Thatch*.
3. With Slide 1 active, insert the **PTLogo.jpg** file from the PowerPointS2 folder. (Use the Picture button in the Images group in the Insert tab.) Change the height of the logo to 4" and then position the logo in the middle of the slide.
4. Make Slide 3 active, select the bulleted text, and then change the line spacing to 1.5.
5. Make Slide 4 active, select the bulleted text, and then change the line spacing to 1.5.
6. Make Slide 2 active and then insert the organizational chart shown in Figure 2.8 with the following specifications:
   - Click the *Hierarchy* option in the left panel at the Choose a SmartArt Graphic dialog box and then double-click *Organization Chart*.
   - Delete and add boxes so your organization chart has the same boxes as the organization chart in Figure 2.8. ***Hint: Use the Add Shape button arrow and click* Add Shape Below *when adding the bottom row of the organization chart.***
   - Type the text in the boxes. (Press Shift + Enter after entering the names.)
   - Change the color of the organizational chart to Colorful Range - Accent Colors 5 to 6.
   - Apply the Cartoon SmartArt style to the organizational chart.
   - Apply the Fill - Light Green, Text 2, Outline - Background 2 WordArt style to the text in the slides (first option from the left in the top row of the WordArt styles drop-down gallery).
7. Make Slide 3 active and then insert the clip art image shown in Figure 2.9 with the following specifications:
   - At the Clip Art task pane, use the word *people* to search for the clip art image shown in Figure 2.9.
   - Change the height of the clip art image to 4".
   - Change the color of the clip art image to Green, Accent color 4 Light (located in the Color button drop-down gallery).
   - Correct the brightness and contast to *Brightness: -20% Contrast: +20%* (located in the Corrections button drop-down gallery).
   - Position the clip art as shown in Figure 2.9.

FIGURE 2.8 Slide 2

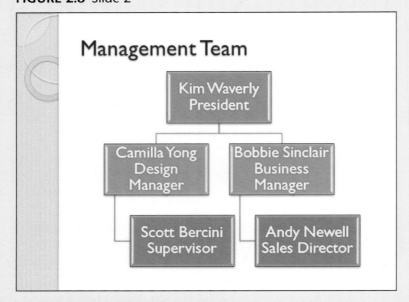

FIGURE 2.9 Slide 3

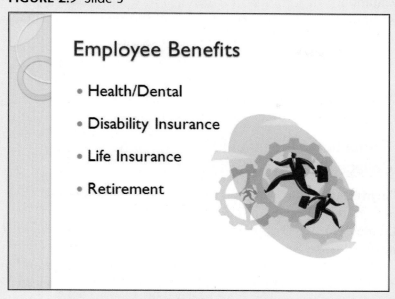

FIGURE 2.10 Slide 5

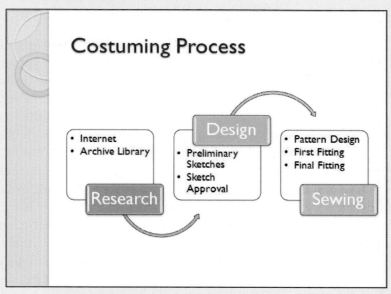

8. Make Slide 5 active and then insert the SmartArt graphic shown in Figure 2.10 with the following specifications:
   - Click the *Process* option in the left panel at the Choose a SmartArt Graphic dialog box and then double-click *Alternating Flow*.
   - Change the color of the graphic to Colorful Range - Accent Colors 4 to 5.
   - Apply the Cartoon SmartArt style to the graphic.
   - Type the text in the boxes as shown in Figure 2.10.
9. Make Slide 2 active, click the organizational chart, and then animate the organizational chart using options in the Animations tab. (You determine the type of animation.)
10. Make Slide 5 active, click the SmartArt graphic, and then animate the graphic using options in the Animations tab. (You determine the type of animation.)
11. Make Slide 3 active, click the bulleted text, and then apply the *Split* animation.
12. Make Slide 4 active, click the bulleted text, and then apply the *Split* animation.

13. Run the presentation.
14. Print the presentation as handouts with all five slides printed horizontally on one page.
15. Save and then close **PS2-R2-PTPres.pptx**.

Skills Assessment

Assessment 1 Formatting a Presentation for Niagara Peninsula College, Theatre Arts Division

1. Open **NPCTheatreArts.pptx** and then save the presentation in the PowerPointEOS folder and name it **PS2-A1-NPCTheatreArts**.
2. Change the theme colors to *Origin* and change the theme font to *Paper*. **Hint: Do not change the design theme, only the design theme colors and font.**
3. Move Slide 7 (*Associate Degrees*) immediately after Slide 2 (*Mission Statement*).
4. Move Slide 6 (*Semester Costs*) immediately after Slide 7 (*Fall Semester Classes*).
5. Make Slide 2 (*Mission Statement*) active, click in the paragraph below the title *Mission Statement*, and then change the alignment to Justify.
6. Change the line spacing to 1.5 for the bulleted text in Slides 5 and 7.
7. Make Slide 5 active, select the bulleted text, and then apply italics formatting.
8. Make Slide 1 active and then insert the logo file named **NPCLogo.jpg** into the slide. Increase the size of the logo and then position it above the column ledge.
9. Make Slide 3 active and then insert a *Radial Cycle* SmartArt graphic (located in the *Cycle* category in the Choose a SmartArt Graphic dialog box) in the slide. Insert the text *Theatre Arts Division* in the middle circle and then insert the following text in the remaining four circles: *Production*, *Acting*, *Set Design*, and *Interactive Media*. Apply a color and SmartArt style of your choosing to the graphic. Apply any other formatting you desire to enhance the visual display of the graphic. Position the graphic on the slide as necessary.
10. Make Slide 4 active and then insert an *Organization Chart* organizational chart (located in the *Hierarchy* category in the Choose a SmartArt Graphic dialog box) in the slide with the boxes and text shown in Figure 2.11. **Hint: To add the extra box along the bottom, click the left box at the bottom, click the Add Shape button arrow, and then click Add Shape Before.** Apply a color and SmartArt style of your choosing to the organizational chart. Apply any other formatting you desire to enhance the visual display of the organizational chart. Position the chart on the slide as necessary.
11. Make Slide 7 active and then insert a clip art image related to *money*. Size, position, and recolor the image so it enhances the slide.
12. Make Slide 3 active and then apply an animation of your choosing to the SmartArt graphic.
13. Make Slide 4 active and then apply an animation of your choosing to the organizational chart.
14. Apply a transition, sound, and transition duration time of your choosing to all slides in the presentation.
15. Run the presentation.
16. Print the presentation as handouts with four slides printed horizontally.
17. Save and then close **PS2-A1-NPCTheatreArts.pptx**.

FIGURE 2.11 Organizational Chart

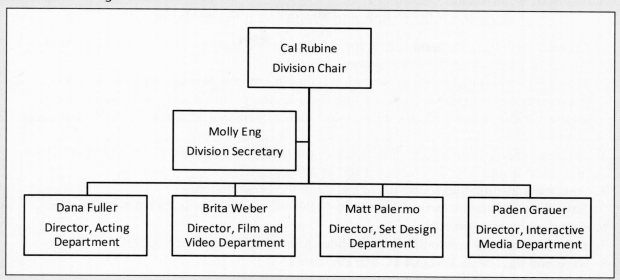

Assessment 2 Formatting a Presentation for First Choice Travel

1. Open **FCTVacations.pptx** and then save the presentation in the PowerPointEOS folder and name it **PS2-A2-FCTVacations**.
2. Change the theme colors to Flow.
3. Change the theme font to Foundry.
4. Increase the font size of the subtitle *Vacation Specials* located in Slide 1 (you determine the size).
5. Apply bold formatting, change the font color to Blue, and change to left alignment for each heading in Slides 2 through 6.
6. Make Slide 1 active and then insert the **FCTLogo.jpg** file into the slide. You determine the size and position of the logo.
7. Apply any formatting you feel is necessary to improve the appearance of each slide.
8. Apply a transition and sound to each slide in the presentation.
9. Run the presentation.
10. Print the presentation as handouts with all six slides printed horizontally on one page.
11. Save and then close **PS2-A2-FCTVacations.pptx**.

Assessment 3 Finding Information on Converting Text to a SmartArt Graphic

1. Open **PS2-A2-FCTVacations.pptx** and then save the presentation in the PowerPointEOS folder and name it **PS2-A3-FCTVacations**.
2. Use the Help feature to learn how to convert text in a slide to a SmartArt graphic.
3. After learning how to convert text, make Slide 4 active and then convert the bulleted text to a SmartArt graphic of your choosing.
4. Apply formatting to enhance the visual display of the SmartArt graphic.
5. Print only Slide 4.
6. Save and then close **PS2-A3-FCTVacations.pptx**.

Assessment 4 Individual Challenge
Locating Information and Preparing a Presentation

1. Connect to the Internet and search for information on your favorite author, historical figure, or someone in the entertainment business.
2. Using PowerPoint, create a presentation with a minimum of four slides on the person you chose that contains a title slide that includes the person's name and your name, and additional slides that includes information such as personal statistics, achievements, and awards.
3. Insert an appropriate screen shot image of the person or something related to the person and insert it into any slide where it seems appropriate.
4. Apply a transition and sound to each slide in the presentation.
5. Save the presentation in the PowerPointEOS folder and name it **PS2-A4-IC-PerPres**.
6. Run the presentation.
7. Print the slides as handouts with six slides printed horizontally per page.
8. Save and then close **PS2-A4-IC-PerPres.pptx**.

Marquee Challenge

Challenge 1 Preparing a Presentation for Worldwide Enterprises

1. Create the presentation shown in Figure 2.12. Apply the Median design theme, the *Trek* theme colors, and the Module theme font. Insert the logo file named **WELogo.jpg** in Slide 1. Insert the clip art images in Slides 3 and 6 using *business* as the search category. Format, size, and position the clip art images as shown. Create and format the SmartArt graphic shown in Slide 5.
2. Save the completed presentation in the PowerPointEOS folder and name it **PS2-C1-WEDist**.
3. Print the presentation as a handout with all six slides on the same page and then close the presentation.

Challenge 2 Preparing a Presentation for The Waterfront Bistro

1. Create the presentation shown in Figure 2.13. Apply the Concourse design theme, the Office theme colors, and the Opulent theme font. Insert the logo file named **TWBLogo.jpg** in Slides 1 and 2. Create and format the SmartArt organizational chart in Slide 3 using the *Hierarchy* SmartArt design. Create and format the SmartArt graphic shown in Slide 4. Insert the clip art image as shown in Slide 6 using *food* as the search category.
2. Save the completed presentation in the PowerPointEOS folder and name it **PS2-C2-TWBInfo**.
3. Print the presentation as a handout with all six slides on the same page and then close the presentation.

FIGURE 2.12 Challenge 1

2/18/2012

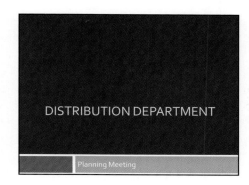

DISTRIBUTION DEPARTMENT

Planning Meeting

Market

- □ Market share
- □ Current market
- □ Future market
- □ Market indicators
- □ Consumer profile

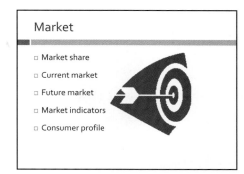

Competition

- □ Current competition
- □ Emerging competition
- □ Competitors' strengths
- □ Competitors' weaknesses
- □ Pricing

Distribution

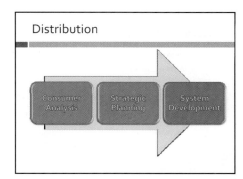

Consumer Analysis

Strategic Planning

System Development

Product Fulfillment

- □ Distribution
  - ◻ Costs
  - ◻ Reliability
  - ◻ System needs
- □ Packaging
  - ◻ Pricing
  - ◻ Appearance
  - ◻ Strengths/weaknesses

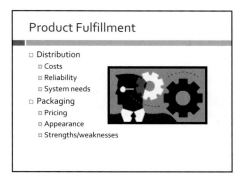

1

FIGURE 2.13 Challenge 2

2/18/2012

Contact Information

▸ Restaurant Manager
  ◦ Dana Hirsch
▸ Location
  ◦ 3104 Rivermist Drive
  ◦ Buffalo, NY 14280
▸ Telephone
  ◦ (716) 555-3166
▸ Web Address
  ◦ www.emcp.net/twfbistro

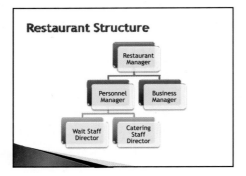

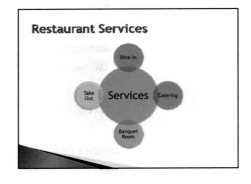

Hours of Operation

▸ Restaurant
  ◦ Monday through Friday, 6:30 a.m. to 10:00 p.m.
  ◦ Saturday, 7:30 a.m. to 11:00 p.m.
  ◦ Sunday, 9:00 a.m. to 7:30 p.m.
▸ Banquet Room
  ◦ Monday through Friday, 5:00 p.m. to 9:30 p.m.
  ◦ Saturday, 5:00 p.m. to 10:30 p.m.
  ◦ Sunday, 3:00 p.m. to 7:00 p.m.

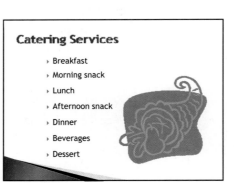

1

Integrating Programs
Word, Excel, Access, and PowerPoint

Skills

- Export Access data to Excel and Word
- Import Excel data to a new table in Access
- Export a PowerPoint presentation to Word
- Export a Word outline to a PowerPoint presentation
- Link an Excel chart with a Word document and PowerPoint presentation
- Edit a linked object
- Embed and edit a Word table in a PowerPoint slide
- Link data to a new Access table and edit linked data
- Embed an Excel worksheet in a Word document

Student Resources

Before beginning the activities in this section, copy to your storage medium the IntegratingBrief folder on the Student Resources CD. This folder contains the data files you need to complete the projects in the section.

Projects Overview

Export grades for AC215-03 from an Access table to an Excel worksheet; import grades for a theatre class from an Excel worksheet into an Access database table; and link grades for TRA220 between an Excel worksheet and an Access database table.

Export data on Canadian distributors from an Access report to a Word document; prepare a presentation for the Distribution Department of Worldwide Enterprises using a Word outline; copy an Excel chart and link it to the Distribution Department meeting presentation and to a Word document and then edit the linked chart; copy a Word table containing data on preview distribution dates, embed it in a PowerPoint slide, and then edit the table.

Create and format a Word document containing information on the annual meeting using data in a PowerPoint presentation.

Copy data in an Excel worksheet on employee payroll and then embed the data in a Word document and then update the payroll hours for the employees for the next week.

Model Answers for Projects

These model answers for the projects that you complete in this section provide a preview of the finished projects before you begin working and also allow you to compare your own results with these models to ensure you have created the materials accurately.

StudentGradesAC215-03.xlsx **is part of the project in Activity 1.1.**

Student_No	Last_Name	First_Name	Grade
111-785-156	Bastow	Maren	B
118-487-578	Andre	Ian	A
137-845-746	Knowlton	Sherri	C
138-456-749	Yiu	Terry	A
146-984-137	Rhodes	Tari	A+
157-457-856	Dwyer	Barbara	C
184-457-156	Van Este	Doranda	B
197-486-745	Koning	Jeffrey	D
198-744-149	Lysenko	Earl	F
211-745-856	Uhrig	Andrew	A
217-458-687	Husson	Ahmad	A+
221-689-478	Bhullar	Ash	D
229-658-412	Mysior	Melanie	A
255-158-498	Gibson	Kevin	A+
274-658-986	Woollatt	Bentley	C
314-745-856	Morgan	Bruce	C
321-487-659	Loewen	Richard	B
325-841-469	Clements	Russell	A
326-945-745	Hodgson	Catherine	C
328-746-985	Porteous	Louis	B
329-685-457	Turpela	Murray	D
344-745-812	Isovski	Alija	C
348-876-486	Ennis	Armado	D
349-856-745	Buziak	Claudette	A+
349-874-658	Retieffe	Susan	F
359-845-475	Collyer	Sandra	D
378-159-746	Gagne	Martine	A

US_Distributors.rtf **is part of the project in Activity 1.2.**

State	City	CompanyName	StreetAdd1	StreetAdd2	ZIPCode	Telephone	Fax
AZ	Phoenix	LaVista Cinemas	111 Vista Road		86355-6014	602-555-6231	602-555-6233
CA	Los Angeles	Marquee Movies	1011 South Alameda Street		90045	612-555-2398	612-555-2377
FL	Tampa	Sunfest Cinemas		341 South Fourth Avenue	33562	813-555-3185	813-555-3177
GA	Atlanta	Liberty Cinemas	P. O. Box 998	12011 Ruston Way	73125	404-555-8113	404-555-2349
IL	Oak Park	O'Shea Movies	59 Erie		60302	312-555-7719	312-555-7381
KS	Emporia	Midtown Moviehouse	1033 Commercial Street		66801	316-555-7013	316-555-7022
KY	Louisville	All Nite Cinemas	2188 3rd Street		40201	502-555-4238	502-555-4240
MA	Cambridge	Eastown Movie House	P. O. Box 429	1 Concourse Avenue	02142	413-555-0981	413-555-0226
MD	Baltimore	Dockside Movies	P. O. Box 224	155 S. Central Avenue	21203	301-555-7732	301-555-9836
MI	Detroit	Renaissance Cinemas	3599 Woodward Avenue		48211	313-555-1693	313-555-1699
NJ	Baking Ridge	Hillman Cinemas	55 Kemble Avenue		07920	201-555-1147	201-555-1143
NY	Buffalo	Waterfront Cinemas	P. O. Box 3255		14288	716-555-3845	716-555-4860
NY	New York	Cinema Festival	318 East 11th Street		10003	212-555-9715	212-555-9717
NY	New York	Movie Emporium	203 West Houston Street		10014	212-555-7278	212-555-7280
NY	New York	Westview Movies	1112 Broadway		10119	212-555-4875	212-555-4877
OH	Dublin	Mooretown Movies	P. O. Box 11	331 Metro Place	43107	614-555-8134	614-555-8339
OR	Portland	Redwood Cinemas	P. O. Box 112F	336 Ninth Street	97466-3359	503-555-8641	503-555-8633
PA	Philadelphia	Wellington 10	1203 Tenth Southwest		19178	215-555-9045	215-555-9048
SC	Columbia	Danforth Cinemas	P. O. Box 22	18 Pickens Street	29201	803-555-3487	803-555-3421
TX	Arlington	Century Cinemas	3687 Avenue K		76013	817-555-2116	817-555-2119
WA	Seattle	Mainstream Movies	P. O. Box 33	333 Evergreen Building	98220-2791	206-555-3269	206-555-3270

The BegThGrades **table within the** Int-NPCStudentGrades.accdb **database is the project in Activity 1.3.**

BegThGrades   1/19/2012

Student No	Last Name	First Name	Grade
102-434-092	Bastow	Maren	B+
173-182-993	Ennis	Amado	B-
205-394-293	Bodine	Rod	A
211-299-348	Gagne	Martine	D
221-295-734	Snowden	Lee	B
312-348-891	Colbert	Sherrie	C-
329-390-655	Yiu	Terry	C
355-293-901	Remy	David	C+

Int-NPCDivPresHandout.docx **is part of the project in Activity 1.4.**

Slide 1

Niagara Peninsula
COLLEGE

Theatre Arts Division

Slide 2

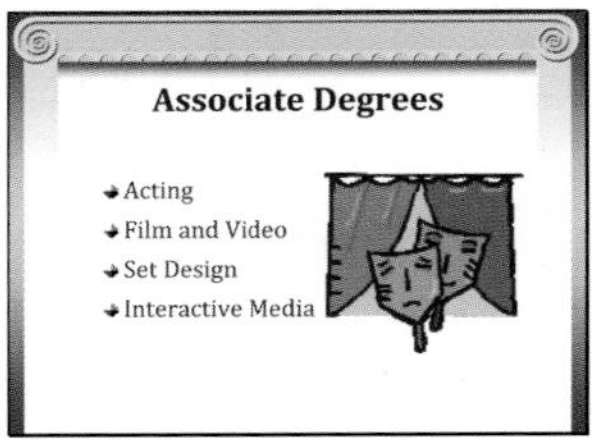

Associate Degrees

→ Acting
→ Film and Video
→ Set Design
→ Interactive Media

Slide 3

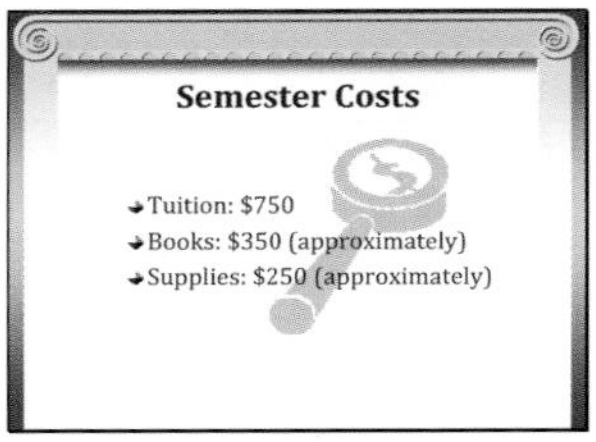

Semester Costs

→ Tuition: $750
→ Books: $350 (approximately)
→ Supplies: $250 (approximately)

Slide 4

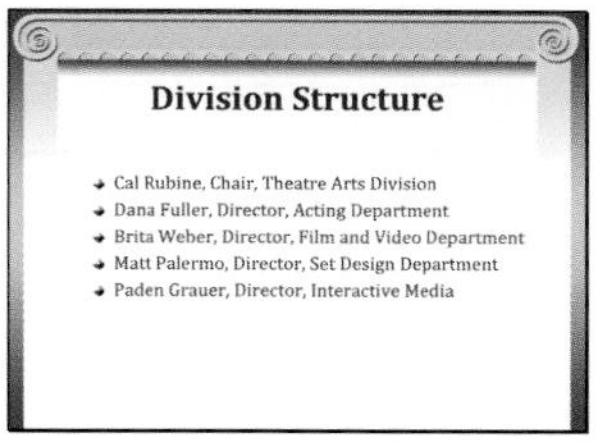

Division Structure

- Cal Rubine, Chair, Theatre Arts Division
- Dana Fuller, Director, Acting Department
- Brita Weber, Director, Film and Video Department
- Matt Palermo, Director, Set Design Department
- Paden Grauer, Director, Interactive Media

_____
_____
_____
_____
_____
_____
_____

Slide 5

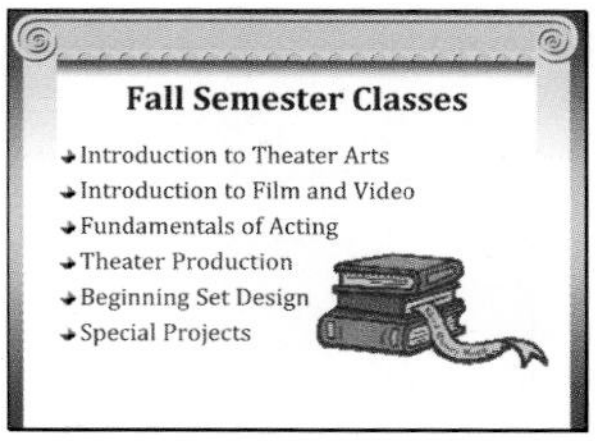

Fall Semester Classes

- Introduction to Theater Arts
- Introduction to Film and Video
- Fundamentals of Acting
- Theater Production
- Beginning Set Design
- Special Projects

_____
_____
_____
_____
_____
_____

Slide 6

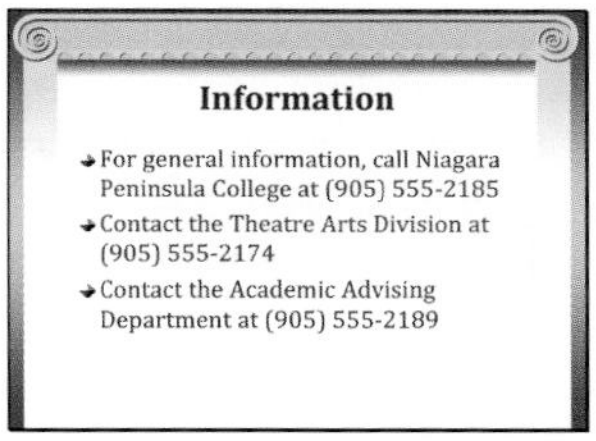

Information

- For general information, call Niagara Peninsula College at (905) 555-2185
- Contact the Theatre Arts Division at (905) 555-2174
- Contact the Academic Advising Department at (905) 555-2189

_____
_____
_____
_____
_____
_____
_____

Int-NPCDivPres.pptx is part of the project in Activity 1.4.

Theatre Arts Division

Niagara Peninsula COLLEGE

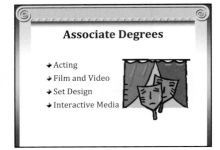

Associate Degrees

→ Acting
→ Film and Video
→ Set Design
→ Interactive Media

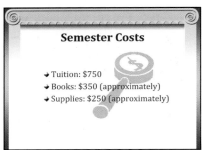

Semester Costs

→ Tuition: $750
→ Books: $350 (approximately)
→ Supplies: $250 (approximately)

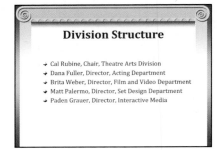

Division Structure

→ Cal Rubine, Chair, Theatre Arts Division
→ Dana Fuller, Director, Acting Department
→ Brita Weber, Director, Film and Video Department
→ Matt Palermo, Director, Set Design Department
→ Paden Grauer, Director, Interactive Media

Fall Semester Classes

→ Introduction to Theater Arts
→ Introduction to Film and Video
→ Fundamentals of Acting
→ Theater Production
→ Beginning Set Design
→ Special Projects

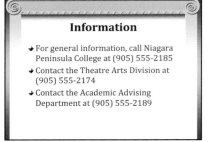

Information

→ For general information, call Niagara Peninsula College at (905) 555-2185
→ Contact the Theatre Arts Division at (905) 555-2174
→ Contact the Academic Advising Department at (905) 555-2189

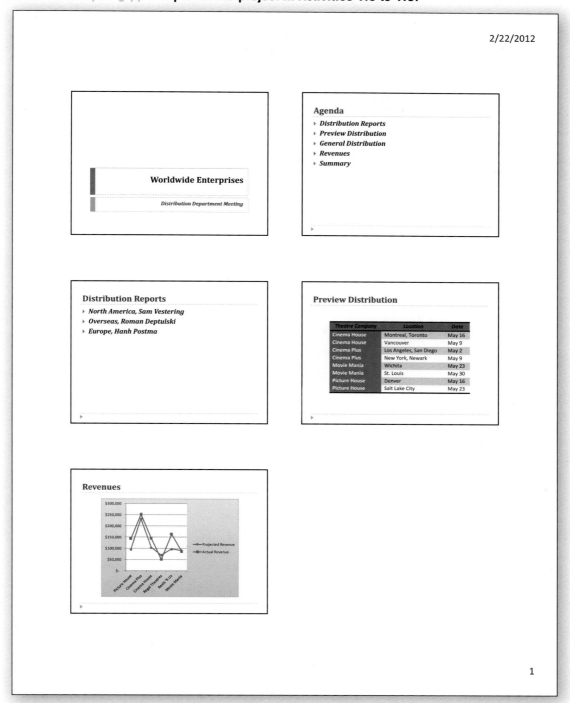

Theatre Company	Projected Revenue	Actual Revenue
Picture House	$ 95,075	$ 143,250
Cinema Plus	$ 231,452	$ 251,812
Cinema House	$ 103,460	$ 144,000
Regal Theatres	$ 69,550	$ 50,320
Reels 'R Us	$ 95,985	$ 163,312
Movie Mania	$ 90,010	$ 85,440

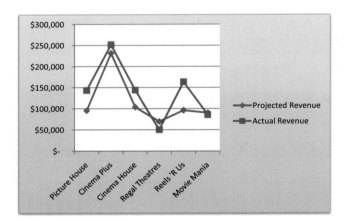

Int-WERevDoc.docx is part of the project in Activities 1.6 and 1.7.

PRODUCT DISTRIBUTION

Projected/Actual Revenues

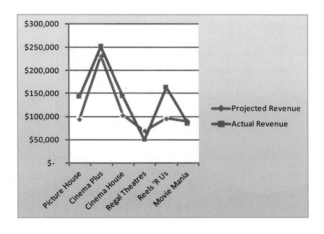

The LinkedGrades table within the Int-NPCStudentGrades.accdb database is part of the project in Activity 1.9.

	LinkedGrades			1/15/2010

Student No	Student	Midterm	Final	Average
111-755-156	Bastow, M.	3.25	2.75	3.00
359-845-475	Collyer, S.	1.50	1.00	1.25
157-457-856	Dwyer, B.	3.50	3.50	3.50
348-876-486	Ennis, A.	2.25	2.00	2.13
378-159-746	Gagne, M.	3.00	3.50	3.25
197-486-745	Koning, J.	2.75	2.50	2.63
314-745-856	Morgan, B.	3.75	3.00	3.38
349-874-658	Retieffe, S.	4.00	3.50	3.75

Int-NPCTRA220.xlsx **is the project in Activity 1.9.**

Student No	Student	Midterm	Final	Average
111-75-156	Bastow, M.	3.25	2.75	3.00
359-845-475	Collyer, S.	1.50	1.00	1.25
157-457-856	Dwyer, B.	3.50	3.50	3.50
348-876-486	Ennis, A.	2.25	2.00	2.13
378-159-746	Gagne, M.	3.00	3.50	3.25
197-486-745	Koning, J.	2.75	2.50	2.63
314-745-856	Morgan, B.	3.75	3.00	3.38
349-874-658	Retieffe, S.	4.00	3.50	3.75

Int-PTWordNov5Pay.docx **is part of the project in Activities 1.10 and 1.11.**

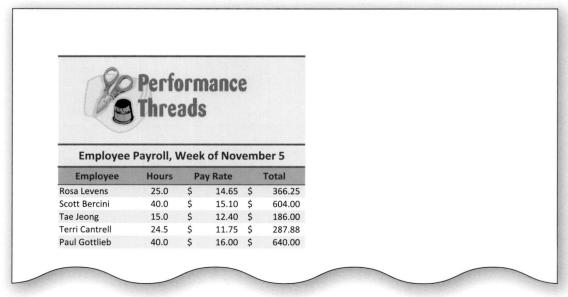

Employee Payroll, Week of November 5

Employee	Hours	Pay Rate		Total
Rosa Levens	25.0	$	14.65	$ 366.25
Scott Bercini	40.0	$	15.10	$ 604.00
Tae Jeong	15.0	$	12.40	$ 186.00
Terri Cantrell	24.5	$	11.75	$ 287.88
Paul Gottlieb	40.0	$	16.00	$ 640.00

Performance Threads

Proudly serving the entertainment industry for over 20 years!

Employee Payroll

Week of November 12, 2012:

Employee	Hours	Pay Rate		Total	
Rosa Levens	40.0	$	14.65	$	586.00
Scott Bercini	40.0	$	15.10	$	604.00
Tae Jeong	40.0	$	12.40	$	496.00
Terri Cantrell	40.0	$	11.75	$	470.00
Paul Gottlieb	40.0	$	16.00	$	640.00
Total				$	2,796.00

4011 Bridgewater Street ✂ Niagara Falls, ON L2E 2T6 ✂ (905) 555-2971

Activity 1.1

Exporting Access Data to Excel

One of the advantages of a suite program like Microsoft Office is the ability to exchange data from one program to another. Access, like the other programs in the suite, offers a feature to export data from Access into Excel and/or Word. Export data using the Excel button in the Export group in the External Data tab. You can export an Access object such as a table, form, and query.

Project

You are Katherine Lamont, Theatre Arts Division instructor at Niagara Peninsula College. You want to work on your grades for your AC-215 class over the weekend and you do not have Access installed on your personal laptop. You decide to export your Access grading table to Excel.

1. Open Access, display the Open dialog box, and then copy the **NPCStudentGrades.accdb** database located in the IntegratingBrief folder into the same folder. Rename the copy **Int-NPCStudentGrades.accdb**.

2. Open **Int-NPCStudentGrades.accdb** and enable the contents.

3. Click the down-pointing arrow in the upper right corner of the Navigation pane and then click *Object Type* at the drop-down list.

4. Click once on the *StudentGradesAC215-03* query.

5. Click the External Data tab.

6. Click the Excel button [icon] in the Export group.

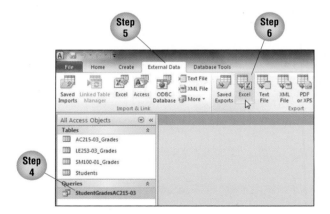

7. At the Export - Excel Spreadsheet dialog box, click the Browse button.

8. At the File Save dialog box, navigate to the IntegratingBrief folder on your storage medium.

   The export wizard automatically inserts the name of the query in the *File name* text box.

9. Click the *File name* text box, press the Home key to move the insertion point to the beginning of the file name, type **Int-** (the file name should appear as **Int-StudentGradesAC215-03.xlsx**), and then click the Save button.

10 At the Export - Excel Spreadsheet dialog box, click the *Export data with formatting and layout* check box to insert a check mark.

11 Click the *Open the destination file after the export operation is complete* check box to insert a check mark and then click the OK button.

Excel opens with the grades from the query in cells in a worksheet in the workbook.

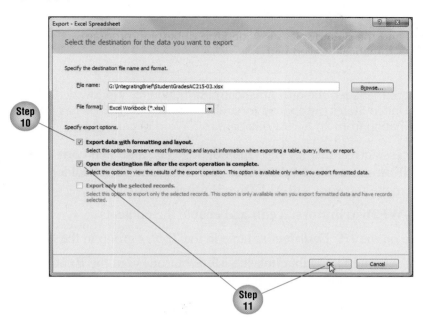

12 If Access is not the active program, click the Access button on the Taskbar.

13 Click the Close button at the Export - Excel Spreadsheet dialog box.

14 Close **Int-NPCStudentGrades.accdb**.

15 Click the Excel button on the Taskbar.

16 In the **Int-StudentGradesAC215-03.xlsx** workbook, insert the following grades in the specified cells in the worksheet:

D4	C
D8	B
D10	F
D14	A
D16	C
D18	B

17 Save, print, and then close **Int-StudentGradesAC215-03.xlsx**.

In Brief

Export Access Table, Form, or Query to Excel
1. Open database.
2. Click desired object in Navigation pane.
3. Click External Data tab.
4. Click Excel button in Export group.
5. At Export – Excel Spreadsheet dialog box, click Browse button.
6. At File Save dialog box, navigate to desired folder, click Save button.
7. Click desired options at Export - Excel Spreadsheet dialog box.
8. Click OK.

In Addition

Exporting Considerations

You can export to Excel a table, form, or query but you cannot export a macro, module, or report. If a table contains subdatasheets or a form contains subforms, you must export each subdatasheet or subform to view them in Excel.

Activity 1.2

Exporting an Access Table to Word

Export data from Access to Word in a manner similar to exporting to Excel. To export data to Word, open the database, select the object, click the External Data tab, and then click the Word button in the Export group. At the Export - RTF File dialog box, make desired changes and then click OK. Word automatically opens and the data displays in a Word document that is automatically saved with the same name as the database object. The difference is that the file extension *.rtf* is added to the name rather than the Word file extension *.docx*. An RTF file is saved in "rich-text format," which preserves formatting such as fonts and styles. You can export a document saved with the *.rtf* extension in Word and other Windows word processing or desktop publishing programs.

Project

Sam Vestering, the manager of North American distribution for Worldwide Enterprises, needs information on United States distributors for an upcoming meeting. He has asked you to export the information from an Access database to a Word document.

1. Make Access active, display the Open dialog box, and then copy the **WEDistributors.accdb** database from the IntegratingBrief folder into the same folder. Rename the copy **Int-WEDistributors.accdb**.

2. Open **Int-WEDistributors.accdb** and enable the contents.

3. Click once on the *US_Distributors* table in the *Tables* group in the Navigation pane.

4. Click the External Data tab, click the More button in the Export group, and then click *Word* at the drop-down list.

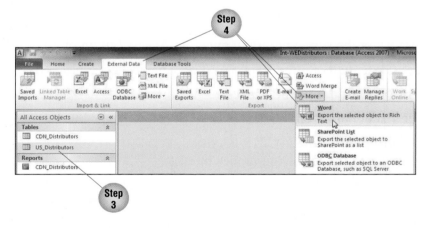

5. At the Export - RTF File dialog box, click the Browse button.

6. At the File Save dialog box, navigate to the IntegratingBrief folder on your storage medium.

   The export wizard automatically inserts the name of the table in the *File name* text box.

7. Click the *File name* text box, press the Home key to move the insertion point to the beginning of the file name, type **Int-** (the file name should appear as **Int-US_Distributors.rtf**), and then click the Save button.

8. At the Export - RTF File dialog box, click the *Open the destination file after the export operation is complete* check box and then click OK.

   Microsoft Word opens and the information for U.S. distributors displays in a Word document.

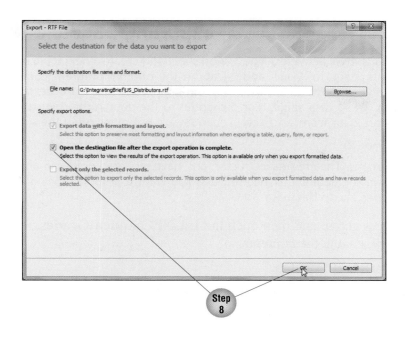

Step
8

In Brief

Export Access Table to Word

1. Open database.
2. Click table in Navigation pane.
3. Click External Data tab.
4. Click Word button in Export group.
5. At Export - RTF File dialog box, click Browse button.
6. At File Save dialog box, navigate to desired folder, click Save button.
7. Click desired options at Export - RTF File dialog box.
8. Click OK.

9 If Access is not the active program, click the Access button on the Taskbar.

10 Click the Close button at the Export - RTF File dialog box.

11 Close **Int-WEDistributors.accdb**.

12 Click the Word button on the Taskbar.

13 Change the orientation to landscape by clicking the Page Layout tab, clicking the Orientation button in the Page Setup group, and then clicking *Landscape* at the drop-down list.

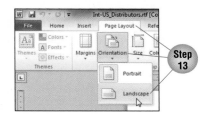

Step
13

14 Click in any cell in the table.

15 Autofit the contents by clicking the Table Tools Layout tab, clicking the AutoFit button in the Cell Size group, and then clicking *AutoFit Window* at the drop-down list.

Step
15

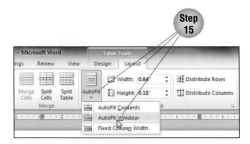

16 Save, print, and then close **Int-US_Distributors.rtf**.

In Addition

Adjusting a Table

In this section, you adjusted the Word table to the cell contents. The Table AutoFit feature contains three options for adjusting table contents as described at the right.

Option	Action
AutoFit Contents	adjusts table to accommodate the table text
AutoFit Window	resizes table to fit within the window or browser; if browser changes size, table size automatically adjusts to fit within window
Fixed Column Width	adjusts each column to a fixed width using the current widths of the columns

Activity 1.3

Importing Data to a New Table

In the previous two activities, you exported Access data to Excel and Word. You can also import data from other programs into an Access table. For example, you can import data from an Excel worksheet and create a new table in a database file. Data in the original program is not connected to the data imported into an Access table. If you make changes to the data in the original program, those changes are not reflected in the Access table.

Project You are Gina Simmons, Theatre Arts instructor, and have recorded grades in an Excel worksheet for your students in the Beginning Theatre class. You want to import those grades into the **NPCStudentGrades.accdb** database.

1. Make Access active and then open the **Int-NPCStudentGrades.accdb** database. If necessary, enable the contents.

2. Click the External Data tab.

3. Click the Excel button in the Import & Link group.

4. At the Get External Data - Excel Spreadsheet dialog box, click the Browse button.

5. At the File Open dialog box, navigate to the IntegratingBrief folder on your storage medium and then double-click *NPCBegThGrades.xlsx*.

6. At the Get External Data - Excel Spreadsheet dialog box, click the OK button.

7. At the first Import Spreadsheet Wizard dialog box, click the Next button.

8. At the second dialog box, insert a check mark in the *First Row Contains Column Headings* option and then click the Next button.

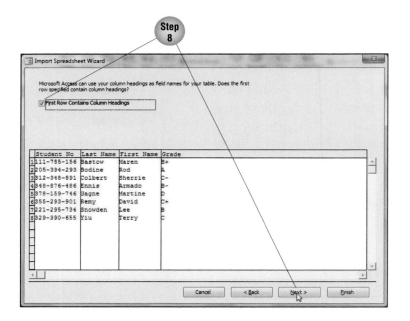

9. At the third dialog box, click the Next button.

10 At the fourth dialog box, click the *Choose my own primary key* option (this inserts *Student No* in the text box located to the right of the option) and then click the Next button.

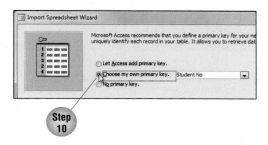

In Brief

Import Data to New Table
1. Open database.
2. Click table in Navigation pane.
3. Click External Data tab.
4. Click Excel button in Import group.
5. Click OK at Get External Data - Excel Spreadsheet dialog box.
6. Follow Import Spreadsheet Wizard steps.

11 At the fifth dialog box, type **BegThGrades** in the *Import to Table* text box and then click the Finish button.

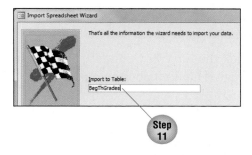

12 At the Get External Data - Excel Spreadsheet dialog box, click the Close button.

13 Open the new table by double-clicking *BegThGrades* in the list box.

14 Print and then close BegThGrades.

15 Close **Int-NPCStudentGrades.accdb**.

In Addition

Importing or Linking a Table

You can import data from another program into an Access table or you can link the data. Choose the method depending on how you are going to use the data. Consider linking an Excel file instead of importing if you want to keep data in an Excel worksheet but use Access to perform queries and create reports. In Access, you can only update linked data in one direction. Once an Excel table is linked to Access, you cannot edit data in the Access table. You can update the data in the Excel file and the Access table will reflect the changes but you cannot update data within Access.

Activity 1.4

Exporting a PowerPoint Presentation to Word

You can send data in one program to another program. For example, you can send Word data to a PowerPoint presentation and data in a PowerPoint presentation to a Word document. To send presentation data to Word, click the File tab, click the Save & Send tab, click the Create Handouts option, and then click the Create Handouts button. At the Send To Microsoft Word dialog box that displays, specify the layout of the data in the Word document, whether you want to paste or paste link the data, and then click OK. One of the advantages to sending presentation data to a Word document is that you can have greater control over the formatting of the data in Word.

Project

Create a handout as a Word document that contains slides from a PowerPoint presentation on the Theatre Arts Division at Niagara Peninsula College.

1. Open PowerPoint.

2. With PowerPoint the active program, open the presentation named **NPCDivPres.pptx**.

3. Save the presentation and name it **Int-NPCDivPres**.

4. Click the File tab, click the Save & Send tab, click the *Create Handouts* option, and then click the Create Handouts button.

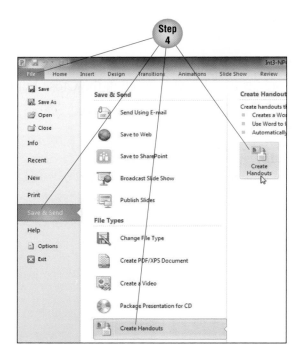

5. At the Send To Microsoft Word dialog box, click the *Blank lines next to slides* option.

6. Click the *Paste link* option located toward the bottom of the dialog box and then click OK.

7. Click the Word button on the Taskbar.

    The slides display in a Word document as thumbnails followed by blank lines.

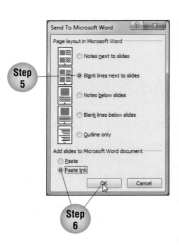

8 Save the Word document in the IntegratingBrief folder on your storage medium and name it **Int-NPCDivPresHandout**.

9 Print and then close **Int-NPCDivPresHandout.docx**.

10 Click the PowerPoint button on the Taskbar.

11 Make Slide 3 active and then change *$650* to *$750*, change *$250* to *$350*, and change *$200* to *$250*.

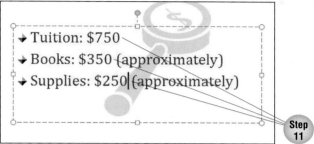

Step 11

In Brief

Export PowerPoint Presentation to Word
1. Open presentation.
2. Click File tab.
3. Click Save & Send tab.
4. Click *Create Handouts* option.
5. Click Create Handouts button.
6. Choose desired options at Send To Microsoft Word dialog box.
7. Click OK.

12 Save **Int-NPCDivPres.pptx**.

13 Click the Word button on the Taskbar and then open **Int-NPCDivPresHandout.docx**. At the message asking if you want to update the document with the data from the linked files, click the Yes button.

14 Scroll through the document and notice that the amounts in Slide 3 reflect the changes you made to Slide 3 in the PowerPoint presentation. (If you do not see the updated amounts, close the document without saving it and then open it again.)

15 Save, print, and then close **Int-NPCDivPresHandout.docx**.

16 Make PowerPoint the active program and then close **Int-NPCDivPres.pptx**.

In Addition

Pasting and Linking Data

The *Paste* option at the Send To Microsoft Word dialog box is selected by default and is available for all of the page layout options. With this option selected, the data inserted in Word is not connected or linked to the original data in the PowerPoint presentation. If you plan to update the data in the presentation and want the data updated in the Word document, select the *Paste link* option at the Send To Microsoft Word dialog box. This option is available for all of the page layout options except the *Outline only* option.

Activity 1.5

Exporting a Word Outline to a PowerPoint Presentation

As you learned in the previous section, you can send data in one program to another program. For example, you can send Word data to a PowerPoint presentation and data in a PowerPoint presentation to a Word document. You can create text for slides in a Word outline and then export that outline to PowerPoint. PowerPoint creates new slides based on the heading styles used in the Word outline. Paragraphs formatted with a Heading 1 style become slide titles. Heading 2 text becomes first-level bulleted text, Heading 3 text becomes second-level bulleted text, and so on. If styles are not applied to outline text in Word, PowerPoint uses tabs or indents to place text on slides. To export a Word document to a PowerPoint presentation, you need to insert the Send to Microsoft PowerPoint button on the Quick Access toolbar.

Project

Prepare a presentation for the Distribution Department of Worldwide Enterprises using a Word outline.

(1) Open Word and PowerPoint.

(2) With Word the active program, open the document named **WEOutline.docx**.

> Text in this document has been formatted with the *Heading 1* and *Heading 2* styles.

(3) Insert a Send to Microsoft PowerPoint button on the Quick Access toolbar. Begin by clicking the Customize Quick Access Toolbar button ⬇ that displays at the right side of the Quick Access toolbar.

(4) Click *More Commands* at the drop-down list.

(5) Click the down-pointing arrow at the right side of the *Choose commands from* list box and then click *All Commands* at the drop-down list.

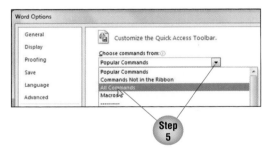

(6) Scroll down the list box that displays below the *Choose commands from* list box and then double-click *Send to Microsoft PowerPoint*.

> Items in the list box display in alphabetical order.

(7) Click OK to close the Word Options dialog box.

> Notice the Send to Microsoft PowerPoint button added to the Quick Access toolbar.

(8) Send the outline to PowerPoint by clicking the Send to Microsoft PowerPoint button 📄 on the Quick Access toolbar.

9. When the presentation displays on the screen, make sure Slide 1 is the active slide. (If the presentation does not display, click the PowerPoint button on the Taskbar.)

The presentation is created with a blank design template.

10. With Slide 1 active, change the layout by clicking the Layout button ▦ in the Slides group in the Home tab and then clicking *Title Slide* at the drop-down list.

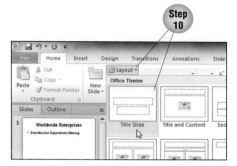

11. Make Slide 4 active and then change the layout to *Title Only*. Make Slide 5 active and then change the layout to *Title Only*. Make Slide 6 active and then change the layout to *Title Only*.

12. Apply a design theme by clicking the Design tab, clicking the More button ▾ at the right side of the Themes thumbnails, and then clicking *Origin*.

13. Save the presentation and name it **Int-WEDistDeptMtg**.

14. Close **Int-WEDistDeptMtg.pptx**.

15. Click the Word button on the Taskbar.

16. Right-click the Send to Microsoft PowerPoint button on the Quick Access toolbar and then click the *Remove from Quick Access Toolbar* option at the shortcut menu.

17. Close **WEOutline.docx**.

In Brief

Insert Send to Microsoft PowerPoint Button on Quick Access Toolbar
1. Click Customize Quick Access Toolbar button at right side of Quick Access toolbar.
2. Click *More Commands*.
3. Click down-pointing arrow at right side of *Choose commands from* list box.
4. Click *All Commands*.
5. Scroll down *Choose commands from* list box, double-click *Send to Microsoft PowerPoint*.
6. Click OK.

Send Word Outline to PowerPoint Presentation
1. Open Word document.
2. Click Send to Microsoft PowerPoint button on Quick Access toolbar.

In Addition

Applying a Style in Word

Heading styles were already applied to the text in the **WEOutline.docx** Word document. If you create an outline in Word that you want to export to PowerPoint, apply styles using options in the Styles group in the Home tab. A Word document contains a number of predesigned formats grouped into style sets called Quick Styles. Display the available Quick Styles sets by clicking the Change Styles button in the Styles group in the Home tab and then pointing to Style Set. Choose a Quick Styles set and the styles visible in the Styles group change to reflect the set. To display additional available styles, click the More button (contains a horizontal line and a down-pointing triangle) that displays at the right side of the style thumbnails. To apply a heading style, position the insertion point in the desired text, click the More button, and then click the desired style at the drop-down gallery.

Activity 1.6

Linking an Excel Chart with a Word Document and a PowerPoint Presentation

You can copy and link an object such as a table or chart to documents in other programs. For example, you can copy an Excel chart and link it to a Word document and/or a PowerPoint presentation. The advantage to copying and linking over just copying and pasting is that you can edit the object in the originating program, called the *source* program, and the object is updated in the linked documents in the *destination* programs. When an object is linked, the object exists in the source program but not as a separate object in the destination program. Since the object is located only in the source program, changes made to the object in the source program are reflected in the destination program.

Project In preparation for a company meeting, you will copy an Excel chart and link it to the Worldwide Enterprises Distribution Department meeting presentation and to a Word document.

1. Open Word, Excel, and PowerPoint.

2. Make Word the active program and then open the document named **WERevDoc.docx**. Save the document with Save As and name it **Int-WERevDoc**.

3. Make PowerPoint the active program, open the presentation named **Int-WEDistDeptMtg.pptx**, and then make Slide 6 the active slide.

4. Make Excel the active program and then open the workbook named **WERevChart.xlsx**. Save the workbook with Save As and name it **Int-WERevChart**.

5. Copy and link the chart to the Word document and the PowerPoint presentation by clicking once in the chart to select it.

   Make sure you select the chart and not a specific chart element. Try selecting the chart by clicking just inside the chart border.

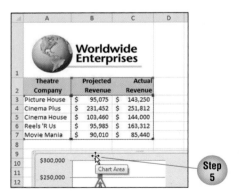

6. With the chart selected, click the Copy button in the Clipboard group in the Home tab.

7. Click the Word button on the Taskbar.

8. Press Ctrl + End to move the insertion point to the end of the document.

9. Click the Paste button arrow and then click *Paste Special* at the drop-down list.

10. At the Paste Special dialog box, click the *Paste link* option, click the *Microsoft Excel Chart Object* option in the *As* list box, and then click OK.

11. Select the chart and then center it by clicking the Center button in the Paragraph group in the Home tab.

12. Save, print, and then close **Int-WERevDoc.docx**.

13. Click the PowerPoint button on the Taskbar.

14. With Slide 6 the active slide, make sure the Home tab is selected, click the Paste button arrow, and then click *Paste Special*.

15. At the Paste Special dialog box, click the *Paste link* option, make sure *Microsoft Excel Chart Object* is selected in the *As* list box, and then click OK.

16. Increase the size of the chart so it better fills the slide and then move the chart so it is centered on the slide.

17. Click outside the chart to deselect it.

18. Save the presentation, print only Slide 6, and then close **Int-WEDistDeptMtg.pptx**.

19. Click the Excel button on the Taskbar and then click outside the chart to deselect it.

20. Save, print, and then close **Int-WERevChart.xlsx**.

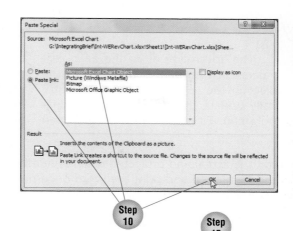

Step 10

In Brief

Link Object between Programs
1. Open source program, open file containing object.
2. Select object, click Copy button.
3. Open destination program, open file into which object will be linked.
4. Click Paste button arrow, *Paste Special*.
5. At Paste Special dialog box, click *Paste link*, click OK.

Step 15

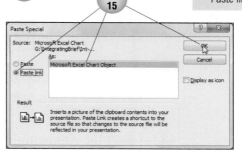

Step 16

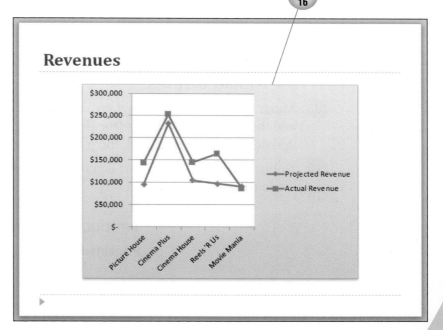

In Addition

Linking Data or an Object within a Program

In this section, you learned to link an object between programs using the Paste Special dialog box. You can also link an object in Word using options at the Object dialog box. To do this, click the Insert tab and then click the Object button. At the Object dialog box, click the *Create from File* tab. At the dialog box, type the desired file name in the *File name* text box or click the Browse button and then select the desired file from the appropriate folder. Click the *Link to file* check box to insert a check mark and then click OK.

Activity 1.7

Editing a Linked Object

The advantage of linking an object over copying data is that editing the object in the source program will automatically update the object in the destination program(s). To edit a linked object, open the document containing the object in the source program, make the desired edits, and then save the document. The next time you open the document, workbook, or presentation in the destination program, the object is updated.

Project

Edit the actual and projected revenue numbers in the Worldwide Enterprises Excel worksheet and then open and print the Word document and PowerPoint presentation containing the linked chart.

1. Open Word, Excel, and PowerPoint.

2. Make Excel the active program and then open the workbook named **Int-WERevChart.xlsx**.

3. You discover that one theatre company was left out of the revenues chart. Add a row to the worksheet by clicking once in cell A6 to make it the active cell. Click the Insert button arrow in the Cells group in the Home tab and then click *Insert Sheet Rows*.

4. Insert the following data in the specified cells:

   A6 **Regal Theatres**
   B6 **69,550**
   C6 **50,320**

5. Click in cell A3.

6. Save, print, and then close **Int-WERevChart.xlsx**.

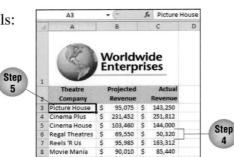

7. Make Word the active program and then open **Int-WERevDoc.docx**. At the message asking if you want to update the linked file, click the Yes button.

8. Notice how the linked chart is automatically updated to reflect the changes you made to the chart in Excel.

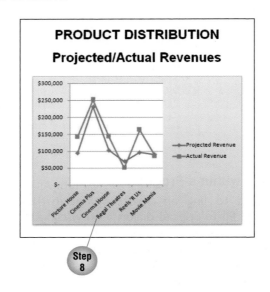

9 Save, print, and then close **Int-WERevDoc.docx**.

10 Make PowerPoint the active program and then open **Int-WEDistDeptMtg.pptx**.

11 At the message telling you that the presentation contains links, click the Update Links button.

12 Make Slide 6 the active slide and then notice how the linked chart is automatically updated to reflect the changes you made to the chart in Excel.

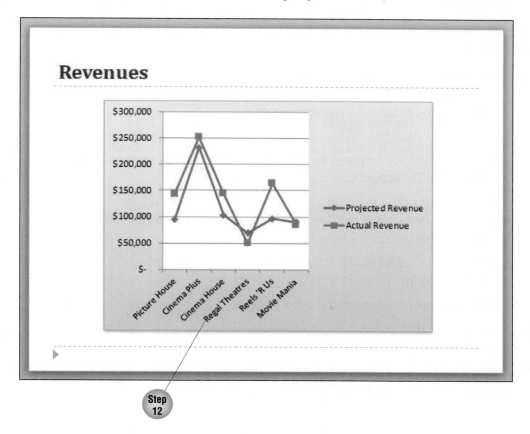

13 Save the presentation and then print only Slide 6.

14 Close **Int-WEDistDeptMtg.pptx**.

In Addition

Updating a Link Manually

You can choose to update a link manually in the destination program. To do this, open a Word document containing a linked object. Right-click the object, point to *Linked (type of object) Object*, and then click *Links*. At the Links dialog box, click the *Manual update* option and then click OK. With *Manual update* selected, a link is only updated when you right-click a linked object and then click *Update Link*, or when you display the Links dialog box, click the link in the list box, and then click the Update Now button.

Activity 1.8

Embedding and Editing a Word Table in a PowerPoint Slide

You can edit an embedded object in the destination program using the tools of the source program. Double-click the object in the document in the destination program and the tools from the source program display. For example, if you double-click a Word table that is embedded in a PowerPoint slide, the Word tabs and ribbon display.

Project Update the distribution dates for an embedded table in the Worldwide Enterprises Distribution Department meeting presentation.

1. Open Word and PowerPoint, make PowerPoint the active program, and then open **Int-WEDistDeptMtg**. At the message telling you that the presentation contains links, click the Update Links button.

2. Make Slide 4 the active slide.

3. Make Word the active program and then open the document named **WEPrevDistTable.docx**.

4. Click in a cell in the table and then select the table. To do this, click the Table Tools Layout tab, click the Select button ⃗ in the Table group, and then click *Select Table* at the drop-down list.

5. With the table selected, click the Home tab and then click the Copy button in the Clipboard group.

6. Click the PowerPoint button on the Taskbar.

7. With Slide 4 the active slide, click the Paste button arrow and then click *Paste Special* at the drop-down list.

8. At the Paste Special dialog box, click *Microsoft Word Document Object* in the *As* list box and then click OK.

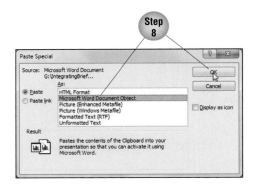

9. With the table selected in the slide, use the sizing handles to increase the size and position of the table so it displays as shown on the next page.

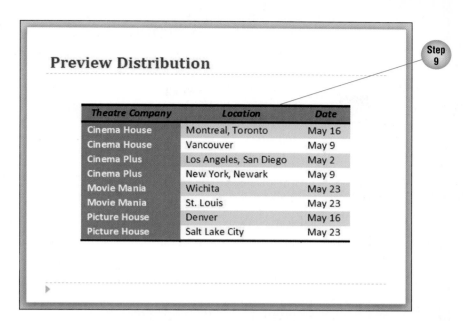

Step 9

10. The distribution date to Movie Mania in St. Louis has been delayed until May 30. Edit the date by double-clicking the table in the slide.

    Double-clicking the table displays the Word tabs and ribbon at the top of the screen. A horizontal and vertical ruler also display around the table.

11. Using the mouse, select *23* after *May* in the *St. Louis* row and then type **30**.

12. Click outside the table to deselect it.

    Clicking outside the table deselects it and also removes the Word tabs.

13. Print Slide 4 of the presentation.

14. Delete Slide 5.

15. Apply a transition and sound of your choosing to all slides in the presentation.

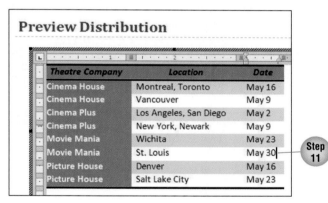

Step 11

16. Run the presentation.

17. Save and then close **Int-WEDistDeptMtg.pptx**.

18. Click the Word button on the Taskbar and then close the document.

In Addition

Display an Embedded Object as an Icon

An embedded object displays in the destination program as it appears in the source program. You can embed an object as an icon in the destination program representing the object. To change the embedded object to an icon, right-click the object, point to *Document Object*, and then click *Convert*. At the Convert dialog box, click the *Display as icon* check box, and then click OK. To view the embedded object in the source program, double-click the icon in the destination program. After viewing the object, return to the destination program by clicking the File tab and then clicking *Close and Return to (file name)*.

Activity 1.9

Linking Data to a New Table

Imported data is not connected to the source program. If you know that you will use your data only in Access, import it. However, if you want to update data in a program other than Access, link the data. Changes made to linked data are reflected in both the source and destination programs. For example, you can link an Excel worksheet with an Access table and when you make changes in the Excel worksheet, the change is reflected in the Access table.

Project

You are Cal Rubine, Theatre Arts instructor at Niagara Peninsula College. You record students' grades in an Excel worksheet and also link the grades to an Access database file. With the data linked, changes you make to the Excel worksheet are reflected in the Access table.

1. Make Excel the active program and then open the workbook **NPCTRA220.xlsx**.

2. Save the workbook with Save As and name it **Int-NPCTRA220**.

3. Print and then close **Int-NPCTRA220.xlsx**.

4. Make Access the active program and then open the **Int-NPCStudentGrades.accdb** database.

5. Click the External Data tab and then click the Excel button in the Import & Link group.

6. At the Get External Data - Excel Spreadsheet dialog box, click the Browse button.

7. Navigate to the IntegratingBrief folder on your storage medium and then double-click **Int-NPCTRA220.xlsx**.

8. At the Get External Data - Excel Spreadsheet dialog box, click the *Link to the data source by creating a linked table* option and then click OK.

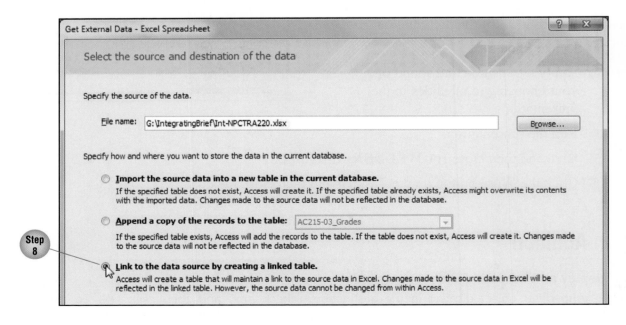

9. At the first Link Spreadsheet Wizard dialog box, click the Next button.

10. At the second dialog box, make sure the *First Row Contains Column Headings* option contains a check mark and then click the Next button.

11 At the third dialog box, type **LinkedGrades** in the *Linked Table Name* text box and then click the Finish button.

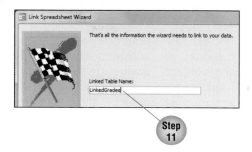

Step 11

In Brief

Link Data to New Table
1. Open database.
2. Click table in Navigation pane.
3. Click External Data tab.
4. Click Excel button in Import & Link group.
5. At Get External Data - Excel Spreadsheet dialog box, click Browse button.
6. Navigate to desired folder, then double-click desired file.
7. At Get External Data - Excel Spreadsheet dialog box, click *Link to the data source by creating a linked table* option, then click OK.
8. Follow Link Spreadsheet Wizard steps.

12 At the message stating the link is finished, click OK.

Access uses different icons to represent linked tables and tables that are stored in the current database. Notice the icon that displays before the LinkedGrades table.

13 Open the new LinkedGrades table in Datasheet view.

14 Close the LinkedGrades table.

15 Make Excel the active program and then open **Int-NPCTRA220.xlsx**.

16 Make cell E2 active, click the AutoSum button arrow, click *Average* at the drop-down list, and then press Enter.

This inserts *3.00* in cell E2.

17 Copy the formula in cell E2 down to cells E3 through E9.

18 Save, print, and then close **Int-NPCTRA220.xlsx**.

19 Click the Access button on the Taskbar and then open the LinkedGrades table and notice the worksheet contains the average amounts.

20 Print and then close the table.

21 Close **Int-NPCStudentGrades.accdb** and then exit Access.

In Addition

Deleting the Link to a Linked Table

If you want to delete the link to a table, open the database and then click the table in the Navigation pane. Click the Home tab and then click the Delete button in the Records group. At the question asking if you want to remove the link to the table, click Yes. Access deletes the link and removes the table's name from the Navigation pane. When you delete a linked table, you are deleting the information Access uses to open the table, not the table itself. You can link to the same table again, if necessary.

Embedding an Excel Worksheet into a Word Document

You can copy an object between documents in a program, link an object, or embed an object. A linked object resides in the source program but not as a separate object in the destination program. An embedded object resides in the document in the source program as well as the destination program. If a change is made to an embedded object at the source program, the change is not made to the object in the destination program. Since an embedded object is not automatically updated as is a linked object, the only advantage to embedding rather than simply copying and pasting is that you can edit an embedded object in the destination program using the tools of the source program.

Project Copy data in an Excel worksheet on employee payroll for Performance Threads and then embed the data in a Word document.

1. With Word open and the active program, open the document named **PTWordNov5Pay.docx**.

2. Save the document with Save As and name it **Int-PTWordNov5Pay**.

3. Make Excel the active program and then open the workbook named **PTExcelNov5Pay.xlsx**.

4. Save the workbook with Save As and name it **Int-PTExcelNov5Pay**.

5. Embed cells into the Word document by selecting cells A3 through D8.

6. Click the Copy button in the Clipboard group in the Home tab.

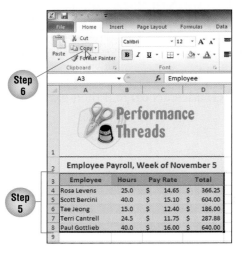

7. Click the Word button on the Taskbar.

8. Press Ctrl + End to move the insertion point to the end of the document (the insertion point is positioned a double space below *Week of November 5, 2012:*).

9. Click the Paste button arrow and then click *Paste Special* at the drop-down list.

10 At the Paste Special dialog box, click *Microsoft Excel Worksheet Object* in the *As* list box and then click OK.

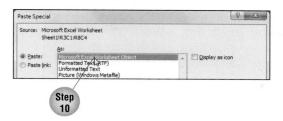

Step 10

In Brief

Embed Data
1. Open desired programs and documents.
2. Select data in source program.
3. Click Copy button.
4. Click button on Taskbar representing destination program.
5. Click Paste button arrow *Paste Special*.
6. Click object in *As* list box.
7. Click OK.

11 If necessary, click outside the table to deselect it.

12 Save, print, and then close **Int-PTWordNov5Pay.docx**.

13 Click the Excel button on the Taskbar.

14 Press the Esc key to remove the moving marquee around cells A3 through D8.

15 Click in cell A2 to make it the active cell.

16 Save and then close **Int-PTExcelNov5Pay.xlsx**.

In Addition

Inserting an Embedded Object from an Existing File

You embedded an Excel worksheet in a Word document using the Copy button and options at the Paste Special dialog box. Another method is available for embedding an object from an existing file. In the source program document, position the insertion point where you want the object embedded and then click the Object button in the Text group. At the Object dialog box, click the Create from File tab. At the Object dialog box with the Create from File tab selected as shown at the right, type the desired file name in the *File name* text box or click the Browse button and then select the desired file from the appropriate folder. At the Object dialog box, make sure the *Link to file* check box does not contain a check mark and then click OK.

Activity
1.11

Editing an Embedded Worksheet

You can edit an embedded object in the destination program using the tools of the source program. To do this, double-click the object in the document in the destination program and the source program tools display. For example, if you double-click an Excel worksheet that is embedded in a Word document, the Excel tabs display at the top of the screen.

Project Update the payroll hours for the employees of Performance Threads for the week of October 18 in the embedded Excel worksheet.

Performance Threads

1. With Word the active program, open **Int-PTWordNov5Pay.docx**.

2. Save the document with Save As and name it **Int-PTWordNov12Pay**.

3. Change the date above the table from *November 5* to *November 12*.

4. Position the arrow pointer anywhere in the worksheet and then double-click the left mouse button.

   In a few moments, the worksheet displays surrounded by column and row designations and the Excel tabs.

5. To produce the ordered costumes on time, the part-time employees worked a full 40 hours for the week of November 12. Make cell B4 the active cell and then change the number to *40*.

6. Make cell B6 the active cell and then change the number to *40*.

7. Make cell B7 the active cell and then change the number to *40*.

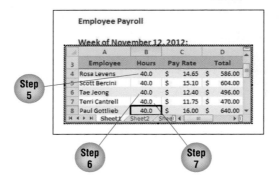

8. Bobbie Sinclair, Business Manager, wants to know the payroll total for the week of November 12 to determine the impact it has on the monthly budget. Add a new row to the table by making cell A8 the active cell and then pressing the Enter key.

9 With cell A9 the active cell, type **Total**.

10 Make cell D9 the active cell and then click the AutoSum button $\boxed{\Sigma}$ in the Editing group in the Home tab.

11 Make sure *D4:D8* displays in cell D9 and then press the Enter key.

12 Increase the height of the worksheet by one row by positioning the arrow pointer on the bottom middle black sizing square until the pointer turns into a double-headed arrow pointing up and down. Hold down the left mouse button, drag down one row, and then release the mouse button.

In Brief
Edit Embedded Object
1. In source program, double-click embedded object.
2. Make desired edits.
3. Click outside object.

13 Using the arrow keys on the keyboard, make cell A3 the active cell and position cell A3 in the upper left corner of the worksheet. (This will display all cells in the worksheet containing data.)

14 Click outside the worksheet to deselect it.

15 Save, print, and then close **Int-PTWordNov12Pay.docx**.

The gridlines do not print.

In Addition

Troubleshooting Linking and Embedding Problems

If you double-click a linked or embedded object and a message appears telling you that the source file or source program cannot be opened, consider the following troubleshooting options. Check to make sure that the source program is installed on your computer. If the source program is not installed, convert the object to the file format of a program that is installed. Try closing other programs to free memory and make sure you have enough memory to run the source program. Check to make sure the source program does not have any dialog boxes open and, if it is a linked object, check to make sure someone else is not working in the source file.

Skills Review

Review 1 Exporting Access Data to Excel

1. Create a new folder on your storage medium and name it IntegratingEOS.
2. Open Access, display the Open dialog box, and then copy the **PTCostumes.accdb** database from the IntegratingBrief folder on your storage medium to the IntegratingEOS folder. Rename the database **Int-PTCostumes**.
3. Open **Int-PTCostumes.accdb** from the IntegratingEOS folder and, if necessary, enable the contents.
4. Click the *CostumeInventory* table in the Navigation pane and then export the data to Excel in the IntegratingEOS folder on your storage medium, and save the workbook as **Int-R1-CostumeInventory**.
5. When the data displays in Excel, make the following changes in the specified cells:
   - C4 Change *110.00* to *120.00*.
   - C5 Change *110.00* to *125.00*.
   - C7 Change *99.50* to *105.00*.
6. Save, print, and then close **Int-R1-CostumeInventory.xlsx**.
7. Click the Access button on the Taskbar.
8. Close the Export - Excel Spreadsheet dialog box and then close the database.

Review 2 Exporting an Access Report to Word

1. With Access the active program, open **Int-PTCostumes.accdb**.
2. Click the *CostumeInventory* report in the Navigation pane and then export it to a Word document in the IntegratingEOS folder, and save the document as **Int-R2-CostumeInventory**.
3. If necessary, make Word the active program, change the page orientation to landscape, and change the margins to *Normal*.
4. Save, print, and then close **Int-R2-CostumeInventory.rtf**.
5. Exit Word.
6. With Access the active program, close the Export - RTF File dialog box and then close the database.

Review 3 Importing Data to a New Table

1. In Access, open the **Int-PTCostumes.accdb** database from the IntegratingEOS folder and, if necessary, enable the contents.
2. Import a worksheet from the Excel workbook named **PTCostumeHours.xlsx** from the IntegratingBrief folder. (Do not make any changes to the first Import Spreadsheet Wizard dialog box. At the second dialog box, make sure the *First Row Contains Column Headings* option contains a check mark. Do not make any changes to the third dialog box. Click the *No primary key* option at the fourth dialog box. At the fifth dialog box, type **DesignHours** in the *Import to Table* text box and then click the Finish button. At the message asking if you want to save the import steps, click the Close button.)

3. Open the new DesignHours table.
4. Print and then close the DesignHours table.
5. Close the **Int-PTCostumes.accdb** database.
6. Exit Access.

Review 4 Exporting a PowerPoint Presentation to Word

1. Open Word and PowerPoint.
2. With PowerPoint the active program, open the presentation named **FCTVacations.pptx** and then save it in the IntegratingEOS folder and name it **Int-R4-FCTVacations**.
3. Send the PowerPoint data to Word as slides with blank lines next to the slides. Click the *Blank lines next to slides* option and the *Paste link* option at the Send To Microsoft Word dialog box.
4. Save the Word document in the IntegratingEOS folder and name it **Int-R4-FCTVacSpecials**.
5. Print and then close **Int-R4-FCTVacSpecials.docx**.
6. Click the PowerPoint button on the Taskbar.
7. Make Slide 4 active and then change *$950* to *$1,050*, change *$1,175* to *$1,275*, and change *$1,215* to *$1,315*.
8. Save the presentation and then print Slide 4.
9. Make Word the active program, open **Int-R4-FCTVacSpecials.docx**, and then click Yes at the question asking if you want to update the link.
10. Print only page 2 of **Int-R4-FCTVacSpecials.docx**.
11. Save and then close the document. Exit Word.
12. Make PowerPoint the active program and then close **Int-R4-FCTVacations.pptx**.

Review 5 Linking and Editing an Excel Chart in a PowerPoint Slide

1. Make PowerPoint the active program and then open **NPCEnroll.pptx**.
2. Save the presentation in the IntegratingEOS folder and name it **Int-R5-NPCEnroll**.
3. Make Slide 4 active.
4. Open Excel and then open the workbook named **NPCEnrollChart.xlsx**.
5. Save the workbook in the IntegratingEOS folder and name it **Int-R5-NPCEnrollChart**.
6. Click the chart once to select it (make sure you select the entire chart and not a chart element) and then copy and link the chart to Slide 4 in the **Int-R5-NPCEnroll.pptx** PowerPoint presentation. (Be sure to use the Paste Special dialog box to link the chart.)
7. Increase the size of the chart to better fill the slide and then center the chart on the slide.
8. Click outside the chart to deselect it.
9. Save the presentation, print Slide 4, and then close the presentation.
10. Click the Excel button on the Taskbar.
11. Click outside the chart to deselect it.
12. Save and then print **Int-R5-NPCEnrollChart.xlsx**.
13. Insert another department in the worksheet (and chart) by making cell A7 active, clicking the Insert button arrow in the Cells group in the Home tab, and then clicking *Insert Sheet Rows* at the drop-down list. (This creates a new row 7.) Type the following text in the specified cells:

    A7 **Directing**   C7 **32**
    B7 **18**   D7 **25**

14. Click in cell A4.
15. Save, print, and then close **Int-R5-NPCEnrollChart.xlsx**.
16. Exit Excel.
17. With PowerPoint the active program, open **Int-R5-NPCEnroll.pptx**. At the message telling you that the presentation contains links, click the Update Links button.
18. Display Slide 4 and then notice the change to the chart.
19. Save the presentation, print only Slide 4, and then close the presentation.

Review 6 Embedding and Editing a Word Table in a PowerPoint Slide

1. With PowerPoint the active program, open **Int-R5-NPCEnroll.pptx**. At the message telling you that the presentation contains links, click the Update Links button.
2. Save the presentation with Save As in the IntegratingEOS folder and name it **Int-R6-NPCEnroll**.
3. Make Slide 5 the active slide.
4. Open Word and then open the document named **NPCContacts.docx**.
5. Select the table and then copy and embed it in Slide 5 in the **Int-R6-NPCEnroll.pptx** presentation. (Make sure you use the Paste Special dialog box.)
6. With the table selected in the slide, use the sizing handles to increase the size and change the position of the table so it better fills the slide.
7. Click outside the table to deselect it and then save the presentation.
8. Double-click the table, select *Editing* in the name *Emerson Editing*, and type **Edits**.
9. Click outside the table to deselect it.
10. Print Slide 5 of the presentation.
11. Apply an animation scheme of your choosing to all slides in the presentation.
12. Run the presentation.
13. Save and then close **Int-R6-NPCEnroll.pptx** and then exit PowerPoint.
14. Close the Word document **NPCContacts.docx** and then exit Word.

Review 7 Linking Data to a New Table and Editing Linked Data

1. Open Excel and then open the workbook **FCTBookings.xlsx** from the IntegratingBrief folder.
2. Save the workbook in the IntegratingEOS folder and name it **Int-R7-FCTBookings.xlsx**.
3. Open Access, display the Open dialog box, and then copy the **FCTCommissions.accdb** database from the IntegratingBrief folder on your storage medium to the IntegratingEOS folder. Rename the database **Int-FCTCommissions**.
4. Open the **Int-FCTCommissions.accdb** database from the IntegratingEOS folder and, if necessary, enable the contents.
5. Link the Excel workbook **Int-R7-FCTBookings.xlsx** with the **Int-FCTCommissions.accdb** database. (At the Get External Data - Excel Spreadsheet dialog box, click the *Link to the data source by creating a linked table* option. At the third Link Spreadsheet Wizard dialog box, type **LinkedCommissions** in the *Linked Table Name* text box.)
6. Open, print, and then close the new LinkedCommissions table.
7. Click the Excel button on the Taskbar.
8. Make cell C2 active, type the formula **=B2*0.03**, and then press Enter.
9. Make cell C2 active and then use the fill handle to copy the formula down to cell C13.
10. Save, print, and then close **Int-R7-FCTBookings.xlsx**.

11. Click the Access button on the Taskbar.
12. Open the LinkedCommissions table.
13. Save, print, and then close the LinkedCommissions table.
14. Close the **Int-FCTCommissions.accdb** database and then exit Access.

Review 8 Embedding an Object

1. Open Word and then open **WERevMemo.docx**.
2. Save the document in the IntegratingEOS folder and name it **Int-R8-WERevMemo**.
3. Make Excel the active program and then open the workbook named **WEExcelRev.xlsx**.
4. Embed the data in cells A2 through D8 into the Word document **Int-R8-WERevMemo.docx** a double space below the paragraph of text in the body of the memo.
5. Save and then print **Int-R8-WERevMemo.docx**.
6. Click the Excel button on the Taskbar, close the workbook, and then exit Excel.
7. With **Int-R8-WERevMemo.docx** open, double-click the worksheet and then make the following changes to the data in the specified cells:
    A2 Change *July Revenues* to *August Revenues*.
    B4 Change *1,356,000* to *1,575,000*.
    B5 Change *2,450,000* to *2,375,000*.
    B6 Change *1,635,000* to *1,750,000*.
    B7 Change *950,000* to *1,100,000*.
    B8 Change *1,050,000* to *1,255,000*.
8. Move the insertion point up to cell A2 and then click outside the worksheet to deselect it.
9. Make the following changes to the memo: change the date from *August 13, 2012* to *September 3, 2012*, and change the subject from *July Revenues* to *August Revenues*.
10. Save, print, and then close **Int-R8-WERevMemo.docx**.
11. Exit Word.

INDEX

WORD

ACCESS

INTEGRATING PROGRAMS

COMMON COMMANDS FOR MICROSOFT 2010 OFFICE SUITE

WORD, EXCEL, POWERPOINT

Feature	Ribbon Tab, Group	Button, File Tab	Shortcut
bold	Home, Font	B	Ctrl + B
Clipboard task pane	Home, Clipboard		
close		X , Close	Ctrl + F4
copy	Home, Clipboard		Ctrl + C
cut	Home, Clipboard		Ctrl + X
exit program	File	Exit	
font	Home, Font	Calibri (Body)	
font size	Home, Font	11	
font color	Home, Font	A	
Format Painter	Home, Clipboard		
Help			F1
hyperlink	Insert, Links		Ctrl + K
italic	Home, Font	I	Ctrl + I
New tab Backstage view	File	New	
open	File	Open	
paste	Home, Clipboard		Ctrl + V
Print tab Backstage view	File	Print	Ctrl + P
save	File	, Save	Ctrl + S
save as	File	Save As	F12
shapes	Insert, Illustrations		
SmartArt	Insert, Illustrations		
table	Insert, Tables		
text box	Insert, Text		
underline	Home, Font	U	Ctrl + U
WordArt	Insert, Text		

WORD

Feature	Ribbon Tab, Group	Button, File Tab	Shortcut
align text left, center, or right	Home, Paragraph		Ctrl + L; E; or R
bullets	Home, Paragraph		
change styles	Home, Styles		
Clip Art	Insert, Illustrations		
columns	Page Layout, Page Setup		
envelopes and labels	Mailings, Create		
footer or header	Insert, Header & Footer		
line spacing, single or double	Home, Paragraph		Ctrl + 1 or 2
Navigation pane	View, Show		Ctrl + F
page break	Insert, Pages		Ctrl + Enter
page number	Insert, Header & Footer		
Page Setup dialog box	Page Layout, Page Setup		
picture	Insert, Illustrations		
Quick Parts	Insert, Text		
screenshot	Insert, Illustrations		
section break	Page Layout, Page Setup		
Spelling & Grammar	Review, Proofing		F7

POWERPOINT

Feature	Ribbon Tab, Group	Button, File Tab	Shortcut
align text left, center, or right	Home, Paragraph		Ctrl + L; E; or R
font size, increase or decrease	Home, Font		Ctrl + Shift + > / Ctrl + Shift + <
list level, increase or decrease	Home, Paragraph		Tab or Shift + Tab
layout	Home, Slides		
new slide	Home, Slides		Ctrl + M
screenshot	Insert, Images		
Slide Sorter view	View, Presentation Views		
Spelling	Review, Proofing		F7

EXCEL

Feature	Ribbon Tab, Group	Button, File Tab	Shortcut
Accounting Number format	Home, Number	[button]	
align text left, center, or right	Home, Alignment	[button]	
apply worksheet theme	Page Layout, Themes	[button]	
borders	Home, Font	[button]	
cell formulas			Ctrl + ~
change margins	Page Layout, Page Setup OR File, Print	Options [button]	Ctrl + Shift + &
column width or row height	Home, Cells	[button]	
Comma Style format	Home, Number	[button]	
create column, line, or pie chart	Insert, Charts	[button]	F11
decimal, increase or decrease	Home, Number	[button]	
delete cell, column, row, or worksheet	Home, Cells	[button]	
fill color	Home, Font	[button]	
filter table	Home, Editing	[button]	
Find and Replace	Home, Editing	[button]	
format, move, copy, or rename worksheet	Home, Cells	[button]	
indent, increase or decrease	Home, Alignment	[button]	
insert cell, column, row, or worksheet	Home, Cells	[button]	
insert comment	Review, Comments	[button]	Shift + F2
insert function	Formulas, Function Library	[button]	
merge and center	Home, Alignment	[button]	
scale page width and/or height	Page Layout, Scale to Fit OR File, Print		
sort	Home, Editing	[button]	
Spelling or Thesaurus	Review, Proofing	[button]	F7; Shift + F7
SUM function	Home, Editing	[button]	Alt + =

ACCESS

Feature	Ribbon Tab, Group	Button, File Tab	Shortcut
add fields to a form	Form Layout Tools Design, Controls	[button]	
add or delete records	Home, Records	[button]	Ctrl + +; Delete
change margins	Print Preview, Page Size OR Page Layout	[button]	
column (field) width	Home, Records	[button]	
conditional formatting in form or report	Form Layout Tools Format, Control Formatting OR Report Layout Tools Format, Control Formatting	[button]	
filter	Home, Sort & Filter	[button]	
Find	Home, Find	[button]	Ctrl + F
Form tool	Create, Forms	[button]	
Group, Sort, and Total pane	Report Layout Tools Design, Grouping & Totals	[button]	
insert or delete fields	Table Tools Design, Tools	[button]	Delete
insert totals	Home, Records	[button]	
labels	Create, Reports	[button]	
landscape orientation	Print Preview, Page Layout	[button]	
primary key	Table Tools Design, Tools	[button]	
print or Print Preview	File, Print	[button]	Ctrl + P
Property sheet	Form Layout Tools Design, Tools OR Report Layout Tools Design, Tools	[button]	Alt + Enter
Query Design or Query Wizard	Create, Queries	[button]	
relationships	Database Tools, Relationships	[button]	
Report tool	Create, Reports	[button]	
run a query	Query Tools Design, Results	[button]	
sort ascending or descending order	Home, Sort & Filter	[button]	
table or table design	Create, Tables	[button]	